Introduction to Behavior Analysis in Special Education

Frank R. Rusch
University of Illinois at Urbana-Champaign

Terry Rose
University of North Carolina

Charles R. Greenwood
University of Kansas

Foreword by Donald M. Baer
University of Kansas

PRENTICE HALL, Englewood Cliffs, New Jersey 07632

Library of Congress Cataloging-in-Publication Data

RUSCH, FRANK R.
  Introduction to behavior analysis in special education.

  Includes bibliography and index.
    1. Special education—United States. 2. Behavioral
assessment—United States. 3. Reinforcement
(Psychology) I. Rose, Terry, [date]
II. Greenwood, Charles R., [date]   . III. Title.
LC3981.R87 1988   371.9   87-17430
ISBN 0-13-478413-8

Editorial/production supervision and
  interior design: Marianne Peters
Cover design: Diane Saxe
Manufacturing buyer: Margaret Rizzi and Peter Havens

 © 1988 by Prentice-Hall, Inc.
A Division of Simon & Schuster
Englewood Cliffs, New Jersey 07632

Printed in the United States of America
10 9 8 7 6 5 4 3 2 1

ISBN 0-13-478413-8

Prentice-Hall International (UK) Limited, *London*
Prentice-Hall of Australia Pty. Limited, *Sydney*
Prentice-Hall Canada Inc., *Toronto*
Prentice-Hall Hispanoamericana, S.A., *Mexico*
Prentice-Hall of India Private Limited, *New Delhi*
Prentice-Hall of Japan, Inc., *Tokyo*
Simon & Schuster Asia Pte. Ltd., *Singapore*
Editora Prentice-Hall do Brasil, Ltda., *Rio de Janeiro*

Contents

Foreword

This book describes an alliance between applied behavior analysis and special education. The alliance is a natural one; most people who have worked in both disciplines find themselves unable to say when they are doing one and when the other. There are two explanations for that: The application of behavior analysis is almost always educational, in the best and broadest sense of the word; and special education is the branch of education that most requires an applicable analysis of behavior in order to teach. Each of these propositions deserves comment, and a foreword may be exactly the place for it, because it is the context rather than the content of a book like this.

Applied behavior analysis is almost always educational, because of three fundamental characteristics: 1) it always begins as a response to a human problem; 2) it analyzes that problem into behaviors, typically underdeveloped skills, or self-disadvantaging, socially undesirable responses (these are the behaviors that, if changed, *solve* the problem); and 3) it changes those behaviors, and in the process it studies the ways that the environment can be used to create behavior changes so that a technology of behavior change results. Isn't that exactly education?

Of these three characteristics, the third, its teaching technology, is most often taken as the hallmark of applied behavior analysis. In truth, however, the second is its greatest contribution: The recognition that what people call problems can always be restated simply as behaviors to be changed. But we can make this contribution a little less simple, much more realistic, and much more valuable. We can do that by recognizing that the behaviors that constitute a problem exist sometimes only in the person who has the problem, sometimes only in the people who see that person as having a problem, but most often in both. This contribution becomes extraordinarily valuable in two instances: 1) when our teaching technology becomes good enough to let us change exactly those behaviors in all those people, and 2) when our professional, personal, and social ethics show us when and how to do that only in the ways that maximize our and their most fundamental personal and social values. (Indeed, one of our best values is to recognize that We and They are the same people.) Characteristically, applied behavior analysis also will recognize that this last consideration—those personal and social values that ought to and usually do determine our professional ethics—are also behaviors, but behaviors that we see not as a problem but as our heritage and our treasure.

Applied behavior analysis is almost always educational, but education is not always behavior-analytic. In the past, it has not needed to be. Education has served its societies for centuries, but across that span of time, it most often served to educate those few most suited to formal education—the best supported, the most resourceful, and the most curious—in other words, those most proficient at teaching themselves once made aware of what there was to learn. It is the very recent history of education that has seen it not only applied to but, in fact, required of the mass of its societies. Universal education is a uniquely modern concept. Thus, educational traditions are based on its interaction with the easiest-to-teach students. But the function of special education is almost the reverse of that tradition: to accomplish useful development in the most-difficult-to-teach students—the least supported, least resourceful, least curious students of our society. It is as if education is finally realizing the deepest of its moral obligations, as summarized in Matthew 25:40 some 2,000 years ago: How we treat the least of us shows us how much we respect our God.

Special education addresses the most difficult to teach, and just because of that, must understand teaching as completely as all of our behavioral sciences will allow. In past centuries, teaching could well consist primarily of pointing out what there was to be learned, explaining those parts that students did not learn simply by trying, and punishing any absence of trying. The students of special education often require a great deal more than that. To teach them, we shall have to understand the structure of what we are teaching. In particular, we shall need to see the following: that what we used to think of as simple lessons are actually complex; that upon analysis these lessons are seen to have basic components, which are the true simple lessons; and that some of those simple components had better be taught before some or the later components will prove to be too complex after all. Then we have to understand the process of our students' learning, even when they are presented with these simple lessons in their proper order. They may learn little of it themselves, because they have not yet been taught the skills of teaching themselves. Often, we are not used to that. Most of the regular education students come to school already in possession of some of those skills, and they quickly learn more in the primary grades. They are a delight to teach, we often say, and what we often mean is that they teach themselves so much. Thus, regular students do not require us to understand very much about teaching; and some special students require us to find out everything about teaching. If we want to truly understand teaching, it is the special students who are the greatest delight to teach. They require us to learn *all* about our profession as teachers, and if teaching is a delight, then teaching very well is a special delight—the more so, because when we teach them well, *they learn what we teach.* They are thereby on the road to learning how to teach themselves, and we are thereby on the road to learning how to teach them to teach themselves. That lesson may make us the most valuable teachers of all, not only for the special students, but for all students.

It is good to be on that road, even if not at its end. This book marks an interesting point along the way, a point when the alliance between applied behavior analysis and special education is advanced enough to be very useful, but still underdeveloped enough to require intensive research in the students and real-life settings of education, and to require intensive ongoing inquiry into our values. It is exactly the right time for such a textbook, because it will report progress so far, teach us how to use it, and spur further progress and further use. Indeed, it will become a tool of that further progress. And so I congratulate its readers on their good fortune to be part of that adventure and to have this tool for it.

Donald M. Baer
Roy A. Roberts Distinguished Professor
of Human Development and Psychology
University of Kansas

Preface

Introduction to Behavior Analysis in Special Education traces the historical development of special education (Chapter 1) and the emergence of applied behavior analysis since before the twentieth century. Over the course of several decades applied behavior analysis has developed principles and methods that have enjoyed widespread growth and adoption. Chapter 2 presents important, early developments, including the identification of principles that describe relationships between behavior and environment. These principles include well-known behaviors that we use in our everyday interactions. For example, we praise our children for attaining educational and personal goals that we believe are important; we also praise our colleagues in the workplace for a job well done. Similarly, we admonish performance that is disruptive in the classroom. How we behave in education, in business, at home, and elsewhere is based upon well-known principles of behavior that have been studied in diverse settings, such as in prisons, in classrooms, on buses, at work, and in the home.

Chapter 3 presents "some commonalities" between special education and applied behavior analysis. These "commonalities" include addressing important educational outcomes, focusing upon the individual, being accountable for our promises to change behavior, and addressing individual's problems versus allowing these problems to direct attention away from relevant goals. Chapter 3 also contributes to setting the groundwork that recognizes special education and applied behavior analysis share mutually-beneficial historical and current philosophical and ideological dimensions.

Chapter 4 overviews contemporary dimensions of applied behavior analysis and incorporates special education by example. This chapter, as well as all remaining chapters in this text, draws from a broad-based literature that exposes diverse special education problems and how applied behavior analysis has addressed and solved these problems. These problems and solutions focus upon children, youth, and adult issues in educational and noneducational settings.

Chapters 5 through 8 introduce and examine various behavior-analytic approaches to assessment that have proven helpful to special educators. To help translate the various principles and theories connected with behavior analysis into practical, day-to-day program planning and assessment, the discussion of each major technique is followed by examples of applications with individuals with mild handicaps and individuals with severe handicaps. The major areas covered include ways to observe and define behavior in natural settings and the relevance of these activities for overall program planning (Chapter 5). Due to their importance for meaningful and appropriate instructional program planning and implementation, two major sections are devoted to measurement in special education and applied behavior analysis—they are broadly divided into intermittent (Chapter 6) and continuous assessment (Chapter 7). For each, the purpose, characteristics, and advantages/disadvantages of assessment are overviewed. Finally, Chapter 8 introduces strategies for evaluating behavioral progress. Particular focus is given to four single-subject designs: ABAB reversal design, multiple-baseline design, changing-criterion design, and alternating-treatments design. The results of assessment using these designs provide necessary empirically-validated data to plan, monitor, and when necessary, adjust individualized education plans. Chapter 8 also introduces withdrawal designs, which are important to our better understanding how to withdraw educational programs without losing control over the target behavior.

Chapters 9 through 15 discuss a variety of principles and practices that have a direct effect on behavior. Chapter 9 discusses the principles of reinforcement, the different classes of reinforcement, and the different types of reinforcers. As in every chapter, a large number of applied examples are provided. The principles and strategies that can be employed to increase the effectiveness of any reinforcement-based intervention, as well as factors that may have a negative effect on the power of any reinforcers, are discussed in Chapter 10. A thorough understanding of reinforcement and the uses of various reinforcers is rarely enough to ensure that an educational program will be effective in the long-term or that the newly learned behavior will develop into a functional one for the individual. Frequently, the schedule on which the reinforcement is delivered is a determining factor regarding the ultimate success of any intervention. Chapter 11 provides a discussion of several types of reinforcement schedules.

As we move into Chapters 12 and 13, a new intervention focus emerges: a focus on antecedent stimuli that are present in the environment before a behavior occurs. Chapter 12 introduces the aspects of stimulus control, describes how to assess for the presence of stimulus control, and discusses the procedures that develop stimulus control most successfully. Chapter 13 focuses on using stimulus control procedures to create new behaviors by providing extensive discussions of modeling, shaping, chaining, and generalization training.

Once again, our intervention focus switches as we begin to read Chapters 14 and 15. This time we switch back to a study of consequences, but this time the consequences are those that will reduce the occurrence of behavior. The principles of punishment, the different types of punishment, its appropriate and effective use, and several reductive procedures (based on the principles of punishment), including overcorrection, response cost, and timeout are discussed in Chapter 14. Another set of procedures that are designed to reduce the occurrence of behavior, but are based on arranging reinforcers so that an alternate, incompatible positive behavior is established, will be reduced to an acceptable limit is described in Chapter 15.

Special education has emerged as a discipline that focuses upon children, youth, and adults who fail to learn at rates equivalent to the majority of society's member. Historically, these individuals have been segregated from the mainstream of society. Children and youth were once denied educational opportunities or provided an education apart from the regular classroom. Adults have been similarly treated. Not long ago adults with handicaps were expected to live and work apart from mainstream residential and employment opportunities. Oftentimes these adults were institutionalized and denied an equal opportunity for employment. Much has changed, however, over the past several years. Special education was permanently altered with the passage of P.L. 94-142. Among other things, P.L. 94-142 emphasized individual's unique needs by stressing the importance of educational services delivered in the least restrictive environment.

Applied behavior analysis has developed into a technology that addresses problems of social importance. A long period of experimental research initially was devoted to studying principles of behavior and the methodology that allowed behavioral scientists to more completely study relationships between behaviors and behavior and setting. Once these principles were more completely understood society's problems were increasingly addressed. Applied behavior analysis is a practical approach to dealing with society's problems. This approach continues to demonstrate its effectiveness in the application of methods for improving individual growth and development. *Introduction to Behavior Anal-*

ysis in Special Education introduces you to an ideologically-relevant and methodologically-contemporary approach to understanding and solving educational problems.

ACKNOWLEDGMENTS

I would like to thank: Dr. Alan C. Repp for his support and encouragement; Kathy Minch for reading and reviewing the entire text; and to Professors Laura Jordan and Robert Henderson for spending time with me to recount the history of special education.

Frank R. Rusch

I would like to acknowledge the people who provided help and support at critical junctures in the development of this book: my wife, Gail, for providing emotional support when it seemed as if the writing would go on forever, and my children, Regan and Randy, for sacrificing the time we couldn't spend together while I wrote.

Terry Rose

I would like to thank: Drs. Judith Carta, David Rotholz, and Debra Whorton for assisting me in conceptualizing and reviewing specific literature; Ms. Dale Walker, a doctoral student, for reading and editing my chapters; Ms. Mary Todd for clerical support; and Ms. Alva Beasley for graphics.

Charles R. Greenwood

chapter 1

Special Education: Development of a Discipline

Throughout history societies have established customs, laws, and moral codes based upon the way the majority behaves. These norms have served to set the goals upon which the education of children is based and the standards according to which individuals are judged. Historically, deviation from these standards or failure to progress toward society's goals has resulted in punishment, incarceration, segregation, and even death. Diverse explanations have been offered to account for deviation and failure to progress including family traits, genetics, environmental influences, and demonic possession. These explanations are important insofar as they have guided societies to adopt certain approaches to educate and treat their members. The earliest conceptions of why some individuals were different from the majority centered around the belief that evil spirits entered the human body. The differences were subsequently considered external manifestations of these evil spirits. Not surprisingly, treatment was directed toward exorcising these demons by praying, by using incantations, by cutting a hole in the skull, or by flogging.

Hippocrates was influential in supplanting the demonological conception of deviant behavior with a disease-oriented conceptual scheme. Early treatments included wholesome diets, hydrotherapy, and bloodletting. Behavior that departed substantially from accepted social, legal, and ethical norms was considered a symptom of an underlying disease. Even today, treatment of social deviance is a medical specialty and "patients" suffering from "mental illness" are treated in medically-oriented "mental health" centers. Indeed, had Hippocrates suggested that behavior differed from the accepted norm due to idiosyncratic environmental influences rather than from an underlying disorder, the conceptualization and treatment of behavioral differences may have taken an entirely different course.

Also throughout history, the education of individuals with behavioral excesses or deficits has centered around mythology, superstition, religion, and fear. Although the historical roots of special education can be traced to the beginnings of human existence, special education as we know it today was not firmly developed until the early nineteenth century. In this chapter we chronicle special education's foundation with a discussion of the pioneering men and women who challenged the wisdom of the church and the widespread belief that individuals were either "possessed" or suffering from disease. Definitions of special education have varied according to the concepts explaining why individuals behave the way they do. For the purposes of this text, *special education refers to the goals and educational techniques incorporated to teach children, youth, and adults who deviate from society's norms and fail to learn at rates equivalent to the majority of society's members.* The practical concern of contemporary special education is to change environments and behavior such that individuals can function effectively within social communities. This orientation departs from those concepts that emphasize "differentness."

In this chapter, we divide the nineteenth and twentieth centuries into five distinct periods, the first period being devoted to an overview of many of the major events that firmly established the foundations of special education in the nineteenth century. For the four periods that follow in the twentieth century we introduce some of the major influences on the treatment of individuals with handicaps, including the efforts to test individual potential, the effects of wars, the introduction of vocational education, the introduction of state legislation, the introduction of labeling and special classroom placement, and a single president's interest in developing and advancing the education of persons with mental retardation which resulted in litigation and federal legislation. Each of these and related events are historically overviewed in

four periods of time which we entitle: (a) 1900–1950: Focus upon the Individual; (b) 1950–1960: Development of a National Concern; (c) 1960–1970: The Growth Period; and (d) 1970–1980: The Judicial Years.

1800–1900: Foundations of Special Education

In the beginning of the nineteenth century, treatment of persons with handicaps began to change dramatically due to the efforts of Jean Itard (1774–1838). In 1799, a 12-year-old boy was captured in the forests of Aveyron, France. Jean Itard, a physician who specialized in diseases of the ear and deaf education, decided to educate this boy, whom he named Victor. Subscribing to the theory that the mind was a blank slate and that one had only to develop the appropriate learning and sensory experiences, Itard began a rigid, 5-year program that made a clinically apparent change in Victor's behavior. When Victor was found in the Aveyron forest, he bit and scratched those who initially attempted to aid him. He was unable to speak. He rocked incessantly, and he was generally animal-like in his actions. Although Itard did not make Victor "normal," he did change his behavior dramatically through gradual, systematic sensory training and environmental interactions. For example, Itard taught Victor to discriminate between hot and cold by having Victor bathe frequently, teaching him the difference between cold and hot water. Today, Itard's emphasis on sensory training can still be found in preschools and in programs for children who are both handicapped and not handicapped. Another of Itard's major contributions was the development of an approach in which education and its effects were systematically recorded. Itard kept written records of his work, which assisted him greatly in determining why he was successful.

Itard's work was continued through one of his students, Edward Seguin (1812–1880), and much of their efforts were reflected in the subsequent work of Maria Montessori (1870–1952). Seguin's educational method embod-

Jean Marc Gaspard Itard.
Photo courtesy of Harvard University Press.

Maria Montessori.
Photo courtesy of American Montessori Society.

Samuel Gridley Howe.
Photo courtesy of Perkins School for the Blind.

ied the two following principles that are still relevant today: (a) a recognition and appreciation of individual differences through individual observation and, (b) an assessment, followed by experimental training on functional tasks that have relevance to everyday life. A physician and educator, Seguin's tenet that even children with severe handicaps have the capability to learn continues to be a major theoretical perspective today.

Seguin left France in 1848 and emigrated to the United States where he established the first educationally oriented institution for persons with handicaps, becoming superintendent of the Pennsylvania Training School for Idiots. Although a title like "idiot" would seem barbaric today, in Seguin's day any effort to educate persons with handicaps was uniquely humane. His educational rather than custodial approach to institutionalization included an emphasis on the whole individual, the need for individualized instruction, and the importance of a good relationship between the teacher and the child. He was elected the first president of the Association of Medical Officers of American Institutions for Idiotic and Feeble-minded Persons in 1876. Today, this association bears the name of the American Association of Mental Deficiency.

By the end of the nineteenth century, the popularity and growth of training programs, such as the Pennsylvania Training School for Idiots, outpaced their financial support and, not surprisingly, hopes diminished with regard to educating people with handicaps in the United States. Training institutions began once again to center upon custodial activities.

In Italy, Maria Montessori had obtained a copy of Seguin's book, *Idiocy and Its Treatment by the Physiological Method* (1866). She translated and copied all 600 pages of this text by hand. Montessori, the first woman to receive a medical degree in Italy, opened the Orthophrenic School for the Cure of the Feeble-minded in Rome, and she achieved spectacular successes in teaching children with mental retardation to read and write. In addition, Montessori extended her program by opening a school in Rome for children who were not handicapped. Subsequently, Montessori moved to the United States. Her efforts directed toward educating children and youths with mental retardation were not well received because of widespread pessimism regarding these persons' potential to become productive members of society. Consequently, Maria Montessori began to extend her work with children who were not handicapped.

Without a doubt, Itard, Seguin, and Montessori had considerable impact upon the edu-

cation of persons with handicaps. Others also played important roles in developing a foundation for special education. Not surprisingly, severe handicaps were the focus of much of the early work reported by these educators and others. It was not until the birth of intelligence tests and enforcement of compulsory education laws that persons with mild handicaps—including emotional disturbances, learning disabilities, and behavior disorders—became a major focus within the American educational system. Before the turn of the century persons with severe handicaps or sensory impairments were easy to identify because they failed to contribute to society in obvious ways unless educated. Because criteria for success throughout much of the nineteenth century included, primarily, the capability to contribute to the survival of the family, only those who required education became the focus of the emerging special programs.

Development of Sensory Education. A number of prominent individuals shaped the formation of sensory education prior to the nineteenth century. Ponce de Leon and Juan Pablo Bonet in Spain, and Spanish-born Jacob Rodriguez Periere and Abbé de l'Epée in France, contributed directly to the formation of deaf education and indirectly to the education and treatment of persons with handicaps (Kanner, 1964). Ponce de Leon is remembered for his successful efforts to teach two brothers to read and write. He taught one of these brothers several languages, which eventually led to this person being ordained. Bonet is well known for his creation of a manual alphabet that bears close resemblance to the American Manual Alphabet. In France, Periere's work influenced the work of Seguin. De l'Epée's work formed in Paris the first school focusing upon deaf education.

In the United States several persons, including Samuel Gridley Howe, influenced the development and growth of sensory education. A graduate of Harvard Medical School, Howe was instrumental in helping establish the Perkins Institute for the Blind, founded in 1832 in Watertown, Massachusetts, and became its first director. In 1837, Howe brought to Perkins an instructor who was visually impaired, John Pringle, from the Edinburgh Institute for the Blind in Scotland. Pringle became the director of what was probably the first sheltered workshop in the United States. Howe's purpose in establishing the workshop was to train persons with visual handicaps to work in their home communities. Interestingly, these persons, however, wished to remain in the workshop and not venture into the community. In an effort to encourage them to leave the Perkins Institute, Howe established a separate workshop a few blocks away and required them to work away from the institution.

One of Howe's major accomplishments was the education of Laura Bridgeman, whom he taught by means of a finger alphabet to read and write. It was this work that eventually resulted in Helen Keller's education by another person with visual handicaps—Anne Sullivan—who entered the Perkins Institute at the age of 14. After receiving a series of eye operations that partially restored her vision, and after having studied the reports on Laura's education, Sullivan left the Perkins Institution to teach Helen Keller. Among the most widely known "miracles" in the history of deaf education is Sullivan's work that eventually led Helen Keller to communicate with those in the world around her, culminating in her graduating *cum laude* from Radcliffe College.

Throughout the nineteenth century, individuals with handicaps largely received their education in segregated facilities, and even today they are often segregated for instructional purposes. Although some educators, such as Howe, believed that education for persons with handicaps should focus solely upon assisting individuals to achieve their maximum potential in schools and community settings, segregation achieved widespread support. Arguments in favor of segregation included instructional convenience, peer acceptance, and lowered costs. Interestingly, industrialization led to the development of a series of events that helped to firmly establish the delivery of instruction in segregated facilities. In the next section, we review these events and, in particular, the considerable influence of intelligence testing and the work of Binet, Goddard, and others upon special education.

1900–1950: Focus upon the Individual

Several historic milestones significantly influenced the quality of life of individuals with handicaps around the turn of the century. Compulsory school-attendance laws and American industrialization significantly shaped the focus of education in the United States with the creation and emphasis on vocational education. Among the most important events around the turn of the century was the development of standardized tests with the Binet-Simon Scale. In 1904, Alfred Binet, a psychologist, was appointed to a commission by the French Minister of Education to study ways of identifying students able to benefit from the standard curriculum offered in the schools. In 1905, the Binet-Simon Scale of mental development was created by Alfred Binet and Theodore Simon, a physician. In 1916, Lewis Terman, an American psychologist at Stanford University, further perfected and standardized the Binet-Simon Test. This improved version was called the Stanford-Binet test.

Most testers, including Binet, modeled their standardized tests on the norms and mores of existing social standards. Alfred Binet (1909) wrote:

An individual is normal when he is able to conduct himself in life without need of the guardianship of another, and is able to perform work sufficiently remunerative to supply his personal needs, and finally when his intelligence does not exclude him from the social rank of his parents. As a result of this, an attorney's son who is reduced by his intelligence to the condition of a menial employee is a moron; likewise the son of a master mason, who remains a servant of thirty years is a moron; likewise a peasant, normal in ordinary surroundings of the fields, may be considered a moron in the city. (p. 266)

The belief that social class differences influenced the performance of individuals on a test fueled the eugenics movement and influenced "tracking" of children in schools. *Eugenics* refers to the science that studies the means to improve a species by controlling hereditary qualities such as mating practices. Arguments by such noted psychologists as Terman and Thorndike helped foster the ability-tracking curricular model in our schools. Children were grouped according to "native "ability and educated accordingly. Terman (1919) believed that it was far more important for the United States to educate its intelligent "stock" than to train its "dullards." Around the turn of the century, according to the developers of the Stanford-Binet Test, Blacks and European immigrants were not considered part of the intelligent stock. Goddard, Terman, and other noted testers called for the sterilization of the "socially inadequate" (including persons with mental retardation), the termination of indiscriminate immigration, and the formation of the tracking system in American schools.

One leader of the eugenics movement in the United States was Charles Davenport. Around the turn of the century, Davenport persuaded several national committees to establish a biological experimental station under the auspices of the Carnegie Institution of Washington. Initially, Davenport studied heredity by breeding animals. As Davenport's interest in animal breeding began to wane, he used his influence to attract others to the study of human heredity. During the period between 1910 and 1918, noted individuals associated with various committees to study heredity included Robert M. Yerkes and Edward L. Thorndike (Committee of Mental Traits), Alexander Graham Bell (Committee on Heredity of Deaf-mutism), and H. H. Goddard (Committee on the Heredity of the Feeble-minded). These committees were successful in lobbying for the passing of sterilization laws in 21 states. This lobbying was responsi-

ble for almost 9,000 sterilizations of institutionalized persons with mental retardation, as well as passage of laws banning "feeble-minded people" from marrying.

Also around the turn of the century, compulsory school-attendance laws began to be enforced. One of the reasons for the development of compulsory school-attendance laws was the industrial demand for an educated working class. Although the first state compulsory attendance law was enacted in 1852 in Massachusetts, not all states adopted such laws until 1918. Most reform-minded educators, following the pedagogic tenets of Rousseau, believed that education should do no more than train the mind and hoped that these compulsory attendance laws would be the much needed antidote for social degeneration. Unfortunately, teachers accustomed to dealing only with children of the more "leisured class" found dealing with working-class children increasingly difficult, and schools began to initiate programs to separate working-class children from their leisure-class classmates.

Compulsory attendance laws, the birth of intelligence tests that supposedly predicted potential, and the emergence of industrialization in the United States led to the development of school curricula that resulted in unequal education. The industrial revolution demanded that a labor force acquire the habits, values, and personality configurations conducive to assembly line techniques. Thus, the rationale for industrial education was based upon the need to "develop in the future industrial worker psychic structures that would increase . . . productivity and diminish . . . alienation" (Violas, 1978, p. 125). Laws were in effect that forced all children to attend school, intelligence tests became the tools to predict probable socio-economic status, and industrialization led to industrial education for lower-class children. As indicated previously, until this time children with mild handicaps were not readily discernible if they fit well into rural or urban communities by contributing to the immediate needs of their families. Compulsory attendance, the testing movement, and industrialization were three primary forces that combined to identify children with unique educational needs and thereby justify their separate education.

Only the great world wars equaled or surpassed the contributions of these three forces in establishing special education programs for persons with handicaps between 1900 and 1950. World Wars I and II resulted in the intensification of industrial education in our schools and the passage of educational legislation. Among the most important of these education laws are the Smith-Hughes Act (1917) and the Vocational Rehabilitation Act Amendments (1943). The Smith-Hughes Act is considered the single most important legislative enactment for vocational education because most of the structure of vocational education was established. The earlier emphasis on industrial education in the United States before 1917, however, was not forgotten. Vocational education subsumed the industrial emphasis and included emerging concerns for education in agriculture, home economics, and the trades. The Smith-Hughes Act also resulted in the creation of the Federal Board of Vocational Education, which had the authority and responsibility for the vocational rehabilitation of returning disabled veterans from World War I. This responsibility led directly to subsequent legislation that supported services for persons with physical disabilities. Pivotal to the growth of special education was the passage of the 1943 Vocational Rehabilitation Act Amendments, which extended services to persons with mental retardation for the first time.

In 1912, Henry Goddard's *The Kallikak Family* appeared and espoused hereditary causation of retardation. In this book, Goddard traced the offspring of two women that Martin Kallikak, a soldier in the American Revolution, had impregnated. One was a "retarded barmaid" with whom Kallikak established a "bad family", the other was his wife, with whom he established a "good family." The children from Kallikak and his wife were described as intelligent and contributing members of society. The "other side" of the family

tree was described by Goddard as composed of children with handicaps, prostitutes, and criminals. Interestingly, the results of this investigation were based upon a case study that was offered by a social worker who accepted hearsay evidence. The view that mental retardation was largely inherited lasted for nearly 70 years, and it was not really challenged in the public mind until John F. Kennedy became president. Then in 1985 D. J. Smith published *Minds Made Feeble: The Myth and Legacy of the Kallikaks*. Smith traced the Kallikak tale back to its very roots and found out who the Kallikaks were, how they lived, where they worked, and how they conducted their lives. His findings are markedly different from those that have been accepted as fact for over 70 years. Smith remarked that the Kallikak story was "an illustration of the power of a social myth." Goddard found characters that he could make fit the tale. The Kallikaks gave human form to a story that the social Darwinists and eugenicists had been developing for decades. The public found in the book a parable they wanted to believe. Politicians, policy makers, and the powerful found evidence in the Kallikak family story that their disregard of the rights of the weak was consistent with the natural order of life and in the best interest of the nation" (Smith, 1985, pp. 8–9).

1950–1960: Development of a National Concern

The 1950s were consolidating years for special education. During this brief period much of what we now associate with it was already subsumed under the term "special education." Some of the major developments that occurred during the 1950s are the establishment of the finances associated with the high cost of special education; the proliferation of special classes; the passing of laws requiring special education in segregated settings; the first beginnings of sheltered workshops; special class placement and related research; and the start of advanced graduate work in special education. Most importantly this period witnessed the development of a national concern for special education because of governmental recognition that education should be the major focus of a free society.

The 1950s began with several states passing new legislation in support of special education. Education of the "intellectually superior," state reimbursement to public schools serving children with handicaps, adjustment of school-age limits, and teacher salaries were among the topics considered. There was also a growing recognition of financial responsibility for the education of persons with handicaps. The emphasis upon early educational experience for children under the age of six years and the willingness of many states to pay the higher cost of education were major advances.

Similarly, advances were being made with adults with handicaps. For example, there were only six sheltered workshops for individual with mental retardation in the United States in 1953, and much of the work in sheltered workshops was not competitive but therapeutic. Trainers were primarily volunteers. Sheltered workshops did not really begin to prosper until the passage of the Vocational Rehabilitation Amendments of 1954, which offered grants to nonprofit agencies to support research and demonstration projects. During the first 10 years after this Act, 151 grants were awarded in support of these efforts (Nelson, 1971).

Throughout the early and mid–1950s, special education became firmly entrenched as a discipline devoted to the study of diverse handicaps. Hearing and speech handicaps, mental retardation, slow learning in the classroom, visual disabilities, and physical disabilities were topics reported on in *Exceptional Children*–the voice of the Council for Exceptional Children (founded in 1923). Other themes also began, many of which are still present today, such as total school planning and team approaches (Pritchard, 1952).

Today, teams of professionals continue to represent alternative approaches to the total school planning service. In 1951, Frederick A. Whitehouse introduced the need for teamwork in special education to serve persons with severe handicaps. Whitehouse urged that "someone from every profession representing a major area of human need" (Whitehouse, 1951, p. 46) be included, suggesting the team be composed of a physician, a psychiatrist, a psychologist, a social worker, and an educator, in addition to a physical therapist, an occupational therapist, a speech therapist, a recreation therapist, a vocational counselor, and a placement specialist. Unfortunately, even today this approach to providing services is not firmly established, as vocational counselors and placement specialists are often excluded from educational teams serving persons with handicaps.

Finances began to plague the growth and development of special education very early in the 1950s. In fact, in 1952 the president of the Council for Exceptional Children, John W. Tenny, noted the need for appropriations in the form of special grants at the federal level to help offset inflation and to help supplement existing state support. In 1952, he suggested:

(1) That our public relations program must be such as to keep influential people aware not only of the needs of exceptional children, but also of the social gains resulting from their proper care and education.

(2) That those of us who work at the state level should keep regulations and reports as simple and brief as possible, consistent with the assurance of sound and adequate programs for exceptional children.

(3) That each of us, in our particular job, review our program and our efforts, to be sure that we are giving the best possible service at the least possible cost. (Tenny, 1952, p. 187)

There was a sudden growth in the number of segregated special classes for children with handicaps immediately following World War II (Goldstein, Moss & Jordan, 1965). The need for increasing numbers of special classes was based on the belief that placing children with handicaps in special classes would be more beneficial to them than keeping them in regular classes. Not surprisingly, the 1950s were also characterized by growing awareness that thousands of children were being placed in special classes. F. E. Lord, president of the Council on Exceptional Children, delivered an address on the topic of special class placement at the first general meeting of that council in Minneapolis in 1956. In his address he alluded to the growth of special classes and problems associated with them, including attracting the child that does not belong there (Lord, 1956).

It was not until *after* the tremendous growth of special classes that educators sought evidence to prove that there were any actual benefits to special class placement. For example, Goldstein et al. (1965) sought to determine the efficacy of special classes for children with mild mental retardation with respect to their intellectual development, academic achievement, and social and personal adjustment. Subjects included 129 children who were identified at the beginning of their first grade experience to have scored between 69 and 85 on an intelligence test. These children were randomly placed into one of four special classes or into their original first grade class. Special class programming was based upon a special curriculum guide and all teachers were certified to teach in the area of mental retardation. The regular classes were taught by teachers certified in elementary education where no specific curriculum was used. All of the children were tested periodically for four years to evaluate the effects of the special and regular class treatment. The results indicated no difference in level of academic achievement between those in special classes and those in regular classes. Children in the lower IQ group (80 or less) showed higher academic achievement in the special class placement. There was higher arithmetic achievement of those children in the regular class in the higher IQ group (81 and above). Goldstein concluded that personal and social adjustment was facilitated in the special class and impeded in the regular class, while IQ scores were differentially influenced. The results of

this study are representative of a number of similar studies that supported special class placement. Unfortunately, these studies suffered numerous methodological shortcomings that were not considered when reporting the results. For example, the tests administered were not valid. The results obtained by invalid tests are expected to vary at different points in time regardless of whether there are actual changes in the children tested. In fact, if a tester administered any one of the tests at two different time periods the probability of obtaining a different score is incredibly high.

All studies investigating the value of special classroom placement have problems that influence their findings. In most studies for example, random selection was not used to decide which children would enter special and regular classes. Thus, one could assume that the children placed in special classes had greater problems. Also, several studies did not control for length of treatment, the curriculum used, or teacher competence. Further, the curricula in the regular classes were not controlled in any of these studies. Additionally, in most of the studies all of the children had some regular class experience. Consequently, we do not know how regular class experience interacted with special class placement to influence the achievement areas studied.

Some definite conclusions, however, may be made about the placement of children from these and similar studies. These studies demonstrated that there was little or no difference in level of academic achievement between children placed in regular classes or children placed in special classes. Cassidy and Stanton (1959) and Goldstein et al. (1965) concluded that the primary benefit of special class placement is that the student shows increased social adjustment. These results are still widely questioned.

Two events, occurring in 1957 and 1958, continue to have profound impact upon special education today. Before 1957 there were no advanced graduate programs in special education; special educators obtained their education and additional degrees in medicine, psychology, educational administration, and related fields. This situation was changed when Samuel A. Kirk (1956) presented the components of a doctoral program in special education at the University of Illinois that he believed should educate individuals to assume leadership positions in the education of teachers, in the conduct of research, and in the administration of education at local, state, and national levels.

Throughout the first half of the twentieth century, there was growing recognition that children and adults with handicaps could benefit from a financial and legal commitment on the part of the federal government. Programs and emphases were not coordinated under a single legislated mandate. This concern was addressed with the passage of the National Defense Education Act of 1958, also known as the Hill-Elliott Act, which contained three titles that resulted in the direct growth of special education through loans to students in institutions of higher education (Title II), national defense fellowships (Title IV), and grants and special programs for guidance, counseling, and testing (Title V). Although the "race to the moon" with the Russians and the launching of Sputnik in 1957 resulted in an increased national concern to identify children with gifts, this event also influenced the swiftness by which the House of Representatives and the Senate passed the Hill-Elliott Act of 1958.

In summary, the 1950s were important for special education for the following reasons: (a) Special education was established for diverse handicaps; (b) Advanced graduate training programs in special education were initiated; and (c) Legislation, both state and federal, was beginniing to impact upon the needs of chilren, youth, and adults with handicaps. This period was also remarkable because such leaders as Lord challenged special and regular education's practice of segregating children, which consequently led to one of the most interesting and controversial efforts in special education—the study of whether special class placements resulted in higher achievement. The following section reviews The Growth Period and concludes with a "challenge" that shaped, quite dramatically, special education practice in the seventies.

1960–1970: The Growth Period

The 1960s were unique to special education as the field grew enormously. In the early 1960s, the study of learning disabilities was begun. Although special educators did not at the time believe that learning disabilities would result in a new educational focus, they eventually utilized the controversy that surrounded learning disabilities (for example, definition, prevalence, assessment) to reexamine the value of all categorical labels. In this section we review the federal government's role, the emergence of the field of learning disabilities, and the continued growth of special classroom placement of labeled children. We also reflect upon the type of services typically offered in the 1960s to individuals with diverse and unique needs. Finally, we conclude with a brief overview of the principle of normalization—a concept that today has no single accepted definition, yet has had a major influence on parents, paraprofessionals, and professionals associated with the education of persons with handicaps.

In 1961, President Kennedy created the President's Panel on Mental Retardation which, in October 1962, offered 95 recommendations for a national plan to combat mental retardation. Shortly thereafter, two bills were passed during the Fall of 1963. They were the Maternal and Child Health and Mental Retardation Planning Amendments (P. L. 88-156) and the Mental Retardation Facilities and Community Mental Health Centers Construction Act (P. L. 88-164). Among the programs resulting from these two legislative acts were the Maternal and Child Health and Crippled Children's Program, the Training of Teachers of Handicapped Children Program, the Research and Demonstration Projects in the area of children with handicaps, and the Division of Handicapped Children and Youth. This latter division obtained the responsibility to administer grants and funds for children with handicaps, including mental retardation, emotional disturbance, physical disabilities and other health impairments, visual handicaps, speech and hearing impairments, and multiple handicaps. Adults with similar handicaps were not omitted from these legislative acts, and many adults qualified for income maintenance benefits through the Social Security Administration. Also, vocational rehabilitation for persons with handicaps gained support through the creation of the Division of Training and the Division of Research Grants and Demonstrations. These combined programs were the result of the recommendations made by the President's Panel on Mental Retardation, and even today, in revised form, they continue to play a major role in efforts to provide special education services to persons with diverse handicaps.

Two related events received widespread recognition and debate during the 1960s. These were labeling and placement in special classes. There was then, and is today, widespread conviction that labeling a person through placement in a special program should be avoided. Placement in special programs, such as in self-contained classrooms, reshapes an individual's opportunities as well as an individual's social and self-expectations in negative ways. A well publicized and controversial study conducted by Rosenthal and Jacobsen (1968) suggested the potential harmful effects of labeling. In their study they indicated to teachers a group of children that, on the basis of an IQ measure, would most likely show greater gains in achievements. When these children were tested again at the end of the year their achievement gains, in fact, surpassed the gains made by their peers. Rosenthal and Jacobsen believed that these gains were a result of expectancy cues transmitted by the teachers to the children. Controversy still surrounds these results because of the failure of numerous investigators' attempts to replicate "expectancy effects."

There should be little doubt that placing a young student in a segregated, special class or school denies this student the opportunity to interact with a student who is not handicapped. These interactions between students with handicaps and without handicaps are just as important as interactions between students with handicaps for many reasons. Foremost among these reasons is recognition among students who are not handicapped that students with handicaps share many qualities, including the ability to enter into friendships.

One of the controversies within special education that began in the 1960s—and is still with us today—is the recognition that large numbers of minority and poor children are over-represented in special classes. Franks (1971), for example, found that the racial composition of programs in Missouri for children with learning disabilities was almost exclusively white, whereas black children constituted one-third of special class enrollments. Similarly, Mercer (1973) found that school psychologists in California were more likely to recommend special class placement for Mexican-American and poor children than for white children living in families earning average incomes.

During this period special educators also began to question their "open arms" attitude of placing children in these segregated "special classes." Lloyd M. Dunn (1968), for example, a long-time advocate of self-contained special classes, switched his position by stating:

I have loyally supported and promoted special classes for the educable mentally retarded for most of the last 20 years, but with growing disaffection. In my view, much of our past and present practices are morally and educationally wrong. We have been living at the mercy of general educators who have referred their problem children to us. And we have been generally ill prepared and ineffective in educating these children. Let us stop being pressured into continuing and expanding a special education approach that we know now to be undesirable for many of the children we are dedicated to serve. (p. 5)

Dunn based his new philosophical stance largely upon the slow academic and social progress of children placed in homogeneous classrooms and the large proportion of poor and minority children found in those classrooms. Much of the impetus for returning children to the regular classroom was based upon the results of research and practice that culminated in the belief that separate is neither equal nor better.

Until the late 1960s, special education experienced rapid growth and acquired an identity which, for the most part, reflected its categories of exceptionality, not its instructional approaches. By 1960, the following categories of exceptionality existed: mental retardation; emotional disturbance; learning disabilities; visual, hearing and speech impairments; orthopedic handicaps; and giftedness. Additionally, each of these, except giftedness, were further broken down into mild and severe levels. For example, mental retardation was distinguished by educable, trainable, and custodial classifications (Robinson & Robinson, 1976).

Since the 1960s categorical special education has been challenged by some that believe that children with handicaps should be served, regardless of their label, on the basis of the goals and education necessary. The common practice of educating children and youth in the schools was to identify these "handicapped children," diagnose the extent of their "handicap," and then place the student in a classroom serving similarly "handicapped children." In his challenge to such practices, Lilly (1970) proposed that every child, once placed in the regular classroom, remain there with assistance offered to the teacher to educate that child. The rationale for this approach was straightforward, that is, to provide the student the assistance necessary for him or her to remain in the normal environment. This rationale was not too different from the one suggested by Itard, Seguin, Howe, and others, who initially sought to return persons from the special training institution to the community. However, as history has indicated, this approach (that is, grouping

children according to need), albeit altruistic in intent, resulted in the massive growth of segregated training settings with little if any movement of individuals from these settings back to the community.

Since the late 1960s, there has been a growing interest in advancing special education noncategorically. *Noncategorical special education refers to serving persons with handicaps on the basis of their individual behavioral excesses or deficits rather than on the basis of their label.* Critics of noncategorical special education maintain that there are too many specialized training techniques associated with the range of handicaps, particularly sensory handicaps, to allow for a noncategorical approach. However, our position is that children, youth, and adults with diverse handicaps can be best served by focusing upon individual needs and applying the universally accepted procedures outlined in subsequent chapters of this text. This is not to suggest that the regular classroom teacher is always aware of these "best practices" when educating, for example, students with mild mental retardation.

Before 1969, the term *normalization* (Nirje, 1969) was unknown to most persons working in educational or rehabilitation settings. The first extensive overview of normalization was developed by Wolf Wolfensberger (1972). The term came from Denmark and refers to "making available to all (people with handicaps) patterns of life and conditions of everyday living which are as close as possible to the regular circumstances of society" (Nirje, 1969, p. 173). Further, the concept has been expanded to suggest that the responsibility of educators is to teach individuals to function within socially accepted boundaries. For example, the normalization approach suggests that a teacher insruct a student to interact with peers in a way that represents the *usual range of performance* acceptable to the peer group, such as playing four square on the playground during recess. Although the term normalization has no single accepted definition, it has undoubtedly led to the recognition that individuals are not best educated by being labeled, but by being educated via procedures that result in acceptable gains.

The segregated classroom is not the expected educational setting for a student, nor is the segregated sheltered workshop the expected employment setting for graduating students. Special education should seek to educate people by identifying their needs on an "individual-by-individual" basis so that the individual may remain in the mainstream of society. Normalization does not imply that people with various handicaps should necessarily do what everyone else does; it does, however, suggest that our efforts should be directed toward education that results in *acceptable* behavior occurring within an *acceptable range* of what our society would expect or value. Normalization continues to challenge the thinking of educators, parents, and others who believe that individuals should be labeled and segregated, and it suggests that labels such as "mentally retarded" and " behaviorally disordered" result in those persons who are labeled being devalued as human beings.

The decade of the 1960s experienced vastly increased funding as a result of legislative action. The 1960s were also noted for the passage of the Elementary and Secondary Education Act of 1965, which resulted in the creation of special programs of assistance to children and youth. In addition, regional instructional-materials centers for innovation and research were established. In 1966, the Bureau of Education for the Handicapped was also created and empowered with the responsibility of providing leadership to states in the conduct of their service responsibilities. Although the 1960s may be remembered as "The Growth Years," they will also be remembered as that period when learning disability was introduced as a new category of exceptionality, and when labeling and the efficacy of special class placements and categorical education were challenged. The introduction of the term "normalization" toward the end of the 1960s signalled the beginning of a challenge to educators to provide normalized services in normalized settings. Each of these

events and many others served to define broadly special education as it entered the 1970s, a decade that we refer to as "The Judicial Years." In our next section, we overview some of the major legislation that recommended that all school-aged children have a right to an appropriate and free education.

1970–1980: The Judicial Years

The responsibility of educators to provide education sufficient to prepare children for active participation in the adult community cannot be disputed. This mission, as old as time itself, is the foundation upon which public instruction is based. During the 1970s, judicial acknowledgments of the right to education and to treatment led professionals and paraprofessionals to take note of one of the most discriminated against groups of people since the adoption of the Constitution of the United States of America—persons with handicaps. The constitutional principles of due process and equal protection, as embodied in the Fifth and Fourteenth Amendments, along with the doctrine prohibiting cruel and unusual punishment under the Eighth Amendment, formed the foundation upon which courts upheld the rights of persons with handicaps.

In the early 1970s, special education classes typically served a range of students. Educational programming for these students varied immensely from social development to instruction in reading, writing, and arithmetic. Toward the mid–1970s, changes occurred in special education classrooms as students began moving back to regular classrooms. New concepts in the educational placement of students, "normalization," and "mainstreaming," were being put into effect. Concurrent with efforts to move students back into the regular classroom, an entirely new group of children was beginning to appear in the schools, those with severe handicaps.

Several litigative cases mandated that all children have the right to education and to treatment regardless of their handicaps. Many old laws were investigated with respect to the rights of students to a free public education. In general, the following rights formed the basis for providing education for all persons with handicaps: the right to racial equality in education; the right to testing, placement, and due process; the right to education; and the right to treatment.

Thirty years ago, education was interpreted by the U. S. Supreme Court to be of such extreme social importance that chilren, regardless of race, could not be denied it (*Brown* v. *Board of Education of Topeka*, 1954). This particular decision stated that education was a *right* and decreed that the opportunity for an education must be equal to all. Over a decade later, a nationwide attack was under way against public schools that denied equal educational opportunities to students with handicaps. Briefly, these denials of equal opportunities included excluding students from public schools, unjustifiably classifying persons as "retarded," funding special education services at lower levels than regular education services, establishing separate criteria for admission of persons with handicaps to school systems, limiting the size of special education classes and the capacity of special educational services, and failing to provide education for homebound or institutionalized persons. Categorically, the courts addressed each of the above discriminatory practices by ruling that excluding students from public schools was unconstitutional. They also ruled that classifying criteria must be revised and that IQ testing and placement be temporarily suspended. It was decided that school budgets be increased or amended to provide education for students with handicaps and that procedural due process be used in all schools' decisions excluding and classifying students. Special education was to be judicially supervised, and alternatives to classroom education were to be implemented.

Concurrent with the development of a right to education was the development in the courts of the right to treatment. This framework was based upon three well-known legal principles: procedural due process, sub-

stantive due process, and equal protection. Briefly defined, *procedural due process* guarantees each citizen the right to be informed about and to protest against government action. *Substantive due process* guarantees that individual rights and privileges may not arbitrarily be taken away; substantive due process also prevents the state from acting unreasonably, arbitrarily, or capriciously in dealing with a citizen. *Equal protection* guarantees the same rights and benefits for all citizens with respect to their government. Procedural due process was applied to prevent unjustified civil commitments of individuals to mental institutions and unjustified transfers of individuals from one type of an institution to another. Substantive due process and equal protection were applied to civil confinement in cases where the nature and duration of confinement bore no reasonable relation to the purposes for which the persons were being confined. Substantive due process and equal protection also applied when there was no rationale or compelling state interest in the classification or confinement. Equal protection further required that confinement be justified only when treatment and rehabilitation were available since confinement affected the fundamental right of personal liberty.

Although a number of cases were decided in many states, the cumulative results of all these decisions had not been enforced by any single state until the passage of Public Law 94–142, the Education for All Handicapped Children Act of 1975. This law authorized grants to states to assist them in initiating, expanding, and improving education programs for students between the ages of 3 and 21. The spirit of P. L. 94-142 was to ensure all school-aged children the following: (a) the right to *a free, appropriate public school education;* (b) the right to *educational placement based upon both informal and formal evaluations with input from the child's parent(s);* (c) the right to *educational programming in the least restrictive environment;* (d) the right to *an individualized educational program tailored to their individual needs*; and (e) the right to *a periodic review of the appropriateness of the educational plan.*

These rights were based upon five principles. The right to a free, appropriate public school education was based, in part, upon the *principle of zero exclusion* (Crowner, 1975). Zero exclusion maintains that every student is due a free, appropriate public education, and it implies that every student is educable regardless of level of functioning. Public Law 94-142 demanded that all individuals who had been excluded from school in the past and were within the state compulsory school-age limits be provided with appropriate educational services by the public schools. This decree challenged the practice of passing students from one agency to another.

The right to educational placement is based, in part, upon the *principle of nondiscriminatory testing*. This principle emanated from several litigative cases that sought to protect children from inappropriate classification. Two significant court cases were *Diana v. State Board of Education* (1973), a suit filed on behalf of nine Mexican-American children who were placed in special classes after being tested in English, and *Larry P. v. Riles* (1972), a suit that sought to eliminate the use of IQ tests in the San Francisco school district for the purpose of placing black children into special classes. The principle of nondiscriminatory testing requires: (a) that students be evaluated by a multidisciplinary team that includes at least one teacher or specialist with knowledge in the area of the specific disability (for instance, a specialist in occupational therapy, physical therapy, or speech therapy); (b) that tests or assessment instruments be administered in the child's native language, (for instance, Spanish) or some other method of communication (for instance, manual signs, communication boards); (c) that no single test or assessment instrument be used as the sole criterion for special education services, and that alternative methods of assessment be used (for instance, direct observation in the home or in the classroom); and (d) that tests

and assessment instruments be validated for the specific purpose for which they are used, and that these instruments serve a prescriptive function and do not merely generate a test score.

The right to educational programming in the least restrictive environment is based upon the *principle that,* to the maximum extent possible, *students should be educated in settings with students who are not handicapped.* This right maintains that students should *only* be segregated *if* the nature or severity of the handicap is such that education in integrated settings cannot be achieved with the use of supplementary aids, or that such supplementary services cannot be supplied satisfactorily. Called the *principle of least restrictive environment,* this principle is one that has led to much confusion. One interpretation has led to transferring students to regular classrooms which, for some children such as those with severe handicaps, has, in practice, been more restrictive than establishing quality services in nonintegrated settings (e.g., in classrooms with only students with severe handicaps). Thurman (1981) argued that "professionals involved in the individual education program (IEP) process must begin to become more aware of the necessity not only to stipulate least restrictive environments, but also to stipulate those environments which contain the physical and attitudinal supports that maximize habilitation" (p. 69). Previously, Thurman (1977) indicated that changing the student's social system is as important as changing the child. The least restrictive principle, then, contends that a student be placed in an educational environment where the student "is given enough support to express whatever competencies he or she possesses but not so much support that dependence results and thus additional learning is stunted" (Thurman, 1981, p. 69). The recommendation that the student be placed in an integrated setting is, unquestionably, an outgrowth of the principle of normalization (Wolfensberger, 1972) and the common knowledge that resulted from years of research on modeling, imitation, and learning (Baumeister, 1981).

The right to an individualized education program tailored to individual needs is based upon the *principle of a free and appropriate education*. The principle of a free and appropriate education is certainly related to the principle of least restrictive setting. No student is appropriately served if that student is not placed in a true learning setting, that is, a setting that requires the student to express his or her competencies and requires the acquisition of additional competencies to enjoy that setting more fully. The principle of appropriate education goes beyond the principle of least restrictive environment by suggesting that all students be provided with appropriate services, personnel, and facilities necessary to meet full educational opportunities. This has consequently included providing appropriate student-teacher ratios, appropriate age ranges within classrooms, normal schoolday hours, normal interactions between students who are handicapped and not handicapped, adequate supportive staff (for instance, occupational therapists and speech therapists), appropriate and adequate materials and equipment, functional curriculum content, adequate data based instruction, and adequate transportation services.

The Individualized Education Plan is a written document that summarizes a learning program tailored to a specific child. The IEP's two major functions are to establish learning goals and to stipulate services that must be provided to meet those learning goals. Both goals and services must be based upon an analysis of a student's strengths and weaknesses. The IEP is established or revised at the beginning of each school year, and all goals and services promised must be reviewed at least annually. P. L. 94-142 requires the IEP to include the following components:

a. A statement of the student's present levels of educational performance;

b. A statement of annual goals, including short term instructional objectives;

c. A statement of the specific education and re-

lated services to be provided to the student, including the extent to which the student will be able to participate in regular education programs;

d. The projected dates for initiation of services and the anticipated duration of the services; and

e. Appropriate objective criteria and evaluation procedures and schedules for determining, on at least an annual basis, whether the short term instructional objectives are being achieved.

Finally, the right to a periodic review of the appropriateness of the education plan is based upon the *principle of parent participation*. Parents have not always been included in decision-making relevant to the service their children will receive. Before P. L. 94-142, there were in fact no safeguards for parents. Children were not evaluated using their native language. And parents were not involved in making recommendations regarding what services their children would or should receive or provided the opportunity to question placement or services. As a result of P. L. 94-142, the principle of parent participation requires that parents give written consent prior to testing and evaluation. Parents must be included in the placement decision making process and be provided the necessary support to utilize whatever steps are necessary to have an impartial due process hearing if they are not in agreement with the decisions of the school board.

Although much of the work of this time was directed toward school-aged persons, adults with handicaps did not go unnoticed during the 1970s. Many adults, particularly those with severe handicaps, resided and worked in segregated facilities or remained in the home. The *principle of normalization, litigation, and research* resulted in changes, both positive and negative, for these individuals. Like education provided in schools, training provided in post-secondary school settings was centered around the existence of a continuum of services. Unfortunately, this continuum has not existed in the majority of our communities, nor has any coordination existed to advance adults from more restrictive to less restrictive residential and employment settings (Rusch, 1981). The seventies ended with 20,000 adults being referred to segregated, sheltered employment settings every year (Whitehead, 1981). Sheltered workshops, which are owned and operated by public and private nonprofit corporations, numbered about 3,000 in 1979 with approximately 200,000 adults receiving services (Whitehead, 1979). Although the growth and expansion of sheltered workshops has been extraordinary since the early 1960s, the majority of adults with handicaps have not been served by these programs (Urban Institute, 1975). Of those employed in workshops the average hourly wage in 1976 was only eighty-one cents (U.S. Department of Labor, 1979). Recent data reported by Bellamy, Rhodes, Bourbeau, and Mank (1986) indicated that if a person were placed into a typical sheltered workshop at the age of 18, this individual could expect to be of retirement age before advancing to competitive employment, based upon the average exiting data.

Since the mid-nineteenth century, when public residential facilities were first established, there has been steady growth in the number of such facilites. The number had increased from 105 in 1960 to approximately 260 in 1976 (Conroy, 1977; Scheerenberger, 1978). The number of persons residing in these settings approximated 150,000 in 1980. Between 1960 and 1980 about 4,000 community residential facilities were established in the United States (Heal, Novak, Sigelman, & Switzky, 1980). These facilities differed from public residential facilities because they were smaller in size and a small number of persons were served. They were located in the communities rather than outside city limits. They served persons largely between the ages of 15 and 30. The growth of community residential facilities was related to the introduction of the principle of normalization and at least three critical types of litigative cases that were decided during the years 1970 to 1980. Pertaining to deinstitutionalization, the courts first placed marked restrictions on who

could be considered eligible for admission to public residential facilities by ruling that no individuals with mild handicaps shall be a resident of an institution (*Wyatt* v. *Stickney*, 1972), unless that person suffers from psychiatric or emotional disorders in addition to his or her mental retardation (*Welsch* v. *Likens*, 1974) or is considered dangerous (*Lessard* v. *Schmidt*, 1972). Second, the courts ruled that no one shall be admitted to a residential facility until all other community resources have been considered and exhausted. And third, the courts ruled that no one shall reside in an institution longer than necessary.

In this period, the rights of adults with handicaps were recognized by the courts as well as by legislation in the form of the Rehabilitation Act Amendments of 1973 (P. L. 93-112). Although this law was passed in 1973, the regulations were not published until 1977. In part, this delay was due to its potential influence on schools and employers. Much of its language and implications were similar and complementary to the requirements of P.L. 94-142. The regulations of P.L. 93-112 applied to preschool, school, and adult level programs and to private facilities that received federal funds. P.L. 93-112 regulates the hiring, training, advancement, and retention of qualified workers with handicaps by employers that are under contract with the federal government for more than $2,500 per year. Section 503 P.L. 93-112, requires empoyers to initiate affirmative action measures for adults with handicaps seeking employment openings. These procedures assure that qualified applicants with handicaps are notified and are provided an equal opportunity to apply and be considered for employment. Section 504, described as the most comprehensive civil rights protection ever extended to persons with handicaps in the United States, challenges the fundamental actions and attitudes of all persons who are not handicapped with the following statement:

No otherwise qualfied handicapped individual . . . shall, solely by reason of his handicap, be excluded from the participation in, be denied the benefits of, or be subjected to discrimination under any program or activity receiving Federal financial assistance. (Section 504, The Rehabilitation Act Amendments of 1973)

The regulations that were finally drafted and issued in 1977 contained four basic regulations significant for persons with handicaps. These required that (a) programs be accessible; (b) individuals be offered a free public education: (c) all new facilities built after 1977, and all facilities by 1980 be barrier free; and (d) all materials and practices that discriminate against individuals be abolished.

The 1970s were good years for children, youth, and adults with handicaps. The 1970s were also very good for the field of special education since special educators were able to affirm the rights of students, employees, and residents by referring to laws rather than relying upon the philanthropy of educators and employers. Significant advances were also made in finding the best practices to follow in order to educate persons with handicaps. Such practices became contained in the legislation of P.L. 94-142 and P.L. 93-112. Zero-exclusion, nondiscriminatory testing, integration, appropriate education, individualized educational plans, and periodic review by the parents or guardians were all considered essential practices and formed the "principles" upon which "rights" were based. Although special education was strengthened by litigation and legislation during the 1970s, there remained significant challenges to be addressed as special education entered the 1980s.

SUMMARY

Special education has historical, philosophical, and legal foundations that prove it to be a vital and necessary addition to our educational and social communities. Historically, special education has been influenced by the superstitious beliefs of the past, the early work of several European physicians, the development of testing, the influences of wars, and the rise of vocational education. Philo-sophically, special education has most recently been dramatically influenced by the principle of normalization. Legally, the courts have affirmed that children, youth, and adults with handicaps have rights and that these rights must be acknowledged and protected. Historically, all professions, and the vast majority of persons associated with these professions, both public and private, have disregarded individuals with handicaps and have practiced discrimination against these individuals. Indeed, discrimination against persons with handicaps may be unsurpassed by other discriminatory practices such as racial and sexual discrimination, which have become well-understood.

Special education is a discipline that has grown from the efforts of educators, employers, and other members of our society to segregate individuals who differed from the majority and from the normal in the classroom, on the job, and in the community. In this chapter, we referred to special education as a discipline that seeks to educate children, youth, and adults who deviate from society's norms and fail to learn at rates equivalent to the majority of society's members. The *goal* of a special education is to integrate children, youth, and adults who deviate from society's norms into society. Today, we can look back and characterize special education as a field that has traditionally been associated with labels and the placement of persons according to those labels. In actuality, however, it is not special education per se but society that has labeled individuals. Special education grew as a field in the context of a society that segregated and discriminated.

This century began with a testing movement that estimated the potential of those with handicaps. It saw the development of vocational education as an alternative to regular education. Special education became well established in the fifties, sixties, and seventies and is today challenged as our society attempts to educate people and to prepare them for entry into normal community life. This chapter has overviewed some of the major events that led to the formation and growth of special education. In ensuing chapters we develop the procedures that are just beginning to characterize one approach to special education—an approach that focuses upon the education of members of our society who have special needs in integrated settings.

REFERENCES

BAUMEISTER, A. A. (1981). "Mental retardation policy and research: The unfulfilled promise." *American Journal of Mental Deficiency, 85,* 449–456.

BELLAMY, G. T., RHODES, L. E., BOURBEAU, P. E., & MANK, D. M. (1986). "Mental retardation services in sheltered workshops and day activity programs: Consumer benefits and policy alternatives." In F. R. Rusch (ed.), *Competitive employment issues and strategies* (pp. 257–271). Baltimore, MD: Paul H. Brookes.

BINET, A. (1909). *Les idees modernes sur les enfants.* Paris: E. Flammarion.

Brown v. Board of Education of Topeka, 347 U.S. 483 (1954).

CASSIDY, V. M., & STANTON, J. E. (1959). *An investigation of factors involved in the educational placement of mentally retarded children: A study of differences between children in special and regular classes in Ohio.* (United States Office of Education Cooperative Research Program, Project 043.) Columbus, OH: Ohio State University.

CONROY, J. W. (1977). "Trends in deinstitutionalization of the mentally retarded." *Mental Retardation, 15,* 44–46.

CROWNER, T. T. (1975). "A public school program for severely and profoundly handicapped students; Zero exclusion." In L. Brown, T. Crowner, W. Williams, & R. York (eds.), *Madison's alternative for zero exclusion: A book of readings* (pp. 112–169). Madison, WI: Madison Public Schools.

Diana v. State Board of Education, Civil No. C-70-37 R.F.P. (N.D. Cal. 1970 and 1973).

DUNN, L. M. (1968). "Special education for the mildly retarded: Is much of it justifiable?" *Exceptional Children, 35,* 5–22.

FRANKS, D. J. (1971). "Ethnic and social characteristics of children in EMR and LD classes." *Exceptional Children, 37,* 537–538.

GODDARD, H. H. (1912). *The Kallikak family.* New York: Macmillan.

GOLDSTEIN, H., MOSS, J. W. & JORDAN, L. J. (1965). *The efficacy of special class training on the development of mentally retarded children.* (United States Office of Education Cooperative Research Program, Project 619.) Urbana, IL: University of Illinois, Institute for Research on Exceptional Children.

HEAL, L. W., NOVAK, A. R., SIGELMAN, C. K., & SWITSKY, H. N. (1980). "Factors that affect the success of community placement." In L. W. Heal and A. R. Novak (eds.), *Integration of developmentally disabled individuals into the community* (pp. 45–74). Baltimore, MD: Paul H. Brookes.

KANNER, L. (1964). *A history of the care and study of the mentally retarded.* Springfield, IL: Charles Thomas.

KIRK, S. A. (1956). "A doctor's degree program in special education." *Exceptional Children, 24,* 50–52, 55.

LARRY, P. v. RILES, 343 F. Supp. 1306 (N.D. Cal. 1972).

LESSARD v. SCHMIDT, 349 F. Supp. 1078 (E.D. Wis. 1972).

LILLY, M. S. (1970). "Special education: A teapot in a tempest." *Exceptional Children. 37,* 43–49.

LORD, F. E. (1956). "A realistic look at special classes." *Exceptional Children, 22,* 321–325, 342.

MERCER, J. R. (1973). *Labelling the mentally retarded.* Berkeley, CA: University of California Press.

NELSON, N. (1971). *Workshops for the handicapped in the United States.* Springfield, IL: Charles C. Thomas.

NIRJE, B. (1969). "The normalization principle and its human management implications." In R. B. Kugel & W. Wolfensberger (eds.), *Changing patterns of residential services for the mentally retarded* (pp. 231–240). Washington, DC: President's Committee on Mental Retardation.

PRITCHARD, M. (1952). "Total school planning for the gifted child, part III." *Exceptional Children, 18,* 174–180.

Education for All Handicapped Children Act of 1975, P.L. 94-142, 20 U.S.C. 1401 *et seq.,* 89 Stat. 773.

Rehabilitation Act of 1973, P.L. 93-112, 87 Stat. 394, as amended by Sec. 19 of P.L. 95-602. 29 U.S.C. Sec. 794, 1977.

ROBINSON, N. M., & ROBINSON, H. B. (1976). *The mentally retarded child.* New York: McGraw-Hill.

ROSENTHAL, R., & JACOBSEN, L. (1968). *Pygmalion in the classroom.* New York: Holt, Rinehart & Winston.

RUSCH, F. R. (1981). "Reaction to work productivity and the developmentally disabled." In J. A. Leach (ed.), *Productivity in the workforce: A search for perspectives* (pp. 89–92). Champaign, IL: Office of Vocational Education, Department of Vocational and Technical Education, College of Education, University of Illinois.

SCHEERENBERGER, R. C. (1978). "Public residential services for the mentally retarded." Madison, WI: National Association of Superintendents of Public Residential Facilities for the Mentally Retarded, Central Wisconsin Center for the Developmentally Disabled. Also available in N. R. Ellis (ed.), *International review of research in mental retardation,* vol. 9. New York: Academic Press, 1978.

SEGUIN, E. O. (1866). *Idiocy and its treatment by the physiological method.* New York: W. Wood.

SMITH, D. J. (1985). *Minds made feeble: The myth and legacy of the Kallikaks.* Rockville, MD: Aspen Systems Corporation.

TENNY, J. W. (1952). "The president's message: Financial problems in special education." *Exceptional Children, 18,* 187.

TERMAN, L. (1919). *The intelligence of school children.* New York: Houghton Mifflin.

THURMAN, S. K. (1977). "The congruence of behavioral ecologies: A model for special educa-tion programming." *Journal of Special Education, 11,* 329–333.

THURMAN, S. K. (1981). "Least restrictive environments: Another side of the coin." *Education and Training of the Mentally Retarded, 16,* 68–70.

Urban Institute (1975). Report of the comprehensive service needs study. Washington, DC: Urban Institute.

U.S. Department of Labor (1979, March). Study of handicapped clients in sheltered workshops (vol. II). Washington, DC: U.S. Department of Labor.

VIOLAS, P. C. (1978). *The training of the urban working class: A history of twentieth century American education.* Chicago: Rand McNally.

WELSCH v. LIKENS, 373 F. Supp. 487 (D. Minn. 1974).

WHITEHEAD, C. (1979). "Sheltered workshops in the decade ahead: Work and wages, or welfare." In G. T. Bellamy, G. O'Connor, & O. C. Karan (eds.), *Vocational rehabilitation of severely hand-icapped persons* (pp. 71–84). Baltimore, MD: University Park Press.

WHITEHEAD, D. (1981). "Employment and training of handicapped individuals." Unpublished manuscript. Washington, DC: Department of Health and Human Services.

WHITEHOUSE, F. A. (1951). "Teamwork, an approach to a higher professional level." *Exceptional Children, 18,* 75–82.

WOLFENSBERGER, W. (1972). *Normalization: The principle of normalization in human services.* Toronto, Ont., Canada: National Institute on Mental Retardation.

WYATT v. STICKNEY, 344 F. Supp. 373 (M.D. Ala. 1972).

chapter 2

Behavior Analysis: Development of a Technology

In Chapter 1 we indicated that different reasons have been used to explain why individuals deviate from established norms. Early explanations ranged from possession by evil spirits to family traits. Medical explanations were often used. More recently, the environment and events within environments have been suggested as contributing to the way individuals behave. Each of these explanations has contributed to the evolution of educational practices and services over time. With this in mind, we defined special education as the application of goals and methods used to teach persons who deviate frrom society's norms or fail to learn at rates equivalent to the majority of society's members. We also indicated that the practical concern of contemporary special education was to change environmental events which would lead to changes in behavior so that individuals could function within integrated social communities. This definition of special education is an important one because it focuses attention upon factors that we have some influence over, that is, environments and behavior.

This chapter introduces applied behavior analysis and chronicles its foundation. *Applied behavior analysis* refers to the selective use of principles of behavior (for example, reinforcement, punishment, and stimulus control) and to the simultaneous evaluation, based upon societal values, of behavior change as a function of manipulating environmental events according to these principles. Special education and applied behavior analysis are related in their intent (education) and in their efforts to evaluate individual behavior with reference to society's values. Their differences lie largely in the principles and methodology that are used to change behavior. Applied behavior analysis exclusively utilizes behavioral principles, whereas special education has tended to borrow from a broader theoretical base including developmental, psychoanalytic, and cognitive psychological theories. Also, special education has focused exclusively upon individuals with handicaps, whereas behavior analysis has been applied not only to persons with handicaps, but also to diverse populations, such as students, parents, athletes, and prisoners.

Today, special education and behavior analysis enjoy widespread use; the marriage between the two has been an important development. The discipline of special education has incorporated behavior analytic methods and has pursued almost endless combinations of these methods to solve problems of decided social importance. Behavior analysis in special education has gained tremendous respectability within the academic community; numerous journals report the use of behavioral approaches to problemsolving in special education.

Traditional approaches to conceptualizing, diagnosing, assessing, and treating deviant behavior have posed challenges to the emergence of applied behavior analysis in special education. Among the traditional approaches, the "medical" or "disease" model has posed the major challenge in spite of the absence of evidence that this model is effective (Eysenck, 1961; Fraley & Vargas, 1986; Levitt, 1963). The medical model, when applied to behavior, implies that deviant symptoms are the result of underlying processes analogous to "diseases." Because biological factors have been shown to be related to deviate behavior, the disease model has been accepted as an appropriate model for all types of deviate behavior. However, when the disease model has been suggested to account for deviate behavior without an identified organic basis, questions have arisen over the veracity of this extrapolation (Kazdin, 1978). Special education and behavior analysis have emerged with a revolutionary new perspective on human behavior, one that by-passes for the most part the traditional theories of underlying processes and inner states of the mind.

In special education, diagnosing a deviate behavior pattern with regard to a label (that

is, an underlying process) and then positing the label as the cause of the behavior has been called *reification* (Whelan, 1972). For example, much of the classical terminology used in special education to describe behavior patterns has evolved from the medical model. The medical model has used terms, such as dyslexia, to represent symptoms of learning problems. Dyslexia is the term often used to represent the partial inability to read characterized by associative learning difficulties. The problem with such labels is that they are used to describe (reify) the cause of the problem. For example, the statement "she reads poorly" leads educators to label the child, that is, the child who cannot read, as "dyslexic." When the teacher is asked, "Why does she read poorly?" the answer is "Because she is dyslexic." The focus of special education has been labeling the child based upon the cause rather than describing the problem in terms of the performance, and performance can be changed. Consequently, people have been labeled based upon terminology borrowed from a medical orientation. These labels have formed traditional categories that are selfsustaining in that they contribute to "reification" of the labels used. The pervasiveness of this medical orientation in special education is evidenced by the implicit embracing of the medical model in the use of such terms as "dyslexia," "treatment," "therapy," "disability," and "rehabilitation."

As will be seen in this chapter, educators who view special education from a behavioranalytic perspective do not see the need to use terminology borrowed from the medical model (for example, Deitz, 1982). This chapter delineates this position and provides an overview of the historical developments leading to the formation of applied behavior analysis, including philosophical and psychological traditions dating from the nineteenth century. Because behavior analysis has a distinctive environmental focus, no attempt is made to review biochemical explanations (Cott, 1972); biophysical explanations (Berry, 1969); developmental explanations (Fine,

1973; Kessler, 1966); or theories of cognitive and moral development (Piaget & Inhelder, 1969). This chapter introduces the experimental foundations of applied behavior analysis by emphasizing the work of physiologists and the development of behaviorism, the experimental foundations of behavior modification, and the subsequent birth of the applied behavior analysis approach. As with Chapter 1, we delineate periods of time that appear to best chronicle the development of applied behavior analysis. We begin with an overview of the nineteenth century. This is followed by the twentieth century divided into four periods: (a) 1900–1950: Focus upon Replication and Refinement; (b) 1950–1960: Extensions of Operant Conditioning to Humans; (c) 1960–1970: Birth of Applied Behavior Analysis; and (d) 1970–1980: Development of a Heart.

1800–1900: Experimental Foundations of Applied Behavior Analysis

Early behavior research consisted largely of observing the individual in his or her natural environment and recording behavior. For example, Charles Darwin's (1877) observation and recording of his own infant's behavior served as a prototype for numerous infant biographies compiled in the 1880s. Today, the case history method of documenting behavior is a direct outgrowth of the methods used by Darwin and others in the late nineteenth century. *Naturalistic observation* provided potentially invaluable information about the behavior of selected individuals. These studies were, however, extremely selective in the choice of who was observed, and they were also characterized by subjectivity in design, both in the choice of behaviors selected for recording and in the definition and criteria used to evaluate behavior change. Later, experimental research methodology began to emerge in laboratory settings and to offer a number of advantages over these earlier naturalistic studies. Laboratory research eliminated variables that might have interfered

with or confounded a study, allowed the systematic presentation and removal of these experimental variables, and precisely measured behaviors under investigation (Moore, 1985).

Behavior has been divided into two separate classes: respondent and operant. *Respondent behavior* refers to behavior, often reflexive, that requires no previous learning and is considered part of the physiology of an individual. *Operant behavior* refers to behavior which has an effect or "operates" on the environment. Toward the end of the nineteenth century, physiologists studied respondent behavior in laboratory settings and developed most of the important laws of respondent behavior that are still with us today. Although examples of operant behavior research are documented throughout the seventeenth, eighteenth, and nineteenth centuries, its principles were not firmly established in laboratory settings until the 1930s. Respondent behavior (respondents) is commonly distinguished from operant behavior (operants) in two ways. First, respondents are controlled by their eliciting stimuli or antecedents, whereas operants are controlled by their consequences (Skinner, 1938). Secondly, respondents are either present at birth (unconditioned or unlearned responses) or are learned. Respondents present at birth are known as *unconditioned reflexes*, such as the knee jerk reflex and pupillary constriction. Unconditioned reflexes, or unconditioned respondents, are elicited by unconditioned stimuli. For example, if a light is shined in a child's eye, the pupil will contract. The unconditioned stimulus is the light shone in the eye and the unconditioned response is the pupil contraction. This relationship was quantitatively studied by physiologists, such as Sir Charles Sherrington at the turn of century.

The most famous account of respondent conditioning was reported by Ivan P. Pavlov, a Russian physiologist. Pavlov's classic experiment with dogs involved pairing food powder (unconditioned stimulus) with a tone (neutral stimulus). Initially, the unconditioned response (salivation) was demonstrated to be elicited by an unconditioned stimulus (food). The tone was initially considered a neutral stimulus because when it was presented it did not elicit an unconditioned response. However, after the neutral stimulus (the tone) had been repeatedly paired with the unconditioned stimulus (the food powder), Pavlov was able to demonstrate that the tone *alone* would elicit salivation. This process is known as *respondent conditioning.* The neutral stimulus (the tone) is called a conditioned or learned stimulus when it is capable of eliciting a conditioned response that is similar to the unconditioned response. When the conditioned stimulus elicits a conditioned response, this new relationship is called a *conditioned reflex.* The major difference between the work of Pavlov and the work of physiologists such as Sherrington was that Pavlov studied reflexes that were formed by the interaction of behavior with environmental stimuli, whereas physiologists such as Sherrington studied reflexes determined by heredity.

These physiologists greatly influenced the foundations of applied behavior analysis. Foremost was their vigorous advocation of the use of objective methods to study the issues of psychology. Their work also led to the establishment of "lawful relations," with regard to animal behavior. This in turn led to the study of similar relationships among humans and the development of some well known processes such as extinction, generalization, and discrimination. These lawful relations were the result of observation, experimentation, and description of natural phenomenon. Discovery of a relation between a variable (such as tone) and a behavior is referred to as a *functional relationship.* The applied behavior analysis approach is concerned with identifying functional relationships.

Concurrent with increased research in the physiology of animals and the study of reflexology in Russia was the development of comparative animal psychology in America, Great Britain, and Europe. In America, Edward L. Thorndike (1874–1949) studied factors affecting learning in cats and dogs that emphasized

"associations" between situations and responses. Thorndike (1905) formulated two laws: (a) the *Law of Effect,* which states that "any response which in a situation produces satisfaction becomes associated with that situation, so that when the situation recurs the (response) is more likely than before to recur . . . " (p. 205), and (b) the *Law of Exercise,* which states "that a response made in a particular situation becomes associated with the situation." The Law of Effect relates directly to the principle of reinforcement and the Law of Exercise relates directly to stimulus control. Briefly, the *principle of reinforcement* in behavior analysis refers to the procedure whereby a stimulus increases the frequency of a response when that response is followed immediately by a consequence, or stimulus, that has reinforcing properties. The *principle of stimulus control* in behavior analysis refers to the procedure whereby a stimulus occasions differential responding in the presence of antecedent events (the stimulus) that are associated with reinforcing and punishing consequences.

In spite of their shared emphasis upon the use of objective, experimental methodology, the work in Russia, in America, and in Great Britain developed independently around the turn of the nineteenth century. Nevertheless the experimental method of studying animal behavior was well established by 1900. The development of this experimental research methodology was especially important because it challenged directly many of the subjective accounts of human and animal behavior.

1900–1950: Focus upon Replication and Refinement

The turn of the century witnessed extensions of respondent conditioning experiments to humans in Russia and America. One of the earliest accounts reported in America was by Edwin B. Twitmyer (1873–1943) at the University of Pennsylvania. While conducting his dissertation research on the knee jerk, Twitmyer serendipitously discovered the conditioned reflex by pairing the stimulation of the tendons in the knee with the ringing of a bell. Twitmyer's work, however, went unnoticed at the time primarily because considerable interest was already focused upon the major work of Pavlov and others in Russia.

Krasnogorski (1907), a colleague of Pavlov's, was one of the first researchers to demonstrate that respondent conditioning was possible with humans. Krasnogorski directly extended Pavlov's salivary conditioning experiment to a 14-month-old child. He presented food as the unconditioned stimulus (US), measured the amount of salivation as the unconditioned response (UR), and conditioned the salivatory reflex by presenting the sound of a bell (neutral stimulus) immediately before the food was presented to the child. Ultimately, the sound of the bell alone was sufficient to elicit salivation (a conditioned response); thus, the bell had become a conditioned stimulus (CS).

Respondent conditioning was also demonstrated to be possible with emotional responses. Watson and Raynor (1920) reported the first laboratory attempt to condition an emotional response in a child named Albert. This experiment began with Albert being shown a white rat, a rabbit, a dog, and several other animals and objects. Initially, Albert showed no fear or emotional reactions (conditioned emotional reactions) to any of the animals or objects. The next step in this experiment was to find an unconditioned stimulus

(US) capable of eliciting an unconditioned emotional response. Watson and Raynor selected a loud tone (produced by striking a steel bar with a hammer) that produced the unconditioned emotional reactions of crying, trembling, and startle in Albert. Given this finding, Watson and Raynor set out to establish a white rat as a conditioned stimulus to which the conditioned response of crying would be formed. The white rat (neutral stimulus) was then presented to Albert and when the child reached for the rat, an experimenter struck the steel bar with a hammer (unconditioned stimulus). At this point, Albert withdrew his hand and demonstrated the unconditioned emotional responses characteristically displayed when the loud tone was presented alone (that is, crying and trembling). Following one week without conditioning, Albert was again presented with the white rat. This time he did not reach for the white rat, but simply stared at it. This reaction led Watson and Raynor to suggest that the pairing of the loud noise with the rat, a week earlier, did produce a change in Albert's behavior (conditioned emotional response).

Subsequent pairings of the white rat and the loud tone firmly established the relationship between the once neutral stimulus (the rat) and the unconditioned stimulus (the loud tone) forming a conditioned emotional response. Further, when Albert was presented with a white dog, a white fur coat, white cotton wool and a white Santa Claus mask, he either cried, turned away, attempted to crawl

KRASNOGORSKI CONDITIONING EXPERIMENT

1. An unconditioned stimulus (US) elicits an unconditioned response (UR).

2. A neutral stimulus, the sound of a bell, is paired with the unconditioned stimulus (food).

3. The neutral stimulus functions as a conditioned stimulus when it becomes capable of eliciting a conditioned response that is similar to the unconditioned response.

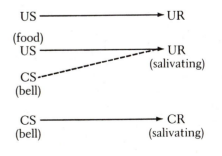

away, or hid his head. These reactions led the investigators to conclude that condtioned emotional responses *generalize*. That is, when presented a second stimulus similar to the conditioned stimulus, the second similar stimulus would elicit the conditioned response. Additionally, the more similar the second stimulus to the conditioned stimulus, the greater the magnitude of the conditioned response. With this experiment, Watson and Raynor provided a clear and simple example of how emotional behavior could be conditioned.

Following this early conditioned experiment, Mary Cover Jones published the results of her efforts to eliminate these same fear responses. Working under Watson's supervision, Jones taught a young child named Peter not to elicit severe anxiety responses when in the presence of furry objects such as feathers, wool rugs, and, especially, white rabbits. She taught him to play affectionately with a white rabbit by slowly and systematically moving the rabbit, contained in a cage, closer to him over the course of several days. Eventually, the rabbit was let out of the cage and allowed to play closer to Peter while Peter was eating. Ultimately, Peter's fear of rabbits and other furry objects disappeared. These accounts are reported in *The Elimination of Children's Fears* and *A Laboratory Study of Fear: The Case of Peter* (Jones, 1924a, 1924b). Watson also reported the treatment of Peter in his text, *Behaviorism*, when he wrote, "Finding that emotional responses could be built in with great readiness, we were eager to see next whether they could be broken down, and if so by what methods" (1924, p. 167).

Jonn B. Watson (1878–1958) was, in particular, responsible for extending the objectivism of comparative psychology to human behavior, and he is generally regarded as the first "behaviorist." His first published paper announcing the behavioral position suggested that psychology was the study of behavior (performance), rather than the study of nonobservable events (mental processes). The following passage from "Psychology as the Behaviorist Views It" is considered a classic:

Psychology as the behaviorist views it is a purely objective experimental branch of natural science. Its theoretical goal is the prediction and control of behavior. Introspection forms no essential part of its methods, nor is the scientific value of its data dependent upon the readiness with which they lend themselves to interpretation in terms of consciousness. The behaviorist, in his efforts to get a unitary schema of animal response, recognizes the dividing line between man and brute. The behavior of man, with all of its refinement and complexity, forms only a part of the behaviorist's total scheme of investigation.

(Watson, 1913, p. 158)

Watson originated the term "behaviorism" (1914), and he rejected data that did not result from observation of overt behavior. He considered such concepts as mind, instinct, thought, and emotion as useless and superfluous, and his view of human behavior was based almost exclusively upon the importance of the environment in determining behavior (Todd & Morris, 1986).

Watson was succeeded by several noted psychologists, including Edwin R. Guthrie, Edward C. Tolman, Clark L. Hull, O. Hobart Mowrer, and B. F. Skinner. Each played an important part in the advancement of behaviorism. Guthrie is known for his introduction of *contiguous conditioning*, which refers to the likelihood of a response recurring in a situation where it was once performed. A most important extrapolation made by Guthrie (1959) was not how learning developed, but how undesirable behaviors could be unlearned. From Guthrie's work came systematic desensitization (Franks, 1969) and implosive therapy (Marks, 1972) which are recent behavior change techniques, used to eliminate fear or anxiety responses. Typically, systematic desensitization is accomplished by pairing an anxiety-inhibiting response (for example, deep muscle relaxation) with gradually increasing intensities of fear-evoking stimuli. In contrast, implosive therapy usually exposes the individual to intense anxiety provoking stimuli. By repeatedly exposing the person to the conditioned stimulus, the stimulus eventually loses its ability to produce the conditioned emotional response of anxiety.

Tolman differed from Watson, and many of his behavioral contemporaries, in what he considered to be the eventual goal of behavioral studies. He believed that individuals did not learn specific responses in larger behavioral chains, but rather, "learned meanings and developed cognitions about various stimuli vis-à-vis a goal" (Kazdin, 1978). He did, however, utilize the major methodological tenets of behaviorism including an emphasis upon objective description, an absolute unit-based measurement system, an experimental approach, and an eventual statement of a functional relation.

Hull accounted for habit formation, as discussed by Thorndike, by suggesting that the relationship between a stimulus and a response was strengthened when the drive for the stimulus was reduced. He implied that learning involved the reduction of basic biological drives, such as hunger and thirst (Dollard & Miller, 1950; Hull, 1943). The reinforcement potential of stimuli having no obvious relation to the basic needs was generally ignored in his *drive reduction theory*, with only those stimuli capable of reducing the more basic biological drives being considered capable of reinforcing behaviors.

Finally, Mowrer, a colleague of Hull's at Yale, integrated Pavlov's and Thorndike's theories in a revision and extension of Hull's drive reduction theory. Mowrer suggested that not all learning could be accounted for by the reduction of drives. In particular, Mowrer pointed out that drive reduction could not easily explain avoidance learning under punishment conditions and implied that the "stamping out" process developed by Thorndike resulted in the development of specific behaviors. For example, an adult punished for speeding learned how to drive (behave) in a particular manner (at a speed approximating the posted speed).

Mowrer (Mowrer & Mowrer, 1938) also pioneered practical applications of learning principles, particularly of respondent conditioning. Between 1934 and 1940, in addition to being on the staff of the Institute of Human Relations at Yale University, Mowrer and his wife (Willie Mae C. Mowrer) were "house parents" of 24 children. Many of these children were enuretic, and the Mowrers were resolved to apply Pavlovian conditioning in an effort to make bladder distention a conditioned stimulus for waking instead of a conditioned stimulus for bedwetting. The Mowrers developed an apparatus and training procedure that was effective in eliminating enuresis in 38 children. The apparatus consisted of a water sensitive pad connected to a battery and a bell. The pad was placed on the bed underneath the child. If the child urinated, the urine completed an electrical circuit that rang the bell. The bell woke the child who then was required to change clothes, bedding, and the covering on the water-sensitive pad. In this experiment, the unconditioned stimulus was the bell; bladder tension, produced by the filling of the bladder with urine, was the neutral stimulus. After the filled bladder (which immediately preceded the ringing of the bell) was paired with the bell, the filled bladder became a conditioned stimulus capable of waking the child. More recently, similar procedures have been tried in toilet training normal children (Mahoney, Van Wegenan, & Meyerson, 1971) and children and adults with mental retardation (Azrin & Foxx, 1971; Foxx & Azrin, 1973).

Like Hull and Mowrer, B. F. Skinner's work was crucial in the formulation of behavior analysis and its applications. After graduating from Harvard University, Skinner embarked upon a highly productive research and teaching career. Among his works are several texts devoted to the experimental analysis of behavior, including *The Behavior of Organisms* (1938), *Science and Human Behavior* (1953), *Verbal Behavior* (1957), *Cumulative Record* (1959), and *Schedules of Reinforcement* (with C. B. Ferster, 1957).

During the early part of Skinner's career, his research was largley confined to the laboratory. It was devoted to the development of principles of operant conditioning and the experimental analysis of behavior. Some of

B. F. Skinner.
Photo by Susan Hogue.

Skinner's original work focused upon respondents and operants, and the two types of conditioning procedures (that is, unconditioned and conditioned) involved in developing operant and respondent responses (Skinner, 1935,

1937, 1938). Pavlov and Thorndike had already introduced the two types of conditioning procedures. Pavlov's procedures stressed the relation between a new stimulus and a reflex; Thorndike's procedure stressed the relation between a given stimulus and a new response. Skinner (1937) introduced two conditioning types, Type S conditioning and Type R conditioning, to distinguish between the two classes of responses, respondents and operants. Pavlov's respondent paradigm was referred to as Type S conditioning because reinforcement was correlated with the *stimulus*. Thorndike's paradigm was referred to as Type R conditioning because the reinforcement was correlated with the *response*. This distinction was important because, until this time, much of the earlier behavioral work focused upon respondent conditioning rather than operant conditioning.

Initially, Skinner's goal was to discover lawful relations between behavior and the consequences of behavior (Skinner, 1956). His earlier work focused upon animal behavior and was free of any theorizing about abstract physiological processes. Skinner used the white rat in his experiments and he designed elaborate, automated experimental equipment in which to study the responses of his rats. His development of automated equipment to record the responses of his rats con-

Skinner's Type S and Type R Conditioning Paradigms

The Law of Conditioning of Type S.	The Law of Conditioning of Type R.
"The approximately simultaneous presentation of two stimuli, one of which (the 'reinforcing' stimulus) belongs to a reflex existing at the moment at some strength, may produce an increase in the strength of a third reflex composed of the response of the reinforcing reflex and the other stimulus." (Skinner, 1938, p. 18)	"If the occurrence of an operant is followed by presentation of a reinforcing stimulus, the strength is increased." (Skinner, 1938, p. 21)
The Law of Extinction of Type S.	The Law of Extinction of Type R.
"If the reflex strengthened through conditioning of Type S is elicited without presentation of the reinforcing stimulus, its strength decreases." (Skinner, 1938, pp. 18–19)	"If the occurrence of an operant already strengthened through conditioning is not followed by the reinforcing stimulus, the strength is decreased." (Skinner, 1938, p. 21)

tinues to greatly facilitate experimental work in operant conditioning.

Skinner continued to refine his experimental equipment until he accomplished the design of a soundproof box that contained a food tray with a reloadable magazine, a light, and a lever that was connected to a cumulative recorder. This apparatus became popularly known as "Skinner's box." White rats were placed into this soundproof box in order to study their lever-pressing responses, which were automatically recorded on a graph. Briefly, a step-wise linear graph was created by a kymograph and vertically moving pen. The slope of the line depicted the rate of response; the steeper the line the higher the response rate. Utilizing the Skinner Box, Skinner identified substantive "principles of operant conditioning." These principles of operant conditioning describe the effects of consequences that follow behavior and include four basic operations: (a) presenting positive or removing aversive stimuli after a response, known as reinforcement; (b) presenting aversive or removing positive stimuli after a response, known as punishment; (c) discontinuing the presenting of a reinforcing stimulus after a response, known as extinction; and (d) reinforcing a response in the presence of one stimulus but not in the presence of another stimulus, known as stimulus control. Each of these operations is described more fully subsequently.

BASIC PRINCIPLES OF OPERANT CONDITIONING

Reinforcement. The *principle of reinforcement* refers to a procedure in which a response produces a stimulus change and, as a result, becomes more probable. The term "reinforce" means to "strengthen," and, therefore, the term *reinforcement* refers to the process of strengthening. There are two operations that can strengthen a response. The first operation, *positive reinforcement*, refers to the procedure that results in increased responding when a stimulus is presented. The second procedure, *negative reinforcement*, results in increased responding when a stimulus is removed. The terms "positive" and "negative" in operant conditioning mean respectively, "to add" something or "to subtract" something. Skinner exemplified these two operations either by delivering food to the white rat contingent upon pressing the level (positive reinforcement), or by terminating an

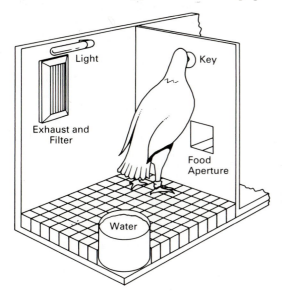

(a) Experimental Chamber

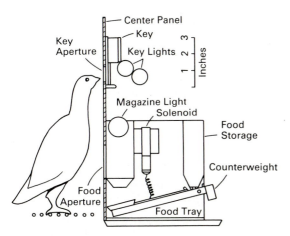

(b) Side view of experimental chamber and associated apparatus

Figure 2.2 "Skinner's Box"

electrical shock contingent upon pressing the lever (negative reinforcement). In these two examples, lever pressing responses increased as a function of food delivery or shock cessation, respectively.

Punishment. The *principle of punishment* refers to the procedure in which responding produces a stimulus change, and, as a result of this change, the responding becomes less probable. Just as there are two types of reinforcement there are two types of punishment, positive and negative. In *positive punishment*, the stimulus change is one in which something is added to the environment. In *negative punishment*, the stimulus change is one in which something is taken away from the environment. *Positive punishment* refers to the procedure of decreasing the probability of a response by presenting a stimulus, such as a shock, when a white rat presses the lever. *Negative punishment* also refers to the procedure of decreasing the probability of a response; however, the stimulus, such as a food source, is removed after a white rat presses the lever.

Extinction. The *extinction principle* refers to the procedure in which a response that was previously reinforced is no longer reinforced. Extinction and punishment both result in decreases in responding. Extinction differs from punishment in that, when the extinction procedure is utilized, there are simply no consequences following the response. In contrast, punishment procedures rely upon either the presentation of a negative event (for instance, shock) or the removal of a positive event (for instance, the food magazine). Both of these are contingent upon responding. With extinction there is no consequence; rather, the previously reinforced response is no longer reinforced. For example, in laboratory research the food is no longer delivered contingent upon lever pressing. Typically, once food no longer follows lever pressing, extinction eventually results in the reduction or complete elimination of the response.

Stimulus Control. Another principle that is very important in behavior analysis is the *principle of stimulus control. Stimulus control* refers to the extent to which an antecedent

---

Paradigms for each of Skinner's Principles of Reinforcement and Punishment

Positive Reinforcement Paradigm	Negative Reinforcement Paradigm
R ⟶ S^{+R}	S^{-R} ⟶ R $\cancel{S}^{R}$
(lever press) (food)	(shock) (lever press) (shock discontinued)
When an operant reponse is followed by a reinforcing consequence, it results in an increase in occurrence of the operant response.	In the presence of an aversive stimulus (S^{-R}), the operant response (R) discontinues the presentation of the aversive stimulus, which results in an increase in the frequency of occurrence of the operant response.

Positive Punishment Paradigm	Negative Punishment Paradigm
R ⟶ S^{-R}	S^{+R} ⟶ R ⟶ $\cancel{S}^{R}$
(lever press) (shock)	(food, magazine) (lever press) (no food magazine)
An operant response is followed by presentation of an aversive event (S^{-R}), which functions to decrease the frequency of that operant response.	In the presence of a positive reinforcer the operant response is followed by the removal of the positive reinforcer, which results in a decrease in the frequency of occurrence of the operant response.

stimulus determines the probability that a particular response will occur. The control that antecedent stimuli exert on the response results from the following: (a) the response being reinforced if it occurs in the presence of a discriminative stimulus (abbreviated SD); (b) the response not being reinforced in the presence of S-deltas (abbreviated S△); and (c) other responses not being reinforced in the presence of the SD. In Skinner's experiments, when the white rat responded differentially to different stimuli, the rat was said to be under *stimulus control*. For example, if the rat depressed the lever in the presence of a red light but not in the presence of a green light, the rat was under stimulus control of the red light. The stimulus conditions (that is, the red light and the green light) exerted control over behavior because of the different consequences with which each stimulus was associated (that is, reinforcement when the light was red versus no reinforcement when the light was green, respectively).

Paradigms for each of Skinner's Principles of Extinction and Stimulus Control

---

Extinction Paradigm

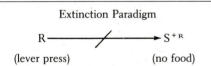

An operant response, which was previously reinforced, ceases to produce reinforcing consequences, and thus decreases to its pre-reinforcement rate.

Stimulus Control Paradigm

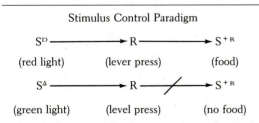

In the presence of a discriminative stimulus (S^D) the operant response is positively reinforced; an operant response that is emitted in the presence of an S-delta (S^△) is not reinforced.

The Experimental Analysis of Behavior

B. F. Skinner's contribution to behavior analysis were methodological as well as conceptual. Skinner stressed a methodological approach to the study of behavior that is referred to as the "experimental analysis of behavior." This approach contains several characteristics that Skinner believed were essential to produce a true science of behavior. These characteristics included: (a) the study of single subjects; (b) a focus upon experimental control of the experimental environment; (c) the recording of behavior as a function of time; (d) a concentration upon an independent variable's influence on the subject's behavior; and (e) the continuous and repeated observation of behavior.

The Single Subject. One of the major elements of any scientific experiment is *control*. *Control* refers to operations that are undertaken that enable us to conclude, after a experiment has been conducted, that factor A led to the results and *not* factors B, C, D, or E. Traditionally, in psychology and education control is achieved by the use of a *control* group. Theoretically, the "control" group represents individuals who are the same in every respect as the "experimental" group, except that the specific manipulation that is under examination is available only to the experimental group. Thus, any differences observed between the experimental group and the control group are ascribed to the experimental manipulation. This assumption, however, has long been known to be untrue (Campbell & Stanley, 1963) because each individual within the group has a learning and maturational history that is unique. These sources of differences between individuals in experimental and control groups cloud the conclusions that can be made, but these sources are all controlled in single-subject research.

In contrast to experiments in which specific groups are used to achieve control, Skinner employed the "subject-as-his-own-control" design. Typically, in the single-subject aproach a small number of subjects are studied. The researcher observes a selected aspect of behavior of the subjects at repeated points in time, and then the researcher introduces an experimental manipulation and observes the selected aspect as it changes the subject's behavior. The purpose of studying the single subject is to reveal behavioral changes of the individual. The single-subject approach asks the question "How does the behavior of the same individual differ under alternative situations?" When control groups are used, the essential question is: "How does the behavior of the control group differ from the behavior of the experimental group?" Data that is based upon groups of subjects represent the "average person", and such data cannot represent the performance of any single person. Because of this Skinner (1950) sought to develop "a science of the individual."

Experimental Control. One of the basic methodological problems of conducting traditional experiments is accounting for the differences between control and experimental groups. Frequently, group differences are caused by factors other than the planned manipulations being studied. To partially combat unwanted external influences, Skinner emphasized the use of a soundproof box that eliminated unwanted external influences and provided an environment whereby the experimenter could control experimental variables very precisely. Skinner also ruled out external influences by applying design features to his experiments. One of these included controlling the order in which independent variables were manipulated, proving that a specific reinforcement schedule, for example, was the important element in changing behavior and not a sequence of one schedule following another in the experiment. The objective of experimental control is to ascribe behavior changes to changes in the environment and not to something else.

Response Rate. The study of the frequency of behavior over time provided a major methodological advance in the experimental analysis of behavior. Response rate

simplified analysis and interpretation of data, which allowed for the quantification of change. All questions of science, including those posed by Skinner, must be made answerable by answering the question in terms of events that are observable and quantifiable. Skinner (1950) focused upon the task of explaining the conditions that dictate response probability, for example, by detailing the influence of various schedules of reinforcement upon rate of responding.

Functional Relations. The credibility of a science of human behavior is tied to the ability to replicate the findings and show them as "real." The importance of Skinner's early work was tied to how reliable his principles were. Skinner realized the necessity for carrying out his work in a manner that allowed others to make the same observations and conclusions. His principles of operant conditioning were the result of his research focusing upon demonstrated functional relationships, and not upon mere theory or hypothesis. *Functional relationships* refer to the effects of experimental treatments (the independent variables) upon the rate of a selected response (for example, the lever press response).

Demonstrating that a particular relationship was replicable served only part of Skinner's aims. Once Skinner completed his work in the area of identifying principles of operant conditioning, he focused his interest upon the generality of his principles. Characteristically, research in operant conditioning tested functional relationships using rats, pigeons, and monkeys. It was not until around 1950 that the generality of Skinner's principles were tested among humans. This research is examined in the next section of this chapter.

Continuous Observation and Recording of Behavior. One of the most important characteristics of the experimental analysis of behavior is its reliance upon the objective recording of behavior over extended time periods. Early research techniques included automated equipment, such as the cumulative recorder, to record behavioral output. This monitoring equipment assisted in the continuous recording of behavior, which allowed researchers to increase the number and complexity of experiments that required hundreds of hours of time. Incorporating the continuous observation and recording of behavior made it possible for researchers to control for human error in assessment by utilizing standardized methods. The principles and methods of Skinner's research methodology and analysis eventually led to the study of human behavior in natural environments (that is, applied behavior analysis). To date, no other approach to the study of human behavior has enjoyed such widespread growth. Nevertheless, before 1950, it was unclear how the results of Skinner's voluminous laboratory work really related to social concerns and contemporary issues regarding human behavior.

Several important events occurred just prior to 1950, which greatly influenced the systematic extension of Skinner's work to nonlaboratory settings. While Skinner was developing his arguments for extensions of operant principles to all types of behavior and social situations, a very simple but interesting experiment was reported by Paul R. Fuller in 1949. Fuller sought to determine if he could teach an essentially inactive, 18-year-old "vegetative idiot" to move using the principles of reinforcement and the use of operant methodology. The subject, a boy weighing 30 pounds, was described by Fuller (1949) in the following manner:

"he lay on his back and could not roll over; he could, however, open his mouth, blink, and move his arms, head, and shoulders to a slight extent. He never moved his trunk or legs ... He had been fed liquids and semi-solids all his life. While being fed, he sometimes choked and would cough vigorously." (p. 587)

Fuller provided small amounts of a warm sugar-milk solution for the boy to drink from a syringe as a consequence (a reinforcement procedure) of the boy lifting his right arm while not appreciably moving his head or shoulders. During an initial 20 minute period, the syringe was placed next to the subject but not operated. The boy's right-arm movements were observed and found to occur less than once per minute. Next, the solution of warm sugar-milk was made available to the boy if he moved his right arm during four consecutive 20-minute sessions. During these periods his arm movements increased threefold, to more than 3 times per minute. Fuller then followed this period with a period in which the solution was not made available, and the behavior decreased (an extinction procedure). This experiment was important because it exemplified the extension of Skinner's research methodology, that is, the "experimental analysis of behavior," to humans.

Other important events that occurred prior to the 1950s included the establishment of organizational structures and associations that provided operant investigators with a means to affiliate and discuss their research. In 1946, faculty and students from Indiana University and Columbia University who were interested in the developing principles of operant conditioning and experimental analysis of behavior held their first formal meeting on these topics at Indiana University. A newsletter that described activities of these faculties and students appeared shortly thereafter.

Another significant development was the formation of a psychology curriculum based upon reinforcement theory (Keller & Schoenfeld, 1949) and the offering of coursework on reinforcement theory at Columbia College. Although considered by some as a "cult" (Wendt, 1949), the program at Columbia College helped to establish reinforcement theory as a viable topic in the psychology curricula.

1950–1960: Extensions of Operant Conditioning to Human Behavior

Major extensions of operant principles to human behavior were primarily conceptual rather than empirical during the period from 1950 to 1960. For example, Skinner asserted that individuals are forced to operate in an aversive system of control, frequently involving the threat of the consequences of failure, and he said that our society must shift to a system that emphasizes positive reinforcement, rather than negative reinforcement or punishment, in order to develop more fully individuals in our schools and in our society. His novel, *Walden Two* (1948) illuminates a society based upon positive reinforcement of human potential. His principles of operant conditioning were also presented as functioning in all types of life situations in his *Science and Human Behavior* (1953), which introduced applications of operant conditioning to government, law, religion, psychotherapy, economics, and education.

There were, however, notable events that helped to demarcate the "Skinnerian approach" as applied to human behavior through empirical methods (Krantz, 1971). These events included (a) the development of an operant laboratory that focused upon "psychotic problems," (b) the formation of the Society for the Experimental Analysis of Behavior, and (c) the study of child behavior and development. Skinner established a laboratory using pigeons. And he started a laboratory at the Metropolitan State Hospital in Waltham, Massachusetts, wishing to extend his research to the study of human behavior. His work with pigeons, in which he was assisted by Charles B. Ferster, is detailed in *Schedules of Reinforcement* (1957). Skinner's work directed toward human behavior suggested the utility of the behavioral approach as a viable alternative to the medical model. His work at the Metropolitan State Hospital, with Ogden R. Lindsley, focused upon the utility of his methods and the generality of his operant principles to the behavior of psychotic patients.

Laboratory research grew rapidly during the 1950s, as did the advanced graduate education of several notable scholars (for example, Ferster and Lindsley). At this time, however, there were no formal publication outlets for research conducted in the laboratories, nor were there professional associations. This situation changed in 1958 with the formation

of the Society for the Experimental Analysis of Behavior (SEAB), which published the *Journal of the Experimental Analysis of Behavior (JEAB)*. *JEAB* was devoted solely to publishing research that focused upon the methodological characteristics of operant research.

During this period there were also extensions of the methodology of operant conditioning to the study of child behavior. At the time that Skinner and Lindsley were conducting their experiments with psychotic patients, Sidney W. Bijou was applying operant methods to the study of child behavior at the University of Washington's Institute of Child Behavior (Bijou, 1955, 1957a, 1957b, 1958a, 1957b; Bijou & Sturges, 1959). Bijou's work focused upon the evaluation of different types of reinforcers (for example, sounds and toys) and responses (for example, dropping marbles, pushing buttons and lights, and pressing levers). At the same time, Bijou also studied the laboratory responses of animals and children with mental retardation (Bijou & Orlando, 1961; Orlando & Bijou, 1960).

During the 1950s there was little concern for the application of operant principles and methods to practical human problems. Almost all research conducted in the later 1950s was basic laboratory experimentation. The purpose of this research was to replicate and extend the basic principles that had been derived from Skinner's initial experiments with animals (1938) and, more recently, from his work with Ferster in 1957 with human behavior. Work during this period was essential in developing a solid data base for conceptualizing extrapolations to humans and in developing methodological applications of operant procedures that would eventually be utilized to solve the "problems of everyday life."

1960–1970: Birth of Applied Behavior Analysis

Early applications of operant conditioning techniques to human beings were directed toward verifying that the principles of operant conditioning that were shown to govern animal behavior also governed human behavior. The use of these principles with humans did not emerge from the laboratory setting until the 1960s. However, once applications of what became known as "behavior modification" made its way out of the laboratory several events occurred which resulted in universal recognition of what we now call "applied behavior analysis." In this section we overview some of the earlier applied work of Sidney W. Bijou, as well as others, and the events surrounding the formal recognition of applied behavior analysis. We conclude with a discussion of how applied behavior analysis differs from behavior modification, by focusing upon the characteristics of applied behavior analysis introduced in the 1960s.

Bijou's work began to focus increasingly upon both the problems of children with mental retardation and children who were not handicapped toward the end of the 1950s. The early 1960s saw applications of the "carefully established empirical laws of behavior" from the laboratory to the practical problems of children with mental retardation. In 1961, Bijou established an experimental classroom at the Rainier School in Buckley, Washington. Jay S. Birnbrauer, Montrose M. Wolf, and others collaborated with Bijou in investigating the relationship betwen antecedent events and academic responding (such as reading, solving arithmetic problems, and spelling), which eventually resulted in the Rainier Reading Program (Bijou, et al., 1966; Birnbrauer, et al., 1965, Birnbrauer, et al., 1964). This group also studied the relation of consequent events to academic responding and was among the first to publish results of a tokeh economy whereby secondary reinforcers were used (Birnbrauer & Lawler, 1964; Birnbrauer, Wolf, Kidder, & Taque, 1965). These secondary reinforcers included poker chips and points that were given to the students for completing assigned work. These tokens were then traded by the children for primary reinforcers, including food, toys, special privileges, and free time to play.

Several other investigators were responsible for the development of operant methods outside the laboratory setting. Donald M. Baer, who after completing his doctoral studies at the University of Chicago, was hired by Bijou and established his own research laboratory focusing upon social development. At the University of Washington, Bijou and Baer collaborated on a general theory that viewed child development in relation to observable environmental events (Bijou & Baer, 1961, 1965, 1967). Around this same time period, O. Ivar Lovaas at the University of California at Los Angeles, Gerald R. Patterson at the University of Oregon, Wesley C. Becker and Leonard Ullmann at the University of Illinois, and Richard and Michael Dinoff at the University of Alabama were embarking upon research programs and training graduate students in the use of operant methods that would shape the direction of applied behavior analysis. Lovaas began a program for children with autism; Patterson focused upon the use of social reinforcement to assist children in adjusting to problems in home and school settings; Becker sought to expand operant techniques in the classroom; and Ullmann contributed directly to the view that learning theory principles could be applied to the treatment of abnormal behavior. The Dinoffs worked with boys with emotional disturbances in a summer camp, called Camp Ponderosa. Certainly, many others also contributed to the growth and spread of behavioral principles in nonlaboratory settings. Their work is detailed in greater depth in Kazdin (1978).

The role of each of these individuals in the proliferation and centralization of operant research may have been most dramatic when tracing their influence upon the careers of others. Baer, who left the University of Washington in 1965, directly influenced several operant researchers to join him at the University of Kansas. These individuals included Montrose M. Wolf, Todd Risley, R. Vance Hall, and Betty Hart. Similarly, Bijou left the University of Washington at about the same time to join the faculty at the University of Illinois. Becker, Bijou, Ullmann, and others were responsible for directly influencing the efforts of several graduate students who continued to contribute to clinical and educational applications, including, Donald Thomas and K. Daniel O'Leary.

In the mid–1960s few people anticipated the enormous impact that the use of Skinner's principles of operant conditioning and his research methods would have upon the everyday lives of people in diverse settings. The application of operant principles, which came to be known as "behavior principles," became so prevalent that a new journal was devoted to reporting these applications of behavior principles to everyday problems and situations. The *Journal of Applied Behavior Analysis* was first published in 1968. In the inaugural edition, Baer, Wolf, and Risley (1968) defined *applied behavior analysis* as the "process of applying sometimes tentative principles of behavior to the improvement of specific behaviors, and simultaneously evaluating whether or not any changes noted are indeed attributable to the process of application" (p. 91).

In the early- to mid-1960s, almost all applications of the principles of operant conditioning and the experimental analysis of behaviors were conducted in laboratory settings and subsequently in experimental settings, such as the Rainier Experimental Classroom established by Bijou and his colleagues. It was not until the mid- to late-1960s that these researchers' students and colleagues began investigating "actual problems of social importance," and applied behavior analysis developed characteristics that were different from the earlier work in laboratory or carefully controlled settings. For example, in 1963 the Juniper Gardens Children's Project was founded as a community-based application of applied behavior analysis (ABA) to the problems of low income and black children and families in the northeast section of Kansas City, Kansas. The black activistists of the 1960s became interested in the potential of ABA as a means for improving services to children within the community. Here, Risley, Wolf, Hall, and Hart developed several lines of ABA research which are frequently cited. These classic studies in the areas of preschool language

(Risley & Hart), classroom behavior management (Hall), and community-based services to young delinquents (Wolf) will be reviewed in subsequent chapters. Further, it is equally important to remember that these earliest efforts were absolutely critical to the credibility of the newly formed area of *applied behavior analysis*. In order for research to qualify as *applied behavior analysis* it had to focus upon problems of social importance; that is, the problems selected for study had to be important to society, not merely convenient to study. *Applied behavior analysis* (ABA), which is distinguished from *behavior modification* discussed subsequently, also focused upon an evaluative system that assisted in determining whether change had been accomplished in terms of meaningful educational goals.

There is a primary distinction between ABA and behavior modification. ABA "involves the systematic variation of behavioral and environmental factors thought to be associated with an individual's difficulties, with the primary goal of modifying his behavior in the direction that, ideally, he himself (or his agent) has chosen" (Brown, Wienckowski, & Stolz, 1976, p. 4). Furthermore ABA "specifically excludes psychosurgery, electroconvulsive therapy, and the administration of drugs independent of any specific behavior of the person receiving the medication" (Brown et al., 1976, p. 3). These latter procedures can be, and have, been associated with the broader term, *behavior modification*. Popular books, most notably *Brave New World* by Aldous Huxley and *A Clockwork Orange* by Anthony Burgess, have conributed greatly to exaggerated accounts of behavior modification. Consequently, behavior modification has been the frequent target of criticism, due largely to terms such as "control," "conditioning," and "modification" that invoke visions of malfeasance not originally considered by Skinner and other earlier researchers.

Applied behavior analysis is more rigorously defined as an educational and evaluative system than behavior modification. It is based upon principles of learning and characterized by the following substantive and methodological criteria (Baer, Wolf, & Risley, 1968):

1. *Applied* behavior analysis concentrates on *socially important behaviors* (Epling & Pierce, 1986). The term "applied" denotes "the interest which society shows in the problems being studied" (p. 92). Applied behavior analysts focus their attention on behaviors that are educationally relevant such as reading and talking. Simultaneously, these behaviors are studied in the context of settings where these behaviors are important. For example, reading might be the focus of study in the classroom and talking the focus of study during a play period. The non-applied researcher would not necessarily study these behaviors because of their applied importance, but might study them because reading relates to hypotheses about compressed speech and talking relates to hypotheses about phonetics. Although theoretically relevant, these investigations are constrained by their failure to focus upon behaviors that are socially important to the individual in the setting where the behavior is a problem.

2. Applied *behavior* analysis focuses upon *quantifiable units of behavior*. Behavior must be defined in terms that allow for direct observation and measurement. To qualify as behavioral, the physical events of an individual must be defined in terms whereby two observers, who were given a list of events comprising the behavior under study, could agree that responding had actually occurred. For example, if aggression in the classroom was the behavior of interest and if it were defined as hitting, biting, kicking, pinching others, then two observers (for example, a teacher and a teacher's aide) should be able to agree that behavior had occurred. "Explicit measurement of [observer agreement] thus becomes not merely good technique, but a prime criterion of whether the study was appropriately behavioral" (Baer et al., 1968, p. 93).

3. Applied behavior *analysis* emphasizes *individual* rather than group *analysis of the effectiveness of programs*. ABA is characterized by replication. The extent to which behavior has been changed and that change is attributable to an educational program is exemplified by the "concept of replication, and replication is the essence of believability" (Baer et al., 1968, p. 95). Skinner emphasized "functional relationships" because of his interest in discovering relationships between behavior and environmental events that eventually allowed statements to be made about the generality of effects. In the traditional sense, an intervention, such as tutoring, is introduced after performance has been repeatedly assessed during a baseline phase in which the behavior is studied in the absence of the planned intervention. Following this assessment, the intervention is introduced and its effects are studied. If performance changes immediately and abruptly, then the intervention's effects are considered. In the case of immediate impact, change due to the intervention usually is more believable than if change is slow or delayed. In either case, judgments are made and confirmed or unconfirmed ultimately by "replication of effect." If performance can be shown to be functionally related to the presence or absence of the program, believability is heightened or lowered, respectively.

Throughout the 1960s, ABA research focused upon the problems of persons with mental retardation, students, predelinquents and delinquents, drug addicts and alcoholics, and medical patients. These people were studied in diverse settings, including hospitals, clinics, classrooms, and institutions. This research continued to demonstrate that the "principles of operant conditioning" and the "methodology of experimental analysis," initially developed by Skinner, had wide utility. Significant developments included the flight from the laboratory, the professional development of several individuals who continued to influence the growth and direction of ABA, the formation of a journal to disseminate applied research, and the publication of the "characteristics of applied behavior analysis." This period gave way to the continued development and refinement of applied behavior analysis, which has almost assuredly resulted in its continued growth and adoption in diverse fields of study and application.

1970–1980: Development of a Heart

The 1970s were characterized by the continued growth and development of ABA in such diverse areas as acting-out behavior in the classroom (Walker et al., 1976; Walker et al., 1975), aggression in the home (Patterson et al., 1973, Wahler, 1976), and delinquency (Braukmann et al., 1975). As discussed previously, ABA is defined by its intent (that is, its application), its focus upon behavior that is quantifiable and observable, and its methodology which is used to evaluate its effectiveness.

Baer et al. included the dimension of "social importance" in their landmark article published in the *Journal of Applied Behavior Analysis* in 1968. In fact, they wrote that applied behavior analysis is constrained to examining behaviors which are socially important and that "if the application of behavioral techniques does not produce large enough effects for practical value, then application has failed" (pp. 92–96). They went on to suggest that people who have a vested interest in change should also be the arbiters of change. They stated that "ward personnel may be able to say that a [person taught] to use 10 verbal labels is not much better off in self-help skills than before, but that one with 50 such labels is a great deal more effective" suggesting that "the opinions of ward aides may be more relevant than the opinions of psycholinguists" (p. 96). In ABA, persons who have a vested interest in the focus and the outcome of an educational program or who are uniquely qualified to evaluate focus and change because of their training are referred to as *significant others*. Interestingly, although the value of significant others was acknowledged in 1968, it was a decade later before this "dimension" of applied behavior analysis was formally acknowledged (Kazdin, 1977; VanHouten, 1979; Wolf, 1978). In this concluding section of Chapter 2, we define the dimension of "social importance" via social validation methodology.

Social validation refers to the social context of education in evaluating needs and expectations (Wolf, 1978). Social validation has two components, the focus of treatment and the intervention effects. Social validation of the *focus of treatment* decides whether a behavior selected for treatment is important in enhancing the target individual's everyday functioning. Social validation of *the intervention effects* examines the acceptability of the magnitude of behavior change. In applied behavior analysis, social validation has become the primary method of choice for combining the basic needs of target individuals, such as students, with the expectations of family members and other significant persons in developing curricular and intervention priorities. Todd Risley (1970) also suggested that both criteria (that is, needs and expectations) are required in validating program intent and effect. The focus upon basic needs has provided a standard for establishing interventions that are necessary for individual growth. The essential question asked is whether the behavioral program results in the student, for example, acquiring a skill (for instance, learning to read) that improves everyday classroom performance (for instance, reading comprehension).

In the 1970s and earlier, procedures were developed to evaluate the social validity of goals and results. These included *social comparison* and *subjective evaluation*. The method of social comparison involves comparison of a target individual's behavior before and after treatment with similar behavior of peers who display acceptable levels of performance. Social validation is demonstrated when, after treatment, the target individual's behavior is as valued as that of the target individual's peers. With the method of subjective evaluation, target behavior is evaluated for importance by experts and significant others with whom the individual has contact (for example, peers, teachers, and friends).

For several decades, our society has been depicted as uncovering a technology of human behavior that would surely bring about our social destruction. This view is particularly true in such novels as *Animal Farm* and *1984* by George Orwell and *Brave New World* by Aldous Huxley. Although Skinner (1953) addressed this issue by suggesting that our technology is neither good nor bad, but neutral, scepticism and fear have prevailed among those who equate all behavioral approaches, including applied behavior analysis, as potentially deceptive and omnipotent. It is our use of this technology, however, that can be good or bad. To discontinue the pursuit of learning why people behave as they do, and to cease developing methods that can be used to help people structure their environments to promote change would be prematurely denying principles and methods that have already greatly improved human functioning. The dimension of social validation, which asks important questions about the need for proposed changes and about our satisfaction with the results of the application process, is based directly upon societal input. Recognition of this dimension of applied behavior analysis was clearly the most significant event in the 1970s.

Summary

In this chapter, we discussed many developments, including philosophical and psychological traditions dating from the nineteenth century, that have helped shape the course that applied behavior analysis has taken. While the roots of applied behavior analysis can be traced to the work of Pavlov, Thorndike, Watson, and others in experimental psychology at the beginning of this century, certainly the most influential and important person in this field has been B. F. Skinner. Skinner argued for a laboratory analysis of behavior radically different from the dominant methodology in psychology through the first 60 years of this century. He also argued for application of behavior analysis to every day affairs and problems. In Skinner's schema, behavior depends upon, or is a function of, the environment. This is the fundamental assumption of Skinner's approach which today seems so "unremarkable" that one would hardly expect arguments about it. Yet this assumption has nevertheless generated a number of criticisms. Some persons view it as an argument against heredity—but it is not; some view it as an argument against humanity—but it is not. It is, instead an argument for a more humane humanity. Given the first

assumption, that behavior is a function of the environment, the second assumption is that we should deal with behavior in its present context. Applied behavior analysts assume that behavior is a function of (a) the immediate environment, (b) the past environment, and (c) genetic contributions. In the applied analysis of behavior, genetic contributions are assumed, but their study remains for physiologists, medical doctors, histologists, and geneticists. In addition, applied behavior analysis does not dwell on the historical environment. In the applied analysis of behavior, we might question what events contributed to the present behavior and whether these events are continuing, or we might question the interpretation a person has of past events, the way he or she talks about those events, and the way the person's interpretation affects present behavior; but, unlike several forms of psychotherapy, ABA does not *dwell* on the historical environment. ABA, instead, deals with the present environment and how it can be arranged to promote and maintain appropriate, healthy, and adaptive behaviors.

In Chapter 3, we introduce "some commonalities" between contemporary special education and applied behavior analysis. These shared commonalities form the basis for developing this text. Applied behavior analysis and special education complement each other in the delineation of goals and methods, based upon societal input, that can be incorporated to educate children, youth, and adults.

REFERENCES

Azrin, N. H., & Foxx, R. M. (1971). "A rapid method of toilet training the institutionalized retarded." *Journal of Applied Behavior Analysis, 4*, 89–99.

Baer, D. M., Wolf, M. M., & Risley, T. R. (1968). "Some current dimensions of applied behavior analysis." *Journal of Applied Behavior Analysis, 1*, 92–97.

BERRY, H. K. (1969). "Phenylketonuria: Diagnosis, treatment and long-term management." In G. Farrell (ed.), *Congenital mental retardation*. Austin, TX: University of Texas Press.

BIJOU, S. W. (1955). "A systematic approach to an experimental analysis of young children." *Child Development*, 26, 161–168.

BIJOU, S. W. (1957a). "Methodology for an experimental analysis of child behavior." *Psychological Reports*, 3, 243–253.

BIJOU, S. W. (1957b). "Patterns of reinforcement and resistance to extinction in young children." *Child Development*, 28, 47–54.

BIJOU, S. W. (1958a). "A child study laboratory on wheels." *Child Development*, 29, 425–427.

BIJOU, S. W. (1958b). "Operant extinction after fixed-intervals. Schedules with young children." *Journal of the Experimental Analysis of Behavior*, 1, 25–29.

BIJOU, S. W., & BAER, D. M. (1961). *Child development: A systematic and empirical theory* (vol. 1). New York: Appleton-Century-Crofts.

BIJOU, S. W., & BAER, D. M. (1965). *Child development: Universal stages of infancy* (vol. 2). New York: Appleton-Century-Crofts.

BIJOU, S. W., & BAER, D. M. (1967). *Child development: Readings in experimental analysis* (vol. 3). New York: Appleton-Century-Crofts.

BIJOU, S. W., BIRNBRAUER, J. S., KIDDER, J. D., & TAGUE, C. F. (1966). "Programmed instruction as an approach to the teaching of reading, writing and arithmetic to retarded children." *Psychological Record*, 16, 505–522.

BIJOU, S. W., & ORLANDO, R. (1961). "Rapid development of multiple-schedule performances with retarded children." *Journal of the Experimental Analysis of Behavior*, 4, 7–16.

BIJOU, S. W., & STURGES, P. T. (1959). "Positive reinforcers for experimental studies with children—consumables and manipulatables." *Child Development*, 30, 151–170.

BIRNBRAUER, J. S., BIJOU, S. W., WOLF, M. M., & KIDDER, J. D. (1965). "Programmed instruction in the classroom." In L. P. Ullmann & L. Krasner (eds.), *Case studies in behavior modification*. New York: Holt, Rinehart & Winston.

BIRNBRAUER, J. S., KIDDER, J. D., & TAGUE, C. F. (1964). "Programming reading from the teachers' point of view." *Programmed Instruction*, 3, 1–2.

BIRNBRAUER, J. S., & LAWLER, J. (1964). "Token reinforcement for learning." *Mental Retardation*, 2, 275–279.

BIRNBRAUER, J. S., WOLF, M. M., KIDDER, J. D., TAGUE, C. F. (1965). "Classroom behavior of retarded pupils with token reinforcement." *Journal of Exceptional Child Psychology*, 2, 219–235.

BRAUKMANN, C. J., FIXSEN, D. L., PHILLIPS, E. L., & WOLF, M. M. (1955). "Behavioral approaches to treatment in the crime and delinquency field." *Criminology*, 13, 299–331.

BROWN, B. S., WIENCKOWSKI, L. A., & STOLZ, S. B. (1976). *Behavior modification: Perspective on a current issue*. Washington, DC: U.S. Department of Health, Education, and Welfare.

COTT, A. (1972). "Megavitamins: The orthomolecular approach to behavior and learning disabilities." *Therapy Quarterly*, 7, 245–258.

DARWIN, C. A. (1977). "A biographical sketch of an infant." *Mind*, 2, 285–294.

DEITZ, S. M. (1982). "Defining applied behavior analysis: An historical analogy." *The Behavior Analyst*, 5(1), 53–64.

DOLLARD, J., & MILLER, N. E. (1950). *Personality and psychotherapy*. New York: McGraw-Hill.

EPLING, F. W., & PIERCE, D. W. (1986). "The basic importance of applied behavior analysis." *The Behavior Analyst*, 9(1), 89–99.

EYSENCK, H. J. (1961). The effects of psychotherapy. In H. J. Eysenck (ed.), *Handbook of abnormal psychology*. New York: Basic Books.

FERSTER, C. B., & SKINNER, B. F. (1957). *Schedules of reinforcement*. New York: Appleton-Century-Crofts.

FINE, S. (1973). "Family therapy and a behavioral approach to childhood obsessive-compulsive neurosis." *Archives of General Psychiatry*, 28, 695–697.

FOXX, F. M., & AZRIN, N. H. (1973). "The elimination of autistic self-stimulatory behavior by overcorrection." *Journal of Applied Behavior Analysis*, 6, 1–14.

FRALEY, L. E., & VARGAS, E. A. (1986). "Separate disciplines: The study of behavior and the study of the psyche." *The Behavior Analyst*, 9(1), 47–59.

FRANKS, C. M. (1969). *Behavior therapy appraisal and status*. New York: McGraw-Hill.

FULLER, P. R. (1949). "Operant conditioning of a vegetative human organism." *American Journal of Psychology*, 62, 587–590.

GUTHRIE, E. R. (1959). "Association by contiuity." In S. Koch (ed.), *Psychology: A Study of a science, Study 1: Conceptual and systematic, Vol. 2: General systematic formulations, learning, and special processes.* New York: McGraw-Hill.

HULL, C. L. (1943). *Principles of behavior.* New York: Appleton-Century-Crofts.

JONES, M. C. (1924a). "A laboratory study of fear: The case of Peter." *Pedagogical Seminary and Journal of Genetic Psychology, 31,* 308–315.

JONES, M. C. (1924b). "The elimination of children's fears." *Journal of Experimental Psychology, 7,* 382–390.

KAZDIN, A. E. (1977). "Assessing the clinical or applied importance of behavior change through social validation." *Behavior Modification, 1,* 427–437.

KAZDIN, A. E. (1978). History of behavior modification. Baltimore, MD: University Park Press.

KELLER, F. S., & SCHOENFELD, W. N. (1979). "The psychology curriculum at Columbia College." *American Psychologist, 4,* 165–172.

KESSLER, J. W. (1966). *Psychopathology of childhood.* Englewood Cliffs, NJ: Prentice Hall.

KRANTZ, D. L. (1971). "The separate worlds of operant and nonoperant psychology." *Journal of Applied Behavior Analysis, 4,* 61–70.

KRASNOGORSKI, N. I. (1907). "The formation of artificial conditioned reflexes in young children." *Russkii Vrach, 36,* 1245–1246. Translated and republished in Y. Brackbill and G. G. Thompson (eds.), *Behavior in infancy and early childhood: A book of readings.* New York: Free Press, 1967.

LEVITT, E. E. (1963). "Psychotherapy with children: A further evaluation." *Behavior Research and Therapy, 1,* 45–31.

MAHONEY, K., VAN WAGEMAN, R. K., & MEYERSON, L. (1971). "Toilet Training of normal retarded children." *Journal of Applied Behavior Analysis, 4,* 173–181.

MARKS, I. M. (1972). "Flooding (implosion) and allied treatments." In W. S. Agrass (ed.), *Behavior modification: Principles and clinical applications.* Boston: Little, Brown.

MOORE, J. (1985). "Some historical and conceptual relations among logical positivism, operationism, and behaviorism." *The Behavior Analyst, 8(1),* 53–63.

MOWRER, O. H., & MOWRER, W. M. (1938). "En-

vresis–a method for its study and treatment." *American Journal of Orthopsychiatry, 8,* 436–459.

ORLANDO, R., & BIJOU, S. W. (1960). "Single and multiple schedule of reinforcement in developmentally retarded chilren." *Journal of the Experimental Analysis of Behavior, 3,* 339–348.

PATTERSON, G. R., COBB, J. A., & RAY, R. S. (1972). "Direct intervention in the classroom: A set of procedures for the aggressive child." In F. W. Clark, D. R. Evans, & L. A. Hamerlynck (eds.), *Implementing behavior programs for schools and clinics.* Champaign, IL: Research Press.

PIAGET, J., & INHELDER, B. (1969). *The psychology of the child.* New York: Basic Books.

SKINNER, B. F. (1937). "Two types of conditioned reflex and a pseudo type." *Journal of General Psychology, 16,* 272–279.

SKINNER, B. F. (1938). *The behavior of organisms: An experimental analysis.* New York: Appleton-Century-Crofts.

SKINNER, B. F. (1948). *Walden two.* New York: MacMillan.

SKINNER, B. F. (1950). "Are theories of learning necessary?" *Psychological Review, 57,* 193–216.

SKINNER, B. F. (1953). *Science and human behavior.* New York: Macmillan.

SKINNER, B. F. (1956). "A case history in scientific method." *American Psychologist, 11,* 221–233.

SKINNER, B. F. (1957). *Verbal behavior.* Englewood Cliffs, NJ: Prentice Hall.

SKINNER, B. F. (1959). *Cumulative record: A selection of papers.* New York: Appleton-Century-Crofts.

SKINNER, B. F. (1969). *Contingencies of reinforcement: A theoretical analysis.* Englewood Cliffs, NJ: Prentice Hall.

THORNDIKE, E. L. (1905). *The elements of psychology.* New York: Seiler.

TODD, J. T., & MORRIS, E. K. (1986). "The early research of John B. Watson: Before the behavioral revolution." *The Behavior Analyst, 9(1),* 71–88.

TWITMYER, E. B. (1902). *A study of the knee jerk.* Philadelphia: Winston.

VAN HOUTEN, R. (1979). "Social validation: The evolution of standards of competency for target behaviors." *Journal of Applied Behavior Analysis, 12,* 581–592.

WHALER, R. G. (1976). "Deviant child behavior

within the family: Developmental speculations and behavior change strategies." In H. Leitenberg (ed.), *Handbook of behavior modification and behavior therapy*. Englewood Cliffs, NJ: Prentice Hall.

WALKER, H. M., HOPS, H., & FIEGENBAUM, E. (1976). "Deviant classroom behavior as a function of combinations of social and token reinforcement and cost contingency." *Behavior Therapy*, 7, 76–88.

WALKER, H. M., HOPS, H., & JOHNSON, S. M. (1975). "Generalization and maintenance of classroom treatment effects." *Behavior Therapy*, 6, 188–200.

WATSON, J. B. (1913). "Psychology as the behaviorist views it." *Psychological Review*, 20, 158–177.

WATSON, J. B. (1914). *Behavior: An introduction to comparative psychology*. New York: Holt.

WATSON, J. B. (1919). *Psychology: from the standpoint of a behaviorist*. Philadelphia, Lippincott.

WATSON, J. B. (1925). *Behaviorism*. New York: Norton.

WATSON, J. B., RAYHER, R. (1920). "Conditioned emotional reactions." *Journal of Experimental Psychology*, 3, 1–14.

WENDT, G. R. (1949). "The development of a psychology cult." *American Psychologist*, 4, 426.

WHELAN, R. J. (1972). "What's in a label? A hell of a lot!" In *The legal and educational consequences of the intelligence testing movement: Handicapped and minority group children*. Columbia, MO: University of Missouri Press.

WOLF, M. M. (1978). "Social Validity: The case for subjective measurement, or how applied behavior analysis is finding its heart." *Journal of Applied Behavior Analysis*, 11, 203–214.

chapter 3

Special Education and Applied Behavior Analysis: Some Commonalities

The 1970s will be remembered as a critical turning point in the history of special education, primarily due to the enactment of the Bill of Rights for the Handicapped—Public Law 94-142 (The Education for All Handicapped Children Act). In the field of applied behavior analysis, the 1970s witnessed the "Development of a Heart." That is, the principles and methods of applied behavior analysis were increasingly influenced by consideration for the expectations and opinions of diverse consumers, including the student. The growth and evolution of special education and applied behavior analysis suggest several commonalities. These "commonalities" include (a) educational relevance; (b) an individualized teaching approach; (c) individualized assessment; (d) accountability; (e) a noncategorical approach; (f) an empirical approach; and (g) pragmatism. Each of these commonalities form a psychology in our society where decisions about special education are made. This psychology is the result of ap-

plied behavior analysis, which seeks relevant and useful methodology and a technology that asks relevant and meaningful questions. In the 1980s there was the beginning of a psychology that approached problems of human development equitably.

As mentioned in Chapter 1, services for individuals with mild handicaps have typically been provided categorically and in segregated classrooms. These classrooms have included a disproportionately high number of male students or representatives of a minority group. For students with severe handicaps, educational services have been offered in segregated settings as well. One of the most unfortunate educational outcomes in the past decade is the finding that the curricula offered to individuals in segregated settings bears little resemblance to curricula offered to individuals in nonsegregated settings. For example, students with severe handicaps oftentimes receive instruction that is age-inappropriate and nonfunctional.

The emergence of social validation, which includes the expectations and opinions of consumers, has been partly responsible for recent trends in questioning the focus of special education (such as whether the curriculum is age-appropriate) and the procedures used to obtain its goals (as when determining whether the curriculum is functional). In part, social support for students with handicaps through passage of legislation has also resulted in widespread discussion of the relevance of special education. Educational relevance is one of several important "commonalities" discussed in this chapter. The various commonalities between special education and applied behavior analysis (ABA) demonstrate that special education as a social movement will be successful and that part of this success will result from special educators' increased recognition of the valuable problem-solving orientation of applied behavior analysis. The following discussion introduces several highly positive and beneficial interrelationships between the two disciplines.

EDUCATIONAL RELEVANCE

When President Gerald R. Ford signed the Education for All Handicapped Children Act (Public Law 94-142) on November 29, 1975, a comprehensive legal framework existed for improving special education services for children, youth, and adults with handicaps. Public Law 94-142 has one major, broad purpose; that is, it is designed to assure that all children and youth with handicaps will receive a free appropriate public education that emphasizes special education and related services designed to meet their unique needs.

Among the provisions of P.L. 94-142, the provision that all chidren will be placed in the least restrictive setting necessary to meet their unique educational needs, in particular, will continue to impact education significantly (Abeson & Weintraub, 1977). This provision requires that each student be placed in an educational environment that is as close to a regular school program as is possible, while still being responsive to the student's educational needs. Establishing relevant educational goals, as required by P.L. 94-142, led to the formulation of instruction that specified the context, the behavior, and the criterion that special educators must attend to in order to assure that students were making educational gains. Today, professionals in both special education and applied behavior analysis are equally convinced of the importance of (a) educating students with handicaps together with students who are not handicapped and (b) taking the social context of education into consideration when evaluating community expectations and satisfaction (Wolf, 1978).

Applied behavior analysis also is based upon behavioral principles that focus upon educational relevance. As a practical approach to dealing with society's problems in such diverse settings as hospitals, classrooms, detention facilities, homes, prisons, and group homes, applied behavior analysis continues to demonstrate its effectiveness in the application of methods for improving individual growth and development. It is widely recognized in applied behavior analysis that multiple perspectives are necessary to assure that students are educated according to curricula whose goals match the expectations of the social context in which they are or will be placed. Incorporation of the beliefs and opinions of significant others has assisted in the identification and evaluation of these socially relevant goals. By combining the basic needs of target individuals (that is, students) and the expectations of significant others (that is, peers, friends, and family members), social validation methodology often results in the delineation of goals that focus upon educational relevance.

AN INDIVIDUALIZED TEACHING APPROACH

Both special education and applied behavior analysis focus upon an individualized teaching approach whereby intervention is *not* prescribed for a specific etiological group such as

Commonality 1: *EDUCATIONAL RELEVANCE*

Contributions from Special Education
- Public Law 94-142 as a mandate for educational relevance
- Goals for individual students

Contributions from Applied Behavior Analysis
- Development of principles to improve behavior
- Emphasis upon social validation

"dyslexics", the "brain damaged", or the "retarded." Rather, programs are implemented according to the total environment of the individual, including such considerations as the parental, school, and home environments. Thus, special education focuses upon the unique problems of students and the development of methods to help these individuals achieve their potential. Applied behavior analysis, in turn, focuses upon the design of individualized teaching programs and the relationships between learning principles and the individualized approach.

Students with handicaps and their non-handicapped peers are unique. One of the problems that confronts special education is choosing a teaching approach that will allow for individual differences. Contemporary special education views the student with handicaps as someone who will live, work, and re-create in several social contexts over a span of many years. Consequently, these future goals form a set of expectations that direct the individualized teaching approach. (Rusch, Chadsey-Rusch, White & Gifford, 1985). Contemporary special education departs from the traditional approach in that the student is taught to function within our complex society. For example, for adolescent students with severe handicaps, the teaching approach focuses upon age-appropriate and functionally individualized activities (for instance, playing checkers rather than playing with blocks). Similarly, adolescent students with mild handicaps learn to read words based upon the expectation that these words are

representative of words that they will be required to read when they get a job—the words are functionally relevant.

Applied behavior analysis has also been involved in designing individualized teaching programs. In these efforts, researchers have been concerned primarily with applications of principles in applied social contexts. In the inaugural volume of the *Journal of Applied Behavior Analysis,* for example, Zeilberger, Sampen, and Sloane (1968) reported on their use of a combined extinction and reinforcement procedure designed to reduce an individual child's aggressive behavior in the home setting. The principles of learning, extinction, and reinforcement were found to have an immediate and lasting effect on behavior. An interesting aspect of this early study was the use of the child's mother to administer extinction and reinforcement procedures. The mother focused on three classes of aggressive behavior, including *physical aggression* (hitting, pushing, kicking, throwing) *yelling,* and *bossing* (directing another child or adult to do something). Immediately following the child's display of one or more of these acts the mother placed her 4-year-old son in "time-out" for 2 minutes. (One of the family bedrooms was modified for this use by the removal of toys and other items of interest to the child.) She also told him what he had done wrong (for example, "You cannot stay here if you fight.") Then she returned her son to his regular activities once the "time-out" period was over. She also reinforced her son's behavior for appropriate play. The use of a mother and child in this study incorporates the components of an individualized teaching approach to fit the situation and the setting.

Individualized Assessment

Although both the fields of special education and applied behavior analysis recognize the importance of assessment, special education has held group assessments, based upon early intelligence testing, in a special high regard. It is generally agreed that the primary purpose of assessment is not to determine if an individual fits a diagnostic category (for example, learning disabilities, behavior disorders, or mental retardation), but to identify behaviors that require modification and, in turn, determine if the effects of education are sufficient. Increasingly, special education acknowledges the need to assess individuals rather than groups. The practice of assessing groups has proven valuable for making decisions about groups. But, if teachers are most often interested in teaching individuals (even if they are usually taught in groups) then assessing individual performance seems most reasonable and, as has been proven, valid for making instructional decisions.

Traditional special education has relied heavily on two types of tests: intelligence tests (to determine potential) and achievement tests (to determine current performance levels). While initially administering group versions of these tests, the move to individual testing has been overwhelming in the past decades. There has also been a great shift in special education from relying on norm-referenced tests (based on group scores) to criterion-referenced tests (which measure the extent to which a student's performance on a particular skill demonstrates mastery of that skill). Applied behavior analysis has always had as a defining characteristic the assessment of an individual's behavior in a natural environment rather than even a small group (Wolf & Risley, 1968). For example, an individual's ability to utilize self-control procedures has been recommended as an important adjunct to instructional programs for students who display disproportionately high rates of talking, rocking, noncompliance, and aggression in the classroom (Walker, 1979) as well as on the job (Rusch & Schutz, 1981). In 1983, Rhode, Morgan, and Young reported on a self-management procedure that effectively reduced the inappropriate classroom behavior of six elementary school students with behavioral handicaps, both in a resource classroom and in the regular classroom. The self-management procedure was introduced into the resource room. Once the students were able to maintain acceptable levels of appropriate behavior with only minimal external reinforcement and to accurately evaluate their own work and behavior, then the self-management procedure was introduced into the regular classroom.

In the Rhode et al. study contemporary special education recognized the importance of focusing upon the *actual improvement of an individual's performance* based upon a criterion that suggested these students instruct

---

Commonality 2: *INDIVIDUALIZED TEACHING APPROACH*

Contributions from Special Education
- Focus upon the unique eduational needs of the student
- Focus upon age-appropriate and funtional instruction

Contributions from Applied Behavior Analysis
- Design of individualized teaching programs
- Application of learning principles in applied social context

Commonality 3:   *INDIVIDUALIZED ASSESSMENT*

Contributions from Special Education
- Recognition of the need to assess individuals, not groups
- Recognition of the need to individualize performance based upon reference criteria

Contributions from Applied Behavior Analysis
- Concentration upon an individual's changing behavior
- Focus upon the individual's behavior in the natural environment

themselves to behave. This focus offers several advantages over the more traditional methods of testing. First, it focuses the teacher upon specific behaviors or skills against which each student is assessed. Second, when a student is found unable to perform a given task (such as self-instructing), the teacher develops a specific criterion referenced test that is used to assess student performance. Finally, assessment of individual performance shows whether the student possesses the behavior.

The Rhode et al. study (1983) exemplifies the evaluation problems encountered in connection with special education. The students were referred to a resource room according to the results of standardized tests including the *Peabody Individual Achievement Test*, the *Woodcock Reading Mastery Tests*, the *Key Math Diagnostic Arithmetic Test*, and the *Slosson Intelligence Test*. At the time of placement, the students were experiencing moderate to severe problems in their natural environment, including disruptive classroom behavior, refusal to complete assigned tasks, aggression toward peers, and bizarre speech. Initially, the special education intervention consisted of evaluating each individual student's performance over time with regard to a specific educational program that assigned the responsibility of classroom behavior to the student. As characteristic of contemporary special education and applied behavior analysis, an effort was then made to evaluate the specific effects of the educational pro-

gram on each student's performance in the natural environment.

ACCOUNTABILITY

Special education and applied behavior analysis share a concern for accountability that results from selecting problems of social importance. In special education the legislative mandates to provide an appropriate education for all students have resulted in an emphasis on accountability in curriculum design, teaching, and administration. Similarly, applied behavior analysis includes methods that once were part of laboratory experimentation but now constitute foundations for evaluating curriculum design, teaching strategies, and educational programs that are educationally relevant.

In general, *accountability* refers to the promise that a person, group of persons, or a profession will be responsive to the promise to deliver service to achieve a preselected outcome. Typically, the outcome must be specified in advance by the parties involved. In special education this recognition of "promise" is important because of two occasions when educators are held accountable. First, they are held accountable for the promised results that are analyzed prior to intervention when, for example, the interdisciplinary team meets to discuss a student's individualized education program. The reviewing body must be convinced that the promised results are worth the time and money needed to achieve them. Second, the teacher is held accountable when the quantitative and qualitative features of the promised results are compared with actual student performance.

Over the past decade, special education and applied behavior analysis have developed instructional techniques derived from the basic study of human behavior. In particular, professionals in the two fields have explored methods for deriving, attaining, and measuring instructional gains within the larger framework of education. These methods include (a) specifying learning outcomes in terms of observable student performance; (b) selecting a range of applied situations for displaying student performances; and (c) specifying criteria for acceptable performances. There is virtually unanimous agreement that specifying learning outcomes enables consumers (such as parents, teachers, and employers) to distinguish the varieties of behavior that are to be modified by instruction.

One of the concerns of contemporary special education is that what is taught in the classroom or in any of several educational settings does not generalize to similar settings. *Generalization of behavior* is synonymous with *functionality*. Special education must ask whether or not the teaching process results in the acquisition of a functional skill. Traditional special education has been interested in getting an indication of mastery of what has been taught; contemporary special education, responding to the often highly general goals of education, wants a measure of transferability of what has been taught. In other words, contemporary special education asks, "Did the student meet the criterion of performance stated by the objective?" and follows this question with "To what degree is the behavior useful?"

The focus on accountability to the consumer in special education requires frequent and extensive performance evaluation (Lessinger, 1970, 1971) based upon a criterion of acceptability (Merrill, 1971) which has been facilitated by applied behavior analysis methods (Kazdin, 1980). For example, Walker and Hops (1976) developed appropriate classroom behaviors such as working on assignments and following instructions in primary grade students. Prior to their participation in special eduation, the students' appropriate behavior was markedly lower than that of their classmates. However, when the subjects finished the program, their appropriate behavior was indistinguishable from that of their classmates. These results suggest that the behavioral changes were both educationally and socially significant because the target behaviors reached a level that represented acceptability. Ultimately, Walker and Hops (1976) sought to achieve a level of acceptability that was consistent with the aim of special education and applied behavior analysis to achieve accountability.

A NONCATEGORICAL APPROACH

Over the past three decades, special education has changed from being a categorical discipline focusing upon a narrow range of mild

---

Commonality 4: *ACCOUNTABILITY*

Contributions from Special Education
- Accountability in curriculum design, teaching, and program administration
- Generalization of behavior

Contribution from Applied Behavior Analysis
- Evaluation of curriculum and teaching strategies
- Identification of learning outcomes, applications of instruction, performance criterion

to moderate handicapping conditions in school-aged children to becoming an increasingly flexible profession that no longer hesitates to cross categorical boundaries and focus upon an ever-widening continuum of individuals of all ages with handicaps of all types. Various states across the country have attempted to eliminate categorization based upon labels (Birch, 1974). Instead, attempts have been made to emphasize the educational needs of the student rather than applying a label that emphasizes the disability category. Attempts have also been made to broaden categories, as in the state of California's use of the term "learning handicaps" for students with mild handicaps. This recent change in special education has its counterpart in applied behavior analysis, which has traditionally concentrated on behavioral improvement and principles of learning that deemphasize a reliance on categories and labels.

Since Dunn's (1968) attack on educational programs that he characterized as often ineffective and over-inclusive of minority children, the special education literature has been filled with articles about categorical special education and the effects of labeling. The labeling issue in special education has primarily centered upon whether or not the negative effects of labeling outweigh the positive effects of being classified. Algozzine and Mercer (1980) suggested two perspectives for studying this issue, including (a) the impact of the label on the perception and behavior of the student, and (b) the impact of the label on the perception and behavior of others who interact with the student. The available literature appears to be equally divided between the two positions.

Regardless of labeling effects, positive or negative, the trend toward noncategorical special education based upon educational need is well established and is sure to gain added momentum as states move toward noncategorical teaching certification and methods of instruction become the basis for delivery of the educational service (Marston, 1987). Hallahan and Kauffman (1977) discussed the significance of the noncategorical movement:

The notion of noncategorical special education has become increasingly popular in the last few years. This movement has occurred for at least two reasons. First, the widespread disenchantment with "labeling" has led many professionals to conclude that placing children in categorically labeled classrooms is *ipso facto* an unacceptable practice. Second, there is no rational basis, in terms of instructional efficacy, for grouping children in accordance with some of the categorical labels now in use. (p. 319)

Traditionally, special education teachers have been educated and certified according to diagnostic categories (Blackhurst, 1981). In recent years, however, teacher education programs have also begun to concentrate upon instructional methods that benefit students with mild and severe handicaps, regardless of their diagnostic labels. In his keynote address at the first annual conference of the Teacher Education Division of The Council for Exceptional Children in 1978, Maynard Reynolds (1979) criticized categorical approaches to teacher education suggesting that such practices embellish the labeling and categorization of students with handicaps. He stated:

Unfortunately, the ways we have been classifying and grouping children in special education and tracking teachers for training in special education . . . have not been fully rational. Despite all our concerns with providing the best education possible for children and training enough teachers to serve them, we have never thought through the question of what is a rational scheme for classifying and grouping children, nor the other side of the coin, what is the best way to organize and conduct teacher-education programs to support such a scheme . . . Let's face it: These categories are neither natural nor rational. (p. 5)

Special education has come to recognize that the categorical approach used to place and track students and to prepare teachers perpetuates negative stereotypes (Will, 1986). For example, regular educators and some special educators have been found to hold lower expectations for students who were labeled than for students who displayed virtually identical behaviors but were not labeled (Gillung & Rucker, 1977). The ultimate consequence of such practices is found when lower expectations result in individual teaching programs that are significantly different and inferior for labeled students.

One of the major questions facing special educators is whether teaching per se is qualitatively different for different categories of students. There appears to be no distinguishing characteristics that recommend teaching students with mental retardation, for example, in a distinctly different manner from that manner used with students demonstrating specific learning disabilities, emotional handicaps, physical handicaps, or no handicaps (Reynolds, 1979). Generally, a four-step process is used in teaching: (a) assessing students; (b) establishing goals and objectives; (c) identifying and using effective instructional methods; and (d) evaluating the result of the instructional process.

In a concentration on behavioral improvement, which has not included the use of categorical labels, applied behavior analysis has arrived at the following basic components associated with effective teaching:

1. *Identification of general goals.* General goals refer to desired outcomes, that is, the behavior the student will demonstrate when he or she has achieved mastery of a given goal. This general goal in education may be identified by (a) social comparisons; (b) societal requirements and expectations (also known as subjective evaluation); and (c) empirical data on learning outcomes, content areas, and personal values. According to the social comparison approach, an individual is compared with others of his or her own age. In respect to assessing successful functioning in society, (Kazdin, 1977), societal requirements and expectations are taken into consideration. Finally, the summative approach emphasizes the evaluation of specific, data-based sources of information such as behaviors that contribute to individual growth; behaviors that must be learned to pursue a given curriculum area; or behaviors that are judged to be personally valuable or desirable.

2. *Screening and selecting general goals.* The screening process provides a means for eliminating inappropriate goals and identifying the relationships that may exist between current and future student needs. By necessity, these goals are different for students with mild and severe handicaps. For students with mild handicaps, the following three domains underlie school activities: (a) the *cognitive* domain, which focuses upon intellectual activities; (b) the *affective* domain, which involves attitudes, emotions, and values; and (c) the *psychomotor* domain, which stresses physical activities and skills (Bloom, 1956; Krathwohl, Bloom, & Masia, 1964). The emphasis for students with severe handicaps, on the other hand, is placed upon the specific requirements of present and future environments with regard to residential, employment, and recreation pursuits (Brown et al., 1983).

Initial goals are selected based on priority judgments from among the goals that remain after the screening process. As a result of P.L. 94-142, these priority judgments include the opinions of (a) parents, (b) the target student when possible, (c) the teacher, and (d) administrative personnel. Final goal selection almost always includes a discussion of necessity and feasibility.

3. *Specification of behavioral objectives.* Objectives are statements of the behaviors a student must perform (including the situations surrounding such performances) to prove that he or she has met a given objective. Behavioral objectives include three primary components: (a) designation of a behavior (usually observable) that is to be performed; (b) inclusion of a situation in which the behavior has applied significance, for example, cooperating with peers during a free-play period versus cooperating with a peer in a simulated, learning setting; and (c) specification of a criterion level of performance that allows for an evaluation of minimal acceptability.

4. *Direct observation of the target behavior over time.* Direct observation or measurement of the student's behavior proceeds through a sequence of steps, which are detailed in this text. Briefly, these steps include (a) using quantitative measures, (b) observing the behavior without changing situational variables, such as antecedent and consequent events, (c) measuring behavior across several situations over time to obtain an estimate of the student's *behavior* in

Commonality 5: *NONCATEGORICAL APPROACH*

Contributions from Special Education
- Moving away from categories and labels
- Recognizing the need for effective teaching strategies

Contribution from Applied Behavior Analysis
- Concentrating on behaviors of importance
- Using behavioral principles with systematic instructional methods to improve student performance

target situations, (d) introducing instruction that is based upon known behavioral principles, and (e) continuing to measure the target behavior during instruction to detect quantitative changes.

An Empirical Approach

The foundations of special education were traced earlier through an overview of the work of Itard, Seguin, Montessori, and others. This early work, which has retained remarkable currency to this day, included efforts (a) to develop educational programs for teaching individuals the necessary skills and behaviors so that they could return to their community and (b) to recognize the need for an association of professionals who would serve as educational advocates of persons with handicaps. Unlike Itard who concentrated on hearing, Seguin worked with several senses, considering touch, hearing, and sight as the most important. Also, Seguin sought to gradually increase the difficulty of tasks (now called "shaping") and to gradually make discriminations less obvious (now called "fading"). Further, Seguin anticipated Skinner's concept of contingencies and the relation of environmental events to responding through his use of antecedent stimuli such as the communication board, which consists of pictures and statements that allow the student to communicate with others, (which he developed), antecedent procedures such as fading, and programmed consequences of responding. Finally, records were kept of Seguin's re-

search to document that his approach was based upon lawful relations.

Although early research also stimulated the objective study of behavior in psychology, objective study of individuals with handicaps lagged considerably until the 1950s and the creation of federal sponsorship of special education research. Many factors may have accounted for the exclusion of persons with handicaps from direct study during the first half of this century, including the conviction that "dull" students could not possibly benefit from the same education as "bright" students. These students, who were excluded from mainstream American education, either received their education in segregated facilities or were denied an education, with their contribution to society being placed upon their future role in the nuclear family. Although significant advances have been made in the education of persons with handicaps, it has not yet been generally recognized that it was critical to adopt an instructional method that is both empirical, that is, based upon objective methods of data collection and self-correcting, whereby programs that appear to be ineffective are improved.

Applied behavior analysis has its roots in philosophical and psychological traditions also dating back to the nineteenth century. For example, Benjamin Franklin demonstrated that behavior could be changed:

We had for our chaplain a zealous Presbyterian minister, Mr. Beatty, who complained to me that the men did not generally attend his prayers and exhortations. When they enlisted they were promised, besides pay and provisions, a gill of rum a day, which was punctually serv'd out to them, half in the morning, and the other half in the evening; and I observ'd they were as punctual in attending to receive it; upon which I said to Mr. Beatty: "It is perhaps, below the dignity of your profession to act as steward of the rum, but if you were to deal it out and only just after prayers, you would have them all about you." He liked the tho't, undertook the office, and, with the help of a few hands to measure out the liquor, executed it to satisfaction, and never were prayers more generally and more punctually attended; so that I thought this method preferable to the punishment inflicted by some military laws for non-attendance on divine service. (Franklin, *American Philosophical Society*. Reprinted by Skinner, 1969, p. 247)

Franklin's analysis and subsequent revision of the method by which rum, a primary reinforcer, was distributed reflects the spirit of everyday adoption of behavioral principles to adjust consequences in order to support socially agreed-upon behavioral goals.

Numerous examples may be cited to illustrate how special education has incorporated applied behavior analysis and its self-correcting, data-based nature to improve educational outcomes. For example, Breyer and Allen (1975) utilized a token economy to improve the behavior of 15 first grade students whose academic and social behaviors were considered too severe to allow them to be promoted into a regular second grade classroom. A program was designed to eliminate disruptive behavior and improve appropriate "on-task" behavior. After baseline observation and re-

cording of the target behaviors, the teacher praised desired student performance. However, praise alone did not result in the gains believed necessary to consider these students as passing the first grade. Consequently, in addition to praise, token reinforcement was used whereby the students received points after specific time intervals depending upon how well they were working. Points were exchangeable for prizes ranging in value from five cents to $1.50, which were obtained at a "good study store" located in the classroom. The effects of the tokens combined with praise were clearly superior to praise alone in improving classroom performance; and, as a consequence several of the students achieved the necessary gains to be promoted into the second grade. The nature of this instructional program illustrates the use of applied behavior analysis in special education settings, and it also shows the way in which the data-based nature of applied behavior analysis allows for necessary improvements in the instructional program to achieve socially significant outcomes.

PRAGMATISM

Traditionally, many educators have viewed a handicap as a problem resulting from psychological forces residing in the individual. Although the cause of these problems vary depending upon specific theories of exceptionality, the behavioral problems and the steps taken toward understanding behavior

---

Commonality 6:   *EMPIRICAL APPROACH*

Contributions from Special Education
- Early emphasis upon empirical research
- Acknowledgment of need for an empirical, self-correcting approach

Contributions from Applied Behavior Analysis
- Empirical nature of Skinner's work
- Emphasis upon data-based instructional programs

are important for indicating the proper approach to education. Thus, *acceptable behavior* generally represents a socially acceptable expression of the psychological forces; *unacceptable behavior,* on the other hand, is often considered to be the result of psychological processes that have gone awry. Students who are excessively active, misbehave, and display obnoxious behavior more than their peers are often said to be "emotionally disturbed", the implication being that their "emotions" are disturbed. But when psychological forces within the student are accorded the crucial role of "the problem", the implication for diagnosis and education resides outside those factors that are immediately available to special educators.

Over the years, exceptional behavior has been viewed in a variety of ways. The intrapsychic approach, the psychoanalytic theory, and the trait theory have had the greatest impact upon the way in which students with handicaps have been assessed and educated.

The *intrapsychic approach* suggests that psychological forces within the individual are responsible for his or her behavior. To understand the behavior of individuals, therefore, proponents of the intrapsychic approach suggest considering underlying psychological processes. However, little agreement exists about the nature of these intrapsychic psychological processes and the way in which they influence behavior.

The *psychoanalytic theory,* in turn, was introduced by Sigmund Freud (1856–1939) in his attempt to explain all behaviors by referring to manifestations of unconscious personality processes. Although psychoanalytic theory has been criticized because of its inability to verify its supporting propositions empirically and its general neglect of social and cultural influences on behavior (Stuart, 1970), it has evolved considerably and remains the major proponent of underlying psychic causes of "abnormal" behavior.

The *trait theory* persists as the major guiding viewpoint in special education today. Like psychoanalytic theory, trait theory also posits underlying personality structures as the cause

for behavior (Mischel, 1971). Traits are inferred from behaviors. For example, a student who behaves aggressively is considered to show the trait of "aggressiveness". Referred to in special education as *reification*, the trait that has been inferred from behavior is used to account for a given behavior; for example, the aggressive student acts the way he or she does because he or she is aggressive in underlying personality structures.

Each of the above models has strongly influenced educational assessment. Thus, rather than observation of behavior directly, assessment of underlying personality is recommended. Further, assignment of labels to students—a major function of current assessment practices—implies that underlying conditions are responsible for the unacceptable behavior. Such labels include "mentally retarded", "learning disabled", "hyperactive", and "emotionally disturbed."

Teaching methods are also directly influenced by these theories. For example, because assessment of underlying personality provides little useful information for educational pruposes, teaching methods tend to be nonspecific or general, making changes in educational programs difficult to evaluate. Further, adherence to these theories has led many educational programs to focus upon maladaptive rather than adaptive behaviors.

In addition to being influenced by theoretical approaches that attempt to relate behavior and personality, special education increasingly has been influenced by applied behavior analysis. In contrast to intrapsychic approaches, applied behavior analysis rejects implied relationships between internal forces and behavior. Applied behavior analysis emphasizes environmental influences on behavior. Consequently, according to proponents of applied behavior analysis the behaviors that need to be learned or altered through application of behavioral principles are the proper subject of special education. Additionally, the social context is afforded heightened importance in determining whether a given behavior is regarded as unacceptable. In this connection, the social norms and expectations of

Commonality 7:   *PRAGMATISM*

Contributions from Special Education
- Theoretical explanation for methods of instruction
- Recognized need to develop methods of teaching

Contributions from Applied Behavior Analysis
- Concentration upon behavior rather than theoretical constructs
- Emphasized the value of behavior in the applied context.

groups and cultures are often studied to determine what is within the range of acceptability. Finally, applied behavior analysis advocates the use of an objective basis for qualitatively distinguishing between acceptable and unacceptable behavior. To achieve this goal, students are provided educationally relevant experiences that reflect our society's goals.

SUMMARY

This chapter introduced several "commonalities" between special education and applied behavior analysis. These commonalities included focusing upon educational improvement by individualizing teaching and assessment. Further, this chapter emphasized the focus upon accountability, noncategorical teaching, empiricism, and pragmatism. It appears that special education and applied behavior analysis have the potential to enhance applications of the teaching process to solve problems of social importance.

There are numerous barriers to full adoption of a behavior analytic approach to special education, however. Special education has undergone much historical development, and some of this history is very positive. Special education combined with applied behavior analysis suggests an evolving psychology. Unfortunately, some of special education's influence upon individuals with handicaps is limiting. For example, the use of testing to identify people as belonging to one disability category or another is not useful to our larger social goals, which include preparing individuals to live, work, and recreate in mainstream society.

REFERENCES

ABESON, A., & WEINTRAUB, F. (1977). "Understanding the individualized education program." In S. Torres (ed.), *A primer on individualized education programs for handicapped children* (pp. 3–8). Reston, VA: The Foundation for Exceptional Children.

ALGOZZINE, B., & MERCER, C. D. (1980). "Labels and expectancies for handicapped children and youth." In L. Mann & D. A. Sabatino (eds.), *Fourth review of special education* (pp. 287–313). New York: Grune & Stratton.

BLACKHURST, A. E. (1981). "Noncategorical teacher preparation: Problems and promises." *Exceptional Children, 48*, 197–205.

BLOOM, B. S., ed. (1956). *Taxonomy of educational objectives; Handbook 1: Cognitive domain.* New York: David McKay.

BREYER, N. L., & ALLEN, G. J. (1975). "Effects of implementing a token economy on teacher attending behavior." *Journal of Applied Behavior Analysis, 8*, 373–380.

BROLIN, D. E. (1976). *Vocational preparation of retarded citizens.* Columbus, OH: Charles E. Merrill.

BROWN, L., PUMPIAN, I., BAUMGART, D., VANDERVENTER, P., FORD, A., NISBET, J., SCHROEDER, J., & GRUENEWALD, L. (1981). "Longitudinal transition plans in programs for severely handicapped students." *Exceptional Children, 47*, 624–631.

DUNN, L. M. (1968). "Special education for the mildly retarded—Is much of it justifiable?" *Exceptional Children, 35*, 5–22.

GILLUNG, T. G., & RUCKER, C. H. (1977). "Labels and teacher expectations." *Exceptional Children, 43*, 464–465.

HALLAHAN, D. P., & KAUFFMAN, J. M. (1977). "Labels, categories, behaviors: ED, LD, and EMR reconsidered." *The Journal of Special Education, 11*, 139–149.

HEWETT, F. M. (1968). *The emotionally disturbed child in the classroom.* Boston: Allyn and Bacon.

KAZDIN, A. E. (1980). *Behavior modification in applied settings.* Homewood, IL: The Dorsey Press.

KRATHWOHL, D. R., BLOOM, B. S., & MASIA, B. B. (1964). *Taxonomy of educational objectives; Handbook 11: Affective domain.* New York: David McKay.

LARRIVEE, B. (1981). "Modality preference as a model for differentiating beginning reading instruction: A review of the issues." *Learning Disability Quarterly, 4*, 180–188.

LESSINGER, L. M. (1970). "Acountability and curriculum reform." *Educational Technology, 10*, 56–57.

LESSINGER, L. M. (1971). "Robbing Dr. Peter to pay Paul: Accountability for our stewardship of public education." *Educational Technology, 11*, 11–14.

MAGER, R. F. (1962). *Preparing instructional objectives.* Palo Alto, CA: Fearon.

MARSTON, D. (1987). "Does categorical teacher certification benefit the mildly handicapped child?" *Exceptional Children, 53*, 423–431.

MERRILL, M. D. (1971). *Instructional design: Readings.* Englewood Cliffs, NJ: Prentice Hall.

MISCHEL, W. (1971). *Introduction to personality.* New York: Holt, Rhinehart & Winston.

PIAGET, J. (1964). "Development and learning." In R. Ripple & V. Rockcastle (eds.), *Piaget rediscovered: A report on the conference on cognitive studies and curriculum development* (pp. 7–20). Ithaca, N.Y.: Cornell University.

REYNOLDS, M. C. (1979). "Categorical vs. noncategorical teacher training." *Teacher Education and Special Education, 2*, 5–8.

REYNOLDS, M. C., WANG, N. C., & WALBERG, H. J. (1987). "The necessary restructuring of special and regular education." *Exceptional Children, 53*, 391–398.

RHODE, G., MORGAN, D. P., & YOUNG, R. K. (1983). "Generalization and maintenance of treatment gains of behaviorally handicapped students from resource rooms to regular classrooms using self-evaluation procedures." *Journal of Applied Behavior Analysis, 16*, 171–188.

RUSCH, F. R., CHADSEY-RUSCH, J., WHITE, D. M., & GIFFORD, J. L. (1985). "Programs for severely mentally retarded adults: Perspectives and methodologies." In D. Bricker & J. Filler (eds.), *Severe mental retardation: From theory to practice* (pp. 119–140). Reston, Virginia: Council for Exceptional Children.

RUSCH, F. R., & SCHUTZ, R. P. (1981). "Vocational and social work behavior: An evaluative review." In J. L. Matson and J. R. McCartney (eds.), *Handbook of behavior modification with the mentally retarded* (pp. 247–280). New York: Plenum Press.

SKINNER, B. F. (1969). *Contingencies of reinforcement: A theoretical analysis.* Englewood Cliffs, NJ: Prentice Hall.

STUART, R. B. (1970). *Trick or treatment: How and when psychotherapy fails.* Champaign, IL: Research Press.

TERMAN, L. M., & MERRILL, M. (1937). *Measuring intelligence.* Boston: Houghton-Mifflin.

TERMAN, L. M., & MERRILL, M. (1960). *The Stanford-Binet Intelligence Scale.* (2nd ed.). Boston: Houghton Mifflin.

WALKER, H. M. (1979). *The acting-out-child: Coping with classroom disruption.* Boston: Allyn and Bacon.

WALKER, H. M., & HOPS, H. (1976). "Use of normative peer data as a standard for evaluating classroom treatment effects." *Journal of Applied Behavior Analysis, 9*, 159–168.

WILL, M. C. (1986). "Educating children with learning problems: A shared responsibility." *Exceptional Children, 52*, 411–416.

WOLF, M. M. (1978). "Social validity: The case for subjective measurement or how applied behavior analysis is finding its heart." *Journal of Applied Behavior Analysis, 11*, 203–214.

WORKMAN, E. A. (1982). *Teaching behavioral self-control to students.* Austin, TX: Pro-Ed.

ZEILBERGER, J., SAMPEN, S. E., & SLOANE, H. N. (1968). Modification of a child's problem behaviors in the home with the mother as therapist. *Journal of Applied Behavior Analysis, 1*, 47–53.

chapter 4

Characteristics of Applied Behavior Analysis in Special Education

In the previous two chapters we presented an overview of events that have led to (a) the development of a discipline that has sought to serve children, youths, and adults with handicaps—special education—and (b) the development of a technology that has allowed for the systematic study of human behavior—applied behavior analysis. Chapter 3 focused on several "commonalities" between special education and applied behavior analysis. These commonalities form the basis for our interest in developing practical approaches to instructional programs for persons who fail to grow and develop according to societal norms. Students with mild and severe handicaps, for example, are often distinguished by their inabilities and their failure to acquire and use the skills needed to survive in the classroom (Walker, 1979), as well as in settings outside the classroom.

Traditional approaches to special education have sometimes forced the transfer of the student with mild handicaps from the reg-

ular to the segregated "special" classroom; or, worse yet, the student with severe handicaps has been transferred to the segregated classroom in the segregated "special" school. The practice of providing instruction outside the mainstream of educational and community activities is now challenged by our developing understanding of the type of instruction to be provided and the setting in which it should be provided. We contend that persons with mild and severe handicaps should not receive an education that highlights their differences, rather, they should receive one in which integration can be achieved supported by effective instructional practices.

In this chapter we introduce the characteristics of applied behavior analysis and provide examples of how teachers have incorporated applied behavior analysis in *integrated settings*. The characteristics of behavior analysis presented include use of (a) conceptual systems; (b) replicable instructional procedures; (c) functional analysis; and (d) analysis of individual performance. Additionally, direct and continuous measurement of behavior and social validation methodology will be discussed. Finally, this chapter concludes with a discussion of natural ecologies which points out the importance of providing instruction in *integrated settings,* that is, settings that are representative of environments that are either frequented by nonhandicapped individuals or in which individuals with handicaps will ultimately be required to live, work, and recreate.

CONCEPTUAL SYSTEMS

Applied behavior analysis is based upon principles of learning, for example, the principle of reinforcement. Skinner elaborated basic behavioral principles that contributed to operant performance. Based upon Skinner's research, a diverse set of instructional techniques has been derived for classroom application. Skinner's conceptual approach toward behavior is reflected in substantive principles introduced in Chapter 2. His methodological approach relates to the "experimental analysis of behavior." Table 4.1 lists these basic principles of behavior, accompanied by indications of the specific operations or procedures and their effect on behavior. These behavioral principles were referred to by Baer, Wolf, and Risley (1968) as essential to the development of *conceptual systems.*

Baer et al. (1968) noted that:

the field of applied behavior analysis will probably advance best if the descriptions of its procedures are not only precisely technological, but also strive for relevance to principle. To describe exactly how a preschool teacher will attend to junglegym climbing in a child frightened of heights is good technological description; but further to call it a social reinforcement procedure relates it to basic concepts of behavioral development. . . . This can have the effect of making a body of technology into a discipline rather than a collection of tricks. (p. 96)

In applied behavior analysis, a *conceptual system* refers to the substantive idea drawn from a class of relationships that result in a generalized concept. For example, positive reinforcement is commonly defined as a procedure in which following behavior with a positive reinforcer will result in an increase of that behavior. Conceptually, following the behavior with a positive consequence has led to the conclusion that positive reinforcers increase the likelihood of that response, if made contingent, that is, withheld until that response (behavior) actually occurs.

An example of the use of positive reinforcement was reported in the *Journal of Applied Behavior Analysis,* when Muir and Milan (1982) described and evaluated a reinforcement program in which parents earned lottery tickets based upon training accomplish-

TABLE 4.1 Summary of Basic Principles of Operant Conditioning

Principle	Characteristic Procedure or Operation	Effect on behavior
Reinforcement	Presentation (removal) of a positive (negative) event after a response	Increases the frequency of the response
Punishment	Presentation (removal) of a negative (positive) event after a response	Decreases the frequency of the response
Extinction	Ceasing presentation of a reinforcing event after a response.	Decreases the frequency of the previously reinforced response
Stimulus control and discrimination training	Reinforcing the response in the presence of one stimulus (S^D) but not in the presence of another (S^Δ)	Increases the frequency of the response in the presence of the S^D and decreases the frequency of the response in the presence of the S^Δ

Source: From *History of Behavior Modification: Experimental Foundations of Contemporary Research,* p. 100, by A. E. Kazdin, 1978, Baltimore, MD: University Park Press. Reprinted by permission.

ments and, subsequently, won prizes for their children's progress during home-based intervention. Three families were included to assess the effects of the lottery ticket prizes on children's mastery of language skills. Results indicated that reinforcing parents for training accomplishments, as evidenced by their children's achievements, produced socially significant increases in the childrens' progress under routine supportive practices. This specific application of positive reinforcement expands the conceptual development of the principle of (positive) reinforcement. First, the approach extended a commonly used procedure, presentation of an event after a response that has an expected outcome on behavior, (that is, it increases the frequency of the responses) because it was applied in a manner that has not been previously widely used. Rather than directly reinforcing the children's responses, the procedure was directed toward the parents in the hope that its effect on behavior would be maintained by a primary change agent, the parent, rather than a secondary change agent, the consulting teacher.

Another example of the use of the principle of reinforcement to modify social behavior was reported by Strain, Shores, and Kerr (1976). Subjects were three 4-year-old boys who had a history of behavior problems including delayed speech, tantrumming, and opposition to and withdrawal from their peers. A combination of verbal and physical prompts, plus verbal praise (the positive reinforcer) contingent on appropriate social behaviors, was used to increase the children's frequency of appropriate social behavior. The prompts included such comments as, "Now let's play with the other children" and "Pass the block" or "You can play house together." Physical prompts consisted of leading the child into the proximity of other children, modeling play with other children, and moving a child in such a way that he interacted with a peer. Teacher praise was given contingent on a target child interacting positively with a peer. Praise was always preceded by the teacher calling the child's name, for example, "Ricky, I like the way you are talking with Mary."

Figure 4.1 displays the frequency of positive and negative behaviors for Dan, Hank, and Ricky—the target children in the Strain et al. study. Whenever the procedure, referred to as "Intervention I" and "Intervention II" was used, the frequency of appropriate behavior increased and the frequency of inappropriate behavior decreased. This program demonstrates the function that prompts can serve by setting the occasion or providing the opportunity for appropriate behavior. When an appropriate behavior occurred, the teacher positively reinforced it with verbal praise. Again, the conceptual system used and evaluated was the principle of (positive) reinforcement.

REPLICABLE INSTRUCTIONAL PROCEDURES

From a replication perspective, applied behavior analysis is characterized by an emphasis upon two dimensions of the instructional process—teaching and learning, that is, student behavior change. In applied behavior analysis *replication* refers to the process of defining teacher and student behaviors sufficiently well that it leads to exact duplication by others. Thus, replicable teaching procedures entail describing the following: (a) antecedent events that occur prior to student responses (including academic and social behavior), (b) the student response, and (c) events that follow student responses. P.L. 94-142 requires that individualized educational programs (IEPs) be developed for all students with handicaps. IEPs take the form of detailing student goals and objectives, including statements of conditions under which student responses should occur and statements of evaluation criteria. The conditions under which student responses should occur include the three teaching procedures listed above. They will be more fully described subsequently.

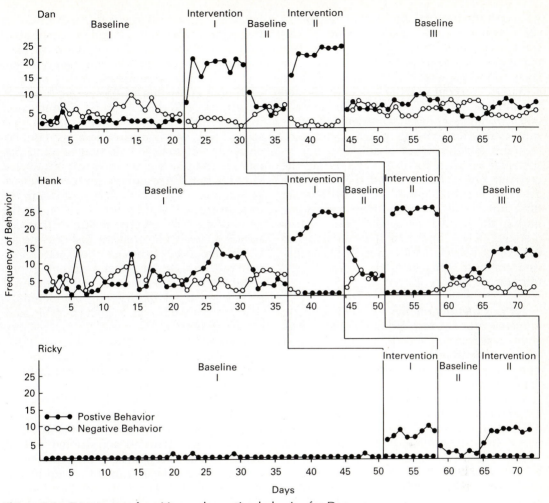

Figure 4.1 Frequency of positive and negative behavior for Dan, Hank, and Ricky across phases.

Source: From "An Experimental Analysis of 'Spill-Over' Effects on the Social Interaction of Behaviorally Handicapped Pre-school Children" by P. Strain, R. Shores, & M. Kerr, 1976, *Journal of Applied Behavior Analysis, 9*, p. 37. Copyright 1976 by the Society for the Experimental Analysis of Behavior, Inc. Reprinted by permission.

Antecedent Events. Teachers may use three types of antecedent conditions to prompt student performance: (a) materials, (b) rate of instruction, and (c) instructional arrangements. An example of the use of *materials* as antecedents in the teaching process was reported by Dunlap and Koegel (1980). In an effort to evaluate the effectiveness of two methods of presenting instructional tasks to two autistic children, Dunlap and Koegel introduced a "constant task" and a "varied task" condition. The former used the common method of presenting a single task throughout a session. For example, if the task was counting objects, the teacher might say, "How many fingers?" until the student performed the task correctly. The varied task condition was identical to the constant task condition (there were no systematic teaching differences) except that the task to be learned was interspersed with a variety of other tasks taken from the children's curricula. The results of this instructional program indicated that the children (ages 5 and 7 years) responded less correctly over time during the constant task condition than they did with the varied task condition, and furthermore they substantially improved their responding during the varied task condition. Consequently, it was concluded that variations in the use of instructional materials may motivate children with autism to correctly perform target tasks.

Rate of Instruction has also been found to influence student responding. Thus, considerable research has shown that rapid pacing of teacher instructions, combined with a clear signal to respond, positively influences student's academic performance in primary grades. Signals are considered valuable in group instruction because they may serve as discriminative stimuli, thereby increasing the occurrence of attending and responding. Teachers also use signals to delay responses by higher ability students until slower students have had the opportunity to formulate an answer and prepare to respond to the signal. For example, the teacher may say, "OK" then pause and ask, "What's the answer?" Such a delay provides all students an opportunity to answer, not just the higher performing students.

Rate of Presentation, also referred to as *pacing,* serves to regulate the quantity of instructional material taught within a given time period and to maintain students' attention to instructional material. Carnine (1976) showed that a faster presentation rate decreases the occurrences of students' off-task behavior, while increasing the occurrence of correct answers and participation. Off-task

behavior, answering correctly, and participation during beginning reading instruction were recorded by Carnine for two low-achieving first grade students during two different rates of teacher presentation. A slow-rate presentation, consisting of presenting a task to the student and then waiting 5 seconds after the student's response before presenting a second task, was compared to a fast-rate, no-delay presentation. In both slow-rate and fast-rate presentations, a new task was introduced after the student responded correctly. Rate of presentation was established by dividing the total instructional time for a session by the number of tasks presented during that session. The results favored the fast-rate, no delay presentation of the next task. Rate of instruction is one of several teaching procedures that has been evaluated in an effort to develop a set of teaching competencies that are defined so as to be replicable and, equally important, that relate to students' academic performance in the classroom.

Handleman (1979) investigated generalized responses to common questions asked of four boys, ages 6 to 7 years, enrolled in a center for developmental disabilities at Rutgers University. Greater generalization was found when the boys received instruction at different locations versus in a restricted setting, that is, in a cubicle similar to the type speech and language clinicians might set up to provide instruction. The different locations included natural school settings including the classroom, a lounge, near the coat cubbyholes, in the bathroom, and at the front door. A measure of generalization included answering questions in a non-trained setting such as the home. In addition, several instructional arrangements in the school setting, rather than single instructional arrangements, were replicated across several school environments to facilitate generalization of learning.

Instructional Procedures. Instructional procedures range from simple verbal commands to varying levels of instructional procedures based upon student performance. Varying levels of instruction have been used by teachers of students with severe handicaps. For example, Vogelsberg and Rusch (1979) taught three school-aged students with severe handicaps to cross streets at intersections. The students were provided preinstruction, instructional feedback, and selective repeated practice to acquire the skills needed to cross the street at partially controlled intersections (stop signs on two of the four corners). Selective repeated practice was introduced only when physical assistance was required on the skills students found particularly difficult to learn. The instructional procedures included telling the students what to do to successfully cross the street. Specifically, the teacher provided the following information before each trial: "I'm going to tell you the correct way to cross the street. First you walk to the corner, stop, look behind you, in front of you, to your left, and to your right; if there are no cars coming, walk quickly across the street, step up on the curb, and stop" (p. 268). After preinstruction, the verbal cue "cross the street" was given.

If the students had difficulty performing any one of the steps required to cross the street, instructional feedback was given in the form of verbal instruction or verbal instruction with a model, with partial physical assistance, or with total physical assistance. Table 4.2 displays the levels of instructions used by teachers in the Vogelsberg and Rusch (1979) study.

Results of this instructional program indicated that instructional feedback was sufficient in teaching "approach" (walking to and stopping on the curb) and "walk" (walking quickly across the street and stopping on the other side) responses; however, selective repeated practice was required to establish the necessary "look" responses. The use of different levels of instructional assistance in the order of least restrictive (no assistance) to most restrictive (total physical assistance) and utilizing specific performance criteria (amount of physical contact and verbal cues) adheres to the requirement of replicable procedures.

Student Responses. Student response is the second aspect of replicable teaching procedures. One of the primary goals of applied behavior analysis has been to describe student behavior in a precise manner. Student behaviors, often referred to as either aca-

TABLE 4.2 Levels of Instructional Assistance*

Code	Level of Assistance	Trainer Performance	Amount of Physical Contact	Verbal Cue
5	No assistance	Trainee completes the task independently in response to the natural environment while trainer observes.	None	None
4	Verbal cue	Trainer stands behind the student and gives verbal cues.	None	LISTEN
3	Verbal cue and model	Trainer models behavior while repeating verbal cue with a point prompt.	None	WATCH ME
2	Verbal cue and partial physical assistance (prompts)	Trainer repeats verbal cue while directing the trainee with small physical prompts.	2 seconds	YOU DO IT
1	Verbal cue and total physical assistance	Trainer repeats verbal cue and physically guides the trainee through the entire behavior.	Total	DO IT WITH ME

*Begin at Code 5, wait 3 seconds, proceed to the next level of assistance if the response is incorrect.

Source: From "Training Severely Handicapped Students to Cross Partially Controlled Intersections" by R. T. Vogelsberg & F. R. Rusch, 1979, *AAESPH Review, 4,* p. 267. Copyright 1979 by the Association for the Severely Handicapped. Reprinted by permission.

demic or social, have been carefully scrutinized. Typically, these behaviors are listed in measurable terms as behavioral objectives. For example, observable behaviors include marking, writing, removing, counting orally, naming, stating, and smiling. In contrast, behaviors such as concentrating, feeling, and understanding are not usually studied and not typically contained in a statement of objective. Since this second set of behaviors is not directly observable, gains reported by one teacher cannot be readily *replicated* by another.

Carnine's (1976) study of presentation rate exemplifies replicability in student response. As mentioned above, Carnine focused upon three student responses, including the social off-task and participation behaviors and the academic answering behavior. Figure 4.2 shows the average duration in seconds for

each session of the slow-rate and fast-rate presentation phases in his study.

Figures 4.3 and 4.4 display the academic and social behavior of the two students in Carnine's study. Carnine described his students' behavior as follows:

If a [student] responded within 1 sec. after the teacher's cue to answer, it was rated as Participation. If the [student] answered after more than 1 sec., it was recorded as nonparticipation. (Nonparticipation was not corrected by the teacher.) Appropriate academic responses were rated as Answering Correctly, even if the response was late and had been rated as nonparticipation. A wrong or no response was rated as incorrect and was corrected by the teacher. "Off-Task" behavior was defined as the occurrence of any of the following behaviors (from Becker, Madsen, Arnold, and Thomas, 1967): Gross motor occurred when the [student's] body left the seat of his/her chair to

Figure 4.2   Average task duration in seconds for each session of the slow- and fast-rate presentation phases. The student teacher taught during the final two phases (Sessions 34 through 38).

Source: From ''Effects of Two Teacher Presentation Rates on Off-Task Behavior, Answering Correctly, and Participation'' by D. W. Carnine, 1976, *Journal of Applied Behavior Analysis, 9,* p. 202. Copyright 1976 by the Society for the Experimental Analysis of Behavior, Inc. Reprinted by permission.

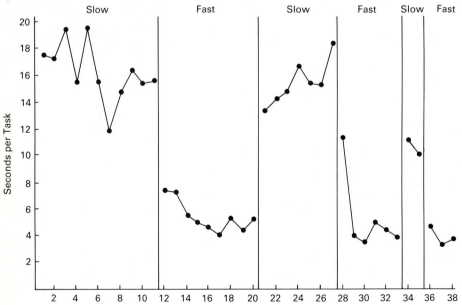

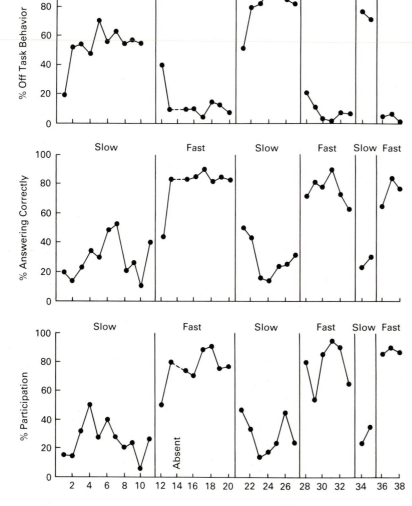

Figure 4.3 Percent occurrence of off-task, answering correctly, and participation for Subject 1 during the slow- and fast-rate presentation phrases. The dotted lines indicate when subject 1 was absent. The student teacher taught during the final two phases (Sessions 34 through 38).

Source: From "Effects of Two Teacher Presentation Rates on Off-Task Behavior, Answering Correctly, and Participation" by D. W. Carnine, 1976. *Journal of Applied Behavior Analysis, 9,* p. 204. Copyright 1976 by the Society for the Experimental Analysis of Behavior, Inc. Reprinted by permission.

engage in an appropriate behavior; e.g., walking around, moving chair, jumping. "Blurting out" occurred when the subject engaged in inappropriate or undirected talking, crying, screaming, laughing loudly, singing, calling "teacher," or blurting out answers before the teacher signalled for a response. "Talking" occurred when the [student] carried on conversations with other children in the group. "Other" occurred when the [student] ignored the teacher or exhibited minor motor behavior, such as foot tapping or other behaviors judged disruptive but that were not included in the previous four categories. (p. 201)

It is desirable to know precisely how the student's behaviors are defined. Carnine's study is an excellent illustration of both replicable teaching procedures and student responses. Thus, a person interested in assessing the effects of presentation rate on a similar student's behavior could readily dupli-

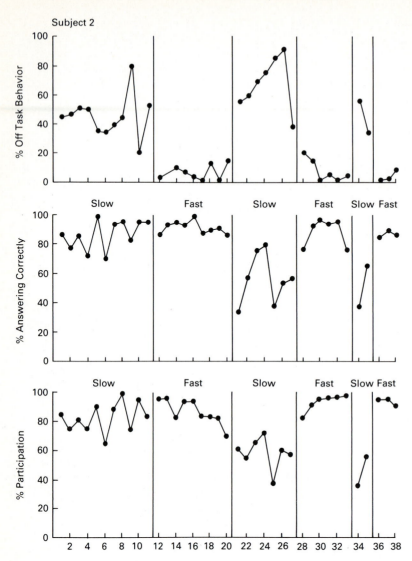

Figure 4.4 Percent occurrence of off-task, answering correctly, and participation for Subject 2 during the slow- and fast-rate presentation phases. The student teacher taught during the final two phases (Sessions 34 through 38).

Source: From "Effects of Two Teacher Presentation Rates on Off-Task Behavior, Answering Correctly, and Participation" by D. W. Carnine, 1976, *Journal of Applied Behavior Analysis, 9*, p. 205. Copyright 1976 by the Society for the Experimental Analysis of Behavior, Inc. Reprinted by permission.

cate the methods and procedures outlined by Carnine because of the high degree of specification of both teacher and student behavior.

Consequent Events. Consequent events are the third aspect of replicable teaching procedures. Numerous articles across a wide range of journals have reported the use of *replicable* consequent events applied in teaching students with mild and severe learning and behavior problems. For example, Fink and Carnine (1975) reported the effects of informational feedback and graphing on reducing the number of arithmetic worksheet errors. Ten first grade students (four males and six females) were included in this study. Students were provided feedback on the number of errors they made by a number written on the top of the worksheet which told how many errors were made. This consequence was followed by a feedback-plus-graphing consequence after the feedback procedure *alone* was studied, that is, the average number of errors made by each student was determined and a written feedback report given. Compared to the written feedback-alone, the feedback-plus-graphing consequence led to a reduced number of errors. Fink and Carnine's results constitute one among many demonstrations showing that use of a replicable consequence procedure which involves feedback and graphing can positively influence student responses.

The use of replicable procedures is a characteristic of applied behavior analysis which insures that others can apply the same *teaching procedures* to the same student *responses*. The teaching procedures include (a) antecedent conditions; (b) student responses; and (c) consequences. In applied behavior analysis the replicability requirement relates directly to functional analysis. Typically, functional relationships between procedures and responses are studied, thereby heightening the importance of incorporating replicability standards.

FUNCTIONAL ANALYSIS

Applied behavior analysis emphasizes relationships between instructional programs and changes in target students' behavior. For example, a previewing procedure such as *listening* might be used to assess a teacher's reading performance. The teacher reads the assigned selection aloud while the student follows along silently. Following this step, the passage is read aloud by the student (Rose, 1984). The teacher evaluates the cause-and-effect or *functional relationship* between the instructional strategy (the independent variable) and the student's behavior (the dependent variable). A functional relationship exists if it can be demonstrated that the dependent variable systematically changes in the desired direction as a result of the introduction of the independent variable.

Experimental Designs. Functional relationships are detected through the use of experimental designs. Numerous designs have been developed to assist in detecting relationships between independent and dependent variables. (These designs are presented and discussed in Chapter 8.) For example, Koegel, Dunlap, Richman, and Dyer (1981) analyzed the relationship between "orienting instructions" (the independent variable) and verbal labeling (the dependent variable) in three children with autism. The three students, who ranged in age from 5 to 7 years, were taught six discrimination tasks in the context of a multiple-baseline design. The tasks, selected by the students' teachers, included specific tasks that each student did not otherwise respond to. Table 4.3 lists the tasks, the referral problems, and the specific orienting cues used with each student who participated in the instructional program. For example, for "Child 1/Task 1" the child was required to respond "yes" or "no" to affirmation questions. The child was presented with a stimulus object (for example, a picture of a dog) and the teacher asked a question such as, "Is this a dog?" or "Is this a cat?" The child was required to answer "yes" or "no."

The multiple-baseline design is one of several designs teachers can use in the classroom to evaluate the effectiveness of instructional programs. In the Koegel et al. (1981) study the *multiple-baseline design* compared the influence of using "nonspecific orienting cues" (baseline) to "specific orienting cues" (treatment) on the behavior of the children.

The nonspecific orienting procedure consisted of a variety of phrases commonly used with the students such as, "Look at the picture," "Listen to me," and "Pay attention" (see Table 4.3). The children regularly responded appropriately to these instructions and were praised for doing so. They would look in the direction of the stimulus materials, look at the therapist's face, and sit erectly. However, when the children responded (for example, looked in the direction of the stimulus materials) when instructed to do so, it was difficult for the therapist to determine if the

TABLE 4.3 Specific Tasks, Referral Problems, and Orienting Cues for Each Child Who Participated in the Koegel et al Study. The Nonspecific Orienting Cues Required Nonspecific Orienting Responses from the Child. The Specific Orienting Cues All Required the Children to Verbally Label a Specific Relevant Cue.

Child/Task No.	Task	Referral Problem	Examples of Nonspecific Orienting Cue(s)	Specific Orienting Cue(s)
Child 1/Task 1	"Is this a ___?"	Child does not look at stimulus cards (i.e., problematic visual cue).	"Look at the picture."	"What is this?"
Child 2/Task 1	"Which is more (less)?"	Child answers a different question (i.e., problematic auditory cue).	"Listen to me."	"Which is more?, and say it." (Child says "more.")
Child 1/Task 2	"Point to more (less)."	Child does not respond differentially to the auditory cues.	"Listen to me." "Pay attention."	"Point to more, and say it." (Child says "more.") "Point to less, and say it." (Child says "less.")
Child 3/Task 1	"Put it by same (different)."	(a) Child does not look at picture, and (b) does not respond differentially to the auditory cues.	(a) "Look at the pictures," and, (b) "Listen to me."	(a) "What is this?" (for each picture) (b) "Put it by same, and say it." (Child says, "same.") "Put it by different, and say it." (Child says, "different.")
Child 1/Task 3	"Touch ___ first, and ___ last."	Child does not respond differentially to the auditory cues.	"Listen to me." "Pay attention."	"Touch ___ first, and ___ last, and say it." (Child says, "___ first, ___ last.")
Child 2/Task 2	"Put it in front (behind)."	Child does not respond differentially to the auditory cues.	"Listen to me."	"Put it in front, and say it." (Child says, "front.") "Put it behind, and say it." (Child says, "behind.")

Source: From "The Use of Specific Orienting Cues for Teaching Discrimination Tasks" by R. L. Koegel, G. Dunlap, G. S. Richman, & K. Dyer, 1981, *Analysis and Intervention in Developmental Disabilities, 1,* p. 190. Copyright 1981 by Pergamon Press, Inc. Reprinted by permission.

child had oriented to relevant cues. For example, it was difficult to tell whether the child was orienting to an entire picture, a part of the picture, or if the child was even clearly focusing on the picture. The same was true when the therapist used instructions such as, "Listen to me". For although the child looked in the therapist's direction, it was difficult to tell exactly what, if any, words the child was listening to in the subsequent target instruction. Therefore, while the nonspecific orienting cues always produced orienting responses, these responses did not yield precise information about the specific cues to which the children were orienting. The baseline condition was continued for 20, 39, 40, 60, 80, and 210 trials for individual child/ task combinations (see Figure 4.5).

The treatment condition was identical to baseline conditions except that prior to responding to the target instruction the children were required to verbally label specific relevant cues which did not appear to be controlling their responding.

When the orienting problem involved a problematic visual cue (for example, the child failed to look at the stimulus materials), then the therapist used a previously taught skill to prompt the child to verbally label the specific relevant visual cue. Then the therapist praised the child. For example, for the task, "Is this a fish?" the following procedure was initiated: Since the child had previously learned to label such pictures, the therapist simply placed the stimulus picture in front of the child, and asked the question, "What is this?" After the child responded by labeling the picture a "fish," the therapist was assured that the child had responded to the specific relevant visual cue (for example, the picture of the fish as opposed to the background). The therapist then presented the target task ("Is this a fish?" "Is this a dog?" and similar questions.) The specific cues used for each child are listed in Table 4.3.

When the orienting problem involved problematic auditory cues, the therapist presented the target instruction and prompted and reinforced the child for repeating the specific relevant words prior to responding in the instruction. For example, for the task, "Put it in front," the therapist might employ the following prompting procedure. First, the therapist would say, "Say 'front,'" and the child would repeat the word "front." The therapist would then say, "Say 'behind,'" and the child would repeat the word, "behind." In order to insure that the child was not merely echoing the last word, the therapist would present a target instruction such as, "Put it in front, and say it," after approximately three trials for each word. The child would then say the specific relevant word, "front," before being allowed to make the target response (of placing the block in front of the box). The treatment condition continued in the same manner as the baseline condition except that

on each trial the child labeled relevant cues prior to making the target response (The specific cues for each child are listed in Table 4.3.) Criterion for successful completion of the experiment was 90 percent correct responses within a given (plotted) block of ten unprompted trials.

The results of the instructional program (see Figure 4.5) show that, for each of the problematic tasks, the introduction of the requirement that the students verbally label relevant cues produced immediate improvements in correct responding. Thus, a *functional relationship* was demonstrated by manipulating *one key variable* (a specific orienting cue) at a time. As illustrated in Figure 4.5, each time the specific orienting cue condition was introduced, the student's behavior changed. Because this condition was introduced to a second and a third student at different times *and* because these students' behaviors, like those of the first student, changed *only* when the treatment was presented, we can conclude that a functional relationship exists.

In applied behavior analysis, the results of instructional programs are graphically displayed. While the graphs may take many different forms, the basic purpose is to plot a horizontal line or abscissa and a vertical line or ordinate. These lines represent the repeated measures over time of the student behavior, respectively. (In Figure 4.5 the lines were labeled "Blocks of Trials" and "Percent Correct Unprompted Responding".) Next, the "baseline" data are plotted, followed by the "treatment" data. These data represent the data points that are connected by a line representing each instructional condition; for example, "non-specific orienting cues" and "specific orienting cues."

Traditionally, data are visually analyzed to determine if a functional relationship exists (Parsonson & Baer, 1978). Visual inspection requires that the data be graphically displayed so that the various characteristics of the data can be readily examined. Visual inspection focuses upon changes in mean, trend, and level. The *mean* for each phase (for example, base-

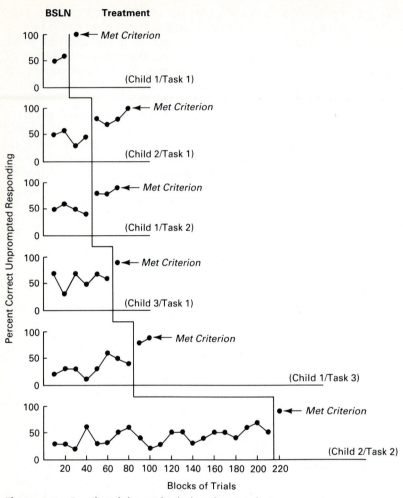

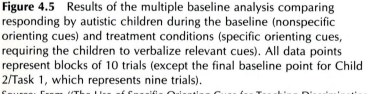

Figure 4.5   Results of the multiple baseline analysis comparing responding by autistic children during the baseline (nonspecific orienting cues) and treatment conditions (specific orienting cues, requiring the children to verbalize relevant cues). All data points represent blocks of 10 trials (except the final baseline point for Child 2/Task 1, which represents nine trials).

Source: From "The Use of Specific Orienting Cues for Teaching Discrimination Tasks" by R. L. Koegel, G. Dunlap, G. S. Richman, & K. Dyer, 1981, *Analysis and Intervention in Developmental Disabilities, 1,* p. 194. Copyright 1981 by Pergamon Press. Reprinted by permission.

line, specific cues) permits evaluation of the effects of the different conditions; that is, it provides a summary statement. The *trend* refers to changes within a condition, thus, a line is drawn to depict any upward or downward shift. Typically, this line is drawn by connecting the first data point in a condition with the last data point in the same condition. Other techniques have been recommended (White, 1974), however. Changes in *level* refer to shifts between the last data point in one condition and the first data point in a subsequent condition. These two data points are not connected in a graph; instead, a vertical line is drawn to indicate a change in conditions. Level is important because it assists in evaluating the immediate impact of a new instructional program. (Each of these terms and graphs are discussed in detail in Chapter 8.)

Applied behavior analysis relies upon the ability of the teacher to determine whether his or her teaching is responsible (functional) for changes in student performances. This is done using experimental designs. While designs, graphs, and judgmental aids—including mean, trend, and level—assist in the detection of such changes, their primary function is to determine functional relationships at the level of the individual.

ANALYSIS OF INDIVIDUAL PERFORMANCE

Because applied behavior analysis focuses on the individual and not the group, the individual's performance is typically monitored weekly, daily, or more frequently over an extended time period. The student's behavior is also studied under alternative teaching conditions. For example, arithmetic errors might be the focus of instructional analysis during a "teacher feedback" condition as well as a "self-monitoring and reinforcement" condition. In addition, the student's performance is analyzed by comparing it to the same student's previous performance.

Dineen, Clark, and Risley (1977) evaluated the effects of peer tutoring on elementary students' spelling performance. The subjects in the Dineen et al. study (1977) were three students, ages 9 to 10 years, who were members of an ungraded, open-environment classroom containing 12 students of normal intelligence, but with a 2-year reading and a 1-year math achievement deficiency. Briefly, these students presented to each other one of six

lists of 15 words to be spelled during a 20-minute tutorial. During the session, the tutor sat facing the tutee across a desk and two boxes large enough to accept the index cards. During the initial assessment period, each of the three students spelled less than 30 percent of the words correctly. After the students began to teach one another, improvement of each student's spelling was nearly equivalent for words on which they tutored another student and for words on which they themselves were tutored (compared to their baseline levels). No performance changes were noted on words on which subjects neither gave nor received instruction. These findings led Dineen et al. (1977) to conclude "that peer tutoring is profitable for the tutor as well as the tutee, [providing] a basis for recommending peer tutoring as one method of individualizing instruction" (p. 231).

Individual subject analyses may also be conducted under varying contingencies (Greenwood, Hops, Delquadri, & Guild, 1974). Specifically, it is possible to completely individualize an instructional program, whereby (a) behavioral criteria are based upon the *individual*, (b) recording behavior is based upon the *individual*, and (c) consequences are based upon *individual* performance. Table 4.4 presents the possible combinations of instructional components (a) when the individual is the focus (cells 1 through 6) and (b) when the individuals are treated as a group (cell 8).

Greenwood et al. (1974) provided an example of (a) the *group* criterion in the form of classroom rules; (b) recording the behavior (duration) of the entire class *group*; and (c) providng a *group* consequence dependent upon the collective performance of the group. The effects of rules, rules-plus-feedback and rules-plus-feedback-plus-group-and-individual-consequences for appropriate behavior were studied in three elementary classrooms during reading and arithmetic periods. The consequences consisted of individual and group praise and group activities such as extra recess and additional reading time. The total intervention program (rules-plus-feedback-plus-group-and-individual-

TABLE 4.4 Possible Combinations of Instructional Components when the Individual Is the Focus of the Analysis

	BEHAVIORAL CRITERIA ESTABLISHED FOR			
	Individuals		Group	
CONSEQUENCES BASED UPON	*RECORDING BASED UPON*		*RECORDING BASED UPON*	
	Individual	Group	Individual	Group
Individual	1	3	5	7
Group	2	4	6	8

Source: From "Group Contingencies for Group Consequences in Classroom Management: A Further Analysis" by C. R. Greenwood, H. Hops, J. Delquardi, & J. Guild, 1974, *Journal of Applied Behavior Analysis, 7*, p. 424. Copyright 1974 by the Society for the Experimental Analysis of Behavior, Inc. Adapted by permission.

consequences) was found to be most effective in increasing class appropriate behavior compared to baseline and prior phases. In contrast, rules alone produced no change in classroom behavior.

DIRECT CONTINUOUS MEASUREMENT

Applied behavior analysis relies upon direct measures of student performance. This approach is in contrast to the tradition of school psychologists who tend to assess performance on one continuum, such as IQ, while making statements about performance on another continuum, such as reading. Thus, *direct measurement* both assesses performance and states performance results on the same continuum. Intelligence tests and achievement tests are examples of direct measurement. As discussed in Chapter 3, the results of intelligence tests are typically used to rank students along a supposed continuum of mental ability. Similarly, the scores obtained on achievement tests are used to rank students. For example, a student who correctly answers 50 percent of the problems on an arithmetic test (a direct measure) may be assigned a score of "fifth grade, sixth month" (an indirect mea-

sure), which is a descriptor of a *different* continuum of skills.

A direct measure, on the other hand, evaluates a particular behavior and focuses on only that behavior. Direct measurement is useful for teachers for assessing objectives. For example, Neff, Iwata, and Page (1980) evaluated the effects of interspersal training versus high-density reinforcement on spelling acquisition and retention. Specifically, they compared an interspersal personal training approach, consisting of inserting words most recently learned by students during training, to a high-density reinforcement procedure, which is frequently used as a means of shaping academic performance in tutorial settings. The subjects were two students with moderate mental retardation and one student with profound deafness.

Direct measurement consisted of checking the students' responses as either correct or incorrect. Each daily spelling session consisted of one trial for each of 20 words selected from the *Dolch Basic Vocabulary* list (Forbes, 1956). The teacher presented a word vocally to each of the two students and a word in sign language to their deaf peer. A correct answer consisted of a written response in which each letter corresponded to the same word from the list. During baseline assessment, words correctly responded to were considered learned; hence they formed an initial pool of "known" words for the student. Words incorrectly responded to constituted a pool of training items.

During baseline assessment correct responses were followed by praise, whereas incorrect responses were corrected by the teacher (a) circling the incorrect letters written by the students; (b) vocalizing or finger spelling the correct spelling; and (c) requiring the student to write the words correctly three times. During "high-density reinforcement," ten reinforcers were delivered each session. For example, on each of the ten trials for a session, students were told, when appropriate, "You're really paying attention nicely," if they were looking at the paper, or "I am proud of you for writing so neatly," if the written response was clearly legible (Neff et al., 1980, p. 154).

During "interspersal training," one interspersal spelling session was instituted daily. Each session consisted of 20 trials—ten trials containing new words and ten trials consisting of known words that were presented in alternating order. As mentioned known words were initially derived from a pool of words spelled correctly on a pretest. These words were later replaced by mastered training words, that is, as a student reached criterion for a training word, that word was placed in the known words pool and a new training word was subsequently added to the list. Each time a training word was mastered, training and known words were rotated.

After a baseline was established, the high-density reinforcement or the interspersal approaches were presented each day in a randomly alternating order. Results indicate that interspersal training was more effective than high-density reinforcement in facilitating acquisition of spelling words. These data, which were obtained via *direct measurement*, have implications for educational practices by revealing that the less effective approach was the approach typically used in the classroom, that is, reinforcement.

This study exemplifies the primary advantage of utilizing direct measurement. By having a direct measure of each student's performance on spelling certain words, the teacher could immediately identify correct words with which to intersperse incorrectly spelled words. In contrast, when using achievement test scores, the teacher must translate a generality into a specific—the generality being the test score, the specific being those words the students spelled correctly or incorrectly. At this level, direct measurement is distinguished from indirect measurement. Direct measurement results in the design of effective teaching programs.

Traditionally, therefore, two types of measurement systems have been used. One is the indirect intermittent system, and the other is the direct continuous system. The former has a long history of use in special education, whereas the latter is a primary characteristic of applied behavior analysis. By directly assessing individual performance, direct measurement provides the teacher information about students' progress on learning tasks in the classroom. The primary methods of obtaining direct measures include completed student products and direct teacher observation of student behavior.

DAILY MEASUREMENT

Individuals behave differently from day to day. For many adults peak work performance falls during the first half of an eight-hour work shift; others perform better during the second half of such a shift. Students may follow similar performance patterns. That is, while reading a student may start out slowly, warmup, and then increase the rate of words read. Eventually, the student may revert back to reading more slowly as fatigue sets in. In addition to fatigue, factors such as maturation and stress may influence performance. Applied behavior analysis acknowledges that performance is unique to the individual, thus the individual is the primary focus of study. Because many different factors may influence performance positively or negatively, applied behavior analysis has emphasized the need to collect data frequently, often daily.

Daily measurement of performance provides a rich source of data on the behavioral process as well as the final product. Because applied behavior analysis stresses observation of performance over a period of time, including baseline and instructional programming, the teacher accumulates considerable information about the behavioral characteristics of students as they change (process).

Traditional evaluation approaches, on the other hand, tend to focus more on the behavioral *result* or the product of the instructional program being studied. Thus, few measurements are taken and evaluation usually entails a single performance measure to aid the teacher in determining how well a given student is doing. Typically student performance is compared to the performance of other students, not to the performance of the individual student alone.

One of the most important reasons for collecting daily measures is that they facilitate decisions about the teaching and the learning process. For example, it would be difficult to evaluate the influence on comprehension of daily drills during reading if only one or a few data points were collected. However, collection of daily measures for several sessions before daily drills were instituted and throughout the trial period would provide a basis for individual analysis. Applied behavior analysis is distinguished from other approaches to teaching students by its reliance upon repeated measures, often collected daily. Because the learning process and the product of the teaching process are critical to contemporary special education services, applied behavior analysts stress the importance of gathering a rich source of performance measures.

SOCIAL VALIDATION

Applied behavior analysis focuses upon problems of social importance. That is, it addresses the essential question: Will the behaviors selected and changed have some impact on the individual's overall functioning in everyday life? Since the inception of applied behavior analysis, methods for identifying the *focus* and the *results* of instructional programs have continued to develop. The term *social validation* generally refers to this developing methodology that assists in determining the focus of instructional programs and whether or not observed behavior changes meet the demands of the social community (that is, needs and expectations) of which the individual is a part. (Kazdin, 1977; Kazdin & Matson, 1981; VanHouten, 1979). Two social validation procedures have been developed to identify the focus and the results of instructional programs. These procedures are referred to as social comparison and subjective evaluation. *Social comparison* entails comparing an individual's behavior before and after instruction with the similar behavior of a peer, that is, somebody who is similar to the target individual but whose performance of the target behavior differs. Typically, the instructional program is considered acceptable when, after treatment, *the individual's range of competence* is indistinguishable from that of targeted nonhandicapped individuals. Using the method of *subjective evaluation,* significant others (that is, persons who have an interest in the educational outcomes, such as parents), for example, evaluate the student's behavior to demonstrate if they view behavior change resulting from the instructional program as significant, that is, as having a meaningful influence on the student's life. The primary difference between the two procedures is that social comparison relies upon direct measurement of identical behavior of, for example, students with handicaps and students without handicaps. Subjective evaluation, on the other hand, usually entails ratings or rankings by significant others.

Identifying the Focus of Instruction. Identifying the focus of instructional programs is important for handicapped students. Behavior has social implications and thereby influences social acceptability. Instructional programs strive to enhance learning by teaching students to acquire and use a variety of behaviors as well as helping them discontinue behaving in ways that draw negative attention from others. Because behavior varies among different individuals and settings, they must be identified at the "local level." For example, Nutter and Reid (1978) utilized social comparison to identify standards for community acceptance. Since appearance is important for community participation and acceptance, these researchers taught five women with severe mental retardation how to select their clothing to coincide with popular fashion. The women were taught to select color-coordinated clothing in accordance with popular fashion based upon local community standards. Normative data were obtained through *direct observation* of over 600 nonhandicapped women residing in the community. Typical combinations of clothing and garments worn were recorded in a variety of settings, such as at a local shopping mall or at a restaurant.

Subjective evaluation is another useful methodology for determining instructional focus. When utilizing this methodology, *opinions* are solicited from persons capable of making meaningful decisions about a student's behavior based on their relationship to the person (for example, a parent or a friend) or their professional expertise (for example, a teacher or a potential employer). The most obvious form of professionals' opinions may be obtained during the IEP development. For example, to identify problem situations for delinquent youths and the responses necessary for handling these situations, Freedman, Rosenthal, Donahoe, Schlundt, and McFall (1978) consulted psychologists, social workers, counselors, teachers, and delinquent boys. Once these situations were identified, the delinquent youths were asked to *rate* whether the situations were problems and how difficult they found it to handle them.

Assessing the Results of Instruction. Social validation methodology is also valuable for assessing instructional effectiveness. As with identification of instructional focus, the assessment of instructional effects is achieved primarily through social comparison and subjective evaluation. In altering conduct problems and deportment in the regular classroom, Walker and his colleagues at the University of Oregon have used social comparison methodology to evaluate the extent to which disruptive students deviate from their nonhandicapped peers in the classroom (Walker, Mattson, & Buckley, 1971) and at home (Walker, Hops, & Johnson, 1975). For example, Walker and Hops (1976a) incorporated social comparison methodology by utilizing normative behavioral observation data as a standard for evaluating the effects of an instructional program designed to reinforce either direct academic performance or survival skills. Prior to utilizing the instructional program, which consisted of token reinforcement, the target students displayed markedly lower rates of appropriate behavior than did their nondisruptive peers. *Direct observation* of both groups of students' behaviors were conducted. When the program was completed and the target students were replaced in their referral classes, behavior (for example, working on assignments and following instructions) fell within the range of acceptability of their nondisruptive peers.

In addition to its value in identifying the focus of instructional programs, subjective evaluation is useful for determining whether instructional results are of sufficient magnitude to alter *opinions*. Rusch, Weithers, Menchetti, and Schutz (1980) utilized subjective evaluation methodology to assess the effectiveness of an instructional program designed to reduce conversational topic repetitions of a male with moderate mental retardation employed in a dormitory kitchen at the University of Illinois. When asked to pinpoint troublesome behavior that required change, supervisors and coworkers indicated that the target employee repeated topics excessively during conversations (Rusch et al., 1980). Consequently, coworkers were provided pre-instruction on how to use instruction, feedback, and mild social censure as a consequence when the employee repeated a topic.

Table 4.5 presents the percentage of coworkers who believed the target employee repeated topics too often and should repeat topics less.

Initially when polled after meals (to establish a baseline) four out of ten coworkers reported that the target employee repeated too often; 50 percent (five of ten) thought he should repeat less. After meal session 20, once coworkers were instructed to deliver the educational program, 60 percent thought the subject should repeat less often. After meal session 39, 70 percent or the majority of those polled indicated that the target employee repeated the same topic too often and should repeat topics less. Following the final day of instruction, after the target employee had not repeated himself during 21 of the 27 meals, *all* coworkers questioned indicated that the employee repeated topics too often and should repeat less. Clearly, there was a discrepancy between direct measurement and subjective evaluations.

Wolf (1978) offered reasons why direct measures do not always coincide with subjective evaluations. These include the possibility that behavior observed and recorded by trained observers may represent a narrower class of responses than behaviors typically rated by peers. For example, in the Rusch et al. (1980) study, topic repetition for the coworkers may have represented a measure that comprised a broader definition than the one used by personnel who utilize applied behavior analysis.

Social validation was introduced in 1968 by Baer et al., but its use has lagged far behind the expectations of applied researchers (Wolf, 1978). This delay between use and development may be related to the fact that what is considered socially important is based upon the expectations of others. Efforts to measure expectations reliably, in turn, have lagged behind the measurement of overt behavior. Social criteria, which are based upon expectations, require that instructional programs be educationally relevant for the individual and valued by society. Social validation criteria extend beyond traditional special education criteria for acceptability because it identifies broader relevant educational and community programs by experimental means. Educational significance is difficult to establish unless significant others or the students themselves determine "acceptable behavior." Social validation ensures that intervention priorities, such as instructional focus and effectiveness of instruction, are not arbitrarily circumscribed. This methodology ensures a consensually valid impact upon individual functioning. Our understanding of what is valid as well as our understanding of what is valued is still emerging.

TABLE 4.5 The Percentage of Co-Workers Who Believed the Target Employee Repeated Too Often and Should Repeat Topics Less

Session	Repeats too often	Should Repeat Less
16 (N = 10)	40%	50%
20 (N = 9)	60%	70%
39 (N = 10)	70%	60%
67 (N = 5)	100%	100%

Source: From "Social Validation of a Program to Reduce Topic Repetition in a Non-Sheltered Setting" by F. R. Rusch, J. A. Weithers, B. M. Menchetti, R. P. Schutz, 1980, *Education and Training of the Mentally Retarded, 15*, p. 213. Copyright 1980 by the Division on Mental Retardation, The Council for Exceptional Children. Reprinted by permission.

NATURAL ECOLOGIES

If the ultimate goal of instructional programs is to help individuals develop to the maximum, then their potential for living, working, and recreating in an integrated community must be carefully assessed to discover *ecological congruencies* (Thurman, 1977). According to Thurman (1977), ecological congruence occurs when an individual's behavior is in harmony with the social norms of his or her environmental context. *Ecological incongruence,* on the other hand, occurs when individuals display behaviors that vary considerably from established social norms or when they lack the skills necessary to function or perform adequately in the normal environmental context. Historically, special education has identified such incongruencies primarily in the classroom setting and has removed deviant students from their *natural* ecology, the regular classroom, to an *unnatural* ecology, the segregated classroom. When ecological incongruencies occur, applied behavior analysts stress that either the student behavior needs to be changed or the environmental context in which the deviant or incompetent behavior occurs needs to be altered. To date, little research has been focused on changing the environmental context to achieve ecological congruence. Instead, research has addressed changing the individual's deviant or incompetent behavior by, primarily, removing the problem from one setting to another.

In this text, the natural ecology is the regular classroom or the community; special education refers to the process of teaching skills and behaviors that enable persons with handicaps to co-exist *with nonhandicapped persons* in the natural ecology. To achieve this purpose, emphasis is placed on (a) behavior interrelationships that occur from participation in special education programs and the impact of such participation upon target behaviors and (b) the impact of physical, social, and cultural contexts on special education.

Behavior Interrelationships. Even though environmental events (antecedents and consequences) play a major role in maintaining a particular behavior, Voeltz and Evans (1983) argued that behavior interrelationships are just as important. *Behavior interrelationships* imply that the operant may not be maintained solely by external environment stimuli but that it may be influenced by other chains or clusters of behaviors displayed by the individual. Thus, multiple, rather than single behaviors, are emphasized, and the possibility that changes in one behavior may affect other behaviors is acknowledged. For example,

Schroeder, Schroeder, Rojahn, and Mulick (1981) emphasized the importance of studying self-injurious behavior (SIB) from this perspective. These authors devoted part of their analysis of self-injurious behavior to covarying response topographies. In their study, the effects of medication change were monitored across a variety of interpersonal behaviors of a 16-year-old youth with severe mental retardation and prone to temper tantrums. Also, a number of instructional programs were assessed when the boy was given the following medications under different circumstances: (a) thioridazine was decreased from 150 mg to 100 mg and accompanied by a time-out program; (b) thioridazine was decreased to 0.0 mg with 5 mg of thiothixene added, and (c) thioridazine remained at 0.0 mg but thiothixene was increased to 10 mg. Results suggested that although temper tantrums were best suppressed at 0.0 mg of thioridazine and 5 mg of thiothixene, the reduction in medication was also related to increased levels of positive behaviors. Furthermore, it appeared that the medication change also affected positive social responses and that changes in these behaviors were related more to one another than to the suppression of tantrum behavior through medication. Schroeder et al. (1978) suggested that if only data on temper tantrums had been collected to the exclusion of other individual and interpersonal (staff) behavior, one might have easily been misled to believe that the reduction of thioridazine was solely responsible for bringing temper tantrums under control.

Setting Influence. A recent focus in applied behavior analysis has been the study of setting events (Wahler & Fox, 1981). The primary reason for acknowledging the setting as functionally related to behavior stems from recent documentation that setting events influence behavior apart from the temporal properties of reinforcement principles. For example, in a preschool environment with nonhandicapped children Krantz and Risley (1977) reported that an antecedent period of vigorous activity set the occasion for reduced attention to the teacher and more disruptive behavior during a subsequent story-reading activity. Interestingly, a rest period antecedent to the story-reading period (the setting event) reduced the number of disruptions while increasing attention. The implication of this type of contingency management procedure for the control of inappropriate and appropriate behavior among students with handicaps is clear—settings influence the behavior of students, including students with handicaps.

Natural ecologies consist of behavior-behavior and behavior-setting interactions. Consequently, since behavior can be influenced by both intrapersonal and setting variables, both sets of variables and their effect on each other must be considered to maximize the success and effectiveness of special education.

SUMMARY

This chapter introduced the following characteristics of applied behavior analysis: (a) adhering to conceptual systems; (b) using replicable instructional procedures; (c) incorporating functional analysis; (d) focusing upon individual performance; (e) obtaining direct, daily measurement of behavior; (f) basing measurement upon social validation methodology; and (g) emphasizing the need to provide instruction in settings representative of environments ("natural ecologies") that are either frequented by nonhandicapped individuals or are settings in which individuals with handicaps ultimately will be required to live, work, or recreate.

REFERENCES

BAER, D. M., WOLF, M. M., & RISLEY, T. R. (1968). "Some current dimensions of applied behavior analysis." *Journal of Applied Behavior Analysis*, 1, 91–97.

CARNINE, D. W. (1976). "Effects of two teacher presentation rates on off-task behavior, answering correctly, and participation." *Journal of Applied Behavior Analysis*, 9, 199–206.

CLOWARD, R. D. (1967). "Studies in tutoring." *Journal of Experimental Education*, 36, 14–25.

DINEEN, J. P., CLARK, H. B., & RISLEY, T. R. (1977). "Peer tutoring among elementary students: Educational benefits to the tutor." *Journal of Applied Behavior Analysis*, 10, 231–238.

DUNLAP, G., & KOEGEL, R. L. (1980). "Motivating autistic children through stimulus variation." *Journal of Applied Behavior Analysis*, 13, 619–627.

FINK, W. T., & CARNINE, D. W. (1975). "Control of arithmetic errors using informational feedback and graphing." *Journal of Applied Behavior Analysis*, 8, 461.

FORBES, C. T. (1956). *Graded and classified spelling list for teachers*. Cambridge, MA: Educators Publishing Service.

FREEDMAN, B. J., ROSENTHAL, L., DONAHOE, C. P., SCHLUNT, D. G., & McFALL, R. M. (1978). "A social-behavioral analysis of skill deficits in delinquent and nondelinquent adolescent boys." *Journal of Consulting and Clinical Psychology*, 46, 1448–1462.

GREENWOOD, C. R., HOPS, H., DELQUADRI, J., & GUILD, J. (1974). "Group contingencies for group consequences in classroom management: A further analysis." *Journal of Applied Behavior Analysis*, 7, 413–425.

HANDLEMAN, J. S. (1979). "Generalization by autistic-type children of verbal responses across settings." *Journal of Applied Behavior Analysis*, 12, 273–282.

KAZDIN, A. E. (1977). "Assessing the clinical or applied importance of behavior change through social validation." *Behavior Modification*, 1, 427–451.

KAZDIN, A. E., & MATSON, J. L. (1981). "Social validation in mental retardation." *Applied Research in Mental Retardation*, 2, 39–54.

KOEGEL, R. L., DUNLAP, G., RICHMAN, G. S., & DYER, K. (1981). "The use of specific orienting cues for teaching discrimination tasks." *Analysis and Intervention in Developmental Disabilities*, 1, 187–198.

KRANTZ, P. J., & RISLEY, T. R. (1977). "Behavioral ecology in the classroom." In S. G. O'Leary & K. D. O'Leary (eds.), *Classroom management: The successful use of behavior modification*. New York: Pergamon Press.

MUIR, K. A., & MILAN, M. A. (1982). "Parent reinforcement for child achievement: The use of a lottery to maximize parent training effects." *Journal of Applied Behavior Analysis, 15,* 455–460.

NEFF, N. A., IWATA, B. A., & PAGE, T. J. (1980). "The effects of interspersal training versus high-density reinforcement on spelling acquisition and retention." *Journal of Applied Behavior Analysis, 13,* 153–158.

NUTTER, D., & REID, D. H. (1978). "Teaching retarded women a clothing selection skill using community norms." *Journal of Applied Behavior Analysis, 11,* 475–487.

PARSONSON, B. S., & BAER, D. M. (1978). "The analysis and presentation of graphic data." In T. R. Kratochwill (ed.), *Single-subject research: Strategies for evaluating change.* New York: Academic Press.

ROSE, T. L. (1984). "The effects of previewing on retarded learners' oral reading." *Education and training of the Mentally Retarded, 19,* 49–53.

RUSCH, F. R., WEITHERS, J. A., MENCHETTI, B. M., & SCHUTZ, R. P. (1980). "Social validation of a program to reduce topic repetition in a non-sheltered setting." *Education and Training of the Mentally Retarded, 15,* 208–215.

SCHROEDER, S. R., SCHROEDER, C. S., ROJAHN, J., & MULICK, J. A. (1981). "Self-injurious behavior: An analysis of behavior management techniques." In J. L. Matson & J. R. McCartney (eds.), *Handbook of behavior modification with the mentally retarded.* New York: Plenum Press.

STRAIN, P., SHORES, R., & KERR, M. (1976). "An experimental analysis of 'spill-over' effects on the social interaction of behaviorally handicapped preschool children. *Journal of Applied Behavior Analysis, 9,* 31–40.

THURMAN, S. K. "Congruence of behavioral ecologies: A model for special education." *The Journal of Special Education, 11,* 329–333.

VANHOUTEN, R. (1979). "Social validation: The evolution of standards of competency for target behaviors." *Journal of Applied Behavior Analysis, 12,* 581–592.

VOELTZ, L. M., & EVANS, I. M. (1983). "Educational validity: Procedures to evaluate outcomes in programs for severely handicapped learners." *The Journal of the Association for the Severely Handicapped, 8,* 3–15.

VOGELSBERG, R. T., & RUSCH, F. R. (1979). "Training severely handicapped students to cross partially controlled intersections." *AAESPH Review, 4,* 264–273.

WAHLER, R. G., & FOX, J. J. (1981). "Setting events in applied behavior analysis: Toward a conceptual and methodological expansion." *Journal of Applied Behavior Analysis, 14,* 327–338.

WALKER, H. M. (1979). *The acting-out child: Coping with classroom disruption.* Boston: Allyn and Bacon.

WALKER, H. M., & HOPS, H. (1976a). "Increasing academic achievement by reinforcing direct academic performance and/or facilitative non-academic responses." *Journal of Educational Psychology, 68,* 218–225.

WALKER, H. M., & HOPS, H. (1976b). "Use of normative peer data as a standard for evaluating classroom treatment effects." *Journal of Applied Behavior Analysis, 9,* 159–168.

WALKER, H. M., HOPS, H., & JOHNSON, S. M. (1975). "Generalization and maintenance of classroom treatment effects." *Behavior Therapy, 6,* 188–200.

WALKER, H. M., MATTSON, R. H., & BUCKLEY, N. K. (1971). "The functional analysis of behavior within an experimental class setting." In W. C. Becker (ed.), *An empirical basis for change in education.* Chicago: Science Research Associates.

WHITE, O. R. (1974). *The "split middle" a "quickie" method of trend estimation.* Seattle, WA: University of Washington, Experimental Education Unit, Child Development and Mental Retardation Center.

WOLF, M. M. (1978). "Social Validity: The case for subjective measurement, or how applied behavior analysis is finding its heart." *Journal of Applied Behavior Analysis, 11,* 203–214.

chapter 5

Defining Behavior

Designing, implementing, and evaluating special education programs is a large and complex undertaking which goes far beyond the confines of the traditional classroom to include everyday life skills such as grooming, feeding, traveling, working, studying, shopping, interrelating, banking, and so forth. Determining and meeting the needs of exceptional students in these areas requires the use of systematic methods and procedures. A sample of topics and domains of behavior frequently included in special education programs (Jorgensen, 1982) is presented in Table 5.1. This represents *one* example of many such schemes for classifying human behavior (compare with Bloom, 1956).

Thus, unlike the natural sciences, for example, which have developed strict definitions of subject matter (Barker, 1968)—chemistry has tables of elements and biology classifications of species—no single classification of human behavior and its settings has gained universal acceptance in the fields of education and psychology. Behavior classification systems do exist, however. For example, the system presented in Table 5.1 is derived from the contents of Individual Educational Programs (IEPs) developed for special education students. Thus, it is not a conceptual but an empirically based system. In other words, Jorgensen's topics and domains (as seen in Table 5.1) illustrate what special educators have focused their instructional programs on in diverse settings. The proposed 16 domains of behavior represent an attempt to organize our knowledge of behavior into manageable units for instruction. These units are molar and, like molecules, each can be broken down further into elementary tasks, behaviors, and skills. In addition, it is possible to conceive of domains not represented here, such as problem solving and conceptual learning. As we design, implement, and evaluate special education, we will need procedures for defining tasks, behaviors, and skills.

TABLE 5.1 Illustrative Topics and Domains Frequently Included in Special Education

Motor Skills:
  gross motor
  fine motor
  locomotion
Self-Help Personal Skills:
  toileting
  feeding
  drinking
  grooming
  dressing
Perceptual Skills:
  sensory perception
  left-right
  auditory perception
  visual perception
  sequencing
Pre-Academic Skills:
  names of common objects
  numbers
  letters (names/sounds)
  colors
  shapes
Language and Speech Skills:
  receptive language
  vocabulary
  listening
    comprehension
  expressive language
    single words (vocab.)
    sentences
  nonverbal communication
    signing
    symbol systems
  speech
    articulation
    voice
Math Skills:
  numbers (reading, writing, counting)
  number-object correspondence
  basic facts (addition, subtraction, multiplication, division)
  fractions
  decimals, percents
  charts, graphs
  geometry
  measurement
    time, money, distance
School Skills:
  following directions
  school attendance
  starts tasks, stays on tasks, completes tasks
  relationships with authority figures
Vocational Skills:
  career awareness
  job interview skills
    production
    task sequencing
    attendance
    compliance
    independence

Consumer Skills:
  budgeting
  banking
  insurance
  permits, licenses
  living space (apartment, house, and so on)
    locating, leasing, renting
  shopping
  getting information
  ads
Leisure Skills:
  individual hobbies
  team sports
  organizations and clubs
  restaurants, cafes, theatres
  movies
Reading Skills:
  phonics-word attack-decoding
  vocabulary
    select word lists
    survival vocabulary
    sight words
  fluency
  comprehension
Writing Skills:
  handwriting
    manuscript
    cursive
    capitalization
    simple sentences
    paragraphs
    creative writing
    reports, stories
    letter writing
Spelling Skills:
  sight words
  phonetically regular words
  word patterns (families)
  words in context
Study Skills:
  outlining, note taking
  dictionary skills
  reference skills
  library skills
Social Skills:
  self-identification
  self-concept
  self-control
  social conversation
  interpersonal relations
Independent Living Skills:
  home management
  telephone skills
  transportation skills
  laundry
  food management
  emergency-safety
  child care

Source: From *Increasing the effectiveness of multidisciplinary teams* (p. 5) by S. Jorgensen, 1982. Des Moines, IA: Drake University, Midwest Regional Resource Center.

IMPORTANCE OF DEFINING BEHAVIOR

Clear and concise definitions of behavior are important for several reasons. First, they are a prerequisite for establishing the behavior(s) to be measured. Second, behavioral definitions provide the means for objective statements about behavior change goals and subsequent evaluation of these goals. Third, behavioral definitions enable us to focus on the proper teaching methods and strategies to accomplish these goals. Each of these areas will be discussed in the following sections.

Prerequisite for Establishing Target Behaviors

Proper measurement of behavior requires *clear* and *unambiguous* definitions. Specifically, this means that after having studied a *written description* of a given behavior, two people can observe a student and, when the target behavior occurs, agree that the behavior did occur. Accurate definitions, therefore, are those on which observers can routinely arrive at the same counts of the behavior being observed. This unique and stringent condition of joint observer agreement on the occurrence of a behavior is the hallmark of behavioral assessment and other forms of scientific measurement. By applying it to the behavioral definitions we construct for students, we insure that our assessments of behavior will be objective, accurate, and meaningful.

Consider for a moment other measurement operations in which we routinely engage. Measuring the length of an object, for example, requires the use of a ruler that has been, for our example, calibrated in feet and inches. One foot is defined as 12 inches. The measuring procedure consists of relating the ruler to some starting point on the object and then marking off some distance, let us say 2 feet 3 inches away from the starting point. If the same procedure and another ruler marked in feet and inches are used, it is highly likely that another person will confirm that exactly 2 feet 3 inches have been marked off. Be-

cause agreement on the measurement of length can be obtained, important tasks can be based upon these measurements, for example, the construction of a table or the building of a ship. Agreement is essential to accurate measurement, thereby preventing the potentially disastrous consequences of inaccurate measurement—a table that is not level or a ship that will not float.

Let's consider our example further and assume that the accuracy of the measurement was checked the second time using a metric ruler instead of a feet and inches ruler. Length now has a new definition—meters, centimeters, and millimeters—and the two measurements would not agree.

Consider a behavioral example of this very problem. Compare the following two statements written by a teacher intending to define the same student response:

> *Definition 1* - Emily raises her hand during the discussion.
> *Definition 2* - Alexia participates in the discussion.

Here, we have two definitions of participation as in the prior case we had two definitions of length. The definitions will lead the assessor to two different conclusions about participation.

The behavioral example entails an additional problem. Rather than being equally specific but different definitions of participation, as in the example of different measures of length (meters versus feet), one definition of participation is too broad. That is, Definition 2 may or may not subsume *specific* behaviors like: asks a question, raises a hand, states the directions to the game, asks players to take their turn, reads the question aloud, passes the card to the person on the left, and so on. All these behaviors could mean participation. Due to the lack of specificity and precision, two observers would most likely obtain low agreement on the occurrence of participation in Definition 2. In contrast, Definition 1 provides a statement of a specific behavior (raises her hand) making observation and, consequently, observer agreement much easier. Only by reading the exact behaviors meant by participation and remembering them can observers successfully meet the agreement criteria. *Thus, we can conclude that all measurement operations must facilitate agreement on what is being measured.*

A major problem in developing universally agreed-upon definitions of behavior relates to the use of ambiguous language. Verbs are the key to unambiguous behavioral definitions because they communicate what we *do*. Consequently, verbs that specify observable behavior should be used when developing behavioral definitions, including such verbs as *to look, to tell, to run, to lift, to say, to jump, to roll, to stand, to raise, to lower, to touch, to sit,* and *to talk.* In contrast, verbs that do not communicate specific actions should be avoided. These include such general and broad verbs as *to participate, to think, to listen, to discuss, to consider, to conceptualize, to know, to understand, to communicate,* and *to teach.*

Objective Statements for Behavior Change Goals and Their Evaluation

Definitions of behavior on which observers can agree provide the basis for objective statements of the student performance goals we wish to establish.

The *objective approach* requires that what we teach be directly observable and verifiable and subject to the observer agreement test. This is different from the subjective approach to teaching whereby students are taught skills which are not verifiable and which may only be apparent to the instructor. The danger of the latter approach is that its unverifiable nature makes it impossible for others to know which skill has been taught and, consequently, whether a change in skill level has really taken place. The objective approach, on the other hand, insures that what we teach is observable to both the student and other interested parties such as parents.

Behavioral objectives are statements about behaviors and skills and the context in which they are to occur; for example, home or school. In addition, some level of competence or proficiency is specified. Based on behaviors that students do not possess prior to teaching, behavioral objectives consist of written descriptions of what students will be able to do as a result of effective instruction. Using behavioral objectives, it is possible to construct the appropriate means for measuring student performance and to confirm when and to what extent teaching efforts have succeeded in establishing new skills. This information is useful in planning the next objective to be taught and how it will be measured.

Focus on Proper Teaching Methods

Behavioral objectives provide a focus for selecting effective teaching procedures by specifying a definite goal. Thus, objectives form the basis of a general teaching method that can be expressed as a continuing cycle which includes: (a) assessing behaviors; (b) planning objectives; and (c) applying appropriate teaching procedures. This method tells us *what to teach, what teaching procedures to use,* and *when we have successfully taught the skill.*

Thus, we define behavior in order to set objective educational goals for students—goals which can be observed by others, including the student. These goals, in turn, enable us to measure the results of our teaching efforts. In addition, we define behavior to insure that instructors know what teaching procedures are most applicable.

DEFINING THE OCCURRENCE OF BEHAVIOR

To measure behavior it is necessary to know when a given behavior has occurred. Three forms of evidence that are widely used to define occurrence of behavior will be discussed. They are: (a) direct observation; (b) machine recording; and (c) permanent products of behavior.

Direct Observation

When using direct observation, a human observer makes some record of the occurrence of a given behavior. A teacher can easily record handraising by simply making a tally mark on a sheet of paper each time a student's hand is raised. This type of record is presented in Table 5.2. At the end of a specified observation time period (for example, spelling period), the frequency of these tallies can be compiled to arrive at a single score that represents the occurrence of handraising during that session. This type of recording could also be carried out with a hand-held digital counter that incrementally increases the count each time the counter is pressed to record a target response. Similarly, a classroom teacher may tally the total number of oral reading errors (for example, hesitations, omissions, and word substitutions) made by a student during a 2-minute oral reading assessment. Figure 5.1 illustrates a procedure for recording the frequency of oral reading errors. While the student is reading, the number of errors observed by the teacher are marked by a slash. In this example, William has made nine errors during the 2-minute reading assessment. The form also allows for other measures to be made, such as the total number of words read and the number of correct words read. All these measures allow calculations such as rate of errors or percent of correct words to be made.

Outside the classroom, students could be directly observed to determine their ability to make a bed or to safely use marked pedestrian crosswalks on the way to work.

An essential aspect of direct observation is application of the agreement test. Since definitions of behavior may not be clear and since human observers are at times inaccurate, the agreement test is used to insure the consistency and objectivity of observation recording. The counts in Table 5.3 demonstrate two outcomes of the agreement tests.

The high-agreement example shows that one observer counted 13, the other 12, that is, a difference of only one count. This level of agreement may be quantified by dividing the larger quantity into the smaller and multiplying the quotient by 100 to form a percentage, $(12/13) \times 100 = 92\%$. In the low-agreement example, one person counted 13 handraises, the other 9, resulting in a percentage agreement of 69%. A rule of thumb in special education states that 80% agreement is the minimum level required to establish agreement on the test.

Machine Recording

Machines also can be reliably used to record occurrence of behavior. For example, Cleary and Packman (1968) added a touch-sensitive screen to a teaching machine involving three-item discrimination tasks. Students registered their selection of one of the three items (for example, a diamond, a circle, or a square) by touching the item on a screen, and this, in turn, caused a count to be made by the machine. For similar purposes, microcomputers and computer-assisted teaching machines are widely used in education. In the classroom, computers can be programmed to record students' behavior while they engage in computer-assisted instruction. For example, the frequency of correct responses to a specific lesson can be recorded. These data can be reported to the teacher by the computer or used by a computer program to adjust the lesson to the student's error pattern (Siegel &

TABLE 5.2 Frequency Recording Example

Student: *Tony*	Date: *5-23*	Session: *2*	Observer: *Ray T.*

Handraising Frequency Tally	Total Frequency Score
*HHt HHt HHt /// *	18

FIGURE 5.1 Sample Reading Rate Observation Form

Name: *William*   Level: *9*   Date: *9/15/84*

This is based upon a 2-minute reading session

          Beginning page: *31* ----- Word: *The*

               Ending page: *32* ----- Word: *at the park.*

.... Errors Tally ....

~~1~~	~~2~~	~~3~~	~~4~~	~~5~~	~~6~~	~~7~~	~~8~~	~~9~~	10
11	12	13	14	15	16	17	18	19	20
21	22	23	24	25	26	27	28	29	30

Total Words Read: *105*
Total Errors: *009*
Total Correct: *096*

Percent Correct: *91%* [(96/105) × 100]
Correct Words per Minute: *048* (96/2min.)
Error Words per Minute: *004.5* (9/2min.)

Source: From *Reading peer tutoring manual,* p. *11–12,* by J. Delquadri, M. Elliott, and V. Hughes, 1981. Kansas City, KS: University of Kansas, Juniper Gardens Children's Project.

Davis, 1986). Student responding can be recorded directly from the computer keyboard, by a touch-sensitive stylus, by a computer "mouse," or by voice activation.

In community settings, machines that include counters or timers are often used. Punching a time clock is one simple and widespread means of recording arrival to and departure from work. A counter mounted on the door can record the number of racks of dishes a dishwashing machine has washed while a student is learning to perform the job during a trial work period. Bailey and Meyerson (1969) reported machine recordings involving an adult with a limited response repertoire due to profound mental retardation in

TABLE 5.3 Possible Agreement-Test Outcomes

High-Agreement Example	
Handraising Frequency Tally	Total Frequency Score
~~HHT~~ ~~HHT~~ /// (Observer 1)	13
~~HHT~~ ~~HHT~~ // (Observer 2)	12
Low-Agreement Example	
Handraising Frequency Tally	Total Frequency Score
~~HHT~~ ~~HHT~~ /// (Observer 1)	13
~~HHT~~ //// (Observer 2)	9

a hospital setting. Specifically, an electronic counter that recorded the frequency of behavior was connected to a lever which the subject pulled.

Permanent Products of Behavior

Permanent products of behavior result from a given behavior and remain following the behavior. For example, math problems solved by a student are a written product of the student's computational behavior. The problems can be graded, counted, analyzed, and treated as direct indices of the students' ability to perform this particular task. In the community, adults working in an electronics firm may assemble electronics parts. The individual electronic parts are the permanent products of their behavior.

Observation, machine recording, and permanent products of behavior provide the objective basis for determining whether or not a behavior has occurred. It can be argued that measurement by machine and permanent product are the most objective records of behavior since the behavior itself actually produces a lasting physical change on the recording medium, whatever it may be—computer memory bank, items made, or written words. Observational recording, in comparison, is mediated by the observer who sees and then records the behavior. Since observers are open to various forms of bias and inexactitude, observational recording requires careful monitoring and use of specified procedures (that is, the agreement test) to insure that reliable and accurate records are being obtained. Chapter 7 includes observational procedures taking into account observer fatigue and other problems associated with direct observation.

We will now turn to a discussion of the dimensions of a behavioral definition in further preparation for writing behavioral objectives. Some sample behavioral definitions used in a rural residential program for youth with severe handicaps are listed in Table 5.4 (Singer, Close, Irvin, Gerston, & Sailor, 1984).

DIMENSIONS OF A BEHAVIORAL DEFINITION

Behavioral definitions can be construed in at least seven dimensions: (a) topography, (b) locus, (c) magnitude, (d) latency, (e) duration, (f) frequency, and (g) accuracy. Whereas topography and locus must be part of all behavioral definitions, the inclusion of magnitude, latency, duration, frequency, and accuracy in any single definition depends upon the nature of the response being defined.

TABLE 5.4 Sample Behavioral Definitions

Definitions of Targeted Inappropriate Behaviors

Physical abuse of others:
  Aggressive behavior directed against other persons. The behavior is a motor behavior such as kicking, hitting, pulling hair, and throwing objects at another. This category does not include verbal behavior.

Physical abuse of the environment:
  Manipulation of objects in such a way that the object must be replaced, repaired, or substantially restored. This category includes breaking dishes, tearing books, dumping the contents of a dresser, feces smearing on household furniture, cutting hoses and cords with knives, breaking windows, and smashing holes in walls.

Physical self-abuse:
  Motor behaviors directed at the client's own person that actually or potentially cause tissue damage. This category includes self-hitting, self-biting, hair pulling, head banging, and placing inedible objects in the eyes, mouth, nose, and ears.

Source: From "An alternative to the institution for young people with severely handicapping conditions in a rural setting" by G. Singer, D. Close, L. Irvin, R. Gersten, and W. Sailor, 1984, *The Journal of the Association for Persons with Severe Handicaps, 9.* 255.

Topography

A response's *topography* refers to its form and content. Thus, topography specifies orientation in space or the angle of movement of various body parts as a response is made. Since behavior is fluid, changing from moment to moment, so is its topography. For example, lifting a fork to one's mouth requires a set of movements that involve scooping food onto the fork, lifting the fork to the mouth, and placing the food into an open mouth. This movement is followed by chewing, swallowing, and the simultaneous replacement of the fork near the plate.

In geography, topography refers to variation in land formations; in behavior analysis, the term specifies the patterning of a response in space and time. Absolute representation of topography of a response may take the form of a photograph or a videotape. In behavior analysis we are rarely interested in defining topography this completely, but there is a focus on critical features which are subsequently incorporated into our definition. As an illustration, consider turning on a light in a room. The topograpy of a "switch-on" response is broad. Conceivably, any response that moves the switch to the "on" setting is appropriate, and the switch can be moved to the "on" position by a sequence of behaviors that might include:

Walking to the switch, touching the switch with two fingers (thumb and index finger), followed by pushing or pulling the switch with the thumb or the index finger, depending on the direction in which the switch is to be moved.

This sequence of switching is called a *response class*. A response class is a set of topographic variations, and, in this simple example, it results in the turning on of the light. In some instances, a narrower response class is necessary—the behavior must be executed in a very specific manner. In others, as in the turning on of the light, we accept a broader response class—the behavior may be executed in any manner, as long as the response results in the light being turned on. As a rule

of thumb, definitions of narrow response classes are more complex, requiring greater specification of acceptable forms of the response than definitions of broader response classes. For example, the way a student grasps a pencil requires a clear, concise topographic description. The correct response may be defined as:

The student grasps the pencil between the thumb and middle finger with the index finger resting on top. With the hand positioned on the desk in preparation for writing, the pencil will form an angle of between 25 to 45 degrees off the horizontal line defined by the desk.

Locus

Locus refers to the object or person to which a behavior is directed. The loci of behavior in the classroom consist largely of the objects and persons in the school and those objects and persons that constitute classroom instruction. Thus, students with mild handicaps may be taught classroom behavior rules (Greenwood, Hops, Delquadri, & Guild, 1974), such as sitting in a chair or desk or correctly using books, curriculum materials, toys and games, audiovisual equipment, and computers. Students with mild handicaps may also be trained to engage in positive relationships with their peers (Greenwood, Todd, Hops, & Walker, 1982; Greshman, 1982). In addition to this type of instruction (Chadsey-Rusch, Karlan, Riva, & Rusch, 1984), students with more severe handicaps may also be trained to use doors, stairs, and prosthetic devices within the school and community setting.

Outside the school students with mild handicaps are frequently trained to comply with parent commands and instructions. Parents, siblings, and friends are common loci of social relations. Objects in the home, ranging from toys to clothing, are frequent loci of programs designed to teach students to clean up their rooms or to learn independent dressing skills. For students with severe handicaps, loci within the home are often those dealing with eating, grooming, toileting, and bathing (Wilcox & Bellamy, 1987). In employment settings, supervisors and coworkers constitute the social loci. When at work, equipment and materials related to work tasks become the common loci; whereas, games and toys and their rules are typical loci in recreational settings.

Magnitude

Magnitude is defined as the intensity of a response, usually in terms of force, pressure, distance, or amplitude. For example, one difference between a pat on the shoulder and being hit on the shoulder relates to magnitude. Magnitude is often measured in terms of force (for example, of force grams per response). Many of the behaviors we take for granted in our daily lives require response magnitudes which are too large for persons with physical handicaps, and, consequently, these behaviors serve as barriers to the equal access of persons with disabilities. Consider the force necessary to push open a door to a large building or the response magnitudes required to hold objects that break easily.

Examples from Classroom Settings. Noise is often a problem in the classroom. Noise magnitude can be defined and measured by a decibel meter. Schmidt and Ulrich (1969) used a decibel meter to measure and set appropriate criterion levels in a noise-reduction program for fourth grade elementary students. Noise within an "open" concept school building and noise originating outside a classroom, from a playground or parking lot, can also be measured in this way.

Examples from Community Settings. For children with handicaps, the magnitude of noise in the home may be a target for assessment. Similarly, the force of handshakes and pats on the back is an important aspect of appropriate positive interactions. Children who are aggressive in their play and in their peer social interaction tend to use excessive force in such settings. Students with severe handicaps often need training in how to control their fine- and gross-motor movements.

Opening doors in homes, school buildings, and automobiles requires specific levels of force. Similarly, managing the force requirements of fine-motor movements such as feeding is often a target for assessment and intervention. Some persons with physical disabilities use excessive force in their fine-motor movements due to their disability, as in the case of cerebral palsy.

Latency

Many important behaviors occur following some signal from the environment. Two types of latencies are of interest to special educators—response latency and interresponse latency. *Response latency* refers to the time between a signal event or stimulus, such as the teacher giving a command to put materials away, and the time when the student begins cleaning up. *Interresponse latency* signifies the interval between completing one response, such as solving a math problem or vacuuming a bedroom and beginning another—solving a second problem or vacuuming the next room. Thus, latency is a measure of the time intervening between an event and a response (response latency) and the time between one response and the next (interresponse latency). Latency length results in different consequences depending upon the particular situation. For example, if students have large latencies, they may fail to be hired for a job, be judged to be less skillful, or fail to acquire academic skills. Since latency is an important dimension of the rate of performance, behavior change efforts often focus upon reducing latency.

Examples from Classroom Settings. The latency between teacher instructions or commands and student compliance is a problem that routinely confronts teachers. For example, with students who have mild handicaps, group compliance is a frequent problem. Consider the latency between the time when the teacher says, "Everyone please line up at the door" and the point when the last child is standing in line. Interresponse latencies are often an issue in regard to student's independent work and study. Low interresponse latencies between looking up definitions of individual words in a dictionary make it unlikely that a student will complete the assignment within the time allowed.

Examples from Community Settings. Persons with severe handicaps must often learn to acquire response latencies that are appropriate for such situations as crossing an intersection (Vogelsberg & Rusch, 1979), exiting an elevator, and departing a stopped bus. In all these instances, the response must begin within a few seconds after the opportunity to respond is present. Appropriate interresponse latencies, in turn, are necessary for meeting production quotas, such as assembling the expected number of products or the bussing of the expected number of dirty dishes from a table. Here, finishing one response is the signal or stimulus to start the next.

Duration

Duration is defined as the period of time in which a response continues. It is most often measured in terms of the elapsed time or the number of short time intervals (for example, the number of 10-second intervals) during which a response occurs. Duration is particularly important for defining behaviors that must be briefly and quickly executed or those that must persist over time. Examples of brief behaviors include the winning times at sports events. Examples of long-duration behaviors include attention to a particular task, time engaged in studying, and so forth. In these instances, a longer time period is generally better.

Examples from Classroom Settings. Attention to task (or the inverse, nonattending to task) is a frequently targeted behavior of students with mild handicaps (for example see Greenwood et al., 1979; Walker & Buckley, 1968). Attention may be measured by observing a child and using a stopwatch to record the total time that he or she engaged in a given behavior. Greenwood et al. (1974)

developed a definition of attention for an entire class of students. Behavior defined in this manner was measured by using a clock and light device (see Figure 5.2). When all students were engaged in the behaviors, the teacher turned the clock and light on. The clock recorded the elapsed time. When at least one student was not engaged in the behavior, the clock and light were switched off. At the end of the session the cumulative time that all students were attending was recorded.

Knapczyk, Johnson, and McDermott (1983) assessed the on-task behavior, work production, and work accuracy of students learning an assembly task in a prevocational educational program for adolescents with severe

Figure 5.2 Clocklight
Source: Adams, G. L. (1984). An inexpensive wireless remote controlled clocklight. *Education and Treatment of Children, 1,* p. 76.

handicaps. Observers tallied 10-second intervals in which on-task behavior occurred for the entire time period and tracked the percentage of intervals that students were on task.

Examples from Community Settings. Students with mild handicaps often need to practice behaviors in order to decrease the time required to dress for school, to clean up one's room, to run an errand, and so forth. More specifically, for students receiving vocational training, attending to task has been defined as any observable physical activity that is job related; for example;

any observable physical activity that is job related during an entire 30 second interval. Time spent not attending is defined as the absence of any job related activity, for instance, standing still, staring out the window, moving hands in pockets, or any behavior without an apparent association with completing any aspect of the job, during any one second period. If there is a hesitation or a moment without task-related activity, the entire 30 second interval is coded as time spent not attending. (Rusch, 1979, p. 403)

Frequency

Frequency refers to the number of specific events that have occurred and which are measured in terms of counts or tallies within a time period. The number of times a student hits his head, the number of microscopes assembled, or the number of salads prepared are examples of frequency. Frequency definitions are also commonly expressed in terms of *rate of response,* which is the ratio of frequency per unit of time (for example, responses per minute). "Frequency definitions are also expressed as the *percentage of momentary time samples* in which a response was observed to occur (for example, percent of intervals). As with duration, magnitude, and latency, high and low frequencies of responding have differential consequences.

Examples from Classroom Settings. For students with mild handicaps, the frequency of academic behaviors are common behav-

ioral targets, such as the number of problems or assignments completed, as are the frequencies of disruptive or inappropriate behaviors, such as being out-of-seat, talking out-of-turn, having temper tantrums, and displaying aggressive responses.

The frequency of rumination was addressed with four students with multiple handicaps in classroom settings (Barton & Barton, 1985). The children in this study were observed by classroom aides and teachers who recorded the frequency of rumination per day for each child. Brady et al. (1984) assessed and increased the frequency of social interactions in a 15-year-old autistic boy who was also severely withdrawn. Their study was conducted in a special education classroom in a regular elementary school.

Examples from Community Settings. For some students, homework completion is a problem. Rosseau, Poulson, and Salzberg (1984) established a homework program for 16 students with records of low academic achievement. As part of the program, the authors defined the number of assignments that students completed by measuring whether the student handed in the assignment within 3 minutes of the time the teacher requested it and by measuring the number of students who chose to rework their assignments. As a minimum criterion, reworking meant that at least one problem was reworked. The 3-minute criterion was used to insure that students had actually completed the work outside of classroom time.

Phillips (1968) reported the frequency of several behaviors, such as the number of bathroom cleaning tasks and the number of "ain't" responses, within a home-style rehabilitation program for predelinquent boys. Sixteen bathroom tasks were defined by partitioning the floor into quarter-inch squares and assessing the absence of dirt with each of these squares. The frequency of "ain't" verbalizations was recorded for a single student during a daily 3-hour period using a silent pressure-sensitive digital counter (Phillips, 1968).

Hanson and Hanline (1985) conducted several experiments to train parents to work with their children in the home. As a means of initiating communication with the parents, one child with both visual and auditory impairments was taught to depress a pressure-sensitive panel that produced an auditory bleep. The response was defined by the frequency of panel depressions. Since the panel had a preset pressure requirement, the response was further defined by the pressure required to activate the switch. With another student, the authors recorded the frequency of vocalizations and smiles. Vocalization was defined as:

"Sound which did not include whines, cries, or sneezes" but did include "coos, gurgles, and giggles."

Smiles were defined as:

"Any instance in which corners of the mouth are upturned. Child's mouth may be open and child may vocalize."

In another study in which frequency recording was used (Breen, Haring, Pitts-Conway, & Gaylord-Ross, 1985), four high school-aged students with autism and other severe handicaps were trained to initiate and maintain social interactions with nonhandicapped peers during breaktimes in two community job sites. The frequency of prosocial behaviors from a task analysis list of behaviors taught to the students was recorded and converted to a percentage score (frequency observed divided by total possible behaviors times 100). The prosocial behaviors that were trained are specified in Table 5.5.

Accuracy

Often behaviors must be performed according to some criterion making them either correct or incorrect. Math problems correctly solved and spelling words correctly written are common examples.

Accuracy is usually expressed as the frequency of correct responses divided by the total number of problems assigned or attempted and expressed as the percentage of correct answers. Rate measurement also may be expressed as either a correct or incorrect percentage. Finally, accuracy may be expressed as the number of trials required for an indivdiual to reach a criterion level of performance. For example, it may take a student five trials to correctly identify all the objects used in a color-discrimination task.

TABLE 5.5 Breaktime Task Analysis of a Social Behavior Sequence

1. S. leaves work area.
2. S. pours a cup of coffee.
3. S. adds 1 spoon/packet of sugar.
4. S. adds 1 ounce of milk.
5. S. takes coffee to any table and sits down.
6. S. asks familiar co-worker/peer, "Hi, how are you?"
7. S. asks peer "Would you like coffee?"
8. S. pours a cup of coffee for peer.
9. S. hands coffee to peer.
10. S. asks peer, "What's new?"
11. S. responds appropriately to peer question, "What have you been doing at work?" (that is, "doing dishes," "raking," "weeding").
12. S. responds to peer statement, "Take it easy" with "Take it easy."
13. S. returns to work.

Source: From "The training and generalization of social interaction during breaktime at two job sites in the natural environment" by C. Breen, T. Haring, V. Pitts-Conway, and R. Gaylord-Ross, 1985, *The Journal of the Association for Persons with Severe Handicaps, 10,* p. 44.

Examples of Classroom Settings. Improved oral reading is a target behavior with many students. Oral reading may be defined as:

"Eyes directed upon the correct page in a reading book, while the student says aloud the words read from left to right across the printed page."

The essential aspects of topography in this definition include looking at the page, orally pronouncing the words on the page, and eyes moving from left to right across the page in relation to the correct words being read in correct sequence. Oral reading errors have been defined as including:

(a) hesitations—defined as a pause in oral reading lasting longer than three seconds,
(b) omissions—defined as failing to read aloud a word that should have been read,
(c) substitutions—defined as stating aloud a word that is not the word that should be read. (Delquadri, Elliot, & Nughes, 1981)

Reading instruction for persons with severe handicaps may involve presenting words or signs that naturally exist in the community, such as stop signs, exit signs, enter signs). In this context, reading may be defined as:

"Student immediately (within 3 to 5 seconds) says/signs the word when it is presented on a 3 by 5 inch flashcard (in a slide depicting the word in its natural location)."

Definitions of a student's correct understanding of the meaning of a survival word, for example, the word "stop," may include the following dimensions:

(a) When asked what the word "stop" means, the student will shake his or her head from side to side.
(b) When asked to demonstrate functional awareness of the meaning of the word the student stops walking across the street when the "wait or stop" walking sign is flashed.

Examples from Community Settings. In the home setting, students may be required to routinely clean their bedroom. This task includes correctly or incorrectly placing books on a book shelf, shoes on a shoe rack, and shirts on hangers in the closet. Accuracy defined as attempted trials to achieve a criterion may be used to establish the correct disposition of each of these single behaviors. The student must learn these entry behaviors in the hope that the student can accurately place the objects in the room before the parent gives a general clean-up command.

In employment settings, starting and stopping numerous tasks is an important skill (Rusch, 1979). The ability to start another task within an allotted time after completing a prior task is usually the criterion for assessing how independent a target employee is. Rusch, Morgan, Martin, Riva, and Agran (1985) taught two employees with moderate mental retardation to work throughout two critical work periods. During lunch and dinner service hours in a large university cafeteria, the two employees needed frequent reminding to get back to work because they stopped working after completing single tasks (such as wiping a counter, stacking plates, or replenishing butter patties. After being taught to instruct themselves to keep working, the target employees were capable of moving from a completed task to the next task within a specified time period. In this case the criterion for success was to move from the completed task to the next task within 5 seconds.

INCORPORATING BEHAVIOR DEFINITIONS INTO BEHAVIORAL GOALS AND OBJECTIVES

The Individualized Educational Program (IEP) required for each student presents the special education teacher with the task of preparing instructional goals and objectives at three levels: (a) annual goals; (b) short-term objectives; and (c) daily or weekly objectives.

TABLE 5.6 Interrelationship Between Goals

[....................... IEP ....] [....................... Lesson Plans ....]

Annual Goal -

        -Short-term goal-- -Weekly goal

                        -Weekly goal

                        -Weekly goal-- -Daily goal
                                          -Daily goal
                                          -Daily goal
                                          -Daily goal
                                          -Daily goal

Whereas the first two are included annually in a student's IEP, the daily or weekly objectives are typically covered within daily lesson plans. Conceptually, the three levels of objectives interrelate to insure that the educational program for a given student is "appropriate." This interrelationship is illustrated in Table 5.6.

Annual goals are achieved by systematically teaching the prerequisite short-term, weekly, and daily objectives. Table 5.7 illustrates how several daily objectives can be traced back to a single annual goal.

Annual goals are general performance statements within particular skill domains, such as language and speech or social interaction; and, as such, they lack important details, including the conditions under which a response will occur and the standard for performance. These components, in turn, are specified in *short-term objectives*. Daily or weekly instructional objectives are behavioral objectives which focus on tasks and skills to be taught on a daily or weekly basis. The distinction between goals and objectives is demonstrated in Table 5.7. For example, at the daily level, the teacher works through a series of exercises to first teach Darrell to pull on his shoes when asked to do so. This step is followed by Darrell learning to close the velcro

TABLE 5.7 Example of Annual, Short-Term, and Daily Goals

Annual Goal

    The student will develop a repertoire of personal self-help skills in the area of dressing.

Short-Term Goal (Quarterly)

    When presented with two types of shoes and fasteners (velcro tabs or laces), and told, "Put these shoes on!" by the teacher, Darrell will put the shoes on his feet and correctly fasten them with 95% accuracy.

    Instructional Goals (Daily)

        Day 1 (Velcro tabs): When presented with an open-tab shoe and told "Darrell, put this shoe on your left (or right) foot," Darrell, with *guided help from the teacher* will insert his foot and pull the shoe on with his hands with 100% accuracy.

        Day 2 (Velcro tabs): When presented with an open-tab shoe and told "Darrell, put this shoe on your left (or right) foot," Darrell, with *no help from the teacher,* will insert his foot and pull the shoe on with his hands with 100% accuracy.

        Day 3 (Velcro tabs): After pulling on the shoe and told to "Lock the tab," Darrell will pull the tab closed with his left hand with 100% accuracy.

strap on command using his left hand. On subsequent days, additional objectives might include putting on, lacing up, and tying shoes with laces. These trials might be followed with others, requiring the student on commands from the teacher to put on and take off two different types of shoes. Successful completion of this stage might complete the short-term objective (see Table 5.7), as well as meet the annual IEP goals.

Goals and objectives enable us to plan what and how we will provide instruction over a given period. We will now consider using the information we have discussed so far to construct behavioral objectives.

ELEMENTS OF BEHAVIORAL OBJECTIVES

Behavioral objectives are performance statements that include a *definition* of the target behavior (*What*), specify the *conditions* under which a behavior will occur (*When, Where, Loci*), and the *criterion* level or standard for the response (*How Much* and *How Well*).

Behavior (What)

The behavior component of an objective consists of a statement of the target response

telling us *what* we expect the student to be able to do after the response has been taught.

In contrast, what the student is already capable of doing is termed *entry behaviors*. *Entry behaviors* refer to the prerequisite skills that are necessary before a new skill can be learned. If our assessments were to indicate that a student lacked a certain entry skill, then this would become the objective to be taught first, rather than the objective as otherwise planned. This adjustment is illustrated in Table 5.8. Before we clarify the dishwashing objective for Brent, we must insure that he can complete all the necessary entry behaviors. Unless Brent was able to bus dishes from the table, for example, we would not be successful teaching him to wash the dishes—if the total objective included the expectation that he buss the tables as well as wash the dishes. The objective might be modified to allow an individual with severe handicaps to participate in many, but not all, the tasks associated with washing dishes, thus sharing the dishwashing task with another person who possesses the necessary skills (compare with Brown et al., 1985).

Conditions (When, Where, Loci)

The conditions of a behavioral objective specify *when* and *where* a behavior should be

---

TABLE 5.8 Entry Behaviors and Their Relationship to an Objective

Behavioral Objective for Brent

In the kitchen after breakfast, Brent will wash the dishes each morning. (Dishes will be considered washed when a random sample of five items in the drainer reveal no observable traces of food or food residue.)

Entry Behaviors for the Objective

Brent is in the kitchen.

Brent can prepare breakfast.

Brent can point to the dish detergent.

Brent can plug the sink drain.

Brent can use both taps to pour hot water (96°F to 120°F) into the plugged sink to a depth of 7 inches.

Brent can bus dishes from the table and load them into sink.

Brent can place washed dishes into a drainer.

Brent can unplug the sink and drain the water.

Brent can wipe the sink and drain board dry with a towel.

Brent can hang the towel to dry.

expected to occur. Since behavior is situation specific, the *loci* or the physical objects and persons toward whom the behavior will be directed must also be incorporated. These conditions provide the individual with the opportunity and the locus for the reponse to follow. Table 5.9 provides a list of conditions that might accompany an objective statement about washing dishes.

Criterion (How Much, How Well)

The criterion component of the behavioral objective states the performance level we expect. The criterion is often expressed as a quantity, for example, the frequency, magnitude, duration, or latency. Or it may be expressed as a quality; for example, *how well* the performance is done. As such, the criterion serves as a performance standard that a student must reach before he or she can be said to have mastered or achieved a given objective. If the student's performance is below the criterion, then we continue teaching the same objective. When the criterion is reached, our teaching efforts are directed toward a new one. Schutz, Jostes, Rusch, and Lamson (1980) included a quality criterion in an objective designed to teach employees to

TABLE 5.9 Example of Conditions

When-Conditions
   In the morning after breakfast (between 6:30 A.M. and 7:30 A.M.)
   In the afternoon after lunch (between 11:30 A.M. and 1:00 P.M.)
   In the evening after dinner (between 5:30 P.M. and 7:00 P.M.)
   When asked to do so by the house parent
   When it is Brent's turn according to the house schedule

Where-Condition
   In the kitchen

Loci-Conditions
   Between the table and the sink
   With the assistance of the house parent
   With the assistance of a skilled peer
   Without any assistance

sweep and mop floors. The target employees were taught to sweep and mop floors during one phase of their instruction; in another phase the instructors asked work supervisors if the floors met industrial standards for cleanliness.

The data graphed in Figure 5.3 illustrate the use of quantity criteria. In this case, where a student is being trained to assemble washers on bolts, errors are defined as:

"Those assemblies on which (a) there are not two washers and (b) there are no washers contained between the head of the bolt and twist-on lock nut."

From a review of the performance of this task by nonhandicapped workers, the teacher has determined that three errors or less in one session is an appropriate error rate. Further, the teacher has decided to require that the student must achieve this level for three days in a row to demonstrate that the skill is firmly acquired. Starting at 14, 15, and 13 errors during the first three sessions, the number of errors steadily declined, dropping below three errors in session 8. Between sessions 8 and 12, all sessions were below three errors. After session 10, the student reached the objective and new objectives were initiated.

Criteria must not be established arbitrarily. Rather, they must be based upon the following considerations: "When building IEP objectives, care should be taken to ensure that (a) functional skills are targeted; (b) there is a high likelihood that these skills will be rewarded in the natural performance settings; and (c) a plan exists for providing regular opportunities to perform the skill after it is learned (Horner, Williams, & Knobbe, 1985). Several of these recommendations were expanded by Sobsey and Ludlow in 1984.

Functional. Criteria must enable a behavior to result in a functional outcome for the student. For example, teaching an individual to come to you when called is not functional without some minimum latency response between your call and his arrival. If Juan's latency is too large, he will not receive either

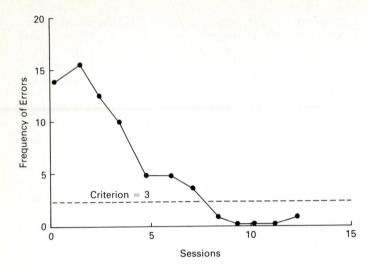

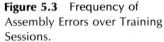

Figure 5.3 Frequency of Assembly Errors over Training Sessions.

the greeting or the instruction you have planned for him.

Naturally Rewarded. Many responses are functional only if they occur at some rate of occurrence in the target setting. For a student to complete his math assignments, for example, he or she must calculate problems accurately at some rate per unit of time. This critical rate is often determined by evaluating the time allowed for math instruction and then by setting a criterion in the student's behavioral objective based upon the math problems that must be solved daily to meet weekly, short-term and annual objectives.

Safe and Socially Acceptable. Criteria must not be so high or low so as to pose danger to the student. The latency set for responding to a cross signal in a controlled intersection is a case in point. The student may be in danger of getting hit by a car if he or she is either too slow or too fast. One error may be fatal. In addition to being safe, criteria must be set at levels that are socially acceptable. A low frequency of many behaviors (for example, tantrums, aggressive responses, math calculation errors) are tolerated and even expected by many teachers and parents. But if the same behaviors are displayed everyday, too frequently, or at high magnitude dur-

ing the day, they will bring the child to the attention of the school psychologist, special education teacher, the assistant principal, or even the police (in case of excessive absenteeism).

Normal. In this case *normal* refers to criteria set at the same levels as for children who are not handicapped. Frequently it is inappropriate for criteria to differ for children with mild handicaps compared to nonhandicapped peers. Walker and Hops (1976), for example, used the rates of social interaction demonstrated by nonhandicapped peers in a classroom setting as the criterion level for similar social interaction among children who were withdrawn. The criterion of normality may include a behavioral range of acceptability. For example, Walker and Hops (1976) could have established a band of acceptability based upon the range of interactions. Fewer interactions would then set the lower range of accept ability, while the higher interactions on a given day could be used to establish the higher level. Interactions that occurred between these levels would then be considered acceptable.

Accurate. Many behaviors such as academic tasks require an accuracy criterion (a percentage of math equations solved correctly or of words spelled correctly). For many behaviors, both rate and accuracy criteria are needed.

Realistic. The criterion for a given behavior also must be realistic, that is there must be some evidence to suggest that the student can reach the criterion in a reasonable amount of time. Some forms of graphed data (for example, Figure 5.1) enable teachers to examine a student's current level or rate of performance and predict the future date, given the rate of progress, on which the criterion is likely to have been reached.

Appropriate for Entry Into The Next Objective. Criteria should be set high enough to guarantee that the corresponding performance is adequate to function as an entry behavior for the next objective. For example, in order to establish dishwashing at home after every meal, bussing of dishes from the table must be trained to also occur after every meal. If dish bussing were only trained to occur every other day, it would serve as an insufficient entry behavior.

Allows for Overlearning. Performing a behavior more frequently than necessary to initially acquire the response is important to maintain that response within the student's behavioral repertoire. The opportunity to respond (Greenwood, Delquadri, & Hall, 1984) or the opportunity to perform (Horner et al., 1985) have been emphasized as being important elements in maintaining responding beyond mere acquisition. By setting high criterion levels, we increase the practice and fluency of the response and thereby the probability of its maintenance over time.

Controls For Random Occurrence. Criteria must take into account that the response needs to be reliably established. Thus, a 100% accuracy requirement based upon only one opportunity to make the response is too prone to chance outcomes in the future opportunities to be a measure of learning. Instead, a series of opportunities, trials, sessions, and so forth must be sampled at a high percentage of success.

Having discussed the conditions, behavioral definitions, and criterion components of behavioral objectives, we now turn to some important issues in writing behavioral objectives.

WRITING BEHAVIORAL OBJECTIVES

To write behavioral objectives it is useful to use a format like the one in Table 5.10. In addition to insuring that the objective includes the three components of behavioral objectives discussed previously, the dates for the beginning and the ending time must be estimated to comply with IEP requirements.

The objectives listed in Table 5.11 illustrate the principles discussed previously. For example, each objective is complete by including conditions, behavior, and criteria. Specifically, the conditions relate to those necessary to evoke or occasion a given response and include the loci. The behaviors to be taught are functional in that they will be instrumental to the student. The topography of each behavior is also stated. Finally, the criteria are specific in terms of frequency, latency, and accuracy, and they address the considerations suggested by Sobsey and Ludlow (1984).

However, these examples are not organized into a coherent plan for accomplishing anything beyond acquisition of the stated responses. When writing objectives, we must plan for elaborated responding to increase the functionality of each response. Elaboration requires that objectives be sequenced to first insure acquisition, then fluency, and finally generalization and maintenance.

Acquisition is defined as the establishment of a response within the context of the original conditions and criteria of the objective. *Fluency* refers to higher levels of rate and accuracy, reflecting skilled performance. *Generalization*, in turn, is defined as the occurrence of a response in the presence of conditions (where, when, and loci) that are different from those stated in the original objective.

TABLE 5.10   Sample Behavioral Objectives

Conditions (When, Where, Loci)	Behavior (What)	Criterion (How Much, How Well)	Date Begin	Date End
On the playground when his name is called by the teacher,	Jim will acknowledge by waving his hand (held above head)	90% of at least 10 opportunities	1/15	1/30
When presented with a choice between red and blue objects by the teacher during one-on-one sessions and asked, "Touch the red one,"	Mary will touch the red object	95% of at least 20 trials	1/1	1/15
When asked to read from a passage in a basal reader (Level A) by the teacher,	David will read orally with	a correct rate of 85 words per minute and an error rate of less than 0.5 words per minute	1/15	2/15
When presented with the words *Stop, Poison, Danger,* and *Exit* on flash cards,	Latashia will read orally each item	with a latency of less than two seconds and 95% accuracy on a minimum of 20 trials per session	2/15	2/30

Thus, handraising taught during a spelling period has generalized when it occurs at the same fluency in reading and math periods. Finally, *maintenance* refers to the continuance of a response in the absence of the original procedures used to teach the response. The response must occur with the same fluency and under the same conditions as stated in the original objective. (Specific training procedures are discussed in Chapter 12).

The example in Table 5.11 demonstrates how objectives can be designed to elaborate responding beyond acquisition by including fluency, generalization, and maintenance. Beginning with the original objective, the teacher defines acquisition at 80 percent of 10 trials. In the second objective, fluency is defined as 90 percent of 30 trials. Generalization is defined as the ability to perform the response in the classroom and the lunchroom

TABLE 5.11   Elaborating a Single Behavioral Objective

Conditions	Behavior	Criteria	Target
On the playground, when his name is called by the teacher,	Jim will acknowledge by waving his hand, walking to the teacher, and asking "You called me?"	80% of at least 10 opportunities	Acquisition
On the playground, when his name is called by the teacher,	Jim will acknowledge by waving his hand, walking to the teacher, and asking "You called me?"	90% of at least 30 opportunities	Fluency
In the classroom, when his name is called by the teacher, or the aide	Same as above	Same as above	Generalization
In the lunchroom when his name is called by the teacher or the aide	Same as above	Same as above	Generalization
At random monthly intervals in the lunchroom, classroom, and on the playground, when his name is called by the teacher or aide	Same as above	90% of at least 10 opportunities	Maintenance

after it was originally taught on the playground. Lastly, maintenance is defined as Jim's ability to perform the response when monthly random opportunities are presented to him in all three settings. Thus, the scope of the original objective has been expanded to include fluency, generalization, and maintenance. At the same time, the student's behavior must (a) occur in several situations where it will be functional, (b) demonstrate high levels of fluency and accuracy, and (c) remain in the student's repertoire of skills over time.

SUMMARY

In this chapter, we have discussed the importance of defining behavior to promote clarity and objectivity, and as a means of focusing our teaching efforts. Occurrence of behavior may be determined by direct observation, machine recording, and by analysis of permanent products. Next, we considered the dimensions of a behavioral definition accompanied by examples for students with mild and severe handicaps in both classroom and community-based settings. The goals and objectives requirement mandated for special education by PL 94-142 in terms of the Individual Educational Program (IEP) was examined in relationship to annual goals and short-term behavioral objectives, as well as the correspondence of these goals with the daily or weekly objectives which make up daily lesson plans. This overview was followed by a discussion of the elements constituting a behavioral objective accompanied by a sample format showing how to prepare behavioral objectives. Finally, the importance of elaborating the scope and impact of behavior change beyond acquisition, by including objectives targeted at fluency, generalization, and maintenance, was emphasized as the ultimate goal of an instructional program. The following chapter will discuss the logical extension of these concepts and procedures as they relate to assessment and evaluation of behavior change.

REFERENCES

BAILEY, J., & MEYERSON, L. (1969). "Vibration as a reinforcer for a profoundly retarded child." *Journal of Applied Behavior Analysis, 2*, 133–137.

BARKER, R. G. (1968). *Ecological psychology.* Stanford, CA: Stanford University Press.

BARTON, L. E., & BARTON, C. L. (1985). "An effective and benign treatment of rumination." *The Journal of the Association for Persons with Severe Handicaps, 10*, 168–171.

BLOOM, B. S. (1956). *Taxonomy of educational objectives handbook I: Cognitive domain.* New York; David McKay.

BRADY, M. P., SHORES, R. E., GUNTER, P., McEVOY, M. A., FOX, J. J., & WHITE, C. (1984). "Generalization of an adolescent's social interaction behavior via multiple peers in a classroom setting." *The Journal of the Association for Persons with Severe Handicaps, 9*, 278–286.

BREEN, C., HARING, T., PITTS-CONWAY, V., & GAYLORD-ROSS, R. (1985). "The training and generalization of social interaction during breaktime at two job sites in the natural environment." *The Journal of the Association for Persons with Severe Handicaps, 10*, 41–50.

BROWN, L., SHIRAGA, B., YORK, J., KESSLER, K., STROHM, B., SWEET, M., ZANELLA, K., VAN DEVENTER, P., & LOOMIS, R. (1985). "Integrated work opportunities for adults with severe handicaps: The extended training option." *Journal of The Association for Persons with Severe Handicaps, 9*, 262–269.

CHADSEY-RUSCH, J. C., KARLAN, G. R., RIVA, M. T., & RUSCH, F. R. (1984). "Competitive employment: Teaching conversational skill to mentally retarded adults in employment settings." *Mental Retardation, 22*, 218–225.

CLEARY, A., & PACKHAM, D. (1968). "A touch detecting teaching machine with auditory reinforcement." *Journal of Applied Behavior Analysis, 1*, 341–345.

DELQUADRI, J., ELLIOTT, M., & HUGHES, V. (1981). "*Reading peer tutoring manual.*" (pp. 11–12). Kansas City, KS: University of Kansas, Juniper Gardens Children's Project.

GREENWOOD, C. R., DELQUADRI, J., & HALL, R. V. (1984). "Opportunity to respond and student academic performance." In W. Heward, T. Heron, D. Hill, & J. Trap-Porter (eds.), *Behavior analysis in education* (pp. 58–88). Columbus, OH: Charles E. Merrill.

GREENWOOD, C. R., HOPS, H., DELQUADRI, J., & GUILD, J. (1974). "Group contingencies for group consequences: A further analysis." *Journal of Applied Behavioral Analysis, 7,* 413–425.

GREENWOOD, C. R., HOPS, H., WALKER, H. M., GUILD, J. J., STOKES, J., YOUNG, K. R., KELEMAN, K. S., & Willardson, M. (1979). "Standardized classroom behavior management program (PASS): Social validation and replication studies in Utah and Oregon." *Journal of Applied Behavior Analysis, 12(2),* 255–271.

GREENWOOD, C. R., TODD, N. M., HOPS, H., & WALKER, H. M. (1982). "Behavior change targets in the assessment and treatment of socially withdrawn preschool children." *Behavioral Assessment, 4,* 273–298.

GRESHAM, F. M. (1982). "Social skills training with handicapped children: A review." *Reviews of Educational Research, 51,* 139–176.

HALL, R. V., DELQUADRI, J., GREENWOOD, C. R., & THURSTON, L. (1982). "The importance of opportunity to respond in children's academic success." In E. B. Edgar, N. G. Haring, J. R. Jenkins, & C. G. Pious (eds.), *Mentally handicapped children: Education and training* (pp. 107–140). Baltimore, MD: University Park Press.

HANSON, M. J., & HANLINE, M. F. (1985). "An analysis of response-contingent learning experiences for young children." *The Journal of the Association for Persons with Severe Handicaps, 10,* 31–40.

HORNER, R. H., WILLIAMS, J. A., & KNOBBE, C. A. (1985). "The effect of 'opportunity to perform' on maintenance of skills learned by high school students with severe handicaps." *The Journal of the Association for Persons with Severe Handicaps, 10,* 172–175.

JORGENSEN, S., ed. (1982). *Increasing the effectiveness of multidisciplinary teams.* Des Moines, IA: Drake University, Midwest Regional Resource Center.

LOVITT, T. C., EATON, M., KIRKWOOD, M. E., & PELANDER, J. (1971). "Effects of various reinforcement contingencies on oral reading rate." In E. A. Ramp & B. L. Hopkins (eds.), *A new direction for education: Behavior analysis* (pp. 54–71). Lawrence, KS: University of Kansas Press.

PHILLIPS, E. L. (1968). "Achievement place: Token reinforcement procedures in a home-style rehabilitation setting for 'predelinquent' boys." *Journal of Applied Behavior Analysis, 1,* 213–223.

ROSSEAU, M. K., POULSON, C. L., & SALZBERG, C. L. (1984). "Naturalistic behavioral intervention with inner-city middle school students." *Education and Treatment of Children, 7(1),* 1–15.

RUSCH, F. R. (1979). "A functional analysis of the relationship between attending to task and producing in an applied restaurant setting." *The Journal of Special Education, 13,* 399–411.

RUSCH, F. R., MORGAN, T. K., MARTIN, J. E., RIVA, M., & AGRAN, M. (1985). "Competitive employment: Teaching mentally retarded employees self-instructional strategies." *Applied Research in Mental Retardation, 6,* 389–407.

SCHMIDT, G. W., & ULRICH, R. E. (1969). "Effects of group contingent events upon classroom noise." *Journal of Applied Behavior Analysis, 2,* 171–180.

SCHUTZ, R. P., JOSTES, K. F., RUSCH, F. R., & LAMSON, D. S. (1980). "Acquisition, transfer, and social validation of two vocational skills in a competitive employment setting." *Education and Training of the Mentally Retarded, 15,* 306–311.

SIEGEL, M. A., & DAVIS, D. M. (1986). *Understanding computer-based education.* New York: Random House.

SINGER, G. H. S., CLOSE, D. W., IRVIN, L., GERSTEN, R., & SAILOR, W. (1984). "An alternative to the institution for young people with severely handicapping conditions in a rural community." *The Journal of the Association for Persons with Severe Handicaps, 9,* 251–261.

SOBSEY, D., & LUDLOW, B. (1984). "Guidelines for setting instructional criteria." *Education and Treatment of Children, 7,* 157–165.

STANLEY, S. O., & GREENWOOD, C. R. (1981). *CISSAR: Code for instructional structure and student academic response: Observer's Manual.* Kansas City, KS: University of Kansas, Juniper Gardens Children's Project.

TROTTER, A. B., & INMAN, D. A. (1968). "The use of positive reinforcement in physical therapy." *Physical Therapy, 48,* 347–352.

VOGELSBERG, R. T., & RUSCH, F. R. (1979). "Training severely handicapped students to cross partially controlled intersections." *AAESPH Review, 4,* 264–273.

WALKER, H. M., & BUCKLEY, N. K. (1968). "The use of positive reinforcement in conditioning attending behavior." *Journal of Applied Behavior Analysis, 1,* 245–250.

WALKER, H. M., & HOPS, H. (1976). "Use of normative peer data as a standard for evaluating classroom treatment effects." *Journal of Applied Behavior Analysis, 9,* 159–168.

WILCOX, B., & BELLAMY, G. T. (1987). *The activities catalog.* Baltimore, MD: Paul H. Brookes.

chapter 6

Intermittent Behavioral Assessment

In this chapter we begin discussing assessment of behavior and introduce measurement devices used in special education and applied behavior analysis. Used for summative purposes, intermittent assessment reflects an individual's current status or comprehensive functioning at a single point in time. Intermittent assessment measures typically cover several domains of performance (Gage & Berliner, 1984) such as academic performance, social competence, or manual dexterity. The results of intermittent assessment measures are expressed as composite scores or patterns of scores called *profiles* across the measured domains. Interpretation of results is made meaningful by comparison to either norms or mastery criteria, and any discrepancies between an individual's scores and the standards are used to define performance.

INTERMITTENT ASSESSMENT

Results of intermittent assessment describe an individual's performance at some point in time (for example, after ten units of instruction, at the end of a course, or after a year in a special education program), thereby revealing abilities in terms of (a) norms, (b) mastery of criteria, or (c) both norms and mastery criteria.

Norm-referenced intermittent measures compare an individual's performance to that of a normative group. Thus, they show whether an individual's scores fall above or below the average for a person's age, race, and sex. Since norm-referenced measures compare what individuals can do in terms of what other individuals are doing, that is, the group norm, they are routinely used in program planning. Assessment of this type is helpful by pointing to areas of performance that may be problematic relative to the norm, however, it does not specify intervention strategies.

The other major type of intermittent assessment is the criterion-referenced measure that determines what a person can do based on performance standards. That is, criterion-referenced assessment is used to reveal what an individual knows or can perform and what he or she needs to learn. For example, a student may display 100 percent of the minimum competencies necessary for high school graduation or for employment as a short-order cook. As opposed to norm-referenced measurement assessment of this type, it is useful for planning and monitoring instruction.

Three familiar intermittent assessment instruments that are used in education are: (a) the standardized achievement test; (b) the intelligence test; and (c) the minimum-competency exam. Standardized achievement tests are designed to assess domains of knowledge that are taught in school, such as reading vocabulary and reading comprehension. Consequently, they are commonly administered in the fall (October) and spring (April) of each school year to evaluate academic progress. The *Metropolitan Achievement Test* (MAT) (Prescott, Balow, Hogan, & Farr, 1978) is an example of an achievement test *battery* since it is composed of several subtests, covering the subjects of vocabulary, language, reading comprehension, mathematics, social studies, and science. The MAT is designed to be administered to several students at the same time. The MAT report illustrated in Table 6.1 shows that reading, mathematics, and language tests were administered to eight students.

Another major type of intermittent assessment instrument is the intelligence tests. The *Kaufman Assessment Battery for Children* (Kaufman & Kaufman, 1983), the *System of Multicultural Pluralistic Assessment* (SOMPA) (Mercer & Lewis, 1979), or the *Wechsler Intelligence Scale for Children-Revised* (WISC-R) (Wechsler, 1967), are tests designed to mea-

sure "general abilities" considered to be acquired through the normal processes of maturation and socialization. Thus, intelligence tests assess domains that are not exclusively covered within the school curriculum. They are administered to individuals no more frequently than every 1 to 3 years. Figure 6.1 presents the summary of results from the *Kaufman* for one student. Scores are presented for *Mental Processing Subtests*, ranging from (1) Magic Window to (10) Photo Series, *Achievement Subtests*, ranging from (11) Expressive Vocabulary to (16) Reading Understanding, and *Global Scales*, ranging from sequential processing to nonverbal.

Minimum-competency exams, the third type of intermittent assessment device, measure specific skills addressed within the school curricula. Such tests vary from district to district and from state to state as they are designed to reflect content mandated by state and local boards of education and contain, for example, the 3- or 4-year high school curricula. For example, in the School District of Kansas City, Missouri, all eighth graders take the state-mandated *Basic Essential Skills Test* (BEST). If they do not pass the math, reading, and social skills areas, courses subsequently taken in high school, then they are given credit only after the student takes the test again and passes. Students must pass the test before they graduate from high school.

An example of the results obtained from a criterion-referenced test of reading readiness is displayed in Table 6.2. The test is administered in a local education agency (LEA) to 5- or 6-year-old children upon entry to school. Scores are the percentage correct within each domain. If the student scores below 85 percent on any one domain, that domain is considered a weakness that should be remediated. The domain is considered mastered when a score of 85 percent is obtained.

Sources of Information

Sources of intermittent assessment information include the student, peers, teachers, parents, employers, professionals, and ar-

TABLE 6.1 Metropolitan Achievement Test

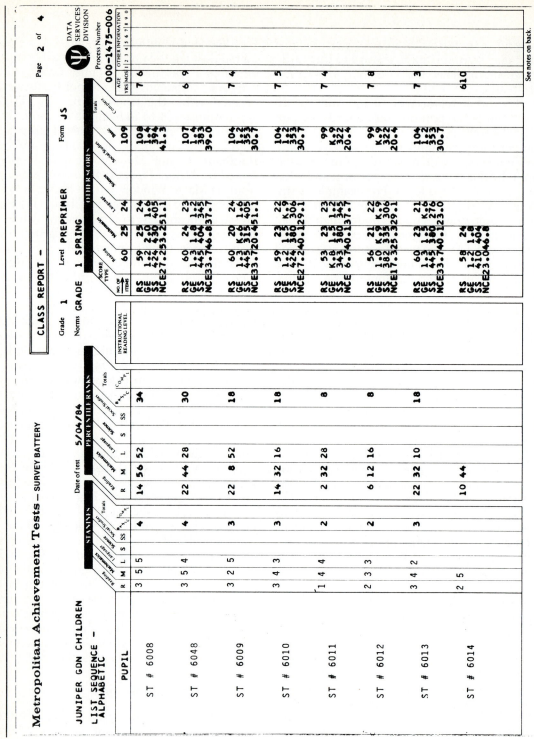

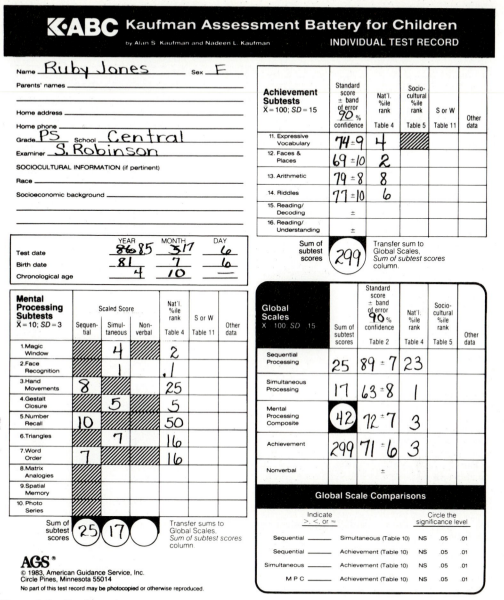

Figure 6.1   Kaufman Inventory

chives. In the case of the student or client, information may be derived either from direct observations or the products of his or her performance. Information may also be obtained through self-reports or self-observations made by the student.

Peers may be in a position to contribute information about an individual's general so-

TABLE 6.2 Sample Results from Criterion-Referenced Test

COMPREHENSIVE SPECIAL SERVICES COOPERATIVE
Summary Sheet

Student No.: _____

Student Name: _____ B.D. _____ C.A. _____ Sex _____

Grade _____ Student Address _____

Student Phone _____ Parents/Guardian _____

School _____ Teacher _____ Dist. # _____

Examiner _____ Date(s) Tested _____

Handedness: Left _____ Right _____ Glasses: Yes _____ No _____

READINESS

Subtest #	# Poss.	# Earned	*Strength + Weakness −
1. Nursery Rhymes	7	7	100
2. Following the Arrows	4	4	100
3. Colors	27	22	81
4. Sequence Stories	4	1	25*
5. Drawing, Cutting, Placing	29	5	17*
6. Categories	15	10	67*
7. Gross Sounds	6	6	100
8. Following Oral Directions	10	6	60*
9. Aud. Attention Unrelated Words	6	6	100
10. Memory for Sentences	12	11	92
11. Directions in Space	10	5	50*
12. Hidden Figures	19	18	95
13. Spatial Relationships	17	15	88
14. Naming Body Parts	16	12	75*
15. Missing Parts	6	2	33*
16. Same or Different	9	2	22*
	197	132	67

*Use 85% as cut-off point (the standard). If the student scores below 85% correct on a subtest, consider this as an area for remediation.

Note: B.D. = Birth Date, C.A. = Chronological Age.

Source: From *Comprehensive special services cooperative tests*, p. 1, by D. L. Welch and L. J. Miller, 1972, Olathe, KS: Educational Modulation Center.

ciometric status (for example, peer relations, friends, and sportsmanship), or specific features of a classmate's social behavior (Hops & Greenwood, in press). Peers supply a unique source of information since they have opportunities to observe, interact, and informally assess aspects of an individual's behavior during parts of a day that are unavailable to teachers, parents, employers, friends, and so on.

Teachers may provide information concerning a student's academic, behavioral, and social and emotional adjustment. The amount of time teachers spend with students is only exceeded by the time parents spend. Thus, teachers observe students' academic and social successes and failures on a daily basis. They also observe the student across multiple settings such as the classroom, the playground, the lunchroom, and the auditorium, and they observe students within various contexts of instruction and curriculum activities.

Generally, parents spend more time than anybody else with their children. Like teachers, they may be immediate observers of a child's behavior. Unlike teachers, however, they are not bound by a single school year. Since their perspective on a child is life-span oriented, ranging in most cases from birth to early adulthood, parents can contribute unique information about the medical history, the developmental milestones, the peer and sibling relationships and friendships, the general academic strengths and weaknesses, and the emotional problems of the child.

Professionals (such as physicians, nurses, and psychologists), while not as familiar or experienced with a child as peers, teachers, or parents, can provide expert information related to their special fields of knowledge. In each of these fields, intermittent assessment devices are routinely used and their results bear directly upon the special education of children with handicaps. For example, routine well-child visits to the pediatrician will result in the developmentally correct screenings for probable diseases and disabilities and in the administration of the appropriate treatments. Similarly, referral of a child with delayed speech language development will result in comprehensive assessments by speech clinicians and audiologists.

Computerized information archives or cumulative records (school records, case records, and agency records) are often the repository of a child's cumulative assessment history and progress during his or her education. With the exception of archives, these sources of information are available for assessment purposes and can be used to help define a child's problem, select the most appropriate special education curriculum, and design and monitor instruction and treatment.

Intermittent Assessment Instruments and Techniques

The instruments used to obtain assessment information from various sources include (a) narrative records, (b) nominations, (c) rankings, (d) checklists, (e) ratings, (f) tests, and (g) observations.

Narrative Records. Narrative records are written descriptions that may include case notes, client histories, standard psychological reports, cumulative data on academic progress, prior IEPs, and so forth. Case notes, for example, include professionals' informal interpretation of visits or observations of the client, interpretation of assessment information, and conclusions of clinical judgments. Client histories consist of interview information concerning the client's developmental strengths and weaknesses. They also include a medical history which summarizes important health information such as genetic family histories, past diseases, operations, reoccurring problems, and allergies to particular drugs. There is also a screening questionnaire covering common symptoms and complaints that may signal current problems.

A standard psychological report will contain a brief case history, results of standardized tests, and a written interpretation of the test results. Concluding with a diagnosis of the student's problem, the report also suggests recommendations for additional assessment, forms of treatment, and curricular modifications.

Nominations. Nominations are the results of clinical, professional, or lay judgments. The most typical nomination is referral of a student to the school psychologist, often as part of a teacher's nomination for potential special education services. With some disabilities, teacher nominations are confirmed a very high percentage of the time (Algozzine, Christenson, & Ysseldyke, 1982). Some peer sociometric instruments also include nomination procedures (Hops & Greenwood, in press) using such items as "list the names of three classmates you most like to play with."

By summing the number of classmate nominations each student receives, a popularity ranking is obtained.

Rankings. Rankings result in student or behavior problem estimates related to their relative importance or magnitude. A ranking developed by Greenwood, Walker, Todd, and Hops (1979) enables a teacher to rank students from low to high in terms of the most "talkative" (see Figure 6.2).

Checklists. In contrast to nominations, which are informal designations of students with certain presumed attributes, and rankings, which order students relative to one another in regard to a specific attribute, checklists provide an actual count of the number of attributes present for a given individual. Thus, checklists are used to detect the presence or absence of a behavior or skill. After reading an item on the checklist, the assessor marks the presence or absence of the specific attribute. Like rankings and nominations, checklists are most often completed by a teacher who is familiar with the target student. At times checklists are completed in the setting of interest, thus being very similar to direct observational assessments. The basic raw score produced on the checklist denotes the number of behaviors or skills present or absent. In Table 6.3 for example, on the *Walker Problem Behavior Identification Checklist* (WPBIC), a domain score is selected, but only if the behavior is present (Walker, 1983). The sum of circled scale scores is used to derive a standard score for the five domains addressed: acting-out, withdrawal, distractibility, disturbed peer relations, and immaturity.

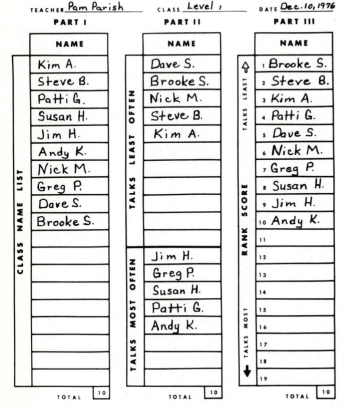

Figure 6.2 Sample Ranking Form

TABLE 6.3 Example Items from the Walker Problem Behavior Identification Checklist

	Scales (Domains)				
Item	1	2	3	4	5
1. Has temper tantrums	2				
2. Has no friends				4	
3. Refers to himself as dumb, stupid, or incapable					3
④. Must have approval for tasks attempted or completed				1	

Note: Scale 1 = Acting Out; Scale 2 = Withdrawal; Scale 3 = Distractability; Scale 4 = Disturbed Peer Relations; Scale 5 = Immaturity. The circle = This item describes the student being evaluated.

Source: From Walker, H. M. (1983). *Walker Problem Behavior Identification Checklist (WPBIC).* Los Angeles: Western Psychological Services, p. 3.

Ratings. Going beyond checklists, ratings indicate both the presence of an attribute and its magnitude. Rating scales are routinely completed by teachers, parents, clinicians, physicians, and peers based upon experiences with a student or client. For example, in evaluating the statement "initiates play with peers," the teacher circles a number on a scale from 1 to 7 to reflect judgment of the extent to which this behavior is manifest, based upon prior observations of the student. Ratings that use this scoring method are called *Likert scaling* (Guilford, 1954). Unlike nominations and rankings for which only a single composite score is obtained, scores from ratings can reflect (a) the composite average over all items rated and (b) the score for each single item (see Table 6.4).

Tests. Tests present the student with one or more tasks for which the response is di-

TABLE 6.4 A Likert-Scaled Item

"Rate the extent that he/she initiates play with peers"

1............ 2 ....3 .... 4............. ⑤ ....6...........7

Never	Average	Often

Note: The circle = The extent to which this item is true for the student being assessed.

rectly observed or recorded. Tests may be commercially prepared or developed by teachers and other school personnel. The topography of the response being assessed in a test varies depending upon the task and the purpose of the test. For example, for the *Snellen Test of Visual Acuity* (Salvia & Ysseldyke, 1985) the student stands at a distance of 20 feet from a printed card and, with one eye covered, reads letters of various sizes.

Other types of tests, such as intelligence tests, measure school ability or aptitude for regular education programs. Items on this test reflect general knowledge, such as the name of the President of the United States. For example, the *Otis-Lennon School Abilities Test* (Otis & Lennon, 1979), a group-administered instrument, is widely used in public school settings.

Academic tests, in sum, are designed to assess mastery of school curricula. Consequently, items tap such areas as reading comprehension, computation skills, and so forth. Academic testing items may require having the student select the correct item from several incorrect ones (multiple choice) identify true from false assertions or provide a written narrative in a short answer or essay format.

Direct Observations. Direct observations may take place during classroom activities as well as in nonclassroom settings. Observations may also occur in contrived settings, that is, settings or situations specifically construed to stimulate everyday activities. Contrived settings may include testing or counseling situations or observations of interactions between mother and child in a play room. Observational assessment may be systematic or informal.

For systematic observation reliably defined behaviors are recorded using standard sampling procedures (see Chapter 5), whereas informal observations use neither reliable definitions nor standard sampling procedures. Since informal observations are based upon expert opinion and experience, they do not yield quantitative information (for example, frequency, rate or percent of responding) but narrative comments about a student's behavior. To increase objectivity, informal observations may employ features of ranking or rating devices.

In both formal and informal observations in special education and applied behavior analysis, observers are careful not to intrude on the situation so as to artificially influence the behavior of the target individual. Thus, efforts are made to conceal *their* presence (for example, using one-way mirrors), and certain procedures are followed to insure their nonparticipation on the behavior being studied.

Uses of Data

Intermittent assessment data serve two primary functions: administrative and instructional.

Administrative. In special education assessment information is principally devoted to such administrative uses as (a) classification of students, (b) program development and staffing decisions, and (c) program evaluation—including teacher evaluations. Some of the specific steps within each of these administrative uses are now discussed.

Student referral and screening, the first steps in the classification process, typically involve intermittent assessment. That is, students are referred or nominated by their teachers or parents for more comprehensive forms of assessment. At this stage measurement is subjective since it is based upon the judgments of those making the referral. *Problem definition* is accomplished after the administration of tests, classroom observations, and other classroom-based measures. At this point data are compiled to provide profiles of scores, rather than a single score, describing a student's overall strengths and weaknesses. These data may be presented as the performance expected of the average student. In areas where there are weaknesses, additional tests related to the presumed problem may be administered.

Program and classroom placement is determined as a result of a series of meetings, as outlined in the regulations of P.L. 94-142, attended by the teacher, the parents, district officials, and other specialists. These meetings review a student's case and are based on intermittent assessment data derived from tests, narrative records, or informal observations. Although continual measures also may be considered, intermittent measures are favored for this purpose because of the breadth of what they measure and the availability of norms. If placement is recommended then an IEP is developed.

To define their *special education populations* and make decisions about the *types of programs* needed in the district, administrators also use summaries of data from intermittent measures. The same data are also used as part of an LEA's *program evaluation* efforts. In order to be accountable, districts must conduct evaluations of the effectiveness of their special education programs. Program evaluation in special education is not easy. Unlike regular education, where all students may be assessed on one or two distinct approved intermittent measures, the diversity of special education students' abilities and skills prevents the uniform use of a single evaluation instrument.

Instructional. The instructional uses of intermittent assessment involve (a) pinpointing behavioral objectives, (b) IEP implementation, and (c) monitoring of individual student progress. As mentioned in Chapter 5, the IEP consists of short-term objectives based upon intermittent measures. Pinpointing behaviors what will be taught in the classroom is often the result of the combined use of criterion-based intermittent assessment and continuous assessment. We discuss continuous assessment in Chapter 6. Similarly, monitoring student progress also relies upon this combined assessment function.

TYPES OF INTERMITTENT ASSESSMENT INSTRUMENTS

Intermittent instruments primarily consist of two forms, norm-referenced and criterion-referenced, which are distinguished by the referencing method employed. *Instrument referencing* refers to a test's method of interpretation or inference and applies to all instruments regardless of format, content, or source of information. Some commercially available instruments employ both norms and criteria referencing.

NORM-REFERENCED INSTRUMENTS

The goal of norm-referenced tests is to display an individual's performance in relation to the norm-group mean. Thus, norm-referenced tests often have national application; that is, they may be administered to any individual in any state, in any district, in any school. Further, they may be meaningfully interpreted at each of these levels. They are restricted, however, to the extent that the normative group can be considered representative of the individual.

Fundamental Principles

The principles underlying norm-referenced tests include validity studies, reliability studies, administration standards, content selection, and norm-referencing standards.

Validity. Validity indicates the extent to which a test measures what it is intended to measure. Validity studies are conducted for all commercially published tests and results are reported in the manual which usually accompanies the test. Validity types and methods differ according to the intended uses of a test. In order to assert that a reading test, for example, has *content validity* or that its items represent the correct domain of information or performance, the developer would use certain procedures to guide the selection of items on the test.

Such procedures might include sampling items from existing reading curricula, polling to determine the appropriateness of items to be selected, or comparing items to those included in other established reading tests. To verify that a reading test assesses abilities that are related to measured intelligence, the developer may measure a sample of students on both the reading test and an intelligence test at approximately the same time and correlate the two sets of scores. The extent to which the students who scored high in reading also scored high in measured intelligence establishes the test's degree of *concurrent validity.*

Establishing the *predictive validity* of a test requires demonstrating that students' scores on a given test correlate highly with later life outcomes. For example, it may be established that high scores on a reading test at elementary grade levels are predictive of above average high school grades. For older students, valid achievement test results should predict future college grades, exemplary performance on college entrance exams, or employability. Similarly, valid interest or aptitude test should predict the future employment or match the interests of individuals to persons within particular occupations.

Reliability. In order for a test to be valid, it must also be reliable. That is, a student should score the same, or nearly the same, on two administrations of the same test when little time intervenes between the two testings. The short intervening time is important to ensure that new learning will not unduly affect the results of a second administration of the test. Test and retest scores are statistically correlated and to the extent that correlations are high (for example, between 0.70 and 1.00 for the Pearson r correlation) reliability is established. Several variations of this basic reliability procedure include alternate forms and split-half reliability procedures. Using the former, two different test forms of equal difficulty are compared at test and retest occasions. With split-half procedures, on the other hand, the scores based on the odd-numbered items on the test are compared to those based on the even-numbered items within a single test administration. Wide discrepancy between scores in such situations would signal that the test is confounded—either the items or the method used to administer the test may be inadequate. In contrast, factors that promote high reliability include selecting items for which the answer cannot be obtained by guessing and testing procedures that are equivalent.

Administration Standards. The validity and reliability of intermittent measures depend heavily on each testing situation being equivalent. Thus, administration standards specify the exact procedures to be used. Adherence to these standards ensures that the scores obtained for a particular individual are comparable to those of the norm-group who were tested under these identical conditions.

Content Selection. Content selection in norm-referenced tests is related to sampling. For example, the content for a national reading test might be identified by examining the 50 leading commercially prepared curricula and subsequently randomly selecting 50 items for inclusion. These items could also be screened for difficulty level and bias.

Norm-Referencing. An individual's performance on a norm-referenced test reflects a comparison to a group norm, that is, the test score indicates a student's deviation from the group mean, referred to as a *standard score* his or her ranking relative to the norm is a percentile rank or stanine score. This kind of comparison is called an *intersubject comparison* because different persons are compared.

There are several types of standard scores. The *z-score*, for example, assigns the value of zero to the mean with a standard deviation from the mean of +1 or −1. In the plus direction, above the mean, +1, +2, and +3 standard deviations are possible. Equivalent negative values are possible below the mean. For example, if an individual's standard score is 1.53, he or she has scored a little over one and one-half standard deviations above the mean. Based on the principle of the normal curve, 68 percent of the group is expected to fall between −1.0 and +1.0, 96 percent between −2.0 and +2.0, and 99 percent between −3.0 and +3.0 (see Figure 6.3).

Traditionally, scores on intelligence tests have been scaled such that the mean equals 100 and the standard deviation is 15. Thus, a score of 85 is one standard deviation below the mean, whereas a score of 115 is one stan-

Figure 6.3　The normal curve and the percentage of cases falling under (+ and −) one, two and three standard deviations from the mean, expressed as z and IQ scores.

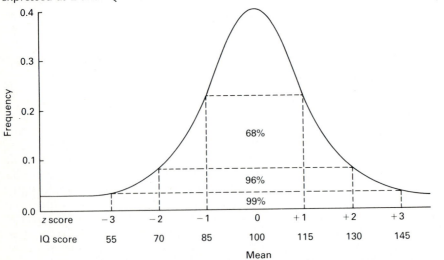

dard deviation above the mean. Based on the normal curve, 68% of the population will have IQ scores falling between 85 and 115.

Rank-ordered scores are also used to express an individual's performance relative to the norm-group. Thus, a student scoring at the 50th percentile scored higher than did 50% of the normative group. Similarly, a stanine score of 5, places the student at the midpoint of a scale ranging from 1 to 10.

Developmental scores indicate an individual's performance relative to specific ages or grade levels. Thus, a student with a mental age (MA) equal to his chronological age (CA) (e.g., 6 years, 5 months) is considered to be at the norm. A student of the same CA = 6 years, 5 months with an MA of 8 years would be performing above the norm. Further, a student with a grade level score of 1.8, or first grade, eighth month, is considered to be at norm if he or she is in the first grade and if the test was administered in April (the eighth month of a standard nine month school year).

The validity of norm-referenced tests is based on the assumption that the normative group consists of persons representative of the general population of which the student taking the test is a member in terms of age, race, sex, socio-economic status, and so forth (Gage & Berliner, 1984). An important part of test development is the *norming process*, which consists of administering a test to a statistically representative sample of students and using their scores as the normative baseline for comparing and interpreting the performance of special individuals.

Traditionally, the best normative samples have been drawn at *random* and given sufficiently large samples drawn at random from a larger population, the mean and standard deviation of the sample will equal the mean and standard deviation of the population" (Kerlinger, 1973 p. 119). Randomization insures that each person in the population is equally likely to be selected, thereby preventing selection bias. In the case of small samples, randomization with stratification by characteristics has been used. *Stratification* enables the developer to target special population charac-

teristics and reflect in them the norm sample (for example, age, race, sex) when only a small number of individuals can be tested and the principle of randomization cannot be expected to operate. In contrast, selection of a norm group by "convenience" is not an appropriate procedure for norm development. (For example, "There just happened to be a preschool next door, so we used them!")

Three types of norms are commonly used: (a) national, (b) local, and (c) special populations. Thus far, we discussed the use of national norms for the development of commercially available tests. Local norms, compiled by LEA personnel, reflect student performance on a given test in prior years. Such norms may be useful in several ways. First, comparisons between the means on local and national norms can provide information about the educational product of the LEA. Second, local high school norms, for example, may be more predictive of a student's success at a local college or university than national norms.

Norms for special populations provide the basis for comparing individuals with specific disabilities or socio-cultural characteristics to individuals with the same disability or characteristics. For example, the educational aptitude of a person with a hearing impairment can be more appropriately determined by comparison to other persons with hearing impairments. Similarly, norms for specific racial or ethnic groups can provide information about a person's performance relative to these specific populations. By comparing performance on certain racial versus national norms, program decisions concerning giftedness, mental retardation, or college admission can be more thoughtfully addressed (Mercer, 1973).

Threats to Validity

Due to the importance of the various elements and considerations that go into developing valid and reliable norm-referenced assessment instruments, any deviation from recommended procedures pose potential threats to the overall validity of test results. In this section we will discuss these major threats.

Violating Administration Standards. If the standards for administering a test are not followed, then the test results become invalid. Although administration standards vary from test to test, they generally include time limits, verbatim instructions to be read by or to the individual, sample items to be completed before the beginning of the test, providing testees with the necessary materials, steps ensuring the testing session is not interrupted, seating arrangements to prevent cheating, a reassuring tone of voice used by the administrator, efforts to make students as relaxed as possible, encouragement to students to try all the items on the test or not to spend too much time on any one problem, and rapidly ending the session to insure an exact termination of the test.

Variations in the use of any of these test administration standards invalidate test results. For example, if the time limits are not exact, some students will have more or less time to complete the test and, consequently, will not obtain a "true" score. Also, consider the effect on the test scores of students who do not have an opportunity to work the example problems before attempting actual test items. Since they are not fully ready for the actual items, they are likely to respond to the test items differently at the beginning of the test than at the end of the test.

Content Taught and Tested Confound. Norm-referenced tests are based on the assumption that what is tested is also taught in the classroom. However, even though the items on commercially produced tests may have been carefully selected by the developer, they sometimes show little overlap with what is taught in a given classroom. The same holds true for tests that focus upon adaptive behavior, employment, and other indices of overall ability. Norm-referenced tests have been criticized repeatedly for their lack of sensitivity in this regard (Gould, 1981). In spite of the most carefully conducted content

validity studies, test developers cannot take into account the instruction in each individual classroom, job, or community. Therefore, selection of norm-referenced tests must take into consideration the match between the actual implementation of the adopted curriculum and the content reflected in the test. This point is particularly important in special education where programs often deviate from the curricula offered to individuals who are not handicapped.

Learning Due to Overtesting. An important issue related to norm-referenced assessment is the possibility that overtesting may result in the tester learning directly from frequent exposure to the same test items. A number of procedures are employed to control this eventuality, including strict test use guidelines and alternate but equal forms of the test. For many standardized academic tests, administration is limited to the fall and spring of a given academic year. Intelligence tests, in turn, are spaced at least one year apart (see Kaufman & Kaufman, 1983).

The use of alternate test forms is predicated upon the test developer's ability to draw sets of items from the same domain of knowledge (for example, reading comprehension) that are of equal difficulty. By creating interchangeable item sets, the separate but equal versions of the test can be made. For example, developing a pool of 100 items and randomly including 30 items on each of three tests is one way to develop alternate but equivalent test forms. Another step in this process involves analyzing item difficulty. Given that all items in the pool of 100 have been administered to a sample of students, items can be matched according to difficulty level by determining the percent of students who missed each item. With this information, the developer can randomly assign items of equal difficulty to different test versions. The final proof of equivalence involves administering several test forms to the same group and checking the equivalence of scores among the different forms of the test. The tests are equivalent if the means are equal and if no statistically significant difference appears among the means.

Norm-Group Inadequacy. For norm-referenced tests o be valid, the roup included in the norming sample must truly represent the individual to be evaluated (Kerlinger, 1973). In spite of adherence to statistical procedures (such as random selection and stratified sampling) that improve the representativeness of a sample, *representativeness* can only be assumed because we cannot test everyone and know the whole population mean. This issue is of particular concern for students with handicaps.

Bias. Testing is invalid and discriminatory when there is evidence that either the items or the norm-group does not adequately represent an individual's cultural background, social history, or physical ability to respond to the test. Thus, norm-reference testing must be based on the assumption that those who take a given test have experienced equal socialization and acculturation. For example, non-English speakers or students who have not been exposed to recent educational practices are often unable to obtain valid results on standardized tests. Another assumption is that all students possess the behaviors and skills required to complete a given test. This may not always be the case, particularly for many students with physical disabilities. For example, tests which require fine-motor coordination are invalid for some individuals with physical handicaps. To remedy this situation, tests have been developed for special populations, or the test administration standards have been adapted to accommodate specific disabilities (see Salvia & Ysseldyke, 1985).

Minority groups, historically, have scored lower on norm-reference tests (Oakland, 1977). Some researchers have attributed this finding to genetic differences in ability between races (Jensen, 1980), others have pointed to historical, political, social, and economic differences in educational opportunity (Oakland & Laosa, 1977). Fishman (1964) concluded that minority students' performance, when compared to essentially white student norms, should be interpreted as an indication of the amount of change required to equal the performance of whites on the test rather than as an example of lower mental functioning or capacity.

Test developers have not always insured that the proper proportions of minorities in the national population (for example, 13 percent blacks and 4 percent Hispanics) were represented in their norm samples. Failure to do so has been repeatedly criticized by minority groups and upheld by the courts as biasing tests against minority-group individuals (Oakland, 1977). This argument has also been supported by the frequent observation that, relative to their proportion in the general population, greater numbers of minority-group children have been placed in programs serving persons with mental retardation (Dunn, 1968; Mercer, 1973) and learning disabilities (Tucker, 1980). Underenrollment of minority-group children in programs for gifted students has also occurred (Sato, 1974). In some cases, this criticism has led to the use of separate norm-groups. (SOMPA, Mercer & Lewis, 1979).

Court rulings in the 1970s and 1980s have challenged the use of tests having inadequate norms. For example, a 1979 ruling in a California case resulted in the following:

> Evidence showed that IQ tests were developed on white populations and were not readjusted or reexamined when it became clear that certain groups, including blacks and Hispanics, received low scores.
>
> The court ordered the state to retest youngsters now assigned to special education.
>
> The court ordered the state to review its assignment criteria and receive court approval before resuming use of standardized intelligence tests on black children for placement purposes (*Kansas City Times*, October 17, 1979).

The widespread use of tests for students in regular education programs has resulted in a number of provisions in P.L. 94-142 to protect and ensure appropriate placement of children with handicaps. Greenwood, Preston, and

Harris (1982, p. 67) presented the following testing practices based upon interpretation of P.L. 94-142:

1. Materials and procedures used for assessment must not be racially or culturally biased.
2. A full evaluation of the child's needs must be conducted prior to placement.
3. Tests and evaluations must be administered in the child's native tongue or other mode of communication.
4. Tests and evaluations must have been validated for the uses in which they are to provide information.
5. Administration must be by trained personnel using proper procedures.
6. Assessments must address specific areas of need or disability and not solely *general* ability. (IQ tests, for example, test general ability.)
7. No single procedure may be used as a sole criterion.
8. Evaluation is to be done by an interdisciplinary team, including teacher and parent.
9. Assessment is to be made in all related areas (for example, academics, hearing, social skills, and so forth).
10. Placement decisions must draw on multiple sources of information.
11. Decisions must be made by a group interpreting the data.
12. Placement must be in the least restrictive environment.
13. An Individualized Education Program (IEP) must be prepared.
14. The IEP must be reviewed annually.
15. A major evaluation is made every three years to review the placement.

These provisions take into consideration not only the adequacy of norm-referenced tests, but decisions related to non-biased placement (Reschly, 1978).

Examples of Norm-Referenced Tests

Norm-referenced tests fall into seven general categories: intelligence, academic achievement, language-speech, perceptual motor, adaptive-behavior, affective-behavioral, and interest-vocational aptitude. Table 6.5 lists examples from each area and a designation of the population for which a given test is designed.

For example, *The Blind Learning Aptitude Test* (Newland, 1969) is intended to assess the intelligence of individuals who are visually impaired. In contrast, The *Kaufman Assessment Battery for Children* (Kaufman & Kaufman, 1983) is used with a wide variety of preschool and school-age children. For additional information about these assessment instruments, the reader is referred to texts on assessment (such as Cronbach, 1984, Salvia & Ysseldyke, 1985, and the *Mental Measurements Yearbook* (Victor, 1985).

Summary

In this section we have discussed the principles underlying the development and administration of norm-referenced assessments and examined potential threats to test validity. We now turn to a similar discussion of criterion-referenced instruments.

CRITERION-REFERENCED INSTRUMENTS

The goal of criterion-referenced intermittent assessment is to display the performance on content taught in an instructional program. Thus, criterion-referenced testing is a measure of an individual's mastery of objectives. Unlike norm-referenced instruments, criterion-referenced ask the question, "What does an individual know or what can an individual do in relation to the ideal?" not "How does the student compare with other students?" Consequently, current performance is interpreted relative to a standard, usually a mastery level of performance. The scores yielded by criterion-referenced tests most often reflect the number of percentage of correct answers. In some cases, a summary score consisting of several items is used as a performance measure. In other instances, scores reflect performance on categories of

TABLE 6.5   Norm-Referenced Test Examples

TARGET POPULATION

	Preschool	Elementary	Secondary	Adult	General Population	Ethnic Minority	Orthopedic Handicap	Visual Impairment	Hearing Impairment	Mild/Moderate Mental Retardation	Severe/Profound Mental Retardation	Language Disability	Learning Disability	Emotional Disturbance	Gifted
Intelligence															
Wechsler Intelligence Scale for Children-Revised (WISC-R) (Wechsler, 1967)		X	X		X	X			X	X			X	X	
The Kaufman Assessment Battery for Children (Kaufman & Kaufman, 1983)	X	X			X	X		X	X	X			X	X	X
Slosson Intelligence Test (Slosson, 1981)	X	X	X	X	X			X		X					
Standford-Binet Intelligence Scale (Terman & Merrill, 1973)		X	X		X					X					
Stanford-Binet Intelligence Test—Fourth Edition (Thorndike, Hagen, & Sattler, 1985)	X	X	X	X	X	X				X	X		X		X
The Test of Nonverbal Intelligence (Brown, Sherbenou, & Dollar, 1982)		X	X	X		X			X	X	X	X	X		
The Nebraska Test of Learning Aptitude (Hiskey, 1966)	X	X	X		X					X					
The Blind Learning Aptitude Test (Newland, 1969)		X						X							
Pictorial Test of Intelligence (French, 1964)	X	X			X		X			X	X	X			
System of Multicultural and Pluralistic Assessment (SOMPA) (Mercer & Lewis, 1979)		X				X									
Academic Achievement															
Iowa Test of Basic Skills (Hieronymus, Lindquist, & Hoover, 1982)		X	X		X	X				X					
Peabody Individual Achievement Test (Dunn & Markwart, 1970)		X	X		X	X	X			X		X	X		X
Wide Range Achievement Test (Jastak & Jastak, 1978)	X	X	X	X	X	X		X		X			X		
Metropolitan Achievement Test (Prescott, Balon, Hogan, & Farr, 1978)		X	X		X	X			X						
The Stanford Achievement Test (Gardner, Rudman, Karlsen, & Merwin, 1982)		X	X		X	X		X	X						
Basic Achievement Skills Individual Screener (BASIS) (Sonnenschein, 1983)		X	X		X	X			X	X			X	X	X
Kaufman Test of Educational Achievement (Kaufman & Kaufman, 1985)		X	X		X									X	

(*continued*)

TABLE 6.5　*(Continued)*

TARGET POPULATION

	Preschool	Elementary	Secondary	Adult	General Population	Ethnic Minority	Orthopedic Handicap	Visual Impairment	Hearing Impairment	Mild/Moderate Mental Retardation	Severe/Profound Mental Retardation	Language Disability	Learning Disability	Emotional Disturbance	Gifted
Language/Speech															
Peabody Picture Vocabulary Test—Revised (Dunn & Dunn, 1981)	X	X	X	X	X		X		X			X			
Clinical Evaluation of Language Functioning (CELF) (Semel & Wiig, 1982)		X	X		X					X		X			
Test of Auditory Comprehension of Language (TACL) (Carron, 1973)	X				X	X				X		X			
Test of Language Development—Primary (Newcomer & Hammill, 1982)		X								X	X	X			
Perceptual Motor															
The Developmental Test of Visual Perception (DTVP) (Frostig, Lefever, & Whittlesey, 1966)	X	X			X					X					
Bender Visual Motor Gestalt Test (BVMGT) (Bender, 1938)		X			X					X			X		
Motor-Free Visual Perception Test (MVPT) (Colarusso & Hammill, 1972)		X			X			X		X			X		
Goldman-Fristoe-Woodcock Test of Auditory Discrimination (Goldman, Fristoe, & Woodcock, 1970)	X	X	X	X	X					X			X		
Adaptive Behavior															
Vineland Adaptive Behavior Scale (Sparrow, Balla, & Cicchetti, 1984)	X	X	X		X			X	X	X	X			X	
AAMD Adaptive Behavior Scale (Nihira, Foster, Shellhaas, & Leland, 1969)	X	X	X	X						X	X			X	
AAMD Adaptive Behavior Scale—School Edition (Lamber & Windmiller, 1981)	X	X	X		X					X					
Adaptive Behavior Inventory for Children (Mercer & Lewis, 1979)		X			X	X				X					
Comprehensive Test of Adaptive Behavior (CTAB) (Adams, 1983)	X	X	X	X						X	X				
Affective/Behavioral Measures															
Walker Problem Behavior Identification Checklist (WPBIC) (Walker, 1983)		X								X				X	
Behavior Problem Checklist (Peterson & Quay, 1979)		X				X			X	X			X	X	

TABLE 6.5   *(Continued)*

Affective/Behavioral Measures	Preschool	Elementary	Secondary	Adult	General Population	Ethnic Minority	Orthopedic Handicap	Visual Impairment	Hearing Impairment	Mild/Moderate Mental Retardation	Severe/Profound Mental Retardation	Language Disability	Learning Disability	Emotional Disturbance	Gifted
Devereux Elementary School Behavior Rating Scale (Spivack & Swift, 1967)		X			X	X		X		X				X	
Interest/Vocational Aptitude															
Kuder Preference Record—Vocational (Kuder, 1976)			X	X	X			X							
The Geist Picture Inventory (Geist, 1975)			X	X					X		X		X		
Strong-Campbell Interest Inventory (Hansen & Campbell, 1985)				X	X	X		X							
Reading-Free Vocational Interest Inventory (Becker, 1981)			X	X						X			X		

objectives within content domains. Either approach reveals the error pattern within a specific objective or domain. Such patterns, in turn, are used to determine what an individual knows and where instruction should begin. Mastery standards are usually set arbitrarily at very high levels (for example, above 90 percent correct) to insure that a given skill is learned. Teaching continues until the standard level is reached.

Fundamental Principles

As with norm-referenced testing, requirements for sound criterion-referenced instruments include validity, reliability, standard administration, and content selection.

Validity. In criterion-referenced testing, which must contain a match between what is tested and what is taught, content validity is demonstrated principally through content selection and consensual agreement by consumers. Unlike norm-referenced measures, content validity here does not relate to sampling but involves careful selection of behavioral objectives and accompanying task analyses. Content validity is demonstrated to the extent that objectives and task analyses are rated "important" or "necessary" skills by teachers, parents, educators, and other consumers such as committees made up of persons with handicaps.

The concurrent validity of criterion-referenced tests is demonstrated when a test correctly discriminates between students that are judged independently by teachers or parents as possessing the requisite skills and those who do not as independently judged by teachers and parents. In this type of study, individuals demonstrating the requisite skills should perform all the tasks on a given test with 90 percent to 100 percent accuracy, whereas those who do not possess the skill would score somewhere between zero and 89 percent.

Predictive validity studies are rarely completed for criterion-referenced tests since the individual's ability to perform the skill (for example, learning to ride the bus to work) is assumed to be of sufficient immediate importance in the student's life to be learned.

Reliability. As previously noted, reliability demonstrates accurate measurement across several test administrations. Reliability is less often assessed with criterion-referenced than norm-referenced tests since many of these are teacher developed rather than commercially published. Test-retest reliability, nevertheless, remains an important indicator of the measurement of quality.

Administration Standards. As for norm-referenced tests, administration standards are important by providing quality control over test administration.

Threats to Validity

Several threats to reliability must be considered with criterion-referenced. These considerations are similar to those reviewed above with norm-referenced tests.

Violation of Administration Standards. As is the case for norm-referenced tests, if administration standards are violated, results become invalid. For example, if different instructions are given to a student on the second administration of a test or if the student were able to cheat on the test because he or she is left unmonitored, the results would be invalid.

Content Taught and Tested Confound. In criterion-referenced testing, test confound is not nearly as great a problem as it is with norm-referenced assessment. With the latter, we are rarely certain that what is tested is actually in the student's curriculum since the content is based upon a sampling process. Theoretically, criterion-referenced testing guarantees correspondence between content taught and content tested. However, the exact extent of this match depends on program implementation. If instruction on a daily basis is guided by the test scores, a match is assured. On the other hand, if results are filed away and not used to plan daily instructional activities, future assessment may be confounded since a student's failure to improve on the next test is partly due to the teacher's failure to pursue the correct course of instruction. To avoid this test confound, therefore, instruction must be based on test information.

Learning Due to Overtesting. Learning due to overtesting is not an issue in criterion-referenced testing since what is measured reflects the instructional content. Thus, criterion-referenced tests may be given frequently without leading to overlearning. Progress to the next set of lessons or repetition of prior lessons is dependent upon the level of tested mastery. If a student is able to reach mastery on the second attempt, even if due to testing alone, it would justify allowing him or her to progress since he or she is demonstrating the prerequisites for what will be learned in the new material.

Bias. Since norms are rarely used in criterion-referenced tests, bias does not pose a very widespread validity threat in this type of testing. However, hybrid tests, those containing both criterion- and norm-referencing, are subject to the same threats to validity as norm-referenced instruments. Thus, the same precautions must be taken to avoid test bias stemming from content and ethnic, sociocultural or handicapping conditions.

Examples of Specific Criterion-Referenced Tests

Table 6.6 contains a listing of published criterion-referenced tests organized into two areas: developmental skills and academic achievement. Instruments listed in the first category are designed for individuals with both mild (*Learning Accomplishment Profile*) and severe (*Callier-Azusa Scale*) handicaps. All three instruments in this area assess daily living skills, gross-motor skills, and speech and language skills.

TABLE 6.6 Criterion-Referenced Test Examples (Commercially Published)

	TARGET POPULATION														
	Preschool	Elementary	Secondary	Adult	General Population	Ethnic Minority	Orthopedic Handicap	Visual Impairment	Hearing Impairment	Mild/Moderate Mental Retardation	Severe/Profound Mental Retardation	Language Disability	Learning Disability	Emotional Disturbance	Gifted
Developmental Skills															
Brigance Inventory of Early Development (Brigance, 1978)	X									X	X				
Callier-Azusa Scale (Stillman, 1978)	X	X						X	X				X		
Learning Accomplishment Profile (Sanford, 1975)	X					X	X	X	X				X	X	
Academic Achievement															
Brigance Inventory of Basic Skills (Brigance, 1977)		X			X							X	X		
Multilevel Academic Skill Inventory (Howell, Zucker, & Morehead 1982)												X	X		
Diagnosis: An Instructional Aid in Reading (Shub, Carlin, Friedman, Kaplan, & Katien, 1973)		X			X							X	X		
Diagnostic Mathematics Inventory (Gessell, 1977)		X			X							X	X		

DEVELOPMENT AND USE OF CRITERION-REFERENCED INSTRUMENTS

Since criterion-referenced measures are bound to specific instructional programs, it is necessary to adhere to certain procedures to determine what should be taught (Zigmond & Miller, 1986). *Task analysis* is the most common basis for developing instructional programs and accompanying tests (Resnick, Wang, & Kaplan, 1973).

TASK ANALYSIS

A *task* signifies a response opportunity for a student or client (Englemann & Carnine, 1982). As such, a task is a specific stimulus

event that occasions a relatively select response or set of responses, for example,

"Bill, go to the store and buy some milk" or
"Bill, roll up the car window" or
"Bill, please fix scrambled eggs for your breakfast this morning."

Tasks are the elements which comprise single behavioral objectives, hence they are not behavioral objectives, such as,

Bill will be able to shop at the grocery market, or
Bill will be able to follow directions, or
Bill will be able to fix his own breakfast.

Tasks are the specific response situations and their associated behaviors that define the set of events which comprise the objective. *Task analysis* is used to plan the situations and behaviors that must be taught and tested to determine if an objective has been mastered.

Uses of Task Analysis

Task analysis may be used to identify: (a) the prerequisite tasks; (b) the sequence of tasks, from simple to complex, that will be taught; and (c) the task selection and organization to enhance generalization of performance to similar but untaught tasks.

Prior to teaching a task, we must ensure that the student is proficient in all entry behaviors (Bijou, 1970). If the task is to "install a Phillips-head screw," the student must be able to select a Phillips-head screw from several alternatives before he or she can be effectively taught the motor behaviors necessary to install the Phillips-head screw" (Englemann & Carnine, 1982, p. 266). *Prerequisite tasks* (selecting the correct screw), then, are those that are trained prior to the primary task (installing the screw).

The *sequence* in which tasks are taught is determined by both a logical and behavioral analysis of what comes first. A logical analysis takes into consideration whether tasks are organized in reasonably correct and consistent fashion. If this order holds up when a skilled individual is observed installing Phillips-head screws (behavioral), the sequence is validated. Otherwise, it is modified in accordance with the correct performance sequence.

A major criticism of traditional task analysis is that, although it is effective for planning specific task and response sequences, it is rarely helpful in planning for generalization as it teaches only a specific task to be taught, for example, "Put the ball on the table." *However, this specific task is only one in a set of similar but different tasks* (Englemann & Carnine, 1982, p. 136). For generalization, Englemann and Carnine suggest using a *transformed task analysis*, which assists in specifying the set of tasks. The transformed task used by Englemann and Carnine (1982) looks like this: "Put the A on the B." By creating a list of feasible objects for the letters A and B, the set of possible tasks can be broadly defined. Thus, the student can be taught to discriminate the differences in the following: "Put the ball on the table," from "Put the knife on the table," or "Put the car on the desk," and so forth. The transformed task also clarifies the difference between identifying essential objects and the motor response required to "Put the A on the B." Further, differences in placing responses, such as "Put the A on the B," or "Put the B on the A," can be made apparent. By teaching subsets of tasks within the universe of such tasks generalization to similar but untaught tasks is optimized.

Another approach to develop generalization is the use of generative response sets (Alessi, 1986; Becker, 1986). For example, the word list in Table 6.7 consists of a set of words that share the root *add* and refer to tasks that involve the concept of addition. Teaching the root and the related words as a set enables students to read or spell some of the remaining words without direct training.

Relevance of Task Analysis to IEP's

As discussed in Chapter 5, specification of long- and short-term IEP objectives is the first step in identifying what students will learn. Task analysis is important in this regard by acting as the instructional planning technique necessary to flesh out what to teach on a day-to-day basis.

Task analysis may be applied to the full

TABLE 6.7 An Example of a Generative Response Set

add		
adds	adding	
	addition	
	additive	
		adder
		added
		addend
		addendum

range of teaching, including (a) specific academic, social, and vocational skills, (b) highly related skills (generalization), and (c) developmental skills. *Specific academic, social, and vocational skills* refer to selected behaviors that normally make up the curricula. For children with mild handicaps these may include academic skills in addition to social skills within the traditional curricula. *Related skills* refer to planning for generalization. Since it is impossible to directly teach all tasks, it is important to select procedures which will optimize students' ability to generalize what they learn so that it can be used with different persons, settings, times, and behaviors. Finally, *developmental skills* refer to those skills normally present in students of a particular age and sex but which are not manifest in the specific individual for whom instruction is being planned. Task analysis here is applied as part of the effort to remediate deficiencies.

For individuals with severe handicaps, task analysis is used to plan the task sequences to be mastered to move students from delayed behavior in self-care, language, or daily living to the target skill. This goal may be accomplished by adapting required performances to accommodate a particular disability (for example, limited physical mobility) thereby enabling the individual to perform a given task using a modified repertoire (such as using a wheel chair instead of walking). Tasks requiring facility with self-care, language, daily living, preacademic, gross- or fine-motor behaviors are considered developmental skills.

Examples of Task Analysis

The task analysis in Table 6.8 illustrates plans for how you might teach an academic task—the long "a" word—to students with mild handicaps.

The teacher establishes a rule about long "a" words, tests the students' use of the rule, and elaborates on the reading of long "a" words by introducing new examples. Next, extensive teacher promptings are faded and independent responding is established, followed by students learning the difference between long and short "a" words. Sequencing of the different sets of tasks which enables incremental building of complex performances and skills is particularly important.

Table 6.9 provides a task analysis of the skills that may be needed by students when acting as peer tutors in spelling. The tutor must (a) present new words for the tutee to spell; (b) check for spelling accuracy; (c) award points depending upon three tutee responses; and (d) implement an error-correction procedure that allows the student to practice a misspelled word. This very specific tutor repertoire has proven to be an effective tutoring procedure (Delquadri, Greenwood, Whorton, Carta, & Hall, 1986). The analysis captures what is necessary to both assess the quality of tutoring (i.e., the behaviors and their sequence) and peer tutors.

Tables 6.10, 6.11, and 6.12 illustrate analyses applicable to persons with severe handicaps. The first shows a behavioral episode used in social skills training of students with autism (Gaylord-Ross, Haring, Breen, & Pitts-Conway, 1984). As illustrated, the sequence of behaviors first considers the approach the student will make to a nonhandicapped student (Steps 1 to 3).

Initiation is made in Steps 4 to 7. If the first initiation is not successful (Step 7), a new approach is made. Otherwise the interaction proceeds with the students sharing the Walkman radio in Steps 8 to 13, until the interaction ends (Step 14).

The next task analysis (Table 6.11) plans assessment and teaching of toothbrushing performance. Following a statement of the terminal objective, the task analysis provides the exact sequence of tasks and responses necessary to complete this complex behavior. In addition to planning the training sequence, this task analysis could be used to assess toothbrushing performance. Observation of a student's errors (such as an incorrect response, omission of a response in the sequence, or a correct response but performed out of sequence) relative to the task analysis would form the bases for determining the step(s) at which instruction should begin.

TABLE 6.8 Task Analysis of Teaching Students to Read Long "*a*" Words

Teacher writes this list of words on the blackboard. All are long "*a*" words:

> *game   lake   fame   scale   fate   case   made*

The teacher next establishes the rule for reading final "*e*" words:

Teacher: "Here's the rule. When there's an '*e*' at the end, say this letter." (Teacher points to the "*e*" and "*a*" in
      game.) "Is there an '*e*' at the end?"
Class: "Yes."
Teacher: "So do I read the letter name?"
Class: "Yes."
Teacher: "What name?"
Class: "*a*"
Teacher: "I'll read the word, *game*. It's still my turn." (Teacher points to *fame*.) "Is there an '*e*' at the end?"
Class: "Yes."
Teacher: "So do I read the letter name?"
Class: "Yes."
Teacher: "What name?"
Class: "*a*"
Teacher: "I'll read the word. *Fame*. Okay, now it's your turn." (Teacher points to *fate*.) "Is there an '*e*' on the end?"
Class: "Yes."
Teacher: "So do you read the letter name?"
Class: "Yes."
Teacher: "What name?"
Class: "*a*"
Teacher: "Read the word."
Class: "Fate."

Practice: The students would then be asked the exact same questions as they were for *fate* through the rest of the
   list—the remaining four words.

Fading Teacher Prompts: Then the teacher would go through another list of six long "*a*" words, providing less assistance. For every word the teacher would ask: "Is there an '*e*' at the end? Read the word."

Practice: Finally the teacher would have the students read six more long "*a*" words independently.

Teach New Discrimination: The next step would be to teach the discrimination between long and short "*a*" words.
   To do this the teacher would go through a list containing both types: *made, mad; late, land; Sam, same.* The
   teacher's instructions would be: "Is there an '*e*' at the end? Read the word."

Source: Adapted from "The pursuit of clarity: Direct instruction and applied behavior analysis" by R. Gersten, D. Carnine,
W. A. T. White in *Focus on behavior analysis in education*, p. 39, 1984.

A similar analysis is presented for how to teach handwashing in Table 6.12.

These preceding examples illustrate task analyses of academic, social, and developmental skills developed for use with individuals who are mildly and severely handicapped. From an assessment standpoint, the task analyses provide the basis for checking what students can do and what they subsequently need to learn to acquire a behavioral objective. We will now discuss teacher and commercially developed criterion-referenced instruments.

TEACHER DEVELOPED INSTRUMENTS

Although many commercial criterion-referenced tests are available, the most frequently used tests are developed by special education teachers. The major considerations in devel-

TABLE 6.9   Task Analysis of Peer Tutoring Skills

Tutor: "Spell CAT."
Tutee: Simultaneously spells the word aloud and writes the word.
Tutor: Checks accuracy of the written word to sample on word list. *If spelling is correct,* tutor says "Good that's right, you get two points." The tutor marks two points on the tutee's point sheet. The tutor now presents the next new word.

or

If spelling is incorrect, tutor says "No, the word is spelled *C A T.* Write it correctly three times."
Tutee: Simultaneously spells the word aloud and writes the word correctly three times, "*C A T C A T C A T.*"
Tutor: Again, the tutor checks the accuracy of the response. "Good, that's right, you get one point." The tutor marks one on the tutee's point sheet. The tutor now presents the next new word.

or

Tutee: Simultaneously spells the word aloud and writes the word with one or more errors, *C A T C A T C E T.*"
Tutor: "No that is incorrect, no points on this word." The tutor presents the next new word.

Source: From Carta, J. J., Greenwood, C. R., Dinwiddie, G., Kohler, F., & Delquadri, J. (1985). *The Juniper Gardens classwide peer tutoring programs for spelling, reading, and math. Teacher's manual.* Kansas City, KS: The Juniper Gardens Children's Project, Bureau of Child Research, University of Kansas, p. 10.

oping these tests involve appropriate content, writing the instruments, and including interpretation of results in classroom use.

Appropriate Content

Criterion-referenced tests are designed to measure mastery of objectives within subject matter and content domains such as units of knowledge or skill within a much broader subject-matter area. Examples of content domains include telling time and meaningful counting. Although assigned to teach large subject areas, teachers must design criterion-referenced tests that reflect smaller units within a subject area. Thus, as expressed in Table 6.13, content domains narrow the field, giving us a manageable set of behavioral objectives and tasks to be taught.

Any content domains adopted by a school program, expressed as goals or objectives, are generally appropriate for task analysis and protocol construction (see Table 5.1). In many cases, task analyses and criterion-referenced

TABLE 6.10   Example of Social Skill Task Analysis (Behavioral Steps)

 1. Student with autism (AS) approaches nonhandicapped student (NS).
 2. AS establishes 1 meter proximity.
 3. AS establishes face forward orientation to NS.
 4. AS says "Hi."
 5. AS waits for a response.
 6. AS says "Want to listen."
 7. AS shows radio to NS. If NS not interested in interacting, AS approaches another student (Step 1).
 8. AS turns on radio.
 9. AS adjusts volume to level 6.
10. AS hands headphones to NS.
11. AS puts on headphones
12. AS selects rock and roll station.
13. AS remains in proximity to NS until termination of interaction.
14. AS says "Bye."

Source: From "The training and generalization of social interaction skills with autistic youth" by R. J. Gaylord-Ross, T. G. Haring, C. Breen, and V. Pitts-Conway, 1984, *Journal of Applied Behavior Analysis, 17,* p. 234.   Copyright 1984 by the Society for the Experimental Analysis of Behavior, Inc.

TABLE 6.11 Task Analysis for Brushing Teeth

Objective: Given a toothbrush, toothpaste, cup, and paper towel, Larry will brush his teeth without verbal instruction according to the task analysis given one trial on each of five consecutive school days.

Task Analysis:

1. The adult trainer says, "It's time to brush your teeth, go over to the sink."
2. One step at a time, the adult instructs Larry to:

a. Turn on the water.
b. Pick up the glass.
c. Fill the glass with water.
d. Set the glass down.
e. Stop the water.
f. Pick up the toothpaste.
g. Open the toothpaste.
h. Put the top down.
i. Squeeze the toothpaste onto the brush.

j. Pick up the top.
k. Put the top on the toothpaste.
l. Put toothpaste down.
m. Pick up the brush.

n. Brush your bottom teeth.
o. Brush your upper teeth.
p. Turn on the water.
q. Rinse your brush.
r. Put your brush down.
s. Turn off the water.
t. Pick up the glass.
u. Rinse your mouth.
v. Spit out the water.
w. Empty glass and put it down.
x. Put the brush in the glass.
y. Rinse and dry your hands.
z. Throw away the towel.

Source: From *Sample activities for the severely multiply handicapped,* p. 15, Kansas State Department of Education, 1984, Topeka: Kansas State Department of Education.

TABLE 6.12 Task Analysis for Washing Hands

1. Locate the sink.
2. Turn on the water.
3. Wet your hands.
4. Pick up the soap.
5. Rub soap on your hands.
6. Put the soap down.
7. Rub your hands together.
8. Rinse your hands.
9. Turn off the water.
10. Pick up the towel.
11. Dry your hands.
12. Throw the towel away.

Source: From *Sample activities for the severely multiply handicapped,* p. 22, Kansas State Department of Education, 1984, Topeka, KS: Kansas State Department of Education.

TABLE 6.13 Relationship Among Subject Matter, Content, Objectives, and Tasks

Element	Example
Subject Matter Area Goal	Preacademic skills
Domain Content Goal	The ABC's
Behavioral Objective	The student will say the ABC's, A through Z, when asked by the teacher without any errors in letters or their sequence.
Tasks	Say "A"
	Say "B"
	Say "A," "B," "C," and so forth.

tests have already been developed for certain programs. In such cases, teachers only need plan their instruction around the proposed objectives and tasks. Otherwise, objectives, task analyses, test protocols, and teaching procedures must be planned before they can be implemented. An example of a complete teaching plan is presented in Table 6.14.

In Table 6.14, the objective, criterion, and task analysis are related to the materials and procedures required to complete the lesson.

Writing Criterion-Referenced Instruments

The following steps are involved in writing criterion-referenced tests: (a) specifying content goals, (b) determining the behavioral objective, (c) performing the task analysis, and (d) writing the protocol. Since content goals and behavioral objectives have been covered in Chapter 5, we will focus here on task analysis.

Performing the Task Analysis. As mentioned, task analysis requires logic, direct observation, and subsequent revision. First, a list is made in order from simple to complex so that prerequisites are always taught first. Second, observe the task actually being performed by a skilled student and compare the sequence of events to your task analysis. Third, based on your observation, revise your list, if necessary, to coincide with what actually happened. You may wish to conduct additional observations to verify the accuracy of your analysis. At this step you may find that highly skilled students always perform the skill in the same order or that some behaviors occur in a different order without apparent effect on mastery of a given task. Fourth, you may wish to pilot test your analysis by assessing students who already possess the target behavior versus those that do not. If you find that the two student groups obtain highly divergent scores (for example, 95 percent versus 20 percent), your analysis is valid.

Writing a Protocol. A protocol is a test or instrument format that contains the tasks to be assessed. In addition, it includes an information heading for writing the student's name, date, other pertinent information, test items, and a space for computing and summarizing scores (see Figure 6.4).

Classroom Use of Teacher-Developed Instruments

When to Administer. Criterion-referenced tests should be administered to (a) assess what a student can do, and (b) monitor the progress of teaching efforts. Frequency of administration will be partly determined by the scope and grain-size of the test. By *scope,* we mean the number of objectives that are assessed in one test; *grain-size* refers to the number of tasks assessed per objective. Thus, tests with a narrow scope and grain-size are administered more often, perhaps upon completion of short units of instruction. Those with wide scope and grain-size—a summative assessment over five units of instruction—are administered less frequently.

How to Administer. A standard administration format should be developed to insure quality of measurement. Such requirements should include necessary instructions to the student, instruction for the arrangement of the student and materials during testing, specified time limits if necessary, and procedures for how to monitor students during the assessment.

Scoring and Interpreting Test Results. As mentioned, criterion-referenced test scores will most likely be expressed as the percentage of total items correct or the percentages for specific domains or objectives included on the test. Depending upon the standard or criterion level of mastery—in our example, 90 percent correct—scores may be used for several purposes.

First, if a test is given with the goal of placing a student into a sequence of instruction, the objectives and tasks at which the student fails to meet the criterion suggests where instruction should begin. Second, if the test is administered to monitor progress, the point

TABLE 6.14   Teaching Plan Including Task Analysis

Behavior: *Brushing teeth—Larry will brush his teeth without verbal instructions according to the task analysis on one trial for five consecutive days.*

Objective	Procedures and Materials	Consequence	Criteria
Given a toothbrush, toothpaste, cup, and paper towel, Larry will brush his teeth without verbal instruction according to the task analysis on one trial for five consecutive school days.	Materials: Toothbrush, toothpaste, cup, and paper towel Procedure: 1. The task is attempted each day after lunch. 2. The adult verbalizes directions while demonstrating each step of the task analysis for five consecutive days. 3. The adult gives verbal directions one step at a time—failure to follow directive results in adult repeating instruction while physically assisting Larry in completing the step.		1/1 for five consecutive days
	Task Analysis: 1. The adult says, "It's time to brush your teeth, go over to the sink." 2. One step at a time the adult instructs Larry to: a. Turn on the water. b. Pick up the glass. c. Fill the glass with water. d. Set the glass down. e. Stop the water. f. Pick up the toothpaste. g. Open the toothpaste. h. Put the top down. i. Squeeze toothpaste onto brush. j. Pick up top. k. Put top on toothpaste. l. Put toothpaste down. m. Pick up brush. n. Brush your bottom teeth. o. Brush your upper teeth. p. Turn on water. q. Rinse your brush. r. Put brush down. s. Turn off water. t. Pick up glass. u. Rinse your mouth. v. Spit out water. w. Empty glass and put it down. x. Put brush in glass. y. Rinse and dry hands. z. Throw away towel.	Pass-proceed to next step. Fail-adult repeats instruction and physically assists Larry to the sink. Pass-adult gives verbal praise intermittently through the steps. Fail-while repeating the step verbally, the adult physically assists Larry in completing the step.	

Source: Taken from the Kansas State Department of Education, 1984.

FIGURE 6.4 Example Protocol

COMPREHENSIVE SPECIAL SERVICES COOPERATIVE
Summary Sheet

Student No.: _____

Student Name: _____ B.D. _____ C.A. _____ Sex _____

Grade _____ Student Address _____

Student Phone _____ Parents/Guardian _____

School _____ Teacher _____ Dist. # _____

Examiner _____ Date(s) Tested _____

Handedness: Left _____ Right _____ Glasses: Yes _____ No _____

READINESS

Subtest #	# Poss.	# Earned	*Strength + Weakness −
1. Name Alphabet from Memory	26		
2. Mns prnt ABC - Memory	104		
3. Mns prnt of ABC - Named	52		
4. Name Mns print ABC	52		
5. Matching Mns ABC	11		
6. Wrt Curs ABC - Memory	104		
7. Wrt Curs ABC - Named	52		
8. Name Curs prnt ABC	52		
9. Dolch Bas. Sight Voc.	220		
10. Aud. Blending Words	12		
11. Init. Cons. Sounds (Pic)	15		
12. Init. Cons. Sounds	38		
13. Init. Cons. Sounds (Aud-Mo)	12		
14. End. Cons. Sounds	12		
15. End. Cons. Sounds	26		
16. End. Cons. Sounds (Aud-Mo)	12		
17. Init. Cons. Blends (Pic)	18		
18. Init. Cons. Blends	36		
19. Init. Cons. Blends (Aud-Mo)	18		
20. Init. Cons. Digraphs	10		
21. Begin. Cons. Digraphs (Aud-Mo)	5		
22. Init. Vowel Sounds	18		
23. Long & Short Vowel Sounds (Aud-Mo)	10		
24. Blend Words	18		
25. Blend Phonetic Elements	22		
26. Double Vowels - Diphthongs	14		
27. Prefixes	18		
28. Suffixes	16		
29. Prefixes-Suffixes	6		
30. Syllabification	11		
TOTAL SCORE	1020		

Source: From Welsch, D. L., & Miller, L. J. (1972) *Comprehensive services tests.* Olathe, KS: Educational Modulation Center, p. 1.

at which the student fails to show mastery at the 90 percent level is compared to his or her previous test performance to reveal the extent of progress. Thus, if the student has mastered eight new objectives since the previous testing, progress is indicated. Again, the point of failure shows where instruction should begin. Third, the error pattern within a task analysis serves as precise diagnosis for planning instruction that avoids redundant teaching efforts. For example, errors on tasks within an objective identify where instruction should be directed. In most cases, teaching is required only on those few missed tasks. After correcting his or her errors, the student should be able to reach mastery of the entire task or objective rather quickly. By directly gearing teaching to specific areas the overall progress will be enhanced.

COMMERCIALLY PREPARED TESTS

When attempting to identify the most appropriate criterion-referenced assessment instrument, users of commercial products typically face the problem of either finding a test that reflects current instructional goals and objectives or of adopting a curriculum so that it contains the necessary criterion-referenced tests.

Selecting Tests to Fit Current Curriculum. Test selection should be an objective process whereby potential tests are matched to the content domains and behavioral objectives within an existing program. This can be accomplished by constructing a checklist that quantifies the match between test content and instructional program.

Beyond teacher-made instruments, criterion-referenced tests are available from commercial publishers, regional laboratories and resource centers, and state departments of education.

Selecting Curricula that Contain Criterion-Referenced Tests. Commercially available mastery-based curricula are designed around

task analyses and contain reading, math, language, corrective reading, and morphological spelling programs (Englemann & Carnine, 1970, 1982). They contain unit mastery tests as well as comprehensive tests covering these content domains. The selection process facing teachers in this case consists of matching the mastery-based curriculum to the content goals of the instructional program being developed.

SUMMARY

In this chapter, we have discussed intermittent assessment starting with a definition based upon its periodic use and its interpretation in terms of global scores and patterns of specific scores. Within intermittent assessment, we distinguished between norm-referenced and criterion-referenced assessment types. After briefly acknowledging the existence of hybrid instruments, those containing both norms and criteria, we noted that the two types of referencing are designed to address fundamentally different purposes. Specifically, norm-referenced intermittent assessment compares a student to other students, usually for the purpose of determining placement in an instructional program. Criterion-referenced intermittent assessment, in turn, compares performance to criteria or mastery standards. For both types of intermittent assessment, we reviewed the underlying principles and assumptions as well as potential sources of test result invalidation. Lastly, we reviewed development and use of criterion-referenced tests with major emphasis on task analysis, a procedure for planning and teaching based on objectives. We discussed issues related to teacher-developed criterion-referenced tests versus commercially available instruments, and concerns related to the former included writing, administering, and interpreting results. For commercially prepared tests, the discussion pointed to the choice between selecting a test to fit an existing curricula or selecting a curriculum to fit existing tests or task analyses within commercially developed programs. In Chapter 7, we explore continuous assessment procedures.

REFERENCES

ADAMS, G. (1983). *The Comprehensive Test of Adaptive Behavior.* Columbus, OH: Charles E. Merrill.

ALESSI, G. (1986). "Generative programming: A strategic approach to the teaching of generalization." In E. S. Shapiro (ed.), *Behavioral assessment and interventions for academic skills.* Symposium presented at the Twelfth Annual Convention of the Association for Behavior Analysis, Milwaukee, WI.

ALGOZZINE, B., CHRISTENSON, S., & YSSELDYKE, J. E. (1982). "Probabilities associated with referral to placement process." *Teacher Education and Special Education, 5,* 19–23.

BECKER, R. L. (1981). *Reading-Free Vocational Interest Inventory.* Columbus, OH: Elbern.

BECKER, W. C. (1986). *Applied psychology for teachers; A behavioral cognitive approach.* Chicago: Science Research Associates.

BIJOU, S. W. (1970). "What psychology has to offer education—now." *Journal of Applied Behavior Analysis, 3,* 65–71.

BRIGANCE, A. (1977). *Brigance Inventory of Basic Skills.* North Billerica, MA: Curriculum Associates.

BRIGANCE, A. (1978). *Brigance Inventory of Early Development.* North Billerica, MA: Curriculum Associates.

BROWN, L., SHERBENOU, R. J., & DOLLAR, S. J. (1982). *Test of Nonverbal Intelligence.* Austin, TX: Pro-Ed.

CARROW, E. (1973). *Test of Auditory Comprehension of Language* (rev. ed.). Austin, TX: Learning Concepts.

CARTA, J. J., GREENWOOD, C. R., DINWIDDIE, G., KOHLER, F., & DELQUADRI, J. (1985). *The Juniper Gardens Classuride peer tutoring programs for spelling, reading, and math. Teacher's Manual.* Kansas City: KS: The Juniper Gardens Children's Project, Bureau of Child Research, University of Kansas, p. 10.

COLARUSSO, R., & HAMMILL, D. (1972). *The Motor-Free Test of Visual Perception.* San Rafael, CA: Academic Therapy.

CRONBACH, L. J. (1984). *Essentials of psychological testing* (4th ed.). New York: Harper & Row.

DELQUADRI, J., GREENWOOD, C. R., STRETTON, K., & HALL, R. V. (1983). "The peer tutoring game: A classroom procedure for increasing opportunity to respond and spelling performance." *Education and Treatment of Children, 6,* 225–239.

DUNN, L. M. (1968). "Special education for the mildly retarded: Is much of it justified?" *Exceptional Children, 35,* 5–22.

DUNN, L., & DUNN, L. (1981). *Peabody Picture Vocabulary Test: Revised.* Circle Pines, MN: American Guidance Service.

DUNN, L. M., & MARKWARDT, F. C. (1970). *Peabody Individual Achievement Test.* Cleveland, OH: The Psychological Corporation.

ENGLEMANN, S., & CARNINE, D. (1970). *(Distar arithmetic: An instructional system* (teacher's guide). Chicago: Science Research Associates.

ENGLEMANN, S., & CARNINE, D. (1982). *Theory of instruction: Principles and applications.* New York: Irvington.

FISHMAN, J. A., ed. (1964). "Guidelines for testing minority group children." *Journal of Social Issues Supplement, 35,* 129–145.

FRENCH, J. L. (1964). *Pictorial Test of Intelligence.* Chicago: Riverside.

FROSTIG, M., LeFEVER, W., & WHITTLESEY, J. (1966). *Administration and scoring manual: Marianne Frostig Developmental Test of Visual Perception.* Palo Alto, CA: Consulting Psychologists Press.

GAGE, N. L., & BERLINER, D. C. (1984). *Educational psychology.* Boston: Houghton-Mifflin.

GARDNER, E. F., RUDMAN, H. C., KARLSEN, B., & MERWIN, J. C. (1982). *Stanford Achievement Test* (7th ed.). Cleveland, OH: The Psychological Corporation.

GAYLORD-ROSS, R. J., HARING, T. G., BREEN, C., & PITTS-CONWAY, V. (1984). "The training and generalization of social interaction skills with autistic youth. *Journal of Applied Behavior Analysis, 17,* 229–247.

GEIST, H. G. (1975). *Manual for the Geist Picture Interest Inventory: Revised.* Los Angeles, CA: Western Psychological Services.

GERSTEN, R., CARNINE, D., & WHITE, W. A. T. (1984). "The pursuit of clarity: Direct instruction and applied behavior analysis." In W. L.

Heward, T. E. Heron, D. S. Hill, & J. Trap-Porter (eds.), *Focus on behavior analysis in education*. Lawrence, Kansas: H & H Enterprises.

GESSELL, J. K. (1977). *Diagnostic Mathematics Inventory*. Monterey, CA: CTB/McGraw-Hill.

GOLDMAN, R., FRISTOE, M., & WOODCOCK, R. (1970). *Goldman-Fristoe-Woodcock Test of Auditory Discrimination*. Circle Pines, MN: American Guidance Service.

GOOD, T. L., & BROPHY, J. E. (1984). *Looking in classrooms* (3rd ed.). New York: Harper & Row.

GOULD, S. J. (1981). *The mismeasure of man*. New York: Norton.

GREENWOOD, C. R., DINWIDDIE, G., TERRY, B., WADE, L., STANLEY, S., & THIBADEAU, S. (1984). "Teacher versus peer mediated instruction: An analysis of achievement outcomes." *Journal of Applied Behavior Analysis, 17*, 521–538.

GREENWOOD, C. R., PRESTON, D., & HARRIS, J. (1982). *Minority issues in the education of handicapped children*. Kansas City, KS: University of Kansas, The Juniper Gardens Children's Project.

GREENWOOD, C. R., WALKER, H. M., TODD, N., & HOPS, H. (1979). "Selecting a cost effective screening measure for assessment of preschool social withdrawal." *Journal of Applied Behavior Analysis, 12*, 639–652.

GUILFORD, J. P. (1954). *Psychometric methods* (2nd ed.). New York: McGraw-Hill.

HANSEN, J. C., & CAMPBELL, D. P. (1985). *Strong-Campbell Interest Inventory*. Palo Alto, CA: Consulting Psychologists Press.

HIERONYMUS, A. N., LINDQUIST, E. F., & HOOVER, H. D. (1982). *Iowa Tests of Basic Skills*. Chicago: Riverside.

HISKEY, M. (1966). *Hiskey-Nebraska Test of Learning Aptitude*. Lincoln, NE: Marshall S. Hiskey.

HOPS, H., & GREENWOOD, C. R. (in press). "Social skills deficits." In E. Mash & L. Terdal (eds.), *Behavioral assessment of child disorders* (2nd ed.).

HOWELL, K., ZUCKER, S., & MOREHEAD, M. (1982). *Multilevel Academic Skill Inventory*. Columbus, OH: Charles E. Merrill.

JASTAK, J., & JASTAK, S. (1978). *WRAT: Wide range achievement test*. Wilmington, DE: Jastak Associates.

JENSEN, A. R. (1980). *Bias in mental testing*. New York: The Free Press.

"IQ tests ruled discriminatory in California," (1979, October 17), *Kansas City Times*.

Kansas State Department of Education (1984). *Sample activities for the severely multiply handicapped*. Topeka, KS.

KAUFMAN, A., & KAUFMAN, N. (1983). *The Kaufman Assessment Battery for Children*. Circle Pines, MN: American Guidance Service.

KAUFMAN, A., & KAUFMAN, N. (1985). *Kaufman Test of Educational Achievement*. Circle Pines, MN: American Guidance Service.

KERLINGER, F. (1973). *Foundations of behavioral research* (2nd ed.). New York: Holt, Rinehart & Winston.

KUDER, F. (1976). *Kuder Preference Record-Vocational*. Chicago: Science Research Associates.

LAMBERT, N., & WINDMILLER, M. (1981). *Diagnostic and technical manual: Revised AAMD Adaptive Behavior Scale—School edition*. Monterey, CA: CTB/McGraw-Hill.

MADDEN, R., GARDNER, E. F., & COLLINS, C. S. (1983). *Stanford Early School Achievement Test* (2nd ed.). Cleveland, OH: The Psychological Corporation.

MERCER, J. R. (1973). *Labeling the mentally retarded*. Berkeley, CA: University of California Press.

MERCER, J. R., & LEWIS, J. F. (1979). *System for multicultural pluralistic assessment* (SOMPA). New York: The Psychological Corporation.

NEWCOMER, P., & HAMMILL, D. (1982). *The Test of Language Development-Primary*. Austin, TX: Pro-Ed.

NEWLAND, T. E. (1969). *Blind Learning Aptitude Test: Experimental Edition*. Urbana, IL: T. Ernest Newland.

NIHIRA, K., FOSTER, R., SHELLHAAS, M., & LELAND, H. (1969). *Adaptive Behavior Scale*. Washington, DC: American Association of Mental Deficiency.

OAKLAND, T., ed. (1977). *Psychological and educational assessment of minority children*. New York: Bruner/Mazel.

OAKLAND, T., & LAOSA, L. M. (1977). "Professional, legislative, and judicial influences on psychoeducational assessment practices in schools." In T. Oakland (ed.), *Psychological and educational assessment of minority children*. (pp. 21–51). New York: Bruner/Mazel.

PETERSON, D., & QUAY, H. (1979). "Behavior Problem Checklist." Available from D. Peterson, 39 North Fifth Ave., Highland Park, NJ 08904.

PRESCOTT, G. A., BALOW, I. H., HOGAN, T. R., & FARR, R. C. (1978). *Metropolitan Achievement Tests: Survey Battery.* Cleveland, OH: The Psychological Corporation.

RESCHLY, D. J. (1978). *School psychological services: Non-biased assessment.* Ames, IA: Iowa Department of Public Instruction.

RESNICK, L. B., WANG, M. C., & KAPLIN, J. (1973). "Task analysis in curriculum design: A hierarchically sequenced introductory mathematics curriculum." *Journal of Applied Behavior Analysis, 6,* 679–710.

SANFORD, A. (1975). *Learning Accomplishment Profile.* Winston-Salem, NC: Kaplan Press.

SATO, I. S. (1974). "The culturally different gifted child—The dawning of a new day." *Exceptional Children, 40,* 572–577.

SALVIA, J., & YSSELDYKE, J. E. (1985). *Assessment: In special and remedial education* (3rd ed.). Boston: Houghton-Mifflin.

SEMEL, E., & WIIG, E. (1982). *Clinical Evaluation of Language Functions.* Columbus, OH: Charles E. Merrill.

SHUB, A., CARLIN, J., FRIEDMAN, R., KAPLAN, J., & KATIEN, J. (1973). *Diagnosis: An Instructional Aid in Reading.* Chicago: Science Research Associates.

SLOSSON, R. (1981). *Slosson Intelligence Test.* East Aurora, NY: Slosson Educational Publications.

SONNENSCHEIN, J. L. (1983). *Basic Achievement Skills Individual Screener.* Cleveland, OH: The Psychological Corporation.

SPARROW, S., BALLA, D., & CICCHETTI, D. (1984). *Vineland Adaptive Scales.* Circle Pines, MN: American Guidance Service.

SPIVACK, G., & SWIFT, M. (1967). *Devereux Elementary School Behavior Rating Scale.* Devon, PA: The Devereux Foundation.

STILLMAN, R. (1978). *Callier-Azusa Scale.* Dallas, TX: University of Texas at Dallas Center for Communication Disorders.

TERMAN, L., & MERRILL, M. (1973). *Stanford-Binet Intelligence Scale.* Chicago: Riverside.

THORNDIKE, R. L., HAGEN, E., & SATTLER, J. (1985). *The Stanford Binet Intelligence Test* (4th ed.). Chicago: Riverside.

TUCKER, J. A. (1980). "Ethnic proportions in classes for the learning disabled: Issues in non-biased assessment." *The Journal of Special Education, 14,* 93–105.

VICTOR, M. J., JR. (Ed.), (1985). *Buros Mental Measurement Yearbook (Vols. 1 & 2).* Buros Institute of Mental Measurement, University of Nebraska at Lincoln, Lincoln, NE.

WALKER, H. M. (1983). *Walker Problem Behavior Identification Checklist* (WPBIC). Los Angeles, CA: Western Psychological Services.

WECHSLER, D. (1967). *Manual for the Wechsler Preschool and Primary Scale of Intelligence.* Cleveland, OH: The Psychological Corporation.

WELSCH, D. L., & MILLER, L. J. (1972). *Comprehensive special services tests.* Olathe, KS: Education Modulation Center.

ZIGMOND, N., & MILLER. S. E. (1986). "Assessment for instructional planning." *Exceptional Children, 52,* 501–509.

chapter 7

Continuous Behavioral Assessment

Continuous assessment is most often used to monitor the progress of teaching or intervention efforts. In this chapter, we resume our discussion of assessment of behavior with particular focus on continuous assessment.

PRECURSORS OF CONTINUOUS BEHAVIORAL ASSESSMENT

Behavior Analysis (Behavioral Assessment)

As discussed in Chapter 2, an early contribution of behavior analysis was the discovery that rate of response, defined as the response frequency per unit of time, was an important means of studying learning (Skinner, 1956). Skinner used a mechanical plotting device which recorded the occurrence of a response on a rotating cylinder covered with graph paper. Each time the subject made a response, the plotting pen moved up one unit, which in effect tallied one new response. This produced a cumulative response curve whose steepness reflected the rate of occurrence.

Cumulative response curves, such as those in Figure 7.1, illustrate the rate of responding in seconds over time. The left panel in Figure 7.1 indicates a much slower overall response rate than the panel on the right. For example, the first response did not occur until Session 6 on the left compared to Session 2 on the right. Overall, three responses were made within a 10-second time period on the left compared to seven in the panel on the right. The plateaus in the graphs mark seconds during which no response occurred, and consequently, no tally was made. This type of graph is called cumulative because each new response is recorded above or, in effect, added to the previous response. Skinner used these curves to study the effects of reinforcement schedules on the responding of laboratory animals.

Lindsley, a student of Skinner's, was one

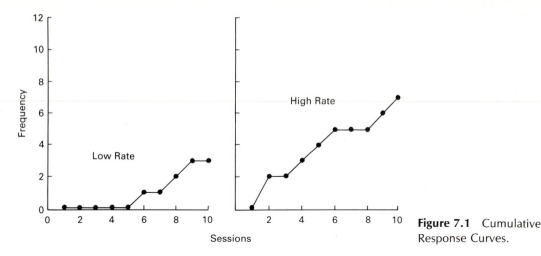

Figure 7.1 Cumulative Response Curves.

of the first to apply continuous assessment procedures to oral reading (Lindsley, 1964). Believing that children were not mentally retarded, but that their behavior in average environments were retarded, Lindsley was a strong advocate of designing "prosthetic" environments that would maximize the behavioral efficiency of exceptional children. Furthermore, he recommended direct measurement of behavior based on time samples under specific environmental conditions.

In his subsequent work, Lindsley has refined the use of continuous rate assessments. Lindsley's "Precision Teaching," refined continuous rate assessment so that any behavior may be measured. This method has been widely described in the literature (for example, White, 1986), and a professional journal, the *Precision Teaching Journal*, has been exclusively devoted to the topic.

Application of continuous rate assessment in special education was described in a now classic article by Lovitt, Kunzelman, Nolen, and Hulten (1968) which appeared in the first volume of the *Journal of Learning Disabilities*. The authors noted that most of the behavioral studies conducted at the time focused on decreasing inappropriate behaviors whereas few focused on accelerating academic behaviors. They described procedures for defining and recording the movement cycles required to write individual letters or

numbers. Data on the rate of academic responding for individual students were recorded and used to evaluate the effects of curricular and instructional decision management.

Similar "classic" applications of continuous assessment to classroom behavior management were those by Hall, Lund, and Jackson (1968) and Walker and Buckley (1968). Rather than rate measures, however, these researchers used interval occurrence observation methods. Both studies assessed classroom attention based on the percentage of 10-second observational intervals during which attention occurred for the entire interval. Figure 7.2 contains the Hall et al. (1968) recording procedure; Figure 7.3 the Walker and Buckley (1968) system.

The Hall data sheet was designed to record four behaviors, two for the student and two for the teacher. For the student, nonstudy versus study behavior were recorded; for the teacher, verbalizations and proximity relative to the student (within 3 feet) were recorded. In Figure 7.2 eight of the eighteen intervals were coded for study behavior 44 percent. The teacher data reveal that the teacher verbalized to the student during six intervals, five of them when the student was engaged in nonstudy behavior, and only once when the student was studying. Finally, during four intervals the teacher was near the student.

Interval Recording Procedure of Hall et al., (1968)

SECONDS ONE MINUTE

10 20 30 40 50 60

N	N	N	N	N	N	N	S	S	S	N	N	S	S	S	S	S	N
		T	T	T						T						T	T
			/	/				/		/							

Row 1 N = Nonstudy Behavior, S = Study Behavior.
Row 2 T = Teacher Verbalization directed toward pupil.
Row 3 / = Teacher Proximity (teacher within three feet).

Figure 7.2 Interval Record Procedures of Hall et al., (1968).

Source: From "Effects of teacher attention on study behavior" by R. V. Hall, D. Lund, & D. Jackson, 1968, *Journal of Applied Behavior Analysis, 1,* p. 2. Copyright 1968 by the Society for the Experimental Analysis of Behavior, Inc.

This type of data was used to examine the effects of systematic teacher attention on study behavior.

The Walker and Buckley (1968) procedure also employed an interval recording system. In this case, a "Z" indicated the first occurrence of student attention. A "Z" followed by a solidus (/) in subsequent intervals (see Figure 7.3) meant that attention was continuing. When the teacher reinforced the student for attending, a dash (–) was recorded. Thus, the data in Figure 7.3 indicated that in over eight intervals, one interval of attention was reinforced.

Attention was scored for 56 percent of the intervals. Furthermore, since the student had to be attending during the entire 10-second interval in order for a "Z" or / to be recorded (whole interval recording), the total time attending was 1 minute 40 seconds. That is, 10 intervals times 10 seconds per interval divided by 60 seconds equal 1 minute 40 seconds.

These two systems illustrate some of the earliest classroom-based approaches to continuous assessment. The widespread interest in these systems and the research they generated led to the establishment of the journal *Behavioral Assessment* in 1979. In its first issue, behavior assessment was described as follows:

"The goals of behavioral assessment are to identify meaningful response units and their controlling variables (both current environmental and organismic) for the purposes of understanding and altering behavior." (Nelson & Hayes, 1979, p. 1)

As reflected in this statement, continuous assessment methods are designed to assist in altering or changing of behavior.

1	2	3	4	5	6	7	8	9	10	11	12	13	14	15	16	17	18
Z	/	/	/	/-							Z	/	/	/		Z	

Each time interval represents 10 seconds.
Z = beginning of a new attending period.
/ = continuation of the same event through successive intervals.
\- = subject reinforcement.

Figure 7.3 Sample Observation Form

Source: From "The use of positive reinforcement in conditioning attending behavior" by H. M. Walker & N. K. Buckley, 1968, *Journal of Applied Behavior Analysis, 1,* p. 248. Copyright 1968 by the Society for the Experimental Analysis of Behavior, Inc.

The most recent stage of the continuous assessment movement is referred to as *ecobehavioral* assessment (Rogers-Warren, 1984). As Bijou and Baer (1978) noted:

The interaction between the child and the environment is continuous, reciprocal, and interdependent. We cannot analyze a child without reference to an environment, nor is it possible to analyze an environment without reference to a child. The two form an inseparable unit consisting of an interrelated set of variables, or an interactional field. (p. 29)

The ecobehavioral approach represents an attempt to assess both the student's response and those temporarily related ecological events, such as the task, materials, or the teacher's behavior, which may be considered elements of the educational program. The data sheet originally developed by Hall et al. (1968) to record student behavior, teacher behavior, and teacher proximity was forward looking because it anticipated the need to assess dimensions of classroom treatment in addition to individual student's behavior.

An ecobehavioral approach requires that student performance be observed and assessed concurrently with specific instructional variables within the classroom environment. As a result, student behaviors can be quantified within very specific contexts of instruction. One can examine how instruction occurs, how it changes over time, and how the observed student response is congruent with the goals of instruction (Carta, Greenwood, & Robinson 1985; Greenwood et al., 1986). In addition to classroom settings, ecobehavioral assessment is also applied to work settings and vocational behaviors (Chadsey-Rusch, 1985; Chadsey-Rusch & Rusch, in press).

Special Education Uses of Curriculum-Based and Community-Based Assessment

Increasingly, continuous behavioral assessment has become an integral component of special education theory and practice (Becker, 1971, Hunt, Goetz, Spears, Rusch, York, & Lilly, 1981; Alwell, & Sailor, 1986). Perhaps most evident has been the application of continuous assessment methods both in the classroom, *curriculum-based assessment,* and in the community, *community-based assessment.* These rapidly developing applications are consistent with the forms introduced in the 1960s. Curriculum-based assessment is defined broadly as "a procedure for determining the instructional needs of a student based upon the student's ongoing performance within existing course content" (Glickling, 1984, p. 4). Tucker (1984), in turn, defined curriculum-based assessment as a "procedure that directly assesses student performance within the course content for the purpose of determining that student's instructional needs" (Tucker, 1984, p. 200).

Community-based assessment is the application of continuous behavioral assessment to important behaviors in the home, on the job, and in areas of life outside of the school and classroom. It can be defined as assessment "focusing on skills most relevant in student's daily lives and which allow them to function as independently as possible in integrated settings" (Brown et al., 1979, cited in Snell & Browder, 1986, p. 2). For example, Rusch and Mithaug (1980) described assessment procedures relevant to competitive employment.

Serving different purposes, curriculum- and community-based assessment differ from criterion-referred assessment in terms of the settings in which the assessment occurs. Curriculum-based assessment employs instruments that allow observation of student performance in the ongoing natural curriculum or lesson, such as daily direct measures of oral reading rate based on text passages or classroom interaction. Thus, daily direct measures of correct performance, such as a task analysis of bathing or fixing meals, are frequent. In contrast, criterion-referenced assessments favor tests and testing situations as the primary context for measurement.

ADVANTAGES OF CONTINUOUS ASSESSMENT

Continuous assessments are objective methods of observing an individual's performance in the natural setting, (for example, observations of work productivity conducted at the employment site). Data yielded in this manner can be used to plan the teaching process on a daily basis so that instructional decisions can be made, a lesson implemented, effects observed, and future educational planning carried out. Continuous assessment methods are cost efficient since they are easy and relatively inexpensive to develop. In addition, they are simple to use. Overall, continuous assessment increases our sensitivity to a student's daily performance, our communications to others about this performance, and our overall knowledge about teaching and learning.

The results of continuous assessment are usually displayed graphically in a relatively easy to interpret format. Furthermore, because these data allow comparisons at different times under different instructional procedures, they emphasize what has worked and what must be done to further improve an individual's performance. In addition, the continuous nature of the data provides an important insight into the stability of an individual's performance over time. Such sensitivity to performance trends is not offered by other types of assessment.

Finally, continuous assessment data provide information on classroom activities which can be used for various purposes. By compiling results from different curriculum-based measures we can develop a comprehensive description of classroom processes and their range. Such data, in turn, can be used as local norms to provide performance criteria or to aid in the selection of specific target behaviors (Germann & Tindal, 1984). To utilize these data, attention must be paid to the validity of the assessment process. The following section briefly overviews some of the fundamental principles of validity relative to continuous assessment.

Several types of validity standards apply to continuous assessment, including ecological, concurrent, and treatment standards.

Ecological validity is demonstrated when continuous assessments are made within natural everyday settings and situations, including the use of the curriculum, the regular classroom schedule (for example, during reading or mathematics instruction), or in training sessions within natural settings (such as on the metrobus or on the job). In contrast, continuous assessment is compromised if settings and situations are simulated and do not reflect performance in natural everyday settings and situations where the student must be able to operate effectively.

Concurrent validity reflects the extent to which continuous assessments are correlates of other measures, such as norm-referenced or criterion-referenced tests. Deno (1982), for example, examined the correlation between curriculum-based measures (that is, the number of correct words read aloud from a basal text) and subtests on the *Woodcock Reading Mastery Test*. Deno found that the word identification subtest correlated at 93 percent (Fuchs & Deno, 1981). Fuchs and Deno (1981) reported that reading aloud from a text discriminated among students in special education programs, students in Title I programs, and regular class students.

The data presented in Figure 7.4 demonstrate the randomly selected groups of students from special education, Title I, and regular education programs produced consistent performance differences at grades one through six in terms of words read correctly during a 1-minute sample. As illustrated, the special education populations consistently performed below Title I students, whose performance, in turn, was below that of regular education students. Recently, Shinn and Marston (1985) have replicated these findings.

Treatment validity is an attribute of continuous assessment when specific measures prove sensitive to change resulting from teaching or another intervention (Nelson & Hayes, 1979). Treatment validity also ad-

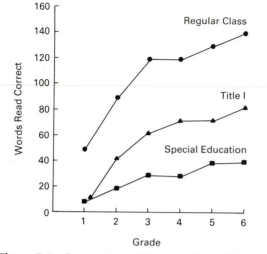

Figure 7.4 Comparison of Regular Class, Title I, and Special Education Students on Curriculum-based Assessment in Reading.

Source: S. L. Deno, 1984, Curriculum—based measurement: The emerging alternative. Taken from *Exceptional Children*, p. 222.

dresses the issue of providing the best means of assessing a behavior to ensure positive treatment outcomes. For example, directly observing a student's attention to instruction has greater treatment validity than using a teacher rating scale after instruction because the direct observation is more sensitive to the actual momentary behavior changes. In contrast, a rating scale is influenced by the teacher's recall of the session.

Another method of obtaining validity is to require that two observers agree upon the occurrence of a target behavior. This type of validation is unique to direct observation and is a major concern in behavior analysis (refer to Chapter 4).

Interobserver Agreement

Interobserver agreement is a reliability factor in continuous assessment. As discussed in Chapter 5, *interobserver agreement* refers to agreement between two observers on the occurrence of behaviors. Such agreement in-

sures that observers apply the same definitions to the behaviors that they record for each student from day to day. As a general rule, an agreement percentage of 80 percent or greater is considered adequate.

Table 7.1 presents several common methods for computing interobserver agreement on behavior.

The first two formulas examine the agreement or disagreement on recording trials within single agreement checks. The last two formulas are based upon total observation scores for all observation sessions. The *percentage agreement for interval data* produces a score ranging from zero to 100 percent and is based upon the number of intervals during the observation period where observers agreed on the occurrence of the behavior. Its clarity and ease of computation have made it the most widely reported observer agreement procedure.

A similar approach, *percentage of non-occurrence for interval data*, is based upon analysis of non-occurrence intervals, that is, where both observers agreed that a given behavior did not occur. The advantages of this approach primarily relate to referencing events which occur infrequently, such as changing classrooms in a junior high or middle school—behaviors that might occur only once per hour.

The *percentage agreement for session* data produces an index ranging from zero to 100 percent, which indicates the agreement between two observers' total session scores. This form of agreement reflects the ratio of behavior recorded by one observer in relation to that recorded by another. Since it is not based upon interval comparisons, percentage agreement for sessions does not provide an interval-by-interval analysis of agreement. Hypothetically, observers could obtain the same total score without observing the same behavior at the same point in time. For example, observer A could record events in the first half of the session and observer B could record events in the second half of the session, yet both could obtain similar totals.

The variable Pearson *r* is a correlation coef-

TABLE 7.1   Summary of Interobserver Agreement Procedures

Agreement Procedure	Formula	References
Interval Agreement		
1. Percent agreement on occurrence =	[100 × (Number Agreements ÷ Number Total Intervals)]	1. Hanson & Hanline (1985) Breen et al., (1985)
2. Percent agreement = Nonoccurrence	[100 (N_1 & 2 ÷ T)]	2. Hopkins & Hermann (1977)

Where N_1 = Number of intervals in which observer 1 records the response as a nonoccurrence, N_2 = Number of intervals in which observer 2 records the response as a nonoccurrence
T = total number of intervals in which records are compared.

Session Agreement

3. Percent agreement on occurrence =	[100 × (smaller ÷ larger)]	4. Rolider & Van Houton (1984)
4. Pearson r = $NEO102 - E01E02 ÷ [\{NE01^2 - (E01)^2\}$ $\{NE0^2 - (E02)^2\}]^{1/2}$		5. Reynolds & Risley (1968)

Where N = the number of paired scores
E = summation of
01 = scores by observer 1
02 = scores by observer 1

---

ficient, which ranges from -1.00 to $+1.00$. High positive values of Pearson r (from 0.70 to 1.00) indicate high levels of agreement. Zero or negative values indicate no agreement or inverse agreement, that is, when one observer records more behavior than the other. The Pearson r, which is usually based upon the scores from at least 10 observer checks, is complex to calculate without computation equipment.

Content

The content of continuous assessment is derived directly from the natural setting, thereby reflecting the curriculum and the social demands of the classroom peer group or the activities and routines that normally transpire at home, in the work place, in a recreational setting, and elsewhere. The behaviors to be assessed are usually related to the curriculum or the repertoires of persons without handicaps who successfully function in the target settings.

Administration

Like all other forms of assessment discussed, continuous assessment requires standard administration to insure that measures obtained on one day are equivalent to those obtained on another day. This principle guarantees that a student's scores on one day can appropriately be compared to those on the next. Standard administration of continuous assessment measures includes such factors as (a) use of the same instructions, (b) continuity in the setting (the same tasks and materials), (c) use of a standard data collection sheet, and (d) assessment for a standard period of time or standard number of trials.

Individual and Peer Referencing (Social Comparison)

Continuous assessment employs both individual and peer referencing procedures to support interpretation of results. *Individual referencing* consists of demonstrating change in a single student's performance over time, such as comparing a student's performance before and after the implementation of a teaching procedure.

In the case illustrated in Figure 7.5, we see that during the baseline Kimkisha wrote as many as eight and as few as five words during a 20-minute session each day. After application of an individualized teaching procedure, however, Kimkisha's writing increased to as many as 20 and as few as 13 words per session. Thus, compared to her early performance, she has made a substantial improvement as a result of the new teaching method. This type of individual referencing or comparison, whereby performance is "compared" at different points in time under different conditions, has been a hallmark of continuous assessment (for more see Rusch, Chadsey-Rusch, White, & Giffon, 1985; Wolf, 1978).

Peer referencing is a means of interpreting a student's performance relative to that of others in the same curriculum or setting (Deno, 1984; Walker & Hops, 1976). If we randomly select Daryl (see Figure 7.6) to serve as a representative peer in Kimkisha's classroom and display their data together in the same graph, several new developments emerge. For example, during the baseline period, Kimkisha not only performed low on the word writing assessment, she was also consistently below Daryl's level of performance. However, during the teaching procedure her performance was improved not only in comparison to her own baseline level, but her performance is now indistinguishable from Daryl's.

Threats to Validity

Contrived Situations or Content. The validity of continuous assessment is based on the assumption that the situations and tasks assessed reflect those in which the student is naturally expected to perform. Therefore, assessment situations that are simulated or artificial, as in standardized testing, increase the likelihood that the measurements do not reflect how the student actually performs in the classroom or community under ordinary circumstances.

Variations of Administration Standards. Variations in administration procedures negate the fundamental assumption that assessment occasions are comparable. For example, if a student is assessed alone by the teacher after usually having been assessed along with other members of the reading group, a substantial difference may be obtained due to the format change.

Figure 7.5   Graphic Display of the Number of Words Written by Kimkisha Before and During Teaching.

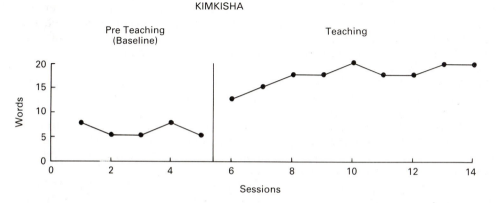

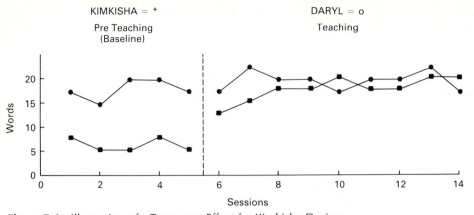

Figure 7.6   Illustration of a Treatment Effect for Kimkisha During Teaching Relative to Pre-teaching and Compared to Peer Normative Data (Daryl).

Low Interobserver Agreement. Low levels of interobserver agreement threaten the validity of results by introducing inaccuracy. According to Hartmann and Woods (1982), 70 to 80 percent agreement or above for complex recording systems reflect acceptable levels of interobserver agreement. Low agreement may result from inconsistent application of behavioral definitions in the recording of behavior. This, in turn, may be due to (a) an inexact behavioral definition, as explained in Chapter 5, or (b) inadequate observer training. If reliability is low, a student's day-to-day scores may differ widely—not as a result of actual student behavior, but due to lack of recording consistency.

Observer Drift. This potential threat to validity refers to a gradual change in the application of a behavioral definition. Drift is a result of inadequate monitoring of observers over time. Reliability checks between observers will remain consistently high even though particular observer pairs change their use of a definition. However, drift may be revealed if these particular observers show low reliabilities when checked against other observers or against a standard, such as a videotaped sample of behavior for which the frequencies of behaviors are known. Drift can be avoided by frequently changing observer pairs or by checking against a videotaped standard.

Complexity. If an observation system is too complex, reliability may be affected (Reid, Skindrud, & Tupline, 1977). Thus, the greater the number of behaviors and the faster the rate of behaviors, the greater the impact on the number of judgments to be made during an observation session. At a certain level reliability will suffer. By keeping the number of behavioral definitions and the rate of behavioral responses at a comfortable level, the negative effects of complexity can be avoided.

Bias. This type of inconsistency in measurement is due to information or events other than those intentionally included in the behavioral definitions. For example, if observers are told that some students are more deviant, retarded, or less academically skilled than others, they may code fewer behaviors than they would otherwise. This is an example of negative bias. Negative bias may operate in very subtle and often unavoidable ways. For example, if observers happen to be parent volunteers or community persons paid as classroom aides, they may hold expectations about some students' abilities that have been formed outside the classroom. To counter observer bias, observers must be informally screened to determine which students they know and what expectations they may hold for specific students.

Bias in a positive direction may be produced when observers know or expect a student is receiving an experimental treatment that they think is designed to improve performance. Bias in a positive direction can also occur when they believe that the students are bright, gifted, or have high IQs. A classic example of the former is the case of college students working in the classroom as observers and knowing that they are evaluating an experimental procedure which they expect to aid the students' learning. Other instances of bias include assigning a volunteer parent to observe his or her own child's performance. This arrangement is not recommended unless parents are specifically being trained to objectively assess their own child's behavior in school and at home. For purposes of data collection, observers should always be unaware of the goals and general procedures associated with their observation assignments.

Reactivity. Sometimes behavior changes because the individual is aware that they are being observed. For example, students may be better behaved than usual when parents are visiting the classroom or when the principal stops by for a visit. Or employees may work more when they are being observed by job coaches (Rusch, Menchetti, Morgan, & Riva, 1984). Reactivity when observers are present confound the validity of continuous assessment by introducing inaccuracy and creating artificial situations.

Reactivity can be controlled in several ways. First, observation of performance should be a routine and not a novel experience in the target setting. Reactivity will be reduced if observation is conducted on a daily basis by teachers, aides, parents, and cross-age or same-age peers. Second, in classrooms where observation is not routine, observation data should not be used until observation has become a classroom routine and students begin to feel comfortable with the arrangement. Third, effort must be made to ensure that the behavior of observers and other assessors is nonreactive. For example, observers should not be so close to students that they interfere with ongoing behaviors. Observers should not stare at students or use looking strategies that appear unnatural or funny. Fourth, if observation is assisted by mechanical devices (for example, counters, watches, tape recorders, or computers), they should be introduced, explained, and demonstrated to students beforehand so that they lose some of their novelty and potential for arousing curiosity.

CONTINUOUS BEHAVIORAL ASSESSMENT PROCEDURES

We will now discuss specific types of continuous behavioral assessment and illustrate them through application of procedures in both classroom and community settings with students presenting mild and severe handicaps. The types of measurement to be discussed include the following: event recording, magnitude recording, duration recording, and interval recording.

EVENT RECORDING

In *event recording* single, discrete events are counted each time they are observed. As a result, event recording yields frequency counts and is the basis for frequency, rate, and accuracy data as described in Chapter 5. Event recording methods are used in direct observation, mechanical observation and permanent product assessments.

Behaviors for Which Event Recording Is Appropriate

Behaviors that can be described as discrete and repetitive lend themselves best to event recording, that is, events with a clear beginning and ending and that reoccur frequently. Examples of the behaviors include hand raising, arithmetic problem solving, table and silverware setting, and episodes of social interacting. In direct observation or applied to an analysis of permanent products, event recording requires little special equipment or materials. Thus, it is highly cost efficient for many educational applications and, consequently, is widely used.

How Educators Use Event Recording

Because of its simplicity, event recording can be used with many behaviors and for both acceleration or deceleration problems. Event recording can be used with a wide array of academic behaviors, with frequencies of completion, and with percentages and rates of accuracy. Event recording may also be applied to behavior management to monitor an extensive range of socially appropriate and inappropriate behaviors. For example, Haavik and Altman (1977) recorded the number of steps made by students in an ambulation training program.

Examples of Event Recording

Classroom Settings. Event recording is often used in the classroom to record tokens or points earned by students with mild handicaps for specific behaviors (cf. Kazdin, 1977). Table 7.2 illustrates a point sheet used by peer tutors to record the points their tutee has earned for correctly read sentences and for completion of an error-correction procedure (Greenwood, Dinwiddie, Terry, Wade, Stanley, Thibadeau, & Delquadri, 1984).

The event data from this sheet can be used in several ways. It shows the number of points earned by the student (21), the number

of sentences read (12), the number read correctly—those slashed as two points (9)—and the number read incorrectly—those earning one point (3). These data can be graphed to reflect progress in reading rate, accuracy, and point earning.

Event recording may be used in combination with public posting of results as a means of motivating improved performance (see Table 7.3). A chart is used to both record and post points earned by students during separate daily tutoring sessions in spelling and arithmetic (Carta, Greenwood, Dinwiddie, Kohler, Delquadri, 1985).

A similar procedure can be used to record and post students' weekly test scores expressed as the percent correct. Using the procedure illustrated in Table 7.4, Monday pretest scores and Fridays posttest scores can be posted so that teachers and students can observe gains and improvements (Carta et al., 1985). This form of public assessment enables the teacher to provide systematic consequences for students' improvements and to plan lesson content based on pretest scores.

In addition to its use with students with mild handicaps, event recording procedures have also been extensively used to assess the instructional performance of persons with severe handicaps. For example, Partington, Sundberg, Iwata, and Mountjoy (1979) used an event recording procedure to assess the effects of time-telling instruction in an educational cooperative for children with multiple handicaps. In this study, each session was defined as the completion of a specified set of time-telling trials. Students' responses were

TABLE 7.2   Peer Tutoring Point Sheet

NAME: Ryan	SUBJECT: Reading	DATE: 11/12/88

–1––––2–	–3––––4–	–5–	–6––––7–	–8–	–9–––10–	–11–				
12–––13–	–14–––15–	–16–––17–	–18–––19–	–20–––21–	22					
23	24	25	26	27	28	29	30	31	32	33
34	35	36	37	38	39	40	41	42	43	44
45	46	47	48	49	50	51	52	53	54	55
56	57	58	59	60	61	62	63	64	65	66

Source: Adapted from Elliott, Hughes, & Delquadri, 1984, p. 25. Reprinted by permission.

TABLE 7.3 Team Point Chart

Teacher: Ms. Walker   Week of: Feb. 10–14, 1987

Name	On Team	Monday S	Monday M	Tuesday S	Tuesday M	Wednesday S	Wednesday M	Thursday S	Thursday M	Friday S	Friday M
Zmark, B.	R	43	22	51	31	68	42	63	85	Test	
Clevon, W.	B	53	43	62	48	71	50	70	80	Test	
Rob Ray, T.	R	22	61	32	63	46	67	59	63	Test	
William H.	B	14	42	19	53	30	63	42	65	Test	
Clarence, T.	R	19	51	30	52	39	53	39	60	Test	
Beverly, H.	B	42	41	48	49	49	48	52	84	Test	
Su Yong, C.	R	45	46	61	59	68	81	63	72	Test	
Kim Su Y.	B	73	70	78	70	80	75	49	58	Test	

R = Red Team; B = Blue Team

Source: From Carta, J. J., Greenwood, C. R., Dinwiddie, G., Kohler, F., & Belquadri, J. (1985). *The Juniper Gardens classwide peer tutoring programs for spelling, reading, and math: Teacher's manual.* Kansas City, KS: The Juniper Gardens Children's Project, Bureau of Child Research, University of Kansas, p. 14. Reprinted by permission.

TABLE 7.4 Weekly Test Score Chart

Dates: Week 1 = Feb. 10–14, 1987   Week 2 = Feb. 17–21, 1987

Students	Spelling Week 1 Pre	Spelling Week 1 Post	Spelling Week 2 Pre	Spelling Week 2 Post	Math Week 1 Pre	Math Week 1 Post	Math Week 2 Pre	Math Week 2 Post
Zmark, B.	23%	78%	34%	85%	56%	95%	58%	88%
Clevon, W.	33%	100%	45%	100%	63%	100%	65%	95%
Rob Ray, T.	55%	78%	58%	85%	35%	61%	38%	72%
William H.	85%	100%	83%	100%	100%	100%	90%	100%
Clarence, T.	36%	96%	42%	92%	55%	100%	62%	100%
Beverly, H.	44%	82%	50%	100%	65%	85%	72%	100%
Su Yong, C.	33%	65%	38%	74%	14%	72%	15%	82%
Kim Su Y.	23%	75%	28%	79%	14%	56%	23%	69%

Source: From Carta, J. J., Greenwood, C. R., Dinwiddie, G., Kohler, F., & Delquadri, J. (1985). *The Juniper Gardens classwide peer tutoring programs for spelling, reading, and math: Teacher's manual.* Kansas City, KS: The Juniper Gardens Children's Project, Bureau of Child Research, University of Kansas, p. 18. Reprinted by permission.

TABLE 7.5 Example Individualized Curriculum Sequence Data Sheet

Student's Name: ___Bernice___

Cues/Prompts	Student Actions	Correction Procedures	%
"Say Baby"	Any Verbal Approximation	Repeat Cue, Phys Prompt	100
"Look at the Baby"	Looks at the Doll	Repeat Cue, Phys Prompt	90
"Take the Baby"	Grasps Baby	Repeat Cue, Phys Prompt	80
"Give Me the Baby"	Gives Baby to Tutor	Repeat Cue, Phys Prompt	
"Look at the Baby"	Looks at Doll	Repeat Cue, Phys Prompt	60
"Say Baby"	Any Verbal Approximation	Repeat Cue, Phys Prompt	50
"Take the Baby"	Grasps Baby	Repeat Cue, Phys Prompt	
"Say Baby"	Any Verbal Approximation	Repeat Cue, Phys Prompt	
"Look at the Baby"	Looks at Doll	Repeat Cue, Phys Prompt	20
"Look at Me"	Looks at Tutor	Repeat Cue, Phys Prompt	10

Date and Teacher Initial columns: 2/3, 2/4, 2/5, 2/6, 2/9, 2/10, 2/11, 2/12, 2/15, 2/16

(Data cells contain hand-recorded marks of x, –, and 0, with a plotted line of circled scores across the dates.)

x = Correct
– = Incorrect
0 = Total correct

Source: Adapted from Holvoet et al, 1980, p. 348. Reprinted by permission.

144

assessed as either correct or incorrect when providing a response to sets of prompts from the trainer, such as "What time is it?"

Durand (1982) assessed the frequencies of two self-injurious behaviors, "hits" and "flicks," in a study of a 16-year-old male with encephalopathy. "Hits" and "flicks" were defined as any touch by the hand to the head and face, excluding the nose. They were usually administered by the boy's fist ("hits") or the back of his hand ("flicks"). Measurements were taken during one-on-one trials. Self-injury was reliably decreased when tasks were easy and hand vibration was made contingent on "hits" and "flicks."

In an event recording procedure described by Holvoet, Guess, Mulligan, and Brown in 1980 (see Table 7.5), verbal prompts to be presented by a trainer were listed in sequence on the left, while the student's response was coded in the recording field to the right. If an item was correct it was marked with an "X," if incorrect with an—. At the end of the session the number of "X"'s was totaled and the correct number circled. The circles were subsequently connected with the circles obtained the following day to generate a graphic display of student progress. Over 11 sessions (see Table 7.5), the number of correct performances increased from a total of two on the first session to a total of ten during each of the last four sessions. The advantage of this procedure is that it yields a complete data collection sheet for each task sequence combined with the graphic display of the student's performance.

Community Settings. Christopherson, Arnold, Hill, and Quilitch (1972) trained the parents of three children to record the frequencies of whining, bickering, and teasing at home. The children included a 9-year-old boy, an 8-year-old girl with mild cerebral palsy who attended a class for students with mild mental retardation, and a normal 5-year-old boy. Behaviors which earned and lost points are summarized in Table 7.6. Behaviors were recorded on cards that the children carried around with them at home. The cards were divided in half with points earned for specific

TABLE 7.6 Partial List of Behaviors and the Number of Points They Gained or Lost and a Partial List of the Activities for Which Licenses were Available and the Price in Points

Licenses Available		Price in Points
Basic Privileges		60
Drive-in Movie		200
Picnic		50
Behaviors That Earned and Lost Points		
George	1) Make bed	10
	2) Hang up clothes	10
Keith	1) Empty trash	20
Dollie	1) Make bed	20
	2) Feed cat	20
	3) Bathe	20
Behaviors That Earned Points		
1) Sweep rug		15
2) Clean bathroom		20
3) Answer telephone		15
Behaviors That Lost Points		
1) Bickering	Each Occurrence	10
2) Teasing		10
3) Whining		10

Source: Adapted from Christophersen et al., 1972, p. 487. Copyright 1972 by the Society for the Experimental Analysis of Behavior, Inc.

behaviors marked on the left along with a designation of who awarded them. The right side contained similar information for points lost. At the end of the day, the points were totaled and the basic privileges for the next day purchased with the points.

The procedure illustrated in Table 7.7 was used in home programming for persons with severe handicaps and was designed to assess a hand-washing task analysis. Each step is scored according to the level of prompting necessary for the response to occur.

Ranging from the most to least intervening, these levels of prompting are in order: physical assistance, demonstration, verbal cue, and independent performance. As illustrated in Table 7.7 in the first session, seven steps required physical assistance, three required demonstration, one required cuing, and one was completed independently. In the eleventh session, however, the student completed the entire sequence independently.

TABLE 7.7   Assessment Protocol

WASHING HANDS

Student   William

Materials   Sink, water, soap, towel

Task Statement   Wash sequence

Teacher   Mrs. Hartmann

Setting   Kitchen

Reinforcement   Walkman Radio Time

Session	1	2	3	4	5	6	7	8	9	10	11
Date	2/14	2/15	2/16	2/17	2/20	2/21	2/22	2/23	2/25	2/26	2/27
1. Locate the sink	0										3
2. Turn on the water	0										3
3. Wet Hands	3										3
4. Pick up soap	2										3
5. Rub soap on hands	1										3
6. Put soap down	0										3
7. Rub hands together	1										3
8. Rinse hands	0										3
9. Turn off water	0										3
10. Pick up towel	0										3
11. Dry hands	1										3
12. Throw towel away	0										3

Summary

	1	2	3	4	5	6	7	8	9	10	11
Number of steps #3	1										0
Number of steps #2	1										0
Number of steps #1	3										0
Number of Steps #0	7										2
Total Training Time											

3 = Independent
2 = Verbal cue or gestural cue
1 = Demonstration
0 = Physical assistance

Source: Adapted from Kansas State Department of Education, 1980, p. 348.

Riordan, Iwata, Wohl, and Finney (1980) assessed the eating behavior of children with moderate levels of retardation who were hospitalized for food refusal and selectivity. The subjects were observed during meals and the frequency of behaviors recorded within 1-minute coding sequences. The number of bites and sips were recorded. In a vocational setting, Chadsey-Rusch, Karlan, Riva, and Rusch (1984) assessed specific social behaviors in adults with moderate mental retardation. These researchers audiotaped samples of interaction while the subjects were on the job and later scored these behaviors in terms of their frequencies during baseline and under intervention. The frequency of topic questions, topic initiations, and topic continuations was tallied.

MAGNITUDE RECORDING

Magnitude recording is defined as recording based upon measures of force, distance, pressure, and amplitude. Generally, magnitude recording requires the use of such devices as a scale, a yard stick, a decibel meter, or a pressure-sensitive meter which yields the appropriate measurements.

Behaviors for Which Magnitude Recording is Appropriate

Since magnitude measures are best used to reflect the intensity of behaviors, they are typically used to assess physical effort and motor movement, such as lifting, running, walking, or standing. Similarly, measures of weight gain or loss are often used as an index of daily eating behaviors and exercise.

How Educators Can Use Magnitude Recording

Problems related to sports, physical development, and rehabilitation are often studied using magnitude measures. Compared to event recording, which requires little instrumentation, the sometimes sophisticated measurement instruments required for magnitude recording put some constraints on widespread use of this recording technique.

Examples of Magnitude Recording

Classroom Settings. Schmidt and Ulrich in 1969 (see Chapter 5) used a decibel meter to monitor the noise level within a classroom. The meter was preset to emit a signal when the level of classroom noise exceeded the criterion. The authors shaped lower noise levels by systematically decreasing the criterion level and reinforcing the group for maintaining the lower level.

Magnitude recording is also frequently used to assess athletic skills in school settings. For example, Wessel (1976) reported a study in which throwing a ball a pre-set distance was measured. The distance was systematically increased over trials.

Similar magnitude assessments are suggested in materials developed by the Special Olympics Sports Skills Instructional Program. For example, in the bowling program the pendulum swinging motion used in throwing the ball is assessed.

Community Settings. Harris and Bloom (1984) used magnitude measures in a weight-loss program for adolescents and adults with mental retardation. They measured the girth in inches of the participants' hips, waist, arms, and thighs, and they measured their weight in pounds. They timed their walking, jogging, and running on a half-mile course. As part of the Riordan et al. (1980) study of food refusal and selectivity, the authors assessed the number of grams of food that subjects consumed during meals. They were able to dramatically increase both the frequency of eating (bites and sips) and the amount of food consumed using contingent positive reinforcement.

DURATION RECORDING

Duration recording is recording based on time. Both duration and latency measures are directly assessed using timing devices. As discussed previously, *duration* refers to the length of time that transpires from the moment a response begins to the moment the same response ends; and *latency* refers to the amount of time that transpires from the point at which the response is prompted to the point the response is actually made. The time a student holds a musical note during an audition is an example of duration; the time a target employee takes to respond to a directive to get to work is an example of latency.

Behaviors for Which Duration Recording Is Appropriate

Behaviors which involve persistence are likely candidates for duration recording. Unlike repetitive, discrete behaviors, which are amenable to event recording, or behaviors of a particular intensity, which lend themselves to magnitude recording, behaviors most appropriate for duration recording can be broadly considered in the class of attention and persistence.

How Educators Can Use Duration Recording

Duration recording is effective for collecting data on attention or task persistence within classroom and community settings. In addition, it is appropriate for recording instances of inappropriate behavior which persist for unacceptable time periods (for example, the duration of tantrums). Since duration recording requires only a timing device, such as the stopwatch or wrist watch with a second hand, it may be used for a number of applications at relatively little cost.

Examples of Duration Recording

Classroom Settings. The duration of individual student's attention or on-task behavior has been directly timed using stopwatches (Hops, Walker, and Hutton, 1973). Using other clock devices (see Greenwood, Hops Delquadri, & Guild, 1974), duration measures can also reflect the on-task or off-task performance of entire groups of students. To record the duration of on-task (or alternatively, tantruming behaviors) for an individual student, it is best to use a stopwatch, and only when the student engages in the behavior should the watch be run.

The data sheet in Figure 7.7 was used by a classroom teacher to record and compute percentage of classroom survival behaviors, a measure of compliance with classroom rules,

Figure 7.7 Teacher's PASS Recording Form
Source: Adapted from Greenwood et al., 1977, p. 130. Reprinted by permission.

Teacher _____ Room _____ School _____

BASELINE

Date: /	Period I	Period II
End Time	9:00	_____
Start Time	8:30	_____
Total Time	:30	_____
Surv. Beha.	:20	_____
Day 1 %	66%	

FULL PROGRAM

Date: /	Period I	Period II
End Time	_____	_____
Start Time	_____	_____
Total Time	_____	_____
Surv. Beha.	_____	_____
Day 4 %		

Date: /	Period I	Period II
End Time	_____	_____
Start Time	_____	_____
Total Time	_____	_____
Surv. Beha.	_____	_____
Day 2 %		

Date: /	Period I	Period II
End Time	_____	_____
Start Time	_____	_____
Total Time	_____	_____
Surv. Beha.	_____	_____
Day 5 %		

based on the duration of this behavior relative to the total length of the observation. The sample sheet outlines the steps for reading the necessary data from a clock.

In this case, the duration of survival behaviors was 20 minutes, the time recorded by the teacher on the clocklight. By dividing the 20-minute survival behavior by the session length (30 minutes), we arrive at the percentage of behavior. Either the duration or the percentage could be used.

Duration can also be measured using whole or partial interval recording procedures. In this case, the number of intervals multiplied by the time per interval yields the total time (whole interval)—or estimate of the total time (partial interval)—that the behavior occurred.

Duration recording procedures have been used with students with severe handicaps in classroom settings. For example, Whitman, Mercurio, and Caponigri (1970) recorded the length of two children's social interactions with peers. These children were mentally retarded and socially withdrawn. Interaction time was reported in minutes per 15-minute observation sessions. The authors also divided total interaction time by the number of interactions to form a score reflecting the average duration of each interaction. Brady, Shores, Gunter, McEvoy, Fox, and White (1984) recorded the duration of peer social interaction of a 15-year-old autistic and severely withdrawn student in a classroom setting. To record the target behaviors, observers spoke the behavior codes into a hand-held tape recorder. The tapes were replayed and scored after the session. A stopwatch was used to record the duration of each interaction and the total time spent interacting. Billingsley and Liberty (1982) applied duration recording to the assessment of holding one's head up. The program, implemented for 10 trials per day, was initiated each time the student was observed with his or her head down. A trial began with the teacher prompting "Head up" or "Look at me". The duration of "head-up" time was recorded using a stopwatch as long as the student's chin was level with the shoul-

der. Based on these data the average duration (the total time in minutes divided by ten trials) was computed.

Community Settings. O'Brien, Azrin, and Bugle (1972) recorded the duration of crawling and walking in a study designed to reduce crawling and increase walking in a child with mental retardation. Utley, Duncan, Strain, and Scanlon (1983) assessed the duration of visual fixation in nonambulatory children with multiple handicaps ranging in age from 1 to 3 years. Assessments were made in each child's bedroom while the child was in the crib.

Billingsley and Liberty (1982) described latency assessment applied to generalized imitation. In this situation, the teacher provided 20 opportunities for the student to imitate her behavior. While the student watched, the teacher prompted by saying, "Do this." The time between the end of the prompt and the beginning of the student's response (latency) was measured by a stopwatch. Average latency per response was computed by dividing the total latency time by 20 opportunities to respond.

INTERVAL RECORDING

Interval time sampling consists of recording either the occurrence or non-occurrence of a behavior during short time intervals. In contrast to event recording where every occurrence of a behavior is counted, only a single occurrence may be recorded in interval time sampling. However, in the latter observation method, an occurrence is defined in several ways, including momentary interval, partial interval, and whole interval.

Momentary interval time sampling requires that a response occur at the beginning of the time interval in order to be recorded as an occurrence. *Partial interval time sampling* requires that a response occur at some time during any part of the interval in order to be scored as an occurrence. Only one response is required. *Whole interval time sampling* requires that a response persist throughout the entire (whole) interval to be scored as an occurrence.

Behaviors for Which Interval Time Sampling Is Appropriate

Interval time sampling recording may be applied to the same situations as event recording (momentary and partial interval sampling) or duration recording (whole interval sampling). Specifically, momentary and partial interval sampling methods are appropriate for assessing discrete, repetitive behaviors, whereas whole interval time sampling lends itself to task-persistent behaviors.

How Educators Can Use Interval Time Sampling Recording

For behaviors that occur at high rates, momentary and partial interval recording methods place fewer demands on the observer to quantify behavior. Once the interval has been designated an interval where behavior is coded, it is not necessary to keep track of subsequent behaviors until the next interval. For this reason, teachers and other observers are often able to increase the number of different behaviors that can be reliably recorded by using momentary and partial interval methods. This is different from whole interval recording which requires that the observer keep track of a response for the entire interval. An advantage shared by all three procedures is that the use of intervals to break up the observational record can facilitate assessment of observer agreement. For example, Leach and Dolan (1985) used momentary time sampling to record reliably the academic performance of all students in a class.

Examples of Time Sampling Recording

Classroom Settings. Hops et al. (1973) described a whole-interval procedure for recording the on-task behavior of students with mild handicaps in classroom settings. The system used is part of the Contingencies for Learning Academic and Social Skills Program (CLASS), whereby a consultant conducts an initial evaluation of the child and the appropriateness of the program for the child. The second sweep hand of the wristwatch was used to time 10-second intervals. Using a data matrix similar to the one in Figure 7.3 the observer marked a plus (+) if the student was on task for the entire interval and a minus (−) if the student was off task for any part of the entire interval.

A more complex procedure (RECESS) was used by Walker, Street, Garrett, Crossen, Hops, and Greenwood (1978) with students engaging in aggressive and negative social behaviors. The system used 5-second intervals represented by the rows of blocks across the sheet in Figure 7.8 which displays a consultant interval recording system similar to the one used by Walker et al. (1978). Number of minutes (one minute per row) is calibrated on the right side of the sheet. If an observation ends in the middle of a 1-minute row, the fraction of a minute is provided by the figures at the bottom of the sheet. Thus, 3′.08′ is equal to 37 intervals of data. The system samples the target student's three behaviors: positive interactions, negative interactions, and rule infractions. It also samples two teacher behaviors, praise and reprimands. Finally, it gives an account of intervals in which none of the behaviors are observed. In the data summary section of the sheet, the rates of behaviors are computed by dividing the number of intervals by the minutes observed.

Another interval sampling procedure, the play check system, developed by Risley and his colleagues (Quilitch & Risley, 1973, 1974), is group based. Unlike systems that provide data on individual students, this system yields a consolidated report on group performance—scores that reflect the percentage of individuals in a specific group who engage in specific behaviors. Recording occurred every minute on the minute. Based on recordings of the number of children playing and also the number playing with other children, the

RECESS

Consultant Interval Recording System

School _____ Child _____ Date _____

Teacher _____ Phase _____ Start Time _____

Recess: A.M.   Lunch   P.M.   Other Observation Period _____

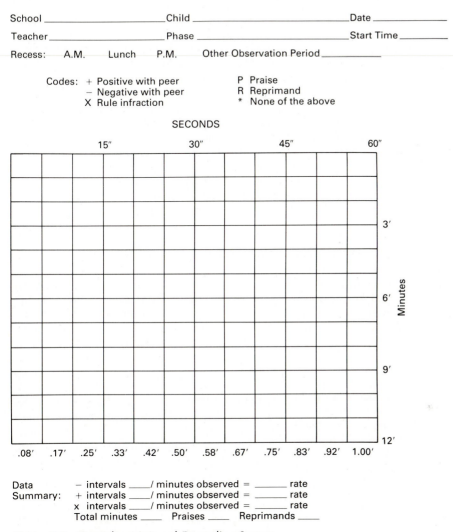

Codes: + Positive with peer   P Praise
          − Negative with peer   R Reprimand
          X Rule infraction   * None of the above

SECONDS

Data
Summary:
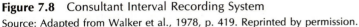
− intervals _____ / minutes observed = _____ rate
+ intervals _____ / minutes observed = _____ rate
x intervals _____ / minutes observed = _____ rate
Total minutes _____   Praises _____   Reprimands _____

Figure 7.8   Consultant Interval Recording System
Source: Adapted from Walker et al., 1978, p. 419. Reprinted by permission.

authors computed the percentage of time the group was engaged in social play.

Interval sampling procedures have been widely used in classrooms for students with severe handicaps. For example, Morrow, Burke, and Buell (1985) taught adolescents with multiple handicaps to observe and self-record their study and on-task behavior. The authors prepared an audiotape on which was recorded tones that occurred at random time intervals. The students were taught to mark one frame in a grid attached to their desk each time they heard a tone. If they were on-task, they marked a plus (+); if they were not on task, they marked a (−). To assure accuracy of the student's recording, an adult observer conducted reliability checks.

The same interval sampling procedure has been used for classroom management whereby the classroom gives feedback by marking a piece of paper for target students. The marks are used both as a measure of classroom behavior and as points that can be spent in a classroom token economy (Sloane, Buckholdt, Jensen, & Crandall, 1979). By using frequent random intervals early in such a procedure and gradually increasing the average interval, it is possible to shape longer periods of on-task behavior using fewer tones per session.

Interval recording methods also have been used in preschool settings to assess students' level of active engagement. For example, the momentary time-sampling procedures developed by Carta, Greenwood, and Robinson (in press) assessed active engagement in terms of the following behaviors: manipulate, self-care, gross-motor, pretend, academic work, and sing or recite.

Community Settings. In employment settings, interval recording has been used to monitor task engagement and time spent on-task (Rusch, Connis, & Sowers, 1978). Rusch et al. (1978) assessed the percent of 1-minute intervals that a woman with mild mental retardation spent working. They calculated the percentage of intervals worked.

Summary

In this section we have reviewed examples of continuous assessment methods based on event recording, magnitude recording, duration recording, and interval recording methods. Our examples covered applications in classroom and community settings. The discussion also suggested the most appropriate behavior for each method and how educators might apply these methods.

RECORDING AND DATA MANAGEMENT PROCEDURES

Conducting continuous behavioral assessment requires both an appropriate instrument and a data management system for dealing efficiently with all the daily records that must be collected, scored, graphed, evaluated, and recorded. The inherent danger with continuous behavioral assessment is that it may produce too much information which may obstruct rather than facilitate daily instructional decision-making. In the following section, we will examine various data collection instruments and procedures and how they may be integrated within a larger classroom data management system.

MEASUREMENT DESIGN

Although individual continuous assessment procedures are cost-effective, teachers, job coaches, and others should resist the temptation to get involved in a too comprehensive project. At the planning stage, a first rule of thumb is to design the simplest instrument possible and measure only those behaviors that are absolutely essential to the goals of instruction. A second rule is, wherever possible, combine steps in the data collection and management process. A prime example here is combining the data collection and graphing steps on one recording sheet.

Recording Sheet

A recording sheet is a prerequisite for conducting systematic and objective observations as it standardizes the observation procedure and serves as the basic summary of the results. The essential elements of any recording sheet include the following: information about the observation period, a recording field, and a score summary section. The information that should be included on every recording sheet includes a section to identify the student observed, the date and session, and the setting or activity during which the observation was made, including the names of the teachers or observers recording the data.

The area of the sheet where student behavior is recorded is called the *recording field.* The format of this area will differ depending upon the type of recording used. For example, if a timer is used, the recording field may have spaces that denote time intervals for recording the behavior of a student over a number of consecutive, equal-length periods of time. If interval recording is used the recording field will consist of numerous interval blocks so that behaviors can be marked as they occur moment-to-moment during the observation.

The *score summary section* is used for computing and recording the actual score values produced during the observation. This process may include computing the percent of intervals, the percent of intervals coded positive, the rates of correct and incorrect responding, the frequency of responding, and so on.

The three major components of a recording sheet are illustrated in Figure 7.9. The sample enables the teacher to record the social interactions in which Antonio engaged during a free-play period. An interaction is defined as any verbal, gestural, or physical behavior directed at a peer. Interactions involving Antonio are recorded in the boxes from left to right. The initiator of an interaction is coded on the left, the responder of an interaction on the right. In the first box, we see that Antonio initiated to Bill (Ant-Bil) and Bill responded (Bil-Ant). Over 15 minutes the total number of interactions for Antonio was eight of which he initiated six. Thus, his interaction rate was eight interactions in 15 minutes (0.53 interactions per minute). His rate of initiations was 0.40 per minute.

When designing a recording sheet, consider the type of recording procedure to be used (for example, duration or interval), the use of the data sheet, the user who will record or observe, the procedures for making of the sheet, the scoring of the sheet, and the storage of the sheet after data collection. To insure efficient use of the data, a data management system is required.

Data Management System

Planning a data management system that is based on the data sheet helps identify all of the steps that are necessary to collect, interpret, and use the data in instructional decision-making. The general design of such a system is illustrated in Figure 7.10. The system consists of two main cycles. The first, the daily instruct-data analysis cycle (see the right side of the table) which includes a number of steps—conducting the instructional session, collecting data, computing of scores, graphing the scores, filing or storing the data sheets, and instructional decision-making in preparation for the next session. This cycle must be completed to guarantee appropriate and sound use of the data.

The second cycle (the left side of the table) shows the steps by which the data management system can be continually reevaluated and changed as conditions change. These steps include designing the recording system, revising the system, and compiling a data base.

ADOPTION AND ADAPTATION OF AVAILABLE INSTRUMENTS

Only few continuous assessment devices are commercially available because they are thought by most publishers to have a limited market. In the absence of commercial products, the best sources of continuous assessment instruments may be found in the behavioral journals dealing with the population and behavior of interest. For students with severe handicaps, for example, the following journals provide the most up-to-date procedures:

Journal of the Association for Persons with Severe Handicaps

Student's Name: Antonio P.   Date: October 12, 1986

Session: Free play   Time start: 9:00 a.m.   Time stop: 9:15 p.m.

                            Elapsed time: 15 minutes

Recording
Field: Social Interactions

Ant-Bil	Bil-Ant	Ant-Sha	Ant-Tyr	Sha-Ant	Ant-Sha	Ant-Bil
Ant-Bil						

Scores Summary: Frequencies and Rates

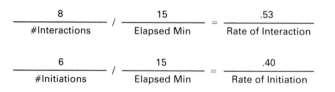

$$\frac{8}{\#Interactions} / \frac{15}{Elapsed\ Min} = \frac{.53}{Rate\ of\ Interaction}$$

$$\frac{6}{\#Initiations} / \frac{15}{Elapsed\ Min} = \frac{.40}{Rate\ of\ Initiation}$$

Interaction Distribution to Among Peers (Who to Who)

	Peer	Frequency	Rate
Antonio and	Bill	4	.27
	Shatasha	3	.20
	Tyrone	1	.07

Figure 7.9   Example Social Interaction Recording Sheet

Source: Adapted from Greenwood, Todd, Walker, & Hops, 1978, p. 31. Reprinted by permission.

Education and Training of the Mentally Retarded
Research in Developmental Disabilities
Mental Retardation

Education and Treatment of Children
Journal of Learning Disabilities
Behavior Disorders

For students with mild handicaps, the following journals should be examined:

From time to time, the following journals report assessment procedures:

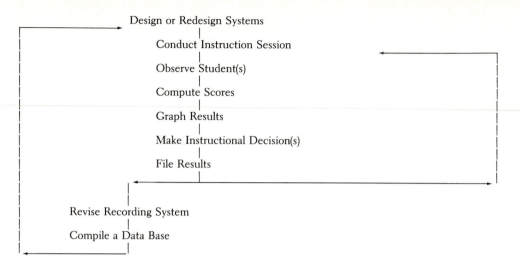

Figure 7.10 — Design or Redesign Systems / Conduct Instruction Session / Observe Student(s) / Compute Scores / Graph Results / Make Instructional Decision(s) / File Results / Revise Recording System / Compile a Data Base

Figure 7.10 Steps in a Data Management System

Journal of Applied Behavior Analysis
Exceptional Children
Behavior Modification
Behavioral Assessment

Another source is texts in applied behavior analysis and special education that include examples of assessment procedures that are directly related to specific target behaviors and applications. A third choice is materials disseminated by regional resource centers, universities, and the discipline divisions of the Council for Exceptional Children (for example, Division of Early Childhood Education, Division for Behavior Disorders, Division for Career Development), or through state departments of education.

Selection Considerations

When selecting among existing procedures, take into consideration the following: First, is the behavior(s) the same as those you wish to assess? Examine the behavioral definitions to make sure they are identical or very close to those you are interested in assessing. If not, determine if it is possible to substitute your own definitions without adversely affecting the procedure. Second, is

the instrument directly applicable to the setting(s) and situation(s) where you plan to apply it? If a commercial system has been used in the same settings and situations as yours, have some assurance that it will provide valid information. If not, you may need to pilot test the procedure in your situation before using it directly. Third, are the behaviors expressed in the correct measurement units, that is, frequencies, rates, magnitudes, and durations that agree with your own definitions of what such units should be? Fourth, what kinds of devices (for example, timers and counters) are necessary and can you easily and inexpensively obtain them? Fifth, is a data sheet provided or is a model described adequately enough so you can recreate it? If it is not, request a copy directly from the author(s). Once a procedure has been published in a journal the authors are expected to provide detailed examples upon request. Furthermore, should you decide to use the author's suggested procedures, it is common practice to ask permission in writing before beginning. Sixth, have the authors' reported interobserver agreement, and is it sufficiently high to support the reliability of the procedure? If agreement levels are low in a published study (where the authors have pre-

TABLE 7.8   Numerical Display

Session	Frequency
1	6
2	4
3	5
4	8
5	6

sumably had opportunity to correct the problem), it will undoubtedly be difficult for you to improve on the reliability without substantial modifications and further testing.

GRAPHING OBSERVATION RESULTS

In this section, we examine the basic elements of graphing and displaying the results of continuous behavioral assessment data. Compared to tables and other numerical methods of presenting data, graphic displays have the advantage of communicating relatively complex events quickly and easily. To substantiate this point, consider the data in Table 7.8 which is presented in a numerical format similar to that used by teachers who keep records in their rollbook. The meaning of these data can be much more clearly communicated when presented in a visual format as shown in Figure 7.11.

Histograms and Linear Graphs

The two following forms of visual display are commonly used (see Figure 7.11) to reflect performance: (a) graphs using bars (histograms) or (b) graphs using lines (line graphs). These two displays are illustrated in Figure 7.13 using the data from Table 7.8. Both graphs display the correlation between the frequency of a behavior, scaled on the vertical axis in each graph, and the session in which this performance was assessed, scaled on the horizontal axis. The bar graph shows that in Session 1 the student produced a score of six compared to a score of four during Session 2. The same data are plotted using points connected with lines in the Figure 7.11 (right panel). Clearly, both daily differences in the behavior, its trend, and its variation over the five sessions are much easier to understand in these two formats than in a numerical table such as Table 7.8.

In graphing continuous assessment data using either bar or line formats, the behavior scale and metric (for example, Z intervals) is always plotted on the vertical axis (referred to as the *ordinate*), whereas the repeated-measures scale and metric (for example, num-

Figure 7.11   Illustrations of Histogram (Left Panel) Versus Line Graph (Right Panel) for the Data in Table 7.8.

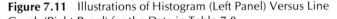
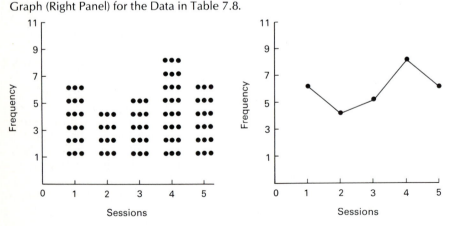

ber of sessions) is plotted on the horizontal axis (referred to as the *abscissa*). This standard feature of graphs always yields a picture of behavior as a function of time.

Although there are no strict conventions for when to use a bar graph versus a line graph format, some informal rules apply. Since they tend to give a simple uncluttered picture of trends, line graphs are frequently used to highlight trends in individual performance over time. Also, compared to bar graphs it is possible to clearly display more than one behavior in the same line graph. Bar graphs, in turn, are frequently used to display magnitude or differences in magnitude, not trends. Bar graphs are more often used to display compiled data, for example, the class mean each day rather the data of individual students. Other than these informal rules, either method can be used depending on which format best communicates the results while being time- and cost-effective.

GRAPHING DATA

Depending on the recording method used, labeling of the vertical axis differs. For example, event recording or duration recording determines the score-metric being graphed (for example, frequencies, rates, percentages, pounds). Thus, the vertical axis in a graph displaying data based on event recording is presented in terms of the frequency or the rate of the behavior compared with sessions or days on the horizontal axis. The frequency of a behavior is simply the number of behaviors

that occurred. The rate of the behavior is the frequency divided by the time observed or frequency divided by time and is expressed as responses per minute. The graph in Figure 7.12 is an example of frequency data.

The graph matrix is scaled by equal units both horizontally and vertically. Equal-interval graph paper in sizes ranging from 4 units per inch to 10 units per inch is commonly used to record data collected. Such graph paper can be used for duration recording expressed in terms of seconds or minutes; magnitude recording expressed in terms of units of force, distance, or amplitude (for example, pounds or decibels); accuracy recording expressed in terms of percent correct; and interval time sampling expressed in terms of the percent of intervals behaviors having occurred.

Rate data may also be graphed using paper scaled in logarithmic units which are not equal intervals (see Figure 7.13).

The advantage of this type of paper is that on a single $8\frac{1}{2} \times 11''$ sheet it is possible to graph rates ranging from zero to 1,000 occurrences per minute. Conceivably, therefore, any behavior of any rate of occurrence can be accommodated using this approach.

INTERPRETING GRAPHED DATA USING VISUAL INSPECTION

We now turn to a discussion of how to interpret graphed data based upon visual inspection—a direct method used in deciding how to proceed with instruction. The statistics

Figure 7.12   Illustration of an Equal Interval Graph Matrix.

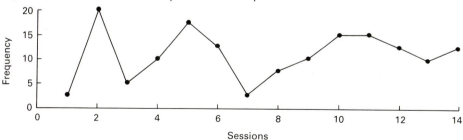

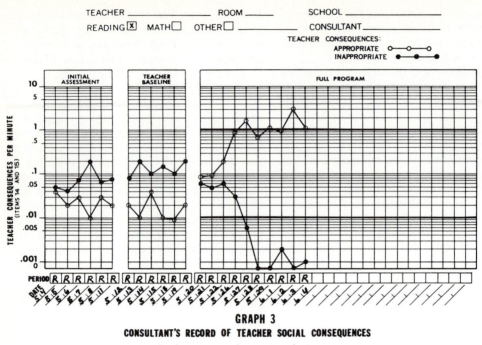

GRAPH 3
CONSULTANT'S RECORD OF TEACHER SOCIAL CONSEQUENCES

Figure 7.13   Rate Data Graphed on Logarithmic Graph Paper.

used to describe graphed data include mean level, trend, and variability.

Mean Level

Mean level is the average performance score. In this case, the average of the points in Figure 7.14 is 11, hence a horizontal line has been drawn. Eleven is the mean level around which all the points vary. This statistic is computed by simply adding all value scores

and dividing the sum by the total number of value scores that have been recorded.

Trend

Trend indicates the direction in which the performance is changing over time, expressed as (a) no trend, (b) an accelerating trend, and (c) a decelerating trend. Each of these conditions are illustrated in Figure 7.15.

In the no trend graph, it is difficult to pro-

Figure 7.14   Illustration of Level in Graphed Data.

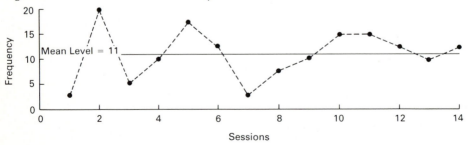

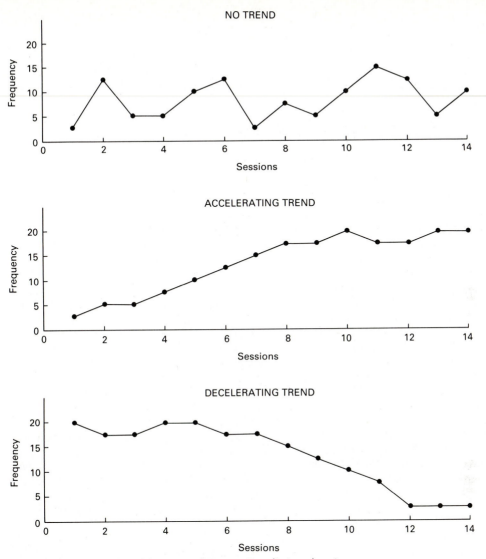

Figure 7.15 Illustration of No Trend (Upper Panel), Accelerating Trend (Middle Panel), and Decelerating Trend (Lower Panel).

ject or predict the direction of the performance in future sessions. Sessions are randomly high or low. Based on the graph showing an accelerating trend, however, we can forecast an increase in performance from one session to the next. Forecasting is also possible of the deceleration example. After the first five sessions the performance trend begins a gradual, systematic decline. Trends suggest that a be-havior is changing and seeking a new mean level.

Variability

Variability is the range of performance from lowest to highest over time (see Figure 7.16).

In this figure, variability is defined by 3,

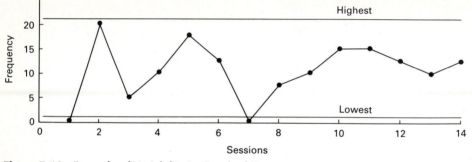

Figure 7.16   Example of Variability in Graphed Data.

the lowest point, and 20, the highest point. Widely variable data are described as *unstable,* meaning that a behavior may change dramatically from one session to the next. Given wide variability, we can assume that a behavior is not well controlled by classroom procedures. In contrast, a graph in which the variability ranges from 3, the lowest, to 7, the highest, may be described as stable, relative to our first example, since its daily variation is three times smaller. In this case, the target behavior can be assumed to be under stimulus control; hence, a consistent performance may be expected from session to session.

The three factors of mean level, trend, and variability take on additional meaning when they are used as the basis for comparing an individual's performance across different conditions of instruction.

INTRASUBJECT COMPARISONS BETWEEN CONDITIONS

We can apply visual inspection to draw a conclusion about the effects of a given teaching procedure. For example, in Figure 7.17, we are comparing a student's performance before (at baseline) and after a time-out procedure was used in an attempt (treatment) to decelerate a behavior. The result of the visual inspection is summarized in Table 7.9. By simply looking at the graphed data during baseline, we can project where performance would probably range in the future by forecasting. However, we notice that the behavior has fallen below the baseline limit. Invoking mean level, trend, and variability statistics we realize that during the baseline period the level was 18.9, no trend was present, and the

Figure 7.17   Example Display of a Treatment Effect in Graphed Data.

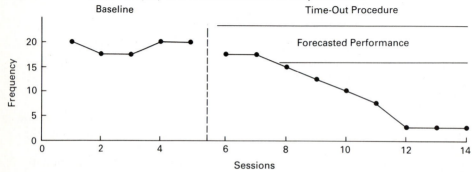

TABLE 7.9 Visual Inspection Summary

Consideration	Baseline	Time-Out
Level	18.9	9.7
Trend	None	Decelerating
Variability	17–20, Range = 3	3–17, Range = 15

data were stable with a range of 3. During the time-out period, however, these factors changed dramatically; that is the level dropped to half, down to 9.7, a clear decelerating trend occurred as evidenced by lower points in each session, and the variability increased to 15. In the last three sessions of the time-out period the level was 3, no trend was apparent, and the range was zero, suggesting that the behavior stabilized at a new level following the systematic decline over the prior six sessions. The conclusion to be drawn from this analysis is that the time-out procedure had a dramatic effect on the frequency of responding, dramatically reducing its frequency compared to the baseline period.

By applying the same procedures to a new set of data we arrive at a different outcome as seen in Figure 7.18.

The result of this visual inspection suggests very little change. In Table 7.10, we have summarized the mean level, trend, and variability information.

The result of the baseline inspection is the same as in the previous example, but the time-out results are highly different. Specifically, the level is 19.1 during time-out compared to 18.9 at baseline, and no trend is discernible during baseline or time-out. The variability has increased to a range of 8 in time-out compared to 3 during baseline. For these reasons, we must conclude that there is no difference, and thus, no effect, for time-out.

One more set of comparisons may be added to this process, as will be seen in the next section.

INTERSUBJECT COMPARISONS

The same procedures can be applied to both individual and peer data within the same graph. As illustrated, during the baseline period, Daryl always obtained more words than Kimkisha. During the teaching period, however, they obtained almost the same number of words with Kim even exceeding Daryl during Sessions 10 and 14. A complete visual inspection will yield a more thorough analysis

Figure 7.18 Illustration of No Treatment Effect Between Baseline and Time-out Procedures.

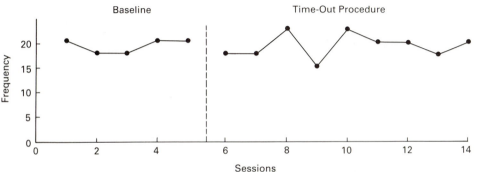

TABLE 7.10   Visual Inspection Summary

Consideration	Baseline	Time-out
Level	18.9	199.1
Trend	None	None
Variability	17–20, Range = 3	15–23, Range = 8

as can be seen in Table 7.11. First, Kim increased her performance during the teaching procedure, thus the number of words tripled from a mean level of 6.2 to 17.8. In addition, her trend changed from no trend to an accelerating trend. Daryl's mean level, however, started out high during baseline and remained high during the teaching period (17.8 versus 20.0). His performance showed no trend in either phase and was stable during both phases (beginning range was 5 and increased to 7).

A comparison between Kimkisha and Daryl reveals that in the baseline phase their mean levels differed, 6.2 for Kimkisha and 17.8 for Daryl, and at no time did Kimkisha score as high as Daryl's lowest score. During the teaching procedure, however, Kimkisha underwent an increasing trend. Her mean level was comparable to Daryl's (17.8 for Kim and 20.0 for Daryl). In fact, Kimkisha regularly scored within the range of Daryl's scores.

Using visual inspection procedures to make both intrasubject and intersubject comparisons, we can conclude that the procedure was highly effective. In this case, it produced change compared to baseline level (intrasubject comparison) large enough to equal that of a normative peer (intersubject comparison). These two effects point to an instruc-tional solution to Kimkisha's initial low baseline performance.

The principles of visual inspection are similar to those of statistical procedures used to describe and analyze differences in performance. However, in visual inspection no single statistic is used to establish that a difference is large enough to be important. Such a conclusion is left to the judgment of teachers, parents, employers and others who are engaged in the instructional program. If a difference cannot be clearly seen or if the difference is small, it is not likely to be an important effect for the student. Consequently, a new intervention should be implemented to change the behavior.

SUMMARY

Continuous behavioral assessment is measurement conducted on a daily or weekly basis and interpreted as trends in individual performance over time. Continuous assessment may also be defined as direct observation of student performance in the curriculum, the classroom, or the community setting. The precursors of continuous assessment may be found in the fields of behavior analysis which contributed the basic concept of behavior as

TABLE 7.11   Visual Inspection Summary

CONSIDERATION	BASELINE		TIME-OUT	
	Kim	Daryl	Kim	Daryl
Level	6.2	17.8	18.8	20.0
Trend	None	None	Accel.	None
Variability	5–8	15–20	13–20	16–23
Range	3	5	7	7

a function of time. The work of Skinner was instrumental in developing this assessment concept, and Lindsley and Lovitt further applied continuous assessment to academic behavior, particularly reading. The efforts of Hall, Walker, and their colleagues led to effective methods for assessing classroom behaviors, more recently continued by Deno and his colleagues who have systematically applied curriculum-based assessment in special education.

In an overview of continuous assessment and its advantages over other forms of assessment, we focused on fundamental principles, assumptions, and threats to validity. Specific applications of continuous assessment instruments were presented, such as event recording, duration recording, magnitude recording, and interval recording. Examples from the literature of the application of continuous assessment procedures were given.

The importance of selecting the most appropriate assessment procedure was stressed (whether adopted or adapted from another source or self-designed) along with the need for a complete data management system. The final section of the chapter contained a discussion of how to interpret the results of continuous assessment.

This chapter concludes our discussion of measurement. In Chapter 8, we will examine single-subject research designs and continuous assessment methods that extend our ability to draw conclusions about the effects of instructional procedures. Now that we have learned how to measure and interpret results, it is important to determine that behavior changes are, in fact, a function of our instruction and not other factors.

REFERENCES

BECKER, W. C. (1971). *An empirical basis for change in education.* Chicago: Science Research Associates.

BIJOU, S. W., & BAER, D. M. (1978). *Behavior analysis in child development.* Englewood Cliffs, NJ: Prentice Hall.

BILLINGSLEY, F. F., & LIBERTY, K A. (1982). "The use of time-based data in instructional programs for the severely handicapped. *The Journal of the Association for Persons with Severe Handicaps, 7,* 47–55.

BLANKENSHIP, C., & LILLY, M. S. (1981). *Mainstreaming students with learning and behavior problems: Techniques for the classroom teacher.* New York: Holt, Rinehart & Winston.

BRADY, M. P., SHORES, R. E., GUNTER, P., McEVOY, M., FOX, J. J., & WHITE, C. (1984). "Generalization of an adolescent's social interaction behavior via multiple peers in a classroom setting." *The Journal of the Association for Persons with Severe Handicaps, 9,* 278–286.

BREEN, C., HARING, T., PITTS-CONWAY, V., & GAYLORD-ROSS, R. (1985). "The training and generalization of social interaction during breaktime at two job sites in the natural environment." *Journal of the Association for Persons with Severe Handicaps, 10,* 41–50.

BROWN, L., SHERBENOU, R. J., & DOLLAR, S. J. (1982). *Test of Nonverbal Intelligence.* Austin, TX: Pro-Ed.

CARTA, J. J., GREENWOOD C. R., DINWIDDIE, G., KOHLER, F., & DELQUADRI, J. (1985). *The Juniper Gardens classwide peer tutoring programs for spelling, reading, and math: Teacher's manual.* Kansas City, KS: The Juniper Gardens Children's Project, Bureau of Child Research, University of Kansas.

CARTA, J., GREENWOOD, C. R., & ROBINSON, S. (in press). "Application of an ecobehavioral approach to the evaluation of early intervention programs." In R. Prinz (ed.), *Advances in the behavioral assessment of children and families* (vol. 3). Greenwich, CT: JAI Press.

CHADSEY-RUSCH, J. (1985). "Community integration and mental retardation: The ecobehavioral approach to service provision and assessment." In R. H. Bruininks & K. C. Lakin (eds.), *Living and learning in the least restrictive environment* (pp. 245–60). Baltimore: Paul H. Brookes.

CHADSEY-RUSCH, J., KARLAN, G. R., RIVA, M. T., & RUSCH, F. R. (1984). "Competitive employment: Teaching conversation skills to adults who are mentally retarded." *Mental Retardation, 22,* 218–225.

CHADSEY-RUSCH, J., & RUSCH, F. R. (in press). "Habilitation program for mentally retarded persons with severe behavior problems." In R. P. Barrett (ed.), *Treatment of severe behavior dis-*

orders: *Contemporary approaches with the mentally retarded.* New York: Plenum.

CHRISTOPHERSEN, E. R., ARNOLD, C. M., HILL, D. W., & QUILITCH, H. R. (1972). "The home point system: Token reinforcement procedures for application by parents of children with behavior problems." *Journal of Applied Behavior Analysis, 5,* 485–498.

DENO, S. L. (1984). "Curriculum-based measurement: The emerging alternative." *Exceptional Children,* 219–232.

DURAND, V. M. (1982). "Analysis and intervention of self-injurious behavior." *The Journal of the Association for Persons with Severe Handicaps, 7,* 44–53.

ELLIOTT, M., HUGHES, V., & DELQUADRI, J. (1984). *Experimental validation and field testing of instructional packages that increase opportunity to respond.* Symposium presented at the 10th Annual Convention of the Association for Behavior Analysis, Nashville, TN.

FUCHS, L., & DENO, S. (1981). *A comparison of reading placements based on teacher judgment, standardized testing, and curriculum-based assessment* (Research Report 56). Minneapolis, MN: University of Minnesota, Institute for Research on Learning Disabilities.

GERMANN, G., & TINDAL, G. (1984). "An application of curriculum-based assessment: The use of direct and repeated measurement." *Exceptional Children, 49,* 244–265.

GREENWOOD, C. R., DINWIDDIE, G., TERRY, B., WADE, L., STANLEY, S. O., THIBADEAU, S., & DELQUADRI, J. (1984). "Teacher versus peer-mediated instruction: An ecobehavioral analysis of achievement outcomes." *Journal of Applied Behavior Analysis, 17,* 521–538.

GREENWOOD, C. R., HOPS, H., DELQUADRI, J., & GUILD, J. (1974). "Group contingencies for group consequences in classroom management: A further analysis." *Journal of Applied Behavior Analysis, 7,* 413–425.

GREENWOOD, C. R., SCHULTE, D., KOHLER, F., DINWIDDIE, G., & CARTA, J. J. (1986). "Assessment and analysis of ecobehavioral interaction in school settings." In R. Prinz (ed.), *Advances in behavioral assessment of children and families* (vol. 2, pp. 69–98). Greenwich, CT: JAI Press.

GREENWOOD, C. R., TODD, N., WALKER, H. M., & HOPS, H. (1978). *Social assessment manual for preschool level.* (SAMPLE). Eugene, OR: University of Oregon, Center at Oregon for Research in the Behavioral Education of the Handicapped.

HAAVIK, S., & ALTMAN, K. (1977). "Establishing walking by severely retarded children." *Perceptual and Motor Skills, 44,* 1107–1114.

HALL, R. V., LUND, D., & JACKSON, D. (1968). "Effects of teacher attention on study behavior." *Journal of Applied Behavior Analysis, 1,* 1–12.

HANSON, H. J., & HANLINE, M. F. (1985). "An analysis of response-contingent learning experiences for young children." *The Journal of the Association for Persons with Severe Handicaps, 10,* 31–40.

HARRIS, M. B., & BLOOM, S. R. (1984). "A pilot investigation of a behavioral weight control program for mentally retarded adolescents and adults: Effects on weight, fitness, and knowledge of nutritional and behavioral principles." *Rehabilitation Psychology, 29,* 177–182.

HARTMANN, D. P., & WOODS, D. D. (1982). "Observational methods." In A. S. Bellack, M. Hersen, & A. D. Kazdin (eds.), *International handbook of behavior modification and therapy* (pp. 109–131). New York: Plenum Press.

HOLVOET, J., GUESS, D., MULLIGAN, M., & BROWN, F. (1980). "Individualized curriculum sequencing model (II): A teaching strategy for severely handicapped students." *Journal of the Association of the Severely Handicapped, 5,* 337–351.

HOPKINS, B. L., & HERMAN, J. A. (1977). "Evaluating interobserver reliability of interval data." *Journal of Applied Behavior Analysis, 10,* 121–126.

HOPS, H., BEICKEL, S. L., & WALKER, H. M. (1976). *Contingencies for learning academic and social skills: Manual for consultants.* Eugene, OR: University of Oregon, Center at Oregon for Research in the Behavioral Education of the Handicapped.

HOPS, H., WALKER, H. M., & HUTTON, S. B. (1973). *CORBEH CLASS Program for acting-out children: Contingencies for learning academic social skills.* Eugene, OR: University of Oregon, Center at Oregon for Research in the Behavioral Education of the Handicapped.

HUNT, P., GOETZ, L., ALWELL, M., & SAILOR, W. (1986). "Using an interrupted behavior chain strategy to teach generalized communication responses." *Journal of the Association for Persons with Severe Handicaps, 11,* 196–204.

KAZDIN, A. E. (1977). *The token economy.* New York: Plenum Press.

LEACH, D. J. & DOLAN, N. K. (1985). "Helping teachers increase student academic engagement rate: The evaluation of a minimal feedback procedure." *Behavior Modification*, 9, 55–71.

LINDSLEY, O. R. (1964). "Direct measurement and prosthesis of retarded behavior." *Journal of Education*, 147, 62–81.

LOVITT, T. C., KUNZELMAN, H. P., NOLEN, P. A., & HULTEN, W. J. (1968). "The dimensions of classroom data." *Journal of Learning Disabilities*. 1, 710–721.

MORROW, L. W., BURKE, J. G., & BUELL, B. J. (1985). "Effects of a self-recording procedure on the attending to task behavior and academic productivity of adolescents with multiple handicaps." *Mental Retardation*, 23, 137–141.

NELSON, R. O., & HAYES, S. (1979). "The dimensions of behavioral assessment." *Behavioral Assessment*, 1, 1–16.

O'BRIEN, F., AZRIN, N. H., & BUGLE, C. (1972). "Training profoundly retarded children to stop crawling." *Journal of Applied Behavior Analysis*, 5, 131–137.

PARTINGTON, J. W., SUNDBERG, M. L., IWATA, B. A., & MOUNTJOY, P. T. (1979). "A task-analysis approach to time telling instruction for normal and educably mentally retarded impaired children." *Education and Treatment of Children*, 2, 17–29.

QUILITCH, H. R., & RISLEY, T. R. (1973). "The effects of play materials on social play." *Journal of Applied Behavior Analysis*, 6, 573–578.

REID, J. B., SKINDRUD, K., & TAPLINE, P. S. (1973). "The role of complexity in the collection and evaluation of observation data." In A. E. Kazdin (ed.), *Methodological issues in applied behavior analysis*. Symposium presented at the 81st Annual Convention of the American Psychological Association, Montreal, PQ, Canada.

REYNOLDS, N. J., & RISLEY, R. T. (1968). "The role of social and material reinforcers in increasing talking of a disadvantaged preschool child." *Journal of Applied Behavior Analysis*, 1, 253–262.

RIORDAN, M. M., IWATA, B. A., WOHL, M. K., & FINNEY, J. W. (1980). "Behavioral treatment of food refusal and selectivity in developmentally disabled children." *Applied Research in Mental Retardation*, 1, 95–112.

ROGERS-WARREN, A. K. (1984). "Ecobehavioral an-alysis." *Education and Treatment of Children*, 7, 283–304.

RUSCH, F. R., CHADSEY-RUSCH, J., WHITE, O. R., & GIFFORD, J. L. (1985). "Programs for severely mentally retarded adults: Perspectives and methodologies." In D. Bricker & J. Filler (eds.), *Severe mental retardation: From theory to practice* (pp. 119–140). Reston, VA: Council for Exceptional Children.

RUSCH, F. R., CONNIS, R. T., & SOWERS, J. (1978). "The modification and maintenance of time spent attending to task using social reinforcement, token reinforcement, and response cost in an applied restaurant setting." *Journal of Special Education Technology*, 2, 18–26.

RUSCH, F. R., MENCHETTI, B. M., CROUCH, K., RIVA, M., MORGAN, T., & AGRAN, M. (1984). "Competitive employment: Assessing employee reactivity to naturalistic observation." *Journal of Applied Research in Mental Retardation*, 5, 332–351.

SCHMIDT, G. W., & ULRICH, R. E. (1969). "Effects of group contingent events upon classroom noise." *Journal of Applied Behavior Analysis*, 2, 171–180.

SHINN, M., & MARSTON, D. (1985). "Differentiating mildly handicapped, low achieving, and regular education students: A curriculum-based approach." *Remedial and Special Education*, 6, 31–38.

SKINNER, B. F. (1956). "A case history in scientific method." *American Psychologist*, 11, 221–223.

SLOANE, H. N., BUCKHOLDT, D. R., JENSEN, W. R., & CRANDALL, J. A. (1979). *Structured teaching.* Champaign, IL: Research Press.

SNELL, M. E., & BROWDER, D. M. (1986). "Community-referenced instruction: Research and issues." *The Journal of the Association for Persons with Severe Handicaps*, 11, 1–11.

SPEARS, D., RUSCH, F. R., YORK, R., & LILLY, M. S. (1981). "Training independent arrival behaviors to a severely mentally retarded child." *Journal of the Association for the Severely Handicapped*, 6, 40–45.

SPECIAL OLYMPICS (n.d.). *Sports skills instructional program: Bowling.* Washington, DC: Special Olympics/Joseph P. Kennedy, Jr. Foundation.

THURSTONE, P., & HOUSE, E. R. (1981). "The NIE adversary hearing on competency testing." *Phi Delta Kappan*, 63, 87–89.

TUCKER, J. A. (1985). "Curriculum-based assessment: An introduction." *Exceptional Children,* *52,* 199–204.

UTLEY, B., DUNCAN, D., STRAIN, P., & SCANLON, K. (1983). "Effects of contingent and noncontingent vision stimulation on visual fixation in multiply handicapped children. *The Journal of the Association for Persons with Severe Handicaps, 8,* 29–42.

WALKER, H. M., & BUCKLEY, N. K. (1968). "The use of positive reinforcement in conditioning attending behavior." *Journal of Applied Behavior Analysis, 1,* 245–250.

WALKER, H. M., & HOPS, H. (1976). "Use of normative peer data as a standard for evaluating classroom treatment effects."*Journal of Applied Behavior Analysis, 9,* 156–168.

WALKER, H. M., STREET, A., GARRETT, B., CROSSEN, J., HOPS, H., & GREENWOOD, C. R. (1978).

Reprogramming environmental contingencies for effective social skills (RECESS): Consultant's manual. Eugene, OR: University of Oregon, Center at Oregon for Research in the Behavior Education of the Handicapped.

WESSEL, J. A. (1976). *I can: Implementation guide.* Northbrook, IL: Hubbard.

WHITE, O. R. (1986). "Precision teaching: Precision learning." *Exceptional Children, 52,* 522–534.

WHITMAN, T. L., MERCURIO, J. R., & CAPONIGRI, V. (1970). "Development of social responses in two severely retarded children." *Journal of Applied Behavior Analysis, 3,* 133–138.

WOLF, M. M. (1978). "Social validity: The case for subjective measurement or how applied behavior analyses is finding its heart." *Journal of Applied Behavior Analysis, 11,* 203–214.

chapter 8

Designs for Evaluating Student Progress

In this chapter we discuss methods that can be used within continuous assessment to validate the effects of teaching and intervention. Often it is important to be able to determine that a certain teaching technique or instructional material used with a student was, in fact, the real reason for change. We are interested in *causes*. To identify causes, we need designs. The designs to be discussed are termed *single-subject*, $N = 1$, or *single-case* designs. They enable a teacher to conclude with a high degree of certainty that a particular teaching procedure was the cause responsible for learning or behavior change. Thus, single-subject designs are a powerful technique for discovering and validating effective teaching methods and procedures.

RATIONALE FOR STUDYING BEHAVIOR

In special education, the behavior of individuals has been investigated for the following reasons: first, to document that special education procedures are effective and that special education contributes directly to students' development; second, to prove accountability and to objectively document the efforts that have been made to teach each student and the results of such efforts; third, to verify the cause and effect of certain specific developmental outcomes; and fourth, to develop effective instructional and training procedures that can be used with children with specific disabilities and performance characteristics.

Related to these reasons for a method of individual analysis is each individual's uniqueness. We all possess a unique physiological make-up and a unique developmental, maturational, and socio-cultural history. Collectively, these factors affect what we know and what we can do. Special education students represent the extreme ranges of these factors, and, as a consequence, we cannot expect all students to respond equally well to the same instructional procedures. A procedure may work well with 95 percent of students in a classroom, but 5 percent will fail to make progress. To find appropriate and effective strategies, we need to study the individual case.

The study of individual behavior must be approached with certainty. We need to rule out a multiplicity of factors that are temporally related to our teaching efforts and that may not directly contribute to behavior change. For example, if we make tokens contingent on the rate of computing math facts and the student's rate doubles immediately thereafter, can we really be certain that it was the token consequences that "caused" the increase in rate? Might not the increase be a result of other factors that just happened to coincide with our use of tokens; perhaps, for example, the teacher gave more precise instructions, or practice was initiated at home by parents, or there was a sudden competition between two students? The designs we will discuss in this chapter have been developed specifically to eliminate troublesome alternative explanations of behavior change like these.

For students for whom standard behavior management procedures are not effective, our mission as teachers is to discover procedures that are effective or, if equally effective, more socially desirable. For example, with head banging and other serious self-injurious behaviors, restraint and electric shock were some of the first effective termination and elimination procedures in the 1960s (Hamilton, Stephens, & Allen, 1967; Tate & Baroff, 1966). However, since that time, research using single-subject designs has provided us with effective procedures of a less restrictive and less aversive nature, including contingent use of mildly distasteful substances like lemon juice (Sajwaj, Libet, & Agras, 1974) and positive-practice overcorrection (Miltenberger & Fuqua, 1981).

Trends in academic instruction also exemplify how single-subject research designs have been used to improve teaching procedures. In the 1970s reinforcement contingencies were commonly used to increase attention and related task engagement as a means of improving students' academic performance. For example, Hall focused on contingent teacher praise (Hall, Lund, & Jackson, 1968), whereas the later work of Walker and his colleagues examined the influence of contingent reinforcement combined with mild punishment on student attention and task engagement (Walker, Hops, & Figenbaum, 1976). More recently, however, single-subject research has demonstrated the importance of frequent opportunities to make academic responses (Greenwood et al., 1984) and the form these opportunities take in the curriculum (Englemann & Carnine, 1982).

OVERVIEW OF DESIGNS

Research in regular and special education has been based largely upon group designs (Campbell & Stanley, 1963). Since much of this research has not been designed to directly address effectiveness, accountability, cause and effect, and individual differences, it is not relevant to our discussion here. Examples of this type of research include the epidemiology of handicapping conditions, which addresses the numbers of students with specific handicaps within the population. Research at this level is actuarial and descriptive. Another example is survey research, intended to sample the opinions and ideas of specific groups (for example, parents and teachers) concerning important issues, such as the quality of special education services in a school district. Yet another line of group-design research focuses on establishing that two or more factors are correlated. For example, one may wish to develop criteria for accepting children into a learning disabilities program based upon the correlation between achievement test scores and intelligence test scores.

When the goal of research turns to the study of effective teaching procedures, only the experiment-control group design applies. Assuming that the response of any one student to treatment is not representative of the "average" response, group-design logic rejects the usefulness of individual subject data. Hence, the group average and the range (lowest and highest performance) becomes the metric for change in these studies. Experimental-control group studies address the question, "Is the average of the experimental group that received special treatment different from the average of the control group that did not receive this treatment?" If the answer is yes, the experimental procedure used is considered important. If the answer is no, the procedure has not proven effective.

The experimental-control design has been criticized for not allowing detailed observations of those students who respond best and worst to the experimental procedure. This drawback is compounded by the use of intermittent forms of assessment, such as pretests and posttests. That is, not only is it impossible to observe the performance of individuals, but the infrequency of measurement further limits the information available for each student. Furthermore, individual scores are not presented as part of the statistical analysis, thereby rendering it impossible to explain why any single student performed in any particular way.

Another criticism of the experimental-control group design, particularly with low-incidence handicapped populations, is that there may not be enough students to conduct an adequate group-design study. Since group designs cannot appropriately be used for many questions about instruction and behavior management, instructional procedures based on this type of research have been few and of limited utility (Greer, 1982).

In contrast, single-subject designs address the criticisms related to use of group design in the study of individual cases, specifically, (a) those criticisms accounting for the variation in individuals' performance over time and (b) those criticisms controlling rival explanations of behavior change.

VARIATION ACROSS INDIVIDUALS

As opposed to group designs in which intermittent measurement is used, single-subject designs account for the variability of a subject's response by continuous assessments of the behavior over time. For example, by measuring the rate of tantrums each day and graphing these data, teachers can portray the day-to-day variation for an individual student. This rate will never be absolutely the same, however, because a number of unknown factors routinely influence it, such as measurement errors (for example, fluctuations in interobserver reliability), situational factors (such as teacher instructions and task difficulty level), factors surrounding the session (such as home environment and interactions with friends or enemies), and physiology (for example, the student may have a cold or has had no breakfast). Given that these events operate continually to influence performance, repeated measurements of a behavior during a specific session or time of day will produce a performance baseline that reveals the impact of these factors. Thus, baselines of this type are routinely used in single-subject research to reflect an individual's typical performance variation as a function of this multitude of factors. In single-subject research designs the subject serves as his or her own control. That is, performance under an experimental procedure is compared to the same student's performance during baseline. To the extent that differences in level, trend, and variation can be detected between baseline and treatment phases, the case for a positive or negative treatment effect can be made for a single subject.

CONTROL OF RIVAL EXPLANATIONS

Single-subject designs control for rival explanations the following ways: (a) by introducing or withdrawing variables, (b) by immediately having and recording effects, and (c) by independently replicating the effects.

Introducing or Withdrawing Variables

A baseline reflecting individual variation is the focus of single-subject designs. Thus, by introducing a new procedure or intervention, an effect beyond that of expected individual variation may be observed. Effects become evident through an increased average level of performance and an accelerating trend in the baseline data immediately after a given procedure was introduced. Effects may also be observed by withdrawing the teaching procedure. The effect of its removal on the data collected during this period is observed and compared to performance during prior conditions.

Immediately Having and Recording Effects

In single-subject designs a manipulation must produce a relatively immediate effect on the baseline (within a session or two) to ensure that treatment and effect are linked in time. If effect delays are greater than two sessions, one must suspect that the procedure was not effective or that some other variable(s) is responsible for any effects that begin after a delay.

Independent Replication of Effects

If experimental effects can be repeated, we can be more certain that the treatment procedure, not random rival events, produced the behavior change. As we will shortly demonstrate, these replications can be produced in a number of ways including repeated presentation and withdrawal of the treatment or introduction of treatments one at a time across several baselines. In contrast to group design, where the generality of experimental effects is demonstrated by replication across many subjects, generalization is demonstrated in single-subject designs by individual replications.

We will now review four classes of single-subject designs: reversal, multiple-baseline and multiple-probe, changing-criterion, and alternating-treatments.

REVERSAL DESIGN

Definition

In the reversal design treatment B is compared to a baseline A, which is characterized by an absence of treatment variables and serves as a control for the treatment. Thus, at the most basic level, comparison of a behavior under a change from A to B and from B to A (ABA) is the basic element of this design, which is based on two assumptions: First, the change from A to B will produce an observable effect on a behavior coincidental with the change. Second, a return to A after B will result in a second coincidental change in behavior but in the opposite direction. Specifically, when B is withdrawn the behavior being measured is expected to return to its original baseline level and trend. To provide a convincing demonstration of causality the full design requires an ABAB sequence (see Figure 8.1). That is, the behavior change produced by B must be demonstrated twice, and it must be returned once to baseline levels when B is removed in order to rule out rival explanations for the observed behavior change (Barlow & Hersen, 1984). Thus, although instructive about what may be influencing a behavior change, AB and ABA designs are not sufficient to be scientifically convincing.

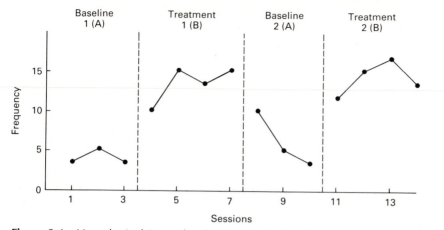

Figure 8.1 Hypothetical Example of Data Graphed to Conform to a Reversal or Withdrawal Design.

Behaviors for Which the ABAB Design Is Appropriate

The ABAB design is appropriate with all behaviors measured as frequencies, durations, latencies, magnitudes, and so forth (see Chapter 5). Exceptions are those few behaviors for which it may be assumed that reversal to baseline level will not occur. For example, if the intervention teaches a child to acquire a skill, such as reading.

The design is most appropriate for behaviors that are influenced by contingencies of reinforcement and punishment, that is, behaviors for which students generally have some capability or proficiency at changing if given the necessary motivation. Thus, we are describing baselines that are greater than zero. However, the class of behaviors requiring academic instruction (for example, how to solve addition or subtraction problems), once learned may not be readily reversible (Sindelar, Rosenberg, & Wilson, 1985). Reinforcement contingencies will have little effect on the number of problems solved if the student does not have the ability to solve any problems of this class. However, once he or she is taught, contingencies can influence both the rate and accuracy of solutions. Behaviors of the latter type are most appropriate for the ABAB design.

Examples from School and Classroom Settings. Carbone, Miller, and Todd (1981) used the ABAB design to investigate the effects of an assignment completion contingency (see Figure 8.2). The purpose of this study was to increase the academic output of a fourth grade child who rarely completed daily assignments and often exhibited crying and tantrums. The number of assignments completed each day was defined as the number of workbook pages completed, plus stories read, plus the number of worksheets completed. A 4-day baseline indicated that the student completed 1.5 assignments on the average (Baseline 1). On Day 5, the teacher introduced a contingency whereby the student could earn 5 minutes to work on building a plastic model airplane by completing an assignment to an accuracy criterion before a time signalled the end of the work period (Treatment 1). During this phase, the number of completed assignments increased to 5.2 on the average. This condition was followed on Day 18 by withdrawal of the contingency and a return to baseline (Baseline 2). The number of assignments dropped to 0.7 per day. On

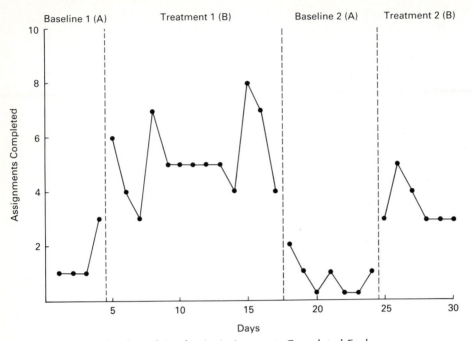

Figure 8.2   The Number of Academic Assignments Completed Each
Day During Baseline and Treatment Phases.

Source: From "Beat the timer game" by V. Carbone, A. Miller, & D. R. Todd,
1981, *Education and Treatment of Children, 4,* p. 57. Reprinted by permission.

Day 24 when the "game" was reinstated, the number of assignments again increased, averaging 3.5 per day. In this design, two replications of the treatment effect were produced. Each time the "game" was in place the number of assignments increased; when the "game" was removed, the number of assignments decreased. These two replications, with change occurring immediately after installing or withdrawing the treatment, enhance our certainty that it is, in fact, the game that is causing the student's change in behavior.

Luiselli (1984) used the ABAB design to investigate the combined effectiveness of brief overcorrection and differential reinforcement of other behavior (DRO). The subject was a 19-year-old female with severe mental retardation who lacked functional expressive language and was unable to perform basic

self-care and daily living activities without assistance. The target behavior was tongue protrusions, which were a constant problem during one-on-one speech therapy. Since the subject's tongue was constantly out of her mouth, the instructor could not physically prompt mouth and lip placements. Furthermore, excessive salivation and drooling inhibited instruction. The use of reprimands had proved ineffective.

During Baseline 1 (A), protrusions (tongue extending past lips) were recorded in the absence of any intervention. The treatment program combined positive-practice overcorrection and DRO. When a protrusion occurred, the positive practice contingency was employed. This consisted of (a) telling her that she must keep her tongue in her mouth, (b) having her take a facial tissue, (c) placing the tissue against her lips, (d) wiping her lips lightly five times, and (e) placing the tissue on the table. Each overcorrection lasted approximately 15 seconds. The DRO procedure reinforced behaviors other than tongue protrusions. If the subject kept her tongue in her mouth, she received an edible each time a bell sounded and she was also lavishly praised by the instructor. The procedures continued to be used, and follow-up observations were made several weeks after the end of the study. As in the prior example, the results indicated that the treatment procedures produced a positive therapeutic change in the student's behavior compared to baseline. A highly variable frequency of protrusions noted during the baseline was reduced to zero in the treatment condition. A subsequent return to baseline accelerated the number of protrusions. The number of protrusions were again reduced when treatment was applied. With the treatment still in place, protrusions remained reduced some weeks later at follow-up observations.

Examples from Community Settings. Jackson, Salzberg, Pacholl, and Dorsey (1981) used the ABAB design to demonstrate the effectiveness of a home-based, bus-riding procedure as seen in Figure 8.3. The student was a 10-year-old male of normal intelligence assigned to a special classroom for students with behavior problems. Due to his disruptive behavior he was about to be excluded from public school bus service. The student's behavior was observed on both the morning trip to school and the afternoon trip home. The duration of these trips was approximately 55 minutes each. Inappropriate bus behaviors included yelling, name calling, spitting, hitting, pinching, and pushing others. The behaviors were recorded by the bus driver and a trained observer who sat behind the bus driver. For Baseline 1 (A) the student's behavior was recorded by both observers. During the first treatment phase, Contingent Privileges 1 (B), the student was able to earn or lose the privilege of playing outdoors and watching television at home. These privileges were either

earned or lost based on a count of the student's inappropriate behaviors as reported to the parent by the bus driver. If he engaged in five or fewer behavior episodes on the bus, according to the driver's record, the privileges were granted. In contrast, more than five episodes meant loss of privileges. This phase was followed by a return to Baseline (A) where the student obtained his privileges regardless of his behavior on the bus. Subsequently, for a second time, Contingent Privileges 2 (B) were started and he had to earn privileges. The last two data points on Figure 8.3 represent a follow-up assessment taken over a 2-week period at the end of the study. The contingency (B) remained in effect during this period. During the Baseline phases, the student's behavior was dramatically more frequent than during the two Contingent Privileges phases. Once in each of the contingency phases, Session 15 and 25, the count exceeded five resulting in loss of privileges.

Hanson and Hanline (1985) used the ABAB design to study the effects of contingent feedback provided at home by parents on the behavior of several children with multiple handicaps. In one experiment, the participant was Marcus, an 8-month-old boy with Down's syndrome who had significant visual and auditory impairments. The baby was taught to signal his parents by using a device that emitted a beep whenever a pressure-sensitive panel was pressed. This device was used because the child did not effectively communicate either vocally or facially. The number of panel depressions, frequency of smiling, and vocalizing, and his state (that is, A = alert as opposed to F = not alert) were recorded.

Following a baseline period when Marcus was placed on the floor for 5 minutes, his father physically prompted him to use the panel. Each panel press was immediately reinforced by the mother who vocalized to him and touched him. Baseline and prompting with feedback were alternated in an ABABA sequence. In the first prompting phase the signalling frequency increased from zero to 3.

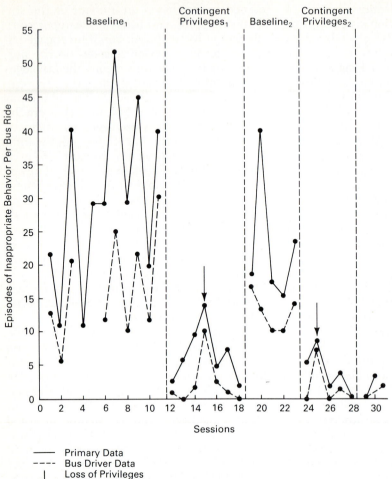

Figure 8.3 Episodes of Inappropriate Behavior During Rides on the School Bus as a Function of a Home-Based Reinforcement Contingency. The two points on the graph reflect follow-up data collected over a two week period.

Source: From "The comprehensive rehabilitation of a behavior problem child in his home and community" by A. T. Jackson, C. L. Salzberg, B. Pacholl, and D. S. Dorsey, 1981, *Education and Treatment of Children, 4*, p. 206. Reprinted by permission.

After Session 10 the rate increased to 7 to 8 responses per session as did the rate of smiling and vocalizing. Subsequent manipulations indicated that Marcus's rate was high during prompting and feedback but returned to the lower baseline level when this contingency was withdrawn. Thus, a causal relationship between the treatment and behavior change was demonstrated.

Issues and Limitations

As noted previously, the ABAB design fails to yield a convincing experimental analysis of behavior when a behavior change does not revert to baseline levels. As mentioned, behaviors which require direct instruction to be established are most likely to fall into this category. Other instances of nonreversibility are evident in the literature too. A change may fail to reverse because variables other than the original B have taken control of the behavior. This may be explained in several ways. First, a variable other than B may have occurred simultaneously with B, thereby, in fact, producing the change. For example, it is conceivable that on the days when token reinforcement contingencies are applied to a student's out-of-seat behavior, an art teaching period was begun which the student found particularly interesting and which caused him to remain seated. In this case, the art instruction is a confounding experimental variable. This may be confirmed by withdrawing and reintroducing the art lessons in an ABAB pattern and observing the effects on in-seat behavior. Second, the variable B may initially have produced the change but other environmental factors subsequently control the behavior (Kohler & Greenwood, 1986). We may here have increased a student's rate of social initiations to peers by using reinforcement contingencies (B), only to discover that his increased rate of initiations is being maintained by his peers' responses to these initiations. As a result, when B is withdrawn, the student's initiation rate with his peers does not return to baseline levels. In these cases, the design fails to yield an analysis or, rather, it demonstrates that we do not yet understand or have control of the variables necessary to achieve the intended results. Consequently, we must redesign the experiment and try again.

In the use of the ABAB design the length of each A or B phase (the number of sessions) is an important issue, as is the question of when to change from one phase to the next. Only rules of thumb apply here. The length of each phase should be determined by inspecting such factors as level change, variation in behavior, and trend. Manipulation of B phases should not occur until the A phase data are stable (that is, the data show a lack of variability and no trend) or until the A phase data show a trend but in the direction opposite to the anticipated effect of B. To decide that the baseline is stable, a minimum of three data points are required for a trend cannot be assessed with fewer that three data points.

If a trend is noted in the same direction as the anticipated effect of treatment, the decision to delay treatment is appropriate. If B is introduced when a trend is already present in the anticipated direction then, it will confound the effect of B. If, however, the trend is in the opposite direction, it is both appropriate and desirable to manipulate B. In this case, a powerful demonstration of the treatment will result if B is able to change the behavior in the opposite direction.

For many potential users of the ABAB design the withdrawal of treatment is viewed as inconvenient, illogical, or unethical. Thus, many teachers do not wish to remove a procedure which seems to be working in order to verify the validity of the treatment. Users of the design who do not appreciate the logic or importance of this type of analysis must select a different design. Some of these options will be discussed later in this chapter.

Another disadvantage of this design is that it may become lengthy if more than two treatment conditions are planned. For example, to analyze the separate effects of verbal prompts (B) and social praise (C) requires an ABAB-CBCB design. The standard design is used to demonstrate the effects of B. In order to look at C, B (verbal prompts) must become the baseline for C, social praise. And C is added to or used with verbal prompts. If the behavior is increased under the combined use of verbal prompts plus social praise (C), we have demonstrated the separate effects of both procedures. Two treatments in the design make for a lengthy process since a minimum of three sessions are required in each phase. Typically, more sessions occur as it often takes a given behavior time to stabilize at optimal levels under the various conditions.

Finally, order effects are not controlled in this design. For example, if we ran the same study in the reverse order, ACACBCBC, we do not know if we would get the same results unless we run both sequences.

MULTIPLE-BASELINE AND MULTIPLE-PROBE-DESIGNS

Definition

Multiple-baseline or multiple-probe designs depend on repeated replications of the treatment effect, A to B, across at least three simultaneously measured baselines at different points in time (Barlow & Hersen, 1984). They do not require a reversal phase to yield a causal analysis. Criteria for the multiple-baseline design include the following: (a) continuous measurement of a response in at least three baselines, (b) lagged introduction of treatment across baselines, (c) immediately observable effects when and where treatment is implemented, and (d) no observable effects in baselines not yet receiving treatment.

The zig-zag line in Figure 8.4 illustrates how the design operates. Treatment (B) is introduced in the first baseline (upper panel) while the other baselines remain under the baseline condition (A). Thus, an AB design occurs in the first baseline. As soon as visual inspection procedures indicate that a change in behavior has occurred, B is introduced into the second baseline while the third baseline remains under the A condition. When behavior change is observed in the second baseline, B is introduced into the third baseline. Thus, the full design is expressed as follows:

ABBB
AABB
AAAB

Across three baselines, introduction of treatment is delayed to provide three independent replications.

The multiple-probe design is a variation of the multiple-baseline design. Although the same criteria apply, the design requires fewer continuous measures or probes. Probes are sampled at least once at the beginning and once at the end of each A and B condition. This probe sequence allows a teacher to demonstrate that a behavior has not changed during the A phase but that change did occur immediately after treatment was introduced. Referring to Figure 8.4, the multi-probe variation would require measurement of the behavior on the first session across all three baselines. Continuous measurement would continue across sessions for the first baseline (top panel). However, the teacher would not measure frequency on Sessions 2 through 6 for the second baseline (middle panel) and on sessions 2 through 10 for the third baseline (bottom panel). Frequency would be measured again on Sessions 7 and 11, just prior to introducing treatment (B). The logic of this design assumes that the behavior is either occurring at stable frequency or not occurring at all (for example, when a target individual has not learned the behavior). After introduction of the treatment, measurement continues in the usual fashion.

Behaviors for Which Multiple-Baseline Designs Are Appropriate

All behaviors are appropriate for multiple-baseline action, including those influenced by contingencies, by academic instruction, or by task analysis, as well as behaviors in need of either acceleration or deceleration. Multiple-baseline design is probably the most frequently reported single-subject design. It is particularly appropriate for use by staff who do not wish to employ reversals and for behaviors which cannot be expected to reverse upon removal of treatment. However, for some problems and situations the design may not be appropriate. For example, for accelerating or decelerating a behavior according to certain criteria, the changing-criterion design may be more appropriate, for example, when a task analysis is used to establish new behavior. Also, the design may not be the best choice when it is undesirable to extend a

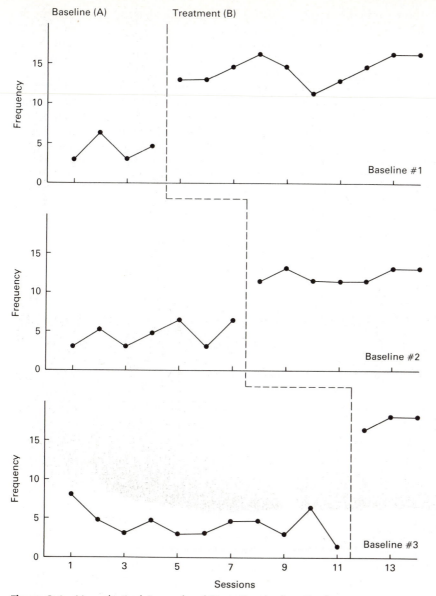

Figure 8.4 Hypothetical Example of Data Graphed to Conform to a Multiple-Baseline Design.

baseline or delay the onset of treatment, for example, when treating for the reduction of self-injurious or destructive behaviors.

A number of options are available for creating the baselines used in the multiple-baseline and multiple-probe designs, including those based on measurements across settings, tasks, responses, persons, and classes and groups. We now turn to examples of designs from each of these options. Each will be illustrated in both classroom and community settings for students with mild as well as severe handicaps.

Multiple-Baselines Across Settings

Classroom Examples. Hall, Cristler, Cranston, and Tucker (1970) used a multiple-baseline design across three settings—morning, noon, and afternoon recess in combination with a reversal design to study the effects of procedures design on reducing tardiness (see

Figure 8.5). Following baseline assessments of tardiness in each recess, the teacher used a chart to post the names of all students who were not tardy. The chart was then used in each of the remaining baselines. Tardiness declined simultaneously with introduction of the chart after each recess, providing a convincing demonstration of the effectiveness of the chart using a multiple-baseline approach. A subsequent withdrawal of the chart across all three baselines was accompanied by increased tardiness. Reapplication of the chart

Figure 8.5 A Record of the Number of Pupils Who Returned Late to Their Fifth-Grade Classroom After Noon, Morning, and Afternoon Recess.

Source: From "Teachers and parents as researchers using multiple baseline designs" by R. V. Hall, C. Cristler, S. S. Cranston, and B. Tucker, 1970, *Journal of Applied Behavior Analysis, 3,* p. 249. Copyright 1970 by the Society for the Experimental Analysis of Behavior, Inc.

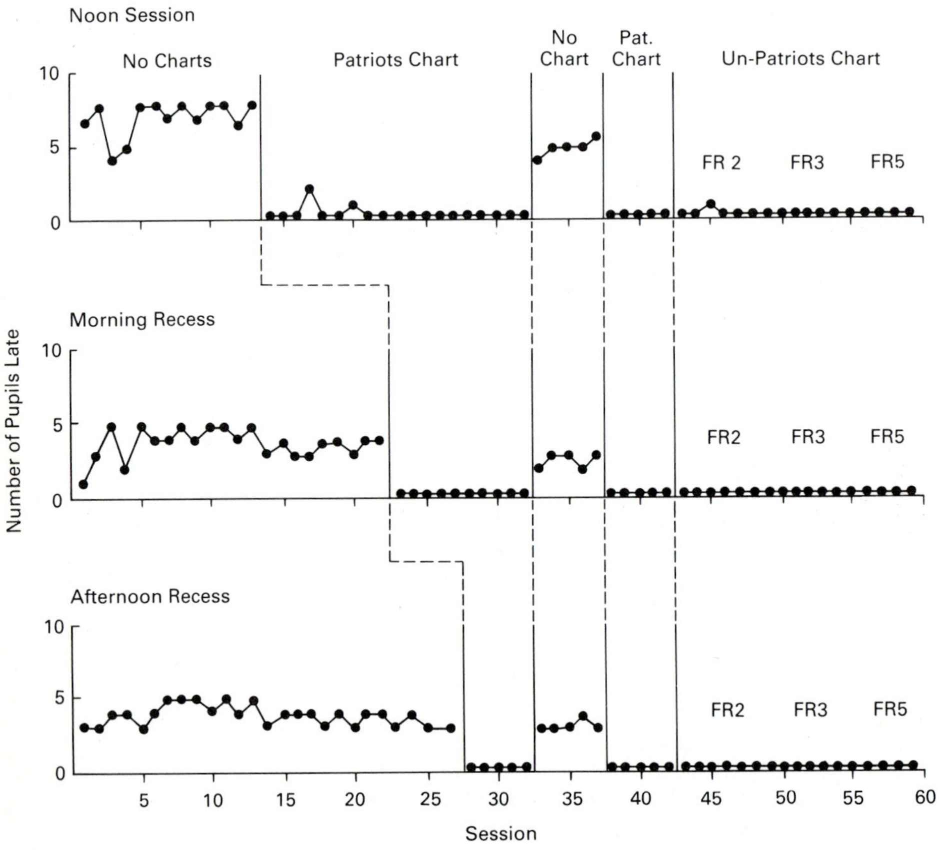

after each recess again reduced tardiness. In the last phase, posting only the names of students who were tardy was employed with positive results; however, this last procedure was not adequately analyzed using this design.

Odom, Hoyson, Jamieson, and Strain (1985) also used a multiple-baseline design across settings in combination with a reversal design to increase the social initiations of children in a mainstreamed preschool class. Baselines were established for the frequency of positive and negative social initiations during 5-minute samples in the three settings of structured play, table work, and learning center. The intervention was implemented by a nonhandicapped peer who was prompted by the teacher to initiate interactions between the target students and Gary, a handicapped peer. An introduction of the procedure increased Gary's positive social behavior only when applied to each setting. Subsequent withdrawal phases revealed that removal of teacher prompts to the nonhandicapped peer confederate reduced Gary's social behavior in all three settings. His initiations recovered when teacher prompts were reinstated.

Community Examples. Dachman, Halasz, Bickett, and Lutzker (1984) employed a multiple-baseline design across settings to evaluate the effects of parent training on a neglectful mother. The mother had been referred to a state agency because she left her son unattended. She had been laid off work and was receiving public aid. She expressed concern to her case worker that she might abuse her son due to his unruly behavior at home and her inability to manage him. In this study, the mother was trained to apply a systematic intervention to her 7-year-old son. Data were collected in the kitchen and living room of the family's trailer home. A counselor and one graduate student served as the therapist and the data collector.

Play, academic, or unstructured settings were created between the mother and son. During the play setting the mother was asked to engage in a preplanned activity with her son for 5 minutes. During the academic set-

tings, a 5 minute academic task was developed by the classroom teacher and used by mother and son. Finally, in the unstructured setting, the mother was asked to engage in any activity with her son as long as both remained in the kitchen or living room. Although several parent and student behaviors were assessed, only data on parent praise are presented in Figure 8.6.

During the baseline assessments, the mother's use of descriptive praise was essentially zero across all three settings. In fact, parent criticism ranged as high as 70 percent of the time. In Phase 1, the parent was taught to use descriptive praising skills prior to each 5-minute session. Then the mother was taught to obtain eye contact with her son, label the behavior being praised, and display enthusiasm while praising. She was then asked to give five praises to her son during the play session. After Phase 1 she received a count of her praises and corrective feedback from the trainers. In Phase 2, the mother was provided only with feedback on her use of praise, whereas in Phase 3 all feedback was withdrawn. Follow-up assessments were made two and six months after the formal end of training.

Results demonstrated that improvements in both descriptive and general praise occurred only when the Phase 1 procedures were introduced. This was true in all three settings, thereby providing a convincing demonstration of a causal relationship between training and the parent's use of praise. The removal of an actual count of behavior (Phase 2) and the removal of corrective feedback (Phase 3) produced only small, if any, decline in the use of praise. The maintenance probes at follow-up also showed a sustained use of praise, but with considerable reduction in the unstructured setting (see Figure 8.6).

Blew, Schwartz, and Luce (1985) used a multiple-baseline design across settings and responses to investigate nonhandicapped peers' ability to train elementary grade students with autism. Task analyses were made of three responses: buying an ice cream cone, checking out a book, and crossing an intersec-

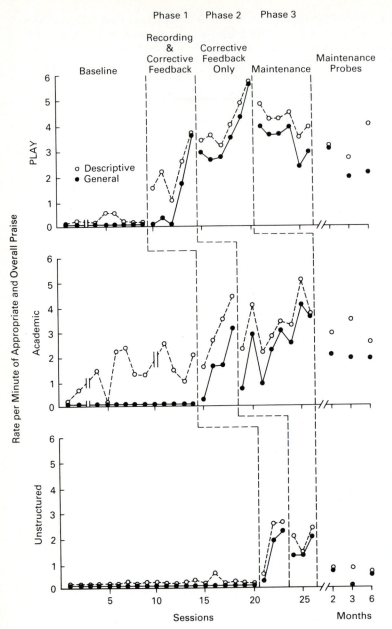

Figure 8.6 Rate of Appropriate and Overall Praise Statements Across Play, Academic, and Unstructured Settings.

Source: From "A home-based ecobehavioral parent-training and generalization package with a neglectful mother" by R. S. Dachman, M. M. Halasz, A. D. Bickett, and J. R. Lutzker, 1984, *Education and Treatment of Children, 7,* p. 190. Reprinted by permission.

tion. And measures were taken on the percentage of steps independently made to carry out these behaviors in a restaurant, at the library, and at an intersection, respectively.

Several procedures were implemented, including peer modeling of the desired responses and training of the tutor prior to tutoring the target student. The procedures were implemented first in the restaurant setting, then at the library, and lastly, in the intersection. In each setting, peer modeling had only limited effects, whereas peer tutoring was clearly the most effective, although some delay was noted in acquiring the street-crossing skill in the intersection setting.

Multiple-baseline Designs Across Situations

Classroom Examples. Murph and McCormick (1985) employed a multiple-baseline design across situations, where situations were defined as groups or sets of road signs each containing three signs. Subjects were five male offenders from 16 to 18 years old, residing at a state correctional facility. Their average reading grade level was 2.5, with a range

from 1.5 to 3.1. The study was conducted in a high school classroom by the teacher. During baseline, students were presented with simulated road signs and asked to read them. Whenever a correct response was given, a plus was recorded next to the sign, otherwise a minus was recorded. During the treatment phase, modeling and instructions were used to teach sight recognition of the words on each sign and what to do when encountering such a sign.

Figure 8.7 presents a multiple-baseline design analysis for one of the students. During the baseline phase this student did not respond correctly to any sign in any of the three sets. When instruction was provided on Session 6 for Set 1 signs, Student 1 responded correctly to all three. However, in the session with Set 2 and Set 3 signs, no improvement

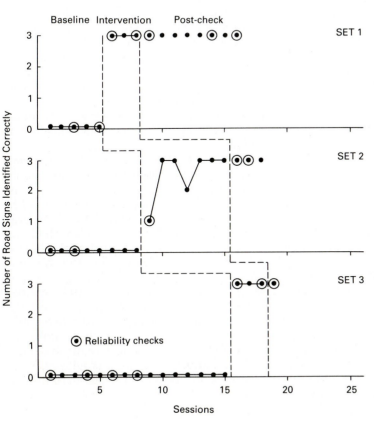

Figure 8.7 Number of Correct Response to Sets of Signs by Student 1.

Source: From "Evaluation of an instructional program designed to teach minimally literate juvenile delinquents to read road signs" by D. Murphy and S. McCormick, 1985, *Education and Treatment of Children, 8*, p. 143. Reprinted by permission.

was noted when instruction was not provided. Improvement for Set 2 signs was observed only when instruction was provided in Session 9. Similarly, improvement was noted for Set 3 signs only when instruction was provided beginning with Session 16. The multiple-baseline design provided the investigators with the information they needed to determine that a causal relationship existed and that this relationship was confirmed by changes occurring coincidentally with introduction of the treatment—in this case across groups of signs to be learned. The causal status of treatment was supported by the three independent replications, all for the same student.

Pancsofar and Bates (1985) used the multiple-baseline design across situations in order to study the effects of instruction on pulling, lifting, and pushing operations associated with handwashing equipment in a school lavatory. A survey of soap dispensing devices in 66 fast-food restaurants in five communities was used to develop a task analysis of responses that pertained to all devices in this group. The devices varied by size, shape, color, location, and procedures for activating them. Lifting, pulling, or pushing were required to use the dispensers.

Soap dispensers that represented all procedures for activation (situations) were then placed in two lavatories in a public school. Four students ranging in age from 9 to 18 years old with multiple handicaps participated. Baselines consisted of the number of machines used independently for the three machines sets (situations)—those requiring lifting, pulling, and pushing responses. Separate baselines where taken in both instructional and generalization (noninstructional) bathrooms that contained identical dispensers.

Prompts and contingent reinforcement were effective in establishing independent use of each type of soap dispenser when applied to each baseline. Generalization to similar dispensers (for example, those requiring pulling responses) was noted to occur after in-

struction was provided on both dispensers requiring the same response.

Examples from the community. Peterson (1984) used a multiple-probe design to examine the effectiveness of training on tasks frequently confronted by "latch key" children. Subjects were normal children left unattended for periods of time during the day when their parents worked. The parents were unable to provide sitters or other forms of childcare. Probes were established across three situations: dealing with emergencies, performing daily habits, and dealing with strangers. The data in Figure 8.8 represent the children's ability to correctly roleplay procedures when confronted with one of these situations.

Examples of specific tasks during emergencies included what to do in case of a fire, a cut, or a tornado. As illustrated, training immediately increased the children's skills with specific tasks. Probes were made at least at the beginning and the end of each baseline to meet the minimum requirement for adequate analysis. In some instances, target behaviors may be difficult to record across treatment sessions, and consequently the behavior is probed during treatment conditions similar to procedures described above relative to baseline.

Riordan, Iwata, Wohl, and Finney (1980) used a multiple-baseline to validate procedures used to increase eating and decrease food refusal and selectivity in a 6-year-old female inpatient at the John F. Kennedy Institute Hospital in Baltimore. This child was moderately mentally retarded and exhibited echolalic speech. This was her fourth admission due to weight loss. Although she possessed self-feeding skills, she exhibited a persistently low and selective food intake. Her body weight and height was five percentiles below children her age. The study took place in the child's dining room. Two meals per day, each 20 minutes long, were employed. Meals consisted of food from the standard hospital menu.

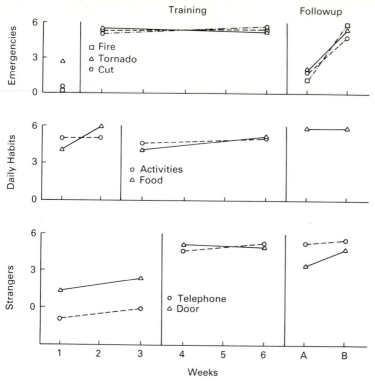

Figure 8.8. Mean Number of Points (maximum = 6) Earned by Subjects in Group 1 in Response to Questions Asked in the Weeks Before and After Training and At One Year Follow-up.

Source: From "The 'safe at home' game: Training comprehensive prevention skills in latchkey children" by L. Peterson, 1984, *Behavior Modification, 8,* p. 486. Reprinted by permission of Sage Publications, Inc.

The multiple-baseline design was created across tasks defined by three food groups: vegetables, meat, and fruit. Results are displayed in Figure 8.9. The graph displays the number of bites and sips taken during each meal (left ordinate) along with the number of grams consumed (right ordinate). During baseline, hardly any chewing or consumption of food was evident across the three food groups. The first intervention was applied to the vegetables baseline. During this condition, when the child took a bite or sipped a vegetable item she was praised by the therapist and immediately given a bite of one of her preferred food items. During subsequent meals, the number of bites of nonpreferred foods required before she was given reinforcement was increased from one to two bites. The second condition consisted of rein-forcement of bites and sips plus swallows. The criterion for reinforcement was increased to three responses before she was given reinforcement. At this point, the bites and sips plus swallow contingency was introduced into the meat baseline. Eleven sessions later it was introduced into the fruit baseline.

This design enabled the experimenters to establish food consumption in the first phase and then increase the response requirement for reinforcement in the following phase. This approach resulted in developing a suitable procedure within the vegetable baseline that was subsequently replicated across the meat and fruit baselines. As in the prior studies, a causal relationship was demonstrated since the change in the patient's eating behavior occurred only after the onset of treatment in each baseline.

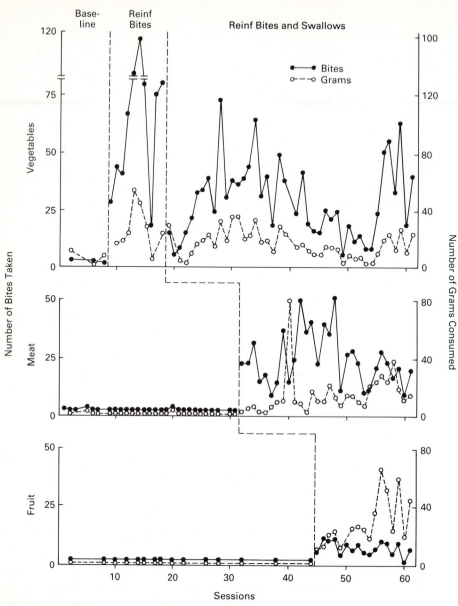

Figure 8.9   Number of Bites Taken (Scaled on the Left) and Grams Consumed (Scaled on the Right) by Amy from Each Food Group Across Experimental Conditions.

Source: From "Behavioral treatment of food refusal and selectivity in developmentally disabled children" by M. M. Riordan, B. A. Iwata, M. K. Wohl, and J. Finney, 1980, *Applied Research in Mental Retardation, 1,* p. 105. Reprinted with permission of Pergamon Press, Ltd.

Examples with Multiple Baselines Across Responses

Classroom Examples. Luiselli, Myles, and Littmann-Quinn (1983) used a multiple-baseline design across both responses and settings in examining the effects of procedures designed to reduce aggressive behavior and the destruction of property. The student was a 15-year-old male diagnosed as having maternal rubella syndrome. He had severe to profound sensorineural hearing loss bilaterally. He possessed partial vision and communicated with one-word and short-phrase sign language. The boy resided in a residential facility for individuals with vision and hearing impairments. The study took place during classroom instruction and in the cottage living unit.

Two behaviors were defined and measured in both settings: aggression, which included punching, slapping, scratching, and head-butting; and destruction, which included ripping, crushing, and breaking objects. At times staff members had to restrain the student since his outbursts were so violent. Some staff members refused to interact with him. Data for aggression and destruction were graphed both for the classroom and for the cottage settings.

The purpose of the study was to compare the effects of reinforcement alone versus reinforcement plus time-out. When reinforcement alone was used, behaviors other than aggression or destruction were reinforced. Tokens (in the classroom) or time intervals without problem behaviors (in the cottage) were exchanged for edibles and privileges. During the reinforcement plus time-out phase, a time-out procedure was added, contingent on the occurrence of either target behavior. Each time aggression or destruction occurred, the student was placed in a time-out room for a 3-minute period.

Reinforcement, introduced in the classroom simultaneously across both behaviors, produced some decrement in both target behaviors. When introduced for both behaviors in the cottage, however, reinforcement was less effective. To this point a multiple-baseline design across settings was utilized. The time-out contingency was applied to each behavior, one at a time. Thus, in the classroom, aggression dropped to near zero following introduction of time-out, while destruction in the same setting remained relatively unchanged. Introduction of time-out for destruction in the classroom several sessions later had a similar decreasing effect. Time-out was then added simultaneously to both behaviors in the cottage with a similar suppressive effect. Follow-up assessments showed no occurrences of the target behaviors when just the time-out contingency was in effect.

The design may suffer from a problem related to the delayed onset of assessments in the cottage. Measurement did not begin in the cottage until 30 measurements had been taken in the classroom. Thus, without assessments during this period, we cannot be assured that treatments in the classroom or any other rival treatment factors may not have exerted some positive effects on the cottage behaviors earlier in the experiment, yet it appears unlikely in this case since the cottage baselines are high and variable. But the lack of probes at the beginning of the phase reduces the design's ability to provide a convincing analysis.

Examples from the Community. Christophersen, Arnold, Hill, and Quilitch (1972) analyzed the effects of token "fines" contingent on three behaviors in a home setting. The 8-year-old subject had mild cerebral palsy and attended a class for students with educable mental retardation. Multiple-baselines were established for bickering, inappropriate behavior at bedtime, and teasing (see Figure 8.10). Intervention involved assessing the boy a 10 point fine when he engaged in inappropriate behavior. Fines were first made contingent on bickering. After bickering had declined and stabilized, the same contingency was applied to inappropriate behavior at bedtime, and subsequently to teasing. In each case, the problem behavior declined when the procedure was applied.

Schleien and Larson (1986) used a multi-

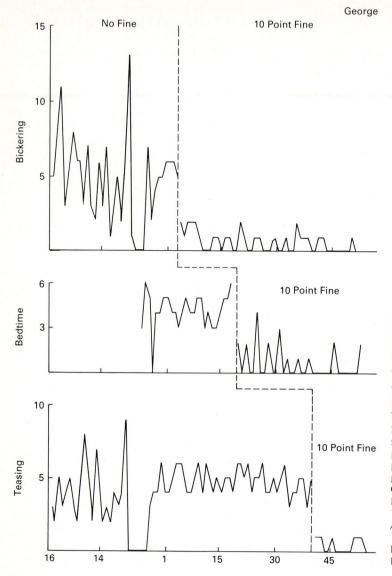

Figure 8.10 Multiple-Baseline Analysis of the Effects of Introducing Point Fines on Antisocial Behaviors of a 9-Year-Old Boy. The arrows indicate when the point system was instituted for maintenance behaviors.

Source: From ''The home point system: Token reinforcement procedures for application by parents of children with behavior problems'' by E. R. Christophersen, C. M. Arnold, D. W. Hill, and H. R. Quilitch, 1972, *Journal of Applied Behavior Analysis, 5,* p. 490. Copyright 1972 by the Society for the Experimental Analysis of Behavior, Inc.

ple-baseline across behaviors designed to assess the effects of a leisure-choice training procedure. Two participants with severe mental retardation attended a program at a community recreation center to learn skills associated with a recreation center. Skills included (a) playing fooseball, a paddleball game, (b) choosing an activity and engaging in it, and (c) walking to and from the community center. Each skill was task analyzed into its constitutent behaviors. Skills consisted of 21, 13, and 13 steps, respectively. The percentage completion of each of these steps served as the dependent measure for each.

Training consisted of two sessions followed by an assessment probe. Instruction with error correction was employed. Specifically, for each step in each skill sequence, a verbal cue was given and the number of steps performed independently was recorded. Each participant received a verbal cue for the step being taught (for example, "Charles, release the ball on to the table.") and was socially reinforced for a correct response. If the response was not performed, the cue was given again and the experimenter demonstrated the response. If the response was still not forthcoming, the experimenter repeated the cue and physically assisted the participant in making the response. Whenever the participant made the correct response, he was socially reinforced. Instruction continued until each participant could make three consecutive independent responses at each step.

Instruction was first introduced for playing fooseball, then for choosing leisure activities, and, lastly, for walking to and from the recreation center. For playing fooseball and walking, an immediate impact was observed on the percent of steps performed independently. Leisure-choice instruction was immediately effective for Charles but somewhat less effective for Lawrence through Session 14. Afterward, both participants rapidly progressed to 100 percent on this skill. Generalization and maintenance probes demonstrated that the skills were used at high levels at one, two, three, and seven months following initial training.

Multiple-Baseline Design Across Persons

Classroom Examples. Perkins and Cullinan (1984) used a multiple-baseline design across students to examine the effects of a direct instruction intervention on fraction skills. Unlike the prior designs in which intrasubject comparisons were made across settings or tasks, in this design intersubject comparisons are made. The subjects were three third graders, two girls and a boy, who could not solve fractions. Daily probe tests were administered covering the content to be taught

by the intervention. The rate of correct and incorrect problem solving served as the dependent measure. No direct teaching of fractions occurred during baseline. The intervention consisted of a set of lessons each with several exercises. Lessons included review of earlier skills and were rapidly paced to prevent boredom. Individual responses consisted of both written and oral forms which were followed by teacher feedback. Progress was individualized by allowing students either to repeat or skip exercises as needed.

The results are illustrated in Figure 8.11. At baseline, all three students produced substantially more incorrect than correct problem solutions per minute. When instruction was provided to Student 1, the rate of errors declined and the rate of correct solutions showed an increasing trend. The same effect was noted for Student 2 five days later when the fractions program was introduced—errors declined and correct solutions increased. A third replication occurred when the program was introduced five days later to Student 3. An additional feature of this design was the return to baseline following fractions instruction, first for Student 1 and five days later for Student 2. On these days, the students received no instruction. In both cases, the rates of correct and error solutions were unchanged, that is, they did not revert to baseline levels. A follow-up assessment was made six days after the end of the study for all three students while no instruction was given. All three students were found to clearly maintain their improved levels of fraction-solving skills.

This example demonstrates how the multiple-baseline design can complete an analysis when a behavior may not be reversible (that is, Student 1 at Baseline 2). Had the ABAB design been employed with just one student, it would have failed. However, the independent and successful replications provided by Students 2 and 3 provide a complete analysis of behavior. Yet, we do not know why the performance of Student 1 and Student 2 was maintained. One explanation is that although instruction was casual in establishing correct performance, other factors (for example, so-

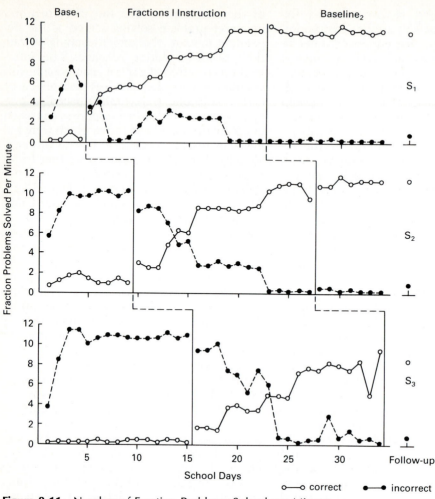

Figure 8.11 Number of Fraction Problems Solved per Minute.

Source: From "Effects of direct instruction intervention for fraction skills" by V. Perkins and D. Cullinan, 1984, *Education and Treatment of Children, 7,* p. 115. Reprinted by permission.

cial contingencies) may have subsequently influenced the use of these skills. As noted earlier, nonreversibility is often related to academic behaviors; therefore, the ABAB design should be used with behaviors only after careful consideration.

Barton and Barton (1985) used a multiple-baseline design to study the effects of treatment for rumination. The students were enrolled in public schools where they received instruction with nonhandicapped students.

The classroom staff used an event-recording procedure to record the number of ruminative responses for each student per day.

Treatment consisted of giving the students 2 to 4 tablespoons of creamy peanut butter upon their arrival at school. Every 2 to 3 hours thereafter for the remainder of the school day the peanut butter was again given. The rationale for using peanut butter was that it is difficult to ruminate and that the effect required to do so would be sufficiently larger than the value of the ruminating behavior to the student. In addition, fluids were reduced to one-half their normal level during meals. The balance of the fluids was provided at other times during the day so that only the distribution of fluids, not their total amount, was manipulated. Because of possible health implications the procedure was monitored by a physician.

Following a reduction in rumination for each student, the frequency and amounts of peanut butter were gradually reduced. Therefore, the ruminative response was totally suppressed. In the case of Student 1, a brief return to baseline occurred and the procedure was reintroduced. Follow-up assessments in the absence of treatment were conducted for all four students. The data indicated zero or near-zero levels of rumination.

Examples from the Community. Rolider and Van Houten (1986) used the same design to validate procedures for reducing bedwetting at home with four children between the ages of 4 and 6 years. The children had continuous histories of bedwetting and in each case the family physician had ruled out medical causes. The number of nights each child had wet the bed was systematically measured. That is, each morning a parent checked the bed linen and the child's clothing to determine whether or not he or she had wet the bed. If the parents could see a wet spot larger than a quarter (a twenty-five cent piece) an instance of bedwetting was scored. Following the baseline phase, a thorough awakening procedure with a nonconsecutive fading criterion was introduced. Parents were instructed to awaken their child 5 hours before the normal awakening time, requiring the child to answer several questions to assure he or she was awake. The child then had to walk to the bathroom where pajama bottoms were lowered and he or she was placed on the toilet. The parent then turned on the sink tap and let the water run as a prompt for urination, while waiting for the child to urinate.

Added to this awakening procedure was a criterion for its removal. For two of the children, the wake-up time was delayed 1 hour when the child had been dry for six nights. This was labeled a *nonconsecutive criterion.* For two other children a *consecutive criterion* was used, which required six days in a row for the awakening to be delayed by 1 hour. A follow-up assessment was made at three, five and eight weeks after termination of the experiment and the procedure.

The results are displayed in Figure 8.12. The treatment was implemented in delayed fashion across Child 1 and Child 2, and simultaneously for Child 3 and Child 4. In each case, the number of bedwetting events declined only with onset of the treatment. No advantage seemed to be offered by consecutive versus nonconsecutive fading of the procedure. Thus, the authors recommended the nonconsecutive procedure since it can be completed faster. Follow-up sessions indicated that no incidence of bedwetting occurred up to eight weeks later.

Breen, Haring, Pitts-Conway, and Gaylord-Ross (1985) used a multiple-baseline design across students in a community work setting. Four students with severe handicaps and autism were trained through a 13-step task analysis of coffee making and initiating social interaction with workers who were on break from work in a retirement complex. A breakdown located at the center of the complex was used by all workers. The percentage of correctly implemented task-analysis steps served as the dependent measure.

Instruction was introduced in a time-lagged fashion to each of the four students after stable performances were noted. Don and Earl were taught to emit the target social behaviors with two or three workers until they achieved generalization to all workers. In each case, the student's performance changed contingent upon introduction of training.

Multiple-Baselines Designs Across Groups or Classes

Classroom Examples. Greenwood, Hops, Delquadri, & Guild (1974) employed a multi-

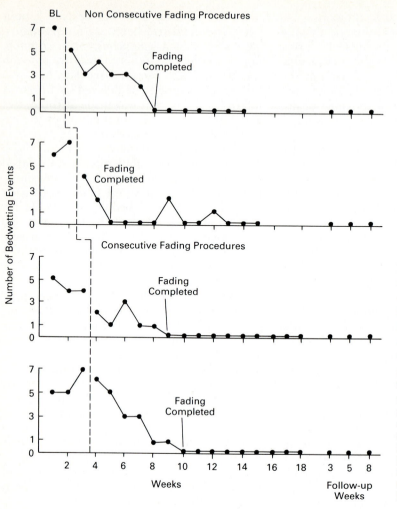

Figure 8.12 The Number of Nights Each Child Wet His or Her Bed During Each Week of the Experiment. The arrows mark when the awakening procedure was completely faded.

Source: From "Effects of degree of awakening and the criterion for advancing awakening on the treatment of bedwetting" by A. Rolider and R. Van Houten, 1986, *Education and Treatment of Children, 9*, p. 139. Reprinted by permission.

ple-baseline design across classes to investigate the effects of rules, rules plus feedback, and rules plus feedback with positive reinforcement on a consolidated measure of classroom appropriate behavior. Three elementary teachers interested in group behavior management techniques and their first, second, and third grade classes participated. A clock-light device was used to record the amount of time all students in the class were either engaged or not engaged in appropriate behaviors. When all students were engaged in appropriate behavior, the teacher activated the clock-light to record duration. When at last one student was not engaged in appropriate behavior, the teacher turned off the clock-light. By dividing the total duration on the clock by the length of the session, a percentage of appropriate behavior baseline was generated and graphed (see Figure 8.13).

Results across classrooms showed that rules alone were ineffective. Rules plus feedback produced some improvement in two of the three classrooms. In all three classrooms the three procedures combined produced strong effects by increasing appropriate be-

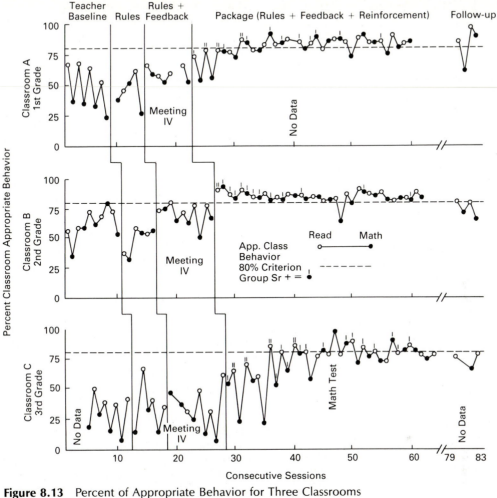

Figure 8.13 Percent of Appropriate Behavior for Three Classrooms Over Experimental Stimulus Conditions (Reading and Math).

Source: From "Group contingencies for group consequences: A further analysis" by C. R. Greenwood, H. Hops, J. Delquadri, and J. J. Guild, 1974, *Journal of Applied Behavior Analysis, 7,* p. 420. Copyright 1974 by the Society for the Experimental Analysis of Behavior, Inc.

havior to 80 percent or above. These effects were maintained in a later follow-up phase with all treatment removed.

Reid et al. (1985) used a multiple-probe design across classrooms to investigate the effects of training teachers to increase the time students with severe handicaps spent engaged in functional educational tasks. Tasks were defined as materials or activities that were either encountered in the students' non-classroom living situation or used by non-handicapped children of the same age group in a nonclassroom setting. Observations were conducted in three classrooms serving 19 students. Each student in each classroom was observed for 40 seconds using a rotational sampling system. The class mean was graphed for each session in each classroom. Baseline data consisted of observations made prior to teacher training.

Teacher training consisted of several components arranged into a single instructional session and several classroom supervision visits by the school principal. The supervision visits provided instructions and feedback. Finally, the last phase of training consisted of follow-up assessments during which the principal continued to make intermittent classroom visits.

Results showed increases in the percentage of on-task intervals during which functional educational tasks occurred after the introduction of teacher training and supervision in each classroom. These results were maintained into the follow-up phase.

Examples from the Community. Barone, Greene, and Lutzker (1986) used a multiple-baseline design across families to evaluate a home safety program for abused and neglected children. Baselines were established for the number of hazardous items observed in the homes of three separate families during repeated home safety checks (see Figure 8.14).

Intervention consisted of an audio-slide show, self-feedback stickers, a home safety review manual, and home safety accessories. These items were designed to cover problems related to poisoning, suffocation, fire, electrical hazards, and firearms. Results indicated that each family dramatically reduced the number of hazards present in the home relative to baseline but only after the program was implemented by each family.

Issues and Limitations

The multiple-baseline design is appropriate for most behaviors including those not expected to reverse when treatment is withdrawn. The design does not depend on a reversal phase. The design is highly flexible and can be efficiently applied to a wide range of problems and situations. The popularity of the design is illustrated by its widespread representation in the literature.

The nature of the design creates a first requirement that treatment be withheld from some baselines until effects have been observed in baselines where treatment has been introduced. Thus, the logic of the design forbids simultaneous introduction of treatment across all baselines. The benefit of this restriction lies in the resulting experimental analysis of behavior. However, in some baselines this restriction may lead to extended delays in treatment, thereby creating an opportunity for students to repeatedly practice inappropriate behaviors. In some cases, the multiple-probe design can be used to reduce the number of baseline sessions held prior to the onset of treatment.

A second design requirement relates to independence of baselines. If effects appear in baselines not being treated, they may compromise the design, particularly if the effects are large. In such instances, variables other than the treatment may be operating.

A third requirement of the design stipulates that effects on behaviors must occur at the same time as there must be a temporal correlation between the treatment and its behavioral effect. The extent to which a delay in effect is noted (that is, the numbers of sessions without results) increases one's skepticism about the causal status of treatment.

According to a fourth requirement, the same treatment (B) must be introduced across the multiple baselines for the purpose of producing replication of effects by the "same" treatment. The extent to which the B varies in quality, fidelity, or quantity across baselines compromises the analysis of behavior.

Changing Criterion Design

Definition. Another variant of the multiple-baseline design, the changing criterion design, is often seen in the two following forms: (a) a single behavior in which criterion steps are incrementally set and achieved (Hartmann & Hall, 1976), or (b) several different performance steps within a task analysis for which a single high criterion is set (for exam-

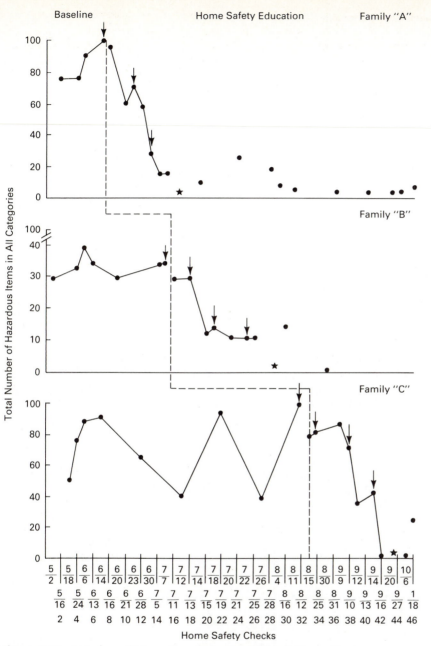

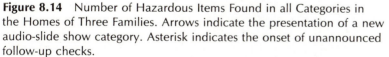

Figure 8.14 Number of Hazardous Items Found in all Categories in the Homes of Three Families. Arrows indicate the presentation of a new audio-slide show category. Asterisk indicates the onset of unannounced follow-up checks.

Source: From "Home safety with families being treated for child abuse and neglect" by V. J. Barone, B. F. Greene, and J. R. Lutzker, 1986, *Behavior Modification, 10,* p. 105. Reprinted by permission of Sage Publications, Inc.

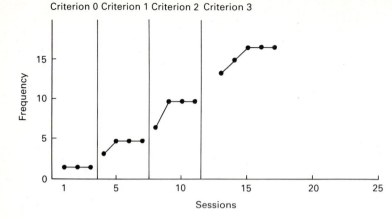

Criterion 0 Criterion 1 Criterion 2 Criterion 3

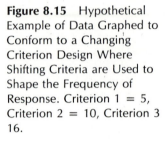

Figure 8.15 Hypothetical Example of Data Graphed to Conform to a Changing Criterion Design Where Shifting Criteria are Used to Shape the Frequency of Response. Criterion 1 = 5, Criterion 2 = 10, Criterion 3 16.

ple, 100 percent correct). These two forms are illustrated in Figures 8.15 and 8.16.

These designs produce replications of effects when treatment is repeatedly applied to changes in criterion levels or task steps. In the first design, the frequency of a response is increased to a criterion level of 5 per minute within a token reinforcement procedure (see Figure 8.15). The data reveal that the behavior has increased and stabilized at the established criterion. After Session 7, it is seen that 10 responses per minute are required for reinforcement. Again, the data demonstrate that the rate has increased and stabilized at criterion level. This effect is replicated a third time with the criterion increased to 16 responses per minute. The noted behavior changes show covariance directly with increments in the criterion, thereby producing a functional analysis (Hartmann & Hall, 1976).

The same logic applies to the design in Figure 8.16. However, hierarchical steps in a task

Figure 8.16 Hypothetical Example of Data Graphed to Conform to a Changing Criterion Design Where Stpes in a 3-step Task Analysis Are Each Mastered to 100% Criterion.

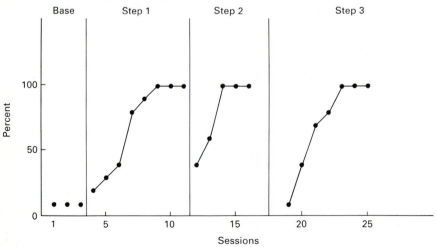

analysis are here taught to a uniform 100 percent criterion level. At Step 1 a chain of behaviors is taught to mastery followed by the training of progressively more complex chains of behavior at Steps 2 and 3. Since a number of successful replications are demonstrated when instruction is applied to each step, a functional analysis is produced.

Behaviors for Which the Changing Criterion Design Is Appropriate. The changing criterion design is most suited for behaviors that require intervention approaches such as academic instruction, shaping, and task analysis (Hartmann & Hall, 1976; Horner, 1971) or for problems that necessitate the establishment of new behavior. In addition, behavior problems that occur at high rates are also appropriately handled by this design when a gradual reduction in behaviors is desired. In special education, behaviors that have absolute zero baseline levels are often appropriate for this design.

Examples from School or Classroom Settings. Partington, Sundberg, Iwata, and Mountjoy (1979) used the changing criterion design to evaluate the effects of a time-telling instructional procedure for both nonhandicapped students (three students) and students with multiple handicaps (two students). Students of widely different levels of functioning were purposely selected to test the effectiveness of the procedures. All students were able to name the written numbers 1 through 12 and to count from 1 to 30. Subjects were taught on an individual basis at a center for children with multiple handicaps or at home.

A task analysis of time-telling produced an instructional program consisting of nine steps or phases with probe sessions between phases and a final generalization phase. During baseline, in the absence of instruction, none of the students made any correct responses. Whenever a probe was lower than a criterion then a remediation phase was conducted. Otherwise, the students were trained on the next step in the task analysis. The results indicated that four of the five children completed

the program. One student (Linda) dropped out of the program when her educational placement changed.

Causality is demonstrated to the degree that performance equaled changes in the criterion. In only three instances did performance fall below the criterion. One of the advantages of this design is that instruction can be focused on small steps, thereby keeping students' error rates at each step low.

Bennett and Ling (1972) used the changing criterion design in combination with a reversal design to investigate the effectiveness of training procedures designed to establish the use of two specific verbal responses—"the" and "is"—with a 3-year-old girl with hearing impairment. One-on-one training sessions were conducted in which trials were presented by the experimenter. A 14-step task analysis was used with probes at the end of each step. The reversal occurred during Steps 8 to 10, when the girl was trained not to use the two verbal responses. Assessments were made on Probes 6 and 7. Retraining took place after Step 10.

Examples from Community Settings. Gardner, Cole, Berry, and Nowinski (1983) evaluated the effects of a self-management intervention package utilizing self-monitoring, self-evaluation, and self-consequences on the levels of disruptive behavior of two adults with mental retardation. The experiment took place in a vocational training program at a residential facility. The design combined reversal and changing criterion procedures (see Figure 8.17).

Self-management phases were separated by baseline conditions in which self-management was not used. Results indicated that self-management with systematic decreases in the criterion for inappropriate verbal behavior systematically reduced disruptive behavior. Reversal phases led to increases in the target behavior.

Horner (1971) used the changing criterion design (both changing criteria steps and withdrawal of reinforcement) to analyze the effects of training on the use of parallel bars

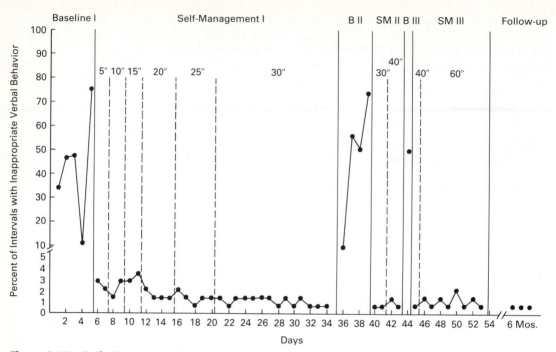

Figure 8.17   Daily Percentage of Intervals with Inappropriate Verbal Behavior During Baseline, Intervention, and Follow-Up Phases for Roger.

Source: From "Reduction of disruptive behaviors in mentally retarded adults" by W. I. Gardner, C. L. Cole, D. L. Berry, and J. M. Nowinski, 1983, *Behavior Modification, 7,* p. 89. Reprinted by permission of Sage Publications, Inc.

and crutches by a 5-year-old male with mental retardation and spina bifida. The student had extensive paralysis of the lower extremities and attempts by a physical therapist to engage him in gait training on parallel bars and crutches had failed. A task analysis of the use of parallel bars resulted in baseline plus six steps. Each step assumed completion of the prior step plus an incrementally more difficult response. For example, Step 0 consisted of

sitting on a stool and gripping the left parallel bar with the left hand and right bar with the right hand in order to receive reinforcement. Step 1 included Step 0 plus pulling to a standing position long enough to consume one tablespoon of root beer . . . Step 5 consisted of 10 walking steps using

the bars for support before being reinforced. (Horner, 1971, p. 18)

The analysis is illustrated in Figure 8.18.

The criterion for advancing in the program was a minimum of 23 successful trials for three consecutive sessions. The student reached criterion and advanced through Steps 1 through 3 rather quickly. On Steps 4 and 5, however, he required two to three times longer to reach the criterion. Following Step 5, reinforcement was withdrawn whereupon performance dropped to zero. Reinstatement of reinforcement resulted in the Step 5 criterion being met immediately for three sessions, suggesting that reinforcement was an essential component in maintaining performance at least within Step 5.

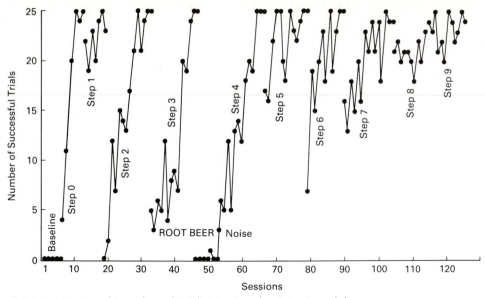

Figure 8.18 Actual Number of Trials Meeting the Criterion of the Appropriate Step Within the Successive Approximation Sequence Establishing Use of Parallel Bars Over Baseline, Acquisition, Extinction, and Reacquisition Conditions.

Source: From "Establishing the use of crutches by a mentally retarded spina bifida child" by R. D. Horner, 1971, *Journal of Applied Behavior Analysis, 4,* p. 186. Copyright 1971 by the Society for the Experimental Analysis of Behavior, Inc.

Issues and Limitations. The changing criterion design assumes immediacy of effects and application of the same treatment procedure to each criterion level or step in the design. Although they may be employed, reversals are not required, and only a single behavior or baseline needs to be recorded.

The length of baseline and treatment phases is a primary issue in this design. That is, phases must be long enough to insure that a behavior has stabilized at the new criterion level and that other variables are not simultaneously operating to support the change. For example, if it were observed that the subject continued to improve rather than maintain performance at the criterion level, which typically occurs, a confounding variable should be suspected. One of the most important outcomes that is expected with the changing cri-

terion design is that the individual performs at the criterion, not above it or below it, to demonstrate a causal relationship. It is also wise to vary the length of each phase to insure that criterion manipulations are unpredictable and cannot be anticipated by the subject(s). For example, the criteria may be adjusted upward in a systematic fashion for three to five successive levels. Then, the criterion could be reduced to a previous level to demonstrate that the individual's performance is under the changing criterion.

Another issue relates to the use of incremental steps. Increments should be based on the general principles of shaping; that is, steps should be small, yet large enough to provide a convincing demonstration of a treatment effect. In a design based on criterion changing, this decision should be based upon performance at the prior step. Thus, step sizes are based upon what the subject can do at that particular time. In a design in which steps are based on a more complex task step or a chain of behavior, the change from one step to another must be small and based on the principle of successive approximation. If the new requirement is too large, the subject will have difficulty meeting the initial step, as evidenced by an inordinately large number of training sessions at a given step. This observation may explain the increased number of sessions required for the subject in the Horner (1971) study to achieve Steps 4 and 5. If Step 5 had been set at seven walking steps rather than 10, fewer sessions would have been needed.

Another consideration involves the minimum number of criterion changes required to yield an adequate behavior analysis. At least three changes are necessary; however, most studies employ more if only to program the many small steps that are required to establish the terminal performance and meet the original training objective.

The efficiency of the changing criterion design is limited somewhat as typically only one treatment is analyzed in a single study. Therefore, alternative treatments are rarely compared within the same design, although several of the examples presented here included a reversal phase (for example, Gardner et al., 1983; Horner, 1971). The number of treatments that can be included in any one design is limited by the number of criterion changes in each treatment condition.

Alternating Treatments Design

Definition. An alternating treatments design is primarily used to compare the relative effectiveness of two or more treatments on the behavior of a single subject (Barlow & Hays, 1979). The design, also referred to as the *multi-element* (Sulzer-Asaroff & Mayer, 1977) and the *simultaneous-treatment design* (Kazdin & Hartmann, 1978), usually contains three phases: baseline, alternating treatments, and replication of the best treatment.

Like the ABAB design, alternation between conditions is essential. However, rather than manipulating a treatment and continuing it long enough for the target behavior to stabilize, as in the ABAB or AB steps in the multiple-baseline design, manipulations in the alternating treatment design occur as frequently as every other session using an unpredictable and often random schedule.

The logic of the design rests upon the ability of different treatments presented in random order to generate differential levels of performance over time. Graphing of the data is somewhat different from that of previously discussed designs. Rather than connecting data from session to session, only sessions under the same treatment condition are connected. These connected points are called elements (see Figure 8.19).

Graphing of data in this way separates a single baseline into two parts which reflect the subject's performance under two specific treatment conditions. In the last phase, the best treatment is applied to all sessions. Replication is evident to the extent that the most effective treatment is applied to both elements in the last phase compared to being applied to a single element in the alternating phase.

Behaviors for Which the Alternating Treatments Designs Is Appropriate. The design is most used with behaviors that do not require shaping to become established (for example, baseline levels greater than zero). Furthermore, it requires that subjects can easily discriminate or switch performance between treatments (Sindelar et al., 1985). For example, behaviors that can be changed by differential exposure to certain instructional procedures can be easily compared using the alternating treatments design. Similarly, problems in stimulus control that involve switching of stimuli (such as colors, word groups or antecedent behaviors) are appropriate for this design as long as the subject's baselines are greater than zero. If the behavior must be shaped, this design is probably not appropriate.

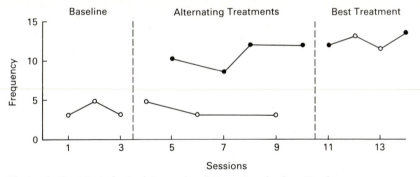

Figure 8.19   Hypothetical Example of Data Graphed to Conform to an Alternating Treatments Design.

Classroom Examples. Rose and Sherry (1984) used the alternating treatments design to compare the effects of two forms of previewing reading material on rates of oral reading. Four male and one female eighth and ninth grade students with learning disabilities participated in a resource room setting. An oral reading baseline was established for the rates of correct and incorrect words read per minute using a 2-minute rate check procedure. Checks assessed the material read the previous day. Following a baseline condition during which the student read a passage aloud without previewing procedures, one of two procedures were introduced on alternate days. On the first day, silent previewing was used, whereas on the alternate day listening previewing was used (see Figure 8.20). During silent previewing the student read the passage silently prior to reading it orally, whereas the listening previewing required him or her to follow along while the teacher read the passage. The student then read the passage aloud. After Session 4 the subjects were randomly presented with these procedures and the baseline procedures.

Results indicated that both previewing procedures were generally better than no previewing for four of the five students. Further, the listening procedure was found to be superior to the silent reading procedure for the same four students. Neither procedure was effective with Student 4.

Singh and Singh (1984) compared the efficacy of positive practice alone and positive practice in combination with reinforcement to no treatment of oral reading errors and the self-correction of oral reading errors by four girls with mental retardation.

The design involved a baseline condition, the alternating treatments phase in which three treatments were compared, and a third phase where the best procedure—positive practice in combination with reinforcement—was used. This last phase was introduced using a multiple-baseline design across subjects. The alternating treatments phase demonstrated that positive practice plus reinforcement was more effective than practice alone and baseline. These effects were replicated in the last phase.

Speigel-McGill, Bambara, Shores, and Fox (1984) used the same design to study the effects of proximity on the social behavior of children with multiple handicaps. Both students in Dyad 1 (Doug, 10-years-old, and Cathy, 12-years-old) were severely retarded and had expressive vocabularies of only three to four words. The students, seated in wheelchairs, were placed across from one another in the corner of the classroom when they were not involved in direct instruction with the teacher or aide. During these sessions, observations were made of their head orientation, vocalization, and gestures using a momentary sampling observation system.

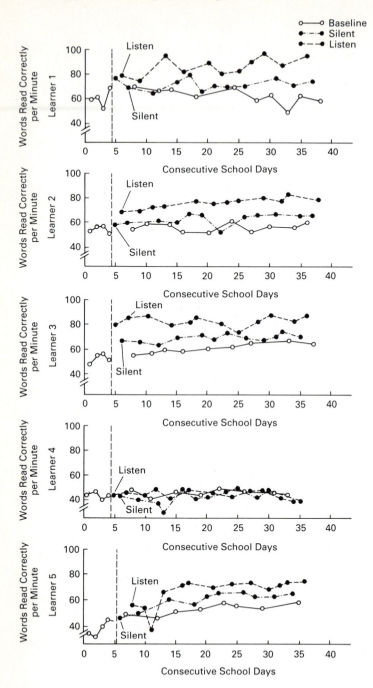

Figure 8.20 Effects of Systematic Previewing Procedures on the Rate of Correctly Read Words.

Source: From "Relative effects of two previewing procedures on LD adolescents' oral reading performance" by T. L. Rose and L. Sherry, 1984, *Learning Disability Quarterly, 7,* p. 42. Reprinted by permission.

Three proximities were evaluated each day, that is, distances of 1, 5, or 10 feet. The students were placed at these distances from each other in a different order each day. For example on one day the order was 1, 5, and 10 feet, the next day 10, 5, and 1 feet, and the next day 5, 10, and 1 feet, and so on. At the beginning of each day, the experimenter prompted the students to interact with each other using modeling and physical guidance to orient the students' faces to each other. The experimenter then removed herself from the two students and data collection began. The results are displayed in Figure 8.21.

For both students, the 1 ft proximity gen-

erated the greatest percentages of socially oriented responding, followed by the 5 ft proximity, with the 10 ft distance having the least facilitating effect. During Sessions 10 through 13, however, the dyad appeared to be equally social at 1 and 5 feet. This was not the case before and after the sessions. Since the three proximities were randomly assigned in each session, the students were unable to predict or anticipate the distances.

Examples from Community Settings. Linton and Singh (1984) evaluated the effects of two training procedures used to teach sign language to four adults with mental retarda-

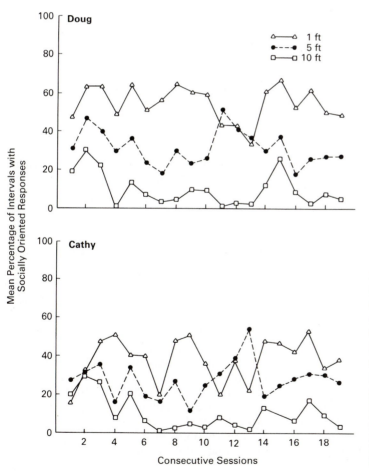

Figure 8.21 Dyad One: Mean Percentage of Combined Socially Oriented Responses (Head Orientation, Vocalizations, and Gestures) at 1 ft, 5 ft, and 10 ft Experimental Proximity Conditions.

Source: From "The effects of proximity on socially oriented behaviors of severely multiply handicapped children" by P. Speigel-McGill, L. M. Bambara, R. E. Shores, and J. J. Fox, 1984, *Education and Treatment of Children, 7*, p. 371. Reprinted by permission.

tion. The study took place in the sitting room of a residential facility. Positive-practice over-correction, positive-practice plus positive-reinforcement, and no treatment were compared in terms of number of correct vocalizations and the number of words signed correctly. The design included baseline, the alternating treatments phase, and a final phase where the best procedure—the combination of positive-practice plus positive-reinforcement—was applied to two of the three word groups being measured.

Issues and Limitations. A primary consideration in the alternating treatments design is the schedule for alternating treatment conditions. Thus, a random procedure for instituting treatments is strongly recommended to ensure that the subject is unable to predict that he or she will be receiving a particular treatment. For classroom teachers, it may be appropriate to choose the procedure just prior to the session to avoid inadvertently communicating advance knowledge to the student(s). Random alternation controls the sequence effects and treatment interaction effects (combined treatment effects) and thereby rules out that one treatment preceding another or their combined effect "caused" a given change, and not any single treatment.

Counterbalancing of rival sources of treatment is also important. For example, if different teachers or times of day or settings are employed, they must be paired with both conditions being alternated to rule out their possible effects. In the case of different teachers, the teachers should be careful to deliver randomly both treatments over the course of the study. If one teacher is always paired with treatment A, another with treatment B, the design fails to provide the necessary level of confidence in the effects of the treatment.

The number of alternations and, therefore, the length of each element within the design is also of importance. The rules of visual inspection (that is, mean level, trend, and variability) ultimately decide this issue (see Chapter 7). It is never advisable to arbitrarily decide the number of manipulations before-

hand. Instead, manipulations should be repeated until either differences between the elements can be clearly seen or until one is convinced that no difference is apparent and present trends do not predict the emergence of a difference.

The number of treatments that can be implemented in the same study also deserves consideration. While there is no absolute limit, more treatments will require more manipulations to obtain a nearly equally number of data points for each element thereby extending the length of the study. Similarly, more than four or five treatment elements displayed on a single graph can be difficult to interpret, particularly if several of them overlap. A rule of thumb, based on our review of the literature, suggests that three to four treatments including a baseline condition is an optimal number in a single study.

The alternating treatments design is thought to suffer from carryover effects from the rapid alternation of treatments. For example, induction is considered to be a positive transfer or generalization effect of one treatment to the other. This potential problem may be ruled out by showing that several studies of the same treatments, but using other designs (for example, ABAB) confirm the findings of the alternating treatments design.

Complex Design Features

We have discussed four single-subject designs, their procedures, and advantages and limitations. We now turn to a discussion of select features that, when added to these designs, increase their power and capacity to generate information.

Combinations. In many of the examples just discussed, researchers combined aspects of two or more designs. Thus, we have seen multiple-baseline designs that employed reversals applied simultaneously across all baselines (Hall et al., 1970), changing criterion designs that employed reversals (Gardner et al., 1983) and alternating treatment designs which employed multiple-baseline procedures across subjects (Singh & Singh, 1984).

The advantage of combining design features is that replications of effects can be produced using different procedures applied to the same subjects(s). By combining design elements, researchers seek to circumvent limitations imposed by a single design. For example, by introducing a treatment in a multiple-baseline design, by withdrawing it, and then by reintroducing it simultaneously across all baselines, cause-and-effect relationships are shown to hold up under two fundamentally different design conditions. Thus, the advantages of both designs are brought to bear in the same analysis, and the effects are even more convincingly demonstrated.

Assessing Generalization across Behaviors, Tasks, Settings, and Persons. For studies in which generalization of performance across behaviors, tasks, settings, and persons is of interest, additional baseline measures must be added and monitored over time. Unlike the multiple-baseline design where all baselines eventually receive treatment, generalization designs may include some measures that go completely untreated or receive only minimal treatment. To the extent that effects are noted in a generalization measure compared to its baseline level and other baselines receiving direct treatment, generalization designs can be evaluated. In a generalization design, therefore, the goal is to document the point at which treatments, in some settings for some behaviors, or for some tasks, is influential enough to produce change in nontreatment settings for nontreated behaviors, or for nontreated tasks.

The most elementary generalization design is one where measures are made only in the generalization setting. For example, Thurston (Hall, Delquadri, Greenwood, & Thurston, 1982) trained parents to teach their children vocabulary words in the evening at home. The same words were pretested and posttested at school by the classroom teacher. The data in an ABAB design are illustrated in Figure 8.22.

During baseline, the student received regular training at school. In the home-tutoring phases, the student performed systematically

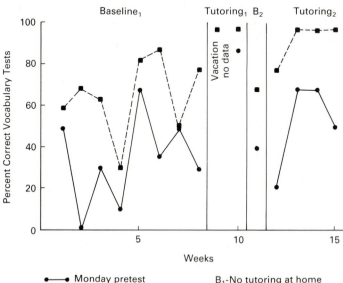

Figure 8.22 Record of Correct Vocabulary Words on Friday Tests Administered by the Teacher at School. The tutoring phases were implemented in the evening at home by the parents.

Source: From "The importance of opportunity to respond to children's academic success" by R. V. Hall, J. Delquadri, C. R. Greenwood, and L. Thurston, 1982. In E. B. Edgar, N. G. Haring, J. R. Jenkins, & C. G. Pious (eds.), *Mentally handicapped children: Education and training,* p. 129. Baltimore, MD: University Park Press. Reprinted by permission.

higher on the vocabulary words at school. During the second baseline, the mother tutored the child on a different set of words than those taught and tested at school. Performance during this week was comparable to the first baseline, and it was lower than the last home-tutoring phase. This design enabled the researchers to demonstrate that home intervention added significantly to the student's school performance.

More complex generalization designs assess treatment and generalization baselines. For example, in a study of parent tutoring of student's oral reading at home, Sasso, Hughes, Critchlow, Falcone, and Delquadri (1981) used a multiple-baseline design across students (see Figure 8.23).

For Student 1 only, the researchers assessed oral rates of reading in two different "readers" of the same difficulty level but by different publishers. The tutoring occurred at home, but oral reading rate was assessed by the teacher at school the following day. Sasso et al. (1981) reported that for all three students reading rate had increased when assessed by the teacher at school immediately after parent tutoring was applied to passages in the original "reader." These results replicated prior findings concerning generalization of home intervention effects to school performance.

In the case of Student 1, gains in one "reader" demonstrated covariance gains in the "reader" that was not taught. Thus, tutoring at home improved performance assessed at school, and, in the case of Student 1 appeared to generalize to reading in a different "reader." Unfortunately, replication of this effect across materials was not completed because additional assessments were not made for the two other students. Therefore, the noted effect was not sufficiently replicated to be convincing.

Hops, Walker, and Greenwood (1979) sought to assess and to program generalization of social skills. A student's percentage of social behavior across two recesses was measured. In the first recess, after screening and baseline assessments, the investigators first

introduced and then gradually withdrew elements of a complex social skills intervention package (see Figure 8.24).

During the second recess, Hops et al. used a simple procedure designed to facilitate generalization. This minimal procedure involved reporting privately to the teacher social episodes made by the target student following the second recess. The data demonstrated that social behaviors generalized to the second recess after the following was done: (a) social skills tutoring and a point-contingency in the first recess and (b) self-reporting by the target student in the second recess. Although this design suffers from several problems, including a lack of reversals or multiple-baseline controls, it does demonstrate a successful effort to assess and program for generalization to a second setting.

Improving on the prior designs, Hops, Greenwood, and Guild (1975) used a complex multiple-baseline design across teachers and settings. After first assessing generalization praising skills by the teacher, they conducted an experimental analysis of the treatment components necessary to program generalization of these skills to the untreated settings (see Figure 8.25).

The teachers were trained to implement a standard behavior management package (Greenwood et al., 1979). For Teacher 1, this occurred during language arts, for Teacher 2 during math, and for Teacher 3 during reading instruction. The packaged program produced large increases in teacher use of praise and decreases in use of disapproval. The data from nontreatment settings (see Figure 8.25) for the same teachers during the same time period revealed small to moderate increases in the use of praise and correlated reductions in the use disapproval statements. However, these generalized changes were much smaller than those obtained in the training settings.

In a second study, the following series of components designed to increase generalization were sequentially introduced: (a) instructions to the teacher to praise in the untrained settings, (b) consultant visits to these settings, (c) consultant visits plus consultant feedback,

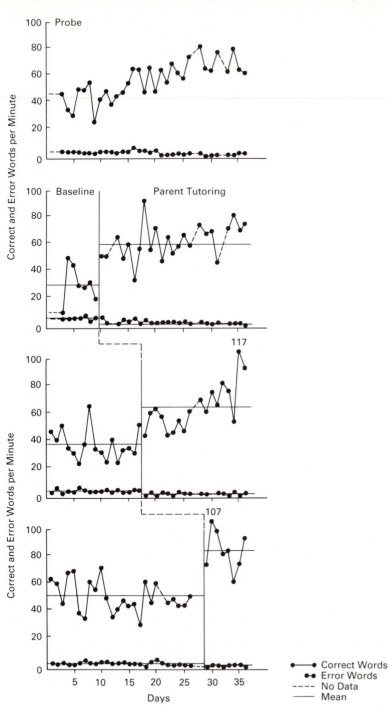

Figure 8.23 The Effects of Parent Home Tutoring on Oral Reading Rates (Correct and Error Words per Minute) Across Three Students.

Source: From "A home tutoring procedure to increase opportunity to respond and increase in-class oral reading skills in LD children" by G. Sasso, V. Hughes, W. Critchlow, I. Falcone, and J. Delquadri, 1981. Paper presented at the CEC Conference on Exceptional Children, New Orleans, LA. Reprinted by permission.

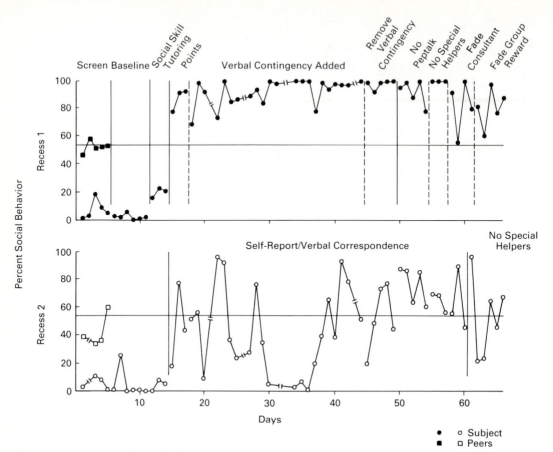

Figure 8.24   Percent Social Behavior Across Two Recess Periods for Subject 1 in Stage II -Year 3 Test of the PEERS Program Package. Shaded area includes + and − 1 standard deviation of mean percent social behavior for grade-level normative group. White lines in Recess 2 represent Recess 1 phase lines.

Source: From "PEERS: A program for remediating social withdrawal in the school setting: Aspects of a research and development process" by H. Hops, H. M. Walker, and C. R. Greenwood, 1979. In *Behavioral systems for the developmentally disabled. I. School and family environments,* L. A. Hammerlynck, ed., p. 76, New York: Bruner/Mazel. Reprinted by permission.

(d) the use of behavior rules for student's behavior, (e) collection of a student behavior baseline, and (f) the use of group reinforcement contingencies. The last phase was a follow-up with all the other procedures removed.

Results indicated that instructions and consultant visits to the classrooms of partici-

pating teachers were only partially effective in generalization. However, the addition of consultant feedback about use of teacher praise was uniformly effective in increasing praise to levels commensurate with those in the training setting. These effects were maintained over subsequent procedures. Differential effects were noted at follow-up, with

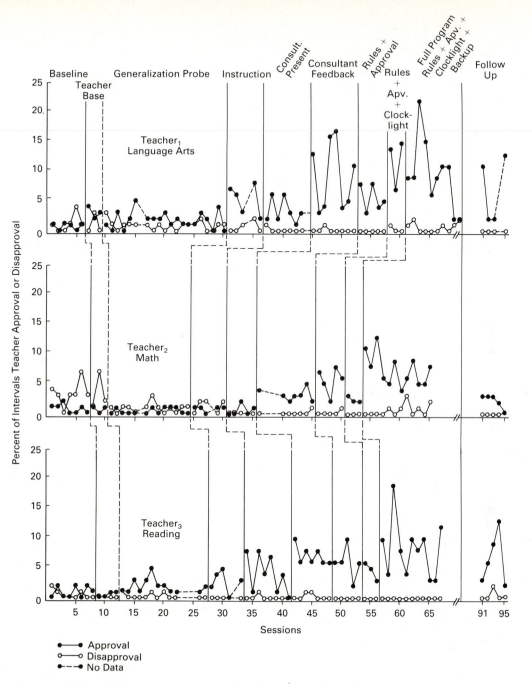

Figure 8.25 Multiple-Baseline Analysis of Across Setting Generalization of Teacher Praising Skills and Component Analysis of Efforts Aimed at Programming Generalization of These Skills.

Source: From "Programming generalization of teacher praising skills: How easy is it" by H. Hops, C. R. Greenwood, and J. Guild, 1975. Paper presented at the Ninth Annual Convention of the Association for the Advancement of Behavior Therapy, San Francisco. Reprinted by permission.

some teachers in some settings returning to baseline levels. In this study, it was possible to identify consultant feedback as a functional variable with respect to the programming of generalized teacher praise; therefore, it was not necessary to implement the entire package to obtain the same effects in the untrained settings.

A similar strategy using a multiple-baseline design on top of another design was used by Pancsofar and Bates (1985). These authors developed treated and untreated baselines within three groups of tasks. In each group, they treated one task, noted a change in performance on the task, and analyzed performance on similar generalization tasks. If the student had not generalized, a second task was taught. Generalization typically occurred within a category after two or three tasks had been directly trained.

The strengths of the last two designs stem from a demonstration of the causal status of efforts to program generalization across settings and tasks. Thus, these designs go beyond the earlier studies that simply confirmed the presence or absence of generalization effects.

Assessing Generalization across Time (Maintenance). As in the examples in this chapter, the maintenance of behavior change over time is frequently reported by the results of follow-up assessments. Such assessments occur at the end of each study, following an experimental analysis of behavior. In some cases, follow-ups are made under the same (Jackson et al., 1981) or reduced (Luiselli et al., 1983) intervention procedures. Sometimes the follow-ups are made in the absence of treatment (Greenwood et al., 1974; Rolider & Van Houten, 1986).

One of the major problems with generalization research is the lack of both effective designs and research results that support experimental analysis of generalization. Rusch and Kazdin (1981) proposed the following three designs for selectively withdrawing training components after behavior control is achieved so as to facilitate the assess mainte-

nance: (1) sequential-withdrawal, (2) partial-withdrawal, and (c) partial-sequential-withdrawal. A sequential-withdrawal design consists of the gradual withdrawal of selected components of the training package in consecutive experimental phases to determine if behavior is maintained. If, during any phase, performance decreases below acceptable levels, the treatment component (or all of the components) is replaced. When the behavior is built back to an acceptable level, a different order of withdrawal is instigated.

Rusch, Connis, and Sowers (1979) applied the sequential-withdrawal design. In their study, prompts, praise, tokens, and response cost comprised the treatment package used to increase an employees' time spent working in a restaurant setting with an ABABCBC design (see Figure 8.26). Once experimental control was established relative to the three combined treatment components, a sequential-withdrawal of single components was initiated. First, response cost contingencies were no longer in effect each day; rather, they were in effect only on predetermined, randomly selected days. Second, a 4-step withdrawal of the token economy was initiated. In a final phase, praise was withdrawn. Within each withdrawal phase no loss in acquired behavior was noted.

The partial-withdrawal design "consists of withdrawing a component of the intervention package or the total package from one of several different baselines (behaviors, persons, or settings) in a multiple-baseline design" (Kazdin, 1982, p. 215). In this design, the intervention is gradually withdrawn across different baselines. If withdrawing the intervention does not result in loss of the desired behavior, then the intervention can be withdrawn from other baselines as well. If the withdrawal results in a loss of behavior, the component(s) is replaced. Following reinstatement to the original performance levels, different withdrawal procedures are attempted while maintaining performance.

Vogelsberg and Rusch's (1979) study demonstrates the value of the partial-withdrawal design in predicting potential maintenance

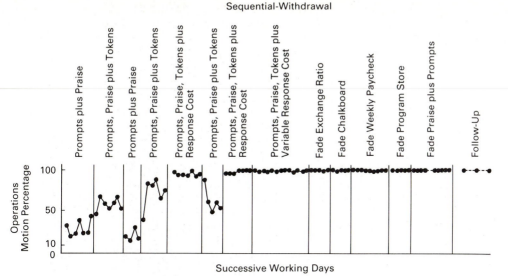

Figure 8.26 Sequential-Withdrawal Assessment of Maintenance of Attending to Task.

Source: From Rusch et al., 1979.

failures before they occur. In their investigation, three individuals with severe mental retardation were trained to cross intersections. When one training component, feedback, was withdrawn from one of the subjects, approaching, stepping, and walking behaviors were maintained (see Figure 8.27). However, a critical feature of crossing, that is "looking" decreased in frequency. These data suggested that a loss in looking might have resulted for all students if a similar withdrawal were introduced for each. Therefore, the investigators undertook a different training strategy with the two remaining students. Behavioral rehearsal and a trainer model resulted in maintenance of each of the criterion behaviors in these two subjects. In addition, this revised strategy was applied to the first subject after successfully rebuilding the diminished looking skills, resulting in successful maintenance. With the partial-withdrawal design, either a single component, several, or all components of a training package are withdrawn from one of the baselines of a multiple-baseline design. This withdrawal strategy is an excellent

means of determining what can happen if similar withdrawals are replicated across the remaining baselines. Once agian, if the withdrawal results in loss of behavior, the components can be replaced. Following reinstatement of the original performance levels, a different withdrawal order may be tried across the same or another baseline (subjects), or the same withdrawal could be replicated across another baseline.

Autonomy and Adaptability. Last, in a partial-sequential-withdrawal design, the two previous strategies are combined. First, all or part of a treatment package is withdrawn from one of the baselines (behaviors, persons, or settings) of a multiple-baseline design. If the behavior is maintained, the withdrawal is advanced to include other components or replicated across other baselines. If the behaviors do not maintain, however, the withdrawn components may be reintroduced simultaneously on one baseline with the withdrawal of the same or different components across one or more of the other baselines.

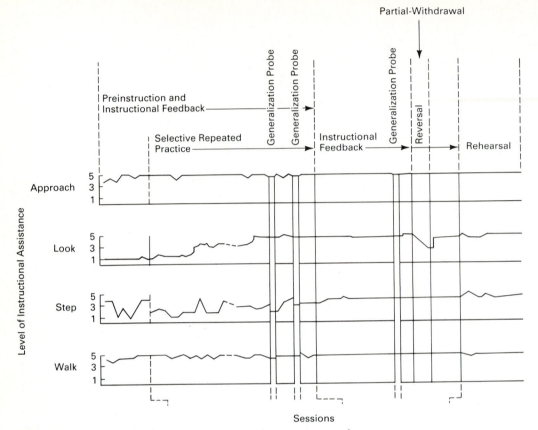

Figure 8.27   Partial-Withdrawal Assessment of Maintenance of
Intersection Crossing Skills.
Source: From Vogelsberg and Rusch, 1979.

Combining the partial and sequential-withdrawal designs allows for the orderly withdrawal of the various components of the treatment package in an effort to decrease the probability that subjects will discriminate the absence or presence of the contingencies. By combining the partial and sequential-withdrawal design strategies investigators can predict, with increasing probability, the extent to which they are controlling the treatment environment as the progression of withdrawals is extended to other behaviors, subjects, or settings. (Rusch & Kazdin, 1981, p. 136)

Martin and Rusch's (in press) assessment of facilitation of meal preparation through the use of pictorial cues incorporated a partial-sequential-withdrawal design (see Figure 8.28). Instructional feedback and preinstruction were included in the treatment package for the three subjects in the study. Following acquisition of the target behavior by the first subject, instructional feedback was withdrawn, followed by withdrawal of preinstruction. Each withdrawal was so successful that a more rapid withdrawal strategy was undertaken with the second subject. Simultaneous withdrawal of both instructional feedback and preinstruction resulted in a minimal loss in performance. A similarly rapid withdrawal strategy was utilized with the third subject. Not only was performance maintained, in

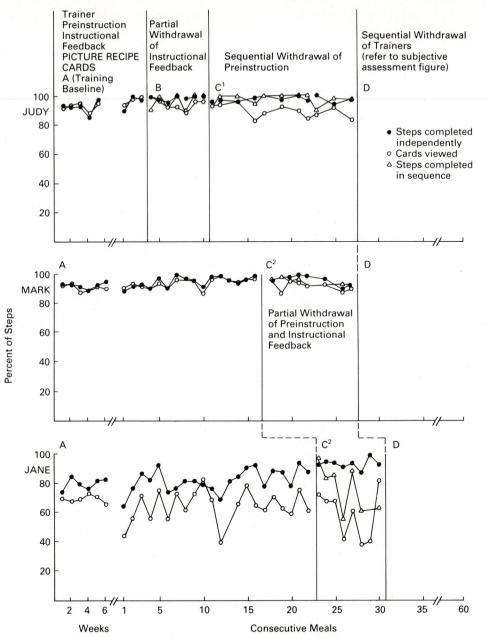

Figure 8.28 Partial-Sequential-Withdrawal Assessment of Maintenance of Meal Preparation Skills.

Source: From Martin and Rusch, in press.

some instances it improved, due in part to the reduction in behavioral outbursts triggered by trainer feedback.

Clearly, withdrawal methodology provides a flexible sequence of procedures for assessing maintenance. The successful implementation of withdrawal methodology is indicated by the presence or absence of change in the dependent measure. Although a plan is needed, withdrawal methodology is "open ended" in the sense that change or lack of change in the dependent measure influences decisions with regard to the sequence of withdrawals. This methodology uses orderly withdrawal of training components to decrease the detection of the absence of those training components by the subject. In summation, these designs can aid behavioral researchers to explore alternative means of terminating interventions without prolonged loss of desired behavior (Kazdin, 1981; Rusch & Kazdin, 1981). In the next section, traditional behavior change methods are characterized. They, like withdrawal strategies, often exploit a gradual transition from training interventions to natural settings.

Including Peer Comparisons. In some cases, social validation of both target behaviors and behavior changes can be facilitated by adding an intersubject comparison within a single-subject design (Kazdin, 1977; Walker & Hops, 1976). For example, during the screening phase, the target individual's baseline level of social behavior may be compared to that of selected peers. In addition, a + and − one standard deviation band around the peer mean (the shaded band) could be provided across days so that the target individual's behavior change can be compared to these data. Accordingly, the individual's level of performance may be: (a) below peer norms in both recesses at screening and baseline, (b) above norm when intervention is implemented, and (c) highly variable when compared to the normative range. Data of this type provide validity for decisions to treat a behavior (showing that it is problematic) and reveal that behavior changes produced

are large enough to be important, that is, the differences in target and peer performance are erased by treatment.

SUMMARY

After introducing the need to study the individual case in special education, this chapter has discussed four single-subject research designs: the ABAB reversal design, the multiple-baseline design, the changing criterion design, and the alternating treatments design. After defining each design and pointing out its most appropriate applications, examples of each from the classroom and community settings were given. These included applications with students with mild and severe handicaps or their caretakers. The issues and limitations of each design were also considered. The last section gave an overview of additional issues which increase both the complexity of the design and increase the information gained from the basic design. These features included reasons for combining research designs in the same study, designs used for the experimental analysis of generalization across behaviors, settings, persons, and time; and the use of peer comparisons to address issues of social validation.

REFERENCES

Barlow, D. H., & Hayes, S. C. (1979). "Alternating treatments design: One strategy for comparing the effects of two treatments in a single subject." *Journal of Applied Behavior Analysis, 12,* 199–210.

Barlow, D. H., & Hersen, M. (1984). *Single case experimental designs: Strategies for studying behavior change* (2nd ed). New York: Pergamon.

Barone, V. J., Greene, B. F., & Lutzker, J. R. (1986). "Home safety with families being treated for child abuse and neglect." *Behavior Modification, 10,* 93–114.

Barton, L. E., & Barton, C. L. (1985). "An effective and benign treatment of rumination." *Journal of the Association for Persons with Severe Handicaps, 10,* 168–171.

BENNETT, C. W., & LING, D. (1972). "Teaching a complex verbal response to a hearing-impaired girl." *Journal of Applied Behavior Analysis, 5,* 321–327.

BLEW, P. A., SCHWARTZ, I. S., & LUCE, S. C. (1985). "Teaching functional community skills to autistic children using nonhandicapped peer tutors." *Journal of Applied Behavior Analysis, 18,* 337–342.

BREEN, C., HARING, T., PITTS-CONWAY, V., & GAYLORD-ROSS, R. (1985). The training and generalization of social interaction during breaktime at two job sites in the natural environment. *Journal of the Association for Persons with Severe Handicaps, 10,* 41–50.

CAMPBELL, D. T., & STANLEY, J. S. (1963). "Experimental and quasi-experimental design for research on teaching." In N. L. Gage (ed.), *Handbook of research on teaching* (pp. 91–176.) Chicago: Rand McNally.

CARBONE, V. J., MILLER, A., & TODD, D. R. (1981). "Beat the timer game." *Education and Treatment of Children, 4,* 53–59.

CHRISTOPHERSEN, E. R., ARNOLD, C. M., HILL, D. W., & QUILITCH, H. R. (1972). "The home point system: Token reinforcement procedures for application by parents of children with behavior problems." *Journal of Applied Behavior Analysis, 5,* 485–497.

CONNIS, R. T., & RUSCH, F. R. (1980). "Programming maintenance through sequential-withdrawal of social contingencies." *Behavior Research of Severe Developmental Disabilities, 1,* 249–260.

DACHMAN, R. S., HALASZ, M. M., BICKETT, A. D., & LUTZKER, J. R. (1984). "A home-based ecobehavioral parent-training and generalization package with a neglectful mother." *Education and Treatment of Children, 7,* 183–202.

DENO, S. (1984). "Curriculum-based assessment: The emerging alternative." *Exceptional Children, 52,* 219–232.

ENGLEMANN, S., & CARNINE, D. (1982). *Theory of instruction.* New York: Irvington.

GARDNER, W. I., COLE, C. L., BERRY, D. L., & NOWINSKI, J. M. (1983). "Reduction of disruptive behaviors in mentally retarded adults." *Behavior Modification, 7,* 76–96.

GREENWOOD, C. R., DINWIDDIE, G., TERRY, B., WADE, L., STANLEY, S., THIBADEAU, S., & DELQUADRI, J. (1984). "Teacher-versus peer-mediated instruction: An ecobehavioral analysis of achievement outcomes." *Journal of Applied Behavior Analysis, 17,* 521–538.

GREENWOOD, C. R., HOPS, H., WALKER, H. M., GUILD, J. J., STOKES, J., YOUNG, K. R., KELMAN, K. S., & WILLARDSON, M. (1979). "Standardized classroom management program: Social validation and replication studies in Utah and Oregon." *Journal of Applied Behavior Analysis, 12,* 235–253.

GREENWOOD, C. R., HOPS, H., DELQUADRI, J., & GUILD, J. J. (1974)."Group contingencies for group consequences: A further analysis." *Journal of Applied Behavior Analysis, 7,* 413–426.

GREER, R. D. (1982). "Countercontrols for the American Educational Research Association?" *Education and Treatment of Children, 5,* 65–76.

HALL, R. V., CRISTLER, C., CRANSTON, S. S., & TUCKER, B. (1970). "Teachers and parents as researchers using multiple baseline designs." *Journal of Applied Behavior Analysis, 3,* 247–255.

HALL, R. V., DELQUADRI, J., GREENWOOD, C. R., & THURSTON, L. (1982). "The importance of opportunity to respond to children's academic success." In E. B. Edgar, N. G. Haring, J. R. Jenkins, & C. G. Pious (eds.), *Mentally handicapped children: Education and training* (pp. 107–140). Baltimore, MD: University Park Press.

HALL, R. V., LUND, D., & JACKSON, D. (1968). "Effects of teacher attention on study behavior." *Journal of Applied Behavior Analysis, 1,* 1–12.

HAMILTON, J., STEPHENS, L., & ALLEN, P. (1967). "Controlling aggressive and destructive behavior in severely handicapped institutionalized residents." *American Journal of Mental Deficiency, 71,* 852–856.

HANSON, M. J., & HANLINE, M. F. (1985). "An analysis of response-contingent learning experiences for young children." *Journal of the Association for Persons with Severe Handicaps, 10,* 31–40.

HARTMANN, D. P., & HALL, R. V. (1976). "The changing criterion design." *Journal of Applied Behavior Analysis, 9,* 527–532.

HOPS, H., & GREENWOOD, C. R., & GUILD, J. J. (1975). "Programming generalization of teacher praising skills: How easy is it?" Paper presented at the ninth Annual Convention of the Association for the Advancement of Behavior Therapy, San Francisco.

HOPS, H., WALKER, H. M., & GREENWOOD, C. R. (1979). "PEERS: A program for remediating social withdrawal in the school setting: Aspects of a research and development process." In L. A. Hammerlynck (ed.), *Behavioral systems for the developmentally disabled: School and family environments* (Vol I, pp. 48–86). New York: Bruner/Mazel.

HORNER, R. D. (1971). "Establishing the use of crutches by a mentally retarded spina bifida child." *Journal of Applied Behavior Analysis, 4,* 183–189.

JACKSON, A. T., SALZBERG, C. L., PACHOLL, B., & DORSEY, D. S. (1981). "The comprehensive rehabilitation of a behavior problem child in his home and community." *Education and Treatment of Children, 4,* 195–215.

KAZDIN, A. E. (1977). "Assessing the clinical or applied importance of behavior change through social validation." *Behavior Modification, 1,* 427–452.

KAZDIN, A. E., & HARTMANN, D. P. (1978). The simultaneous treatment design. *Behavior Therapy, 9,* 912–922.

KOHLER, F. W., & GREENWOOD, C. R. (1986). "Toward a technology of generalization: The identification of natural contingencies of reinforcement." *The Behavior Analyst, 9,* 19–26.

LINTON, J. M., & SINGH, N. N. (1984). "Acquisition of sign language using positive practice overcorrection." *Behavior Modification, 8,* 553–556.

LUISELLI, J. K. (1984). "Effects of brief overcorrection on stereotypic behavior of mentally retarded students." *Education and Treatment of Children, 7,* 125–138.

LUISELLI, J. K., MYLES, E., & LITTMAN-QUINN, J. K. (1983)."Analysis of a reinforcement/time-out treatment package to control severe aggression and destructive behaviors in a multihandicapped, rubella child." *Applied Research in Mental Retardation, 4,* 65–78.

MILTENBERGER, R. G., & FUQUA, R. W. (1981). "Overcorrection: A review and critical analysis." *The Behavior Analyst, 4,* 123–141.

MURPHY, D., & McCORMICK, S. (1985). "Evaluation of an instructional program designed to teach minimally literate juvenile delinquents to read road signs." *Education and Treatment of Children, 8,* 133–151.

ODOM, S. L., HOYSON, M., JAMIESON, B., & STRAIN, P. S. (1985)."Increasing handicapped preschooler's peer social interactions: Cross-setting and component analysis." *Journal of Applied Behavior Analysis, 18,* 3–16.

PANCSOFAR, E. L., & BATES, P. (1985). "The impact of the acquisition of successive training exemplars on generalization." *Journal of the Association for Persons with Severe Handicaps, 10,* 95–104.

PARTINGTON, J. W., SUNDBERG, M. L., IWATA, B. A., & MOUNTJOY, P. T. (1979). "A task-analysis approach to time telling instruction for normal and educable mentally impaired children." *Education and Treatment of Children, 2,* 17–29.

PERKINS, V., & CULLINAN, D. (1984). "Effects of direct instruction intervention for fraction skills." *Education and Treatment of Children, 7,* 109–117.

PETERSON, L. (1984). "The 'safe at home' game: Training comprehensive prevention skills in latchkey children." *Behavior Modification, 8,* 474–494.

REID, D. H., PARSONS, M. B., McCARN, J. E., GREEN, C. W., PHILLIPS, J. F., & SCHEPIS, M. M. (1985). "Providing a more appropriate education for severely handicapped persons: Increasing and validating functional classroom tasks." *Journal of Applied Behavior Analysis, 18,* 289–301.

RIORDAN, M. M., IWATA, B. A., WOHL, M. K., & FINNEY, J. (1980). "Behavioral treatment of food refusal and selectivity in developmental disabled children." *Applied Research in Mental Retardation, 1,* 95–112.

ROLIDER, A., & VAN HOUTEN, R. (1986). "Effects of degree of awakening and the criterion for advancing awakening on the treatment of bedwetting." *Education and Treatment of Children, 9,* 135–141.

ROSE, T. L., & SHERRY, L. (1984). "Relative effects of two previewing procedures on LD adolescents' oral reading performance." *Learning Disability Quarterly, 7,* 39–44.

RUSCH, F. R., & KAZDIN, A. E. (1981). "Toward a methodology of withdrawal designs for the assessment of response maintenance." *Journal of Applied Behavior Analysis, 14,* 131–140.

SAJWAJ, T., LIBET, J., & AGRAS, S. (1974). "Lemon-juice therapy: The control of life threatening rumination in a six-month-old infant." *Journal of Applied Behavior Analysis, 7,* 557–566.

SANFORD, F. L., & FAWCETT, S. B. (1980). "Consequence analysis: Its effects on verbal statements about an environmental project." *Journal of Applied Behavior Analysis, 13,* 57–64.

SASSO ,G., HUGHES, V., CRITCHLOW, W., FALCONE,

I., & DELQUADRI, J. (1981). "A home tutoring procedure to increase opportunity to respond and increase in-class oral reading skills in LD children." Paper presented at the CEC Conference on Exceptional Children, New Orleans, LA.

SEEKINS, T., & FAWCETT, S. B., (1987). *Effects of passenger safety laws in seven states.* Lawrence, Kansas: University of Kansas.

SCHMIDT, G. W., & ULRICH, R. E. (1969). "Effects of group contingent events upon classroom noise." *Journal of Applied Behavior Analysis, 2,* 171–179.

SHAPIRO, E. S., & SHAPIRO, S. (1985). "Behavioral coaching in the development of skills in track." *Behavior Modification, 9,* 211–224.

SCHLEIEN, S. J., & LARSON, A. (1986). "Adult leisure education for the independent use of a community recreation center." *Journal of the Association for Persons with Severe Handicaps, 11,* 39–44.

SINDELAR, P. T., ROSENBERG, M. S., & WILSON, R. J. (1985). "An adapted alternating treatments design for instructional research." *Education and Treatment of Children, 8,* 67–77.

SINGH, N. N., & SINGH, J. (1984). "Positive practice overcorrection of oral reading errors." *Behavior Modification, 8,* 23–37

SKIBA, R. J., CASEY, A., & CENTER, B. A. (1986). "Nonaversive procedures in the treatment of classroom behavior problems." *Journal of Special Education, 19,* 459–481.

SPEIGEL-MCGILL, P., BAMBARA, L. M., SHORES, R. E., & FOX, J. J. (1984). "The effects of proximity on socially oriented behaviors of severely multiply handicapped children." *Education and Treatment of Children, 7,* 365–378.

SULZER-AZAROFF, B., & MAYER, G. R. (1977). *Applying behavior-analysis procedures with children and youth.* New York: Holt, Rinehart & Winston.

TATE, B. G., & BAROFF, G. S. (1966). "Aversive control of self-injurious behavior in a psychotic boy." *Behavior Research and Therapy, 4,* 281–287.

VOGELSBERG, T., & RUSCH, F. R. (1979). "Training severely handicapped students to cross partially controlled intersections." *AAESPH Review, 4,* 264–273.

WALKER, H. M., & HOPS, H. (1976). "Use of normative peer data as a standard for evaluating classroom treatment effects." *Journal of Applied Behavior Analysis, 9,* 159–168.

WALKER, H. M., HOPS, H., & FIGENBAUM, E. (1976). "Deviant classroom behavior as a function of combinations of social and token reinforcement and cost contingency." *Behavior Therapy, 7,* 76–88.

chapter 9

Reinforcement

Students in special education classes are exposed to more tests than perhaps any other group of students. Ms. Keller was aware of this and the possibility that the students in her class were becoming both "test-wise" and "test-weary." In September, she had pretested her students on several standardized measures, including the *Key Math* (Connolly, Nachtman, & Pritchett, 1971). But during the school year, Ms. Keller discovered that one of her new students, 11-year-old Dan, could solve several types of math problems that were more difficult than those he had missed on the *Key Math* pretest. This was disconcerting to Ms. Keller because she thought Dan had tried to do his best on the pretest. As she began the posttest evaluations in May, Ms. Keller decided to see how well Dan could really do on the *Key Math* or, as she asked, "How well did he fool me?" She told Dan that if he answered correctly ten more problems than he answered in September, she would buy a soda in the teacher's lounge for him to

drink in class. She did not tell Dan how many problems he answered correctly in September. After scoring Dan's posttest, she found that he exceeded the required ten problems. In fact, she found that he gained 4.4 grade levels in only 7 months! While her principal was duly impressed with her apparent abilities to teach math, Ms. Keller thought that Dan's increased performance might have been related to the promise of a soda, which was a rare treat in her class.

Ms. Keller apparently demonstrated the effective use of a *reinforcer*, the soda, to increase the level of Dan's responses. *Reinforcement* is frequently the critical component of programmatic attempts to teach new behaviors, to increase existing behaviors that are occurring too infrequently, or to maintain behaviors at acceptable levels. The application of reinforcement is apparently so simple that a teacher may be deluded by this "common sense approach" and implement reinforcement procedures in ways that will lead ultimately to failure. Reinforcement, like many issues dealing with human behavior, is complex, and its effective use requires knowledge of its various intricacies.

The next three chapters will define, explain, and illustrate the various components that, when combined, will enable a teacher to use reinforcement effectively in the classroom. Procedural suggestions will be offered, and factors that must be considered before implementing each procedure will be thoroughly explained.

POSITIVE REINFORCEMENT

Definition

Positive reinforcement refers to the process of presenting a stimulus as a consequence of a response that results in an increase in the probability that the behavior will increase in the future.

The definition of positive reinforcement has two major parts: (a) the reinforcer becomes available *after* a particular response has occurred, and (b) the reinforcer increases the probability of that behavior occurring again in similar situations. In addition to these major parts, there are several important components of the positive reinforcement principle. These include the stimulus, the contingency, the response, and the effect that the stimulus has upon the response when contingently applied.

Stimulus. Virtually any environmental event or object is a stimulus, and may influence behavior. An individual usually interacts with stimuli through one or more sensory modalities (for example, visual, auditory, tactile, kinesthetic, and olfactory). Stimuli may be internal events (for example, an increased pulse rate, leg cramps, and thoughts) or external events (for example, a stop sign, points awarded for completed assignments, posted names of students with perfect attendance, or a smile). Internal events include self-selection, internal regulation, and self-regulation processes. External stimuli include stimuli

that (a) can be observed reliably by two or more persons and (b) are easier to manipulate directly by a teacher in order to facilitate behavioral change.

Teachers may influence behavior by presenting, withholding, or eliminating stimuli. The term *stimulus*, as used in the definition of positive reinforcement, means that a stimulus is withheld until a specified response occurs. Other uses of stimuli to affect behavior will be discussed in subsequent chapters.

The stimulus that follows a behavior and increases the level of that behavior is called a *positive reinforcer*. It is important to note the difference between positive reinforcement and a positive reinforcer. *Positive reinforcement* refers to the *procedure* whereby behavior is increased or maintained by delivering a positive reinforcer after the behavior occurs, whereas *positive reinforcer* refers to the *stimulus* itself. There are different arrangements, called *schedules of reinforcement*, which provide for different ways to deliver reinforcers. (Schedules of reinforcement are discussed in Chapter 11.)

Reinforcement Contingency. The concept of a contingency is crucial to understanding much of applied behavior analysis. A contingent relationship (contingency) between a response and a reinforcer is accurately reflected in an "if-then" statement. *If* a response occurs, *then*, and only then, will the reinforcer be delivered. The reinforcer is *available* prior to and during the response, but it is *delivered* only after the response. Watching a sunset from a beach may be reinforcing to us, but we receive that reinforcer only *if* we drive to the beach. The sunset at the beach is available everyday, but we may only gain access to it if we perform a specific response (drive to the beach). This is an example of a natural contingency or one that makes use of naturally occurring reinforcing events. Natural contingencies teach individuals a great deal about their environment; for example, saying "hello" to others oftentimes results in an exchanged greeting.

We may also purposefully arrange contingencies. For example, four preschool boys with IQs ranging from 37 to 51 were rarely attentive during certain class periods. The students were considered attentive when they were in their seats and actively manipulating various fine-motor equipment. In order to increase the levels of this behavior, the teacher began to praise each child after he was attentive for 20 seconds. (For example, she said, "Danny, you're doing a good job.") Attentive behavior increased from approximately 35 percent of the time during baseline to between 80 percent to 85 percent of the time during the verbal praise period (Strain & Pierce, 1977). In this case, verbal praise was consistently available, but withheld until the students had been attentive for at least 20 seconds. Then the reinforcer was delivered, thereby forming a contingent relationship between being attentive for 20 seconds and receiving verbal praise from the teacher.

Response. Reinforcement can be a very powerful environmental consequence and controls a good deal of our responses. Any response may gain access to a reinforcer if the environment has been so arranged. This is true for inappropriate responses as well as those we consider appropriate. In fact, the use of reinforcement without an awareness of the response that actually gains access to a reinforcer is quite often the cause of the inappropriate response. Several studies have found that teachers attend to inappropriate behavior more often than to appropriate behavior (Thomas, Presland, Grant, & Glynn, 1978; White 1975). And the studies have shown that, by altering the focus of their attention from inappropriate to appropriate responses, the teachers could cause the appropriate behavior to increase and the inappropriate behavior to decrease (Becker, Madsen, Arnold, & Thomas, 1967; Hasazi & Hasazi, 1972; Thomas, Becker, & Armstrong, 1968; Zimmerman & Zimmerman, 1962). Many more examples of teachers, other professionals, and parents who were mistakenly reinforcing the wrong response could be listed. The best safeguards against reinforcing

wrong or inappropriate responses are to develop an accurate operational definition of the target response and to observe what happens following an inappropriate response in order to identify the reinforcers for that response.

In most cases, only the *specific* targeted response will be changed by contingent reinforcers. Therefore, we should not expect the reinforcer to automatically alter any other response. For example, Jenkins, Barksdale, and Clinton (1978) found that reinforcing oral reading rate had no effect on comprehension, nor did reinforcing comprehension increase reading rate.

Reinforcement of a specific response may, however, influence other responses that are related in some way (for example, topographically) to the target response (Reynolds, 1968). This effect is known as *response generalization*. Response generalization may be most beneficial to the teacher because it can decrease the amount of instructional time that must be spent on the related skills.[1] For example, Blankenship (1978) found that nine elementary school students made systematic inversion errors occurring where the larger number is subtracted from the smaller regardless of position, (for example, when the 3 is subtracted from the 6 in $73 - 26 = 53$) on at least 90 percent of the subtraction problems requiring borrowing. After training, which involved modeling and feedback, on problems of the 2-digit minus 1-digit type, the students were tested daily on the trained type and eight other types of subtraction problems, which ranged up to 3-digit minus 3-digit numbers with borrowing. Response generalization was demonstrated in varying degrees by eight of the nine students. Furthermore, instruction required an average of only 35 seconds per day per pupil. Contingent reinforcement has also resulted in generalized handwriting (Lahey, Busemeyer, O'Hara, & Beggs, 1977) and in phonics skills and oral reading rate and

---

[1]Response generalization is also most helpful for shaping procedures, which are discussed in Chapter 10.

accuracy (Lovitt & Hurlbert, 1974). Response generalization has not received much attention from applied researchers (see reviews by Rose, Koorland, & Epstein, 1982; Stokes & Baer, 1977).

Response-Level Increases or Maintains. Whether or not a contingently presented stimulus functions as a positive reinforcer is determined solely by observing future occurrences of the target response. The stimulus is a positive reinforcer if, and only if, the target response increases over its baseline levels. Thus, if the responses were to decrease or to remain the same, then the stimulus is *not* a reinforcer. This is true regardless of the value we may place on a stimulus or whether we think it is a reinforcer.

Many objects or events are commonly considered to be "positive" and, thus, reinforcing, including candy, money, and free time. Nevertheless, for certain individuals, these stimuli may not prove to be reinforcers. A penny for each addition problem solved correctly may not reinforce the affluent child who routinely receives a $10 allowance. Even free time, considered by many to be a "universal" reinforcer, may not reinforce every student (Billingsley, 1977). In these two examples, the target responses decreased following the contingent delivery of the stimulus. For these students, the stimuli may not have been reinforcing despite the teacher's best intentions.

Conversely, students may often be reinforced by objects or events that most teachers would never consider to be reinforcing. Verbal disapproval of certain behaviors is one of the most common ways teachers try to decrease inappropriate behaviors. Interestingly, evidence has repeatedly shown that disapproving remarks may be reinforcers for certain students because the target responses increased (Budd, Green, & Baer, 1976; Thomas et al., 1968). In fact, Becker, Engleman, and Thomas (1975) have identified this reinforce-by-disapproving situation as the "criticism trap," which accurately reflects the dilemma many teachers face when they do not evalu-

ate stimulus effects. Even though we may think a particular stimulus should reduce behavior, it may function as a reinforcer for a particular student. The key is its effect on behavior.

The increase of a particular response must be demonstrated reliably before a stimulus can be considered a reinforcer. Let us reconsider Dan's performance on the *Key Math* test. The soda served as a reinforcer because the number of Dan's correct responses increased, but can we be certain that the soda was *functionally* related to that increase? Upon closer inspection, we see that Ms. Keller actually employed an AB design which may have only demonstrated a coincidental or accidental behavioral relationship. Ms. Keller may believe that she had discovered a powerful reinforcer for Dan; however, Dan could have been enrolled in a year-long, remedial math program. Thus, Dan may have done better on his math test because he was taught to work these problems, not because of the soda. We always need to determine whether the selected stimulus (for example, the soda) reliably increases responses when awarded contingently.

The points raised in this section are critical to the effective use of positive reinforcement. Whether any stimulus is a positive reinforcer is determined by its reliable effect on behavior. This criterion is used to classify a consequent stimulus. Evaluation of this criterion must be based on students' response levels and not influenced by any preconceived notions of the pleasantness or "positiveness" of the stimulus to oneself or others. This careful evaluation facilitates the precise use of the term *positive reinforcer* to identify those objects or events that increase or maintain particular responses for particular students.

Just as we must use terminology precisely to describe the interactions between environmental stimuli and behavior, we should also avoid terms that prohibit these precise descriptions. For example, *reward*, which is often used synonymously with a positive reinforcer, refers to any object or event that *should* be liked by the individual to whom it is delivered, *regardless of the effect it has on the individual's behavior.* The essential difference between a reward and a reinforcer has been described by Miller (1980), who advised that a positive reinforcer may be thought of as a "proven reward," because it has demonstrated an effect on the target response. A reward, on the other hand, does not necessarily have a predictable influence on behavior.

NEGATIVE REINFORCEMENT

The previous discussion focused on positive reinforcement, which is one procedure for increasing or maintaining particular responses. *Negative reinforcement* accomplishes the same behavioral effect.

Definition

Negative reinforcement refers to the procedure of removing an aversive stimulus as a consequence of, or contingent upon, a response resulting in an increase in the rate of that particular response in the future.

The definition of negative reinforcement has two major parts: (a) the stimulus is present prior to the occurrence of the particular response, and (b) the response removes or withdraws the stimulus, thereby increasing the probability that the response will recur. Several components of negative reinforcement are the same as those of positive reinforcement, for example, the presence of a contingent relationship, the response, and the effect on behavior. But there are differences, as reflected in the definition of negative reinforcement, that are discussed below.

Aversive Stimulus. An *aversive stimulus* may be thought of in nontechnical terms as an unpleasant event or object (for example, extreme cold), something that the individual will actively seek to avoid or escape. These may be presented through any of the sensory modalities, external or internal, just as any other stimuli. The aversive stimulus that pre-

ceeds the response, and whose removal results in an increase in that response, is known as a *negative reinforcer*. The difference between negative reinforcement and a negative reinforcer is the same as that between positive reinforcement and a positive reinforcer. *Reinforcement*, whether positive or negative, refers to the procedure employed to manipulate stimuli contingent upon a response that results in an increase in that behavior.

The term *aversive stimulus* often creates unnecessary confusion because it is used as a synonym for *negative reinforcer*. An aversive stimulus is neutral until its effect on an individual's behavior is observed. A stimulus becomes aversive only when the individual emits responses that will reliably allow the individual to avoid or escape that stimulus. We may observe this relationship in two ways. First, in the case of negative reinforcement, the stimulus is presented and the individual responds in a way that removes that stimulus. For example, Tess does not enjoy learning her basic addition facts and she begins to cry and whine each time her teacher assigns an addition worksheet. Tess is sent from the classroom and told to stay in the hallway until she can "act like an 8-year-old." Tess continues to cry and whine each math period, which allows her to avoid her addition assignments. Crying and whining are responses that allow Tess to escape the aversive stimulus which is the addition worksheet. The second relationship between an aversive stimulus and behavior may be seen when the stimulus is presented as a *result* of a particular response, a procedure known as punishment (further discussed in Chapter 14). The contingent presentation of an aversive stimulus (a punisher) results in a *decrease* in behavior. Thus, we may see that the term *negative reinforcer* refers to a specific relationship between a stimulus and a response. The term *aversive stimulus*, however, does not clearly describe the effect on behavior or the interaction between the stimulus and a response. Therefore, we will avoid the use of *aversive stimulus* as a synonym for *negative reinforcer*.

Temporal Relationship Between Stimulus and Response. Reinforcing stimuli are related to responses by their availability in time. Preresponse aversive stimuli, which may be avoided by a response, are negative reinforcers. Postresponse positive stimuli are positive reinforcers. In other words, if the reinforcer is presented before the response, the relationship is termed *negative reinforcement*; if the reinforcer is presented after the behavior, the relationship is termed *positive reinforcement*. Table 9.1 presents a clear example of this relationship.

We can assume that the rate of "listening to teacher" increased in both examples in Table 9.1, consequently reinforcers were present in both examples. But, in the first example, the stimulus (aversive) was present before the target response and was removed by the target response. In the latter example, the stimulus (positive) was presented after the target response. The direct effect on the target response was the same—an *increase* in its rate of occurrence.

Sources of Confusion

The concept of negative reinforcement is a confusing one. Apparently, it is no less confusing to many professionals—it is not uncommon to hear or read descriptions of procedures such as punishment which are referred to as negative reinforcement. There are two major sources for this continued confusion that deserve expanded attention. Historical events have been and, perhaps, will remain sources of confusion. Originally, Skinner used the term "negative reinforcement" to describe a reductive effect on behavior (1938). Today we refer to that effect as "punishment," but the confusion over the interchangeable use of these two terms continued until the mid-1960s (Michael, 1975). Since many professors and textbook authors received their training during this time, or were trained by those who did, it is reasonable to expect continuing confusion regarding the use of the term negative reinforcement. However, accepted usage is based on a clear difference between these terms based upon the effect on behavior. If a procedure decreases behavior, it can *never* be a reinforcement procedure.

A second source of confusion arises from the apparent contradiction in terms of "negative" and "reinforcer." We suspect that a major emphasis has been placed on the word "negative" rather than the word "reinforcer." While these terms may appear contradictory, it is helpful to remember that the term *reinforcer* refers to an event that increases the level of a behavior. The descriptors "positive" and "negative" refer to whether the response "earns" a stimulus (positive) or removes a stimulus (aversive).

To Use or Not To Use?

Negative reinforcement is a phenomenon that occurs routinely in our daily lives. Natural sources of negative reinforcement are pervasive; for example, when we put on sunglasses to avoid the glare of a bright, sunny day, we are reinforced by the cessation of the

TABLE 9.1 Temporal Relationship of Reinforcement Procedures

	Preresponse Stimulus	Response	Postresponse Stimulus
Negative reinforcement	While waiting for student to attend to directions, teacher is quiet, frowns, and stares at student.	Student is quiet and looks at teacher.	Teacher stops frowning and staring and begins talking.
Positive reinforcement	Teacher begins talking.	Student is quiet and looks at teacher.	Teacher praises student for listening.

glare. Negative reinforcement may also result from events that are arranged, such as putting on an automobile seatbelt to avoid the sound of the buzzer or obeying a stop sign to avoid receiving a traffic citation. School-based examples also abound, as in the example of the chronically absent student who is truant because school has become so aversive. In spite of the presence of so many sources of negative reinforcement and their obvious effect on behavior, you are encouraged to view negative reinforcement from an analytic rather than a programmatic stance. In other words, one should be aware of the presence of and potential for negatively reinforcing events, but one should avoid purposefully programming these events. There are at least two reasons for cautioning the special education teacher against relying on negative reinforcement, which will be discussed subsequently.

Potential Side Effects. A critical component of negative reinforcement is the presence of an aversive stimulus. The desired effect of this arrangement is the increase in a response that avoids or escapes that particular stimulus, but, as we shall see in Chapter 14, there are also potential undesirable side effects that may result from a reliance on aversive stimuli. These side effects may include escape and avoidance of the situation in which the aversive stimulus is presented (Azrin, Hake, Holz, & Hutchinson, 1965; Azrin & Holz, 1966). The aversiveness of the programmed stimulus may generalize to the whole setting so that the teacher, the classroom, and even the school may become aversive. The principle of negative reinforcement will still work, but now the student will effectively avoid these new aversive stimuli by not coming to school. There is also evidence suggesting that aversive stimuli, whether programmed or not, may increase aggressive responses by the student (Azrin & Holz, 1966). In short, these collateral responses (avoidance, escape, or aggression) may occur, and the result of deliberately introducing aversive conditions to your classroom may be more problematic than those you sought to remediate.

Interactive Relationships. Planning and conducting a "pure" negative reinforcement program is extremely difficult. Invariably, positive reinforcers become available to the student for inappropriate behaviors. Suppose, for example, that a student can avoid missing recess by completing his morning assignments at his desk. But on the first day of this programmed arrangement, he fails to complete his assignment and must remain inside at his desk during recess. As the student begins his work during the missed recess, the teacher must be extremely careful not to provide extra encouragement, verbal praise, increased instructional attention, or any other potentially reinforcing events. This is important because the ultimate effect on the student's behavior may be a continued decrease in finished assignments because the student receives positive reinforcers during the time that he is missing recess, but receiving the teacher's undivided attention.

Teachers also must be aware of the potential interaction effects on their own behavior, possibly to the detriment of their students. Rose (1981), for example, has described potential sources of reinforcement that may encourage teachers to send the student out of the classroom. Using his analysis, let us re-examine Tess, who was sent from the room for crying and whining during math period. We may conclude quite readily from this examination that Tess may have been negatively reinforced for disrupting the math class because those responses allowed her to escape the aversive stimulus (addition worksheets). But the teacher may have also received negative reinforcement for sending Tess to the hallway because that response (sending Tess out of the room) removed the aversive stimulus (Tess's crying and whining). Finally, we may also conclude that Tess's crying and whining may have also gained positive reinforcement from two sources. When the teacher told her to "stay in the hall until she could act like an 8-year-old," the teacher was providing attention contingent upon her inappropriate behavior. As we have seen, attention can be a powerful reinforcer. Also, knowing what we do of school hallways, there is every reason to believe that Tess's hallway contains numerous stimuli that may prove to be reinforcing to her (for example, the bulletin boards, attention from peers, and attention from other teachers). We may conclude that there are many potential sources of reinforcement, both positive and negative, available to Tess that become available only when she is sent from the classroom. This last point is critical because the teacher is the one who allows Tess to gain access to those reinforcers. Thus, negative reinforcement of one teacher response may provide the conditions necessary for a host of other reinforcers to become available. The net result of these interactive relationships is probably continued inappropriate behavior by Tess and an increasingly frustrated and puzzled teacher.

Teachers should be aware of negative reinforcers and their potential effects. By carefully analyzing the environmental conditions present in a classroom, we may avoid the problems discussed above when planning other interventions. This is the analytic function referred to earlier. Naturally occurring negative reinforcers may be employed quite effectively, once they have been identified and carefully analyzed. But the teacher is cautioned against relying too heavily on programmed negative reinforcement because it requires a planned introduction of aversive stimuli to the classroom setting. Many classroom-based stimuli that have been repeatedly paired with student failure have already become aversive to students with handicaps. Why plan to systematically introduce even more aversive stimuli to the classroom?

CLASSIFICATION OF REINFORCERS

Reinforcers may be classified along two dimensions: unconditioned-conditioned and artificial-natural. The accurate classification of any given reinforcer is an important (but often overlooked) component of any reinforcement program because the ultimate goal of independent functioning may only be attained when the different classes of reinforcers are arranged and sequenced properly. Accurate reinforcer classification requires a careful analysis of the interactions between a response and each individual's environment. The following sections provide discussions of classification dimensions, guidelines for accurately classifying reinforcers, and suggestions for the most effective uses of the various classes of reinforcers.

Unconditioned and Conditioned Reinforcers

An *unconditioned* or *primary reinforcer* is one that is "naturally" reinforcing. It is a reinforcer even when a student has had no identifiable history or experience with that reinforcer. Many objects or events have reinforcing properties which, because they require no training of the individual in order to acquire those properties, may be classified as primary reinforcers. Sex, food, warmth, and water are considered primary reinforcers.

Conditioned reinforcers are objects or events that are initially neutral but acquire reinforcing properties through association with stimuli that are reinforcing. For example, very few of us would work very long in order to gain access to small pieces of colored paper. Yet, we do exactly that because those slips of colored paper, which we have labeled "money," allow us to gain access to a variety of other reinforcers. The paper itself is neutral and essentially useless until we learn that it is associated with other objects or events that are reinforcing. Thus, we can see that when a stimulus indicates that reinforcement is forthcoming, that stimulus acquires reinforcing properties. Checkmarks and stars placed on a student's paper and letter grades are all examples of conditioned reinforcers.

Many reinforcing events that we might

consider to be unconditioned are, in fact, conditioned. Verbal praise, for example, begins to acquire reinforcing properties very early in most children's lives. Infants emit certain responses that result in parents picking them up, feeding them, and changing their diapers. Food may be classified as a primary reinforcer, but parents also do other things while performing those parental responsibilities, such as smiling, talking, and hugging their baby. These parental responses become conditioned reinforcers because they are consistently paired with primary reinforcers. Eventually, the baby emits a response, such as smiling upon seeing the parent, and the parent lavishes verbal praise for that response. This chain of events is a simplified version of how verbal praise begins to acquire reinforcing properties. There are also children for whom this example does not apply—children who did not receive consistent, contingent verbal praise at this stage or any other stage of their life. Verbal praise, then, is not going to be an effective reinforcer for that child because it has not been associated with other reinforcers. Therefore, we may conclude that verbal praise is a conditioned rather than an unconditioned reinforcer. Physical contact, such as a hug, and free time are other examples of conditioned reinforcers which may be confused with unconditioned reinforcers.

Certain types of conditioned reinforcers, such as tokens, points, or checkmarks, may be accumulated and exchanged later for other reinforcers, called *secondary* or *back-up reinforcers*, which may be either conditioned or unconditioned reinforcers. Reinforcers that can be accumulated can become *generalized conditioned reinforcers* because they can be associated with a large variety of other reinforcers. A generalized conditioned reinforcer, such as money, will probably be effective most of the time for most individuals because it is not necessary to deprive the student of all sources of reinforcement (Whaley & Mallott, 1971). (Deprivation is a factor that contributes to a reinforcer's effectiveness and is discussed in more detail in Chapter 10.)

Unconditioned and conditioned reinforcers may be used effectively in diverse settings. Generally, unconditioned reinforcers should only be used when more natural, conditioned reinforcers are not effective. However, more natural reinforcers should be consistently paired with the unconditioned reinforcer to promote the reinforcing properties of the newly conditioned reinforcer. For example, while food has been shown to be an effective unconditioned reinforcer in a variety of settings with individuals with handicaps (for examples see Christy, 1975; Craig & Holland, 1970; Hopkins, 1968; Madsen, Madsen, & Thompson, 1974; Mulhern & Baumeister, 1969; Zegiob, Jenkins, Becker, & Bristow, 1976), many more studies have effectively conditioned a reinforcer, such as social reinforcers, by pairing it with food (see Kazdin & Erickson, 1975; Levy, 1974; Madsen et al., 1974; Piper, 1974; Twardosz & Sajwaj, 1972; Wells, Forehand, Hickey, & Green, 1972). The goal should be to provide the reinforcers that are most *natural* for the particular response and setting.

Before we discuss the artificial-natural dimension, let us review the key points regarding the unconditioned-conditioned dimension.

1. A conditioned reinforcer is a stimulus (object or event) that has acquired its reinforcing properties through association with other conditioned or unconditioned reinforcers.
2. Unconditioned reinforcers do not require any prior association with other reinforcers in order to acquire reinforcing properties.
3. If a conditioned reinforcer is not occasionally associated with another reinforcer, it may eventually lose its reinforcing effect.
4. Generalized conditioned reinforcers have become effective because of their association with a variety of other conditioned and unconditioned reinforcers. They will be effective most of the time.
5. Unconditioned reinforcers may be used early in an intervention program when other consequences are not effective. Always develop an association between the unconditioned rein-

forcer and the stimulus you want to become a reinforcer. Also try to eliminate an unconditioned reinforcer as soon as possible.

Artificial and Natural Reinforcers

Natural reinforcers are those events that occur as a consequence of the target response in the natural environment. In many cases, natural reinforcers become available even when no one has deliberately programmed their delivery. Reading signs, for example, can be reinforced by finding correct objects or locations. Feeding oneself is reinforced by the taste of food. Arriving at work on time is reinforced by continued employment.

Reinforcers may be classified as artificial under either of the two following conditions: (a) when natural reinforcers are manipulated by other individuals (such as teachers, parents, co-workers) so they are not available on the same schedule as they would be in a natural environment, or (b) when the reinforcer is not a natural reinforcer for the particular response. The latter condition is the more common in educational and other settings such as group homes, factories, and grocery stores.

The distinction between artificial reinforcers and natural reinforcers is an important one for special educators, for at least two reasons (Ferster & Culbertson, 1982). First, the distinction becomes critical in a practical sense when we consider the difficulties that are encountered when we search for responses to generalize to new settings or situations. When reinforcement is not delivered as a natural result of a response, then the response is not likely to produce the artificial reinforcers in the new setting. Another practical consideration refers to the flexibility of the response. Responses trained with artificial reinforcers tend to be topographically narrow, probably because the response is specified by the teacher and the reinforcers are, too. Therefore, it is only when the specified response occurs that the reinforcer is delivered.

When using natural reinforcers, however, many responses that differ topographically may gain reinforcement. For example, there are many ways for an employee to greet a co-worker and elicit a return greeting. Any of these topographically different responses will gain access to the natural reinforcer, which may be a returned "hello" or the avoidance of someone shaking their head in puzzlement over why the person with a handicap seemed to be off in a different world. By allowing for variability, we are ensuring the employee with a handicap that he or she will be reinforced by emitting any one of several reinforcers (in this case, greetings to co-workers).

The second reason for distinguishing between artificial and natural reinforcers is moral. When discussing this reason, Ferster, et al. (1975) argued that most artificial reinforcers are used for the benefit of the instructor rather than the student. Artificial reinforcers may be useful for the teacher for a relatively long period of time, but they may not be especially useful for the student because the student's behavior is being maintained only when the teacher or other staff is present. No other reinforcer that is related to the student's performance is available when the teacher is absent.

An incident described by John Holt (1967) clearly illustrates the differences in types of responses which may be expected from natural and artificial reinforcement conditions. Holt contrasted the persistence of a young child attempting to assemble a mechanical pen with a child experiencing frustration and distress at insignificant failures in the classroom. The former child's responses were reinforced by the successful completion of the task, whereas the latter child was probably reinforced by teacher attention. In the latter case, the successful completion of the task is an important goal but only when the teacher is present.

We should note that any reinforcer may be either natural or artificial, depending on the natural consequences of the response. Food, for example, is a natural reinforcer for eating, but it is an artificial reinforcer for tying a shoe. Verbal praise is a natural reinforcer for returning a lost book to its owner, but it is an artificial reinforcer for solving an addition problem correctly. We cannot arbitrarily classify any particular reinforcer as natural or artificial. In order to classify any reinforcer, the natural consequences of the particular response must be analyzed.

In many cases, artificial reinforcers must be employed in an intervention program, either because it is more convenient for the teacher or because the student is not reinforced by the natural consequences of a particular response. Identifying a natural reinforcer and devising a viable plan for shifting control from the artificial to the natural reinforcer is critical. This may be done by (a) pairing the artificial with the natural reinforcer; (b) emphasizing the reinforcing properties of the natural reinforcer; (c) allowing some flexibility in the student's performance; and (d) gradually reducing or thinning the amount of the artificial reinforcer or the frequency of its delivery.

Consider the following example: A parent offered her child a piece of candy. The candy is in a jar with the lid placed on top so that all the child had to do is to remove the lid and get the candy. The next time the lid was screwed on about one-half a turn. On each successive presentation the lid was tightened more securely, the child learning to unscrew the lid more each time (Ferster, et al., 1975, p. 252). Is the reinforcer in this example natural or artificial? The reinforcer in this example is candy, but it is a natural reinforcer because the response (unscrew the jar lid) is one that may be reinforced in many settings by food. Also, the response and acquisition of the reinforcer did not require arbitrary intervention by the parent. But, what if the situation were slightly altered. The child is given the jar with the lid being tightened sequentially in the manner described above, but the parent now delivers the candy following each successful response. The candy is not in the jar, but comes from the parent. Is the candy a natural reinforcer in this example? No, it is not, because the natural consequence of unscrewing

a lid on a jar is not having candy handed to you by a parent. Which arrangement would we expect to maintain the response longer and in new situations?

TYPES OF REINFORCERS

There are innumerable objects or events which may serve as reinforcers. In this section potential reinforcers have been categorized according to type: edible, tangible, exchangeable, activity, social, and sensory. Each type of reinforcer will be discussed in terms of its characteristics and potential uses. In addition, there will be presented practical factors for teachers to consider before choosing each type of reinforcer and successful examples of each reinforcer type in programs with students with a variety of handicapping conditions.

The six types of reinforcers are presented in roughly hierarchical arrangement, according to its potential for intrusion into or disruption of the instructional environment. We should remember, however, that this reinforcer hierarchy may not be accurate for all circumstances, nor should the use of a particular type of reinforcer be thought of as inappropriate just because it is a type that occurs near the top of the hierarchy. The teacher should remember two things when beginning a reinforcement program: (a) carefully plan to shift the emphasis gradually from more intrusive to less intrusive types of reinforcers, and (b) plan to begin the program with the least intrusive type of reinforcer that works with the individual student. After completing this section, the reader should be able to select those types of reinforcers that will be the most effective and the least intrusive for a wide variety of situations.

Edible Reinforcers

Edible reinforcers are a potentially powerful type of reinforcer; so powerful, in fact, that many people have relied on them too much. Even today, people often think of applied behavior analysis as "M&M therapy." Nevertheless, in our efforts to provide sophisticated interventions, we should not overlook the effectiveness of edible reinforcers simply because of a preconceived notion regarding the use of edibles that is based on peer pressure or misuses in the past by others. Edibles may be a most appropriate treatment for a particular student and overlooking them may be as wrong as overlooking any other viable intervention.

Edible reinforcers have been used effectively by instructors to teach a variety of skills to children with mild to severe handicaps. Some of the skills taught or augmented with edible reinforcers include: (a) increased selection of nonreversed letters by students with learning disabilities (Sidman & Kirk, 1974), (b) increased rates of speech acquisition and the wearing of prescribed eyeglasses by a boy with autism (Wolf, Risley, & Mees, 1964), and (c) acquisition of independent walking skills by a girl with mental retardation (Meyerson, Kerr, & Michael, 1967). More specific examples are provided subsequently.

Edible Reinforcers with the Mildly Handicapped. Lisa was a 5-year-old child with learning disability (LD) who had great difficulty learning to write her name correctly. Bits of hard candy were delivered for each letter which was formed correctly and in the correct sequence. Eventually, the edible reinforcers were delivered only for the correct completion of her whole name, rather than for individual letters. After two weeks of training, Lisa was consistently able to correctly write her name. Christy (1975) reported the results of a study in which edible reinforcers were available to two groups of preschool children for staying in their seat during a fine-motor activity. Using a multiple-baseline design across subjects with reversals, Christy found the students increased substantially the duration of their in-seat behavior when the edible reinforcers were available. Mark, a 5-year-old boy with mild mental retardation, was "uncontrollable" when his mother took him shopping with her. In order to increase

Mark's appropriate behavior, his teacher suggested a procedure, based on a study by Barnard, Christophersen, and Wolf (1977), in which the mother would deliver edible reinforcers to Mark during the time they were in the supermarket. A variety of edible reinforcers were delivered at the beginning and middle of each aisle, including pieces of pretzel sticks and dry-roasted shelled peanuts. These were available to Mark only if he had stayed within 2 feet of his mother's shopping cart during the previous one-half aisle. The duration of Mark's staying-near-his-mother increased from 55 percent to 95 percent of the time.

Edible Reinforcers with the Severely Handicapped. Students in three classes at a state residential school for the deaf were signalled with a light flash when they had been attending visually for 10 seconds (Craig & Holland, 1970). Each light flash signalled the delivery of edible reinforcers, either M&M's or pieces of breakfast cereal. Visual attending increased by at least 50 percent in all three classes. Kazdin and Erickson (1975) employed edible reinforcers (candy coated cereal) and praise to increase the rate of responding to instructions by 21 institutionalized females (ages 9 to 22 years) during a play activity. Using a multiple-baseline design, Kazdin and Erickson found that the rate of responding to instructions during play behavior at least doubled for each group during the edible reinforcement conditions. Appropriate eating behavior was taught to a 10-year-old boy with multiple handicaps (Thompson, Iwata, & Poynter, 1979). The student emitted high rates of pathological tongue thrusting (reverse swallowing) which prevented appropriate eating and chewing responses. By combining a reinforcement procedure in which food was delivered only when his tongue was in his mouth, and a mild punishment in which his tongue was pushed back into his mouth, Thompson et al. obtained substantial increases in appropriate chewing together with decreases in tongue thrusting and food expulsion.

Factors to Consider. Edible reinforcers may be very powerful, but there are several factors which must be considered before implementing an intervention which makes use of edibles. First, parents must be consulted before using edibles, because allergies or other health problems (for example, diabetes) may preclude the use of certain types of edibles. Second, there is a tendency for many teachers to select food items that are lacking in nutritional value, such as candies or sugar coated cereals. A good idea is to replace these with edibles that are more nutritional, such as raisins, nuts, or granola. Third, consider only those edibles that are not messy. Many food items become sticky when held or are messy to eat. These items usually lead to extra clean-up work for the teacher and may also lead to inappropriate responses by the student, such as smearing the edible on furniture, paperwork, or peers. Fourth, satiation occurs more readily with edible reinforcers than with any other type of reinforcer. (Satiation refers to the reduced power of a reinforcer after repeated presentations and is discussed in more detail in Chapter 10.) To avoid satiation, you should make small portions of the edible reinforcer available. Thus, you should usually select an edible reinforcer that can be easily divided into small portions. Fifth, select an edible reinforcer that is safe for the student. Students who are young or who have severe handicaps may choke on certain foods, for example, nuts or popcorn. Sixth, you must be able to keep the edibles out of the student's reach because many students, especially those who are chronologically or developmentally young, will attempt to grab them and disrupt your teaching activities. Seventh, edible reinforcement is usually artificial in most special education settings; therefore, shift as soon as possible to other, more natural types of reinforcers. Plan for this swift, but gradual, shift before beginning any intervention using edibles.

Table 9.2 lists several food items that may be effective reinforcers. The items on this list are only suggestions; you should not feel restricted to just these items.

TABLE 9.2 Potential Edible Reinforcers

Milk	Cookies
Chocolate milk (instead of white milk)	Marshmallows (the smallest size)
Dry cereal	Pickles
Candy (small pieces)	Cheese
Potato chips	Nuts
Fruit juice	Popcorn
Raisins	Peanuts
Pretzels	

Tangible Reinforcers

Tangible reinforcers are those which are immediately useful to the individual (for example, pens, games, and toys) or are objects which have achieved reinforcing properties, such as stars. They do not require that the student exchange points or tokens in order to receive the tangible reinforcer. Tangibles are delivered directly as a consequence of the targeted response. (Exchangeable reinforcers may be tangible, but their use involves several differences that are discussed subsequently.)

Tangible reinforcers may be very powerful and useful reinforcers, especially when less intrusive or artificial techniques have been unsuccessful. In many instances, they may prove to be the "sparks" that get an intervention started. Rarely, however, have tangible reinforcers been used by themselves in controlled studies. Rather, they have most often been paired with exchangeable reinforcers whereby the child may earn a specified number of checkmarks, for example, which may then be exchanged for the tangible reinforcer. (This use of tangible reinforcers will be discussed in more detail in the section on exchangeable reinforcers in this chapter.) Examples of successful interventions which used tangible reinforcers are described below.

Tangible Reinforcers-Mild Handicaps. Andrew, a 12-year-old boy with behavior disorders, had great difficulty writing cursive letters. The letters and words were usually an incorrect size, extending beyond the top or bottom lines, and frequently illegible. Andrew's teacher allowed him to use a felt-tip pen with blue ink during his handwriting practice. The teacher told him that he could keep the pen when he met a predetermined legibility criteria for the first 13 letters of the alphabet. He could then earn another pen, this time with red ink, after he met criteria on the remaining 13 letters. Within four weeks Andrew had earned both pens.

Tangible reinforcers have also been successfully used to increase staying in-seat, completing task, and saying nonabusive statements to peers. Tangibles earned by students with mild handicaps in these programs included coloring books, posters, vegetable-dye tattoos, and star stickers.

Tangible Reinforcers-Severe Handicaps. Debbie, a 14-year-old student with mental retardation who attended a residential school, rarely remembered to zip the fly on her pants. One day, her teacher noticed that Debbie was very interested in a photo display cube that was on the teacher's desk. An arrangement was made, in which Debbie could keep the photo-cube at her table for as long as her pants were zipped. In addition, Debbie's teacher replaced one of the pictures in the cube every few days with a snapshot of Debbie, contingent upon "perfect zipping." When Debbie's pictures had replaced all the pictures in the cube, indicating approximately 24 days of perfect zipping, Debbie was allowed to keep the picture cube and take it to her cottage.

Factors to Consider. Before you begin a reinforcement program which employs tangible reinforcers, there are several factors to consider. These factors are of two basic types: procedural and ethical.

Several procedural issues or concerns must be considered. First, as with other reinforcers, tangibles are more effective when used with a student who has had restricted access to that particular reinforcer. For example, a child who has a large variety of toys at home may be less responsive to an inexpensive trinket. On the other hand, a child who has very few toys or other personal objects may find the same trinket a very powerful reinforcer. Sec-

ond, you may encounter difficulties in delivering tangible reinforcers, especially if the selected item is large or expensive. You may try to avoid this problem by requiring more work or longer periods of appropriate behavior before delivering the reinforcer, but this procedure will probably be ineffective, especially during the early stages of an intervention because the student may "give up" before receiving any reinforcers. Alternative solutions may involve the student earning parts of the total item. (For example, a model plane may have as many as 50 parts which can be earned separately until the whole model kit is delivered.) Another alternative is a "surprise" bag or box, in which small inexpensive items, or slips of paper specifying particular items, are placed. We have found both of these alternatives to be effective. Third, tangible reinforcers may be most appropriate for younger students because older students typically require more expensive items as reinforcers. Finally, all tangible reinforcers are extrinsic and, with few exceptions, artificial. As with edible reinforcers, you must plan to reduce, as soon as possible, the student's expectation and your reliance on tangibles and begin to provide more natural reinforcers. Tangibles are probably most useful during the initial stages of an intervention program with chronologically or developmentally young students.

There are also ethical concerns to consider, which may apply not only to tangibles but to other reinforcers such as edibles and exchangeables. One objection is the notion of "bribery." "Why should we bribe students to do the things they *should* do?" is the common refrain. There are at least two rebuttals to this question. First, bribery refers to delivering a bribe, of which the most accepted definition is something of value for which a person in a position of trust will pervert his judgment or corrupt his conduct. Thus, we may clearly see that bribery is quite different from earning something of value as a result of some appropriate behavior. The second rebuttal to this question deals with reinforcing students "to do things they should do." This portion of the often asked question makes an accurate, but superficial point. The problem lies in the discrepancy between what they *should* do and what they *actually* do. Learning to "behave properly" is no different than any other kind of learning. Teaching appropriate behavior, whether academic or social, requires the careful arrangement of consequent events, so the student may learn the relationship between his responses and the consequences of those responses.

Another ethical concern refers to treating children differently. A parent may ask, "Why should Wallace receive that _____(fill in a reinforcer of your choice) when my child does not?" A related concern is that the student's peers will become upset by the inequality of these arrangements. First, there is nothing inherently wrong with treating individual students differently, as a matter of fact, doing so describes individualized instruction, to which few would be opposed. The difference is that we are discussing consequent arrangements rather than grouping arrangements or curricular materials, which are somehow viewed differently. Also, reinforcement procedures and appropriate reinforcers are critical components of an individualized program. Second, classmates may be upset, at least initially, by this apparent favoritism. But our experience has indicated that this need not be a serious problem if several things are considered prior to the intervention. Students, even students with handicaps, are usually more astute socially than we give them credit for being and, consequently, they know who is having which particular behavioral problems. Quite often a class meeting can use the students' knowledge to eliminate problems regarding the intervention, if the teacher is open and honest about the individual student's needs or problems and the planned program. They will recognize the problem and may offer a good deal of support. In addition, specific reinforcement programs for an individual student may result in an improvement in the whole class (Christy, 1975). Briefly then, intervention programs do not have to be mysterious or treated as top secret;

in fact, most successful interventions are those which are not treated this way.

Table 9.3 lists some tangible items that may prove to be effective reinforcers. Remember, however, that these are only suggestions and that any tangible item may prove to be reinforcing for a particular student.

Exchangeable Reinforcers

Exchangeables are reinforcers which may be traded, or exchanged, for other more valued *secondary* or *back-up* reinforcers. Exchangeables are similar to tangible reinforcers in many respects, but they usually are not of particular value by themselves. Their reinforcing power comes from the individual's opportunity to exchange them for other types of reinforcers, for example, edibles, tangibles, or activities. Exchangeable reinforcers often are called *tokens* and may include money, poker chips, sticks, or checkmarks.

Token programs have proven to be very successful for a variety of responses in different settings, including: (a) various adaptive responses in a psychiatric setting (Ayllon & Azrin, 1965; 1968), (b) daily living skills for females with mental retardation living in an institution (Thomas, Sulzer-Azaroff, Lukeris, & Palmer, 1977), and (c) various academic skills in public schools (O'Leary & O'Leary,

TABLE 9.3   Potential Tangible Reinforcers

Books	Felt-tip markers
Records	Puzzles
Toys	Jump rope
Hair ribbons	Baseball or football cards
Make-up	Yo-yo
Comb	Models
Art materials	Play money
Toy cars	Positive notes to parents
Comic books	Vegetable-dye tattoos
Marbles	Prizes for work
Pencil or pen	Balls
Eraser	Gold stars
Note pads	Certificates
Dolls	Good work awards
Crayons	Balloons

1976). Token programs have proven to be so effective and popular that the number of studies employing this type of reinforcer has increased dramatically. The effective use of token programs will be discussed fully in Chapter 10. Examples of some use of exchangeable reinforcers, however, are provided below.

Exchangeable Reinforcer-Mild Handicaps. Five students with behavior disorders attending a therapeutic summer camp could earn token reinforcers for improved arithmetic performance in a programmed arithmetic text. Tokens were available when they completed a predetermined number of frames in the text and "bonus" tokens could be earned for satisfactory performance on the periodic in-program tests. Compared to a no-token baseline period, arithmetic productivity increased substantially when the token contingencies were applied (Rickard, Clements, & Willis, 1970).

Three high school boys were often ridiculed by their peers for being "smelly" and "dirty." Their resource room teacher instituted a token reinforcement program to increase personal hygiene habits such as cleaning the hair, body, finger nails, and teeth. The resource teacher rearranged the boys' schedules so that they had physical education class followed by a shower immediately before their special education class. Points were awarded for the completion of each component response of a personal hygiene program, and these points could be exchanged for preferred items or activities, such as snacks and listening to a radio during class.

Mothers of three boys, ages 5 to 6 years, were trained in the delivery of tokens and verbal praise for their son's appropriate shopping behavior, which included staying close to the mother and not disturbing products on the shelves. Both responses increased after tokens were used and subsequent follow-up observations indicated that the behaviors continued to be maintained, even though the procedures had been altered by each mother.

In addition, mother-child interactions were much more positive after the program began (Barnard, et al., 1977).

Exchangeable Reinforcers-Severe Handicaps. An instructional package, including modeling and corrective feedback as well as exchangeable reinforcers, was used to increase the use of adjectives and adverbs in the written responses of four students with hearing impairments and aphasia. The students exhibited poor written language skills and rarely included modifiers in their sentences. During subsequent phases, correct sentences earned each student one point. Two points were awarded for correct sentences containing prenominal adjectives (for example, a *red* truck). A correct sentence containing adverbs earned three points. Finally, correct sentences containing both a prenominal adjective and an adverb earned four points. Following the implementation of this program, the students demonstrated significant increases in response rate, accuracy, and percentage of correct sentences with modifiers (Heward & Eachus, 1979).

Token reinforcers have also been used to increase the frequency of the play behaviors of five institutionalized children with mental retardation. Points and praise were available to the students for initiating either cooperative or competitive play with their peers. The points could be exchanged either immediately after the play period for games or activities, or they could be saved for larger secondary reinforcers, such as field trips. During the token program, the students dramatically increased their cooperative and competitive play to higher levels (Knapczyk & Yoppi, 1975).

Factors to Consider. Exchangeable reinforcers, especially token reinforcement systems, have been among the most widely used interventions. Consequently, exchangeables have received a good deal of attention from researchers, and several potential advantages have been identified in their use. Exchangeables can easily transcend the delay that is often necessary between the reinforced response and the availability of the secondary reinforcer. They can allow the teacher to reinforce responses at any time, so that performance is not interrupted by the delivery of the secondary reinforcer. Consequently, exchangeables facilitate the reinforcement of sequences of responses. They have also been shown to maintain responses effectively over long periods of time when the back-up reinforcer cannot be delivered. These advantages are somewhat related and their relevance to your instructional programming is clear. Other advantages of exchangeables are their resistance to satiation effects and their potential to simplify your reinforcing activities because they allow you to deliver the same reinforcer to a number of students even though their preferences of secondary reinforcers are very different.

From the above discussion, you may find yourself thinking that you have finally found the magic cure-all for your reinforcement needs. Unfortunately, this conclusion is not necessarily accurate. There are several procedural factors which must be considered before you begin a program using exchangeables. These factors may be centered on the program itself, on the teacher, or on the students (Drabman & Tucker, 1974).

Several issues must be resolved before beginning the token program or else it may be doomed to failure. First, you must clearly establish the target behaviors—which behavior will gain exchangeable reinforcers and which, if any, will lose exchangeables for the student. Second, during how much of the school day should the procedure be in effect? Usually a token program can be employed for only part of the day. You must decide which part. Third, you must also decide how often to distribute the exchangeable reinforcers. This decision must account for two very important factors: (a) the number of reinforcers necessary to improve a student's behavior and (b) the demands on your time that delivering exchangeables will make. Fourth, should you use material tokens, such as poker chips, or representational tokens like check marks or

stars? For example, material tokens, because they are like money, may allow a student to gain reinforcement from her peers because she is "wealthy." On the other hand, material tokens may be stolen, extorted, traded, or thrown (Bushell, Wrobel, & Michaelis, 1968). Fifth, what kind of secondary reinforcers should be used? Secondary reinforcers for younger students will be very different from those selected by older students. Usually activities and tangible reinforcers work best, but you must decide what the specific secondary reinforcers will be. Sixth, you must decide how much each secondary reinforcer will cost. Pegging its value to its real-life value may be a good idea, but you must also consider the value it has for the student. Quite often a cheap trinket will be more highly valued than a more expensive item.

Teacher-centered factors relate to the actual implementation of the program. First, you must be consistent. Once you decide to employ exchangeables, you must live by the same rules you have established for your students. For example, you should not change the program from day to day or forget about it for a period of time. Second, you should keep accurate data on your students' performance and use these data to make any changes in the program. If you cannot commit yourself to consistency and data collection, you should probably avoid using exchangeable reinforcers.

Another area of concern involves student-centered factors. Should you employ exchangeables with a whole class or with individual students? The answer to this question can only be determined by you, but, depending on the circumstances, both approaches have been effective. Group reinforcement may not be as effective if your class is too heterogeneous. If you are to use a group contingency with a heterogeneous group, you may want to divide the class into smaller, more homogeneous groups. You must also carefully monitor your newly created economy to detect signs of inflation or depression. If exchangeables are too easy to earn, they may lose their reinforcing power through satiation. If they are too difficult to earn, the intervention is also likely to fail because the students may become frustrated.

All of these issues must be resolved either before or during the program, if you are to be successful. As you can see, there are many potential stumbling blocks to the successful use of exchangeables. While there are very clear advantages of exchangeables, you must remember that a token program is a rather artificial and intrusive type of reinforcers for most classrooms. Quite often, other more natural reinforcers will be just as effective and, in many cases, more efficient. We must conclude, then, that exchangeables should be used only when more natural procedures have failed.

Table 9.4 lists several items that have proven to be successful exchangeable reinforcers. You are reminded, however, that these are only a sampling of items that may be successfully used in your classroom.

Activity Reinforcers

Any activity that is enjoyable or that a student may choose to do may be a very effective reinforcer. If you allow a student to engage in these favored activities after he performs a particular behavior, you are using that activity as a reinforcer. Virtually any activity may be reinforcing for a particular student, as demonstrated by the successful use of such varied activities as free time, extra recess time, or being "teacher's helper."

Activity reinforcers may be natural to the settings in which they are used, such as class-room responsibilities (McLaughlin & Malaby, 1972), access to classroom games (Ayllon & Roberts, 1974), or free time (Marholin, McInnis, & Heads, 1974). They may also be artificial in a particular setting, such as background music on a school bus (McCarty, McElfresh, Rice, & Wilson 1978) or a radio in a classroom (Wilson & Hopkins, 1973). However, even in the case of artificial activity reinforcers, this type of reinforcer is usually less intrusive than edible, tangible, or even exchangeable reinforcers. Satiation also may be less likely to occur with activity reinforcers.

Several programs rely heavily on activity reinforcers. For example, Achievement Place, in Kansas City, KS, (a residential community for predelinquents) makes activities such as shopping trips and recreational activities contingent upon the student's successfully completing tasks or responsibilities (Phillips, Fixsen, Phillips, & Wolf, 1979). Other specific examples of the successful use of activity reinforcers are discussed subsequently.

Activity Reinforcers-Mild Handicaps. Marholin et al. (1974) used free time as a reinforcer for the reading, English, and arithmetic performance of three boys with behavioral disorders. At first, free time was only available if the students met or exceeded their baseline median for reading accuracy. Later, free time was contingent upon meeting or exceeding baseline median accuracy in any one of the three academic subjects, but the subject for that particular day was randomly selected so the students could not predict what subject they had to do well that day. Marholin et al. found that reading accuracy increased when free time was contingent upon that behavior, and, furthermore, free time was an effective reinforcer for all three academic subjects when the students could not predict the subject upon which it was contingent.

Activity Reinforcers-Severe Handicaps. Six girls with hearing impairments, whose IQs ranged from 53 to 74, were rarely in their seats during academic sessions. By providing free time activities contingent upon progressively increased durations of in-seat behavior,

TABLE 9.4 Potential Exchangeable Reinforcers

Badges to be worn during day to alert staff to provide positive attention	Note to parent
	Stars
	Grades
Points	Honor roll
Charted progress toward an activity	Poker chips
	Gift certificates
Checkmarks	Money for snacks
Smiley faces	at school store
	or canteen

Osborn (1969) taught the girls to stay in their seats for at least 25 minutes at a time.

The bus drivers for a special school for disturbed children reported almost constant fighting and out-of-seat behaviors on their buses. Using a multiple-baseline design, McCarty et al. (1978) introduced radio music on the buses. The music was contingent upon appropriate behavior and was turned off for a brief period whenever a student fought or got out of his or her seat. The contingent music proved to be a successful reinforcer for the targeted appropriate behaviors.

Factors to Consider. One of the most important considerations to make when choosing activity reinforcers is the match between activities and the student. As with any other type of reinforcer, those which are not attractive to the student will not have much power as reinforcers. One of the easiest ways to determine which activities appeal to which students is to provide a variety of activities and watch the students. The activities that the students enthusiastically select and do are probably those which will be most effective as reinforcers. You may also simply ask the students what they would like to do. This is probably the easiest selection method, but it may not be too accurate because what we say we like to do and what we *actually* do are quite often not the same.

Another method for identifying reinforcing activities was first identified by Premack (1959). Following a series of laboratory studies, Premack concluded that those activities which a person chooses may be used to reinforce other responses that occur at a low frequency. This procedure, called the *Premack principle*, requires that access to preferred, high frequency behavior be made contingent upon the performance of a less preferred, low frequency behavior. An interesting example of the Premack principle was reported by Homme, DeBaca, Devine, Steinhorst, and Rickert (1963). In their study, a class of nursery school students were observed running and screaming around the classroom for quite long periods of time. Homme and his colleagues arranged to have periods of unrestricted running and screaming contingent upon periods of sitting quietly. The proportion of time the students spent sitting quietly increased dramatically.

The use of the Premack principle is certainly not new. Parents and teachers have probably always used it. The major contribution by Premack to our systematic use of this

TABLE 9.5 Potential Activity Reinforcers

"Gossip" time	Plant a garden
Finger paint	Part-time job
Feed pet	Games with teacher
Play with magnet	Decorate classroom
Talk into tape recorder	Help in cafeteria
Use colored chalk	Have parents visit
Water the plants	Make gift for parent
Use a typewriter	Pick seat on bus
Pick up litter on school grounds	Crafts
Distribute materials	Message runner
Use an overhead projector	Tutor another student
Grade papers	Chew gum in class
Get to time self with a stopwatch	Have picture taken
	Demonstrate hobby to class
Extra recess	Go home early
Group leader	Plan personal daily schedule
Library time	
Hall monitor	Collect lunch tickets
Field trips	Help custodian
Sharpen pencils	Construct bulletin board
No homework	
Choice of seating arrangements	Help librarian
	See films
Raise flag	Party
Free time	Story time
Early dismissal from class	Academic contests
	Organized recreation
Erase boards	Cafeteria helper
Making noises (rattles, bells)	Nature walk
	Time alone with counselor or staff member
Play on playground equipment	
Play with clay or flour and water	Lunch with teacher or other staff member
Rocking in a chair	
Stay up late	Swimming
Line leader	Cookouts
Television	Crafts
Weekend pass	Collect lunch tickets
Games with peers	Art projects (coloring or painting)
Having visitors	

principle was his emphasis on objectively verifying that certain behaviors or activities are, indeed, high frequency or preferred. Too often, we rely on "reinforcers" that appear to be preferred but in reality may not be preferred by a particular student. For example, "Finish your homework and then you can talk on the telephone for a half hour" may not be an effective arrangement if the student has no desire to talk with friends.

Activity reinforcers, especially if we use the Premack principle, are very popular and useful in most classroom settings because there are almost always preferred activities that may be available in the environment. Even sitting at a desk and daydreaming may be used as a reinforcing activity. Unfortunately, some preferred activities may not be appropriate in a particular setting, for example, playing soccer in the classroom. If an activity is a powerful reinforcer but is also inappropriate at a particular time or in a particular setting, we might issue some form of token which can be exchanged at a later time for the preferred activity.

Social Reinforcers

Social reinforcers may be presented by any other person in the classroom setting. Attention, words, smiles, gestures, a pat on the back, or a hug may all be thought of as social reinforcers. Social reinforcers are generally the most natural type of reinforcers and are usually the most readily available in most classroom settings.

The effectiveness of social reinforcers has been documented by a large number of studies. Increased rates of paying attention (Kazdin, 1973; Kazdin & Klock, 1973; Strain & Pierce, 1977), persisting on a task (Hill & Strain, 1977), playing on playground equipment (Hall & Broden, 1967), and writing numerals correctly (Hasazi & Hasazi, 1972) are only a few of the appropriate responses that have been increased with the use of contingent social reinforcement. The following examples discussed in more detail represent only a few of those that are available to demonstrate the effectiveness of social reinforcers.

Social Reinforcers with Mildly Handicaps. Hasazi and Hasazi (1972) reported a study in which the numeral reversals made by a child with learning disabilities are reinforced by the teacher's attention. As may be seen in Figure 9.1, when reversed numerals were ignored by the teacher and correctly formed numerals were attended to with a smile, a pat on the back, and verbal praise, the proportion of correctly written numerals increased remarkably. Another example concerns a 3 and a half-year-old boy enrolled in an experimental preschool classroom who exhibited dangerously aggressive responses to his peers, including choking, biting, and hitting. In addition, he rarely initiated any appropriate interactions with his peers. Typically, the teacher responded to his aggressive behavior with verbal admonitions, such as "We don't do that here" or "You can't play here until you can be a good boy." During treatment, the teacher ignored his aggressive behavior and the victim of his aggression received the teacher's attention. During several reversal treatment conditions the investigators found that a large porportion of the student's aggressive responses were being reinforced by the teacher's attention. When the aggressive behavior was ignored it decreased. In a later phase, the teacher attended to him whenever he initiated peer interactions and these interactions began to increase significantly (Pinkston, Reese, LeBlanc, & Baer, 1973).

Social Reinforcers with Severely Handicaps. Two preschool boys with mental retardation were verbally praised when they had attended to a manipulative task for 20 consecutive seconds. Descriptive verbal praise had a pronounced affect on the boys' attention-to-task responses (Strain & Pierce, 1977). Gray and Kasteller (1969) reported the results of a study in which foster grandparents were used to train institutionalized students with mental retardation to perform basic self-care skills, such as dressing and eating, and simple aca-

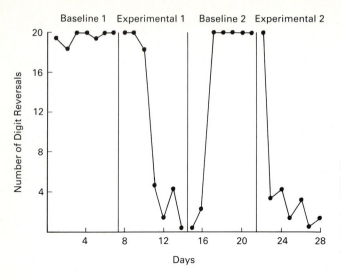

Figure 9.1 Number of Digit Reversals per Day Under Baseline and Experimental Conditions.

Source: J. E. Hasazi, & S. E. Hasazi in "Effects of teacher attention on digit-reversal behavior in an elementary school child." *Journal of Applied Behavior Analysis, 12,* 391–400.

demic responses, like number identification. Whenever a student emitted a correct response, one of the foster grandparents would verbally praise him and give him a hug or a smile. After one year, the students who worked with the foster grandparents demonstrated a statistically significant increase in a variety of skills when compared to a control group.

Factors to Consider. There are two basic pitfalls to avoid when you arrange contingencies using social reinforcers. First, you must remember that you are only one of several possible sources of social reinforcement. Attention and other social reinforcers from peers may be particularly powerful, especially with older students. In fact, peer reinforce-

ment may be so powerful for an inappropriate response that they may increase despite your social reinforcement of a competing appropriate response (O'Leary, Becker, Evans & Saudargas, 1969). The second pitfall is the tendency for teachers to be rather nonspecific in their social reinforcement. Saying "Good" may often be effective, but a more effective approach would be to describe what the student did to earn that praise, such as saying, "I like the way you raised your hand" (Bernhardt & Forehand, 1975; Drabman, 1976; Drabman & Tucker, 1974). By using *descriptive* and *specific* praise you are restating the contingencies, helping the student discriminate reinforced from nonreinforced responses, and prompting the student to perform the desired response again.

There are several impressive advantages to the use of social reinforcers. They can be delivered immediately and consistently to groups of students as well as to individuals. Social reinforcers are very resistant to satiation effects, especially when they are delivered sincerely. They are also very efficient both in terms of teacher time and monetary cost. Another benefit of social reinforcers is that other people who may be important to the student (for instance, peers) may participate in their delivery. Finally, *incidental* social

TABLE 9.6 Potential Social Reinforcers

Smiles	Bragging to someone
Verbal praise	else about their be-
Eye contact	havior
Phone call to parents	Tickles
Pat on the back	Winks
Good papers on bulletin	Physical contact (hugs,
board	pats, or touches)
Being on school patrol	Clapping hands
Positive comments writ-	Sit on teacher's lap
ten on paper	

reinforcers may be arranged. For example, a student achieves criterion on a target behavior and earns both social reinforcers (praise and hugs) and a "good work award" certificate which is signed by the teacher and sent to the student's parents. The teacher, however, also escorts the student to the principal's office and brags profusely about the student's performance. The principal then offers her congratulations and also signs the award certificate. This example illustrates "programmed bragging," but you may also provide incidental social reinforcement by bragging about the student in his presence when he thinks you do not know he is listening.

Because of the obvious advantages of social reinforcement, you should include them in all reinforcement programs, regardless of the other classes of reinforcers being used. You can easily pair social reinforcers with the delivery of any other type of reinforcer. This will serve to make the other types of reinforcers more effective and also help to make the withdrawing artificial reinforcers easier.

Sensory Reinforcers

Sensory reinforcement refers to the unconditioned characteristics of sensory events that increase the probability of the behaviors that they reinforce (Kish, 1966). Sensory reinforcers are those stimulus events that are consequences of a particular response and serve to increase or maintain that response. Typically, they include auditory, visual, tactile or proprioceptive stimuli. While edible reinforcers may be classified as sensory because they interact with the olfactory (smell) and gustatory (taste) senses, they are not included in the category of sensory reinforcers because many of the characteristics of edible reinforcers differ from the characteristics of sensory reinforcers. For example, edible reinforcers are often artificial in a particular setting while, as we shall see, sensory reinforcers are usually natural consequences of particular responses.

The effectiveness of sensory reinforcers with humans was first documented with nor-

mal populations, including infants (Siqueland, 1968), children (Stevenson & Odom, 1961), and adults (Benton & Mefford, 1967). More recent investigations have also demonstrated their effects with handicapped populations, including persons with mental retardation and children with autism (Rincover, 1978).

Sensory reinforcers have been used most frequently with children who have severe handicaps, and their uses have evolved from increasing evidence that self-stimulatory behaviors, such as rocking, finger flicking, and spinning objects are reinforced by the sensory events they produce (Lovaas & Newson, 1976). This conceptualization has led investigators to study the reinforcing effects of sensory feedback of several modalities, including visual (Fineman, 1968; Frankel, Freeman, Ritvo, Chikami, & Carr 1976; Rincover, Newsom, Lovaas, & Koegel, 1977; Rincover, Cook, Peoples, & Packard, 1979), auditory (Rincover, et al., 1977, 1979), and tactile or proprioceptive (Baily & Meyerson, 1969; Favell, McGimsey & Jones 1978; Nunes, Murphey; & Ruprecht, 1977; Rehagen & Thelen, 1972; Rincover, et al., 1979; Wolery, 1978).

The work of Rincover and his associates present the most elegant demonstrations of the reinforcing power of sensory events. For example, Rincover described the preferred sensory stimuli for each of four children with autism in the following way: (a) auditory for one child because he repeatedly engaged in activities that produced auditory feedback, such as playing with toys that made a variety of sounds and adjusting the volume on a radio; (b) visual-movement for one child because he would rhythmically weave objects back and forth in front of his eyes; and (c) visual-flicker for the remaining two children because they engaged in activities that produced a flickering type of visual feedback, such as turning light switches on and off rapidly. In a laboratory setting, the children were trained to press a bar which was connected to an instrument panel. Brief presentations of each child's preferred sensory event (for example, musical tape, windshield wiper movement, or low-frequency strobe lights) were contingent on correct bar-pressing responses. Their results demonstrated conclusively that sensory stimulation reinforced high levels of responding. Furthermore, these high levels of responses were maintained for long periods of time and the children did not become satiated (Rincover et al., 1977).

Rincover and his colleagues in 1979 reported the results of a particularly thorough study which systematically identified the sensory reinforcers for the self-stimulatory behaviors of another four students with autism. In a second experimental phase, they used identified sensory events to teach the children to play appropriately with specific toys. Following two days of careful observation, the following self-stimulatory responses and their suspected reinforcing stimuli were identified: (a) hand flapping, in which the arms were held out to the side with the fingers, wrists, and arms in constant motion—proprioceptive feedback as the reinforcer; (b) twirling objects, such as a plate, on a hard surface and leaning toward the object apparently to listen to the object—auditory reinforcer; (c) throwing feathers, lint, or small pieces of string into the air and waving the hands under it, apparently to keep it afloat—visual reinforcer; (d) finger-flapping in front of her eyes—visual or proprioceptive reinforcer.

At this time in the investigation, the maintaining stimulus events were only guesses, but Rincover and his associates took the next important step and objectively verified their guesses. They attempted to eliminate the particular sensory consequences of a given response. This procedure has been called *sensory extinction* (Rincover, 1978).[2] If the

removal of the sensory event leads to a reduction in the particular response, then the investigators could be sure they had identified the reinforcing sensory feedback for that behavior. During the sensory extinction phase, the following procedures were implemented: (a) for proprioceptive feedback, a small vibrator was taped to the back of the child's hand; (b) for auditory feedback from the plate-spinning, the table top was carpeted in order to eliminate the sound; (c) for visual feedback from finger-flapping, the child was blindfolded for brief periods of time; and (d) for visual feedback from "feather floating," the lights were turned off for brief periods. The researchers found that when these conditions were present, the rate of self-stimulation for each child was greatly reduced. Of more importance, however, they had identified sensory events that were apparently reinforcing for each child.

The final phase of this experiment involved selecting toys which provided the appropriate sensory feedback for each child and then providing some initial training in their appropriate use. The toys selected were a music box (auditory) to substitute for "plate spinning", interfacing building blocks (proprioceptive), beads and string (proprioceptive) for hand flapping, and a bubble-blowing kit (visual) as a substitute for the "feather floating" behavior. Following a brief training period regarding the appropriate use of each toy, both the self-stimulatory and toy-play responses of each child were observed. In general, the self-stimulatory responses decreased significantly and the play responses increased dramatically. Figure 9.2 displays these effects for one of the subjects of this study.

Factors to Consider. There appear to be several advantages to the use of sensory reinforcers. First, they are typically naturally occurring events, and, therefore, they should produce durable behaviors that will generalize to new settings more readily. Second, they are also relatively easy to identify (Rincover & Koegel, 1977). Third, they are relatively resistant to satiation effects. For example, Rin-

---

[2]Extinction refers to the principle of decreasing behavior by removing the reinforcers for that behavior. Extinction has been proven to be an effective technique for reducing behavior and is discussed in more detail in Chapter 14. In the case of sensory extinction, the sensory events that are maintaining a particular behavior are removed, thus reducing the frequency of the behavior. If the removal of the sensory event does not lead to a reduction in behavior, then that sensory event was not a reinforcer of that behavior.

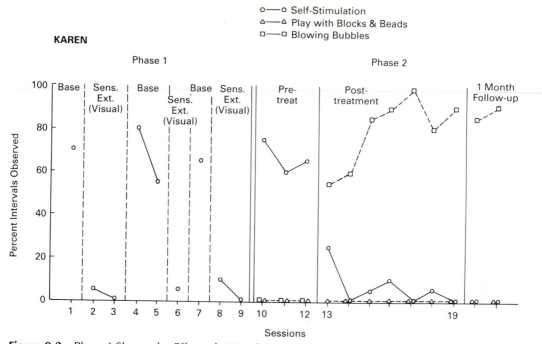

KAREN

Phase 1   Phase 2

Source: A. Rincover, R. Cook, A. Peoples, & D. Packard (1979) in "Sensory extinction and sensory reinforcement principles for programming multiple adaptive behavior change." *Journal of Applied Behavior Analysis, 12,* 221–233.

Figure 9.2 Phase I Shows the Effect of "Visual Sensory Extinction" on Karen's Self-stimulatory Behavior. Phase 2 shows the percentage of self-stimulation, play with the visual toy (bubbles), and play with the proprioceptive toys (beads and blocks) before ("Pretreatment") and after ("Posttreatment") she was taught to play with each of the three toys.

cover et al. (1977) found that the subjects of their study never became satiated in the general area of their preferred sensory stimulation, such as music. Moreover, whenever they became satiated on a particular event, such as a specific song, then a minor change in that event (switching to a new song) maintained the responses at the previously attained high level of responding.

As a result of the use of sensory reinforcers, we may be able to rely less on artificial reinforcers, such as edibles, in programming for students with handicaps. There are several procedural steps which will enhance your chances of successfully using sensory reinforcers. First, you must carefully observe the child's responses. Second, you must deter-mine the probable sensory event(s) that are reinforcing those responses. This determination is to be based on your observations and must be considered to be a "best guess" until it is verified objectively. Third, you must objectively verify the reinforcing power of each stimulus event. Sensory extinction procedures appear to be the simplist way to accomplish this verification. Fourth, you must select events to be used as reinforcers that yield sensory stimulation which is similar to the naturally occurring stimuli. Finally, you must try the intervention and collect data on its effects. Any decision you make regarding the continuation or alteration of your program should be based on data.

Table 9.7 lists several sensory reinforcers

TABLE 9.7 Potential Sensory Reinforcers

Vibration to neck and shoulders	Television
Rubbing skin with hand, feather, fur, or towel	Slide projector
	Soap bubbles
	Music
Jumping	Toys that make various noises
Crawling	Spinning tops
Patting skin	Squeezable toys
Bouncing on teacher's knee	Self-stimulation (via the Premack principle)
Trampoline	
Flickering lights	

that have proven to be effective. Virtually any sensory event may prove to be reinforcing to a particular student, so do not be limited by these suggestions.

SUMMARY

Reinforcement was identified as one of the most powerful behavioral principles for increasing or maintaining response levels. Positive reinforcement was defined, and its major components were identified as stimulus, response contingency, response, and the effects of a reinforcer on a response. Negative reinforcement was also defined, and aversive stimuli was identified as being a necessary component of any negative reinforcer. The temporal relationship between the presentation of a stimulus and its effect on behavior was presented as a means for discriminating between positive and negative reinforcement. Because the principle of negative reinforcement is often confusing, two sources of this confusion were examined, that is, historical events and the apparent contradiction inherent in the terms "negative" and "reinforcement." A discussion of several issues regarding the use of negative reinforcement concluded that section.

Reinforcers were grouped into two classifications: unconditioned-conditioned and artificial-natural. These types were defined and thoroughly discussed. Six types of reinforcers were arranged in a roughly hierarchical order, from most intrusive to least intrusive in a typical classroom setting. The different types of reinforcers identified were edible, tangible, exchangeable, activity, social, and sensory. Each type of reinforcer was discussed in terms of its characteristics and its potential uses. Examples of the successful uses of each type were presented, and the factors that a teacher should consider before using any type of reinforcer were delineated.

Upon completion of this chapter, the reader should have a thorough understanding of the basic principles of reinforcement, the various types of reinforcers, and the specific use of reinforcers. Chapter 10 will extend this knowledge by discussing various strategies and methods that will enable the reader to use reinforcement most effectively.

REFERENCES

AYLLON, T., & AZRIN, N. H. (1965). "The measurement and reinforcement of behavior of psychotics." *Journal of the Experimental Analysis of Behavior*, 8, 357–383.

AYLLON, T., & AZRIN, N. H. (1968). *The token economy: A motivational system for therapy and rehabilitation.* New York: Appleton-Century-Crofts.

AYLLON, T., & ROBERTS, M. D. (1974). "Eliminating discipline problems by strengthening academic performance." *Journal of Applied Behavior Analysis*, 7, 73–81.

AZRIN, N. H., HAKE, D. G., HOLZ, W. C., & HUTCHINSON, R. R. (1965). "Motivational aspects of escape from punishment. *Journal of the Experimental Analysis of Behavior*, 8, 31–44.

AZRIN, N. H., & HOLZ, W. C. (1966). "Punishment." In W. K. Honig (ed.), *Operant behavior: Areas of research and application.* New York: Appleton-Century-Crofts.

BAILEY, J., & MEYERSON, L. (1969). "Vibration as a reinforcer with a profoundly retarded child." *Journal of Applied Behavior Analysis*, 2, 135–137.

BARNARD, J. D., CHRISTOPHERSEN, E. R., & WOLF, M. M. (1977). "Teaching children appropriate shopping behavior through parent training in the supermarket setting." *Journal of Applied Behavior Analysis*, 10, 49–59.

BECKER, W. C., ENGELMANN, S., & THOMAS, D.

R. (1975). *Teaching I: Classroom management.* Chicago: Science Research Associates.

BECKER, W. C., MADSEN, C. H., ARNOLD, C. R., & THOMAS, D. R. (1967). "The contingent use of teacher attention and praise in reducing classroom behavior problems." *Journal of Special Education, 1,* 287–307.

BENTON, R. G., & MEFFORD, R. B. (1967). "Projector slide changing and focusing as operant reinforcers. *Journal of the Experimental Analysis of Behavior, 10,* 479–484.

BERNHARDT, A. J., & FOREHAND, R. (1975). "The effects of labeled and unlabeled praise upon lower and middle class children." *Journal of Experimental Child Psychology, 19,* 536–543.

BILLINGSLEY, F. F. (1977). "The effects of self- and externally-imposed schedules of reinforcement on oral reading performance." *Journal of Learning Disabilities, 10,* 549–559.

BLANKENSHIP, C. (1978). "Remediating systematic inversion errors in subtraction through the use of demonstration and feedback." *Learning Disabilities Quarterly, 1,* 12–22.

BUDD, K. S., GREEN, D. R., & BAER, D. M. (1976). "An analysis of multiple misplaced parental social contingencies." *Journal of Applied Behavior Analysis, 9,* 459–470.

BUSHELL, D., WROBEL, P. A., & MICHAELIS, M. L. (1968). "Applying 'group' contingencies to the classroom study behavior of preschool children." *Journal of Applied Behavior Analysis, 1,* 55–63.

CHRISTY, P. R. (1975). "Does use of tangible rewards with individual children affect peer observers?" *Journal of Applied Behavior Analysis, 8,* 187–196.

CONNOLLY, A., NACHTMAN, W., & PRITCHETT, E. (1971). *Manual for the Key Math Diagnostic Arithmetic Test.* Circle Pines, MN: American Guidance Service.

CRAIG, H. B., & HOLLAND, A. (1970). "Reinforcement of visual attending in classrooms for deaf children." *Journal of Applied Behavior Analysis, 3,* 97–109.

DRABMAN, R. S. (1976). "Behavior modification in the classroom." In W. E. Craighead, A. E. Kazdin, & M. J. Mahoney (eds.), *Behavior modification: Principles, issues, and applications.* Boston: Houghton Mifflin.

DRABMAN, R. S., & TUCKER, R. D. (1974). "Why classroom token economies fail." *Journal of School Psychology, 12,* 178–188.

FAVELL, J. E., McGIMSEY, J. F., & JONES, M. L. (1978). "The use of physical restraint in the treatment of self-injury and as positive reinforcement." *Journal of Applied Behavior Analysis, 11,* 225–241.

FERSTER, C. B., CULBERTSON, S., & BOREN, M. C. (1975). *Behavior principles (3rd).* Englewood Cliffs, NJ: Prentice-Hall, pp. 131–133, 139–142.

FINEMAN, F. R. (1968). "Shaping and increasing verbalizations in an autistic child in response to visual-color stimuli." *Perceptual and Motor Skills, 27,* 1071–1074.

FRANKEL, F., FREEMAN, B. J., RITVO, E., CHIKAMI, B., & CARR, E. (1976). "Effects of frequency of photic stimulation upon autistic and retarded children." *American Journal of Mental Deficiency, 81,* 32–40.

GRAY, R. M., & KASTELLER, J. (1969). "The effects of social reinforcement and training on institutionalized mentally retarded children." *American Journal of Mental Deficiency, 74,* 50–56.

HALL, A. V., & BRODEN, M. (1967). "Behavior changes in brain-injured children through social reinforcement." *Journal of Experimental Child Psychology, 5,* 463–479.

HASAZI, J. E., & HASAZI, S. E. (1972). "Effects of teacher attention on digit-reversal behavior in an elementary school child." *Journal of Applied Behavior Analysis, 5,* 157–162.

HEWARD, W. L., & EACHUS, H. T. (1979). "Acquisition of adjectives and adverbs in sentences written by hearing impaired and aphasic children." *Journal of Applied Behavior Analysis, 12,* 391–400.

HILL, A. D., & STRAIN, P. S. (1977). "The effects of teacher-delivered social reinforcement on the task persistent behavior of educable mentally retarded children." *Psychology in the Schools, 14,* 207–212.

HOLT, J. (1977). *How children learn* (p. 25). New York: Pittman.

HOMME, L. E., DeBACA, P. C., DEVINE, J. V., STEINHORST, R., & RICKERT, E. J. (1963). "Use of the Premack principle in controlling the behavior of nursery school children." *Journal of the Experimental Analysis of Behavior, 6,* 544.

HOPKINS, B. L. (1968). "Effects of candy and social reinforcement instruments and reinforcement schedule leaning on the modification and maintenance of smiling." *Journal of Applied Behavior Analysis, 1,* 121–129.

JENKINS, J. R., BARKSDALE, A., & CLINTON, L.

(1978). "Improving reading comprehension and oral reading: Generalization across behaviors, settings, and time." *Journal of Learning Disabilities, 11,* 607–617.

KAZDIN, A. E. (1973). "The effect of vicarious reinforcement on attentive behavior in the classroom." *Journal of Applied Behavior Analysis, 6,* 71–78.

KAZDIN, A. E. (1977). *The token economy: A review and evaluation.* New York: Plenum Press.

KAZDIN, A. E., & BOOTZIN, R. R. (1972). "The token economy: An evaluative review." *Journal of Applied Behavior Analysis, 5,* 343–372.

KAZDIN, A. E., & ERICKSON, L. M. (1975). "Developing responsiveness to instructions in severely and profoundly retarded residents." *Journal of Behavior Therapy and Experimental Psychiatry, 6,* 17–21.

KAZDIN, A. E. (1973). "The effect of nonverbal teacher approval on student attentive behavior." *Behavior Therapy, 4,* 386–391.

KISH, G. B. (1966). "Studies of sensory reinforcement." In W. K. Honig (ed.), *Operant behavior: Areas of research and application.* New York: Appleton-Century-Crofts.

KNAPCZYK, D. R., & YOPPI, J. O. (1975). "Development of cooperative and competitive play responses in developmentally disabled children." *American Journal of Mental Deficiency, 80,* 245–255.

LAHEY, B. B., BUSEMEYER, M. K., O'HARA, C., & BEGGS, V. E. (1977). "Treatment of severe perceptual-motor disorders in children diagnosed as learning disabled." *Behavior Modification, 1,* 123–140.

LEVY, J. (1974). "Social reinforcement and knowledge of results as determinants of motor performance among EMR." *American Journal of Mental Deficiency, 78,* 752–758.

LOVAAS, O. I., & NEWSOM, C. D. (1976). "Behavior modification with psychotic children." In H. Leitenberg (ed.), *Handbook of behavior modification and behavior therapy.* Englewood Cliffs NJ: Prentice Hall.

LOVITT, T. C., & HURLBURT, M. (1974). "Using behavior analysis techniques to assess the relationship between phonics instruction and oral reading." *Journal of Special Education, 8,* 57–72.

MADSEN, C. H., MADSEN, C. K., & THOMPSON, F. (1974). "Increasing rural head start children's consumption of middleclass meals." *Journal of Applied Behavior Analysis, 7,* 257–262.

MARHOLIN, D., McINNIS, E. T., & HEADS, T. B. (1974). "Effect of two free-time reinforcement procedures on academic performance in a class of behavior problem children." *Journal of Educational Psychology, 66,* 872–879.

McCARTY, B. C., McELFRESH, C. T., RICE, S V., & WILSON, S. J. (1978). "The effects of contingent background music on inappropriate bus behavior." *Journal of Music Therapy, 15,* 150–156.

McLAUGHLIN, T. F., & MALABY, J. (1972). "Intrinsic reinforcers in a classroom token economy." *Journal of Applied Behavior Analysis, 5,* 263–270.

MEYERSON, L., KERR, N., & MICHAEL, J. L. (1967). "Behavior modification in rehabilitation." In S. W. Bijou & D. M. Baer (eds.), *Child development readings in experimental analysis* (pp. 214–239). New York: Appleton-Century-Crofts.

MICHAEL, J. (1975). "Positive and negative reinforcement, a distinction that is no longer necessary; or a better way to talk about bad things." In E. Ramp & G. Semb (eds.), *Behavior analysis: Areas of research and application.* Englewood Cliffs, NJ: Prentice Hall.

MILLER, L. K. (1980). *Principles of everyday behavior analysis* (2nd ed.) Monterey, CA: Brooks/Coles.

MULHERN, T., & BAUMEISTER, A. A. (1969). "An experimental attempt to reduce sterotype by reinforcement procedures." *American Journal of Mental Deficiency, 74,* 69–74.

NUNES, D. L., MURPHEY, R. J., & RUPRECHT, M. L. (1977). "Reducing self-injurious behavior of severely retarded individuals through withdrawal of reinforcement procedures." *Behavior Modification, 1,* 499–516.

O'LEARY, K. D., BECKER, W. C., EVANS, M. B., & SAUDARGAS, R. A. (1969). "A token reinforcement program in a public school: A replication and systematic analysis." *Journal of Applied Behavior Analysis, 2,* 3–13.

O'LEARY, K. D., & DRABMAN, R. (1971). "Token reinforcement programs in the classroom: A review." *Psychological Bulletin, 75,* 397–398.

O'LEARY, S. G., & O'LEARY, K. D. (1976). "Behavior modification in the school." In H. Leitenberg (ed.), *Handbook of behavior modification and behavior therapy.* Englewood Cliffs, NJ: Prentice Hall.

OSBORN, J. G. (1969). "Freetime as a reinforcer of classroom behavior." *Journal of Applied Behavior Analysis, 2,* 113–118.

PHILLIPS, E. L., FIXSEN, D. L., PHILLIPS, E. A., & WOLF, M. M. (1979). "The teaching family model: A comprehensive approach to residential treatment of youth." In D. Cullinan & M. H. Epstein (eds.), *Special education for adolescents.* Columbus, OH: Charles Merrill.

PINKSTON, E. M., REESE, N. M., LeBLANC, J. M., & BAER, D. M. (1973). "Independent control of a preschool child's aggression and peer interaction by contingent teacher attention." *Journal of Applied Behavior Analysis, 6,* 115–124.

PIPER, T. J. (1974). "Effects of delay of reinforcement on retarded children's learning." *Exceptional Children, 38,* 139–145.

PREMACK, D. (1959). "Toward empirical behavior laws: I Positive reinforcement." *Psychological Review, 66,* 219–233.

REHAGEN, N. J., & THELEN, M. H. (1972). "Vibration as a positive reinforcer for retarded children." *Journal of Abnormal Psychology, 80,* 162–167.

REYNOLDS, G. S. (1968). *A primer of operant conditioning.* Glenview, IL: Scott, Foresman.

RICKARD, H. C., CLEMENTS, C. B., & WILLIS, J. W. (1970). "Effects of contingent and noncontingent token reinforcement upon classroom performance." *Psychological Reports, 27,* 903–908.

RINCOVER, A. (1978). "Sensory extinction: A procedure for eliminating self-stimulatory behavior in psychotic children." *Journal of Abnormal Child Psychology, 6,* 299–310.

RINCOVER, A., COOK, R., PEOPLES, A., & PACKARD, D. (1979). "Sensory extinction and sensory reinforcement principles for programming multiple adaptive behavior change." *Journal of Applied Behavior Analysis, 12,* 221–233.

RINCOVER, A., & KOEGEL, R. L. (1977). "Some recent advances and future directions in the education of autistic children." In B. Lahey & A. E. Kazdin (eds.), *Advances in child psychology.* New York: Pergamon Press.

RINCOVER, A., NEWSOM, C. D., LOVAAS, O. I., & KOEGEL, R. L. (1977). "Some motivational properties of sensory reinforcement in psychotic children." *Journal of Experimental Child Psychology, 24,* 312–323.

ROSE, T. L. (1981). "The corporal punishment cycle: A behavioral analysis of the maintenance of corporal punishment in the schools." *Education and Treatment of Children, 4,* 157–169.

ROSE, T. L., KOORLAND, M. A., & EPSTEIN, M. H. (1982). "A review of applied behavior analysis interventions with learning disabled children." *Education and Treatment of Children, 5,* 41–58.

SIDMAN, M., & KIRK, B. (1974). "Letter reversals in naming, writing, and matching-to-sample." *Child Development, 45,* 616–625.

SIQUELAND, E. R. (1968). "Reinforcement patterns and extinction in human newborns." *Journal of Experimental Child Psychology, 6,* 431–442.

SKINNER, B. F. (1938). *The behavior of organisms.* New York: Appleton-Century-Crofts.

STAATS, A. (1973). "Behavior analysis and token reinforcement in educational behavior modification and curriculum research." In *Behavior modification in education: The 72nd yearbook of the National Society for the Study of Education.* Chicago: University of Chicago Press.

STEVENSON, H. W., & ODOM, R. D. (1964). "Visual reinforcement with children." *Journal of Experimental Child Psychology, 1,* 248–255.

STOKES, T. F., & BAER, D. M. (1977). "An implicit technology of generalization." *Journal of Applied Behavior Analysis, 10,* 349–367.

STRAIN, P. S., & PIERCE, J. E. (1977). "Direct and vicarious effects of social praise on mentally retarded preschool children's attentive behavior." *Psychology in the Schools, 14,* 348–352.

THOMAS, D. R., BECKER, W. C., & ARMSTRONG, M. (1968). "Production and elimination of disruptive classroom behavior by systematically varying teacher's behavior." *Journal of Applied Behavior Analysis, 1,* 35–45.

THOMAS, J. D., PRESLAND, I E., GRANT, M. D., & GLYNN, T. L. (1978). "Natural rates of teacher approval and disapproval in grade 7 classrooms." *Journal of Applied Behavior Analysis, 11,* 91–94.

THOMAS, C. M., SULZER-AZAROFF, B. LUKERIS, S., & PALMER, M. (1977). "Teaching daily self-help skills for 'long-term' maintenance." In B. Etzel, J. LeBlanc, & D. M. Baer (Eds.), *New developments in behavioral research: Theory, method, and application.* Hillsdale, NJ: Erlbaum.

THOMPSON, G. A., IWATA, B. A., & POYNTER, H. (1979). "Operant control of pathological tongue thrust in spastic cerebral palsy." *Journal of Applied Behavior Analysis, 12,* 325–333.

TWARDOSZ, S., & SAJWAJ, T. (1972). "Multiple effects of a procedure to increase sitting in a hyperactive retarded boy." *Journal of Applied Behavior Analysis, 5,* 73–78.

WELLS, K. C., FOREHAND, R., HICKEY, K., &

GREEN, K. D. (1977). "Effects of a procedure derived from the overcorrection principle on manipulated and nonmanipulated behaviors." *Journal of Applied Behavior Analysis, 10,* 679–687.

WHALEY, D. L., & MALLOTT, R. W. (1971). "*Elementary principles of behavior.*" New York: Appleton-Century-Crofts.

WHITE, M. A. (1975). "Natural rate of teacher approval and disapproval in the classroom." *Journal of Applied Behavior Analysis, 8,* 367–372.

WILSON, C. W., & HOPKINS, B. L. (1973). "The effects of contingent music on the intensity of noise in junior high home economics classes." *Journal of Applied Behavior Analysis, 6,* 269–275.

WOLERY, M. R. (1978). "Self-stimulatory behavior as a basis for devising reinforcers." *AAESPH Review, 3,* 23–29.

WOLF, M. M., RISELY, T. R., & MEES, H. L. (1964). "Application of operant conditioning procedures to the behavior problems of an autistic child." *Behavior Research and Therapy, 1,* 305–312.

ZEGIOB, L. E., JENKINS, J., BECKER, J., & BRISTOW, A. (1976). "Facial screening: Effects on appropriate and inappropriate behaviors." *Journal of Behavior Therapy and Experimental Psychiatry, 7,* 355–357.

ZIMMERMAN, E. H., & ZIMMERMAN, J. (1962). "The alteration of behavior in a special classroom situation." *Journal of the Experimental Analysis of Behavior, 5,* 59–60.

chapter 10

Using Reinforcement Effectively

Shortly after Michael arrived for his first day in his early-intervention class his teacher, Mr. Lopez, observed that Michael was spitting several times a minute. Having identified a target behavior that was inappropriate for the classroom, Mr. Lopez counted and found that Michael spit as frequently as 240 times during one 30-minute observation period. Mr. Lopez also observed that Michael had very limited expressive language skills and he seemed to spit in situations that would normally require a verbal response. For example, when the teacher's aide greeted Michael, he responded with a burst of spitting.

Armed with this information, Mr. Lopez designed an intervention plan that would increase Michael's verbalizations and at the same time reduce his spitting. As conceived, the plan was simple and seemed destined for quick success. Mr. Lopez and his staff would attend to Michael only when he emitted some verbal sound. Any verbal emission would be satisfactory at this point because

Michael rarely engaged in verbal responses, and Mr. Lopez wanted to increase the frequency of those responses. He would work on their quality at a later time. The staff were also instructed to ignore Michael when he engaged in spitting as a substitute for verbalizations. Mr. Lopez was optimistic about the probable success of this intervention because he had not only identified an appropriate response to reinforce but he thought he had also identified a natural reinforcer for that response.

As the program began, the staff usually "caught" Michael responding appropriately and responded to his verbalizations. At times, however, Mr. Lopez and his aide were both busy with other students and when Michael "spoke" he could not be attended to at that moment. Although the staff conscientiously attempted to respond to Michael promptly, occasionally Michael would be spitting when one of the staff arrived to reinforce Michael's verbalizations.

Mr. Lopez's optimism soon turned into despair because his well-designed intervention did not seem to be producing any significant gain in Michael's verbal responses. In fact, the data indicated that Michael's spitting was increasing at about the same rate as his verbalizations. The intervention was discontinued shortly thereafter, probably because Michael's behavior during the intervention did not reinforce Mr. Lopez's efforts.

As we may see from this example, the accurate identification of a target response and the selection of appropriate kinds of reinforcers are only part of a successful intervention. Several other factors, including the immediacy, frequency, consistency, and magnitude of reinforcement, must also be considered. Strategies must be developed that allow the most effective use of reinforcers. Each of these aspects is discussed in this chapter.

Reinforce Immediately

Immediate reinforcement occurs either while the student is still responding or before he or she has an opportunity to make another response. Immediate reinforcement is much more effective than delayed reinforcement, especially when one is initiating a program that is designed to strengthen a weak response (that is, a response that occurs infrequently). The major reason for immediately reinforcing a desired response is to teach the student to discriminate between those responses that gain reinforcement and those responses that do not. Delayed reinforcement allows the student to emit additional responses between the target response and the reinforcer, and, as a consequence, any intervening responses are also reinforced. In effect, we may be teaching the student to emit the target response and some other response rather than the target response alone (Reynolds, 1968). In our example, Michael's verbalizations were reinforced by attention, but so were his spitting responses because the staff often attended to him either while he was spitting or immediately after he finished.

Was Mr. Lopez inadvertently teaching Michael to speak and then spit or just to speak?

Delivering reinforcement immediately is sometimes difficult in a classroom, especially if the reinforcer is an activity, a tangible, or an edible. Fortunately, students easily learn to tolerate delayed reinforcers when the delays are introduced *gradually*, after the student has learned to discriminate reinforced from nonreinforced responses. Deliver reinforcers immediately when beginning an intervention, however. How rapidly the delays can be introduced will be determined by each individual student; in any case, the data on the student's performance are your best source of guidance.

Reinforce Frequently

Each time you reinforce a response you strengthen that response. Consequently, the more often you reinforce, the more you can change the target response (within certain limits that are explained below). Quite often small amounts of any reinforcer may be more effective than large amounts of the same reinforcer, providing the reinforcer is available frequently. For example, frequent smiles, hugs, and winks may be much more effective than a 5-minute verbal compliment that is delivered only once a day.

Frequency of reinforcement refers either to the number of reinforcers delivered, in a given amount of time or to the number of reinforcers that are delivered relative to the total number of target responses that occur. For example, Mrs. Bellah gives Calvin a checkmark if he is sitting in his seat when a kitchen timer rings that has been set to go off every 5 minutes. Calvin may exchange five checkmarks for 10 minutes of free time away from his seat. In this case, we can describe the reinforcer frequency as one reinforcer every 5 minutes. If Mrs. Bellah has also arranged to deliver "bonus" checkmarks for every five arithmetic problems solved correctly, we can describe this reinforcer frequency as one for every five responses. In the first example, reinforcer frequency depends on the passage of time. In the second example, the frequency of reinforcement depends on the number of correct responses by the student. Reinforcer frequency, also referred to as reinforcer *density,* is a defining characteristic of the various schedules of reinforcement that are discussed in Chapter 11.

The teacher must reinforce more frequently during the initial stages of an intervention because he is teaching the student to discriminate correct responses from incorrect responses. Gradually the frequency may be reduced so that a higher number of responses or longer periods of sustained responding are reinforced. For example, Mr. Lopez had planned to respond to Michael every time he verbalized. This high frequency reinforcement would have been gradually reduced after Michael's verbalizations were strengthened sufficiently. Because no one receives attention each time he or she speaks, progressively lower frequencies of reinforcement would eventually have allowed Michael's verbalizations to be maintained by the natural environment.

Reinforce Consistently

In order for any reinforcer to be effective it must occur consistently. The contingent availability of reinforcement teaches the student to discriminate between appropriate and inappropriate behavior. As with any other learning, if the feedback, in this case a reinforcer, is inconsistently delivered, the student will not learn efficiently. For example, after successive presentations, a student who is learning the basic addition facts responds to the problem $5 + 3 = ?$ in the following ways: 9, 12, and 8. If his teacher were to provide the same feedback for each answer (for example, a smile), how would the student learn which answer was correct? Thus, consistency refers not only to delivering reinforcers for appropriate responses but also to withholding reinforcers for inappropriate responses.

The principle of delivery reinforcers con-

sistently is extremely important, regardless of the frequency of reinforcement (the reinforcement schedule). If you decide to reinforce all correct responses, then strive to reinforce consistently *each* correct response. If you decide to reinforce each tenth correct response, then consistently reinforce *every* tenth response. Students will learn to tolerate delays in reinforcement, but it is difficult for them to learn appropriate or correct responses when reinforcers are delivered inconsistently.

Reinforcer Magnitude

The magnitude or amount of a reinforcer to deliver depends upon several factors: (a) the conditions of deprivation (that is, the time elapsed since the student received a reinforcer of a particular type), (b) the level of satiation (that is, the degree to which a reinforcer has lost some of its effectiveness because the student has recently received a sufficient amount), (c) the type of reinforcer to be used, and (d) the amount of work to be performed in order to gain reinforcement.

Certain types of reinforcers, especially edibles, lead to satiation much more quickly than others. If a reinforcer is more susceptible to satiation effects, deliver small amounts of that reinforcer. Other types of reinforcers, such as social may usually be delivered with less regard for their magnitude, even though they may occasionally be overdone (for example, an obviously phony smile that is out of proportion to the student's response).

More reinforcers will be required to maintain hard work than to maintain easy work (Sulzer-Azaroff & Mayer, 1977). For example, the student who has poor visual tracking skills may find it very difficult to catch a ball that is rolled to him. For this student, catching a ball is hard work, and each success may earn powerful reinforcers. On the other hand, the same student may be very proficient in determining the main topic of a story. This response is relatively easy for him and may be reinforced by brief verbal praise or a smile.

Each of these factors must be considered both individually and, because of their interactions, collectively. However, there is only one way to determine whether or not you are delivering the proper amount of reinforcement; you must try the procedure and collect data regarding its effect. The goal is to deliver the minimum amount of reinforcement that will still increase or maintain the target response. By varying the frequency or magnitude of the reinforcers, you can readily determine when a satisfactory amount is being delivered.

STRATEGIES FOR EFFECTIVE REINFORCEMENT

Selecting an effective reinforcer for any student may seem overwhelming in view of the many factors that are part of that decision. For example, should you use natural or artificial reinforcers? Which type of reinforcer should you select? Will it be possible to reinforce immediately, consistently, frequently, and to use the right amount of any selected reinforcer? These decisions are not as discrete as they may seem at first, and experience in using reinforcement procedures will enable you to make many of these decisions with a minimum of effort. In addition, several strategies have been found to be very helpful when many of these decisions must be made. The combination of one or more of the strategies discussed in this section and your own experience will enable you to use reinforcement procedures so that they are most effective for your students and most efficient for you.

Selecting Reinforcers

Although a certain amount of trial and error may be involved in selecting an effective reinforcer for a particular student, the use of a reinforcer survey may help reduce both confusion, and time involved. A *reinforcer survey* is often a quick and effective way to determine potential reinforcers that are either available in your classroom or may be effective for an individual student. An example of a reinforcer survey is show in Figure 10.1.

This survey has proven to be effective in a variety of settings and is readily adaptable to your particular situation.

Reinforcer Sampling

Usually reinforcers are selected because they are known to have reinforcing properties for the individual student. For example, candy may be selected because the student has previously been observed eating candy, or the opportunity to run and yell outside could be selected because we have observed this to be a preferred activity by a particular student. Occasionally a student may not have had experience with a particular reinforcer, such as a new game or a different looking food. The reinforcing power of these new or different stimuli is unknown to the individual, and, consequently, he or she will not make the responses necessary to earn those stimuli.

A technique known as *reinforcer sampling* has been developed which will allow the student to experience the reinforcing properties of the new stimulus (Ayllon & Azrin, 1968a,b; Holz, Azrin, & Ayllon, 1963). With reinforcer sampling, the student samples the reinforcer briefly in the situation in which it will be used. The sampling should be accomplished without any contingencies; in other words, the student has free access to the new stimulus. Suppose, for example, that you have just purchased an electronic game that has multi-colored flashing lights and produces various sounds. To employ the reinforcer sampling procedure, make the game available to the student for a brief period of time and perhaps play the game with him. If he enjoys playing the game, the reinforcing properties of the game have become known to him, and you may then use the game as a reinforcer by restricting access to it until the appropriate time. Then the student may play with the game only when he has successfully performed the target response.

Teachers and researchers sometimes use a

Figure 10.1 Reinforcer Survey

Read each item and consider your answer carefully before responding. Based on your experience with or knowledge of the student, do you expect the particular item to be a reinforcer for that student? After completing the survey, review your answers and select the reinforcers that are the most natural, or least intrusive, for the student and the setting.

Edible Reinforcers

Snacks: popcorn _____
cereal _____   specify _____
nuts _____   specify _____
potato chips _____
candy _____   specify _____
cookies _____   specify _____
other _____

Drinks: milk _____
juice _____   specify _____
soft drinks _____   specify _____
other _____

Meals: specify _____
_____
_____

Tangible Reinforcers

Toys: play money _____
jump rope _____
baseball or football cards _____
dolls _____   "hot wheel" cars _____
marbles _____   yo-yo _____
balls _____   vegetable-dye tattoos _____
balloons _____   puzzles _____
models (cars, planes) _____   movie-characters toys _____
other _____   (for example, "Star Wars" figures)

Art Materials:
crayons _____   felt-tip markers _____
erasers _____   pencils _____
pens _____   note pads _____
paint set _____   other _____

Books:
biography _____   specify _____
fiction _____   specify _____
science _____   specify _____
sports _____   specify _____
comic _____   specify _____
other _____

Records _____   specify _____

Personal Items:
make-up _____   specify _____
hair ribbons _____   specify _____
combs _____   specify _____
other _____

Miscellaneous:
good-work award _____   note to parents _____
certificates _____   stars _____
flower _____   other _____

(continued)

Figure 10.1   *(Continued)*

Exchangeable Reinforcers

badges _____	points _____
checkmarks _____	poker chips _____
money _____	smiley faces _____
stars _____	other _____

Note: Exchangeables must be paired with secondary reinforcers selected from other categories in the reinforcer survey.

Activity Reinforcers

lunch with principal (or other staff) _____
free time _____

finger paint _____	play with toys _____
water plants _____	play with tape recorder _____
grade papers _____	play with calculator _____
extra recess _____	line leader _____
raise flag _____	television time _____
other _____	

Social Reinforcers

smiles _____	verbal praise _____
pat on the back _____	clapping hands _____
physical contact (hug) _____	tickle _____
phone call to parents _____	attention from peers _____
other _____	

Sensory Reinforcers

vibration _____	jumping _____
rub skin _____	specify material (for example, hand, feather) _____
bouncing _____	
visual _____	specify _____
auditory _____	specify _____
other _____	

technique that is similar to reinforcing sampling in which the reinforcer is shown to the student before the emission of the target response. This technique is known as *reinforcer display* to differentiate it from reinforcer sampling. Risley and Wolf (1967) used reinforcer display by holding a spoonful of food directly in front of the student's face while awaiting the targeted verbal response. Other examples of reinforcer display include displaying a new book to be read during storytime and arranging the items that can be used in the free time area of the classroom. The difference between display and sampling should be clear; display is probably not as effective as sampling when novel stimuli are introduced.

Reinforcer sampling may be quite suscep-

tible to satiation effects. Therefore, it is important to make sure that the samples are only offered in quantities that are enough to enable the student to begin to enjoy the stimulus. The sample quantities must be just enough to leave the student wanting more. In addition, Ayllon & Azrin (1968a) have suggested that reinforcer sampling may be most useful when employed with reinforcers that are earned infrequently. Reinforcers that are delivered frequently actually serve as a sample in themselves for subsequent deliveries, so a sampling for a frequently delivered reinforcer has little impact. An exception to this may be with very young or low-functioning students, for whom several sampling episodes may be necessary.

Use Novelty Reinforcers

The old familiar adage, "Variety is the spice of life," may easily be paraphrased as "Novelty is the spice of reinforcement." If other things are proceeding well, most individuals probably prefer novel experiences or situations (Krumboltz & Krumboltz 1972; Millenson, 1967), so we find it no surprise that many successful teachers use novel reinforcers. The element of surprise is a valuable ally when designing a reinforcement program. Although many reinforcing events are relatively predictable—such as being called on when a hand is raised—an element of surprise can often dramatically increase the rate of response and, in general, spice up the day.

The novel reinforcer may be related to the target response, or it may be totally unexpected. For example, the student who successfully completes an arithmetic worksheet may typically receive verbal praise and free time. The related novel reinforcer for completing a worksheet may be appointing the student to be the one who then checks the other students' work. A reinforcer may also be novel because it is unrelated to the target response. In our worksheet example, the student may unexpectedly be allowed to run an errand for the teacher or to help the janitor for 30 minutes. The individual student may earn the novel reinforcer, but it can often be effective to allow the individual's reinforcer to include another student, a small group, or the whole class. You may surprise the class, for example, by allowing everyone to participate in free time because Martha has successfully tied her shoes—a cause for celebration.

Novelty may be introduced regardless of the type of reinforcer that is most appropriate for the individual student. For example, a "surprise box" may be used in a variety of ways. Inexpensive tangible reinforcers such as animal-shaped erasers and plastic trinkets may be drawn from the box. Or the box may contain slips of paper with various activities listed such as "Take a break," "Wash the chalkboard," "Color a picture," or "Read a maga-zine." You are limited only by your imagination.

Several words of caution must be interjected, because novelty is so appealing. If novelty is overdone, the stimuli will, of course, no longer be novel, so use novel reinforcers sparingly in order to maintain the elements of surprise. You may also need to arrange reinforcer sampling for individual students because they may lack experience with the particular stimulus. As with any other contingency program, the student's performance data should guide you in your decision to maintain or change a novel stimulus. Remember whose behavior is supposed to be reinforced and remember that novelty in classroom settings may be very reinforcing for the teacher regardless of its effects on a particular student.

Move to Natural Contingencies

Many classroom-based reinforcement programs require the teacher or staff to be the source of the reinforcers. Although this relationship may promote desirable changes in the student's behavior, an unfortunate side effect may be the student's dependence on the teacher for those reinforcers. Thus, the newly acquired or strengthened response may only occur in the presence of the teacher (or whoever is the dispenser of reinforcers). Clearly, this is not a desirable situation because the goal is to develop durable skills that the student can generalize to new or different situations.

In order for a reinforcement program to provide for generalization, there should be a gradual shift from teacher-controlled consequences to natural consequences. Often this transfer occurs without a great deal of special planning. As previously discussed, a student who receives consistent reinforcement for a particular response will begin to like performing that response. However, you may have to plan deliberately for sources of reinforcement other than those directly under your control.

The gradual shift of teacher-controlled to

more natural consequences depends on two components: First, the schedule of reinforcement must switch from a continuous schedule (where every target response is reinforced) to an intermittent schedule. (Those schedules of reinforcement are discussed in Chapter 11). Second, most natural reinforcers for the target response must be identified. (Chapter 9 reviews the discussion of natural reinforcers.) The reinforcing behaviors of other people (for example, peers or parents) are a powerful source of reinforcers that are not under the teacher's personal control. Although the attention or approval of others is not always contingent on particular responses, it is a reinforcing consequence that often occurs and can be every bit as powerful as any teacher-controlled reinforcer, and, therefore, we may consider the attention of others to be a source of natural reinforcers.

Once the target behavior is fairly well established under conditions of teacher control, the teacher can begin to plan for the gradual shift to more natural contingencies. One way to do this may be to reduce the student's dependence on the teacher by gradually delivering reinforcers less often. For example, the student who completes an assembly task may expect to receive praise each time the task is completed. Gradually begin to reinforce fewer occurrences of the completed task so that perhaps every other completed task gets some attention. Another way to provide more natural consequences is to encourage the other students to become sources of reinforcement; for example reinforce other students for delivering reinforcers to their peers. Arrange it so that their approving comments about others may earn them more free time. Eventually this contingency can be removed because the natural consequences of positive interactions with their peers become powerful reinforcing events. An additional way to provide a shift to more natural consequences may be to allow the student to assume more responsibility for his or her behavior, such as teaching him to budget his time, to keep his own performance records, and perhaps even to evaluate his own performance.

Relinquishing your control of reinforcers and transferring control to more natural sources is not easy. And identifying more natural sources of reinforcement can be difficult, but the long-term results are worth the effort.

Vicarious Reinforcement

A frequent suggestion to teachers who are attempting to manage behavior problems in the classroom is that a teacher can develop the desired behavior in one student by reinforcing the same behavior of a nearby student (Ackerman, 1972; Becker, Engelmann, & Thomas, 1971; Bootzin, 1975; Buckley & Walker, 1970). This procedure is called *vicarious reinforcement,* and it means the reinforcing effect on an observer when another person receives reinforcement. For example, Carlos sits next to David, who is frequently inattentive. Periodically and systematically, the teacher approaches Carlos to tell him, "I really like the way you're working, Carlos." If David after hearing this also begins to attend to his assignments, then we may conclude that vicarious reinforcement has occurred.

Vicarious reinforcement may have important implications for teachers. If these carry-over effects of reinforcement occur consistently, then the teacher can increase efficiency by planning for these effects. Much time and energy may be saved by reinforcing the target student's neighbors. In effect, two or more students may be reinforced at the same time and many negative statements ("Jerry, sit down right now!") may be avoided.

The effects of vicarious reinforcement have been documented in several studies with mildly and moderately handicapped students (Broden, Bruce, Mitchell, Carter, & Hall, 1970; Drabman & Lahey, 1974; Kazdin, 1973; Kazdin, Silverman, & Sittler, 1975; Strain, Shores, & Kerr, 1976), and anecdotal reports have also suggested its effectiveness (Bolstad & Johnson, 1972; Hall, Lund, & Jackson, 1968). Although these experimental and anecdotal reports are relatively few in number, several important findings have been reported. Verbal praise or attention has been consistently effective as a reinforcer, whereas nonverbal attention, such as a pat on the back, has been found to be relatively ineffective for the nonreinforced student unless it is paired with some type of verbal prompt to direct the nonreinforced student to look at the student who will receive the reinforcer (Kazdin et al., 1975). For example, the teacher might say, "Becky, look at Jenny," directing Becky's attention to the target student, Jenny, who will be reinforced. Strain et al. (1976) have found that reinforcing two target students rather than only one produced a more powerful positive effect on the nonreinforced student than reinforcing only one student.

Nevertheless, vicarious reinforcement may not be effective in all situations for all students. Relatively little is known about the mechanisms underlying its effect. Modeling, the reduction of a source of distraction for the nonreinforced student by reinforcing the target student, the reinforcement history of the students, the students' imitative abilities, and the possibility that reinforcing one student is a discriminative stimulus that lets the other student know reinforcers are available (see Chapter 12) have all been advanced as possible explanations for the effects of vicarious reinforcement (Kazdin, 1973; Strain et al., 1976; Weisberg & Clements, 1977). In addition, the effects of vicarious reinforcement on students with more severe handicaps are unknown at this time. Consequently, the often repeated caution to collect data on students and be guided by these data applies to the use of vicarious reinforcement. Vicarious reinforcement may be effective for many of your students, but you must be aware that some students may not respond.

Individual Peer Contingencies

In the natural classroom environment, peers are probably one of the most powerful sources of reinforcement (and punishment) for other students (O'Leary & O'Leary, 1977). Most intervention programs rely on staff members, including teachers, aides, and parents, to monitor behavior and deliver consequences, but a number of programs are beginning to use peers as reinforcing agents.

Peers have been used extensively at Achievement Place, a program for predelinquents. Investigations of the effectiveness of peer reinforcers have included their use as speech therapists (Bailey, Timbers, Phillips, & Wolf, 1971), administrators of a token economy (Phillips, 1968; Phillips, Phillips, Wolf, & Fixsen, 1973), and as participants in a form of self-government (Fixsen, Phillips, & Wolf, 1973). Classroom uses of peer reinforcing agents have been reported by several investigators who focused primarily on appropriate social and academic responses in preschool and elementary students (Drabman, 1973; Long & Madsen, 1975; Siegel & Steinman, 1975; Solomon & Wahler, 1973; Willis, Morris, & Crowder, 1972; Winnett, Richards, & Krasner, 1971).

The use of individual peers as reinforcing agents appears to offer several advantages. Peer attention has been clearly demonstrated to be a powerful source of reinforcement. However, as Solomon and Wahler (1973) reported, peer attention is often directed toward inappropriate behavior, thereby increasing or maintaining those behaviors. Thus, the redirection of peer attention to appropriate behaviors allows the teacher to focus a powerful source of reinforcement on responses that harmonize with effective instruction. Furthermore, if the target behaviors are most likely to occur in the presence of peers, then the students (peer reinforcing agents) may be in a better position to observe and to reinforce those target behaviors. Also the reinforcing peer should be able to deliver the reinforcers more immediately and frequently than a staff member (Kazdin, 1977; O'Leary & O'Leary, 1977). In addition, generalization of the target behaviors may be promoted because the target students learn to respond appropriately in the presence of a variety of conditions and reinforcing agents (Johnston & Johnston, 1972). When peers deliver reinforcers to each other, especially when social reinforcers are paired with every other type of reinforcer, social interaction is likely to be increased. For many handicapped studens, increasing social interaction is a significant therapeutic goal (Abrams, Hines, Pollack, Ross, Stubbs, & Polyot, 1974). There appears to be a reciprocal arrangement between the peer reinforcer and those whose responses are being reinforced. Not only do the target students' behaviors improve, but also there is evidence that the peer reinforcing agent's behavior improves as well, even when no direct reinforcement has been contingent upon that improvement (Graubard, Rosenberg, & Miller, 1974; Rosenberg & Graubard, 1975; Siegel & Steinman, 1975). (This effect may be related to vicarious reinforcement.) Training students to deliver contingent reinforcers may contribute to the successful mainstreaming of those students. For example, seven students with behavior disorders in a self-contained classroom were trained to modify the behavior of regular classroom teachers with whom they were mainstreamed (Rosenberg & Graubard, 1975). The students were taught to provide verbal and nonverbal reinforcers contingent upon appropriate teacher behavior and to ignore negative teacher behaviors. As a result of these procedures, a significant increase in positive teacher-student contacts was reported. (In a second experiment, the students were similarly taught to improve the behavior of their nonhandicapped peers.) Although in this experiment the favorable changes in the teachers' behavior were not maintained after the students ceased their reinforcement procedures, other reports (for example, Polirstok & Greer, 1977) indicate that these positive changes in teacher behavior can be durable. If successful mainstreaming placements are found to be related to positive teacher-student interactions, then the use of student reinforcing agents may prove to be an effective technique to facilitate those interactions.

When peer contingency managers are used in an educational setting, they must receive adequate training. Skills in observation, reinforcer delivery, and, perhaps, data collection can be learned easily by students (e.g., McLaughlin & Malaby, 1972a). Teaching techniques such as modeling, discussion, role-playing, and corrective feedback appear to be most efficient. An additional instructional and programmatic consideration that appears to be critical to the success of a peer management system is the opportunity for the peer reinforcing agent to earn some kind of reinforcement for his or her efforts (Greenwood, Sloane, & Baskin, 1974). Greenwood et al. (1974) found that merely instructing students in the delivery of points and social approval was not effective in developing their contingent delivery of those reinforcers. When points were made available to the peer managers for their correct administration of the contingencies, their performance improved considerably. Perhaps we should not be surprised to find that in apparently successful peer management systems contingent reinforcement is available to all the participants, not just the target students.

The use of peer managers requires the teacher's awareness of several potentially serious procedural pitfalls. Because peer influence can be a powerful source of reinforcement, the teacher should be especially careful in selecting the peer manager and equally careful in monitoring the peer manager's performance. Power over another individual is a heady wine, and the possibility of the abuse of that power by peers is a reality that you should not dismiss lightly. For example, Willis et al. (1972) found that peer managers may be unduly harsh in their judgments of their peers' performance. Phillips et al. (1973) found that several precautions, including possible fines for the peer manager or election of peer manager by the target students, may avoid many of these power-struggle problems. An added procedural safeguard may include securing parental consent before you implement a peer management system. Finally, the peer manager, as with other staff, must be encouraged to deliver reinforcement consistently (Long & Madsen, 1975).

Group Contingencies

Group contingencies refer to reinforcement programs in which earning the reinforcer is contingent upon the performance of a group of students, typically the whole class or subgroups of the class. The successful use of group contingencies has many features that make it perfectly attractive for teachers. Group contingencies can be economical, practical, and convenient (Litow & Pumroy, 1975).

Several variations of group contingency programs have been identified (Kazdin, 1977; Litow & Pumroy, 1975). The most common variation is probably the *whole group* procedure, in which the performance of each student determines the availability of reinforcers to the whole group, and the performance of the group as a whole determines the availability of reinforcers to each student. For example, free-time activities may be contingent upon the class identifying an average of eight out of ten environmental words (for example, the words "men," "women," and "exit"). If the class fails to achieve this average, then no class member is allowed to participate in free-time activities. Another popular application of the whole group procedure omits the averaging process. In this variation, each member of the group must meet the minimum criterion in order for the whole group to earn reinforcers. Thus, even the lowest performing member of the group must meet the criterion, rather than having his or her performance balanced by a student who performs well above the criterion level (Koch & Breyer, 1974; Wilson & Williams, 1973). Using the previous example, *every* member of the class would have to identify eight environmental words in order for the whole group to gain free time.

A second variation of group contingencies is the *team approach,* which is frequently known as the *Good Behavior Game* (Barrish, Saunders, & Wolf, 1969). The group, or class, is divided into two or more subgroups which will function as teams. Each of these teams becomes a separate group within which the individual student still earns or loses reinforcement for the team and the reinforcement he or she receives depends on the performance of the team. In this respect the team approach resembles the whole group procedure. The teams, however, compete with each other, and the reinforcer is delivered to the team with the best performance. The results of their use of the Good Behavior Game are presented in Figure 10.2. Lutzker and White-Blackburn (1979) provided another example with older students when they evaluated the effects of a team approach, called the good productivity game in a sheltered workshop setting. Institutionalized clients who sorted boards by size were placed on teams that engaged in pseudocompetition in that the teams were paired against each other, but both teams always "won". Reinforcers were candy and early work termination. The team contingency resulted in performance levels that were almost twice as high as baseline. Thus the competition among teams may vary from strictly competitive, in which only one team wins, to pseudocompetitive. A compromise frequently used in classrooms stipulates that any or *all* teams may gain reinforcers if they achieve the predetermined criterion.

Another variation of group contingency arrangements focuses on the performance of a *selected group or member.* The "member" may actually be more than one student or even a particular subgroup, but it is always less than the entire group or class. The selected member approach may be accomplished in several ways. First, the availability of reinforcers for the group may be determined by the best performance of the day or an average of the top performers. (The number of top performers is selected by the teacher.) Second, reinforcers may be made contingent on the lowest performance or on an average of the lowest performers. In either of these instances, the performance level must meet or exceed a preselected criterion which, of course, will vary depending on whether the highest or

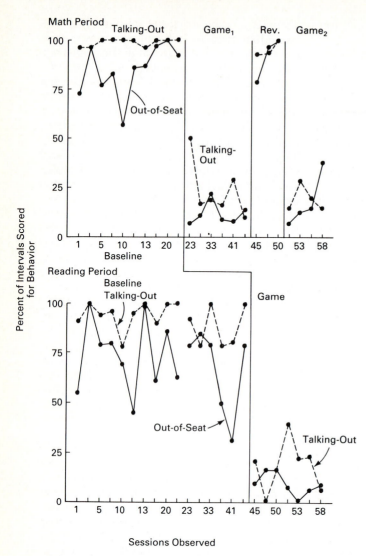

Figure 10.2 Percent of 1-min intervals scored by an observer as containing talking-out and out-of-seat behaviors occurring in a classroom of 24 fourth-grade school children during math and reading periods. In the baseline conditions the teacher attempted to manage the disruptive classroom behavior in her usual manner. During the game conditions out-of-seat and talking-out responses by a student resulted in a possible loss of privileges for the student and his team.

Source: H. H. Barrish, M. Saunders, & M. M. Wolf (1969) in "Good behavior game: Effects of individual contingencies for group consequences on disruptive behavior in a classroom." *Journal of Applied Behavior Analysis, 2,* 119–124.

lowest performers are selected. For example, a class has an average rate for solving basic addition problems of 22 per minute, with a range of 8 to 28 correct per minute. The criterion level for the high performer might be 30; whereas, for the low performer the criterion might be 10 correct per minute. A third approach to the selected-member varation is to select randomly a member of the class and to deliver reinforcement if this student's performance exceeds the criterion (Drabman, Spitalnik, & Spitalnik, 1974; Hamblin, Hathaway, & Wodarski, 1974).

Each variation of the group contingency procedures has been shown to be effective for whole groups, subgroups, and the individuals that constitute those groups. However, little is known of the relative effectiveness of each variation; that is, how well do they compare with each other? Results from comparisons of team approaches and whole-group approaches have been ambiguous. Several researchers have found no apparent differences (Axelrod, 1973; Drabman et al., 1974) and others have found the team approach superior to the whole-group approach (McNamara, 1971). So, although current research indicates that group contingencies may be more effective than individual contingencies (Alexander, Corbett, & Smigel, 1976; Lutzker & White-Blackburn, 1979), there appears to be no consensus regarding which variation of the group contingency plan is most effective.

Several beneficial side effects seem to occur frequently when group contingencies are used. For example, Hamblin et al. (1974) found that when the group's reinforcers were contingent on the lowest three scores in the class, several of the higher-performing students began to tutor the lower-performing students. These tutoring efforts, which had not been prompted by the teacher, resulted in superior achievement by the class as a group. Other potential benefits may include peer encouragement or reinforcement, which would certainly contribute to generalization of the responses and to a shift from teacher-controlled to more natural reinforcers.

Unfortunately, the observed side effects of group contingency arrangements have not always been positive. Peer pressure on individual students to behave in ways that will gain reinforcement for the group may become unpleasant and include threats or actual punishment for those not earning the available reinforcers (Axelrod, 1973; Harris & Sherman, 1973). O'Leary and Drabman (1971) urge teachers to be cautious when implementing group contingency programs because (a) a given student may not be able to perform the target behavior and (b) the class may exert undue pressure on any nonperforming student. Care must be taken to monitor both any negative side effects and improvement in the target behaviors when a group contingency program is used.

Public Posting

Feedback is an inherent component of any reinforcement program. When a student receives any type of reinforcer, the corresponding interaction with the environment provides feedback to the student that the particular response was appropriate for the current conditions. Conversely, the absence of a reinforcer also conveys information regarding the appropriateness of a specific response. Given this feedback component of any reinforcing event, the question of the effects of enhancing this feedback component may be very important in certain situations. For example, in a class of adolescents with behavior disorders, does enhancing, or highlighting, feedback about appropriate performance also enhance the reinforcing properties of the reinforcing event or contribute in any way to the increased performance of appropriate behaviors by the members of the class? Evidence is beginning to accumulate that enhancing the feedback component is a quick, inexpensive, and easily available way to increase a reinforcer's efficiency.

The effectiveness of *public posting*—performance feedback in the form of a public display of students' performance data—has been documented in a number of studies, including public posting on a daily basis (Fink & Carnine, 1975; Hall, Cristler, Cranston, & Tucker, 1970; Van Houton, 1979; Van Houton, Hill, & Parsons, 1975; Van Houton & McKillop, 1977; Van Houton, Morrison, Jarvis, & McDonald, 1974; Van Houton & Van Houton, 1977) or on a weekly basis (Van Houton & LaiFatt, 1981).

Public posting is a simple procedure that apparently may be used in conjunction with, or even in place of, many other types of reinforcement programs. The major requirement that seems to be uniform in most public posting procedures is the use of a chart to post students' performance data. These charts may be large enough for the whole class to see from their seats, or they may be small enough to fit on the top of a student's desk. They may list data from every student in the class, subgroups of students, or just individuals. Charts may reflect data in a bar graph, a line graph, or a simple matrix in which scores are posted without graphics. A great deal of variability is possible, which enables one to adapt public posting to most special education settings and still retain its effects on behavior. In a typical public posting procedure a chart that lists each student's name is placed on a classroom wall. The purpose of the chart is to record the rate of words correctly read orally each day. After each reading session, or probe, the student (or teacher) plots the data for that session. The teacher encourages each student to try to exceed the previous day's score, and reinforcement may be contingent on this improved performance. A number of variations of public posting are possible, including the following: (a) the chart may be individualized, (b) the chart may be placed on a student's desk or in a smaller work area, and (c) the chart and subsequent contingencies may emphasize the group's performance rather than an individual's performance. None of these variations appears to detract from the effectiveness of the public posting procedure.

In addition to the flexible arrangements discussed above, several advantages of public posting have been noted with mildly handicapped and nonhandicapped students of varying ages. Public posting seems to encourage and facilitate more immediate feedback to the student regarding his or her performance. Further, in at least one study the poorer students showed the greatest gain when public posting was in effect (Van Houton & Lai-Fatt, 1981). Another advantage is that there appears to be no increase in negative verbal responses regarding any individual's performance during public posting. Conversely, there seems to be an increase in positive or supportive statements (Van Houton, 1979). Finally, public posting may be less intrusive and more easily managed (whether by student or teacher) than some other reinforcement programs, such as the edible or exchangeable reinforcers.

There are, however, several potential disadvantages to public posting. Although there appears to be no evidence that negative remarks increase after public posting, Van Houton and his colleagues (1977, 1979, 1981) caution that an emphasis on the individual student or the class as a single team may be responsible for the absence of negative comments. If, on the other hand, the public posting procedure was arranged in a way that promoted competition, either among teams or individuals, we might expect to see an increase in derogatory comments. In addition, students may complain occasionally about having their scores or other performance measures posted publicly. Evidence exists, however, that their complaints are rather short-lived and disappear once improvement in performance is displayed (Van Houton & LaiFatt, 1981). If this invasion of privacy appears to be a problem for one or more students in a given setting, coding the students' names may resolve the problem. Public posting displays such as charts may be occasionally destroyed by the students (for example, during a tantrum.) More durable displays can be constructed. For example, Carroll (1977) has described how to construct a durable chart display out of plywood and Plexiglas for a modest cost per student. (Older students may enjoy constructing these chart displays themselves, and this activity might even be an effective reinforcer for some other prosocial behavior.) Finally, although public posting has been shown to be effective for academic and social responses with mildly handicapped and nonhandicapped students, little is known of its effects with moderately to severely developmentally disabled students.

In summary, public posting appears to be an efficient way to increase a reinforcer's effectiveness. The advantages of the procedure seem to outweigh the disadvantages. Of equal importance, the potential disadvantages can be avoided with sufficient planning.

Additional Factors: Deprivation, Satiation, and Competing Contingencies

Three additional factors can either increase or seriously reduce the reinforcing power of any environmental stimulus or event: deprivation, satiation, and competing contingencies. These factors are critical for any classroom-based reinforcement program and must be considered and assessed before one begins to deliver reinforcers systematically.

Deprivation

Most reinforcers are more effective if the student has not had access to them before the intervention. For example, one of the author's former students, Scott, a 10-year-old with a behavior disorder, as part of a token economy, could earn various tangible secondary reinforcers such as toy cars, models, and assorted trinkets. Each of these items was inexpensive, but nevertheless the items were effective for other students in the class. However, Scott's target behaviors were unaffected by these contingencies. After several weeks of investigation, the teacher found that Scott was a proficient shoplifter, whose favorite target was a toy store in a shopping mall near his home. Consequently, Scott had acquired numerous popular and expensive toys contingent upon several behaviors that were most certainly not the ones identified by his teacher. Quite clearly the tangible reinforcers available to Scott at school were not powerful enough because Scott was not deprived of toys. In the same class were several students who lived in the most impoverished home environments. The tangible reinforcers available at school were most powerful for these students because they had very few other toys and very few opportunities to acquire toys in any other way. Obviously, the difference in the effectiveness of these same reinforcers was a result of varying levels of deprivation.

Deprivation can result from a variety of circumstances. Baldwin and Baldwin (1986) have identified three causes of deprivation: natural, deliberate, and compulsory. *Natural deprivation* occurs when the student is engaged in particular behaviors that earn one type of reinforcer but deprive the student of other types of reinforcers. For example, a student who is playing a board game with several classmates is probably receiving social and activity reinforcers. During this game, she is unaware that she is being deprived of edible reinforcers. However, when the game ends, she may be surprised at how hungry she has become and may anxiously begin awaiting lunch or emit a number of behaviors that will gain access to food. *Deliberate deprivation* occurs when a student deliberately abstains from gaining access to a reinforcer. For example, a student who receives tokens for completing various steps of an assembly task may choose to abstain from purchasing any back-up reinforcer until he has accumulated a large number of tokens. He may then go on a buying spree that becomes highly reinforcing because he has self-imposed a state of deprivation. *Compulsory deprivation* occurs as a result of circumstances that are imposed in the environment. For example, Wolf, Risley, and Mees (1964) had a great deal of difficulty in identifying a reinforcer that was effective for persuading an autistic child to wear his glasses. Having the child wear his glasses was critically important because the student's vision was deteriorating. In this situation the child was deprived of television viewing time after dinner. Then, the child was offered the opportunity to view the television if he would wear his glasses for a prescribed period of time.

The idea of deprivation causes concern in many people, and the issues surrounding deprivation are many and complex (Kazdin, 1977). One may argue, for example, that special education students are in a deprived state when they are placed in any educational setting that segregates them from their nonhandicapped peers. Institutionalized students are deprived of "normal" community living, friends, and many of the freedoms of choice regarding their lives. Underachieving adolescents are deprived of employment opportunities and leisure activities. However, many effective interventions that contribute to the remediation of these problems depend on some relatively short-term deprivation. These deprivations are instituted so that reinforcers can acquire sufficient power to persuade the individual to acquire the skills necessary to overcome long-term deprivations.

Due to the complexities of the issue, the teacher is faced daily with situations that relate to deprivation levels, and a few general guidelines may prove helpful in dealing with those situations. There is a general agreement, adequately supported by judicial decisions, that events necessary for survival or continued existence (such as, food, water, and shelter) should not be purposefully restricted. Withholding nonessential reinforcers, however, may be viewed as possibly therapeutic, depending on the duration of the deprivation and the changes in the student's behavior. Thus, preplanned deprivation should be relatively brief and supported by data that indicate a change in the student's behavior. Severe deprivation (for example, restricting access to regularly scheduled reinforcement) should only be used when it is clearly supported both ethically and legally. In most instances, deprivation is not a variable that will require manipulation; rather, the goal will probably be one of identification. If a reinforcer does not appear to be effective, then some investigatory work is indicated. As in the example of Scott, the teacher must try to identify those sources of reinforcement that are competing with the selected reinforcer and deprive the student of the competing reinforcer to enhance the chosen reinforcer's effectiveness.

Satiation

Satiation may be viewed as the opposite of deprivation. Satiation refers to a condition in which the student has experienced the reinforcer to such a degree that its use is no longer effective. The student who has eaten a bag of candy and will not respond at levels sufficient enough to earn more candy may be experiencing satiation.

Any type of reinforcer is susceptible to satiation effects, although edibles and tangibles may be most susceptible. The surest guide to avoiding satiation is to balance deprivation delicately with several other factors discussed previously in this chapter, such as novelty and reinforcer magnitude. Several other procedural considerations may also be helpful. For instance, consider the type of reinforcer being used. When using edible reinforcers, use the smallest portion that is effective. For example, give the student one piece of presweetened cereal for each reinforcer rather than a handful. Many kinds of tangible reinforcers can be earned piece by piece, for example, a car model assembly kit. Other kinds of reinforcers, such as social, may be controlled so that relatively few occur that are not contingently arranged. Also, plan teaching sessions that don't conflict with naturally occurring reinforcers. For example, do not use edible reinforcers immediately after lunch or the morning snack. Similarly, do not use activity reinforcers immediately after recess. Remember to collect and respond to data. If the student is not earning enough reinforcers, he may be on the satiation rather than the deprivation side of the scale.

Competing Contingencies

Like any human environment, the classroom environment is complex, with many contingencies available for most types of responses. A student who has written an assignment may receive a reinforcer from the teacher for completing the task. Before completion of the assignment, the student may have also received some attention from the teacher for staying on-task and working hard. However, the student may also have received social reinforcers from his classmates for making faces at the work, yawning, or demonstrating in other ways that he couldn't care less about completing the assignment. On the other hand, the student may be negatively reinforced for not completing the assignment; the student may wish to avoid the ridicule of his classmates for obeying the class rules. The teacher may also gain access to a negative reinforcer by sending the student out of the room for his inattention and, therefore, removing an aversive stimulus (the student). As we can see, the journey from direction to completion of the assignment is not as simple as it might appear.

If the classroom environment were a system of social vacuums in which each student interacted with just the teacher, then we might expect that any reinforcement program would be effective because the teacher would be the major, if not the only, source of reinforcement. Obviously this situation does not, nor will it ever, exist in a classroom. Many other sources of reinforcement are available to every student for appropriate and inappropriate behaviors. These *competing contingencies* may either enhance or negate the most carefully planned reinforcement program.

The control of effective reinforcers requires the teacher to assess those contingencies that are currently available to each of the students. When competing reinforcers encourage behaviors that are opposed to the target behavior, more powerful reinforcers must be identified and employed. If this identification and substitution process does not occur, the most carefully planned program will not be effective and much time and energy will be wasted. The concept of competing contingencies is not more readily apparent in laboratory settings, nor does it occur only in isolated instances. Given that behavior does not occur in the absence of reinforcement, any behavior that we seek to change is currently being maintained by one or more reinforcers. Consequently, the potential for a competing contingency is present whenever a reinforcer is introduced that will increase a competing behavior.

The critical question, then, is not whether competing contingencies are present, but rather, what is their power and how can their power be overcome? Remember that the target student will indicate the relative power of reinforcers by the change, or lack of change, in his or her behavior. Collect data on the student's behavior in the absence of the intervention (when the natural reinforcers are present) and after beginning the intervention (when the newly introduced reinforcer(s) are competing with the ones already available). If

the rate of duration of the behavior changes in an adaptive or prosocial direction, then you have identified a more powerful reinforcer. If, on the other hand, no change or a change in a maladaptive direction is observed, then you have not selected a reinforcer with enough power to compete against the already established reinforcers in this situation.

Several techniques are available that may enhance the power of your selected reinforcer. Involving the student's peers is probably the surest route to success. For example, the classmates of an on-task student may be reinforced for ignoring his off-task behaviors, whereas, at the same time the student is reinforced for being on-task. Several students might be identified as tutors who can earn reinforcement contingent on the student's behavior as well as their own. Alternatively, the whole class might earn reinforcement as a result of his performance; for example, when he finishes his assignment they can all go outside for recess. As surprising as it may seem, sometimes a class meeting in which the target student's need for extra help is frankly discussed can be quite helpful; in most cases, this need for extra help will probably come as no surprise to his peers.

More severely handicapped students may present other, more complex, identification and substitution tasks for the teacher. For example, if the student is receiving sensory reinforcement for a particular behavior (for example, visual stimulation as a consequence of finger-flicking), then simply involving the student's peers will probably have no effect. Here the teacher must identify alternative sources of a similar reinforcer that can be delivered as a consequence of the target behavior. The search for these competing contingencies may require a sophisticated analysis of the environmental stimuli available to the student. Often, a good deal of trial and error may be required, but the collection and analysis of performance data will facilitate your efforts.

Finally, many of the procedural considerations discussed previously in this chapter may contribute to an increase in the power of any selected reinforcer that must compete with those already available to the student. Reinforcer sampling, following a reinforcer survey, may be most beneficial. Novel, vicarious, peer, and group contingencies may also be effective in overcoming a competing contingency. A final word of advice concerns the planned move to naturally occurring contingencies. Because competing contingencies are most often natural contingencies that can maintain behavior in a variety of situations, the importance of the identification of natural contingencies that can maintain the target behavior cannot be overemphasized. Although artificial reinforcers are frequently most helpful in the beginning stages of most interventions, remember the situation-specific limits of those reinforcers and consistently plan to move to more natural reinforcers. This is the surest route to overcoming competing contingencies as well as to achieving the goals of any intervention program. Keep in mind that the goal of intervention is the generalization of the target behavior to new situations and the maintenance of that behavior for long periods of time. Remember, too, that a student may fail to earn a reasonable number or amount of the particular reinforcer because he or she didn't go long enough without it or had too much of it before the session began. Or perhaps a more powerful competing contingency has maintained an incompatible response. There may also be other problems with a procedure, but the point is that when the student is not earning the reinforcer then something should be changed—something is wrong with the intervention procedure, not with the student.

SUMMARY

Factors that should be components of any reinforcement program are: immediate reinforcement, frequent reinforcement, consistent reinforcement, and the appropriate amount, or magnitude, of any reinforcer.

Strategies for implementing reinforcers effectively are identified in this chapter, and specific problems are described that each strategy may be helpful in overcoming. Efficient and effective methods for implementing each strategy are discussed, and successful examples of these methods are presented. The characteristics and advantages of each strategy that a teacher should consider before using a particular strategy are discussed.

Three procedural factors are identified as critical to the power of any reinforcer: deprivation, satiation, and competing contingencies. Each of these factors is discussed in terms of its effects on any teacher-selected reinforcers. Suggestions are given for using each of these procedural factors to enhance, rather than detract from, a reinforcer's power.

After reading this chapter, the reader should understand the qualities of reinforcers, the factors that allow them to be maximally effective, the various strategies that can enhance a reinforcer's effectiveness, and those procedures that have an impact on a reinforcer's power. The next chapter provides schedules of reinforcement and discusses their characteristic effects on behavior.

REFERENCES

ABRAMS, L., HINES, D., POLLACK, D., ROSS, M., STUBBS, D. A., & POLYOT, C. J. (1974). "Transferable tokens: Increasing social interaction in a token economy." *Pychological Reports, 35,* 447–452.

ACKERMAN, J. M. (1972). *Operant conditioning techniques for the classroom teacher.* Glenview, IL: Scott, Foresman.

ALEXANDER, R. N., CORBETT, T. F., & SMIGEL, J. (1976). "The effects of individual and group consequences on school attendance and curfew violations with predelinquent adolescents." *Journal of Applied Behavior Analysis, 9,* 221–226.

AXELROD, S. (1973). "Comparison of individual and group contingencies in two special classes." *Behavior Therapy, 4,* 83–90.

AYLLON, T., & AZRIN, N. H. (1968a). "Reinforcer sampling: A technique for increasing the behavior of mental patients." *Journal of Applied Behavior Analysis, 1,* 13–20.

AYLLON, T., & AZRIN, N. H. (1986b). *The token economy.* New York: Appleton-Century-Crofts.

BAILEY, J. S., TIMBERS, G. D., PHILLIPS, E. L. & WOLF, M. M. (1971). "Modification of articulation errors of predelinquents by their peers." *Journal of Applied Behavior Analysis, 4,* 265–281.

BALDWIN, J. D., & BALDWIN, J. I. (1986). *Behavior principles in everyday life* (2nd ed.). Englewood Cliffs, NJ: Prentice Hall.

BARRISH, H. H., SAUNDERS, M., & WOLF, M. M. (1969). "Good behavior game: Effects of individual contingencies for group consequences on disruptive behavior in a classroom." *Journal of Applied Behavior Analysis, 2,* 119–124.

BECKER, W. C., ENGELMANN, S., & THOMAS, D. R. (1971). *Teaching: A course in applied psychology.* Chicago: Science Research Associates.

BOLSTAD, O. D., & JOHNON, S. M. (1972). "Self-regulation in the modification of disruptive classroom behavior." *Journal of Applied Behavior Analysis, 5,* 443–454.

BOOTZIN, R. B. (1975). *Behavior modification and therapy: An introduction.* Cambridge, MA: Winthrop.

BRENT, G. (1977). "Precision teaching: Principles and applications." *Education and Treatment of Children, 1*(1), 35–46.

BRODEN, M., BRUCE, M., MITCHELL, M., CARTER, V., & HALL, R. V. (1970). "Effects of teacher attention on attending behavior of two boys at adjacent desks." *Journal of Applied Behavior Analysis, 3,* 199–203.

BUCKLEY, N. K., & WALKER, H. M. (1970). *Modifying classroom behavior: A manual of procedure for classroom teachers.* Champaign, IL: Research Press.

CARROLL, P. J. (1977). "A durable recording and feedback system." *Journal of Applied Behavior Analysis, 10,* 339–340.

DRABMAN, R. S. (1973). "Child versus teacher administered token programs in a psychiatric hospital school." *Journal of Abnormal Child Psychology, 1,* 68–87.

DRABMAN, R. S., & LAHEY, B. B. (1974). "Feedback in classroom behavior modification: Effects on the target and her classmates." *Journal of Applied Behavior Analysis, 7,* 591–598.

DRABMAN, R. S., & SPITALNIK, R., & SPITALNIK, K. (1974). "Sociometric and disruptive behavior as a function of four types of token reinforcement programs." *Journal of Applied Behavior Analysis, 7,* 93–101.

FINK, W. T., & CRANINE, D. W. (1975). "Control of arithmetic errors using informational feedback and graphing." *Journal of Applied Behavior Analysis, 8,* 461.

FIXSEN, D. L., PHILLIPS, E. L., & WOLF, M. M. (1973). "Achievement Place: Experiments in self-government with predelinquents." *Journal of Applied Behavior Analysis, 6,* 31–47.

GRAUBARD, P. S., ROSENBERG, H. E., & MILLER, M. B. (1974). "Student applications of behavior modification to teachers and environments or ecological approaches to social deviancy." In R. Ulrich, T. Stachnik, & J. Mabry (eds.), *Control of human behavior.* (vol. 3, pp. 421–432). Glenview, IL: Scott, Foresman.

GREENWOOD, C. R., SLOANE, H. N., & BASKIN, A. (1974). "Training elementary aged peer-behavior managers to control small group programmed mathematics." *Journal of Applied Behavior Analysis, 7,* 103–114.

HALL, R. V., CRISTLER, C., CRANSTON, S. S., & TUCKER, B. (1970). "Teachers and parents as researchers using multiple baseline designs." *Journal of Applied Behavior Analysis, 3,* 247–255.

HALL, R. V., LUND, D., & JACKSON, D. (1968). "Effects of teacher attention on study behavior." *Journal of Applied Behavior Analysis, 1,* 1–12.

HAMBLIN, R. L., HATHAWAY, C. H., & WODARSKI, J. (1974). "Group contingencies, peer tutoring, and accelerating academic achievement." In R. Ulrich, T. Stachnik, & J. Mabry, *Control of human behavior.* (vol. 3, pp. 333–340). Glenview, IL: Scott, Foresman.

HARRIS, V. W., & SHERMAN, J. A. (1973). "Use and analysis of the 'Good Behavior Game' to reduce disruptive classroom behavior." *Journal of Applied Behavior Analysis, 6,* 405–417.

HOLZ, W. C., AZRIN, N. H., & AYLLON, T. (1963). "Elimination of behavior of mental patients by response-produced extinction." *Journal of the Experimental Analysis of Behavior, 6*(3), 407–412.

JOHNSTON, J. M. & JOHNSTON, G. T. (1972). "Modification of consonant speech-sound articulation in young children." *Journal of Applied Behavior Analysis, 5,* 233–246.

KAZDIN, A. E. (1973). "The effect of vicarious reinforcement on attentive behavior in the classroom." *Journal of Applied Behavior Analysis, 6,* 71–78.

KAZDIN, A. W. (1977). *The token economy: A review and evaluation.* New York: Plenum Press.

KAZDIN, A. E., SILVERMAN, N. A., & SITTLER, J. L. (1975). "The use of prompts to enhance vicarious effects of nonverbal approval." *Journal of Applied Behavior Analysis, 8,* 279–286.

KOCH, L., & BREYER, N. L. (1974). "A token economy for the teacher." *Psychology in the Schools, 11,* 195–200.

KOORLAND, M. A., & MARTIN, M. B. (1975). *Elementary principles and procedures of the standard behavior chart* (3rd ed.). Gainesville, FL: Learning Environments.

KRUMBOLTZ, J. D., & KRUMBOLTZ, H. B. (1972). *Changing children's behavior.* Englewood Cliffs, NJ: Prentice-Hall, Inc.

LINDSLEY, O. R. (1972). "From Skinner to precision teaching: The child knows best." In J. B. Jordan and L. S. Robbins (eds.), *Let's try doing something else kind of thing: Behavior principles and the exceptional child* (pp. 1–11). Arlington, VA: Council for Exceptional Children.

LITOW, L., & PUMROY, D. K. (1975). "A brief review of classrom group-oriented contingencies." *Journal of Applied Behavior Analysis, 8,* 341–347.

LONG, J., & MADSEN, C. H. (1975). "Five-year-olds as behavoral engineers for younger students in a day-care center." In E. Ramp & G. Semb (eds.) *Behavior analysis: Areas of research and applications* (pp. 341–356). Englewood Cliffs, NJ: Prentice Hall.

LUTZKER, J. R., & WHITE-BLACKBURN, G. (1979). "The good productivity game: Increasing work performance in a rehabilitation setting." *Journal of Applied Behavior Analysis, 12,* 488.

MCLAUGHLIN, T. F., & MALABY, J. E. (1972). "Intrinsic reinforcers in a classroom token economy." *Journal of Applied Behavior Analysis, 5,* 263–270.(a)

MCLAUGHLIN, T. F., & MALABY, J. E. (1972). "Reducing and measuring inappropriate verbalizations in a token economy." *Journal of Applied Behavior Analysis, 5,* 329–333.(b)

MCLAUGHLIN, T. F., & MALABY, J. E. (1974). "Set of procedures to improve accuracy of performance and decrease time to complete mathematics problems." *Psychological Reports, 35,* 1092.

MCLAUGHLIN, T. F., & MALABY, J. E. (1974). "Note on combined and separate effects of token reinforcement and response cost on completing assignments." *Psychological Reports, 35,* 1132.

MCNAMARA, J. R. (1971). "Behavioral intervention in the classroom: Changing students and training a teacher." *Adolescence, 6,* 443–440.

MILLENSON, J. R. (1967). *Principles of behavior analysis.* New York: Macmillan.

O'LEARY, K. D., & DRABMAN, R. (1971). "Token reinforcement programs in the classroom: A review." *Psychological Bulletin, 75,* 379–398.

O'LEARY, K. D., & O'LEARY, S. G. (1977). *Classroom management: The successful use of behavior modification* (2nd ed.). New York: Pergamon Press.

PENNYPACKER, J. S., KOENIG, C. H., & LINDSLEY, O. R. (1972). *Handbook of the standard behavior chart.* Kansas City, KS: Precision Media.

PHILLIPS, E. L. (1968). "Achievement place: Token reinforcement procedures in a home-style rehabilitation setting for 'pre-delinquent' boys." *Journal of Applied Behavior Analysis, 1,* 213–223.

PHILLIPS, E. L., PHILLIPS, E. A., WOLF, M. M., & FIXSEN, D. L. (1973). "Achievement place: Development of the elected manager system." *Journal of Applied Behavior Analysis, 6,* 541–561.

POLIRSTOK, S. R., & GREER, R. D. (1977). "Remediation of mutually aversive interactions between a problem student and four teachers by training the student in reinforcement techniques." *Journal of Applied Behavior Analysis, 10,* 707–716.

REYNOLDS, G. S. (1968). *A primer of operant conditioning.* Glenveiw, IL: Scott, Foresman.

RISLEY, T. R., & WOLF, M. M. (1967). "Establishing functional speech in exholalic children." *Behavior Research and Therapy, 5,* 73–88.

ROSENBERG, J. E., & GRAUBARD, P. (1975). "Peer usage of behavior modification." *Focus on Exceptional Children, 7,* 1–10.

SIEGEL, L. J., & STEINMAN, W. M. (1975). "The modification of a peer-observer's classroom behavior as a function of his serving as a reinforcing agent." In E. Ramp & G. Semb (eds.), *Behavior analysis: Areas of research and application* (pp. 329–340). Englewood Cliffs, NJ: Prentice Hall.

SOLOMON, R. W., & WAHLER, R. G. (1973). "Peer reinforcement control of classroom problem behavior." *Journal of Applied Behavior Analysis,* 6, 49–56.

STRAIN, P. S., SHORES, R. E., & KERR, M. M. (1976). "An experimental analysis of 'spillover' effects on the social interaction of behaviorally handicapped preschool children." *Journal of Applied Behavior Analysis,* 9, 31–40.

SULZER-AZAROFF, B., & MAYER, G. R. (1977). *Applying behavior analysis procedures with children and youth.* New York: Holt, Rinehart & Winston.

VAN HOUTON, R. (1979). "The performance feedback system: Generalization of effect across time." *Child Behavior Therapy,* 1, 219–236.

VAN HOUTON, R., HILL, S., & PARSONS, M. (1975). "An analysis of a performance feedback system: The effects of timing and feedback, public posting, and praise upon academic performance and peer interaction." *Journal of Applied Behavior Analysis,* 8, 449–457.

VAN HOUTON, R., & LAIFATT, D. (1981). "The effects of public posting on high school biology test performance." *Education and Treatment of Children,* 4, 217–226.

VAN HOUTON, R., & MCKILLOP, C. (1977). "An extension of the effects of the performance feedback system with secondary school students." *Psychology in the Schools,* 14, 480–484.

VAN HOUTON, R., MORRISON, E., JARVIS, R., & MCDONALD, M. (1974). "The effects of explicit timing and feedback on compositional response rate in elementary school children." *Journal of Applied Behavior Analysis,* 7, 547–555.

VAN HOUTON, R., & VAN HOUTON, J. (1977). "The performance feedback system in a special education classroom: An analysis of public posting and peer comments." *Behavior Therapy,* 8, 366–376.

WEISBERG, P., & CLEMENTS, P. (1977). "Effects of direct, intermittent, and vicarious reinforcement procedures on the development and maintenance of instruction-following behaviors in a group of young children." *Journal of Applied Behavior Analysis,* 10, 314.

WHITE, O. R., & HARING, N. G. (1980). *Exceptional teaching* (2nd ed.) Columbus, OH: Charles E. Merrill.

WILLIS, J. W., MORRIS, B., & CROWDER, J. (1972). "A remedial reading technique for disabled readers that employs students as behavioral engineers." *Psychology in the Schools,* 9, 67–70.

WILSON, S. H., & WILLIAMS, R. L. (1973). "The effects of group contingencies on first graders' academic and social behaviors." *Journal of School Psychology,* 11, 110–117.

WINETT, R. A., RICHARDS, C. S., & KRASNER, L. (1971). "Child-monitored token reading program." *Psychology in the Schools,* 8, 259–262.

WOLF, M. M., RISLEY, T. R., & MEES, H. (1964). "Applications of operant conditioning procedures to the behavior problems of an autistic child." *Behavior Research and Therapy,* 1, 305–312.

chapter 11

Schedules of Reinforcement

Mr. Lopez and his staff have completed an inservice program designed to identify procedures that relate to a reinforcer's effectiveness and to study strategies that teachers can use to enhance their students' reinforcers. He is now convinced that he and his staff are equipped to successfully increase Michael's verbalizations and, at the same time, decrease Michael's spitting. The staff begins the intervention procedure again, this time being very careful to deliver the reinforcers immediately, consistently, and especially, frequently. Michael's verbalizations increased, his spitting decreased, and the staff are very pleased with his (and their) performance.

Mr. Lopez soon became aware of another potential flaw in the intervention that he designed for Michael. As Michael continued to emit verbal responses at higher rates each day, Mr. Lopez and his staff were kept increasingly busy reinforcing Michael's verbal responses with their attention. In fact, the intervention was becoming disruptive to the classroom routine and more importantly, was beginning to deprive other students of the staff's attention. Mr. Lopez realized that no one gets reinforced everytime they do something in the "real world," yet that was exactly what he had planned and successfully employed with Michael. Mr. Lopez wanted to reduce the frequency of the reinforcers, but he was concerned that stopping them abruptly would reduce the rate of Michael's verbalizations. His problem was to find a way to reduce the frequency of reinforcement to a more natural level without disrupting Michael's behavior.

The essence of Mr. Lopez's dilemma involves, on the one hand, the schedule of reinforcement that he arranged for Michael and, on the other hand, the proposed switch to a different schedule that will be likely to maintain Michael's performance. The concept of *schedules of reinforcement* is based on the frequency with which the environment delivers reinforcement or, as Reynolds (1968) wrote "the rule followed by the environment . . . in determining which among the many occurrences of a response will be reinforced" (p. 60). Numerous investigators have focused their attention on the effects of various schedules of reinforcement on the acquisition and maintenance of behavior. The most elegant studies have been conducted in laboratory settings and most of our knowledge of schedule effects are based on these laboratory findings. However, many researchers are actively investigating schedule effects on people in applied settings (for example, classrooms). These studies allow us to generalize our conclusions about the effects of the various schedules of reinforcement and, consequently, we are able to design intervention programs more likely to successfully achieve their goals. These goals may be the acquisition of a new skill, the increase in the proficiency, mastery, or fluency of a previously acquired skill, or the maintenance of a skill over long periods of time.

There are two major classes of schedules of reinforcement: continuous and intermittent. Each class of schedules has certain characteristics and may be expected to have differing effects on behavior. Consequently, schedules of each class have different uses in applied settings, depending on the target behavior's characteristics that are most beneficial to the individual and the level of skill performance that the individual brings to the situation. Each of these schedules, their characteristics, their effects on behavior, and their appropriate uses are explained and discussed in this chapter.

CONTINUOUS REINFORCEMENT

A continuous schedule of reinforcement (CRF) exists when each correct or appropriate response is reinforced. In our example above, Michael's verbalizations were on a CRF schedule because every verbalization resulted in attention from the staff.

Continuous reinforcement is most useful in the initial stages of an intervention if one of two behavioral conditions are present. In the first condition, the target behaviors (in special education classes) are quite often selected because they are not part of the student's repertoire. For example, a student who cannot correctly identify colors needs to learn those skills. In this case, each correct response should be reinforced so the student can learn to accurately discriminate correct from incorrect responding in the presence of certain stimuli. If each response was not reinforced, then incorrect responses could occur and not be punished, thereby lengthening the learning process and reducing instructional efficiency. In the second condition, a target behavior may be selected because, although it is part of the student's repertoire, it occurs so infrequently as to be nonfunctional. For example, the student can solve basic addition problems with only 10 percent accuracy and at a speed of two problems per minute. In this example, each correct response should be reinforced, in order to facilitate discrimination and to increase the rate of correct responses. If each correct response was not reinforced, the student, because of his slow speed, may gain access to so few reinforcers that the frequent reinforcement rule may be violated. In other words, the student responds so infrequently that he will never gain sufficient reinforcement unless and until every response is reinforced.

We may conclude, then, that CRF schedules are most useful for reinforcing new or very weak behaviors. Because these are quite often the types of behaviors taught in special education classes, we might expect to find a large number of CRF schedules in special education classrooms. However, there is an inherent danger in the use of CRF schedules, because, as Mr. Lopez discovered, CRF schedules are not very realistic. The relatively artificial nature of CRF schedules means that these must be eventually eliminated for at least three reasons. In order to discuss the first of these reasons we must pause briefly to discuss *extinction,* a process by which a behavior that was once reinforced no longer gains reinforcement. No reinforcers are available for that behavior or response, and, as a consequence, the response eventually ceases to occur. It may be helpful to view extinction as being the opposite of CRF. (Extinction is discussed fully in Chapter 14.) The importance of extinction to CRF schedules is that different behaviors have different resistances to extinction effects, depending on the schedule under which reinforcement was earned. In other words, a given behavior may be more or less durable in the absence of reinforcement as a result of the schedule of reinforcement that was maintaining that behavior. Behaviors reinforced on a CRF schedule are not very durable. A student who is used to receiving a reinforcer for each correct response will soon stop emitting that response if the reinforcers are no longer available. Consequently, the teacher must plan to shift to a schedule that is consistent with the environment as soon as possible in order to increase behavioral durability.

A second reason for eliminating a CRF schedule is the specific nature of CRF schedules. Rarely will the target behavior gain access to continuous reinforcement in any setting other than the specific one in which instruction is occurring. In effect, extinction or near-extinction conditions prevail in virtually every other situation the individual may encounter. Behaviors taught exclusively under CRF conditions simply will not generalize readily to new settings or situations.

The third reason for moving from CRF to intermittent schedules is more pragmatic in nature. As Mr. Lopez found, it becomes increasingly difficult to deliver reinforcers on a CRF schedule once the student begins to be more proficient in the target behavior. You will find you are spending a larger proportion of your time *delivering* reinforcers and less time teaching. The problem is compounded dramatically if more than one student is receiving CRF at the same time. For example, what happens if three students simultaneously emit a target behavior correctly? Worse still, what if these students are in different areas of the classroom?

We may conclude that a CRF schedule is most useful during the initial stages of an intervention. Its usefulness declines, however, as the individual becomes more fluent or proficient with the target behavior. As proficiency increases, a switch to some type of intermittent reinforcement must be accomplished. Careful planning must precede any shift of reinforcement schedules. The methods used to accomplish the schedule change and the selection of a schedule appropriate to the task must be specified in advance of the change. The various intermittent schedules and effective strategies for changing schedules are discussed in the next section.

INTERMITTENT SCHEDULES

Intermittent reinforcement refers to a procedure in which some, but not all, occurrences of the target behavior are reinforced. For example, Calvin earns a new pencil and the teacher's praise for staying in his seat for 5 minutes. Or, Luther earns twenty-five cents for every 50 ball-point pens he assembles. Each of these examples reflects a particular type of intermittent schedule, of which there are several, that will be discussed later in this section. First, however, the several advantages of intermittent schedules of reinforcement will be presented, followed by a discussion of the most effective ways to switch from a continuous schedule to one of the intermittent schedules.

Advantages of Intermittent Schedules

Intermittent and continuous schedules are useful for very different purposes. As discussed previously, continuous reinforcement is most efficient during the early stages of an intervention when the individual is initially acquiring a new skill, but it is inefficient for maintaining a target behavior once the individual has demonstrated some proficiency. Intermittent schedules, on the other hand, are quite effective and efficient for maintaining behavior and increasing the likelihood of its generalizing to new situations. There are several reasons for these effects of intermittent reinforcement, and they are discussed in the subsequent sections.

Satiation Is Delayed. As discussed in Chapter 10, satiation occurs when the student receives so much of a particular reinforcer that it begins to lose its reinforcing power and is, at least temporarily, no longer reinforcing. Responses on a CRF schedule quite obviously will earn responses more often than responses on an intermittent schedule. For example, when Roger was initially learning to say consonant sounds his teacher delivered a check mark for each correct response. As Roger became more proficient, the frequency of tokens (delivered on a CRF schedule) increased at the same rate as Roger's correct responses. Eventually, Roger earned such a large quantity of tokens that he was temporarily unwilling to work for more.

Because an important educational goal is to teach behaviors that are durable and will continue to be emitted long after any intervention has stopped, it is important to avoid satiation effects. By using an intermittent schedule, we arrange to deliver proportionately fewer reinforcers for the same amount of student work. Consequently, it will require more responses, usually over longer periods of time, before satiation effects are evident. In fact, if the intermittent schedule is arranged optimally, so that the amount of available reinforcement closely matches the individual's capabilities, satiation effects may be avoided altogether. If Roger's teacher had arranged to deliver one token for every five correctly spoken consonant sounds, Roger would have had to say five times as many consonant sounds to earn the prior quantity of tokens. As a result, satiation is delayed.

Behavior Is Maintained Under Extinction Conditions. Intermittent schedules of reinforcement require longer periods of maintained emissions of the target behavior in order to earn the reinforcer. Intermittent schedules of reinforcement also require proportionately more responses for a given number of reinforcers. In either case, the individual learns not to expect a reinforcer for each response. Conditions such as these are much more representative of real-life situations. On a more specific level, these arrangements also mirror the environmental conditions and expectations found in progressively less restrictive educational settings, where reinforcement is typically not available for every correct response. Conversely, behavior maintained on a CRF schedule is much more susceptible to extinction conditions because, in part, the individual has never learned to tolerate an absence of reinforcement for that particular response.

Learned Behaviors Are Maintained. A behavior that has been learned to some degree of proficiency can be more easily maintained on an intermittent schedule than on a CRF schedule. As you may imagine, trying to maintain an ever increasing repertoire of behaviors in any number of students on a CRF schedule will become increasingly burdensome. Soon there will be no time to teach any additional responses because so much time will be spent delivering the reinforcers that maintain those previously learned behaviors. In addition, the maintenance of the response is quite artificial and it is incredibly unlikely that the target behavior would earn continuous reinforcement in any other setting. Maintaining the target behavior on an intermittent schedule that approximates those found in less restrictive settings may enhance the generalization of that response to new settings as well as maintain it in the setting in which it was learned (Rose & Gottlieb, 1981; Rose, Lessen, & Gottlieb, 1982).

Switching From Continuous to Intermittent Reinforcement

Up to this point, our discussion of CRF and intermittent schedules has focused on their differences and relative advantages. Implicit in this discussion has been the notion that the most efficient uses of these differing schedules involves using CRF first and then switching to an intermittent schedule of reinforcement when the need arises. This switch from a CRF to an intermittent schedule is not automatic, nor is it necessarily easy to accomplish. In fact, reducing reinforcement *density* (the ratio of reinforcer to response) can be one of the trickiest, most sophisticated procedures that a teacher will face. If reinforcement density is abruptly reduced, the student may begin to emit the behavior less often or stop entirely. Switching to an intermittent schedule requires great care on the teacher's part and increased attention by the teacher to the student's behavioral data. Fortunately, there are several procedures that have proven to be effective in helping the teacher to accomplish this switch to a less dense reinforcement schedule without disrupting the student's behavior. Progressive and gradual changes, supplemented with various cues, are the keys to success and are discussed in the following sections.

Progressive Changes. The ultimate goal for any reinforcement program is to match behaviors to naturally occurring reinforcers that will maintain those behaviors for a very long time. A critical component of that goal is attaining a schedule of reinforcement that closely approximates the naturally occurring schedule that is arranged by the environment. In pursuit of these goals, we must often begin an intervention with artificial reinforcers delivered on an artificial schedule (CRF). Eventually, as the student begins to emit the target behavior more frequently and reliably, we begin to rely less on the artificial reinforcers and gradually shift control to more natural reinforcers. At the same time, we must begin to progressively reduce the reinforcer density, so that a systematic progression from artificial schedules to more natural schedules occurs. The concept of a progressive switch in schedules requires that the teacher consistently keep trying to reduce the reinforcer density, or *thin* the schedule of reinforcement. You must consistently try to get more responses over longer periods of time for the same amount of reinforcement. Stated another way, you are trying to get to the point where

the student is putting forth maximum effort for the least possible amount of reinforcement. At some point in this progression, a schedule that approximates the natural environment's schedule for that particular response may be reached, and your reinforcement thinning efforts may cease. Until that point is reached, however, you must consistently and progressively attempt to reduce the density of reinforcement. For example, Michael was initially reinforced with teacher and staff attention each time he verbalized instead of spit. As his verbalizations increased in rate and began to occur more reliably, Mr. Lopez began to thin Michael's schedule of reinforcement. First, Mr. Lopez ignored one verbalization in every five. After observing no reduction in Michael's speaking over a period of three days, Mr. Lopez began to ignore every third verbalization. By progressively reducing the number of responses that earned reinforcement, Mr. Lopez eventually reached the point where approximately only one of every ten of Michael's verbalizations were consistently reinforced. If the situation required more staff attention, such as when Michael was actively engaged in a lesson, then more attention was provided. At other times, such as during rest time, no attention was provided for Michael's speaking. By progressively reducing the reinforcement density, Mr. Lopez created a much more natural situation that allowed Michael to more normally interact with his environment. Michael began speaking to his peers and gaining their attention on an intermittent schedule that was arranged naturally.

Mr. Lopez focused on two other procedural considerations prior to and during his progressive reduction in Michael's reinforcer density. First, he observed his staff as they interacted with other students following the students' verbalizations. These data indicated that most students received staff attention after about 10 to 15 verbalizations, except during instructional periods when the attention rate was much higher. Mr. Lopez established his criteria for Michael based on these data, thereby insuring a relatively natural schedule for Michael. Second, Mr. Lopez monitored Michael's response data very closely during the thinning process. Any abrupt drop in Michael's rate of verbalizations would have indicated that the thinning process was proceeding too quickly, and Mr. Lopez would have immediately slowed the progression.

Gradual Changes. Changes in reinforcement density must be made gradually as well as progressively. Even though these two procedural considerations appear to be similar in their requirements, there are important differences. A progressive change in the density of reinforcement does not automatically mean that the change is to be gradual. For example, an autistic student is being taught to make eye contact with his teacher. Initially, each time the child makes eye contact, he receives a reinforcer. After a period of time, the student's performance data indicate that he is consistently and reliably making eye contact and a decision is made to thin his reinforcement schedule. The teacher makes these changes progressively: 1 of every 10 responses is reinforced, then 1 of every 20 responses, and finally 1 of every 30 responses. If the teacher had thinned the schedule progressively *and* gradually, then the sequence may have been as follows: 3 of every 4 responses are reinforced, then 2 of every 4 responses, then 1 of every 4, then 1 of every 5 responses, and so on. Eventually an optimal schedule would be achieved and, by gradually making the changes in the schedule, the teacher would ensure that no disruption in performance would occur.

The gradual nature of any systematic reduction in reinforcement schedules cannot be overemphasized. If the reduction is too quick or abrupt, a disruption in performance is very likely to occur. When a behavior abruptly begins to occur less frequently or ceases to occur and this reduction in performance is accompanied by apparently emotional responses, such as tantrums, then most certainly the changes in reinforcement schedules have been made too quickly. In this case,

you should begin to provide a more dense schedule of reinforcement; in effect, return to a previously successful level. Further thinning of the schedule will have to occur even more gradually and slowly. Conversely, behavior can reduce or cease to occur if the thinning process occurs too slowly. When behavior decreases, even though a dense schedule of reinforcement is in effect, satiation may be occurring. In this case, you may either change the reinforcer or begin to thin the schedule a little more quickly.

Additional Cues or Prompts. Cues and prompts are verbal or physical antecedent stimuli that can remind the student that particular responses will be reinforced. (Cues and prompts are subsets of a broader category of antecedent stimuli known more technically as *discriminative stimuli.* Discriminative stimuli gain their power to set the occasion for certain behaviors by their past association with reinforcers. They are discussed in detail in Chapter 12.) Teachers have control of a large number of cues or prompts that can maintain response levels in the presence of progressively thinner schedules of reinforcement. Verbal cues, such as "When you finish reading ten pages in your reading book, you can go to the free play area," are probably the most efficient cues a teacher can use. Other cues that have proven useful include physical contact (for example, touching a student's shoulder to remind him to continue writing), written instructions, gestures, and signals (for example, holding up your hand when it's time to listen to directions). In each situation, the cue is designed to remind the student of the response requirements and to alert him to the continued availability of reinforcement.

In order for the use of cues to be effective during any thinning procedure, four guidelines to their use should be adhered to. First, it is a good idea to begin to use cues quite early in the reinforcer program, while the schedule is still relatively dense. This will allow the student to learn to associate a particular cue with a reinforcer. Second, it is important to use any cue consistently. Third, the cue should be used frequently. Fourth, you should plan to gradually reduce the use of the cue, using the same guidelines as used when thinning the reinforcer schedule. The process is the same, but the timing will differ. Usually cues will be faded out of a program after the schedule of reinforcement has been thinned to more natural levels because the cues are used to reach those natural schedules of reinforcement. We have now considered issues related to switching to intermittent schedules. We now examine the type of intermittent schedules.

There are two types of intermittent schedules of reinforcement: ratio and interval. *Ratio schedules* are those that arrange to deliver reinforcement based on specified number of responses. *Interval schedules* arrange for the delivery of reinforcement based on the emission of the target behavior and the passage of specified amounts of time. The remaining sections of this chapter present discussions of these types of intermittent reinforcement schedules.

RATIO SCHEDULES

As discussed earlier, intermittent schedules of reinforcement are similar to the schedules that are present in the natural environment. Establishing an intermittent schedule depends on your control of the ratio of reinforcers either to the number of responses that must be emitted or to the length of time that must pass between responses before those reinforcers are available to the student. Thus, schedules of reinforcement can be either *response based* or *time based*. Ratio schedules are response based. (Interval schedules are time based and will be discussed later in this chapter.) Therefore, whenever reinforcement is contingent upon the student emitting a certain number of responses (the target behavior) before a reinforcer is delivered, we can identify that schedule as a *ratio schedule*.

There are two types of ratio schedules: fixed ratio and variable ratio. *Fixed ratio* (FR) schedules require that a fixed number of re-

sponses occur before the next instance of the target behavior is reinforced. For example, a student working in a sheltered workshop is paid after packaging every twenty-fifth packet of plastic tableware. In this case the student is credited with twenty-five cents after placing a plastic knife, spoon, and fork in each of 25 packets, providing, of course, that all of the 25 packets were packaged correctly. *Variable ratio* (VR) schedules, while also providing for reinforcement to be contingent upon the emission of the target behavior following a number of correct responses, specify that the number of responses necessary to gain reinforcement varies. Under a variable ratio schedule, our student who is packaging plastic tableware may still be paid after an average of 25 responses, but the reinforcer will be delivered on a variable basis. Therefore, the student is never certain which specific response will be reinforced; for example, credit, (the reinforcer) may be given after the *twenty-seventh, fifty-fourth, seventy-fifth,* and *one-hundreth* response as long as the average remains one reinforcer for every twenty-five responses.

Students whose behaviors are being reinforced on ratio schedules tend to respond in characteristic ways. In general, relatively high and consistent rates of responding can be achieved when a ratio schedule is used, and the behaviors will continue to be emitted when reinforcement is stopped (extinction). However, there are likely to be differences in performance characteristics depending on whether a fixed ratio or a variable ratio schedule is used.

Fixed Ratio Schedules

As mentioned above, the reinforcer follows a predetermined number of responses in a fixed ratio schedule. Quite often the "FR" designation of a fixed ratio schedule will include the number of predetermined responses necessary to gain reinforcement, so that a "FR5" schedule indicates that each fifth response is to be reinforced. You may have already noticed that a continuous reinforcement schedule is equivalent to a FR1 schedule because the number of predetermined responses in a CRF schedule is one.

You may expect two characteristics of a student's performance to emerge under an FR schedule. First, he is likely to respond at a relatively high rate until the reinforcement is delivered. This is quite logical, since the more rapidly an individual responds under an FR schedule, the sooner he will gain the reinforcer. This results in accumulating more reinforcers within a given period of time. Second, we may expect slightly less consistent responding under an FR schedule than under a VR schedule because a student may tend to pause momentarily following the delivery of the reinforcer. Although this post-reinforcement pause has been well documented in laboratory studies with animals, it is not consistently observed with humans in applied settings. If this brief pause were to occur, the student may display any number of non-target behaviors, such as day-dreaming, going to the restroom, or talking to a neighbor. Despite a lack of evidence that humans are affected by this phenomenon, it is probably best to allow for the possibility of its occurrence until data are obtained for the individual student.

When a FR schedule is ended (extinction), a student's performance is likely to be characterized by bursts of responses (perhaps as rapid as during the FR conditions) followed by progressively longer periods of nonresponding. Eventually, the rate of the target behavior may approach zero. Thinner FR schedules (that is, those requiring more responses per reinforcer) are likely to result in more total responses during extinction conditions. For example, an FR50 requires 50 responses before the student will discover that no reinforcer is forthcoming, while an FR5 requires only 5 responses before this information is learned.

Implementing an FR schedule is fairly easy, especially if the guidelines for switching from CRF to intermittent schedules are followed. In addition, three basic rules should improve your chances of success. First, observe and determine the student's present performance level. Second, select an FR that allows reinforcement after a relatively few responses. Third, increase the number of responses required to gain reinforcement (thin the schedule) while monitoring the student's performance data. If the behavior starts to decrease gradually or stops abruptly, you have increased the number of responses either too quickly or by too large a number; drop back to a previously successful ratio and continue the process in a more gradual fashion.

The use of an FR schedule is illustrated by the work-study experience of Kyle, who was enrolled in a high school EMR class. Kyle began working in a small factory manufacturing chrome automobile bumpers. Kyle's job was to polish each chromed bumper with a buffer. Even though he was earning $3.00 per hour, Kyle's employer reported a notable lack of success in getting Kyle to work as fast as his other employees. Typically, an average worker could buff 40 bumpers per hour, but Kyle was only buffing 10 bumpers per hour. Ms. Robinson, Kyle's teacher, arranged for his employer to pay Kyle on an FR schedule, so that he would earn a certain amount for a given number of bumpers. Since Kyle consistently completed 10 bumpers per hour, the initial ratio was established at 12 bumpers per hour (FR12). A "production sheet" was designed on which the foreman placed a checkmark each time Kyle buffed 12 bumpers correctly. Kyle initially earned $3.00 for each 12 bumpers.

After one week, Kyle was polishing 29 bumpers every 2 hours (the length of his workday) whereas his baseline indicated that 20 per "shift" was Kyle's norm. So, a decision was made to thin the schedule to an FR16. After some initial lack of success, Kyle began to exceed his production goal within eight working days. Again, the schedule was thinned, to an FR21. Now Kyle had to polish 21 bumpers before earning his $3.00 (and 42 bumpers during his 2-hour shift in order to earn the same $6.00 he earned previously when being paid by the hour). By the end of the week, Kyle was consistently meeting his goal. To his employer's delight, Kyle had more than doubled his productivity within three weeks, and it didn't cost the employer any additional wages.

Gradually, the FR schedule continued to be thinned until Kyle was being paid on an FR40 schedule. The FR40 was equivalent to the average worker's productivity. The employer agreed to continue to pay Kyle $3.00 for every 40 polished bumpers regardless of the time. So, under these more natural conditions, Kyle could now earn more than $6.00 for his two hours of work. For example, if he worked extra hard, he could buff 120 bumpers in 2 hours, thereby earning $9.00 instead of his usual $6.00.

Variable Ratio Schedules

When the number of responses necessary to receive a reinforcer varies, the reinforcer is being delivered on a variable ratio schedule. As with FR schedules, the designation of a variable ratio schedule is often abbreviated to indicate the average number of responses necessary to gain the reinforcer. For example, a student who is being reinforced on a VR5 schedule will gain the reinforcer on the average of every fifth response. The actual responses gaining reinforcement will vary, however. So, a VR5 schedule may account for reinforcers being delivered after the second, eighth, ninth, sixteenth, and twenty-fifth responses (25 responses ÷ 5 reinforcers = 5 responses per reinforcer).

Variable ratio schedules are generally more natural than FR schedules, natural reinforcers occur most often in a variable manner. Gambling is a classic example of a VR schedule; the gambler is reinforced, but he or she never knows which lever-pull on the "one-armed bandit" will be a winner. Imagine the gambler's response if slot machines were on an FR schedule.

As with FR schedules, the VR schedules are related to rapid responding. A crucial difference, however, becomes apparent when we consider the consistency of responding. When the ratio is fixed, the student quickly learns how many responses are required to earn the reinforcer. It's predictable. A VR schedule, on the other hand, promotes more consistent responding because the student is never sure which particular response will earn the reinforcer. A reinforcer cannot be predicted. So, *each* response *may* be reinforced. We may conclude that a VR schedule can be characterized by rapid *and* consistent responding.

Behaviors reinforced on a VR schedule are very durable. That is, they continue for a relatively long time under extinction conditions. This durability is related to the variable and unpredictable nature of the schedule. Since the student can never be sure which response will be reinforced, he or she is likely to continue responding for quite awhile in anticipation that the next response will be the one to earn the reinforcer.

Using a VR schedule requires one extra step than does an FR schedule; the schedule will probably be most effective if arranged prior to its use. So, while the teacher using a VR schedule must first determine the student's present performance and, second, choose an average number of responses that will promote success, the teacher must also decide the specific responses that will be reinforced. This decision is easiest to accomplish when planned in advance. As with an FR schedule, the last step is to gradually increase the number of responses required to earn reinforcement; however, with a VR schedule the *average* number of responses required for reinforcement are gradually increased. The specific responses that are reinforced continue to be selected randomly, as long as they result in the correct VR schedule (average number of responses). It may be noted that some teachers consider this extra step to be an added burden. If rapid and consistent responding is the goal for a particular student, then the benefits of the VR schedule will probably be worth this extra effort. Fortunately, like many other skills, experience and practice will reduce the apparent burden of arranging a VR schedule.

An excellent classroom application of a VR

schedule was demonstrated by one of the author's students, Ms. Pope, who taught an elementary cross-categorical class. One of her students, Lynn, was learning her basic multiplication facts. As part of her daily work, Lynn was expected to complete a 30 problem computation worksheet. Lynn earned five minutes of free time upon completion of the work-sheet (an FR30 schedule). However, Ms. Pope noticed that Lynn was frequently off-task, engaging other students in conversation or doodling on her worksheet. Then, as the end of the math period approached, Lynn would begin working quite diligently until she completed her worksheet.

Ms. Pope wanted to decrease these off-task behaviors and decided to achieve this goal by increasing Lynn's productivity. She remembered that a VR schedule facilitates more consistent responding than does the FR schedule. So she switched Lynn to a VR6, with an average of every six problems completed correctly earning one minute of free time. (This yielded the same amount of free time Lynn had been earning previously). Immediately, Ms. Pope noted an increase in Lynn's on-task behavior and a decrease in the total amount of time Lynn spent on the worksheets. Lynn began to work on each worksheet much more consistently and rapidly because she never knew which response would earn the reinforcer.

Advantages of Ratio Schedules

There are several advantages in using ratio schedules, whether fixed or variable. Briefly, both FR and VR schedules provide the following:

1. They generate rapid rates of responding.
2. They are relatively simple to use.
3. They are inexpensive because only a few responses are reinforced.
4. They are especially useful if the target behavior yields a permanent product.
5. They reflect more accurately natural classroom levels of reinforcement.
6. They generate durable behaviors that will per-

sist even though the schedule has been terminated (especially true of VR schedules).

In addition, consistent responding is an advantage of the VR schedule but may not be an advantage of the FR schedule.

Differential Reinforcement of High Rates

As we have seen, ratio schedules are very effective for producing behaviors that occur at a relatively high rate. While the value of high speed responding is quite obvious in factories or on assembly lines, we in education often discuss speed as only an incidental educational goal. Yet, it is becoming increasingly clear that speed, especially in "tool" or prerequisite basic skills, is an important element in a student's proficiency with higher level skills. For example if a student can write only 13 numerals per minute, he will never be able to complete more than 10 to 13 addition problems (with single digit answers) per minute even though he may know many more. An obvious solution to this situation is to simply give the student more time, because we really want to assess "how much he knows." However, allowing the student more time has the effect of masking his lack of proficiency, rather than tapping his knowledge. If a student cannot perform many basic tasks rapidly *and* accurately, a progressive and cumulative cycle of deficient performance levels will begin as the student is introduced to higher and more complex tasks. Data illustrating these speed related proficiencies for several academic tasks are presented in Table 11.1.

Let's use some of these data to further explore the importance of high rate responding in educational settings. Assume that Willie, a second grade student in an EMR resource room, can write 13 numerals per minute and answer 8 basic addition facts per minute. Upon his return to his regular class, how does he compare to his peers on these tasks? (Use Table 11.1 to find rates for these skills at the second grade level). If his regular class teacher allots 10 minutes for practicing basic addition facts, how many problems is Willie likely to

TABLE 11.1 Academic Skill Proficiency Criteria

Task	Expected Grade Level	Proficiency Criteria
Writes numerals 0–9	mid-1st	70 responses per min.
Writes add facts, sums 0–9	mid-2nd	60 rpm
Writes add facts, sums 10–18	mid-3rd	60 rpm
Writes multiplication facts 0–9	mid-6th	90 rpm
Writes upper case letters	mid-1st	70 rpm
Writes lower case letters	early-2nd	70 rpm

Source: Cited in Koenig, C. H., & Kunzelmann, H. P., 1980, *Classroom learning screening: Handbook.* Columbus, OH: Charles E. Merrill, pp. 14–15.

complete in that amount of time? If we assume a typical student will perform at 70 percent proficiency during practice sessions, how many can we expect his "average" peer to complete? So, we can easily compute that Willie is gaining access to only about 19 percent of the problems that an average peer will get to practice each day. If we project this lack of practice over an entire school year and assume an equal discrepancy across a variety of computational skills, we should not be surprised that Willie is falling farther and farther behind his classmates? We should now be able to agree that speed (high-rate responding) is often an important instructional objective.

A most effective method for producing high response rates is a schedule of *differential reinforcement of high rates* or *DRH*. Under DRH conditions, reinforcement is delivered only when the target response has occurred at a rate higher than a preestablished rate. Reinforcement is said to be delivered differentially because *only* high rates will gain reinforcement; rates lower than the preestablished rate, while just as accurate, will not be reinforced. DRH schedules teach that both accuracy *and* speed are important.

Implementing a DRH schedule is similar in almost every way to implementing an FR schedule. The first step requires collecting baseline data. The second step establishes a performance level that is attainable, but requires a certain effort by the student. The third step gradually and progressively increases the number of responses required to gain reinforcement, and the teacher continues to monitor the student's performance.

To illustrate the use of a DRH, let's return to Willie, who, in reality, was one of the authors' students during his public school teaching days. Quite a lot of effort was expended trying to get Willie to respond more rapidly on his basic addition worksheets, however there was no significant gain in Willie's performance. Eventually, his teacher decided to investigate Willie's numeral writing proficiency. As you can see during the baseline phase of Figure 11.1, Willie never exceeded 13 numerals per minute. (The logical relationship between Willie's rate for this response and his rate on basic addition facts was explained previously.) A DRH schedule was implemented, during which Willie was "tested" each day by having him write numerals "as fast as he could" for one minute. Willie could earn access to an overhead projector that he could draw and doodle upon, each time he could "beat" his goal. On days when he did not beat his goal, he was thanked for his effort, told how close he had come, and told to begin his next assignment. As may be seen in Figure 11.1, Willie's performance increased gradually and progressively, with earlier "steps" being smaller than those occurring later in the program.

A potential disadvantage of the DRH schedule derives from its effectiveness. Because of its effectiveness, a student's rate of response may be increased to such an extent that the response is no longer accurate topographically. For example, if you try to read aloud a passage from a book as fast as you can, you will notice that many of the words are no longer comprehensible to a listener. Therefore, using reasonable performance expectations for your students should be a guiding principle when implementing a DRH schedule.

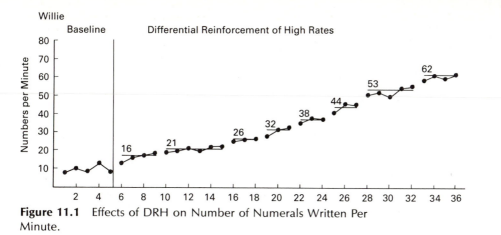

Figure 11.1   Effects of DRH on Number of Numerals Written Per Minute.

INTERVAL SCHEDULES

In the preceding section, we saw that ratio schedules are response based because reinforcement is contingent upon a certain predetermined number of responses being emitted. Interval schedules, however, are time based because reinforcement is contingent upon the passage of a specified amount of time as well as the performance of the appropriate response. Under an interval schedule, the learner is reinforced for performing the target behavior the first time after a certain amount of time has elapsed.

There are two types of interval schedules: fixed interval and variable interval. A *fixed interval* (FI) schedule requires that a certain, fixed amount of time elapses before an emission of the target behavior will earn reinforcement. For example, a student working on increasing the amount of written work while in her seat earns an extra minute of free time if she is writing when a timer rings, signaling the end of a five minute interval. Extra free time is not available until five minutes has elapsed. If she is working after the 5-minute interval elapses, then she earns extra free time. *Variable interval* (VI) schedules also specify that a certain amount of time must elapse before reinforcement is delivered, but the length of the interval will vary, rather than being fixed as with a FI schedule. Re-

turning to our student who is completing written work while seated, if she were being reinforced under a VI schedule, the timer would be set for an average of every five minutes, but the actual length of the interval would vary from interval to interval. So, for example, she may earn extra free time after four minutes, nine minutes, and two minutes. (In our example, 4 + 9 + 2 = 15 minutes. Fifteen minutes divided by 3 opportunities for reinforcement equals an average of one reinforcer every 5 minutes.)

Interval schedules are particularly useful when the target behavior is one of two types. First, if the target behavior lasts for a period of time, such as "on-task" or "in-seat" behavior, then an interval schedule may prove easier to use because on-going instances of the response may be reinforced systematically. For example, if a student were on-task when an interval ends (thus, receiving a reinforcer) and continues to be on-task into and throughout the next interval, the usefulness of an interval schedule of reinforcement becomes apparent. Second, a target behavior may be difficult to observe precisely in an instructional situation, especially due to subtle beginning and ending points for the particular response. (For example, "on-task" may be defined, in part, by where the student's eyes are looking—a difficult behavior to monitor.) In this case, an interval schedule of reinforcement allows accurate and systematic reinforcement of a target response even when the observation of the beginning of a particular episode of that response may require more observational diligence than most teachers will have time to accomplish.

Students who are earning reinforcement under interval schedules tend to respond differently from students operating under ratio schedules. In general, responses under interval schedules will be relatively slower than responses maintained under ratio schedules. There are, however, some similarities in response characteristics. There are also some similarities between interval ratio schedules that depend upon the type of interval schedule (fixed or variable) being used.

Fixed Interval Schedules

At least three student performance characteristics are typical under an FI schedule. First, you are likely to find slower rates of performance, especially as compared to performance levels generated under ratio schedules. This phenomenon is understandable when we consider the basic tenet of the FI schedule is that a certain amount of time must pass before any response will be reinforced. Whether the student works throughout the interval or only at the end of the interval makes no difference. So, a student might perform consistently for only the last 30 seconds of a 5-minute interval and still receive the reinforcer. However, there is some evidence that students will perform at higher rates if the intervals are relatively short (Skinner, 1953). For example, even if a student only responds during the last 30 seconds (hopefully an extreme case), an FI5 schedule will require more frequent responding than will an FI10 schedule. Second, you will find that fixed interval schedules are often associated with inconsistent performance for the same reason just discussed regarding speed. In fact, a phenomenon known as the *fixed interval scallop* has been consistently identified in laboratory studies, in which the individual "takes a break" after being reinforced and gradually

increases his or her performance level until the rate of responding is fairly high towards the end of the interval. (This type of performance should be very familiar to any college student because it is an accurate description of how term papers are completed: not much activity early in the term followed by quite a lot of activity just before the deadline.) Third, you will find that the performance generated under an FI schedule is quite durable; that is, it maintains for relatively long periods of time under extinction conditions. Students whose behaviors have been maintained under FI schedules will respond differently to extinction conditions depending on the density of the FI schedule. The rate of responding will be higher for short rather than longer intervals under extinction. This is because during short intervals the student has not learned to respond as long without reinforcement. A student on an FI5 schedule has learned to expect reinforcement to become available approximately every 5 minutes, while an FI15 schedule teaches the student to expect reinforcement no more often than every 15 minutes.

An FI schedule is probably easier than an FR schedule to implement by a teacher; this is mainly because you do not have to count responses in order to arrange for reinforcement. Rather, you only need to monitor the amount of time a student spends performing the target response (baseline), then, using that information to establish the interval length, set a timer for the approximate number of minutes, and reinforce the first response to occur after the timer sounds. Several other steps will prove useful. First, the guidelines for switching from CRF to any intermittent schedule should be remembered. Second, use the baseline data to establish an interval length that will suit the student's particular needs. If the response is of a type that should be performed at a relatively faster rate (keeping in mind that it will probably be a slower rate than would be produced by a ratio schedule), then start with a shorter interval. On the other hand, if low to moderate rates of responding are acceptable for the particular response, you may choose a longer interval. As an example, a student will perform at a higher rate under an FI5 schedule (reinforcement available after 5 minutes) than he or she would under an FI20 schedule (reinforcement available after 20 minutes). Third, regardless of whether you have begun with a shorter or longer initial interval, maintain the response rate by gradually and progressively increasing the length of the interval. As with ratio schedules, if the behavior starts to deteriorate, return to a previously appropriate interval length and continue the process in a more gradual manner.

Let us return to Ms. Pope's elementary cross-categorical class. She has become convinced of the power of reinforcement schedules and has observed another opportunity to increase a student's performance using an appropriate schedule. She has assigned a project to several of her students that require them to write a report. The report is due in two weeks, but Ms. Pope has noticed that very little has been accomplished after three days, despite allocating 30 minutes each day for the students to work in class on their reports. She has defined working on the project as reading related material, writing, or talking to other group members about the project. She has observed very little reading or writing and a disproportionately large amount of talking (none of which has been about the project unless she prompts with the words "project talk"). Since Ms. Pope is not interested in particularly high rates of responding, she decides to implement an intervention that makes use of an FI schedule.

Ms. Pope explains the intervention to the students so they understand that if they are "working" when the timer rings (every 5 minutes) they will earn an extra minute of free time. She noticed improvements immediately. Virtually every student in the group earned extra free time because they were working when the timer rang or emitted the target behavior within a minute or two after the timer rang. She may have considered the intervention a complete success except that she also noticed an unexpected, but consistent, response pattern by her students. They stopped working for a brief period of time (usually 2 or 3 minutes) after they received the reinforcer, and then as the end of the interval drew near they began to work much more diligently. In addition, she observed that even if a student was not working when the timer rang, she would still have to deliver the reinforcer whenever the student did begin to work—even if it took several minutes for this to occur. Was this a curious phenomenon, or should Ms. Pope have expected this response pattern?

Variable Interval Schedules

As discussed at the beginning of the section on interval schedules, a reinforcer is being delivered on a variable interval (VI) schedule when it is earned for the first target response after an interval of time which varies in length. VI schedules are generally more natural than FI schedules and some authors have even described the VI schedule as being the most desirable of all reinforcement schedules in classroom settings (Foxx, 1982).

While any interval schedule will probably produce slower rates of responding than ratio schedules, the VI schedule produces relatively higher rates of responding than the FI schedule. This is a similarity that VI schedules share with VR schedules. Another similarity between responses reinforced under VI and VR schedules is the consistency of performance maintained by those schedules. When the interval is fixed, the student will determine the approximate interval length and schedule his responses to match the interval length. However, when the interval varies, the student can never be sure when reinforcement will become available. Therefore, responding becomes more frequent and more consistent with the increased probability that reinforcement will follow responding at the end of one of these variable intervals. Therefore, we may conclude that a VI schedule will produce relatively rapid *and* consistent responses.

VI schedules are related to very durable responses. Under extinction conditions, that is when reinforcement is no longer available, the student may be expected to continue to respond in a consistent and regular manner. As with any schedule of reinforcement, the durability of a response maintained by a VI schedule will increase depending on the length of the interval; that is, a behavior maintained under a VI20 schedule will be more durable than one maintained by a VI5 schedule. In addition, the unpredictable nature of the VI schedule probably contributes to increased durability.

Implementing a VI schedule involves essentially the same steps as does an FI schedule. The major consideration involves the same type of preplanning required when implementing the VR schedule: you must choose an average interval length *and* the specific interval lengths you will use. For example, you may decide, using baseline data, to use a VI10—reinforcement available for the first response following intervals that *average* 10 minutes. Next, you calculate which specific interval length will be used that session, for example, reinforcers may be delivered after 6 minutes, 14 minutes, 4 minutes, 8 minutes, 16 minutes, and 12 minutes. Notice that the total number of minutes is 60. Sixty divided by the number of intervals averages out to intervals 10 minutes long. (6 + 14 + 4 + 8 + 16 + 12 = 60; 60 ÷ 6 = 10.) While this extra step may seem burdensome, the VI schedule is actually much easier to implement than the VR schedule and the extra step becomes rather automatic after only a few experiences. Finally, the gradual and progressive lengthening (thinning) of the schedule are key steps along the road to successful implementation and the eventual withdrawal of the program so that the behavior is maintained by natural consequences.

Meanwhile, back in the classroom, Ms. Pope has discovered that a VI schedule will provide many of the same benefits that the FI schedule provided. Furthermore, it is easier to use and avoids many of the disadvantages of the FI schedule. After switching to a VI5 from an FI5, Mrs. Pope observed that not only were her students producing more work

on their project, but they were working more consistently during each interval. When the timer rang, the students received their checkmarks indicating extra free time and almost immediately resumed work on their projects. There was no pause or "rest period" after each interval. Ms. Pope had purposely planned this by arranging several short intervals early in the first day of the new intervention. [For example, reinforcement was available after 1 minute, 3 minutes, 8 minutes, 1 minute, 8 minutes, and 9 minutes. These six intervals totaled 30 minutes, for an average interval of 5 minutes (VI5)]. However, the students were still not working as quickly as she would have liked because they occasionally took their time emitting the target behavior after the timer rang.

Advantages of Interval Schedules

There are several advantages to using interval schedules, whether fixed or variable.

1. They are easy to implement.
2. They are inexpensive because only a few responses are reinforced.
3. They are especially useful if the target behavior's beginning and ending points are difficult to observe while teaching.
4. They reflect more accurately natural sources of reinforcement.
5. They generate durable behaviors that will persist even though the schedule has been terminated (especially VI schedules).

In addition, more consistent and relatively faster responding are related to the VI schedule rather than the FI schedule.

Limited Hold Schedules

Interval schedules, especially VI schedules, produce consistent response patterns and are exceptionally easy to use. However, they produce rates of responding that may be less than those generated by ratio schedules. How can a teacher gain both the ease of implementation and consistency of responding of a VI schedule and the speed of responding of a ratio schedule? One way to increase response rate when using an interval schedule is to impose an additional requirement on the performance; that is the reinforceable target response (the first one to occur after the interval elapses) must occur within a specified time period. This added requirement, the *limited hold,* ensures that the student will have to work more rapidly (emit the target response more often) in order not to lose the opportunity to receive the reinforcer.

For example, under a typical interval schedule, the following sequence of events occurs: the interval ends, the student responds, then reinforcement is delivered, and a new interval begins. However, there is nothing that specifies when or *how soon* the response must occur. In an extreme case, the interval may end and the student may delay emitting the target behavior for 5 minutes or more. Consequently, the schedule is interrupted because no reinforcers are being earned and a new interval cannot begin until the reinforcer is delivered.

A limited hold imposes a time period that immediately follows the end of an interval. Reinforcement can be earned by responding during and only during that limited hold interval. When the limited hold interval elapses, a new FI or VI interval begins. Therefore, under a limited hold, the following sequence of events occurs: the interval ends, the student *responds* within a specified period of time, reinforcement is *delivered,* and a new interval begins. Or the following sequence may occur: the interval ends, the student *does not* respond within a specified period of time, reinforcement is *withheld,* and a new interval begins. Therefore, by restricting the amount of time during which reinforcement is available, the student must respond during that time or lose that particular opportunity to earn the reinforcer.

Returning to Ms. Pope's classroom one more time, we find that she has eliminated the last of her problems with her students' performance on the project and her use of interval schedules. She imposed a 30 second limited hold. Her students now must demonstrate that they are "working" within 30 seconds of the end of any VI interval in order to receive the extra free time available for that interval. After which Ms. Pope calmly announces that a new interval is beginning, "I'm setting the timer again," and the students have learned that this is the signal that means the extra free time is no longer available.

SUMMARY

Two major classes of reinforcement were discussed: continuous and intermittent. Continuous reinforcement (CRF) is most useful during the early stages of a reinforcement intervention, especially if the target behavior is not part of the student's repertoire (when the teacher wishes to create a new behavior) or when the behavior is occurring so infrequently as to be nonfunctional (when the teacher wishes to strengthen a weak behavior). The disadvantages of continuous reinforcement are the following: (1) The behaviors produced are not very durable. (2) Satiation can occur. (3) CRF is not very realistic. (4) It is expensive, because reinforcers are delivered very frequently. (5) Generalization is not likely to occur because very few new settings will provide continuous reinforcement.

Intermittent schedules allow the teacher to overcome the disadvantages of CRF by delivering reinforcement for some, but not all responses. There are two types of intermittent reinforcement: ratio and interval. Ratio schedules are said to be response dependent because reinforcement is delivered after the student has emitted a prespecified number of responses. There are two types of ratio schedules: (a) fixed ratio (FR), in which the number of responses required to earn reinforcement is fixed and does not vary; and (b) variable ratio (VR), in which an average number of responses required to earn reinforcement is established, but the actual number for any particular reinforcer will vary.

Differential reinforcement of high rates of responding (DRH) is a procedure that enhances the effects of ratio schedules. Reinforcement is delivered contingent upon increased speed. Therefore, although a response may be accurate, it will not earn reinforcement unless it occurs at or above a predetermined speed.

Interval schedules are said to be time dependent because reinforcement is delivered contingently upon the emission of the target behavior at or during a specified amount of time. There are two types of interval schedules: (a) fixed interval (FI), in which the interval length (or amount of time) is fixed and does not vary, and (b) variable interval (VI), in which the interval length is based upon an average amount of time, but the actual interval length for any particular reinforcer will vary.

Limited hold is a procedure that may increase the response rate produced by interval schedules. Reinforcement is delivered contingent upon the occurrence of the target behavior within a predetermined period of time following the end of the scheduled interval. The response may be accurate, but unless it occurs within the limited hold interval, it will not earn reinforcement.

Intermittent schedules are: (1) easy to use, (2) inexpensive, (3) more natural, and (4) generate more durable behaviors. Ratio schedules are especially useful when the target behavior yields a permanent product. Variable ratio schedules produce more consistent levels of response that do fixed ratio schedules. Interval schedules are especially useful when the target behavior's beginning and ending points are difficult to observe accurately or if the teacher is engaged in other teaching procedures at the same time. Variable interval schedules are related to faster and more consistent performance levels than are fixed interval schedules.

REFERENCES

Foxx, R. M. (1982). *Increasing behaviors of severely retarded and autistic persons.* Champaign, IL: Research Press.

Koenig, C. H., & Kunzelman, H. P. (1980). *Classroom learning screening: Handbook.* Columbus, OH: Charles E. Merrill.

Reynolds, G. S. (1968). *A primer of operant conditioning.* Glenview, IL: Scott, Foresman.

Rose, T. L, & Gottlieb, J. (1981). "Transfer of training: An overlooked component of mainstreaming programs." *Exceptional Children, 48,* 175–177.

Rose, T. L., Lessen, E. I., & Gottlieb, J. (1982). "A discussion of transfer of training in mainstreaming programs." *Journal of Learning Disabilities, 15,* 162–165.

Skinner, B. F. (1953). *Science and human behavior.* New York: Macmillan.

chapter 12

Stimulus Control

Lamar, a 20-year-old man who was moderately retarded, was almost ready to be placed in a job in the community by Mr. Heller, his special education teacher and job coach. Lamar was able to perform work-related skills with very little difficulty, but he was having difficulty with certain "access" skills, such as appropriate behaviors during break time at his new job site. For example, he could perform many of the responses necessary to operate the soda machine, such as counting the correct amount of change, putting the money in the correct slot, and pushing the correct button for the type of drink he wanted, but Lamar displayed little ability in knowing when his drink selection was empty. He became flustered whenever his money was returned rather than receiving a can of soda. Because these behaviors drew unfavorable attention to Lamar and had a negative effect on his relationships with his co-workers, Mr. Heller began to teach Lamar how to distinguish when a particular type of soda was available and when it was empty. A red light shown above the selection button when that selection was empty. Mr. Heller told Lamar to look for the red light, "When the red light is on, the machine is empty of that flavor soda. You have to choose another flavor, Lamar." Then Mr. Heller directed Lamar to put his coins in the machine and choose a flavor whose red light was illuminated. As expected, no drink was forthcoming and Lamar's change was returned. Lamar tried it again and once again, he received no drink. Next Lamar selected a flavor whose red light was not illuminated, and he received his can of soda. After a few more trials, Lamar learned that an unlit red light "set the stage" for receiving reinforcement for his other responses (putting money in the machine and pressing the correct selection button). He also learned that no reinforcer (the can of soda) would be received if the same behaviors occurred in the presence of the red light. Lamar's "soda selection" behavior had come under the stimulus control of the red light.

The previous three chapters discussed the nature, arrangement, and effective uses of reinforcement to promote behavior change. If we reflect upon the previous discussion of the three-term contingency (of the "ABC's" of behavior), you will remember that reinforcers are part of the consequences of behavior, specifically those consequences that increase response levels. Consequences are the "C" in the ABC's of behavior. (Other "C's" that reduce behavioral levels are discussed in subsequent chapters) You will also remember that the "B" in the ABC's represents a behavior that we have targeted for observation and, perhaps, modification. However, behaviors do not occur and are not reinforced in an environmental vacuum; antecedent stimuli precede behaviors and often "set the stage" for the occurrence of particular behaviors. Antecedent stimuli, the "A" in the ABC's of behavior, are those stimuli that a student responds to; if the response is correct or appropriate, then the consequences of that response should be reinforced. In this fashion, the student learns which behavior is appropriate when a particular stimulus is present. When there is a high probability that the response will occur in the presence of the particular stimulus, we say that *stimulus control* exists. For example, we often teach students to respond in certain ways to certain stimuli that our society has adopted, such as written symbols. If we write the numeral "3" on the chalkboard and ask our students to name that numeral, we expect them to respond by saying "three." When this occurs reliably, we can conclude that stimulus control has been achieved. Or, when a male student reads "MEN" over a doorway and he walks into that bathroom rather than the one labeled "WOMEN," we can conclude again that the particular behavior is "under the control" of that particular antecedent stimulus.

Stimulus control can be used in many ways by special education teachers, such as teaching new behaviors or teaching behaviors that are appropriate only when they occur in the presence of certain antecedent stimuli. The remainder of this chapter discusses several important aspects of stimulus control, including the assessing stimulus control and the procedures for developing and applying stimulus control in your classroom.

ASPECTS OF STIMULUS CONTROL

Antecedent Stimuli

Virtually any environmental stimulus may become an antecedent stimulus for a particular behavior. In that respect, antecedent stimuli are similar to reinforcing stimuli because people must *learn* to respond to most antecedent stimuli. For example, a common experience for visitors to a residential facility is to have at least one of the clients "cling" to their legs or other parts of their bodies. The clients have learned that clinging (response) to a visitor (antecedent stimuli) oftentimes results in their receiving any of several types of reinforcers (for example, candy, gum, hugs, or conversation). Consider your own behavior as you enter a college classroom. You have learned to sit in desks facing the front of the room or a lectern. (Many of you have also learned to sit as far away from those stimuli as possible.) Each person who enters the room and sits in the "student section" receives your attention, but the individual who enters the room and takes his or her position at the front of the classroom is identified immediately as the instructor for the course. During the time the instructor is arranging his or her materials, you are doing the same—opening your notebook and finding a pen or pencil. When the instructor begins speaking, you prepare to or begin to write. What were the antecedent stimuli to which you responded? (Hint: consider the physical arrangement of the environment, the location of individuals, and the behavior of other individuals.) How did you know to respond to these stimuli? You knew how to respond because you have learned through previous experience (learning trials) that certain college-classroom behaviors are reinforced and others are not.

Although the previous examples demonstrate the similarity between antecedent and consequent stimuli, in that they both must be learned, the examples also serve to demonstrate an important difference between stimulus control and reinforcement. Reinforcers are delivered following a response and increase the probability of that response occurring in the future. Stimulus control, on the other hand, is developed when certain consequences have followed a response in the presence of particular antecedent stimuli. When that response occurs predictably in the presence of the particular stimulus, then stimulus control has been attained (Rilling, 1977). In other words, an antecedent stimulus is presented, a individual responds in a certain way in its presence, and then the response is reinforced (although it may also be punished). The antecedent stimulus does not "cause" a certain behavior to occur, rather it sets the occasion for the behavior to occur. The presence of an antecedent stimulus may inform the student that a particular response to that stimulus will result in reinforcement, whereas other responses to the same stimulus may result in punishment and other responses may have no effect on the environment. If we return to the "clinging" clients discussed previously, we can see that several of them have learned that clinging to a stranger often leads to reinforcers. This, in turn, strengthens that response in the presence of other visitors. They may also have learned that masturbating in the presence of visitors will lead to some form of punishment or restriction, and, therefore, they are not likely to engage in that behavior in the presence of that particular antecedent stimulus.

STIMULUS GENERALIZATION

Two behavioral processes are critical to your using antecedent stimuli to change your students' behavior effectively: generalization and discrimination. *Stimulus generalization* occurs when a student responds in the same way to a new stimulus that has some of the same characteristics of the previously learned stimulus. Many social and academic behaviors become more adaptable when the student learns to respond in the same way to similar antecedent stimuli. For example, we may teach a learner to respond to the written stimulus "B" by saying "buh." Later, we would also like the individual to say "buh" when we write "B," but we teach the individual to respond to a slightly different stimulus when we begin teaching cursive handwriting and the writing of the letter "B." When a hyperactive child is taught to stay in her seat in her resource room, we want her to stay in her seat in her regular class, too. We can agree that stimulus generalization may be a crucial aspect of educational planning. Stimulus generalization will be discussed in more detail in subsequent sections of this chapter when we examine procedures for developing and applying stimulus control.

STIMULUS DISCRIMINATION

While teaching stimulus generalization may frequently be a worthy educational goal, we must first teach handicapped students to discriminate among stimuli. *Discrimination* occurs when a given antecedent stimulus prompts, or sets the occasion for, a particular response, while other antecedent stimuli prompt other behaviors. The particular antecedent stimulus that prompts a particular behavior is called a *discriminative stimulus* (abbreviated s^D). As we discussed previously, stimulus control is established by reinforcing particular responses that occur in the presence of particular stimuli. Discriminative stimuli set the occasion for responses that will be reinforced, whereas the same response in the presence of another set of stimuli, *S-deltas* (abbreviated $S^\triangle$), will not be reinforced. For example, when teaching a student to say "buh" following a presentation of the printed stimulus "B," we may present the following:

ANTECEDENT STIMULUS	REPONSE	CONSEQUENCE
"B" (S^D)	"buh"	"Good job"
"C" ($S^\triangle$)	"buh"	"No"

Going in Catania here.

Teaching of this type is called discrimination training. After a period of time, the response will occur reliably in the presence of the S^D and rarely, if ever, in the presence of $S^\triangle$. the S^D is then said to occasion the response and stimulus control is established. Discrimination training will be discussed in much more detail later in this chapter.

When stimulus control is well developed, the casual observer may conclude that the S^D is causing the behavior, leading to the use of such descriptions as "perceiving" or "being aware of" a difference. These are inaccurate and incomplete descriptions of a relationship between a stimulus and an individual's history of reinforcement in the presence of that stimulus. Antecedent stimuli do not "cause" anything , but they do increase the likelihood that a particular behavior will occur because it has been reinforced in the past when it occurred in the presence of the same stimuli.

Sometimes stimulus control is not complete because it was developed with imprecise reinforcement. Using the phonics training example above, the student may have responded to the letter "B" by saying "aaa," even after a good deal of training. If complete stimulus control describes a situation in which virtually every presentation of the S^D occasions the appropriate response, then saying "aaa" in the presence of "B" would appear to be incomplete stimulus control. However, this response might also indicate that the student has not learned to make the appropriate response (saying "buh") regardless of the antecedent stimulus. In either case, the prudent teacher should investigate the situation to determine whether stimulus control is indeed incomplete or if some other problem will explain the student's behavior.

ASSESSING FOR STIMULUS CONTROL

Most classroom behaviors, whether academic or social, occur in the presence of antecedent stimuli that teachers hope are either S^D's or $S^\triangle$'s. However, virtually every student enrolled in special education classes has some problems demonstrating appropriate academic and social responses to a wide range of antecedent stimuli. For example, Mark (who yells as loud and plays as roughly in the classroom as he does on the playground) or Wanda (who cannot compute simple addition facts even after repeated and intensive instruction) may both be demonstrating that the antecedent stimuli we expect to influence their behaviors have not become S^D's and that stimulus control has not been achieved. But, these behaviors may also be evidence of some other "causes." Since antecedent stimuli play such an important part in our lives, there may be some temptation to assume that whenever any behavior does not occur reliably, the problem can be attributed to a lack of stimulus control. If this conclusion is not accurate in every case, and it most assuredly is not, then how can we determine whether the current situation is related to a lack of stimulus control or to some other programmatic difficulty? Is the behavior not occurring because stimulus control has not been achieved or because the student cannot perform the expected response? Answering these questions are crucial for effective instructional programming. Two assessment procedures have proven helpful to special education teachers as they try to answer these questions.

VARY THE STIMULUS MODALITY

Antecedent stimuli are presented through the sensory modalities (taste, smell, touch, sight, and hearing) and the student's response to those stimuli will also rely on sensory modalities. This sensory input-output arrangement is very important for instructional and assessment purposes. For example, written material is presented to the student visually. His response to that material may be oral (reading aloud) or kinesthetic (writing, pointing, and performing). These "see-say" or "see-do" relationships explicitly describe differing responses to the same stimuli and also imply those types of behaviors that will be judged correct or incorrect. The relationship between most antecedent stimuli and expected responses can be characterized in this way. Several examples are given in the following:

ANTECEDENT STIMULI	EXPECTED RESPONSE	RELATIONSHIP
Printed words (see)	Sue reads aloud (say)	See-Say
Printed words (see)	Sue writes answers (write)	See-Write
Printed words (see)	Sue follows directions (do)	See-Do
Spoken words (hear)	John spells words aloud (say)	Hear-Say
Spoken words (hear)	John takes spelling test (write)	Hear-Write
Spoken words (hear)	John points to incorrectly spelled words (do)	Hear-Do

If a student cannot respond appropriately to an antecedent stimulus of a particular modality, then several investigative options become available to the teacher. First, informal tests or probes should be employed to determine if the student is having consistent difficulty with a particular sensory input-output relationship. For example, if an active response (do) to a verbal stimulus (hear) is expected, then various "tests" of this type should be given. Therefore, observing the student's responses following "Hang up your coat," "Turn to page 41," or "Color the triangle orange" may provide information regarding the specific sensory relationship. Next, vary the sensory modality through which the antecedent stimulus is presented. For example, change the above verbal stimuli to written stimuli (see) and observe the student's responses to similar stimuli, such as writing on the chalkboard or verbalizing "Hang up your coat," "Turn to page 52," or "Color the squares red." By systematically varying the sensory input modalities, you can determine whether the behavior is performed in the presence of only certain types of stimuli (which may indicate a stimulus control problem) or if the student cannot perform the behavior (which may indicate a problem not involving stimulus control). You should note that although this assessment procedure was illustrated with rather broadly defined S^D's, the process works equally well with specific S^D's.

For example, Wanda cannot compute basic addition facts with any degree of accuracy. In fact, her answers seem to be random, such that her incorrect response to five plus three might be fifty-three. ("5 + 3 = 53.") Two diagnostic and instructional possibilities are available to explain her performance: Either she does not know her basic addition facts, or certain antecedent stimuli are not occasioning the desired response. Let's investigate the latter possibility first. Four written stimuli are present in this problem. Two are numerals, but we know from previous work that Wanda recognizes these numerals. The remaining potential S^D's are the plus sign ($+$) and the equal sign ($=$). Since Wanda is writing her answer in the correct location (immediately following the " $=$ "), we may eliminate the possibility that the equal sign is the problem. In order to investigate the degree of stimulus control exerted by the visual symbol " $+$ "— as opposed to the operation "plus," we present several basic addition problems verbally to Wanda. If she correctly answers these "hear-write" problems (for example, "What is six plus two?" or "What does six plus two equal?"), then we may conclude that the " + " symbol has not become a discriminative stimulus for addition.

When assessing for stimulus control, remember that stimulus control is not an "all or nothing" situation. There are degrees of stimulus control that may be reflected in inconsistent performance. Therefore, even if you modify the sensory modalities and begin to conclude that you have identified the problem, conduct other informal assessments designed to investigate the degree of stimulus control. Use other instructions, prompts, or demonstrations before concluding that stimulus control is absent, rather than incomplete or poorly developed. For example, when Wanda answers a basic addition problem incorrectly, you may point to the " + " and remind her of its meaning. If she responds correctly following those prompts, then you can realize that your task is to teach her to respond to the appropriate antecedent stimulus, rather than teaching Wanda the basic addition facts.

INVESTIGATE ALTERNATIVE EXPLANATIONS

When a behavior does not occur reliably in the presence of certain antecedent stimuli, the problem may not always be a lack of stimulus control. Several other alternative explanations may be plausible and these should be investigated. One such explanation may be that the response is under the control of an appropriate S^D, but it may be also under the control of other S^D's that may be interfering in a particular situation. For example, illustrations are found in virtually all basal, remedial, and high-interest, low-vocabulary texts. Further, reading methods textbooks often recommend using illustrated word cards to teach sight words or for other word recognition activities. The appropriate S^D's for reading are the printed words; illustrations are ancillary stimuli that should be used to enhance the printed word, but not in place of the printed word. Unfortunately, evidence is beginning to

accumulate that a number of learning disabled students have difficulty responding to the appropriate S^D (that is, the printed word) when less demanding stimuli, such as illustrations, are present (Rose 1986; Rose & Furr, 1984: Rose & Robinson, 1984). Rose and Furr (1984) found that LD students learned new words better when the word alone was presented than when the word and a black-ink illustration were presented together. An equal number of unknown words were taught using word cards with illustrations and without illustrations. As may be seen in Figure 12.1, when students read the words arranged randomly on word lists that were not illustrated, the words that had been presented without competing S^D's (illustrations) were those the students read most rapidly and correctly.

A rich variety of competing S^D's are present in any classroom setting. The importance of identifying these competing antecedent stimuli cannot be overestimated. The competing S^D's may be people, objects, or activities. In many cases, providing a period of time for the student to adapt to the new program or stimulus is the easiest remedy. In other instances, you must actively determine which antecedent stimuli may be the competing S^D's. Careful observation of the student's performance, paying particular attention to any antecedents that the student attends to should yield valuable information.

A second alternative explanation for an apparent lack of stimulus control has to do with the reinforcing properties of the available consequences in a given setting. In other words, the behavior may be under stimulus control at other times and in different places, but because the currently available consequences are not reinforcing, the antecedent stimuli do not act as S^D's. For example, Charles may have learned that when the teacher points to a word on the chalkboard and looks at him, he is to say the word. His teacher then usually told him what a big boy he was whenever he learned new words. But, in his new class, when the teacher points to the word and he reads it, she either corrects his pronunciation or moves immediately to

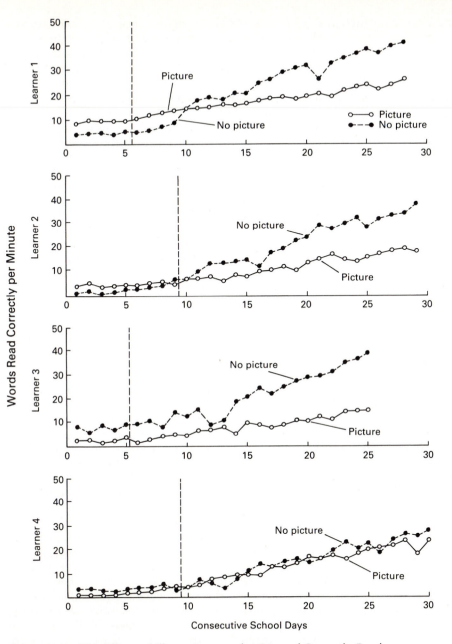

Figure 12.1   The Effects of Illustrations on the Rates of Correctly Read
Words in Isolation.
Source: From Rose & Furr, 1984, pp. 334–337. Reprinted by permission.

another student. In a situation such as this, if the behavior is not reinforced, the S^D will not exert as much influence as previously and the behavior may decrease.

A related situation occurs when the most powerful reinforcers are available but the student does not respond to the S^D. Using the same example, when the new teacher points to the word on the chalkboard, Charles misreads it (even though he knew it), and the other students laugh and disrupt the lesson. Given your knowledge of reinforcement, what do you think Charles is likely to do the next time this instructional activity takes place?

If you have established that the response is part of the student's repertoire, then a third explanation for an apparent lack of stimulus control may have to do with the student's reinforcement (or learning) history. Suppose, for example, that Lydell's previous teacher had yelled at him for going into the wrong restroom at a restaurant. Now even though he has begun to learn to read the words "MEN" and "WOMEN," he may be very hesitant about walking into a room with the stimulus "MEN" above the door without his teacher showing him the correct doorway because of the effective punishment he received earlier in his training program. Situations such as these can be remedied by remembering the principles of effective reinforcement; in this case, gentle guidance into the restroom and abundant praise should overcome Lydell's previous negative experience after a few trials.

Finally, an apparent problem with stimulus control may be explained medically. Various physiological impairments, whether long-term problems, such as visual or motor impairments, or short-term problems, such as a prostrate infection that hinders bladder control, may prevent an individual from responding appropriately to various antecedent stimuli. Special instructional procedures have been developed for those with sensory or motoric handicaps (for example, using a Kurziwell reader instead of printed text for a visually impaired student). Teachers using these adapted instructional procedures will have to train different S^D's, but the procedure will be similar. Individuals who do not appear to have any sensory or motoric impairments, yet continue to display behaviors that are difficult to diagnose behaviorally should probably be examined by a physician.

Once these stimulus control assessment procedures have been employed, you will face an instructional decision. If none of the assessment procedures discussed above have been successful in prompting the target behavior, then you will probably have to respond to that behavior as a new one that must be taught. Effective reinforcement practices and, perhaps, discrimination training (to be discussed later in this chapter) should be implemented. If, on the other hand, the behavior does occur under any of these assessment conditions, but continues to occur inconsistently, then the problem is probably one of stimulus control. Appropriate stimulus control will have to be developed.

DEVELOPING STIMULUS CONTROL

Many times, the stimuli we wish to teach students to respond to are very easily distinguished. Several academic examples have been used previously in this chapter, such as responding appropriately to "3" or " + " or "B." Frequently, nonacademic stimuli are also clear and easy to discriminate. For example, when the telephone rings, Marsha will be reinforced for lifting the receiver and saying "Hello" by someone speaking to her. On the other hand, if Marsha opens the front door when the phone rings she is not likely to find anyone there. However, most academic and nonacademic stimuli are much more subtle than these examples. These subtle stimuli are often the ones that we respond to most often, and they may, in fact, contribute to the presence of behaviors we consider inappropriate. Consider the number of ways we can smile and the different meanings each type of smile conveys. We can express genuine humor or affection, and we can also express sarcasm with different types of smiles. The child who responds to a genuine smile as if it were sarcastic is likely to be viewed as a "grump." There is some indication that the set of problems known as *social perception* disabilities, which can afflict learning disabled individuals, may be conceptualized better as a problem in stimulus control rather than as a result of any internal, psychological difficulties (Rose, 1987).

There are an almost infinite number of stimuli to which we respond. How can we teach a learner to respond to every variation? We can't. However, we can teach individuals to pay attention to several factors that will allow them to respond appropriately to stimuli. Teachers are required to clearly identify the critical properties of the stimulus, focus the learner's attention on the relevant factors and stimuli, and use effective reinforcement procedures when the desired response is emitted in the presence of the stimulus. The remainder of this section provides a discussion of how to clearly identify the critical properties of stimuli and how to focus the learner's attention on the relevant stimuli. Using reinforcement effectively when developing stimulus control most often requires the use of differential reinforcement, which will be discussed in detail later in this chapter.

ATTENTION TO STIMULUS ASPECTS

When developing stimulus control, it is important to identify stimuli that are very distinctive or have properties that can be emphasized during training so the properties become distinctive. The teenager driving a car learns that a red traffic signal at an intersection means to begin a series of responses, lifting the right foot off the accelerator, placing the right foot on the brake pedal, and so on. Performing this series of responses in the presence of a green traffic signal is not going to receive reinforcement from either the driver education teacher or the drivers behind the student driver. When these behav-

iors occur reliably, the red light has become an S^D for stopping and the green light an $S^\triangle$. The shape of the traffic signal and its position are irrelevant stimulus characteristics. The kindergarten child learning to tie his shoes also learns that the shape of the shoe and the location of the arch support are critical characteristics that indicate which foot that shoe fits. Wearing his shoes on the wrong feet is not reinforced, either socially or naturally (because they feel uncomfortable). The color of his shoes is not an important stimulus characteristic and should become an $S^\triangle$ for putting the right shoe on the right foot. In both cases, the student's attention had to be drawn to the stimulus characteristics that were relevant for the specific behavior. Several strategies have been proven effective for achieving this training objective.

Identify Relevant Stimulus Properties.

Because delivering reinforcement depends on the proper response in the presence of a certain stimulus or stimulus conditions, it is extremely important that you are aware of the specific properties of these stimuli. Stimuli may vary from one another along several topographical dimensions; that is, they vary in location, position, size, color, sensory modality, and so forth. If, for example, Tanya is learning the concept of "red," various red-colored items may be presented along with items of several other colors. Since the discriminative stimulus (S^D) is the color red, these items may vary by size (both large and small red items), shape (red circles and squares), and texture (fuzzy and smooth red items). Tanya should select the red items only in order to receive reinforcement. The size, shape, or texture are not relevant stimulus properties. While this example is rather obvious, it illustrates a critical question you must answer as you begin stimulus control training: What properties or characteristics of a given stimulus will be found in all instances of the stimulus? Consider the following example. Reversals are a problem for a number of learning disabled students. One such student frequently confuses the letters "b" and "d." You've decided to teach her to discriminate between a "b" and a "d." What are the relevant stimulus characteristics of these letters?

Many times a student will need to learn complex skills or behaviors, for example, problem solving skills, certain motor skills, or creative responses. Although the differential reinforcement procedures are the same for simple or complex skills, it may become increasingly difficult to identify the stimulus properties that set the occasion for responding. While special education teachers are expected to know many things, no one is expected to become expert in everything. Do not hesitate to consult a subject-matter specialist when planning to teach complex behaviors.

Specify Instructions

Instructions or directions to the student should be related specifically to the relevant stimuli and should specify the discrimination to be made (Gersten, Carnine, & White, 1984). Many teachers will attempt to help a student by providing detailed and superfluous instructions to the student. For example, when teaching a learner to recognize a dime (as opposed to, say, a nickel), a teacher may discuss the value of the dime, what it will buy, how many dimes equal one dollar, and so on. A simpler, more direct approach reduces the distractions by using specific instructions for the learner: "This is a *dime*" and "Say *dime*" and point to the dime and "Point to the dime." Keeping the instructions simple and direct increases the chances that the learner will focus on the relevant stimulus. Once he or she has learned to identify a dime and to discriminate a dime from other coins, then the student can begin to learn all the other aspects of a dime, such as its purchasing power or relative value.

Focus Learner's Attention

Once the relevant stimulus and the specific stimulus properties have been identified, we must consider one important point. Even

though the stimulus is clear to you, it may not be so obvious to the learner. If we do not ensure that the learner is attending to the appropriate stimulus, we may be actually promoting ineffective stimulus control.

The *salience* of a stimulus is a factor that should be considered regarding the learner's attention to that stimulus. Cooper, Heron, and Heward (1987) described salience as the prominence of the stimulus in the learner's environment. Essentially, the issue of stimulus salience asks how noticeable is the stimulus. Sensory capabilities may play a major role in determining the salience of any stimulus for a particular learner. For example, if the student has visual acuity problems, then visual stimuli are less likely to be salient (noticeable for the student). As mentioned in a previous section of this chapter, if you suspect a learner suffers from a sensory modality impairment, a medical examination is recommended.

In other cases, however, competing stimuli, in the absence of any modality impairment, may "overpower" the stimulus to which you are attempting to focus the learner's attention. For example, Marcie may pay attention to the new toys in the free-play area of your classroom rather than to the stimuli you are presenting. In these cases, *masking* or *overshadowing* may be affecting the salience of the instructional stimulus (Mackintosh, 1977). *Masking* refers to a situation in which stimulus control has been achieved, but another stimulus overcomes that control. Ms. Poteet noticed the effects of masking in her class of predelinquent youths, many of whom were gang members. This peer group reinforced noncompliance in almost every form, so even though Carl knew the answer to the math problem she presented, he would not respond in the presence of his peers. *Overshadowing*, on the other hand, refers to the situation in which one stimulus condition interferes with another. Marcie's attention to the new games instead of the new sight words the teacher is presenting is a good example of overshadowing. Cooper et al. (1987) have suggested three ways to overcome masking and overshadowing: (a) change the physical environment (for example, turn Marcie's chair until she cannot see the free play area), (b) highlight and intensify the presentation of the instructional stimuli (for example, increase the speed of the presentation), and (c) deliver reinforcement consistently in the presence of the instructional stimulus.

Many methods are available for your use when assisting the learner to focus on the relevant stimulus or its critical characteristics. Students may be asked to trace the outline of a particular stimulus, such as a geometric shape or a number. We may add a variety of temporary prompts that draw attention, for example, highlighting a new consonant blend in a reading list. Prompts that help the learner discriminate relevant stimulus characteristics by focusing his or her attention to its essential characteristics are called *stimulus prompts*. These stimulus prompts alter the characteristics of the S^D to highlight essential characteristics and, thereby, prompt correct responses. Stimulus prompt strategies are discussed in more detail later in this chapter when *errorless learning* is described.

Excellent examples of the potential problems that may occur when the learner's attention is not focused on the relevant stimulus are found in studies having to do with a phenomenon known as *stimulus overselectivity*. First described in 1971 by Lovaas, Schreibman, Koegel, and Rehm, stimulus overselectivity refers to an individual's paying attention to only one dimension of a complex stimulus or to incidental and irrelevant stimuli. In the first of two classic studies illustrating this phenomenon, Schreibman and Lovaas (1973) demonstrated how stimulus overselectivity in autistic children may explain their extremely deficient social behaviors. Groups of normal and autistic children were trained to point to either a "Ken" or a "Barbie" doll when told to "point to the boy doll or the girl doll." After the training, the researchers exchanged individual items of the dolls' clothes and the heads of the dolls so they could determine which stimulus component or components had triggered the chil-

drens response. The nonhandicapped children typically responded to the doll's head, but could also respond correctly when the clothing was switched. The autistic children selected on the basis of only one component or a combination of minor or unreliable stimulus components. One autistic boy, for example, used shoes as the basis for discrimination; if the doll wore boy's shoes, it was a boy.

Rincover and Koegel (1975) trained autistic children to respond to simple commands, such as touching their nose or raising their hand. After training, the students were taken out of the training room and given the previously learned command by a stranger. Very little generalization occurred. Further investigation found that several of the children were overselective and had attended to an incidental or meaningless stimulus in the training room. For example, the source of stimulus control for one child was the teacher's brief arm movement given during the command "touch your nose." The child responded appropriately in the presence of that arm movement, regardless of what was spoken, and did not respond appropriately if the arm movement did not occur. Another child was under the "control" of the presence of the table and chairs in the training room in addition to the verbal stimulus. So, when he was out of the training room, the child would touch his nose only when the table and chairs were present and the verbal command was given too. This even extended to outside the building: when the table and chairs were placed under the trees, the child would respond correctly.

While overselectivity seems to exist mainly among more severely handicapped populations (Lovaas, Koegel, & Schreibman, 1979; Smeets, Hoogeveen, Striefel, & Lancioni, 1985), there is some evidence that this selective attention to certain stimulus properties is a problem for those with more mild handicapping conditions (Bailey, 1981). For example, the student who calls every blue car a Chevrolet and every red car a Ford may be showing evidence that he or she is not responding to the relevant stimulus characteristics. In any case, the examples provided previously demonstrate the problems that may develop if we do not take care to focus the learner's attention on the relevant stimulus characteristics.

Opportunity to Respond

Greenwood and his colleagues have defined *opportunity to respond* as the interaction between instructional antecedent stimuli (instructional materials, prompts, and questions) and their success in facilitating the emission of the target response (Greenwood, Delquadri, & Hall, 1984). A significant amount of research, conducted primarily at the Juniper Gardens Children's Project in Kansas City, KS, has consistently indicated that establishing stimulus control while increasing a learner's opportunity to respond results in increased performance (Hall, Delquadri, Greenwood, & Thurston, 1982). The opportunity to respond studies have found that several instructional practices are most effective. First, the teacher should arrange antecedent stimuli so that each student has an opportunity to make a correct response. We've all seen classes where one or two students monopolize a lesson while the rest of the class have effectively become observers. Second, learning situations should be arranged so that learners will respond at high rates of correct behavior. Merely responding more often is not enough. One or more learners may be responding incorrectly. Practicing incorrect responses is probably worse than too little opportunity to respond. Third, learning situations should provide for active, rather than passive, responding. Active responses may include pointing to a shape, reading orally, or writing answers to math problems. Passive responding incudes watching another student do anything or listening to a lecture. Although these passive skills may help to ensure "school survival," they do not seem to be strongly related to increases in academic performance. Whereas most opportunity to respond research has focused on academic responses, we may be justified if we generalize the findings discussed to nonacademic behav-

iors. Opportunities to practice any given behavior certainly seem related to improved performance.

ATTENTION TO RESPONSE ASPECTS

Consider the case when you have identified the relevant antecedent stimulus, its critical properties, and an effective reinforcer. Further, you have designed a strategy to focus the learner's attention on those stimulus characteristics. But, the response fails to occur. At this point, you have two options. You can wait until the response is emitted, which might be difficult to justify educationally because it may not occur for quite awhile, or you can implement a method that is useful in "priming the pump" and getting the response to occur initially. Several procedures that have proven to be quite effective are discussed subsequently.

Prompting

Except in rare instances, such as interpersonal interactions or certain language skills, the goal of a stimulus control instructional procedure is to ensure that the response occurs only in the presence of the specific appropriate stimulus or stimuli. Stated another way, we are teaching the learner to do the right thing at the right time in the right places. In those instances when the behavior does not occur reliably under those conditions, then the critical stimulus can be supplemented *temporarily* with additional stimuli that help to set the occasion for the behavior to be emitted. These supplementary stimuli are known as *prompts*, which increase the probability that the S^D will set the occasion for the desired response (Billingsley & Romer, 1983; Snell, 1983). For example, Ms. Hutchins has a problem with Darren, a student in her developmental preschool class. Darren is supposed to wipe his feet on the doormat every time he returns from the playground. Ms. Hutchins has spent a great deal of time teaching all her students that the doormat is an S^D to wipe their feet. Everyone but Darren is very proud of their new "grown-up" behavior, which Ms. Hutchins reinforces consistently. However, the doormat holds little significance for Darren until he is in the classroom, having muddied the carpet. Ms. Hutchins would rather not keep catching Darren "being bad" and reprimanding his behavior. But Darren does not wipe his feet unless she verbally reminds him, which is not always possible when eight handicapped preschoolers are entering the classroom. Ms. Hutchins decides to use a prompt to draw Darren's attention to the doormat. She places a small rubber duck under the doormat that squeaks when squeezed or stepped on. When Darren steps on the doormat, it squeaks. He looks down at the mat, Ms. Hutchins (also alerted by the squeak) reminds Darren to wipe his feet. Two days later, Ms. Hutchins no longer has to say anything to Darren; the squeak alone prompts Darren to wipe his feet. By the middle of the next week Ms Hutchins has removed the duck and replaced it occasionally, but gradually she stops using the duck entirely. Darren had learned to attend to the doormat (the discriminative stimulus) because the duck's squeak (the prompt) has focused his attention. Eventually the prompt is gradually removed (a process called *fading*) as the S^D began to exert more influence on Darren's behavior (stimulus control).

A prompt, then, is (or can be) virtually any stimulus that increases the chance that the appropriate response will occur in the presence of the S^D. Prompts are instructional aids that increase your teaching efficiency. You can use these cues to increase the chances that the student will respond to the appropriate stimulus, rather than just waiting for the response to be emitted. Once the student begins responding, whether correctly or incorrectly, teaching may begin by reinforcing correct responses to S^D's and the responses to $S^\triangle$'s in another way. When teaching complex tasks, each step in the task can be used as a prompt for the next step (using prompts in this manner is particularly useful in chaining

and shaping procedures, which are discussed in detail in the next chapter). Prompts that help increase the chances of the behavior occurring are called *response prompts*. In other words, when using response prompts the S^D remains the same and prompts are added to occasion the appropriate behavior. Remember our discussion of stimulus prompts and compare response prompts to stimulus prompts. A variety of response prompts are used frequently in special education classrooms.

VERBAL PROMPTS. Language is a wonderful thing for any number of reasons. One reason in particular is our ability to use language as a short-cut to establishing stimulus control by using verbal prompts. Several types of verbal prompts are employed in teaching situations (Cuvo & Davis, 1980). Each of these has a wide variety of applications, including the teaching of academic, social, life, and career skills.

Instructions. Instructions are not always used as directions. Many times we use instructions as prompts to alert an individual or a class that a behavior or set of behaviors is expected, such as telling the class "Look at the clock. What do we do at 11 o'clock?" (The class goes to lunch.) This may be a prompt to put their materials away and line up at the door. We may use instructions as part of a teaching strategy. For example, when teaching regrouping in addition, we observe Randy adding the numbers in the "one's place." When it is time to carry the number to the "ten's place," we say "Remember where that '1' goes." Collozzi and Pollow (1984) used verbal instructions as prompts to teach a group of moderately to severely handicapped elementary students to walk independently to their classroom upon arrival at school. Before training, each student would wait in the lobby until all arrived and then be led to their classroom by a teacher. The students learned to walk to their class by themselves in an average of less than 7 days for each student.

When using instructions as prompts, remember that you are making some assumptions about the learner's abilities. As Alberto and Troutman (1986) have indicated, the first assumption is that the instructions are clear, concise, and accurate. As adults, it is easy for us to assume too much knowledge on the part of students and employ instructions based on this faulty assumption. Think, for a moment, about instructions you've received in the past that were confusing. A second assumption we make when using instructions is that the student is capable of following instructions. Many handicapped (and nonhandicapped) students do not attend to or follow instructions well. These assumptions must be dealt with before you can expect instructions to be effective prompts for an individual student. Practice giving short, concise, unambiguous instructions and give your students practice in following instructions. Frequently games are excellent vehicles to provide this kind of practice for you and your students.

Rules. A large amount of our behavior is governed by rules, and rules can play an important role as a prompt in a stimulus control program. Simple rules, such as "i before e, except after c" for spelling or "when two vowels go walking, the first one does the talking" for word attack skills, are very helpful. Mnemonic strategies and verbal (and subverbal) problem solving strategies make use of rules to prompt desired behaviors. More complex behaviors and conceptual behaviors, such as honesty, may be more easily taught using rules as prompts.

Added Emphasis. Sometimes providing a verbal emphasis to a particular aspect of the behavior or task may serve as a useful prompt. An example is when Ms. Williams tells Jamal, "Listen to me count. One, two, three, four, FIVE. What number did I count to, Jamal?" (Five is said the loudest.) Or when taking your class to the library, giving instructions in a quiet voice or whisper may serve as a prompt for quiet talking in the library.

PHYSICAL PROMPTS. Occasionally, a targeted behavior lends itself to a physical prompt. When Colozzi and Pollow taught

their students to walk to class independently, they supplemented their verbal prompts with brief physical prompts to keep the students moving in the desired direction (1984). A touch on the right shoulder to prompt "raise your right hand," pointing at the correct location for a response (for example, the upper right-hand corner of paper is where name is written), or lightly turning a student's head toward the appropriate stimulus may all be useful physical prompts. The instructional techniques of Direct Instruction (for example, Carnine & Silbert, 1979; Engelmann, Becker, Carnine, Meyers, Becker, & Johnson, 1975; Engelmann & Osborn, 1975) rely heavily on physical prompts. For example, the "attention signal" prompts the students to stop what they're doing, look at the teacher, and listen because it's the teacher's turn to talk. All this is accomplished by the teacher holding his hand up, with the palm facing the students (similar to the motion for "stop"). Of course, the students have to be taught to attend to this prompt, which initially requires verbal prompts and consistent reinforcement before the physical prompt is taught. Mercer and Mercer (1981) have suggested the following procedure for prompting a correctly written (nonreversed) lower-case letter "b": Have the learner raise her left arm in front of her and grasp her left elbow with her right hand; when she looks down, she will see a correctly formed "b." There may be a potential for overlapping in procedures when providing a physical prompt, modeling, and physical guidance, because each procedure makes use of a physical activity designed to occasion a desired response. However, remember the intent of the procedure: modeling and physical guidance actually demonstrate how the response should be accomplished; physical prompting only provides a cue that supplements the S^D.

VISUAL PROMPTS. Visual prompts are as useful and pervasive as verbal prompts. A large number of instructional procedures make use of one or more visual prompts. Margin notes in textbooks; colored, highlighted, or underlined words and phrases; or illustrations in basal readers—all may be useful visual prompts. Many handwriting programs make use of visual prompts, such as arrows indicating the direction of writing strokes or a green dot indicating where to begin writing a particular stroke and a red dot to indicate stopping the stroke. One of the authors of this text and his colleagues taught moderately to severely handicapped adolescents to cook independently by prompting their responses with sequentially arranged picture cues (Martin, Rusch, James, Decker, & Trtol, 1982).

Errorless Learning

Prompts may be arranged in two ways: (a) by beginning with relatively weak prompts and gradually increasing the intensity of the prompts; or (b) by beginning with prompts that are significant and gradually decreasing the intensity of the prompts until they are as weak as possible. Csapo (1981) has labeled the first technique the *increasing assistance* approach and the second technique the *decreasing assistance* approach. Our discussion of prompts to this point has emphasized the increasing assistance approach. The decreasing assistance approach is more frequently known as errorless learning.

Errorless learning is a procedure that was created to develop stimulus control by carefully arranging a sequence of discriminative stimuli so that the chances for making errors is reduced or eliminated. The S^D is altered, using stimulus prompts, in order to accentuate the differences between it and the $S^\triangle$. Discrimination training then is provided, with the stimulus prompts being gradually faded as the student responds accurately with no errors. The rationale for errorless learning rests on our knowledge that once errors (or incorrect responses) are made, they tend to be repeated (Bereiter & Engelmann, 1966), especially in situations where independent practice is planned. An example of using stimulus prompts to arrange an errorless learning program was employed by one of the authors when teaching a student to make correctly formed letters (the nonreversed letter "b"). Marion did not discriminate the lower case "b" from "d" or "p" from "q" with any degree of accuracy. The stem of the letter ("stick") was colored on Marion's worksheets and the areas where the stem connected to the circle part of each letter was darkened. Gradually these prompts were reduced (faded), by using paler shades of color and thinner lines at the intersections, until they were eliminated. Mosk and Bucher (1984) taught multiply handicapped students to hang their toothbrushes and washcloths on pegs when they were finished using them. Only one peg was provided at first. Gradually more pegs were added to the board, but initially they were too short to hang anything on, so only the original peg could be used. Eventually, the newer distractor pegs were gradually lengthened until the pegboard contained a typical arrangement of pegs; each student had learned to use only his peg by then. Altering the stimuli (stimulus prompting) proved to be more effective than prompting alone. In other words, the decreasing assistance approach was more effective than the increasing assistance approach.

There is evidence that stimulus prompting when associated with certain aspects of errorless learning is more effective (for example, Foxx & Azrin, 1973; O'Brien, Bugle, & Azrin, 1972). For example, Schreibman and Charlop (1981) found that the efficacy of errorless training is improved when only the S^D is modified, while the $S^\triangle$ is held constant. The prompting strategy of choice may depend on the student's learning stage for the particular discrimination being learned. Evidence is beginning to indicate that errorless training (decreasing assistance) strategies are more successful at the acquisition level (Csapo, 1981; Gentry, Day, & Nakao, 1979) and the increasing assistance strategies are more effective for students at the fluency or proficiency building stages (Csapo, 1981). But, some researchers have found that there may be little relationship between the prompting sequence and learning (Walls, Crist, Sienick, & Grant, 1981).

However, several authors have suggested that difficulties may arise if we rely too heavily on errorless learning strategies. Several authors have found that *time delay* (to be discussed later in this chapter) may be more effective than errorless learning procedures (Bradley-Johnson, Johnson, & Sunderman, 1983; Gentry, et al., 1979; Touchette & Howard, 1984). Others suggest that eliminating errors may eliminate opportunities for learning and establish an artificial environment because the student may not develop a frustration tolerance which makes mistakes in the real world tolerable (Terrace, 1966, Spooner & Spooner, 1984). On the other hand, intermittent reinforcement during training may help alleviate some of the problems associated with errorless learning by enhancing persistent responses (Rodewald, 1979).

Modeling

Imitative behaviors are among the earliest to be reinforced in an infant's life. Playing peek-a-boo, smiling, and making eye contact are all examples of behaviors that are reinforced heartily by parents and are, consequently, learned early in life. As children enter school, teachers demonstrate certain behavior. This procedure, *modeling,* is useful when verbal, physical, or visual prompts have proven ineffective, impractical, or inappropriate. In many cases, modeling is the best procedure for occasioning a response in the presence of a discriminative stimulus. Think for a moment about trying to teach a student to use a personal computer without being able to demonstrate any responses.

As a teacher, an important point to remember is that students quite frequently imitate the behaviors of their peers, especially as they pass into and through adolescence. The presumed power of modeling as a learning device is one of the major points proponents use to argue for mainstreaming handicapped students into settings with nonhandicapped age-appropriate peers. Theoretically, the handicapped students will imitate the behaviors of

their nonhandicapped peers, thereby enhancing their learning experience.

Most students learn a variety of behaviors by imitating models. Imitation is a critically important learning skill throughout life because learning a large number of behaviors, such as engaging in social interactions, speaking any language, or performing a variety of physical skills, requires effective imitative skills. Even though most people learn throughout life to imitate quite effectively, some individuals rarely imitate the behavior of others. Thus, before we can use modeling as a teaching procedure, we must first ensure that generalized imitative responding is within the learner's repertoire. Thus, your "premodeling" training will reinforce imitation in a variety of circumstances because learners who are reinforced for imitating others' responses will also begin to imitate unreinforced responses (e.g., Baer, Peterson, & Sherman, 1967; Charlop & Walsh, 1986). For example, when Charlop and Walsh (1986) trained autistic children to respond in an affectionate way to a hug (by saying, "I like you") using modeling and time delay, they also noted that eye contact occurred more frequently during the modeling intervention period.

Once we are sure that a student has acquired imitative responses, several other factors that can affect the chances of any modeling (or demonstration) procedure must be considered before beginning.

Similarity between Learner and Model. A model that shares something in common with the learner (for example, age, sex, interests, or experiences) is more likely to be successful than one who does not share any similarity to the learner (Bandura, 1969). Therefore, even though a teacher may serve as a model, other students are obviously much more similar to the learner. We may conclude that the peer group may provide more powerful models. However, as Sulzer-Azaroff and Mayer (1977) noted, this should not imply that individual differences should be minimized; too much similarity may hinder generalization. Further, telling the learner about the similarity between the model and himself is likely to increase the probabilities that imitation will occur for the similarities may not be readily apparent to the student at first.

Model's Prestige. Prestigious individuals within a group or class are likely to be effective models. The best athlete, the friendliest student, or the best-looking student may have a high status within the group. Nevertheless, some similarity must exist between a prestigious model and the learner in order to enhance the chances of imitation occurring.

Simple Responses. Imitative behaviors will be learned more quickly if the stimulus is relatively simple and the presentation is relatively slow. It helps if the stimulus contains some elements or components that the learner has already acquired (Bandura, 1965). Of course a model may demonstrate a complex response, but, to maximize effectiveness, complex responses are learned, and imitated more readily if they are subdivided into smaller, component responses.

Reinforce the Model's Behavior. Reinforcing the model's behavior, in addition to the learner's, will increase the imitative behavior of the learner. The use of this vicarious reinforcement factor has resulted in positive effects on imitative behavior, as shown in several studies (Gershuri, 1972; Guralnik, 1976). Available evidence indicates that reinforcing the model either in the presence of the learner or in such a way so that the learner can observe or be informed of the reinforcement increases the power of the procedure.

Competence of the Model. When the model has previously engaged in some cooperative activity with the learner, and when the learner has observed that the model is competent in the behaviors or skills being modeled, then the learner appears more likely to imitate that model. Apparently this willingness to imitate the model is increased even more if the learner has also had a history of

failure in performing the target behavior. For example, Kevin and Rich have been in the same homeroom for two years, during which Kevin has always held a part-time job after school. Rich has repeatedly tried, but failed, to get a job. Mr. Beattie, the vocational counselor, asks Kevin to "work with Rich and help him learn to complete a job application." As a result of Kevin's help, the quality of Rich's applications increased dramatically and Rich landed a job. If Rich were not interested in finding a job and had not known Kevin, then Kevin's efforts would probably have not been too successful.

Combine with Other Prompts. Combining modeling with other types of prompts, such as verbal prompts, increases the chance that imitative learning will occur. Verbal instructions and modeling are especially powerful when used together. For example, showing a student how to "boot" a program on a personal computer may be helpful, but, adding a verbal prompt makes it much easier to remember the sequence of steps. Pairing modeling with other, less intrusive prompts also will facilitate fading the modeling procedure, which will be discussed later in this chapter.

Modeling can be a very effective procedure, but it may also have some limitations. Modeling is frequently difficult to establish, especially when using peer models, because the models have to be trained and monitored closely. A less intrusive prompting procedure will probably be easier to fade. Furthermore, some behaviors are difficult to imitate. The interested reader is referred to Peck, Cooke, and Apolloni (1981) for an excellent review of the research regarding peer modeling.

Physical Guidance

When less intrusive prompting procedures have proven unsuccessful, when a student is seriously delayed, or when a response has been practiced but is still inaccurate (perhaps topographically), then using physical guidance may be appropriate. Physical guidance has been described by Snell (1983) as "putting the learner through" the response. Snell stresses how different this procedure is from doing it for the learner. For example, Striefel and Wetherby (1973) taught a profoundly retarded student to follow instructions such as "Raise your hand" by using physical guidance paired with instructions (verbal prompts). Securing the learner's cooperation is critically important in order for the physical guidance procedure to be effective. A tense, resisting student will not attend to the kinesthetic cues that are the reason for providing physical guidance in the first place. Sulzer-Azaroff and Mayer (1977) recommend relaxation training for students who have difficulty. Finally, transferring stimulus control to the appropriate or more normal S^D by fading the intrusive physical guidance procedure should be accomplished as quickly as possible.

Fading

When we rely on a prompt in order for a behavior to occur, then that behavior is not under stimulus control. Prompts must be withdrawn gradually and progressively until the response occurs in the presence of the natural S^D and in the absence of any prompt. This procedure is called *fading*. Effective fading transfers stimulus control from an "intermediate" S^D (the prompt) to the more natural or appropriate S^D. Prompts must be faded carefully. If they are removed too quickly or abruptly, the behavior may cease to be emitted. If they are faded too slowly, they may actually become S^D themselves.

We can increase our chances of effectively fading a prompt by proceeding toward less intrusive prompts. When beginning a training procedure, consider the least intrusive prompt for any given behavior and decide what type of prompt you would use next if the original one were not successful. Plan in this way for the entire procedure. When fading the prompts, this process is reversed.

Other fading specific procedures, identified by Wolery and Gast (1985), are discussed subsequently.

Graduated Guidance. A physical prompt must be faded as soon as possible. Very early in the training program, demonstrations or instructions should be paired with physical prompts, so that the physical prompts can be removed gradually while the instructions remain. While this procedure may be quite successful with most students, there remains a step in the training where all physical prompting must cease for the first time. For some students, this is too big a step. In many cases, *graduated guidance* (Foxx & Azrin, 1972) is a procedure that is effective at this step. At first, the teacher provides as much physical guidance as necessary, but the minimum amount needed to complete the motion. Guidance is focused on the body part concerned, for example, the hand, in the motion of waving. Gradually the guidance is reduced and the location of the guidance is moved farther away from the body part that is the locus of action. For example, when teaching Carla to wave, the initial physical prompt was rather intrusive and involved the teacher virtually waving Carla's hand. Gradually the pressure on Carla's hand and the vigor of the teacher's movement was reduced. Next, the teacher lightly touched Carla's forearm. Then, after a period of time, a light touch on Carla's shoulder was sufficient. Remember to fade these prompts gradually and progressively. The student's behavior will tell you if you are fading the prompts too quickly. Please note, however, the use of graduated guidance with violent or uncooperative students may be counterproductive and is generally not recommended.

Time Delay. When using the time delay procedure, the prompt remains the same, but its presentation is gradually and progressively delayed (Halle, Marshall, & Spradlin, 1979). Therefore, instead of presenting the prompt immediately, the teacher waits for a predetermined amount of time to allow the student to respond in the presence of the S^D (and in the absence of the prompt). Delays are usually short, perhaps only a few seconds, and may stay the same, that is, constant (Kleinert & Gast, 1982) or gradually lengthen (Charlop & Walsh, 1986). Time delay has been used to fade a variety of prompts, such as visual, verbal, or physical. Charlop and Walsh (1986) taught autistic children to spontaneously vocalize "I like you" or "I love you" in response to a hug. A progressive time delay, beginning with a 2 second delay, was used. The students were hugged; if they did not respond by saying "I like you" within 2 seconds, the mother modeled the verbal response and reinforced the child's imitation. The intervals were gradually lengthened by progressively adding 2 seconds to the delay interval. Billingsley and Romer (1983) reviewed and synthesized the available research on fading prompts and concluded that the time delay procedure may hold great promise. However, since most of the research they reviewed was done with severely handicapped students, we should be cautious when generalizing this conclusion in our treatment of mildly handicapped students.

Most to Least Prompts. This procedure is recommended most often for behaviors such as dressing, using motor skills, self-feeding, and vocational task assembling. It is typically used with individuals who are severely handicapped. To implement the most-to-least procedure, the teacher guides the learner physically through the entire response and then gradually reduces the amount of physical assistance provided during each successive training session. Ideally, the physical assistance is gradually removed totally until other prompts, such as visual or verbal prompts, serve the same purpose. For example, Luyben et al. (1986) taught three adults with severe retardation to use a side-of-the-foot soccer pass by successfully transferring stimulus control by using the most-to-least procedure.

Initially, the trainers demonstrated each response and then provided verbal directions and a "strong" physical prompt, in which the trainer held the learner's body and positioned it appropriately. The next training level reduced the intensity of the physical prompt so that the trainer guided the learner's body without holding. Later training levels included replacing the physical prompts with imitative prompts, which were replaced, in turn, with gestures and finally with verbal prompts. By the end of the training sessions, all prompts had been faded from the program.

Least to Most Prompts. This is probably the most recommended fading procedure and it may also be appropriate for the widest range of behaviors (Snell, 1983). Using the least-to-most procedure, the learner is allowed to emit the targeted response with the least amount of prompting. If he or she is unsuccessful with that level of prompting, then on successive trials greater levels of prompting are provided until the individual can perform the response correctly. A constant latency period, such as 5 seconds, is used between the presentation of the S^D and the opportunity to emit the response. If the response does not occur correctly during the latency period, then the next level of prompt (for example, verbal prompts) should be provided. Several guidelines to follow when using this procedure were suggested by Wolery and Gast (1985). They recommended that the trainer should (a) present the S^D at each prompt level; (b) provide a constant latency period; (c) increase the prompt level only as needed; and (d) deliver reinforcers after each correct response, even if that response was prompted.

Several advantages and disadvantages of the least-to-most procedure have been identified. Advantages include allowing the learner to respond in the presence of the natural S^D on every trial and permitting the learner's behavior to determine the level of prompting provided. Potential disadvantages may include higher error rates and slower acquisition rates. As with virtually all intervention procedures, the individual learner's performance data should guide your decision regarding the continued use of this procedure.

Using Prompts Effectively

Using prompts to facilitate the development of stimulus control demands that you observe several guidelines that have been proven to increase the effectiveness of any prompting procedure.

1. Use the weakest prompts possible, unless establishing an errorless learning program. Although there is little information available regarding a hierarchical arrangement of prompts, a good rule to follow is that the weakest, least intrusive prompts available should be used first. If these are not successful, more powerful and obvious prompts can always be tried later. Since there are no hierarchies available, think about the progression by which a particular prompt will be faded and select a prompt as close to the end of that progression as possible. If, for example, a verbal instruction, such as "look at the plus sign," works effectively as a prompt for a student when teaching simple addition, then there is no need to color the " + " sign.

2. The discriminative stimulus must always precede the prompt. Never present a prompt unless the stimulus has been presented first. For example, while teaching letter recognition, Ms. Dykes tells Andrew, "Here's that funny looking letter again" (prompt) and then shows Andrew the letter "h." Andrew doesn't have to even look at the "h," he can respond to the "funny looking letter" prompt which Ms. Dykes is inadvertently training to be the S^D. A better procedure would have Ms. Dykes showing Andrew the "h," then saying, "There's that funny looking letter again." Andrew would then have to attend to the letter and use the prompt to help remember its name.

3. Use prompts that focus the learner's attention on the S^D. Do not detract attention from the relevant stimulus. For example, illustrations are used extensively in basal readers to facilitate comprehension and word recognition. However, a number of studies have found that illustrations may actually detract from the stimuli most important to successful reading—the printed word (Rose, 1986; Rose & Furr, 1984; Rose & Robinson, 1984). In these and other studies, mildly handicapped students were found to learn new words and comprehend written passages better when illustrations were not used as prompts. This situation may be made worse when a teacher actively uses the illustrations as prompts by directing a student to study a picture in word attack or comprehension training. An excellent discussion of the misuse of prompts in educational curriculum materials was provided by Vargas (1984), in which Vargas provides some questions to ask regarding these curricular prompts.

   a. Can students use pictures or diagrams instead of text to complete an exercise?
   b. Does highlighting or physical layout give away answers, making it unnecessary to read through an assignment?
   c. Are students able to answer questions on a passage without reading it?
   d. Do all of the problems on a page require the same process for solution, making it unnecessary to discriminate between strategies?
   e. Can comprehension questions be answered using grammatical cues alone? (Vargas, 1984, p. 130)

4. Fade prompts as quickly as possible. Fading, as discussed earlier, involves the gradual withdrawal of the prompt. Remember, the goal is to create stimulus control by establishing the discriminative stimulus, not to make the prompt a discriminative stimulus. The prompt is used only to facilitate the student's learning the S^D. If a prompt continues to be used too long, the student may begin to rely too much on the prompt.

Teachers can fool themselves into thinking that their students know more than they really do; more precisely, that their stimulus control has been established when it really has not. We must take care to avoid providing prompts unnecessarily or unconsciously. For example, asking a "yes" or "no" question with a certain inflection can allow the student to answer without knowing what was asked.

If he can discriminate the question type ("yes" or "no" answer) from the inflection, then he has a "fifty-fifty" chance of answering correctly, even if he doesn't know what was asked. Be careful when providing hints; they may actually be prompts to attend to irrelevant stimuli; for example, telling a student, "You can think of that word if I tell you it's an animal that says 'bow-wow.'" Using such an obvious hint allows the student to say the correct word without reading the word, which should be the S^D.

DIFFERENTIAL REINFORCEMENT

As discussed previously, the most basic example of the development of stimulus control occurs when a selected response is emitted under specific stimulus conditions (discriminative stimuli or S^D) and when that response is reinforced. When those stimulus conditions are not present or in effect (S-delta or $S^\triangle$), the response is not reinforced (Terrace, 1966). Providing or withholding reinforcers depending upon the stimulus conditions in which the response occurs is known as *differential reinforcement*. Therefore, when a child sees the stimulus "CAT" written on a flashcard and responds by saying "cat," the child will receive praise or some other type of reinforcement. If the child responds by saying "car," he or she may be corrected or ignored, but the individual will not be reinforced. Another example involves a group of severely retarded students who consistently did not follow simple instructions such as "Sit down." Their teacher began to reinforce them with food and praise each time they followed an instruction correctly. When the instructions were not followed, the teacher provided physical guidance to complete the behavior and then delivered the reinforcers. Later, reinforcers were earned for unguided correct responses only and incorrect responses were ignored. After a while, the students learned to follow simple instructions when the instructions were given without physical guidance. Their behavior had come under the "control" of the verbal instructions (S^D) (Kazdin & Erickson, 1975). The principles of effective reinforcement discussed earlier in this text still hold, but the reinforcer is delivered only when a response occurs in the presence of certain stimuli. Differential reinforcement is the most efficient way to teach a student to discriminate correct from incorrect responses.

If you stop to think about it for a moment, you will realize that teaching students to respond appropriately to particular stimuli is a basic part of a teacher's job. Some would suggest that that may be an excellent definition of teaching. We are expected to teach students to respond to a variety of visual stimuli, such as the written symbols we use for language and mathematics, as well as to obey rules, and to behave in socially acceptable ways in a variety of settings, and so on. Each of these teaching activities are based on establishing stimulus control.

Differential reinforcement requires that we consider several factors. First, we must identify the target behavior. Second, we must identify the specific stimulus or stimuli to which we expect the student to attend. This stimulus will become the discriminative stimulus. (Refer to our previous discussion of stimulus aspects when identifying this stimulus.) Finally, we must plan a reinforcement strategy. Of course, this step requires you to identify an effective reinforcer, but you also must consider the delivery strategy. Remember, there are two operations when using differential reinforcement. The target behavior is emitted in the presence of the specified stimulus (S^D) and is reinforced. The same behavior is not reinforced when it is emitted in the absence of the S^D or in the presence of the $S^\triangle$. As the response is reinforced a number of times in this manner, the antecedent stimulus will begin to occasion the occurrence of the target behavior and stimulus control will begin to exist.

As you may have already guessed, an $S^\triangle$ for one response may become an S^D for a different response and the previous S^D may become an $S^\triangle$. For example, learning that the symbol "3" should occasion the verbal response "three," the student might also learn that "6" is an $S^\triangle$ for the same response (saying "three"). But, the symbol "6" is, or will be, an S^D for saying "six." Many skills are developed efficiently in this manner, for example, the learning of sorting or classification behaviors.

At other times, several varied stimuli may be expected to occasion the same response. For example, discriminating verbs from non-verbs requires responding to a number of words and discriminating which are verbs. Responses of this type are called *concepts*. A number of stimuli are categorized into a particular concept on the basis of some intangible property that is common to all of the antecedent stimuli in that group or concept. This common property is known as an *abstraction*. For example, when teaching the color "red," the texture, shape, size, or location of each antecedent stimulus are irrelevant. The abstraction, or common property, for the concept "red" relates to the tone or light waves of the stimuli. Training the student to discriminate is accomplished by providing many examples of "redness," that is, red-colored antecedent stimuli, and non-red stimuli. A critical feature of concept training is differential reinforcement. Concept training in this manner has been proven to be an efficient methodology for a wide variety of basic concepts (Engelmann & Carnine, 1982).

SUMMARY

The ABC's of behavior are a convenient abbreviation for the major components of applied behavior analysis. Antecedent stimuli (the "A" in the ABC's) are a component that must receive attention in classroom settings. As teachers, we have always worked with antecedent stimuli, but frequently we have dealt with antecedent stimuli with little knowledge of their power or the sophistication needed to teach stimulus discriminations to achieve stimulus control. Knowledge of stimulus control procedures allows teachers to teach most efficiently and are beginning to be viewed as critical to effective instruction in special education classes.

Stimulus control was described in Chapter 12. Several aspects of stimulus control, including antecedent stimuli, stimulus generalization, and stimulus discrimination, were defined and discussed. The procedures most useful for assessing for the presence or absence of stimulus control and several possible alternative explanations for an apparent absence of stimulus control were described. Finally, several procedures for developing stimulus control, including attending to aspects of the antecedent stimulus and aspects of the response itself were presented in detail. Differential reinforcement and discrimination training were also described.

REFERENCES

ALBERTO, P. A., & TROUTMAN, A. C. (1986). *Applied behavior analysis for teachers* (2nd ed.). Columbus, OH: Charles E. Merrill.

BAER, D. M., PETERSON, R. F., & SHERMAN, J. A. (1967). "The development of imitation by reinforcing behavioral similarity to a model." *Journal of the Experimental Analysis of Behavior, 10,* 405–417.

BAILEY, S. L. (1981). "Stimulus overselectivity in learning disabled children." *Journal of Applied Behavior Analysis, 14,* 239–248.

BANDURA, A. (1969). *Principles of behavior modification.* New York: Holt, Rinehart & Winston.

BANDURA, A. (1965). "Vicarious processes: A case of no-trial learning." In L. Berkowitz (ed.), *Advances in experimental social psychology* (vol. 2, pp. 1–55). New York: Academic Press.

BEREITER, C., & ENGELMANN, S. (1966). *Teaching disadvantaged children in the preschool.* Englewood Cliffs, NJ: Prentice-Hall, Inc.

BILLINGSLEY, F. F., & ROMER, L. T. (1983). "Response prompting and the transfer of stimulus control: Methods, research, and a conceptual framework." *Journal of the Association for the Severely Handicapped, 8,* 3–12.

BRADLEY-JOHNSON, S., JOHNSON, C., & SUNDERMAN, P. (1983). "Comparison of delayed prompting and fading for teaching preschoolers easily confused letters and numbers." *Journal of School Psychology, 21,* 327–335.

CARNINE, D., & SILBERT, J. (1979). *Direct instruction reading.* Columbus, OH: Charles E. Merrill.

CHARLOP, M. H., & WALSH, M. E. (1986). "Increasing autistic children's spontaneous verbalizations of affection: An assessment of time delay and peer modeling procedures." *Journal of Applied Behavior Analysis, 19,* 307–314.

COLOZZI, G. A., & POLLOW, R. S. (1984). "Teaching independent walking to mentally retarded children in a public school." *Education and Treatment of the Mentally Retarded, 19,* 97–101.

COOPER, J. L., HERON, T. E., & HEWARD, W. L. (1987). *Applied behavior analysis.* Columbus, OH: Charles E. Merrill.

CSAPO, M. (1981). "Comparison of two prompting procedures to increase response fluency among severely handicapped learners." *Journal of the Association for the Severely Handicapped, 6,* 39–47.

CUVO, A. J., & DAVIS, P. K. (1980). "Teaching community living skills to mentally retarded persons: An examination of discriminative stimuli." *Gedrag, 8,* 14–33.

DYER, K., CHRISTIAN, W. P., & LUCE, S. C. (1983). "The role of response delay in improving the discriminative performance of autistic children." *Journal of Applied Behavior Analysis, 15,* 231–240.

ENGLEMANN, S., BECKER, W., CARNINE, D., MEYERS, L., BECKER, J., & JOHNSON, G. (1975). "Corrective reading program: Teacher's management and skills manual." Chicago: Science Research Associates.

ENGELMANN, S., & CARNINE, D. (1982). *Theory of instruction: Principles and applications.* New York: Irvington.

ENGLEMANN, S., & OSBORN, J. (1975). *DISTAR: An instructional system.* Chicago: Science Research Associates.

FOXX, R. M., & AZRIN, N. H. (1972). "Restitution: A method of eliminating aggressive-disruptive behavior of retarded and brain damaged patients." *Behavior Research and Therapy, 10,* 15–27.

FOXX, R. M., & AZRIN, N. H. (1973). *Toilet training the retarded.* Champaign, IL: Research Press.

GENTRY, D., DAY, M., & NAKAO, C. (1979). "The effectiveness of two-prompt sequencing procedures for discrimination learning with severely handicapped individuals." Moscow, ID: University of Idaho.

GERSTEN, R., CARNINE, D., & WHITE, W. A. T. (1984). "The pursuit of clarity: Direct instruction and applied behavior analysis." In W. L. Heward, T. E. Heron, D. S. Hill, & J. Trap-Porter (eds.), *Focus on behavior analysis in education* (pp. 38–57). Columbus, OH: Charles E. Merrill.

GESHURI, Y. (1972). "Observational learning: Effects of observed reward and response patterns." *Journal of Educational Psychology, 63,* 374–380.

GREENWOOD, C. R., DELQUADRI, J. C., & HALL, R. V. (1984). "Opportunity to respond and student academic achievement." In W. L. Heward, T. E. Heron, D. S. Hill, & J. Trap-Porter (eds.), *Focus on behavior analysis in education* (pp. 58–88). Columbus, OH: Charles E. Merrill.

GURALNIK, M. H. (1976). "The value of integrating handicapped and nonhandicapped preschool children." *American Journal of Orthopsychiatry, 42,* 236–245.

HALL, R. V., DELQUADRI, J. C., GREENWOOD, C. R., & THURSTON, L. (1982). "The importance of opportunity to respond in children's academic success." In E. B. Edgar, N. G. Haring, J. R. Jenkins, & C. G. Pious (eds.), *Mentally handicapped children: Education and training* (pp. 107–140). Austin, TX: Pro-Ed.

HALLE, J. W., MARSHALL, A. M., & SPRADLIN, J. E. (1979). "Time delay: A technique to increase language use and facilitate generalization in retarded children." *Journal of Applied Behavior Analysis, 12,* 431–439.

KAZDIN, A. E., & ERICKSON, L. M. (1975). "Developing responsiveness to instructions in severely and profoundly retarded residents." *Journal of Behavior Therapy and Experimental Psychiatry, 6,* 17–21.

KLEINERT, H. L., & GAST, D. L. (1982). "Teaching a multihandicapped adult manual signs using a constant time delay procedure." *Journal of the Association of the Severely Handicapped, 6(4),* 25–32.

LOVAAS, O. I., KOEGEL, R. L., & SCHREIBMAN, L. (1979). "Stimulus overselectivity in autism: A review of research." *Psychological Bulletin, 86,* 1236–1254.

LOVASS, O. I., SCHREIBMAN, L., KOEGEL, R. L., & REHM, R. (1971). "Selective responding by autistic children to multiple sensory input." *Journal of Abnormal Psychology, 77,* 211–222.

LUYBEN, P. D., FUNK, D. M., MORGAN, J. K., CLARK, K. A., & DELULIO, D. W. (1986). "Team sports for the severely retarded: Training a side-of-the-foot soccer pass using a maximum-to-minimum prompt reduction strategy." *Journal of Applied Behavior Analysis, 19,* 431–436.

MACKINTOSH, N. J. (1977). "Stimulus control attentional factors." In W. K. Honig & J. E. R. Staddon (eds.), *Handbook of operant behavior* (pp. 481–513). Englewood Cliffs, NJ: Prentice Hall.

MARTIN, J., RUSCH, F., JAMES, V., DECKER, P., & TRTOL, K. (1982). "The use of picture cues to establish self-control in the preparation of complex meals by mentally retarded adults." *Applied Research in Mental Retardation, 3.,* 105–119.

MERCER, C. D., & MERCER, A. R. (1981). *Teaching students with learning problems.* Columbus, OH: Charles E. Merrill.

MOSK, M. D., & BUCHER, B. (1984). "Prompting and stimulus shaping procedures for teaching visual-motor skills to retarded children." *Journal of Applied Behavior Analysis, 17,* 23–34.

O'BRIEN, F., BUGLE, C., & AZRIN, N. H. (1972). "Training and maintaining a retarded child's proper eating." *Journal of Applied Behavior Analysis, 5,* 67–72.

PECK, C. A., COOKE, T. P., & APOLLONI, T. (1981). "Utilization of peer imitation in therapeutic and instructional contexts." In P. S. Strain (ed.), *The utilization of classroom peers as behavior change agents* (pp. 69–100). New York: Plenum Press.

RILLING, M. (1977). "Stimulus control and inhibitory processes." In W. K. Honig & J. E. R. Staddon (eds.), *Handbook of operant behavior* (pp. 432–480). Englewood Cliffs, NJ: Prentice Hall.

RINCOVER, A., & KOEGEL, R. L. (1975). "Setting generality and stimulus control in autistic children." *Journal of Applied Behavior Analysis, 8,* 235–246.

RODEWALD, H. K. (1979). *Stimulus control of behavior.* Baltimore, MD: University Park Press.

ROSE, T. L. (1986). "Effects of illustrations on reading comprehension of LD students." *Journal of Learning Disabilities, 19,* 542–544.

ROSE, T. L. (1987). *A reassessment of social perception in terms of stimulus control.* Manuscript submitted for publication.

ROSE, T. L., & FURR, P. M. (1984). "Negative effects of illustrations as word cues." *Journal of Learning Disabilities, 17,* 334–337.

ROSE, T. L., & ROBINSON, H. H. (1984). "Effects of illustrations on learning disabled students' reading performance." *Learning Disability Quarterly, 7,* 165–171.

SCHREIBMAN, L., & CHARLOP, M. H. (1981). "S$^+$ versus S$^-$ fading in prompting procedures with autistic children." *Journal of Experimental Child Psychology, 34,* 508–520.

SCHREIBMAN, L., & LOVAAS, O. I. (1973). "Overselective response to social stimuli by autistic children." *Journal of Abnormal Child Psychology, 1,* 152–168.

SMEETS, P. M., HOOGEVEEN, F. R., STRIEFEL, S., & LANCIONI, G. E. (1985). "Stimulus overselectivity in TMR children: Establishing functional control of simultaneous multiple stimuli." *Analysis and Intervention in Developmental Disabilities, 5,* 247–267.

SNELL, M. E. (1983). *Systematic instruction of the moderately and severely handicapped* (2nd ed.). Columbus, OH: Charles E. Merrill.

SPOONER, F., & SPOONER, D. (1984). "A review of chaining techniques: Implications for future research and practice." *Education and Training of the Mentally Retarded, 19,* 114–124.

STRIEFEL, S., & WETHERBY, B. (1973). "Instruction-following behavior of a retarded child and its controlling stimuli." *Journal of Applied Behavior Analysis, 6,* 663–670.

SULZER-AZAROFF, B., & MAYER, G. R. (1977). *Applying behavior analysis procedures with children and youth.* New York: Holt, Rinehart & Winston.

TERRACE, H. S. (1966). "Stimulus control." In W. K. Honig (ed.), *Operant behavior: Areas of research and application.* New York: Appleton-Century-Crofts.

TOUCHETTE, P. E., & HOWARD, J. S. (1984). "Errorless learning: Reinforcement contingencies and stimulus control transfer in delayed prompting." *Journal of Applied Behavior Analysis, 17,* 175–188.

VARGAS, J. S. (1984). "What are your exercises teaching? An analysis of stimulus control in instructional materials." In W. L. Heward, T. E.

Heron, D. S. Hill, & J. Trap-Porter (eds.), *Focus on behavior analysis in education* (pp. 126–144). Columbus, OH: Charles E. Merrill.

WALLS, R. T., CRIST, K., SIENICKI, D. A., & GRANT, L. (1981). "Prompting sequences in teaching independent living skills." *Mental Retardation, 19,* 243–246.

WOLERY, M., & GAST, D. L. (1985). *Effective and efficient procedures for the transfer of stimulus control.* Unpublished manuscript, University of Kentucky, Lexington, KY.

chapter 13

Applying Stimulus Control

Kevin had been identified as learning disabled, primarily on the basis of a severe spelling deficit. Despite the best efforts of his sixth grade teacher, Kevin continued to spell words incorrectly at a very high frequency, regardless of whether he was writing the words in isolation or in context. Kevin's tutor, Ms. Sullivan, decided to try a different approach—one that was based on some recent stimulus control research. Ms. Sullivan implemented a time delay prompting procedure (as discussed in the previous chapter), using printed spelling word cards as the prompt for Kevin to write each word correctly. Initially, Ms. Sullivan showed each card to Kevin without any delay—she said the word "color" and immediately showed Kevin the card with "color" printed on it. After he demonstrated that he could write each word correctly using the prompts with no delay, Ms. Sullivan began to delay the presentation of the prompt cards for 5 seconds. Ms. Sullivan would say

the word, Kevin was then expected to begin to write the word correctly. If, after 5 seconds, Kevin did not respond, Ms. Sullivan showed Kevin the word card. After several hours of instruction spaced over several weeks, Kevin learned over 90 percent of the words on his spelling list, which was composed of words Kevin did not know before Ms. Sullivan began to work with him. In addition, Kevin was able to generalize the correct spelling of these new words to new settings such as his classroom and his home. He also generalized his correct spelling to new responses, (i.e., spelling the new words correctly in sentences). Ms. Sullivan was quite pleased that the procedure worked so well in so little time. She thought maybe there really is something to be gained from reading those journals her professors kept assigning to her. Meanwhile, Kevin was proud of himself for winning the "game" Ms. Sullivan created, writing the word correctly before he had to be shown the card. (The foregoing example is based on a study by Stevens and Schuster completed in 1987.)

One of the most important goals of any behavior change intervention is to provide learning experiences that allow the individual to emit his newly learned behavior in a variety of settings and contexts. While arranging behavioral interventions so that the teacher controls the contingencies is almost always more efficient than other (perhaps more natural) arrangements, an inherent shortcoming of this approach is that the individual may not receive much opportunity to interact with the naturally occurring contingencies for any particular response. However, the teacher who pays attention to antecedent programming, especially those procedures that develop appropriate stimulus control, is helping to ensure that his students will be able to use their newly acquired social or academic behaviors in ways that are relevant to their life.

The idea that acquired behavior should become generalized is one of the underlying principles of special education. We assume that the specialized teaching techniques and materials in special education classes facilitate the acquisition of adaptive social and academic behaviors. We further assume that these improved behaviors will allow the handicapped student to demonstrate continued gains through her participation in a less restrictive educational environment. These assumptions have contributed to the continued acceptance of mainstreaming (Gottlieb, Rose, & Lessen, 1983). In 1986 approximately two-thirds of the handicapped students enrolled in special education receive the majority of their education in regular education classes (Executive Committee, 1986) despite inconsistent evidence of this policy's effectiveness (e.g., Budoff & Gottlieb, 1976; Gottlieb, et al., 1983).

An inherent assumption in most mainstreaming programs is that generalization will occur spontaneously (Rose, Lessen, & Gottlieb, 1982). Extensive evidence indicates, however, that expectations of naturally occurring generalization are in error; rather, it appears that transfer of training rarely occurs unless it has been purposefully programmed (Jenkins, et al., 1978; Kazdin & Bootzin, 1972; Lovitt, 1977; O'Leary & Drabman, 1971; Stokes & Baer, 1977). The mounting evidence that generalization is an overlooked component of many intervention programs has resulted in an increasing number of professionals calling for increased research efforts regarding generalization (Koorland, 1986; Rose, Koorland, & Epstein, 1982; Test & Rose, 1987). Bursuck and Epstein (1987) reported the results of a survey of important research issues in learning disabilities, as identified by leading researchers in the field. Their report revealed that generalization of interventions across settings were identified by 29 percent of these researchers and long-term effects (maintenance) were identified by 36 percent. Although interest in generalization continues to grow, the number of studies that address generalization continues to remain relatively low (Bursuck & Epstein, 1987). Fortunately, an increasing amount of research has begun to be reported that indicates that an emphasis on stimulus control, as it relates to environmental stimuli found in special and regular education classes, may prove to be a critical missing link in the success of intervention programs (Ellis, Lenz, & Sarbonie, 1987; Emshoff, Redd, & Davidson, 1976; Gerber, 1986; Jackson & Wallace, 1974; Koegel & Rincover, 1974; Rivera & Smith, 1987).

We may conclude, then, that attention to antecedent programming may produce significant benefits for the individual as well as contribute to the success of programmatic efforts, such as mainstreaming handicapped students into regular education classes. Several of the general principles of establishing stimulus control were discussed in the previous chapter. The remainder of this chapter will expand upon those principles and discuss procedures that have proven to be successful when teachers plan for antecedent programming to establish stimulus control.

CREATING BEHAVIORS

Using antecedent programming to develop stimulus control and, later, to develop generalization is most useful for developing behaviors that are not currently in the student's behavioral repertoire or appear so infrequently as to be nonfunctional. Several antecedent programming procedures have proven useful, including modeling, shaping, chaining, and generalization training. These procedures are discussed in detail in the remainder of this chapter.

Modeling

The ability to imitate a model's behavior is obviously critical for the acquisition of many appropriate and inappropriate behaviors, such as a variety of socialization responses and many uses of language. Modeling tactics have proven to be effective in such subject areas as arithmetic (Hendrickson, 1980; Lovitt, 1976), reading (Hansen & Eaton, 1978; Idol-Maestas, 1981), spelling (Grimes, 1981a; Kauffman, et al., 1978), language (Rogers-Warren & Warren, 1980), and handwriting (Stowitschek & Stowitschek, 1979). Learners who are not able to benefit from imitation are among the most difficult to teach and almost always suffer from severe handicapping conditions.

Learners acquire behaviors through modeling like any other operant behavior. First, a model is presented that serves as a prompt for a similar response by the learner (Zane, Walls, & Thvedt, 1981). Then, following the presentation of the model, the target response is emitted within a certain period of time (for example, 5 seconds). Finally, the imitative response is differentially reinforced. If we pause to consider these three environmental interactions, we will recognize the latter two from previous discussions of positive reinforcement and differential reinforcement. But, as we begin to discuss modeling in more detail, it is important to remember to distinguish between modeling as a prompt and modeling as a discriminative stimulus. The physical act of providing a model may become an S^D that sets the occasion for the learner to imitate that behavior and, thus, gain access to reinforcement. But, this aspect of modeling should occur primarily during the training sessions, and modeling should serve as an S^D for only as long as necessary to establish the imitative response. Modeling should actually serve as a prompt for the imitative response *in the presence of* the naturally occurring S^D. We want to teach the learner to respond appropriately to a variety of similar stimuli, eventually in the absence of the model, rather than to the model. For example, we may model the behaviors required to enter a city bus, put the correct change in the correct place, and choose an appropriate (unoccupied) seat. The actual stimuli that we would like to develop as S^D's probably include the bus itself, the front door of the bus, the coin receptacle, and unoccupied seats. Since we are interested in training the learner to use these skills independently, it is clear that our modeling should serve as prompts for this stimulus control training, rather than as an S^D that sets the occasion for the correct behaviors.

USING MODELING EFFECTIVELY. As discussed in the previous chapter, several factors are related to an increase in the effectiveness of any modeling procedure: (a) the similarity between the learner and the model, (b) the model's prestige (c) the selection of a simple response, (d) the reinforcing of the model's behavior, (e) the competence of the model, and (f) the combining of the modeling procedure with other prompts.

Modeling, as with any other instructional procedure, should be related directly to the goal of instruction and be selected with the learner's current level of functioning in mind. In some cases prerequisite skills, such as attending and imitating, must be developed before modeling can be expected to be effective.

When implementing the modeling procedure, Striefel (1974) identified four significant procedures to be used: probe sequence, training trials, putting through, and alternating sequences. First, each session should begin with a *probe sequence* which allows the teacher to assess the learner's current performance level and to provide data regarding whether or not the learner is acquiring the new response. A probe sequence consists of a certain number of presentations (for example, 3 to 5) in random order of each behavior to be taught during that session. If the learner can perform the target behavior correctly after each presentation of the model, then you may conclude that the particular response has been acquired and should not be included in the training session.

Second, following the probe sequence, *training trials* are begun. Each training trial is a series of consecutive presentations of the model, the learner's response, and the reinforcement for either correct responses or approximations of the correct response. The first behavior trained should be either the response that was most often imitated (but not imitated often enough to meet the criterion) during the probe sequence, or, if no responses were emitted correctly, the behavior that most closely approximated a correct response. Striefel (1974) suggests that each training trial continue until the learner imitates the model five times consecutively. Once the learner meets this criterion, the alternating sequence procedure (to be discussed) is implemented. If the learner responds incorrectly three times in succession or does not respond at all after three training trials, then the teacher should begin using physical prompts.

After the probe sequence, the third procedure, the use of *physical prompts* begins. Using physical prompts (see the previous chapter for a more detailed discussion) has been called *putting through* by Striefel (1974). As you may expect, this procedure will be more effective for certain classes of behavior than for others because physical prompting is not appropriate or efficient for many behaviors. (Other examples of modeling that do not depend upon physical prompting are discussed later in this section.) However, when physical prompts are indicated, the putting through

procedure seems to be quite effective. When the learner continues to have difficulty performing the imitative response, the teacher should begin to guide the student through the target response or movement and then reinforce his or her behavior. Gradually and progressively fade the physical prompts, so that you physically guide the learner through the response up to the last component of the response, which he or she should emit without help. On successive trials, remove the physical prompt at successively earlier steps of the behavior. For example, if you were teaching a learner to eat with a spoon, you may follow these steps:

1. Begin the putting through process by placing your hand over the learner's hand to hold the spoon.
2. Scoop food into the spoon and move the spoon to the learner's mouth.
3. Put the spoon into the learner's mouth.
4. Place your other hand on the learner's chin.
5. Remove the spoon by pulling it slightly upward and out.
6. Push the learner's chin upwards to close his mouth.

On the next trial, you should prompt the behavior by doing Steps 1 through 5 and allow the learner to perform Step 6 by himself. On successive trials, you would guide the learner through Step 4, allowing him to emit steps 5 and 6 by himself, and so on. Eventually, the physical guidance can be faded entirely and the learner may perform the entire sequence of responses without the model. At this point, the presence of food and a spoon should serve as an S^D for this sequence of responses. As discussed above, once the learner performs this behavior correctly in five consecutive training trials, he is ready for the alternating sequence procedure.

The fourth procedure, using *alternating sequence*, allows you to further evaluate the learner's performance and to provide some additional training trials to help ensure maintenance of the newly learned responses. Several newly learned behaviors are selected as well as an equal number of previously learned behaviors (for example, five newly learned and five previously learned responses). The training trial procedure is used to evaluate how well the skills have been acquired and whether any important components of the responses are not being emitted accurately. If an error occurs, you may use the putting through process briefly again. Striefel (1974) recommends a criterion of at least 14 correct responses out of 15 trials, with training to continue if this criterion is not met.

In addition to the above training sequence, several other practices have been proven to increase the effectiveness of modeling. First, *short training sessions,* usually no longer than 10 minutes each, are more effective than longer sessions. In fact, two short sessions during the same day are probably more effective than one long session (Heward, 1978).

Second, you should use *effective reinforcement* procedures, including the schedule of reinforcement and the various types of reinforcers. You may, for example, begin a modeling procedure using a continuous reinforcement schedule (CRF), but—as with any other reinforcement-based intervention—you should gradually thin the CRF schedule until a more natural schedule is attained. Even if you begin the training with artificial reinforcers, such as edibles, remember to move to more natural reinforcers (for the particular response) as soon as possible. Social and verbal praise should always be paired with any artificial reinforcers. Remember, too, that a deterioration in performance may be a result of satiation, rather than a flaw in your training procedure.

Third, *be patient.* Be prepared to move back to an earlier teaching step if the learner's performance deteriorates. Also, be prepared to modify your teaching sequences if the learner's behavior deteriorates or begins to plateau at a level below the criterion. (You may have progressed through the teaching stages too quickly or your teaching sequence may be incomplete and lacking an important step.)

Fourth, if generalization of newly learned responses is a particular problem for certain learners, then you should carefully plan the modeling procedure to enhance the generalization process. For example, employing multiple models (for examples, Bandura & Menlove, 1968) and *in vivo* training using multiple models and settings (for examples, Stokes, Baer, & Jackson, 1974) have proven to increase the probability that generalization will occur.

Some Examples. Kauffman and his colleagues (1978) used an innovative aspect of modeling to teach spelling skills to learning disabled youngsters. They compared the effectiveness of modeling the correct spelling of a word following the learner's error to the same modeling procedure plus an imitation of the learner's mistake, in which the learner's error was repeated by the teacher before the correct response was modeled. In the modeling only sessions, the following instructional sequence was followed" Praise followed each correct response. After each misspelled word the teacher *said,* "Here is the way you wrote the word," and the teacher shows the student the mistake. Then the teacher says, "Here is the correct way to spell the word," and the teacher shows the correct way to spell the word. During the modeling plus imitation sessions, praise again followed each correct response. The teacher responded to each error by *saying,* "This is how you spelled _____" and then the teacher *wrote* the misspelled word exactly as the child spelled it. Then the teacher said, "But, this is the correct way to spell _____." The teacher then writes the word correctly. The learner was then instructed to write the word correctly. Kauffman and his colleagues found the modeling plus the imitation of errors to be especially effective for teaching words that are spelled phonetically.

Building upon this study and related studies, Grimes (1981b), in a discussion of oral feedback following spelling errors, provided three examples of how a teacher can use models to prompt a correct spelling response:

1. Model the Complete Response
    Teacher: "Tomorrow" (says word)
    "t-o-m-o-r-r-o-w" (spells word orally)
    Learner: "Tomorrow"
    "t-o-m-o-r-r-o-w"
2. Model Partial Response
    Teacher: "Tomorrow"
    "t-o-m-o-r-____"
    Learner: "Tomorrow"
    "t-o-m-o-r-r-o-w"
3. Repeat an Error
    Teacher: "t-o-m-m-o-r-r-o-w?"
    Learner: "t-o-m-o-r-r-o-w"

Traditional early intervention procedures for parents of seriously handicapped infants usually involve discussion of unique or difficult child care behaviors. An innovative approach was reported by Minor, Minor, and Williams (1983) which used modeling to train parents of developmentally delayed infants to perform a number of child care behaviors, in such areas as gross-motor, fine-motor, self-help, and language skills. During the modeling training, a staff member explained the rationale and purpose for every step in the teaching sequence to be modeled. The parent rehearsed each response, without the child, and any questions were answered. Then the parent demonstrated the modeled activity with the child while being observed by the teaching staff member. When errors occurred, the activity was stopped by the staff member, who then guided the parent through the modeled response again. Social and verbal reinforcers were delivered frequently. Minor and his colleagues reported the success of this procedure, as measured by the children's developmental gains, as well as a reduction in parental anxiety and an increase in the parents' skill levels.

FACTORS TO CONSIDER. Even though modeling has proven to be an effective procedure for creating behaviors that were not previously in a learner's repertoire, there are several factors to consider before beginning imitation training. Models may be unplanned as well as planned (Striefel, 1981). As we have seen, a planned model demonstrates exactly what behavior is expected. An unplanned model, however, may have the same effect on behavior. Unplanned models are not specifically programmed, rather they are present in everyone's environment at all times. For example, a particulary prestigious classmate may greatly influence a learner's behavior—for good or bad. The teacher is an especially powerful unplanned model. For example, if you are consistently tardy for the beginning of class or lose your temper when frustrated, then what behaviors are you indirectly teaching your pupils? On the other hand, what are you teaching if you are consistent in your interactions with students and are prepared and ready to go when class begins?

Finally, modeling is not always an appropriate intervention. Repp (1983) has written emphatically that modeling is not appropriate when teaching even simple tasks to learners functioning at low developmental levels. Although supporting the use of demonstrations (for example, showing a learner how to brush her teeth), Repp argues against relying on modeling alone for individuals with low-function levels. Combining physical guidance, shaping, or chaining with modeling may be recommended for these learners.

Shaping

Modeling rests on the assumption that an individual is able to perform the various components of a target behavior, even if some prompting is necessary. Many times, unfortunately, the behavior that a teacher wants a learner to emit is not part of the learner's repertoire. In this case, a different procedure is required.

Shaping is defined as the process of differentially reinforcing successive approximations of the specified target behavior. In other words, "Shaping fosters the gradual development of a new behavior by repeatedly reinforcing minor improvements or steps toward that behavior. Instead of waiting for a new behavior to occur in its final form, we reinforce every resemblance of that new behavior" (Panyan, 1980, p.1). For example, a special education teacher may use shaping to increase eye contact between a child with autism and the teacher by differentially reinforcing looking in the direction of the teacher, looking at the teacher, looking at the teacher's face, and, finally, looking at the teacher's eyes.

Before proceding with a discussion of shaping, further consideration of two key components of the definition should prove helpful. First, *differential reinforcement* refers to reinforcing the emission of a specific member of a response class, while other members of the same response class are not reinforced. This function of differential reinforcement is somewhat different from its use in previous discussions of differential reinforcement in developing stimulus control. When developing stimulus control, the delivery of reinforcement depends upon the learner emitting the correct response in the presence of an S^D; the same response in the presence of an $S\Delta$ is not reinforced. Therefore, differential delivery of reinforcement is related to the antecedent stimuli. When implementing a shaping procedure, however, the differential delivery of reinforcement depends upon the learner emitting responses that are successively more similar to the target behavior. So a response that earns reinforcement early in the shaping program will not earn reinforcement later in the program. Using the eye contact example, initially the child may earn reinforcement for looking in the teacher's direction. Once that response occurs reliably, the child will earn reinforcement for looking at the teacher, but looking in the teacher's direction will no longer be reinforced.

A second component of the shaping definition refers to *successive approximations*. As you may have surmised, a successive approximation is a response that is either a prerequisite component of the target behavior or a more functional level of the same response class. A prerequisite component of the target behavior is one that must be topographically accurate in order for the target behavior to be mastered. For example, a learner must be able to grasp objects in order to perform several

self-help skills (for example, brushing his teeth or using silverware). In a shaping procedure, these prerequisite responses would be taught and differentially reinforced first. A more functional level of the same response class is one in which the topography of the behavior is the same, but other behavioral dimensions differ in intensity, frequency, duration, and so forth. For example, a child may pet a live puppy using the same intensity and force that she uses when she pets a stuffed animal (for example, gripping the puppy's skin painfully, squeezing the puppy too tightly, or pulling the puppy's ear). These responses are topographically similar, but a shaping program may provide differential reinforcement for touching the puppy more gently.

There are several advantages to using shaping. First, as mentioned above, shaping is one of the most effective procedures for teaching new behaviors. Second, shaping is a positive procedure in which reinforcement is available differentially for behaviors that gradually approximate the target behavior, while behaviors that do not approximate the target behavior are extinguished. Third, it can be combined effectively with a variety of other procedures to increase the efficiency of each component procedure.

USING SHAPING EFFECTIVELY. At this point, shaping may appear to be a relatively simple, straightforward procedure. But its use requires a thorough understanding of many behavioral principles and a great deal of skill in implementing those procedures. Several critical procedural steps have been identified.

First, define the target behavior. Trying to implement a shaping procedure without a careful definition of the target behavior may be likened to driving from New York to California when you have no map and do not know in which direction to drive. A related issue demands that the target behaviors be prioritized. Most handicapped individuals have multiple behavioral deficits. It is important to select the first (or most important) behavior to be shaped—"first things first."

While this decision is inherently an individual one that depends on many ecological variables, the following two alternatives have proven helpful: The teacher should (a) select a behavior that is likely to increase the learner's chances of receiving reinforcement from the natural environment (Allyon & Azrin, 1968; Heward, Dardig, & Rossett, 1979; Bailey & Lessen, 1984) or (b) select an "access" behavior, one that will increase the probability of the learner's acceptance in less restrictive environments (Hawkins, 1986). (Many self-help skills, such as wiping one's nose, fall under this guideline.) Regardless of how you decide which behavior to begin shaping first, an overriding issue is the age-approriateness of the response.

Second, define the response that the learner can emit which is related to the target behavior. In other words, decide where to begin. Carefully selecting this beginning response will allow you to avoid waiting for "something to happen" and also allow you to begin differentially reinforcing the learner's behavior much sooner.

Third, sequence the responses that will lead to the target behavior. This sequence will become the steps in the shaping procedure. Several sources are available to help you sequence the responses. You can seek expert opinion from journals (Van Houten, 1979), texts (Snell, 1983), commercially available materials (Brown & Hammill, 1983), your colleagues, and your state and local educational agencies. You can also observe a peer of the learner who is competent in the particular behavior and record the responses he or she performs. In addition, perform the behavior yourself and record the responses necessary to achieve the target behavior. In most cases the entire task sequence may not be needed because you only have to sequence the behaviors from the point at which you will begin the shaping procedure. You do not have to be concerned about responses occurring earlier in the response sequence because the shaping procedure depends upon successive approximations toward the target behavior.

Fourth, determine a success criterion for each step in the response sequence. There are no guidelines that clearly specify how many correct responses are required before beginning to differentially reinforce the response at the next step. The teacher must make this decision. The learner must remain at each step long enough to demonstrate competence, but not so long that the particular response earns too much reinforcement. If too much reinforcement is given there is a danger that the response step will become too firmly established. If that occurs, then when you begin to differentially reinforce a behavior that more closely approximates the target behavior (consequently, ignoring the previously reinforced behavior), the extinction process of the old behavior will be much more difficult. If this happens, it may become difficult to motivate the student to move on to the next step (Foxx, 1982).

Fifth, proceed gradually. Consider the size of the steps that lead to the target behavior. A recurring theme throughout this book has been that the learner's behavior is your best guide. You must be prepared to shift to new steps at any time because some responses will be learned quicker than others. Each response that is a closer approximation to the target behavior must be reinforced, whether or not you planned on that behavior occurring at that time. Conversely, a learner emitting the response at a given step does not guarantee that the behavior at the next step will occur immediately.

A classic study reported by Horner (1971) illustrates each of the above procedural guidelines. Horner designed a program to teach a child with mental retardation and spina bifida to use crutches—the more traditional efforts by a physical therapist had resulted in six months of tantrums and physical resistance. While the program involved two stages, first using parallel bars and then using crutches, we will focus on the program to train parallel bar use. First, the target behavior (using parallel bars for self-ambulation) was analyzed to determine each of the steps necessary to proceed from the child's current performance level. Six steps were identified:

1. Sit on a stool, grip the left parallel bar with the left hand, and grip the right parallel bar with the right hand.
2. Step 1 and pull to a standing position on parallel bars and maintain standing position long enough to drink one tablespoon of root beer (reinforcer).
3. Steps 1 and 2 and take one step using the parallel bars for support in order to earn the reinforcer.
4. Same as Step 3, but three steps must be taken using the parallel bars for support.
5. Same as Step 3, but five steps must be taken using the parallel bars for support.
6. Same as step 3, but ten steps must be taken using the parallel bars for support.

A criterion of 23 or more successful trials per session (out of 25 trials) for three consecutive sessions was established for each step in the shaping process. Finally, Horner proved adept at being willing to respond to the child's response data rather than adhering rigidly to preset criteria or conditions. As may be seen if Figure 13.1, success at one step did not insure immediate success at the next level.

Only three sessions were required at Step 3 (which meant Horner had to be ready quickly to differentially reinforce a different response). As Figure 13.1 shows the criterion was not an inflexible requirement at Step 4.

FACTORS TO CONSIDER. Even though shaping is one of the most effective procedures for teaching new behaviors, it is not always the procedure of choice. Shaping should be selected when other, quicker procedures, such as reinforcement, prompting, chaining,

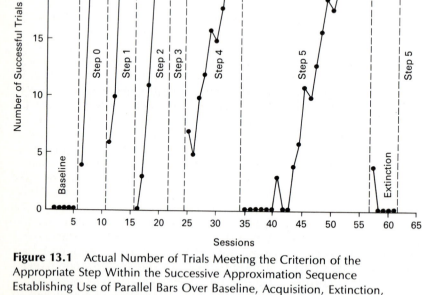

Figure 13.1   Actual Number of Trials Meeting the Criterion of the Appropriate Step Within the Successive Approximation Sequence Establishing Use of Parallel Bars Over Baseline, Acquisition, Extinction, and Reacquisition Conditions.

Source: R. D. Horner (1971) in "Establishing use of crutches by a mentally retarded spina bifida child." *Journal of Applied Behavior Analysis, 4,* 183–189. Copyright 1971 by the Society for the Experimental Analysis of Behavior, Inc.

or a combination of these, have not or will not produce the target behavior. Shaping is a time-consuming procedure which often requires an extended training period. Careful record keeping and observations are frequently necessary to identify subtle changes in the learner's behavior that might indicate that he or she is ready to move to the next step. Therefore, while shaping can be most effective, you might be wise to save it for when it is really necessary.

Chaining

Up to this point, the discussions of the various stimulus control procedures have implied that the behaviors you will be concerned with most often are relatively simple and discrete. They seem to be behaviors that occur in the presence of a discriminative stimulus and are then reinforced. But many of the behaviors we want learners to acquire involve several of these discrete behaviors combined. They must be performed in a rapid and accurate sequence following the presentation of the discriminative stimulus. These sequences of responses are *behavior chains*. More precisely, each response in the sequence occurs in the presence of an S^D for that particular response. Eventually, each response in the chain serves as feedback as well as an S^D for the next response in the sequence. Any behavioral chain can be defined by three components: First, a specific set of discrete responses must be performed. Second, each response interacts with the environment so that some conditioned reinforcement becomes available and serves as a discriminative stimulus for the next response in the sequence. Third, the set of responses must be emitted in a specific sequence.

Figure 13.2 presents a graphic explanation of this sequential relationship between each stimulus and response in a chain. Notice that once the first response is emitted in the presence of the original S^D it becomes an S^D for the next response in the chain. The second response, in turn, becomes an S^D for the third response and so on.

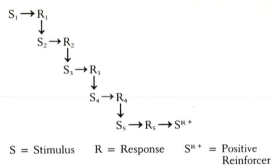

$$S_1 \rightarrow R_1$$
$$\downarrow$$
$$S_2 \rightarrow R_2$$
$$\downarrow$$
$$S_3 \rightarrow R_3$$
$$\downarrow$$
$$S_4 \rightarrow R_4$$
$$\downarrow$$
$$S_5 \rightarrow R_5 \rightarrow S^{R+}$$

S = Stimulus   R = Response S^{R+} = Positive Reinforcer

Figure 13.2 Relationship Between Each Discriminative Stimulus, Responses, and Reinforcer in a Behavior Chain. Note that each response becomes a discriminative stimulus for the following response in the chain.

As an example, refer to Figure 13.3 when you consider the following sequential responses necessary to find the sum of a 2-column addition problem. First, identify the operation by looking at the operational symbol (+). The plus sign is S_1; looking at the symbol is R_1. Looking at the symbol identifies the operation and prompts the next component of the sequence, that is R_1 becomes S_2 for the next response, which is adding the numerals in the one's place (R_2). That response, in turn, becomes an S^D (S_3) for writing the answer in the proper location (R_3). Writing the answer for the one's place becomes an S^D (S_4) for adding the numerals in the ten's place (R_4). Finally, adding the numerals in the ten's place sets the occasion (S_5) for writing the sum of the tens place in the correct location (R_5) which results in verbal praise from the teacher. As you can tell, a proficient learner will emit each of these responses quite rapidly, but each response must occur in the presence of a particular stimulus and in a particular sequence or the final behavior may be inaccurate. As you can also tell, teaching such complex sequences requires a more complex instructional procedure than more usual stimulus control procedures, such as prompting or shaping.

Frequently, the distinction between shaping and chaining is confusing. Kazdin (1975) has clarified this distinction. Usually, shaping

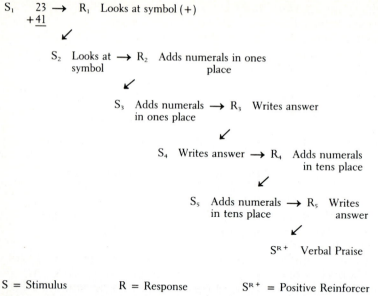

S_1 23 $\rightarrow$ R_1 Looks at symbol $(+)$
    $+\underline{41}$

S_2 Looks at $\rightarrow$ R_2 Adds numerals in ones
    symbol   place

S_3 Adds numerals $\rightarrow$ R_3 Writes answer
    in ones place

S_4 Writes answer $\rightarrow$ R_4 Adds numerals
                                        in tens place

S_5 Adds numerals $\rightarrow$ R_5 Writes
    in tens place   answer

S^{R+} Verbal Praise

S = Stimulus   R = Response S^{R+} = Positive Reinforcer

Figure 13.3   Relationship Between Each Discriminative Stimulus, Responses, and Reinforcer in the Behavior Chain "Adding 2-Column Problem." Note that each response becomes a discriminative stimulus for the following response in the chain.

is used to develop new behaviors and prompts may be used to facilitate responses that are increasingly more similar to the target behavior. Chaining, on the other hand, is generally used to develop a sequence of behaviors when the responses in that sequence are already part of the learner's behavioral repertoire. In other words, the goal of shaping is to develop the target behavior, and the responses developed along the way are not apparent when the shaping process is completed and the goal has been attained. The component responses in a behavioral chain, even those developed very early in the training procedure, will still be apparent when the training is completed.

TASK ANALYSIS. A behavior chain is composed of a number of responses that must be performed in a particular order. The process of identifying the component responses for any given target behavior and then ordering them so they lead to the target behavior is called *task analysis.* Performing a task analysis

is an important instructional step not only because it allows the teacher to identify the instructional content and sequence, but also because it answers two other questions crucial to effective teaching: "Where do I begin?" and "What do I teach next?"

Although a thorough discussion of task analysis is beyond the scope of this book, several important components will be presented. (The interested reader is referred to Bailey and Wolery, 1984; Gold, 1976; Howell, Kaplan, & O'Connell, 1979; Moyer & Dardig, 1978; Rose, 1985; Smith, Smith, & Edgar, 1976; and Snell, 1983 for more complete discussions of task analysis and procedures.)

Several methods have been identified to develop a task analysis and to verify the accuracy of its sequence. First the response components are sequenced after observing competent individuals perform the target behavioral chain (Cuvo, Leaf, & Borakove, 1978; Foster & Keilitz, 1983; Horner & Keilitz, 1975). Second, component responses may be identified and sequenced after consulting with experts in the subject matter (Schleien, Wehman, & Kiernan, 1981; Wilson, Reid, Phillips, & Burgio, 1984). Third, you may actually perform the responses, such as assembling a piece of equipment or tying ones own shoes, and record the discrete responses necessary to successfully achieve the target behavior (Bellamy, Horner, & Inman, 1979; Snell, 1983).

Regardless of the method used to develop a task analysis, you must remember that most response sequences will require some revisions, usually because some important functional steps were omitted. For example, Foster and his colleagues (1976) developed an apparently comprehensive response sequence, composed of 20 steps, for use in teaching women with developmental disabilities to use sanitary napkins. Some years later, after experience with the original task analysis, they revised the sequence until it included 35 steps (Foster & Keilitz, 1983).

CHAINING PROCEDURES. While the term behavioral chain refers to the entire sequence of responses leading to a particular target behavior, *chaining* refers to the actual process by which each of the responses are linked to one another to form the behavioral chain. Chaining is the most frequently used method of applying task analysis to complex tasks (Sailor & Guess, 1983). There are two basic types of chaining: forward chaining and backward chaining. These two basic chaining procedures yield four programmatic options for the teacher: forward chaining, total task presentation (a variation of forward chaining), backward chaining, and backward chaining with leap aheads.

Forward Chaining. Once the response sequence has been identified through a task analysis, the component behaviors are taught according to that sequence. Therefore, the learner begins with Step 1 and reinforcement is delivered once that behavior has met the predetermined criterion. Next, the learner will perform Step 1 and Step 2 in sequence, with reinforcement being dependent upon success on Steps 1 *and* 2. As the training pro-

gresses, the learner is expected to perform all preceding steps in the sequence plus the new step before receiving reinforcement (known as differential reinforcement). Thus, in the later stages of training the learner practices each step of the response sequence during each training session.

For example, you may use the following response sequence to teach a child to drink from a cup. He or she would receive reinforcement when the first step, reaching for the cup, is performed accurately. Before moving forward to Step 2, some criterion for mastery, such as accurate performance on 3 consecutive trials, should be required. But, during the training process, the reinforcer should be available on a very dense schedule, perhaps a CRF. From then on, reinforcement would only be available if the child performs Step 1 and Step 2 in order. Once mastered, then Steps 1, 2, and 3 would be required—and so on, until all seven steps are performed quickly and sequentially.

1. Extend arm toward cup.
2. Grasp opens as arms near cup.
3. Place hand around cup.
4. Tighten grasp around cup.
5. Lift cup.
6. Pull arm with cup toward face.
7. Place cup to mouth and tilt.

In addition to using forward chaining to develop chains of specific responses, Bellamy and his colleagues (1979) have suggested that several chains may be linked together to form a larger chain, a "chain of chains." In effect, the chain itself is modifiable because reinforcement is still contingent upon the emission of the target behavior, which only results when the component responses are performed accurately. Therefore, by sequencing the target behaviors of several chains, these chains can be viewed as the equivalent of discrete responses, and a new chain can be created. For example, Wilson, et al. (1984) taught four institutional residents to eat in a family-style manner. They identified 12 premeal, 9 meal, and 9 postmeal "skill clusters," which are actually smaller behavioral chains. Once the learner was in the dining room and told to eat, the first skill cluster had to be completed within 3 seconds or the trainer guided the learner's movements to complete the response. This procedure was followed, using a forward chaining procedure, until all the steps were mastered and all the learners had become virtually independent eaters.

Sailor and Guess (1983) have suggested that there are two primary advantages to using forward chaining. First, delivering reinforcement systematically is relatively easy. Second, evaluating the outcome of each step in the chain is relatively objective and straightforward. A third advantage may result from these first two advantages: teaching trainers, including paraprofessionals, to use forward chaining is simplified.

Total Task Presentation. While the order of the response sequence remains the same as in forward chaining, when using the total task presentation the learner is trained on every step in the sequence every session. The teacher provides assistance for each response the learner is not able to emit accurately. Training continues until the learner is able to perform the chain at the mastery level (Gold, 1976; Spooner & Spooner, in press).

Using total task presentation to teach the response sequence above for teaching a child to drink from a cup, training would begin with the first step and proceed through the last step during each training session. Various prompts, such as verbal directions or physical guidance, may be used as needed. Reinforcement becomes available after each step in the sequence.

Spooner and his colleagues (Spooner, 1984; Spooner, Lee, & Spooner, 1984; Spooner & Spooner, in press; Spooner, Weber, & Spooner, 1983) have speculated that the total task presentation may be related to increased rates of learning for two reasons. First, the learners are exposed to the relevant stimuli more frequently because each step in the response sequence is practiced every session. Conversely, forward chaining procedures pro-

vide more practice on the earlier steps in each sequence that those closest to the target behavior. The second reason is based on research that indicates that learning occurs more rapidly in conditions in which errors are more probable (Graf, 1980; Lindsley, 1981, 1983; Liberty & Wilcox, 1981). High error rates are easily created in total task training procedures because there is a greater opportunity to make incorrect responses than with either forward chaining or backward chaining.

Backward Chaining. When using backward chaining, the response sequence identified in the task analysis is the same as if forward chaining were to be used. Procedurally, the teacher completes all the responses, except for the last response in the chain. The learner performs that response and then receives a reinforcer. Once that step has been mastered, then the teacher performs all but the last two responses in the chain, and the learner must perform the last two responses in sequence in order to receive the reinforcer. Using our drinking from a cup response sequence, the sequence remains the same. The teacher performs Steps 1 through 6 for the learner, who then must perform Step 7, placing the cup to the mouth and tilting (drinking), for which reinforcement is earned. After she has mastered that step, you perform Steps 1 through 5, and the learner must perform Steps 6 and 7 in order to receive the reinforcer. Next, you perform Steps 1 through 4, the learner emits Steps 5, 6, and 7, and so on until the learner is performing the whole behavior chain from Step 1 through 7.

An implication of this procedure is that the identified response sequence may not be the same as the instructional sequence. Even though the behavioral chain must be performed in the correct sequence, we may teach the individual steps in the chain in a different order as long as the learner practices the chain in the correct sequence. Figure 13.4 clarifies this apparent contradiction. As may be seen, the response sequences for each chaining procedure, as identified by a task

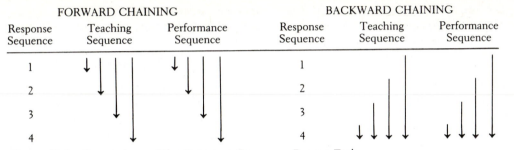

Figure 13.4 Comparison of the Response Sequence From a Task Analysis and the Instructional and Learner Performance Sequences for Forward Chaining and Backward Chaining Procedures.

analysis, are the same. The teaching sequences differ, however. In forward chaining, the teacher begins with Step 1, then teaches Steps 1 and 2, and so on. In backward chaining, the teacher begins teaching Step 4, then teaches Steps 3 and 4, and so on. The learner's performance sequence is similar, but in forward chaining he begins with Step 1, then Steps 1 and 2, and so on. The learner begins with Step 4, then Steps 3 and 4, and so on in when being taught using backward chaining. Regardless of the teaching procedure employed, the learner's performance sequences are the same and also match the response sequence when training is completed.

Spooner (1984) described a backward chaining procedure with eight severely and profoundly retarded adults. Each person was taught to assemble two pieces of hardware that had seven component parts each. During the backward chaining instruction, each learner was presented with a completed assembly of one piece of hardware, except for the last step. After the learner performed that step correctly six consecutive times (the predetermined mastery criterion), he or she moved to the next to last step. In this manner, the task was presented to the learner with all but the "training step" being completed at each successively higher level in the response sequence. The learner then had to complete the remainder of the response sequence independently. The results indicated that the backward chaining procedure was an effec-

tive procedure for teaching these complex assembly tasks to institutionalized individuals.

Backward chaining is advocated by many because the learner gains access to the natural reinforcer for the particular behavior chain much quicker than in forward chaining. The last step in the chain is reinforced by the natural consequences. The next-to-last step becomes an S^D for the response that will gain the natural reinforcer. Therefore, especially during the early training stages, the natural reinforcers for the particular behavior chain are much more immediate and a functional relationship between the responses in the chain and the natural consequences of those responses is developed more readily. For example, if we were to teach a child to tie his shoes, the first training step in a backward chaining procedure would be to "pull the loops in the bow away from each other and tighten." The learner would immediately receive the natural reinforcers for that chain—his shoes would feel more comfortable, they would stay on his feet, his socks would not bunch up in his shoes, etc. If we were to use the forward chaining procedure, the first step taught would be to "pinch the lace." Obviously, some type of artificial reinforcer would have to be programmed for this and a number of the other early steps in that chain.

Backward Chaining with Leap Aheads. A variation of backward chaining, backward chaining with leap aheads, has been suggested as a way to accelerate learning (Eaton & Wittman, 1982; Spooner, et al., 1986). One criticism of chaining's focus on training individual steps has been that training only one step in a response sequence can slow the learning process (Liberty & Wilcox, 1981). Using leap aheads, several steps are combined into functional clusters of steps which are then trained in the same manner as in backward chaining. Spooner, et al. (1986) have described the following leap ahead procedure using a vocational task that requires the learner to put on and tighten a nut.

The steps of picking up the nut, orienting it to the bolt, and threading the nut may be combined into one cluster. This allows more than one step to be taught at a time. With a training task that had been broken down into 25 steps, the 25 individual steps might comprise 5 functional units or clusters. Instead of training each of the 25 steps individually to a specific criterion, the trainer starts with the last step, trains that step to criterion, then leaps ahead to the next functional cluster of steps. The trainer trains each cluster in the sequence, until the learner is performing all of the original 25 steps. (p. 124)

The leap ahead procedure seems to hold promise for response sequences that are most appropriately taught using a backward chaining procedure. Research efforts regarding the best ways to cluster steps in a behavior chain into functional units and further comparisons of the efficiency of the leap ahead procedure will add greatly to its usefulness for teachers. You might consider using the leap ahead procedure as a variation to backward chaining.

USING CHAINING EFFECTIVELY. Several factors have been identified that will increase the effective use of any chaining procedure.

Quality of the Task Analysis. A complete, detailed, and thorough task analysis is a critical prerequisite for a successful chaining procedure. In order to ensure the quality of the task analysis, you must attend to developing the task analysis or locating an already existing task analysis before you begin training. Also, remember that the original task analysis

may need to be modified, either by adding, combining, or deleting steps, during the training process.

Use Effective Reinforcement Procedures. Remember the reinforcement principles discussed earlier in this book. Several key points are especially germane to chaining procedures. Reinforcers have the most effect on the behaviors that immediately precede their delivery. Behaviors that occur relatively close to the end of a response sequence also occur closest in space and time to the delivery of the reinforcer. Therefore, behaviors near the "end" of a behavior chain are more likely to be strengthened than those occurring during the initial steps in the chain. The longer the chain becomes (that is, the more responses required), the more this effect may be noticed. The early steps in the behavior chain may, in effect, be under extinction conditions. Moreover, the more work required, the more powerful the reinforcer must be to maintain the level of responding. Longer chains imply more work. Therefore, plan the schedule of reinforcement carefully and consider the amount of effort required by the learner when establishing the schedule of reinforcement. The move from a continuous schedule of reinforcement to an intermittent schedule is a delicate process in chaining procedures.

Vary the Stimuli. To the extent possible, plan to use as many variations of the initial stimulus as is feasible. The same behavior chain may appropriately use a variety of similar stimuli. For example, using different types of shoes (for example, high-top sneakers as well as leather dress shoes) when teaching shoe tying, or using different types of toothpaste dispensers (e.g., tube or pump) when teaching tooth brushing will increase the generalizability of the behavior chain.

As the initial stimulus varies, some specific responses in the behavior chain may vary, for example, squeezing a tube of toothpaste as opposed to pushing the bottom on a pump dispenser are different responses. As training continues, providing for more and more generalization of the chain, remember to be sensitive to the potential for varying responses. In effect, this may require some slight, and perhaps transitory, change in the task analysis.

Generalization Training

Teaching one example never automatically instills a concept, a rule, or a habit. Learning one aspect of anything never means that you know the rest of it. Doing something skillfully now never means that you will always do it well ... Thus, it is not the learner who is dull, learning disabled, concretized, or immature, because all learners are alike in this: no one learns a generalized lesson *unless a generalized lesson is taught.* (Baer, 1981, pp. 1–2)

In order for any behavior to really be significant for the learner, teachers must attend to the generalization of the behavior change. Baer, Wolf, and Risley (1968) described a generalized behavior change as one that endures over time, appears in a wide variety of settings, or appears in a wide range of related behaviors. More recently, Stokes and Baer (1977) wrote that generalization has taken place if the trained behavior occurs in different places and times without being retaught or if it results in new related behaviors occurring without additional training. As these descriptions imply, there are three types of generalization: stimulus generalization, maintenance, and response generalization.

STIMULUS GENERALIZATION. Stimulus generalization occurs when a response that has been reinforced in the presence of one stimulus occurs with increased frequency in the presence of a different, but similar, stimulus (Sidman, 1960). Generally, the more similar the stimuli, the more we may expect responses to generalize to those stimuli. A group of stimuli that we may expect to be similar enough to occasion the same response is known as a *stimulus class*. Extending this notion of stimuli along the lines suggested by Stokes and Baer (1977) allows us to describe stimulus generalization as the degree to which the learner performs the target behavior in environments that differ from the

one in which training was provided. For example, Wrestling, Koorland, and Rose (1981) found that 82 percent of surveyed special education teachers in a variety of settings reported using a one-to-one instructional grouping for more than one-third of the day for each student. Consequently, we may expect some degree of stimulus generalization to occur in the regular class during individualized instruction, but probably not during larger group instruction. However, Kaufman, Agard, and Semmel (1983) reported observations where individualized educational groupings occurred only 12 percent of the time in regular education classes. We might conclude, then, that a handicapped learner who is used to receiving individual instruction for at least one-third of the day may encounter some generalization problems in a regular class because the controlling stimuli would be very different.

Stimulus generalization was assessed along two dimensions in a study by McGee, Krantz, & McClannahan (1986). They evaluated the effectiveness of an incidental teaching procedure on the acquisition and generalization of functional sight word reading skills. Using prompts and stimulus fading, the teachers presented labels to preferred toys until each learner could match the word card with the preferred toy. First, stimulus generalization was assessed by arranging five boxes in the free play area. Each box contained a toy and was labeled with a word card. Three boxes were labeled with target (trained) words; the other two were distractors and labeled with words unknown to the child. Second, the printing on the word cards was changed by making the print smaller and using different style letters (typewritten as opposed to hand lettered). The effects of the procedure and the degree to which the learners generalized across different stimulus conditions may be seen in Figure 13.5.

MAINTENANCE. Maintenance refers to the continued occurrence of a behavior after the arranged (or programmed) training contingencies have been removed (Kazdin, 1977). Main-

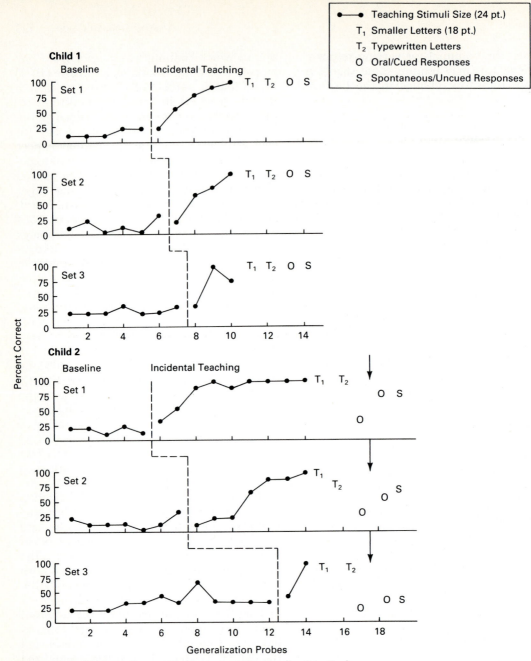

Figure 13.5 Percent Correct Responses on Generalization Probes Involving Novel Stimulus Materials and Response Modalities. Arrows indicate the point at which Child 2 received special oral reading sessions.

Source: G. G. McGee, P. J. Krantz, & L. E. McClannahan (1986) in "An extension of incidental teaching procedures to reading instruction for autistic children." *Journal of Applied Behavior Analysis, 19,* 147–157. Copyright 1986 by the Society for the Experimental Analysis of Behavior, Inc.

tenance occurs when the natural contingencies in the natural (nontraining) environment are sufficient to maintain the behavior at this current level. Conversely, a lack of maintenance may occur when extinction conditions or punishers are the consequences of the trained behavior being emitted in the natural environment (Whaley & Malott, 1971).

Three students with moderate handicaps were taught to initiate and expand on conversational topics with their nonhandicapped peers by Haring and his colleagues (1986). Conversational prompts were obtained from actual conversations with nonhandicapped peers, and the learners were taught to initiate conversations using these conversation "starters," such as "What television show did you watch last night?" The learners were also taught to expand upon these conversations when initiated by another student. The learners' performance levels were evaluated for twelve days following the end of the training sessions and found that each learner continued to initiate and expand upon conversations.

RESPONSE GENERALIZATION. Response generalization refers to the situation in which a particular stimulus, which has set the occasion for reinforcement of a specific response, also sets the occasion for a similar but different response (Sidman, 1960). A number of different responses, in addition to the trained response, may be functional in the presence of the same S^D. Using a demonstration procedure and feedback, Blankenship (1978) taught nine LD learners a correct algorithm that overcame the inversion errors they were making systematically in subtraction problems. An inversion error occurs when a learner subtracts the minuend from the subtrahend in subtraction problems requiring borrowing, for example:

$$
\begin{array}{r}
42 \\
-\ 8 \\
\hline
46
\end{array}
\qquad
\begin{array}{r}
321 \\
-147 \\
\hline
226
\end{array}
$$

Instruction focused on one type of subtraction problem: two digits minus one digit with regrouping from the tens place to the ones

place (the example on the left in the previous example). Daily measures of learner performance on nine classes of subtraction problems ranging from the instructed problem to three digits minus three digits with regrouping from hundreds place to tens place and from tens place to ones place (the example on the right in the previous example), were obtained daily on five sets of randomized subtraction worksheets containing five problems of each type. Therefore, no learner received instruction or feedback on any other problem type except the originally instructed problem type. Following this systematic instruction, Blankenship found that five learners demonstrated some degree of response generalization to each of the noninstructed problem types, three learners generalized to between two and seven problem types, and only one student failed to generalize at all. Figure 13.6 presents data for one learner's responses to the instructed problem type and his response generalizations.

PLANNING FOR GENERALIZATION. We must remember that generalization is rarely, if ever, a spontaneous event. As a result, we must plan carefully how a behavior may generalize once our instruction is completed. Baer (1981) has suggested several factors to consider when planning for generalization.

Which Behaviors Need to be Changed? Consider the learner first. Decide upon and list all the forms of the target behavior that may need to be changed. Although this will be a relatively difficult task, once you have finished you will have some guidance regarding the particular intervention you may implement. More importantly, you will have a much better basis to make a critical instructional decision: You must decide which behaviors need to be taught directly and which need to be included in your generalization plan. Suppose, for example, we have selected saying "Excuse me" as the target behavior because it is an appropriate way to interrupt another's conversation. Do you want the student to smile when she says "Excuse me"? Do you want the student to make eye con-

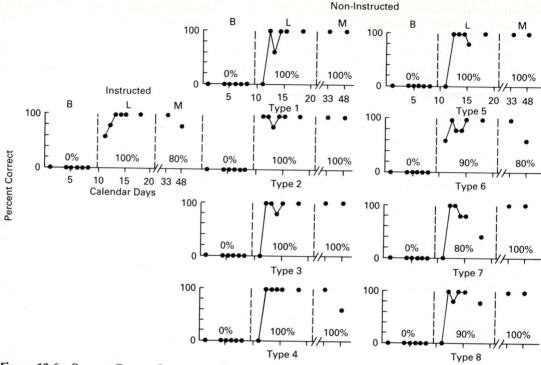

Figure 13.6   Percent Correct Scores on All Problem Types for Joe During Baseline (B), Intervention (I), and Maintenance (M).

Source: C. S. Blankenship (1978) in "Remediating systematic inversion errors in subtraction through the use of demonstration and feedback." *Learning Disability Quarterly, 1,* 12–22.

tact, touch one of the other individuals gently on the arm or shoulder and say, "Excuse me"? Should she learn to wait for a brief period of time before interrupting, regardless of whether she says "Excuse me" or not?

What Are the Situations, Settings, and Places the Needed Behavior Changes Should Occur? With Whom? You should list each environment in which the learner should emit the newly learned response once generalization is complete. In our polite interruption example above, you might consider at least the following. Should the student say "Excuse me" to friends or to strangers or to adults? Should the behavior occur on the playground, in the cafeteria, in class, at work, or home?

Once these situations have been listed,

Cooper, Heron, and Heward (1987) suggest some further thought and actions. This list should be prioritized so that the setting in which the behavior is most likely to occur, or in which it presents the biggest problem, is listed first. It is recommended that consideration be given to the potential stimuli available in each setting, as well as possible reinforcers and possible schedules of reinforcement.

What Are the Behaviors That Must Be Emitted by Significant Others and In What Situations? Implicit in any plan for generalization is that other people in other settings will have direct influence on the learner's behavior. "Everyone in contact contributes to everyone else's behavior, both to its changes and its maintenance" (Baer, 1981, p. 12).

When considering these other people, Baer suggests that they may fall into two categories: (a) those who may only be expected to tolerate and not act against the new behavior and (b) those who will need to assume either an active or supportive role. For each group of individuals, a list should be made of the behaviors they must display or not display and in which settings. For example, several key individuals may be identified to participate in the appropriate interruption example above. These individuals may be asked to respond to the student saying "Excuse me," even if the student doesn't get it quite right at first. Others, who may not interact with the learner very often, may be informed of the procedure, but not asked to behave any differently.

Benefits of Planning. Baer (1981) has listed several possible benefits for engaging in the admittedly time-consuming and demanding process required in order to plan for generalization to occur. First, you can see the scope of the problem facing you as well as the requirements of your teaching program. Second, you may choose to teach less than the full scope of the problem, but this must be an informed decision rather than one that occurs because you overlooked an important component. Third, you will not be surprised if a less than complete teaching program results in a less that complete set of behavior changes. Fourth, you can decide to teach less because of practical considerations (there is only so much time in the day). But, nevertheless, you can decide what *is* important to teach directly and in ways that will enhance the chances that other desired responses will generalize to new settings. We may conclude reasonably that if we do not develop a systematic plan, we are forced to rely on the "train and hope" approach to generalization (Stokes & Baer, 1977).

Effective Generalization Strategies

Once a distinction has been made between those behaviors you will teach directly and the settings in which they will be taught and those behaviors and settings for which you will plan for generalization to occur, you are ready to begin the planned intervention. Baer (1981) identified the following six effective strategies for producing generalized behavior change.

AIM FOR NATURAL REINFORCERS. As early as 1968, behavior analysts were recommending that we select target behaviors that will be maintained by natural reinforcers in the natural environment (Ayllon & Azrin, 1968). Inherent is this recommendation is the expectation that the natural contingencies for all other learners will eventually be sufficient to maintain the behavior of our learner. For example, toilet training to eliminate enuresis (bedwetting) may often be a trying effort that requires such training procedures as prompting and artificial reinforcers, such as edibles, during the early training stages. The target behavior is probably maintained after these artificial reinforcers are removed because both physcial and social discomfort can be avoided (for example, Azrin, Sneed, & Foxx, 1973).

In many cases, unfortunately, it is difficult to identify behaviors that will generate reinforcement in the natural environment that is sufficient to maintain the target behavior. Nevertheless, we must remember that all behaviors, regardless of where or when they are emitted, occur and continue to occur because they result in some type of reinforcement. We may have difficulty in identifying these natural reinforcers because they seem so natural to us (Baer, 1981).

Baer (1981) has identified two problems that teachers frequently must address when attempting to identify naturally occurring reinforcers. The first problem may be that the behavior is simply not well established; it has not been learned well enough to be functional. If this is the case, teaching to a higher level of fluency should solve this problem.

A second problem may occur when individuals in the natural environment are not actively delivering reinforcers for the behaviors the learner is emitting. For example, we tend to pay little attention to the learner who is at his desk working quietly, but we probably spend a great deal of time attending to the child who disrupts the class. We cannot assume that the natural environment, or even a less restrictive environment, will provide reinforcers on an appropriate schedule. We may, however, use this knowledge to our benefit. Stokes, Fowler, and Baer (1978) taught eight preschool children to recruit reinforcers from their teachers. They taught the children to emit several aspects of the behaviors considered to be "good work" in a preschool, such as working quietly and erasing mistakes. Then they taught the children to prompt the teacher to attend to their good work and to provide reinforcers for that work. The children were taught to prompt their teacher by saying several things designed to recruit reinforcers, such as "Have I been working carefully"? The children used these prompts appropriately and consequently received verbal praise from the teacher at much higher rates. When considering this type of procedure, you should carefully decide upon the topography of the recruiting behavior and how often the learner will emit the behavior. Otherwise, you may end up with a learner who is too loud, interruptive, and persistent in his prompting of the teacher's attention.

INCLUDE ENOUGH EXAMPLES. If a goal of your intervention is for the learner to emit the newly learned behavior in a variety of settings and situation, then, obviously, you should teach the student in a variety of settings and situations. Or, if you want the learner to respond to similar stimuli in various ways, then you should teach the learner the various responses that would be appropriate. This sounds simple enough and it would certainly eliminate many of the problems involved in training for generalization. Alas, it is rarely practical or efficient. Rather, you must decide which behaviors (in which settings or situations) to teach directly and which to monitor to see if they generalize.

One way to promote generalization without trying to teach everything to everybody is to rely on *general case programming* (Becker, Englemann, & Thomas, 1975; Becker & Engelmann, 1978). A major emphasis of general case programming is using sufficient members of a class of stimuli to increase the chances that a learner will respond appropriately to any member of the same stimulus class. Teaching the "general case" to students must include examples of the appropriate stimulus class (that is, the characteristics of one stimulus are the same for all members of that class) *and* nonexamples of the appropriate stimulus class (that is, those characteristics that are sufficiently different so that the stimulus is not a member of that class). These examples must also teach the range of variability within a stimulus class that define the parameters of that class (Engelmann & Carnine, 1982). For example, if we are teaching a child to recognize the color *blue*, we will include a variety of examples (blue plastic chips, blue wooden chips, blue material, blue eyes, large blue objects, and so forth) and nonexamples (red plastic chips, yellow wooden chips, green material, brown eyes, small red objects, and so forth) to ensure that the defining characteristics of the stimulus class are learned. These characteristics have to do with the various hues of the color blue, but do not include the texture, size, function, or location of the training material.

Even though general case programming was originally developed to teach language and other academic skills to mildly handicapped learners, it has been used successfully with a wide range of behaviors for both mildly and severely handicapped learners. For example, Horner and his colleagues have employed general case programming to teach moderately to severely handicapped high school students to use virtually every type of soda vending machine (Sprague, & Horner, 1984) and vocational skill (Horner & McDonald, 1982). Other successful uses of general case programming have been found for teaching functional skills (Wilcox & Bellamy, 1982) as well as appropriate social behaviors (Engelmann & Colvin, 1983) to severely handicapped youth.

TRAIN LOOSELY. Paradoxically, although you have been advised to control and standardize your teaching procedures and to increase efficiency and evaluate effects, Baer (1981) has suggested that this structure may restrict the generalization of the behaviors being learned. This view holds that complete stimulus control and discrimination may inhibit generalization, and, therefore, an effective strategy for promoting generalization may be to vary as many dimensions of the antecedent stimuli as possible. Although there have been few studies of this procedure, Baer (1981) has offered the following several suggestions:

Use two or more teachers

Teach in two or more places

Teach from a variety of locations (for example, in front of the learner, beside the learner)

Vary your tone of voice

Vary your choice of words

Show the stimuli from a variety of angles, using one hand then the other (if appropriate)

Have other persons present at some times and not other times

Vary the reinforcers

Vary the lighting conditions

Teach sometimes in noisy conditions, sometimes in quiet

Vary the decorations, the furniture and its locations

Vary the time of day when you teach the particular skill

Vary the temperature in the teaching setting

Do all of this as often and unpredictably as possible (Baer, 1981, p.25)

You would be a rare teacher indeed if you could routinely accomplish all of these variations. Consider these to be guidelines or reminders to vary the teaching environment as much as possible. If these nonessential stimulus components are varied, you should reduce the likelihood that any of them begin to exercise any control over the behavior being taught.

PROGRAM COMMON STIMULI. The degree of similarity between the stimulus used in training and any stimuli found in a generalized setting will influence the amount of stimulus generalization that occurs. The more different they are, the less stimulus generalization we may expect to take place. Therefore, if we can include some stimuli from the generalized setting during training, we may be able to increase the likelihood that stimulus generalization will occur. For example, the differences between special classes and regular classes are readily apparent along a number of dimensions (for example, class size, instructional groupings, or frequency of reinforcement). Rose, et al., (1982) have recommended that various stimuli present in the regular classroom that are different from the special classroom, such as classroom rules, curricular materials, types of directions, or schedules of activities, should be emulated in the special class to the maximum extent that is feasible. Instructional groups may be gradually increased in size, perhaps by adding children from the regular class to which the learner will be mainstreamed. Perhaps, the regular class teacher could begin to assume instructional responsibility for certain instructional activities in the special class. Anderson-Inman (1982) demonstrated the potential of this approach by teaching spelling to a special education student in the resource room using the materials, procedures, and words that would be used in the regular class. The results indicated that by using these common stimuli, the student increased her correct spelling responses to the point where she was achieving at the same rate as her nonhandicapped peers.

USE SIMILAR REINFORCEMENT SCHEDULES. When creating new behaviors or strengthening behaviors already present in the learner's repertoire, it is necessary to deliver reinforcement very frequently (perhaps every time the response is emitted). It has been demonstrated quite clearly, however, that more durable responses are created by switching to intermittent reinforcement. Intermittent schedules of reinforcement are more likely to promote generalization because behaviors trained under intermittent schedules are much more resistant to extinction.

Sometimes, however, a learner may not be able to distinguish which particular behaviors may be reinforced in a given setting. This may be especially true when a learner moves from a special education class, which is typically characterized by a relatively dense schedules of reinforcement, to a regular class in which reinforcement is delivered less often and, perhaps, less consistently. Perhaps one way to ensure that responses will generalize is to observe the schedules of reinforcement available in less restrictive or other generalized settings and to begin to gradually thin the training reinforcement schedule until it approximates that found in the generalized setting.

TEACH SELF-MANAGEMENT TECHNIQUES. Self-management is a set of procedures that has obvious value when programming for generalization. When a learner is able to manage his own behavior effectively, the programmed intervention may essentially be in effect in all settings or conditions in which the learner finds himself or herself. Although self-management is a rather generic term that describes several procedures, with respect to generalization it refers to any process that teaches an additional behavior (besides the original response) that serves as a prompt and reinforces the targeted behavior change across settings and behaviors at all times. But self-management procedures are not a panacea. Baer and Fowler (1984) caution us that merely training some self-management response does not ensure that the learner will use it. They remind us that self-management is a response, not unlike any other response, that also needs generalization and maintenance. The practice of training one behavior to "mediate the generalization of another behavior may succeed—but it may also represent a problem in guaranteeing the generalization of two responses, where before we had only the problem of guaranteeing the generalization of one" (p. 149). Nevertheless, the development of self-management procedures continues to gain favor with teachers as well as researchers, which is probably as it should be. The remainder of this chapter provides a discussion of self-management procedures.

Advantages of Self-Management. Several advantages of self-management procedures have been identified by Cooper, et. al., (1987) and Kazdin (1975).

1. An external change agent (for example, a teacher) may not notice or respond to occurrences of appropriate behavior. A large number of responses are being emitted at any given time in any classroom. No one expects the teacher to observe and respond to every response. But the effect on the learner whose behavior is overlooked may be negative. A lack of consistency is the result.

2. Students with self-management skills can help operate a more efficient classroom. Traditionally, teachers have assumed the responsibility for assessing and consequating learners' behaviors. The more a learner can assess and consequate her own behavior, the more time is available for the teacher to attend to other aspects of the curriculum or other instructional responsibilities. Recent findings that increased opportunities for learners to respond result in higher rates of learning (Greenwood, Delquadri, & Hall, 1984) bring both good news and bad news to teachers. The good news is that the learners in their class can learn more, quicker; the bad news is that it results in even more time being spent grading and evaluating learner performance. Self-management procedures may prove of significant value in solving this dilemma.

3. Self-management may be helpful when competing contingencies are relatively strong. For example, the peer group becomes a powerful source of reinforcement, especially as learners move into their teenage years, and the power of the peer group as sources of reinforcement may override the progressively weaker reinforcers available from teachers. Certain maladaptive behaviors may be reinforced by the peer group, such as nonresponsiveness. Self-man-

agement strategies may prove useful in maintaining responses that might otherwise be extinguished.

4. A learner's contribution to a self-management plan may result in better performance under self-selected conditions or reinforcers than when these are determined by others, (for example, Billingsley, 1977; Glynn, Thomas, & Shee, 1973).
5. Self-management is reinforcing because being in control is reinforcing.
6. The teacher may become an S^D for the target behavior, rather than some more relevant environmental stimulus. Self-management can help prevent this.

Self-Management Strategies Self-management strategies may be composed of four major procedures that may be used in varying degrees: stimulus control procedures, self-monitoring, self-reinforcement or self-punishment, and verbal mediation. Whenever any or all of these procedures are implemented, some degree of self-management is in effect.

STIMULUS CONTROL PROCEDURES. Manipulating antecedent stimuli seems to be a logical aspect of self-management because this procedure plays such a large part in externally managed intervention programs. Our daily lives offer many examples of providing prompts to ourselves for performing certain behaviors, for example, the music student who places his instrument case beside the front door so he will remember to take the instrument to school that day or the dieter who tapes a picture of a slim and trim model on the refrigerator door. Despite the clear appeal of using stimulus prompts for self-management, there are virtually no applied studies that support its use for special education students.

SELF-MONITORING. Monitoring one's behavior requires self-observation and self-recording. These procedures are as important to self-management programs as they are to externally managed programs, for all the same reasons.

In addition to information about the effects of the intervention, self-recorded data

may serve as an intervention by having a *reactive effect*. A change in behavior may occur simply as a result of the self-observation process and, more significantly, this change is often therapeutic (for example, Broden, Hall, & Mitts, 1971; Hundert & Bucher, 1978; Kneedler & Hallahan, 1981; Lovitt, 1973; Rosenbaum & Drabman, 1979). However, the changes that occur as a function of self-recording tend to decrease over a relatively short period of time unless some other self-management procedures are also implemented (McLaughlin, 1976; O'Leary & Dubey, 1979). O'Leary and Dubey (1979) following a thorough review of self-management procedures have concluded that self-recording may be an effective initial intervention. Beyond the initial stages, self-recording seems to promote maintenance of behaviors that were initially modified by more traditional teacher-managed interventions (O'Brien, Riner, & Budd, 1983).

O'Leary and Dubey (1979) suggested the following components be included whenever you teach students to self-record:

1. Select target behavior
2. Define target behavior
3. Select data collection system (for example, adaptations of event recording, time sampling, or permanent product recording)
4. Teach use of the data collection system
5. Monitor practice data recording sessions
6. Employ self-recording independently

An example of a successful self-recording procedure with three hyperactive children was reported by Barkley, Copeland, and Sivage (1980). Each student was given a card to record whether they were behaving in accordance with posted class rules (that they helped to develop). The rules were "stay in your seat, work quietly, raise your hand if you need help, don't space out, and don't bug others." A tape recorder signaled the end of a variable interval (VI1 for the first week and VI3 for the next two weeks). The learners then evaluated their behavior at that point in time and recorded whether they were obeying the rules or not. Bonus points for accuracy were awarded to ensure honesty. The procedure proved to be quite successful for increasing the amount of time the learners spent on-task.

This study also highlights an issue that many teachers raise when considering implementing a self-recording program: honesty. On one hand, this may not be too important because it appears that regardless of whether the learner is honest and accurate or not in self-monitoring, the procedure may nevertheless serve as an effective behavior change intervention (Rosenbaum & Drabman, 1979). On the other hand, students have been shown to be accurate and reliable observers of their own behavior (Santogrossi, O'Leary, Romanczyk, & Kaufman, 1973; Glynn, et al., 1973). Nevertheless, training learners to be more accurate has been a relatively simple process when accuracy has been reinforced (Hundert & Bucher, 1978; Nelson, Lipinski, & Boykin, 1978), but increasing accuracy has proven to be no guarantee that performance on the target will be enhanced as a result (O'Leary & Dubey, 1979).

SELF-REINFORCEMENT OR SELF-PUNISH-MENT. Reinforcement, whether teacher-determined or self-determined, has a long history of effectiveness. There are some indications that self-determined reinforcers and self-determined schedules of reinforcement may sometimes be more effective (for example, Billingsley, 1977). One of the first demonstrations of the relative effectiveness of allowing learners to select their own reinforcement contingencies was reported by Lovitt and Curtiss (1969). Certain academic responses were identified by the teacher along with the amount of free time that could be earned for the successful completion of each task. Later the learner was allowed to establish his own free-time contingencies for the same academic responses. Results indicated that the learner increased his academic response rate by 44 percent during the self-selected rein-

forcement phase as compared to the teacher-selected contingencies.

Self-punishment usually takes the form of a response cost condition that is added to an existing token system (Humphrey, Karoly, & Kirschenbaum, 1978). Humphrey, et al., (1978) implemented a self-imposed response cost system and a self-reinforcement system in an especially disruptive second grade class. Some students earned tokens for obeying the class rules and meeting the guidelines for earning reinforcement. Other learners began their day with a full quota of tokens and fined themselves for inaccurate work, according to the response cost guidelines. Both self-management systems were found to be related to an accelerated rate of academic responses and both were related to a maintained level of accuracy. The researchers concluded that, although the self-punishment procedures were effective, the self-reinforcement procedures were slightly more effective.

VERBAL MEDIATORS. While growing up, we always heard that "crazy" people talked to themselves and if you talked to yourself, people would think you were crazy, too. Now we know that everyone talks to themselves quite often. We remind ourselves to do a certain task ("Don't forget to pick up the sweaters at the dry cleaners"), encourage ourselves ("Come on. You can return this guy's serve"), and congratulate ourselves ("I knew I could do it"). Verbal statements such as these can affect the observable responses to which they are directed. This basic process has been elaborated upon and has been called *verbal mediation, cognitive modeling,* or *cognitive behavior modification.*

Most studies of the effectiveness of verbal mediation have used training procedures that are either adaptations of a training sequence developed by Meichenbaum and Goodman (1971) or the actual sequence they proposed, as follows:

1. The teacher models the task while talking himself through the procedure;

2. The learner performs the task while the teacher provides verbal instructions;
3. The learner performs the task while talking herself through the procedure and the teacher whispers the steps of the procedure;
4. The learner performs the task while whispering the steps of the procedure;
5. The learner performs the task while making lip movements but no sound;
6. The learner performs the task with no verbal behavior, while guiding her performance with covert instructions.

The initial step in this sequence was seen by Meichenbaum as critical if a student was to learn an effective strategy. He suggested that several skills that are relevant to the performance be included in Step 1 listed previously—initial verbal behavior that guides the modeling (Meichenbaum, 1977).

1. Problem definition ("What is it I have to do?")
2. Focus attention and guide the response ("Carefully . . . draw the line down")
3. Self-reinforce ("Good, I'm doing it right")
4. Self-evaluate, cope, and error-corrections ("That's okay . . . Even if I make an error I can go slowly") (p. 23)

The results of research that investigated this procedure has been somewhat inconsistent. Bornstein and Quevillon (1976) reported positive and lasting effects after they trained hyperactive youngsters to stay on-task. But two other studies failed to reproduce these results (Billings & Waskik, 1985; Friedling & O'Leary, 1979). However, others have found procedures based on Meichenbaum's work to have been related to positive behavior changes (Barkley, et al., 1980; Burgio, Whitman, & Johnson, 1980; Kosiewicz, Hallahan, Lloyd, & Graves, 1982).

A relatively new use of the cognitive modification procedures first espoused by Meichenbaum and Goodman (1971) has been the development of the *learning strategies* approach at the University of Kansas Institute for Research in Learning Disabilities (KU-

IRLD). The term learning strategies is rather broad but is typically used to describe strategies that teach learners to talk their way through a problem by using sets of steps. Each strategy is composed of a set of self-instructional steps that serve as prompts for specific operant responses or covert responses. These steps then prompt the learner to use specific cognitive strategies (for example, self-questioning) that have been trained previously. In addition, the learning strategies approach relies heavily on mnemonic devices to assist the learner in remembering the steps in the problem solving strategy (Ellis, et al., 1987). For example, the CAN-DO mnemonic for learning the content information of the problem solving strategy is presented in the following:

C = Create a list of items to be learned
A = Ask self if the list is complete
N = Note the main ideas from details using a tree diagram
D = Describe each component and how components relate
O = Overlearn the main parts first, supporting details last (Ellis, et al., 1987, p 7)

Learning strategies are most often designed to facilitate the acquisition, the storage, the expression, and the demonstration of the newly learned information, and they were specifically developed to apply to learning disabled adolescents. Deshler and his colleagues (Deshler, Schumaker, Lenz, & Ellis, 1984; Deshler, Warner, Schumaker, & Alley, 1983; Schumaker, Deshler, & Ellis, 1986) have reported major improvements in academic responding as a result of implementing the learning strategies approach in a series of studies at the KUIRLD. Whereas the initial studies seem to hold promise for this approach, the relative newness, the virtual absence of empirical studies performed by individuals not associated with the KUIRLD, and the apparent limited applicability to learning disabled adolescents should instill caution, at least for the time being, in the teacher who is considering using the learning strategies approach.

SUMMARY

Stimulus control procedures may be most useful when implementing a behavioral intervention program that is designed to either create new behaviors or to promote the generalization of previously acquired responses. A variety of procedures for creating stimulus control were discussed in Chapter 13, including modeling, shaping, and chaining. Each of these procedures was discussed in terms of its defining characteristics. Examples of each procedure's use were given. The factors to consider when implementing the specific procedure and the known advantages and disadvantages of each procedure were discussed. Chapter 13 concluded with a thorough discussion of generalization training, including a discussion of the different types of generalization and the different ways in which stimulus control procedures may be used to promote generalization, including such procedures as self-management.

REFERENCES

ANDERSON-INMAN, L. (1981). "Transenvironmental programming: Promoting success in the regular class by maximizing the effect of resource room assistance." *Journal of Special Education Technology, 4,* 3–12.

AYLLON, T., & AZRIN, N. H. (1968). *The token economy: A motivational system for therapy and rehabilitation.* New York: Appleton-Century-Crofts.

AZRIN, N. H., SNEED, T. J., & FOXX, R. M. (1973). "Drybed: A rapid method of eliminating bedwetting (enuresis) of the retarded." *Behavior Research and Therapy, 11,* 427–434.

BAER, D. M. (1981). *How to plan for generalization.* Austin, TX: Pro-Ed.

BAER, D. M., & FOWLER, S. A. (1984). "How should we measure the potential of self-control procedures for generalized educational outcomes?" In W. L. Heward, T. E. Heron, D. S. Hill, & J. Trap-Porter (eds). *Focus on behavior analysis in education* (pp. 145–161). Columbus, OH: Charles E. Merrill.

BAER, D. M., WOLF, M. M., & RISLEY, T. R. (1968). "Current dimensions of applied behavior analysis." *Journal of Applied Behavior Analysis, 1,* 91–97.

BAILEY, D. B., & WOLERY, M. 1984). *Teaching infants and preschoolers with handicaps.* Columbus, OH: Charles E. Merrill.

BAILEY, S. L., & LESSEN, E. I. (1984). "An analysis of target behaviors in education: Applied but how useful?" In W. L. Heward, T. E. Heron, D. S. Hill, & J. Trap-Porter (eds.), *Focus on behavior analysis in education* (pp. 162–176). Columbus, OH: Charles E. Merrill.

BANDURA, A., & MENLOVE, F. L. (1968). "Factors determining vicarious extinctions of avoidance behavior through symbolic modeling." *Journal of Personality and Social Psychology, 8,* 99–108.

BARKLEY, R., COPELAND, A., & SIVAGE, C. (1980). "A self-control classroom for hyperactive children." *Journal of Autism and Developmental Disorders, 10,* 75–89.

BECKER, W. C., & ENGELMANN, S. E. (1978). "Systems for basic instruction: Theory and applications." In A. Catania & T. Brigham (eds.), *Handbook of applied behavior analysis: Social and instructional processes* (pp. 57–92). Chicago: Science Research Associates.

BECKER, W. C., ENGELMANN, S., & THOMAS, D. R. (1975). *Teaching 2: Cognitive learning and instruction.* Chicago: Science Research Associates.

BELLAMY, G. T., HORNER, R. H., & INMAN, D. P. (1979). *Vocational habilitation of severely retarded adults.* Austin, TX: Pro-Ed.

BILLINGS, D. C., & WASIK, B. H. (1985). "Self-instructional training with preschoolers: An attempt to replicate." *Journal of Applied Behavior Analysis, 18,* 61–67.

BILLINGSLEY, F. F. (1977). "The effects of self- and externally-imposed schedules of reinforcement on oral reading performance." *Journal of Learning Disabilities, 10,* 549–559

BLANKENSHIP, C. S. (1978). "Remediating systematic inversion errors in subtraction through the use of demonstration and feedback." *Learning Disability Quarterly, 1,* 12–22.

BORNSTEIN, P. H., & QUEVILLON, R. P. (1976). "The effects of a self-instructional package on overactive preschool boys." *Journal of Applied Behavior Analysis, 9,* 179–188.

BRODEN, M., HALL, R. V., & MITTS, B. (1971). "The effect of self-recording on the classroom behavior of two eighth-grade students." *Journal of Applied Behavior Analysis, 4,* 191–199.

BROWN, L. L., & HAMMILL, D. D. (1983). *Behavior Rating Profile: An ecological approach to behavioral assessment.* Austin, TX: Pro-Ed.

BUDOFF, M., & GOTTLIEB, (1976). "Special class EMR students mainstreamed: A study of an aptitude (learning potential) x treatment interaction." *American Journal of Mental Deficiency, 81,* 1–11.

BURGIO, L. D., WHITMAN, T. L., & JOHNSON, M. R. (1980). "A self-instructional package for increasing attending behavior in educable mentally retarded children." *Journal of Applied Behavior Analysis, 13,* 443–459.

BURSUCK, W. D., & EPSTEIN, M. H. (1987). "Current research topics in learning disabilities." *Learning Disability Quarterly, 10,* 2–7.

COOPER, J. O., HERON, T. E., & HEWARD, W. L. (1987). *Applied behavior analysis.* Columbus, OH: Charles E. Merrill.

CUVO, A. J., LEAF, R. B., & BORAKOVE, L. S. (1978). "Teaching janitorial skills to the mentally retarded: Acquisition, generalization, and maintenance." *Journal of Applied Behavior Analysis, 11,* 345–355.

DESHLER, D. D., SCHUMAKER, J. B., LENZ, B. K., & ELLIS, E. S. (1984). "Academic and cognitive interventions for LD adolescents: Part II." *Journal of Learning Disabilities, 17,* 170–187.

DESHLER, D. D., WARNER, M. M., SCHUMAKER, J. B., & ALLEY, G. R. (1983). "Learning strategies intervention model: Key components and current status." In J. D. McKinney & L. Geagans (eds.), *Current topics in learning disabilities* (vol. 1, pp. 254–284). Norwood, NJ: Ablex.

EATON, M., & WITTMAN, V. (1982). "Leap ups: Acceleration of learning through increasing material difficulty." *Journal of Precision Teaching, 3*(2), 29–33.

ELLIS, E. S., LENZ, B. K., & SARBONIE, E. J. (1987). "Generalization and adaptation of learning strategies to natural environments: Critical agents." *Remedial and Special Education, 8*(1), 6–20.

EMSHOFF, J. G., REDD, W. H., & DAVIDSON, W. S. (1976). "Generalization training and the transfer of treatment effects with delinquent adolescents." *Journal of Behavior Therapy and Experimental Psychiatry, 7,* 141–144.

ENGELMANN, S., & CARNINE, D. (1982). *Theory of instruction: Principles and applications.* New York: Irvington.

ENGELMANN, S., & COLVIN, G. (1983). *Generalized compliance training: A direct-instruction program for managing severe behavior problems.* Austin, TX: Pro-Ed.

EXECUTIVE COMMITTEE OF TEACHER EDUCATION DIVISION OF COUNCIL OF EXCEPTIONAL CHILDREN (1986). "Comments on regular education initiative." *TED Newsletter* (p. 11).

FOSTER, C. D., BILLIONIS, C. S., & LENT, J. R. (1976). *Using a sanitary napkin,* Northbrook, IL: Hubbard.

FOSTER, C. D., & KEILITZ, I. (1983). "Empirical bases for program revisions of task analysis." *Journal of Special Education Technology, 6*(3), 13–23.

FOXX, R. M. (1982). *Increasing behaviors of severely retarded and autistic persons.* Champaign, IL: Research Press.

FRIEDLING, C., & O'LEARY, S. G. (1979). "Effects of self-instructional training on second- and third-grade hyperactive children: A failure to replicate." *Journal of Applied Behavior Analysis, 12,* 211–219.

GERBER, M. H. (1986). "Generalization of spelling strategies by LD students as a result of contingent imitation/modeling and mastery criteria." *Journal of Learning Disabilities, 19,* 530–537.

GLYNN, E. L., THOMAS, J. D., & SHEE, S. M. (1973). "Behavioral self-control of on-task behavior in an elementary classroom." *Journal of Applied Behavior Analysis, 6,* 105–114.

GOLD, M. W. (1976). "Task analysis of a complex assembly task by the retarded blind." *Exceptional Children, 43,* 78–84.

GRAF, S. (1980). "Remembering people a minute a day." *Journal of Precision Teaching, 1,* 31–35.

GREENWOOD, C. R., DELQUADRI, J. C., & HALL, R. V. (1984). "Opportunity to respond and student academic achievement." In W. L. Heward, T. E. Heron, D. S. Hill, & J. Trap-Porter (eds.), *Focus on behavior analysis in education* (pp. 58–88). Columbus, OH: Charles E. Merrill.

GRIMES, L. (1981). "Computers are for kids: Designing software programs to avoid problems of learning." *Teaching Exceptional Children,* 49–53.(a)

GRIMES, L. (1981). "Error analysis and error correction procedures." *Teaching Exceptional Children,* 17–20.(b)

HANSEN, C., & EATON, M. (1978). "Reading." In N. Haring, T. Lovitt, M. Eaton, & C. Hansen, (eds), *The fourth R: Research in the classroom* (pp. 41–92). Columbus, OH: Charles E. Merrill.

HARING, T. G., ROGER, B., LEE, M., BREEN, C., & GAYLORD-ROSS, R. (1986). "Teaching social language to moderately handicapped students." *Journal of Applied Behavior Analysis, 19,* 159–171.

HAWKINS, R. P. (1986). Selection of target behaviors. In R. O. Nelson & S. C. Hayes (eds.), *Conceptual foundations of behavioral assessment* (pp. 331–385). New York: Guilford Press.

HENDRICKSON, J. (1980). *Peer-mediated system: Mathematics, Part I and II.* Nashville, TN: Continental Learning Systems.

HEWARD, W. L. (1978). "How to teach a child to imitate." *The Exceptional Parent,* 50–57.

HEWARD, W. L., DARDIG, J. C., & ROSSETT, A. (1979). *Working with parents of handicapped children.* Columbus, OH: Charles E. Merrill.

HORNER, R. D. (1971). "Establishing use of crutches by a mentally retarded spina bifida child." *Journal of Applied Behavior Analysis, 4,* 183–189.

HORNER, R. D., & KEILITZ, I. (1975). "Training mentally retarded adolescents to brush their teeth." *Journal of Applied Behavior Analysis, 8,* 301–309.

HORNER, R. H., & McDONALD, R. S. (1982). "A comparison of single instance and general case instruction in teaching a generalized vocational skill." *Journal of the Association for the Severely Handicapped, 7,* 7–20.

HOWELL, K. W., KAPLAN, J. S., & O'CONNELL, C. Y. (1979). *Evaluating exceptional children: A task analysis approach.* Columbus, OH: Charles E. Merrill.

HUMPHREY, L. L., KAROLY, P., & KIRSCHENBAUM, D. S. (1978). "Self-management in the classroom: Self-imposed response cost versus self-reward." *Behavior Therapy, 9,* 592–601

HUNDERT, J., & BUCHER, B. (1978). "Pupils' self-scored arithmetic performance: A practical procedure for maintaining accuracy." *Journal of Applied Behavior Analysis, 11,* 304.

IDOL-MAESTAS, L. "Increasing the oral reading performance of a learning disabled adult." *Learning Disability Quarterly, 4,* 294–301.

JACKSON, D. A., & WALLACE, R. F. (1974). "The modification and generalization of voice loudness in a 15-year-old retarded girl." *Journal of Applied Behavior Analysis, 7,* 461–471.

JENKINS, J. R., BARKSDALE, A., & CLIFTON, L. (1978). "Improving reading comprehension and oral reading: Generalization across behaviors, settings, and time." *Journal of Learning Disabilities, 11,* 217–222.

KAUFMAN, M. J., AGARD, J. A., & SEMMEL, M. I. (1983). *Mainstreaming: Learners and their environment.* Unpublished manuscript: University of California-Santa Barbara.

KAUFFMAN, J. M., HALLAHAN, D. P., HAAS, K., BRAME, T., & BOREN, R. (1978). "Imitating children's errors can improve their ability to spell." *Journal of Learning Disabilities, 11,* 217–222.

KAZDIN, A. E. (1975). *Behavior modification in applied settings.* Homewood, IL: Dorsey Press.

KAZDIN, A. E. (1977). *The token economy: A review and evaluation.* New York: Plenum Press.

KAZDIN, A. E., & BOOTZIN, R. R. (1972). "The token economy: An evaluative review." *Journal of Applied Behavior Analysis, 5,* 343–372.

KNEEDLER, R. D., & HALLAHAN, D. P. (1981). "Self-monitoring of on-task behavior with learning disabled children: Current studies and directions." *Exceptional Education Quarterly, 2(3),* 73–82.

KOEGEL, R. L., & RINCOVER, A. (1974). "Treatment of psychotic children in a classroom environment: I. Learning in a large group." *Journal of Applied Behavior Analysis, 7,* 45–49.

KOORLAND, M. A. (1986). "Applied behavior analysis and the correction of learning disabilities." In J. K. Torgeson & B. Y. Wong (eds.), *Psychological and educational perspectives on learning disabilities* (pp. 297–328). New York: Academic Press.

KOSIEWICZ. M. M., HALLAHAN, D. P., LLOYD, J. W., & GRAVES, A. W. (1982). "Effects of self-instruction and self-correction procedures on handwriting performance." *Learning Disability Quarterly, 5(1),* 71–78.

LIBERTY, K., & WILCOX, B. (1981). "Forum: Slowing down learning." *Newsletter of the Association for the Severely Handicapped, 7(2).*

LINDSLEY, O. R. (1981). "Current issues facing

standard celeration charting." Paper presented at the Winter Precision Teaching Conference, Orlando, FL.

LINDSLEY, O. R. (1983). Keynote address at the Winter Precision Teaching Conference, Orlando, FL.

LOVITT, T. C. (1973). "Self-management projects with children with behavioral disabilities." *Journal of Learning Disabilities, 6*, 138–150.

LOVITT, T. C. (1976). "Applied behavior analysis techniques and curriculum research: Implications for instruction." In N. Harring and R. Schiefelbusch (eds.), *Teaching special children* (pp. 112–156). New York: McGraw-Hill.

LOVITT, T. C. (1977). *In spite of my resistance I've learned from children.* Columbus, OH: Charles E. Merrill.

LOVITT, T. C., & CURTISS, K. A. (1969). "Academic response rate as a function of teacher- and self-imposed contingencies." *Journal of Applied Behavior Analysis, 2*, 49–53.

MCLAUGHLIN, T. F. (1976). "Self-control in the classroom." *Review of Educational Research, 46*, 631–663.

MCGEE, G. G., KRANTZ, P. J., & MCCLANNAHAN, L. E. (1986). "An extension of incidental teaching procedures to reading instruction for autistic children." *Journal of Applied Behavior Analysis, 19*, 147–157.

MEICHENBAUM, D. H. (1977). *Cognitive-behavior modification: An integrative approach.* New York: Plenum Press.

MEICHENBAUM, D. H., & GOODMAN, J. (1971). "Training impulsive children to talk to themselves: A means of developing self-control." *Journal of Abnormal Psychology, 77*, 115–126.

MINOR, S. W., MINOR, J. W., & WILLIAMS, P. P. (1983). "A participant modeling procedure to train parents of developmentally disabled infants." *The Journal of Psychology, 115*, 107–111.

MOYER, J. R., & DARDIG, J. C. (1978). "Practical task analysis for educators." *Teaching Exceptional Children, 11*, 16–18.

NELSON, R. O., LIPINSKI, D. P., & BOYKIN, R. A. (1978). "The effects of self-recorders' training and the obtrusiveness of the self-recording device on the accuracy and reactivity of self-monitoring." *Behavior Therapy, 9*, 200–208.

O'BRIEN, T. P., RINER, L. S., & BUDD, K. S. (1983). "The effects of a child's self-evaluation program on compliance with parental instructions in the home." *Journal of Applied Behavior Analysis, 16*, 69–79.

O'LEARY, K. D., & DRABMAN, R. (1971). "Token reinforcement programs in the classroom: A review." *Psychological Bulletin, 5*, 379–398.

O'LEARY, S. G., & DUBEY, D. R. (1979). "Applications of self-control procedures by children: A review." *Journal of Applied Behavior Analysis, 12*, 449–465.

PANYAN, M. (1980). *How to use shaping.* Austin, TX: Pro-Ed.

REPP, A. C. (1983). *Teaching the mentally retarded.* Englewood Cliffs, NJ: Prentice Hall.

RIVERA, D. M., & SMITH, D. D. (1987). "Influence of modeling on acquisition and generalization of computational skills: A summary of research findings from three sites." *Learning Disability Quarterly, 10*, 69–80.

ROGERS-WARREN, A., & WARREN, S. (1980). "Mands for verbalization: Facilitating the display of newly trained language in children." *Behavior Modification, 4*, 361–382.

ROSE, T. L. (1985). "Assessment of arithmetic performance. In A. F. Rotatori & R. Fox (eds.), *Assessment for regular and special educators* (pp. 183–211). Austin, TX: Pro-Ed.

ROSE, T. L., KOORLAND, M. A., & EPSTEIN, M. H. (1982). "A review of applied behavior analysis interventions with learning disabled children." *Education and Treatment of Children, 5*, 41–58.

ROSE, T. L., LESSEN, E. I., & GOTTLIEB, J. (1982). "A discussion of transfer of training in mainstreaming programs." *Journal of Learning Disabilities, 15*, 162–165.

ROSENBAUM, M. S., & DRABMAN, R. S. (1979). "Self-control training in the classroom: A review and critique." *Journal of Applied Behavior Analysis, 12*, 467–485.

SAILOR, W., & GUESS, D. (1983). *Severely handicapped students: An instructional design.* Boston: Houghton Mifflin.

SANTOGROSSI, D. A., O'LEARY, K. D., ROMANCZYK, R. G., & KAUFMAN, K. F. (1973). "Self-evaluation by adolescents in a psychiatric hospital school token program." *Journal of Applied Behavior Analysis, 6*, 277–287.

SCHLEIEN, S. J., WEHMAN, P., & KIERNAN, J. (1981). "Teaching leisure skills to severely handicapped adults: an age-appropriate darts game." *Journal of Applied Behavior Analysis, 14*, 513–519.

SCHUMAKER, J. B., DESHLER, D. D., & ELLIS, E. S. (1986). "Intervention issues related to the education of LD adolescents." In B.Y.L. Wong & J. K. Torgesen (eds.), *Psychological and educational perspectives and learning disabilities* (pp. 329–365). New York: Academic Press.

SIDMAN, M. (1960). *Tactics of scientific research.* New York: Basic Books.

SMITH, D. D., SMITH, J. O., & EDGAR, E. (1976). "Research and application of instructional materials development." In N. G. Haring & L. Brown (eds.), *Teaching the severely handicapped* (vol. 1). New York: Grune & Stratton.

SNELL, M. E., (ed. 1983). *Systematic instruction of the moderately and severely handicapped* (2nd ed.) Columbus, OH: Charles E. Merrill.

SPOONER, F. (1984). "Comparisons of backward chaining and total task presentations in training severely handicapped persons." *Education and Training of the Mentally Retarded, 19,* 15–22.

SPOONER, F., LEE, C. R., & SPOONER, D. (1984). "Comparisons of total task and modified backward chaining: Backward chaining with leap-aheads." In R. P. West, & K. R. Young (eds.), "Precision teaching: Instructional decision making, curriculum and management, and research." Proceedings from the National Precision Teaching Conference. Park City, UT: Utah State University.

SPOONER, F., & SPOONER, D. (in press). "A review of chaining techniques: Implications for future research and practice." *Education and Training of the Mentally Retarded.*

SPOONER, F., WEBER, L. H., & SPOONER, D. (1983). "The effects of backward chaining and total task presentation on the acquisition of complex tasks by severely retarded adolescents and adults." *Education and Treatment of Children, 6,* 401–420.

SPRAGUE, J. R., & HORNER, R. H. (1984). "The effects of single instance, multiple instance, and general case training on generalized vending machine used by moderately and severely handicapped students." *Journal of Applied Behavior Analysis, 17,* 273–278.

STEVENS, K. B., & SCHUSTER, J. W. (1987). "Effects of a constant time delay procedure on the written spelling performance of a learning disabled student." *Learning Disability Quarterly, 10,* 9–16.

STOKES, T. F., & BAER, D. M. (1977). "An implicit technology of generalization." *Journal of Applied Behavior Analysis, 10,* 349–367.

STOKES, T. F., BAER, D. M., & JACKSON, R. (1974). "Programming the generalization of a greeting response in four retarded children." *Journal of Applied Behavior Analysis, 7,* 599–610.

STOKES, T. F., FOWLER, S. A., & BAER, D. M. (1978). "Training preschool children to recruit natural communities of reinforcement." *Journal of Applied Behavior Analysis, 11,* 285–303.

STOWITSCHEK, J. J., & STOWITSCHEK, C. (1979). "Evaluating handwriting performance: The student helps the teacher." *Journal of Learning Disabilities, 12,* 203–206.

STRIEFEL, S. (1974). *Behavior modification: Teaching a child to imitate.* Austin, TX: Pro-Ed.

STRIEFEL, S. (1981). *How to teach through modeling and imitation.* Austin, TX: Pro-Ed.

TEST, D. W., & ROSE, T. L. (1987). "A review of applied behavior analysis interventions with handicapped adolescents." Manuscript submitted for publication.

VAN HOUTEN, R. (1979). "Social validation: The evolution of standards of competency for target behaviors." *Journal of Applied Behavior Analysis, 12,* 581–591.

WRESTLING, D. L., KOORLAND, M. A., & ROSE, T. L. (1981). "Characteristics of superior and average special education teachers." *Exceptional Children, 48,* 357–363.

WHALEY, D. L., & MALOTT, R. W. (1971). *Elementary principles of behavior.* Englewood Cliffs, NJ: Prentice-Hall.

WILCOX, B., & BELLAMY, G. T. (1982). *Design of high school programs for severely handicapped students.* Baltimore: Paul H. Brookes.

WILSON, P. G., GEID, D. H., PHILLIPS, J. F., & BURGIO, L. D. (1984). Normalization of institutional mealtimes for profoundly retarded persons: Effects and noneffects of teaching family-style dining. *Journal of Applied Behavior Analysis, 17,* 189–201.

ZANE, T., WALLS, R., & THVEDT, J. (1981). Prompting and fading guidance procedures: Their effect on chaining and whole task teaching strategies. *Education and Training of the Mentally Retarded, 16,* 125–135.

chapter 14

Punishment

It is difficult to imagine a setting in which punishment is not employed at one time or another. Parents use various forms of punishment to guide their children's behavior. For example, a father may apply mild social censure, such as a verbal reprimand, to the misbehavior of a child who repeatedly attempts to touch a freshly painted wall. Similarly, teachers use varying forms of punishment in the classroom. A teacher may ask a student to leave the classroom for disobeying requests to remain quiet. Regardless of the form punishment takes, the intent is always the same—to decrease inappropriate behavior. Thus, *punishment* refers to either the presentation of an aversive event or the removal of a reinforcing event, which is contingent upon a certain behavior in an attempt to decrease the probability of that behavior occurring in the future.

As with reinforcement, two types of punishment are commonly used—positive and negative. *Positive punishment* requires that an aversive stimulus be presented or added to the environment (see Cell 2, Table 14.1). Related to positive punishment are such procedures as aversive conditioning, verbal reprimands, physical reprimands, and overcorrection. In the second type of punishment, *negative punishment,* a reinforcing stimulus is removed from the environment or the offender is removed from the reinforcing situation (see Cell 3, Table 14.1). Two common negative punishment procedures that have proven useful in managing behavior, *response cost* and *time-out,* are discussed in this chapter. This chapter is divided into two sections. The first section overviews positive punishment. The second section introduces response cost and time-out which are two common examples of negative punishment. Before punishment is discussed, however, this chapter introduces aversive conditioning procedures.

TABLE 14.1   Overview of the Types of Reinforcement and Punishment When a Stimulus is Either Presented or Removed After a Response

Operation Following a Response	TYPE OF STIMULUS	
	Reinforcing Stimulus	Aversive Stimulus
Presented	1 — Positive Reinforcement	2 — Positive Punishment
Removed	3 — Negative Punishment	4 — Negative Reinforcement

Aversive Conditioning

In *aversive conditioning* a student who makes an inappropriate response is punished by the presentation of a negative stimulus. Thus, she or he might receive a lower grade on a spelling test by failing to correctly spell words that have been practiced. Or a student with severe handicaps who incorrectly assembles a microscope may be reprimanded by an employer or supervisor. Aversive stimuli may be classified as either unconditioned or conditioned. These classifications are important because they help us to understand how a stimulus functions to decrease responses.

Unconditioned aversive stimuli refer to a class of stimuli that are inherently aversive, and, when presented following a response, serve to decrease the likelihood of that response in the future. Typically, these stimuli include shock, loud noises, physical assault (for example, spankings), and extreme heat and cold.

Numerous examples may be given of the use of unconditioned aversive stimuli in the classroom. For instance, Luce, Delquadri, and Hall (1980) required elementary school students with severe emotional disturbance to exercise after a verbal or aggressive response. The exercise routine, which required the students to stand up and sit down on the floor 5 to 10 times contingent on an inappropriate behavior, was found to dramatically decrease the inappropriate responses.

Blount, Drabman, Wilson, and Stewart (1982) reduced with a punishment procedure the percent of time two women with profound mental retardation, ground their teeth (referred to as *bruxism*). For the 32-year-old woman, grinding typically took place while she was in or around her bed, whereas the 16-year-old woman ground her teeth while working at a table. On the average, the two women, a 32-year-old and a 16-year-old, ground their teeth 63 percent and 67 percent of the time respectively. They were observed prior to implementation of an "icing" procedure. The icing procedure consisted of a brief tactile application of an ice cube to the cheeks, chin, and under the chin when the grinding occurred. Three 15-minute icing periods and two 5-minute generalization periods were observed 5 days per week. At the conclusion of the 6 month program both women had reduced their teeth-grinding by approximately 90 percent of the time or more. Furthermore, bruxism decreased dramatically during generalization periods.

Conditioned aversive stimuli refer to classes of stimuli that acquire their aversive properties from being paired with stimuli that are already aversive (that is, unconditioned aversive stimuli). This type of stimulus typically includes verbal reprimands (such as exclaiming, "No!") paired with an unconditioned aversive stimulus (such as a spanking). In the classroom, for example, reprimands and statements of disapproval are made to reduce students' playing, being out of their seats, or disrupting others during instructional lessons. Disruptive student behavior can often be decreased or eliminated by saying "No" after each instance of disruptive behavior (Hall, Fox, Willard, Goldsmith, Emerson, Owen, Davis, & Porcia, 1971).

Aversive stimuli reduce behavior by being produced (presented) when the target person behaves inappropriately. Unfortunately, this type of stimuli, especially verbal reprimands, are incorrectly presumed to have general utility. For example, a teacher might presume that correcting a student's behavior by verbally directing it would result in reducing the behavior. In a classic example, Madsen, Becker, Thomas, Koser, and Player (1970) tried such a procedure by using "Sit down!" commands as a consequence for students standing and being out-of-seat. Rather than decreasing these behaviors, the reprimands increased the frequency of standing, and, hence, served as a positive reinforcer for one of the behaviors they were designed to suppress.

Summary. In applied behavior analysis several forms of punishment have been developed based upon whether or not aversive stimuli are presented. Some of the techniques used are familiar because of their widespread use, such as verbal reprimands. The basic punishment paradigm used for weakening an inappropriate response is to follow it by an aversive stimulus, either unconditioned or conditioned. In all cases the punisher is defined by its effectiveness in decreasing the occurrence of a given response.

INTRODUCTION TO POSITIVE PUNISHMENT

Positive punishment refers to any procedure used to decrease responding by adding or presenting an aversive stimulus to the environment. Three basic positive punishers are commonly used: (a) verbal punishers, (b) physical punishers, and (c) punishers that require students to practice appropriate forms of behavior.

Verbal Punishers

Verbal statements, including reprimands, warnings, disapproval, and saying, "No," are widely used to reduce behavior in applied settings. Such statements are frequently exchanged between teachers and students, parents and children, spouses, friends, siblings, and enemies. Although verbal statements may act as punishers, they may also have op-

posite or transitory effects until paired with other aversive consequences. Interestingly, research findings have indicated that reprimands that are presented quietly and privately to students, rather than loudly and publicly, have sustained reductive effects on disruptive behavior (O'Leary, Kaufman, Kass, & Drabman, 1970). Until recently, little was known about the true effects of reprimands. The results of two classic studies by Becker and his colleagues (Thomas, Becker, & Armstrong, 1968; Madsen et al., 1970) suggested that reprimands did not naturally serve as effective punishers when used in classroom settings. However, Van Houten, Nau, Mackenzie-Keating, Sameoto, and Colavecchia (1982) found that verbal reprimands delivered with eye contact and a firm grasp of the offender's shoulders reduced behavior to a greater extent than did verbal reprimands delivered without these accompanying behaviors.

Location has also been shown to influence the effectiveness of reprimands. Thus, Van Houten et al. (1982) demonstrated that reprimands delivered from one meter away were more effective than reprimands delivered from seven meters away. Also, the effects of reprimands have been shown to generalize to nonreprimanded students. For example, in the final of a series of studies completed by Van Houten and his colleagues, reprimands delivered to one pair of students reduced not only the disruptive behavior of the target pair but also that of a second pair of disruptive students.

Other forms of verbal punishers have been proven effective in reducing inappropriate behavior. Threats, for example, often signal that an aversive consequence will be presented if certain target behavior(s) are not discontinued. For example, Schutz, Rusch, and Lamson (1979) sought to reduce the aggressive behavior of three adults who participated in a community-based, competitive employment training program. As illustrated in Figure 14.1, each employee was verbally abusive to her co-workers and supervisors several times a day for many weeks. As part of their

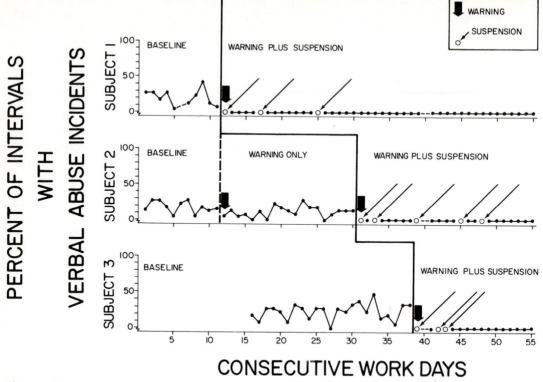

Figure 14.1
Source: From Schutz, Rusch, and Lamson, 1979.

training program, the authors sought to reduce verbal abuse in advance of competitive employment. To identify a behavior management program for the employees that would approximate the employment setting, potential employers were asked how they managed similar behavior on the job. The employers indicated that they would verbally warn or reprimand their employees once; if the target behavior occurred again, they would ask them to leave the premises.

Based on this information, verbal threats in the form of warnings were presented to two of the participants. They were told that they would be "fired for the day" if they verbally abused a fellow worker or supervisor. Only one participant (see Figure 14.1, top panel) was sent home; the other participant was similarly warned without being sent

home. As shown in Figure 14.1, verbal threats were more effective after the promised consequences were delivered. Ultimately, all three participants stopped verbally abusing their co-workers and supervisors after they had been threatened and "fired for the day."

Readily available and easy to use, verbal punishers serve an important function in our society, by controlling inappropriate behavior. Often such punishers are introduced to prevent behavior that may result in more intrusive forms of punishment. For example, parents verbally punish their children for straying too close to the street so that the inappropriate behavior, straying toward the street, comes under the control of verbal punishers rather than physical punishers, for example, being hit by a passing motorist.

A primary limitation of verbal punishers is

their inconsistent effects on behavior. Since most verbal threats used in everyday life are not backed by unconditioned aversive consequences they lose their effectiveness (Kazdin, 1971; Phillips, 1968; Phillips, Phillips, Fixsen, & Wolf, 1971). Thus, over time verbal punishers that are not occasionally backed up have been shown to serve no function, as is the case in classrooms where teachers rely almost solely upon verbal disapproval (White, 1975). To improve the effectiveness of verbal punishers, other behavior management techniques should be considered. (See Chapter 15, "Decreasing Behavior Using Positive Reinforcement and Stimulus Control.")

Physical Punishers

Even though punishers have been shown to effectively change behavior, a number of difficult questions remain unresolved as to the generality of their effectiveness and side effects associated with their use. Physical punishers, such as shock, have been used to control a wide range of behavior, including smoking (Powell & Azrin, 1968), drinking (Wilson, Leaf, & Nathan, 1975), vomiting (Kohlenberg, 1970; Linscheid & Cunningham, 1977), self-injury (Lovaas & Simmons, 1969), and sneezing (Kushner, 1968). In every case the target behavior has been reduced rapidly. The procedure, however, is painful and usually is not used until alternative procedures have proven unsuccessful. For example, Linscheid and Cunningham (1977) attempted to eliminate chronic ruminative vomiting in a 9-month-old infant who was hospitalized with severe weight loss, malnutrition, and secondary medical complications, behaviors judged to be potentially life threatening by a pediatric staff.

Initial efforts to reduce the vomiting included thickening the infant's food and continuous attention by the mother. Subsequently, shock was delivered at 0.5 second intervals when a ruminating sequence was observed beginning. The shock was terminated when the ruminating ceased. The intensity of the shock caused a startle response and produced fussing but without eliciting crying. As a result of treatment, ruminating dropped from a 5-day baseline average of 114 incidents to a single instance 3 days after shock was introduced. To facilitate generalization, and help the infant to abstain from vomiting in settings beyond the specific treatment situation and in the presence of individuals other than the person administering the shock, the treatment location and the individuals interacting with the baby were systematically varied. Generalized reductions in vomiting resulted in the infant gaining weight, and progressing developmentally. The infant was discharged from the hospital, and a follow-up evaluation almost a year later indicated that the behavior remained reduced.

Although shock has been shown to be the most effective aversive procedure studied in laboratory (Azrin & Holz, 1966) and applied settings, it is viewed as the most socially unacceptable among alternative procedures to reduce inappropriate behavior (Kazdin, 1980). Because of the difficulties associated with administering shock (that is, the use of special equipment, the ethical objections, and the availability of other potentially effective physical punishers) the procedure is used only rarely. These rare cases primarily consist of situations that warrant extreme procedures, such as instances in which severe physical harm or death may otherwise result.

The role of physical punishers in the classroom has also generated controversy and discussion in recent years. Corporal punishment (spanking, paddling, and slapping) is one means of reducing student behavior in the classroom. Although the legal foundation for the use of corporal punishment has been affirmed by the United States Supreme Court, its application by school personnel is not justified as a method of reducing student behavior. Not only can spanking and paddling be easily abused and result in injury, but the person who spanks will be reinforced and may unduly expand his or her criteria for administering punishment to include less severe student behavioral incidents. Furthermore, the emotional side effects can result in the students failing to perform appropriately in the presence of certain other students or school personnel. Because other behavior management procedures, such as directly reinforcing incompatible, appropriate behavior, have been shown to be effective, these alternatives should be advocated first, before physical punishment.

A number of physical punishers, besides shock and corporal punishment, have been effective in reducing inappropriate behavior. These include tickling, the presentation of aromatic ammonia, and the contingent use of lemon juice. Greene and Hoats (1971) reported two cases where aversive tickling was used to reduce self-destructive head-banging and a variety of attention getting behaviors, including aggression. Self-destructive head-banging, which lasted as long as 90 minutes during tantrum-like episodes, were displayed by a 13-year-old girl with mental retardation. These episodes occurred at least once a day and resulted in reddening and swelling of the girl's cheeks and temples.

[Greene and Hoats] reduced the head-banging behavior by setting up a contingency between each head-banging occurrence and the aversion tickling procedure (Green & Hoats, 1971, p. 390). The tickling procedure involved approaching the girl from the rear and tickling her forcefully beneath the arms in a serious and deliberate fashion. Figure 14.2 shows the effects of the aversive tickling upon the frequency of head-banging. Although some increase above her baseline rate was observed for two sessions following the introduction of the tickling contingency, the girl's self-destructive episodes eventually declined.

The second subject was also a 13-year-old girl with mental retardation. In addition, she was also blind. This girl displayed a variety of problem behaviors including pinching, scratching, biting, hitting, pulling hair, banging on walls, urinating on the floor, and pretending to have seizures. Using procedures similar to those described for head-banging, Green and Hoats applied tickling for approximately 3 to 5 seconds. Figure 14.3 displays the results of this procedure on the various misbehaviors. As illustrated in Figure 14.3, the misbehaviors decreased in number as a result of treatment; however, they were not eliminated.

Tanner and Zeiler (1975) tried punishing self-injurious behavior using aromatic ammonia. The subject in their investigation was a 20-year-old woman diagnosed as autistic who slapped herself repeatedly. Although shock had been used a year previously to eliminate

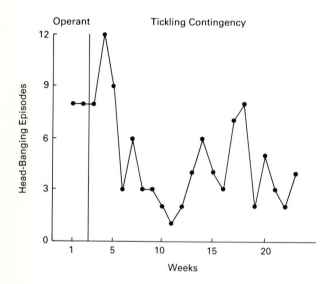

Figure 14.2 The Effect of Aversive Tickling upon the Frequency of Head-Banging Behavior. The elevation of rate during the 17th and 18th weeks was apparently related to a painful dental problem.

Source: From Greene & Hoats, 1971, p. 390.

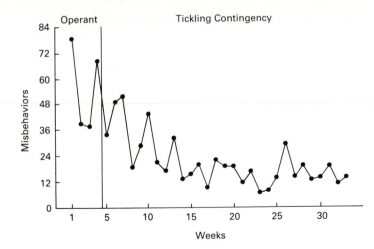

Figure 14.3 The Effect of Aversive Tickling upon the Frequency of Misbehavior.
Source: From Greene & Hoats, 1971, p. 390.

her slapping, this behavior gradually reappeared to such an extent she was slapping herself an average of 34 times per minute. Other attempts to reduce her self-injurious slapping, including restraining her to a chair, having her wear a helmet, and changing her prescribed medication, also met with limited success.

In a further effort to reduce this woman's slapping, aromatic ammonia was tried. Although its fumes were considered unpleasant, they produced no lasting ill effects when used in a diluted form (Goodman & Gilman, 1965). (The fumes from household ammonia, in contrast, are destructive to the nasal mucosa.) The relative safety of ammonia capsules, their cost (approximately 3 cents per capsule), and the convenient size recommended their use by all educational personnel associated with this woman. Tanner and Zeiler believed that if all staff members concealed capsules on their person, the woman would not be able to discriminate between those carrying the capsules and those who did not, thus extending their general effectiveness.

Figure 14.4 displays the results of the punishment procedure, which consisted of crushing a capsule and placing it under the woman's nose when she slapped herself. The ammonia was withdrawn when the woman discontinued slapping. The rate of slapping

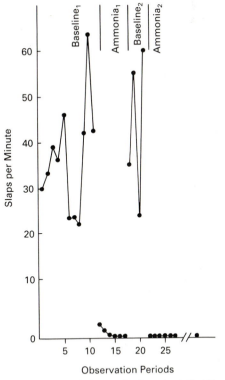

Figure 14.4 A Record of an Autistic Woman's Face Slapping during Experimental Sessions under Baseline and Punishment Conditions.
Source: From Tanner & Zeiler, 1975, pp. 53–57.

decreased immediately upon application of the ammonia and eventually ceased during the last three sessions of the Ammonia 1 phase. Returning to Baseline 2 resulted in a complete return to Baseline 1 slapping levels, suggesting that the ammonia capsules were effective. Their effectiveness was further confirmed when the capsules were reintroduced in the Ammonia 2 phase. Unfortunately, slapping outside the experimental sessions was not eliminated *because personnel used the ammonia capsules inconsistently.*

Sajwaj and his colleagues at the University of Mississippi Medical Center (Sajwaj, Libet, & Agras, 1974) eliminated life-threatening rumination in a 6-month-old infant by squirting a small amount of lemon juice into her mouth whenever rumination or its precursors were detected. A 10-second, whole-interval observation and recording procedure was used to measure the percent of ruminating intervals. As in the Linscheid and Cunningham (1977) study reported previously, weight gain was also measured. Figures 14.5 and 14.6 display the results of the lemon juice procedure. As

can be seen from Figure 14.5, squirting 5 cc to 10 cc of lemon juice into the infant's mouth with a 30 cc medical syringe as soon as vigorous tongue movements (such as thrusts) were detected, eventually resulted in low rumination levels.

Sandra, the infant in the Sajwaj et al. study, continued to gain weight. At the time of her discharge from the hospital she weighed about 12 lb and 5 oz, a 54 percent increase over her pretreatment weight. Sajwaj et al. also reported that

concurrent with the reduction of rumination and with the increase of weight, changes in other behaviors were observed in the hospital. Sandra became more attentive of adults around her, smiling appeared, and she began grabbing at objects near her. Babbling also appeared to increase. During the follow-up visits, it was evident that motor, social, and speech development had continued. The *Denver Developmental Screening Test* and the *Vineland Social Maturity Scale*, given 10 months after discharge, when Sandra was about 19 months old, indicated only a slight developmental delay. (p. 561)

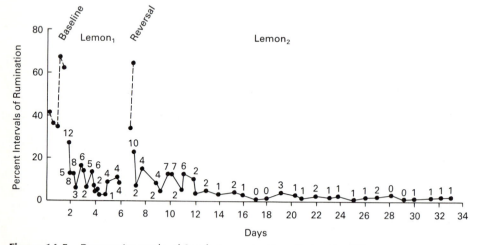

Figure 14.5   Percent intervals of Sandra's rumination during the 20-min postfeeding periods during baseline (BL), lemon-juice therapy periods (LEMON), and brief cessation of therapy (RV). The numbers over the data points refer to the number of applications of lemon juice after each feeding session.

Source: From Sajwaj, Libet, & Agras, 1974, p. 560. Copyright 1974 by the Society for the Experimental Analysis of Behavior, Inc.

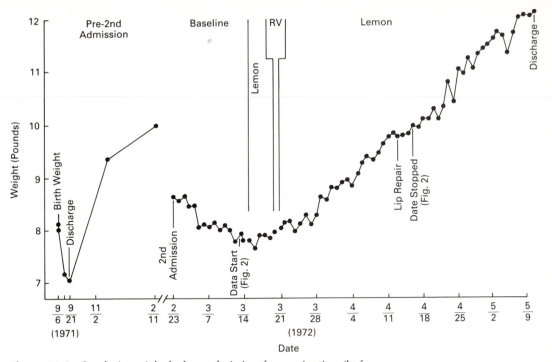

Figure 14.6 Sandra's weight before admission for rumination (before second admission), during baseline before lemon-juice therapy, during lemon-juice therapy (LEMON), and during brief cessation of therapy (RV). Data shown in Figure 1 were obtained between March 13 and April 16, 1972.

Source: From Sajwaj, Libet, & Agras, 1974, p. 561. Copyright 1974 by the Society for the Experimental Analysis of Behavior, Inc.

Punishment through Practice

Discouraging inappropriate behavior while encouraging appropriate behavior is commonly referred to as *overcorrection*. Overcorrection, which combines verbal reprimands, verbal instruction, and manual guidance (if necessary), requires that an offender overcorrect his or her misbehavior. Two types of overcorrection have been reported. There is "*restitutional overcorrection,* in which the individual restores a disturbed setting or situation to a state vastly improved from that existing prior to the disruption, and *positive practice overcorrection,* requiring that the individual practice appropriate modes of responding several times following inappropriate be-

havior" (Rusch & Close, 1976, p. 32). Essentially, both forms of overcorrection may be used concurrently to discourage inappropriate behavior and encourage appropriate behavior.

Overcorrection procedures combine a number of behavior management procedures, which singly or in combination may bring about behavior change. For example Epstein, Doke, Sajwaj, Sorrell, and Rimmer (1974) advocated use of the following procedures (a) telling the student that he or she misbehaved, (b) stopping the ongoing activity, (c) providing systematic verbal instructions, (d) forcing practice of described forms of the behavior, and (e) returning the student to his or her appropriate activity.

Agosta, Close, Hops, and Rusch (1980) decreased the percent of intervals a 37-month-old child bit and mouthed his left hand, which had resulted in reddening and had caused callouses in the area between the thumb and the index finger. Using a multiple-baseline design to evaluate the effects of overcorrection, the authors found that overcorrection led to reductions in both biting and mouthing during two separate periods in a preschool setting. Overcorrection consisted of

reprimanding the [student] immediately upon biting and mouthing (i.e., "Tom, don't bite your hand"). After the reprimand, he was given these instructions: "Now, go to the bathroom and brush your teeth." As was the case throughout the entire study, once instructions were given, the [teacher] waited approximately 3 seconds for compliance. Noncompliance resulted in prompts and/or manual guidance so that the [student] inevitably followed the instructions. In the bathroom, the [teacher] took a toothbrush that had been soaked in an oral antiseptic [Listerine] and presented it to the (student) with these instructions, "Brush your teeth." After 2 minutes had elapsed, the [teacher] instructed the [student] to "Put the toothbrush down." The second component of the training sequence was then begun with the instructions, "Now, Tom, wash your hands." The [teacher] engaged the subject in handwashing, including soaping, rinsing, and toweling for 2 minutes. The [student] was then returned to the setting in which the hand biting and mouthing had been observed. Once in that setting, training was then begun with the instructions, "Now, let me show you something you can do with your hands. Take the pegs from the peg-board and put them in the bowl." The pegboard was a blue 5 cm x 15 cm square with holes to fit any one of 24 plastic pegs of varying color. They were small enough so that they could be grossly manipulated by either of the subject's hands. This activity was modeled for the [student] as the instructions were given. This activity continued for 2 minutes, after which the [subject] was returned to whatever activity he was engaged in at the time biting and mouthing was observed. If, at any time during the overcorrection sequence, the problem behavior was again observed, the entire procedure was begun anew. The combined proce-

dure lasted between 6 and 8 minutes. (Agosta et al., 1980, p. 8)

Although the overcorrection procedure greatly reduced the child's hand biting and mouthing in both preschool periods, the behavior was never reduced to a zero level in the initial overcorrection phase. A reversal and reintroduction of overcorrection established unequivocally that reduction in the self-abusive behavior was attributable to the overcorrection. Thus, when the overcorrection procedure was used throughout the school day, the behaviors were reduced to zero during the instruction period for the remainder of the study.

Generalization across settings from preschool to home was not evident in the Agosta et al. study. However, the authors suggested that such generalization might occur if the parents become involved. For example, after having learned to apply the intervention strategy in the school, the parents could have tried the same procedures in the home setting, thereby increasing the probability of generalization (Stokes & Baer, 1977).

The previous example illustrates how the following overcorrection components, separately and in combination, can account for dramatic behavioral change: (a) feedback (telling the person he or she behaved inappropriately), (b) time-out (stopping the person's ongoing activity), (c) developing compliance (providing systematic verbal instructions and requiring practice of desired forms of appropriate behavior), and (d) negatively reinforcing appropriate behavior by returning the person to a previous, ongoing activity.

Restitutional overcorrection does not require teaching appropriate forms of behavior but does require that (a) all objects (such as furniture) within the immediate area of the disruption be straightened, but not merely the originally disturbed objects; (b) *all* persons present must receive an apology in addition to the victim of the social misbehaviors; (c) a thorough cleansing of the mouth with an oral antiseptic following unhygienic oral contacts,

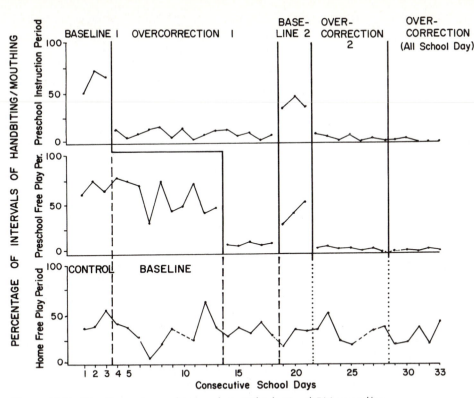

Figure 14.7 The Percentage of Intervals in Which Hand Biting and/or Mouthing was Observed during Each Observational Period. Arrows indicate periods in which agreement checks were made.

Source: From Agosta et al., 1980, p. 9. Reprinted by permission.

such as biting people or chewing objects; (d) wounds be cleansed and medicated after various forms of aggression which have resulted in injury; and (e) a period of quiet time be reserved following commotions, such as shrieking or screaming.

Various types of disruptive behavior have been reduced or eliminated through overcorrection. Overcorrection has been used to provide (a) household orderliness training in instance where objects have been rearranged or disturbed, (b) social reassurance training in the form of an apology when someone has annoyed or frightened others, (c) oral hygiene training for self-inflicted oral infections, such as the example described previously, (d) medi-

cal attention training to care for the effects of aggression, and (e) training for quiet behavior (bedrest) in cases of agitation (Foxx & Azrin, 1973).

In each of the applications cited here, verbal instructions and graduated guidance were typically used to insure that the offender performed the desired restitutional movements. Physical guidance was used only as needed until the person began to perform the movements based on verbal instructions alone. Verbal instructions, in turn, were discontinued when the offender performed the correct behavior(s) independently.

Positive practice overcorrection has been reported to successfully reduce inappropriate behavior and teach alternative forms of behavior. For example, Azrin and Foxx (1971) developed a procedure that rapidly taught nine persons who were profoundly mentally retarded to remain continent. The features of the procedure included: artificially increasing the frequency of the subjects' urinations, positively reinforcing correct toileting, delaying any response from the teacher when there had been "accidents," shaping independent toileting, and requiring cleanliness training. Other important examples of positive practice overcorrection include eliminating self-stimulation (Azrin, Kaplan, & Foxx, 1973) and sprawling on the floor (Azrin & Wesolowski, 1974).

Azrin & Powers (1975) extended the use of positive practice overcorrection to the management of classroom disturbances. Six boys, aged 7 to 11, participated in a six-week special summer school class for the purpose of learning to behave. Each of the students had been identified by his teacher, principal, and school psychologist as severely deficient in academic skills and extremely disruptive in the classroom.

Four separate procedures were applied in an ABCD design. During the initial condition (A), the teacher warned the boys at the start of each class to behave, reminded them when they misbehaved, and praised them for constructive classwork. During this first condition each student disrupted the classroom approximately 29 times during five 20-minute periods. Loss of recess (B) followed the first condition; the students were warned that any misbehavior would result in their having to remain in the classroom between academic periods. Although this condition reduced disruptions significantly, each student continued to disrupt the class about 11 times during the day. Finally, delayed (C) and immediate (D) positive-practice were introduced. The primary difference between *delayed* and *immediate* positive practice was that during the former condition the students practiced during the recess period; during the latter condition, the students were required to practice immediately following any disruptions. *Delayed positive practice* resulted

in a second significant drop in disruptions, decreasing to about two disruptions per day. Subsequently, the *immediate positive practice* condition resulted in fewer than two disruptions per day. The positive practice procedure consisted of the following steps: (a) the teacher asked the student to state the correct procedure for talking in class or leaving one's seat; (b) the student recited the correct procedure; (c) the student raised his hand and waited until the teacher acknowledged him by name; (d) the student asked for permission; (e) the teacher acknowledged the student had practiced correctly and told him, "Let's practice again"; and (f) the student practiced the entire procedure several times during a 5-minute period.

Utilizing the *resource consulting teacher model* (Bornstein, Hamilton & Quevillon, 1977), a 9-year-old boy who was considered behaviorally handicapped, was treated with a positive practice procedure in order to reduce his out-of-seat behavior in the classroom. Because the student and teacher lived in an isolated rural area, professional involvement required long-distance consultation. Similar to Azrin and Powers (1975), Bornstein, et al. required the student to remain in the classroom during a recess period and (a) practice reciting, upon request, the classroom rule, "Do not get out of your seat without permission," and (b) practice raising his hand and, upon being acknowledged by the teacher, asking permission to leave his seat. The results of the program clearly demonstrated the effectiveness of positive-practice.

Overcorrection procedures, which combine several mild punishment techniques, such as verbal reprimands and exaggerated training, have proven to be effective in reducing various types of misbehavior. While two major forms of overcorrection have emerged—restitution versus positive practice—these are not always combined. It appears, however, that overcorrection procedures that actively alter inappropriate behaviors and increase adaptive behaviors offer significant contributions to educational programs. Consequently, utilization of procedures such as those incorporated by Agosta et al. (1980) is encouraged.

INTRODUCTION TO NEGATIVE PUNISHMENT

Negative punishment may be accomplished by arranging a decrease in the contingent reinforcement of a response (response cost), or it may be accomplished by removal of an individual from a situation where reinforcers are available to a situation where the reinforcers are no longer available (time-out from a positive stimulus). The use of negative punishment in everyday life is quite common. The use of response cost is illustrated when a toddler has a toy removed, a child has TV privileges removed, an adolescent has his or her allowance stopped, and an adult pays a fine for driving while under the influence of alcohol. Time-out from positive reinforcement is exemplified by the same toddler being placed in a playpen, the child being sent to bed, the adolescent being "grounded" for the weekend, and the adult being placed in jail or having driving privileges removed. The remainder of this chapter provides several examples and considerations for the use of response cost and time-out.

Response Cost

Response cost is a negative punishment procedure that refers to the loss of a reinforcing stimulus. There are numerous examples of response cost in everyday life. Examples of response cost include the loss of a monetary deposit associated with rental property, the loss of part or all of a child's television viewing time, and the loss of yardage associated with playing football. Table 14.2 shows the positive reinforcer that was lost and the response that resulted in the lost reinforcer for these previous three examples.

Response cost is not always based upon money. However, response cost procedures require that some level of positive reinforcement be present in order that the individual be punished when the reinforcer is withdrawn. If the response cost procedure results in the desired behavior's reduction, then withdrawal of the positive reinforcer from the individual functions as a punisher.

There are situations whereby the loss of a reinforcer is less obvious. Often times these situations are associated with fines that are, for example, associated with speeding, penalties for stealing, or costs associated with use of a system. In the situation where fines are levied for speeding or overtime parking, for example, the civil authority may levy a fine based upon some inappropriate behavior. The levying of the fine is not the stimulus that results in a decrease in future speeding or illegal parking; rather it is the contingent loss (removal) of conditioned reinforcers that have been earned, that is, money. The time between the response and the removal of the positive stimulus during response cost may not always be immediate; in fact, in many cases it is delayed.

There are several examples in the applied behavioral literature that illustrate response

TABLE 14.2   Examples of Everyday Situations in Which Response Cost Typically Occurs.

Response	Positive Reinforcer Removed	Type of Reinforcer
Failure to clean an apartment upon departure	Money	Monetary
Failure to clean a room or obey parent's request	Television viewing time	Privilege
Off-sides, clipping, and illegal block during football	Yardage	Nonmonetary

cost that is delayed and that is based upon the removal of reinforcers that our society has identified and used as conditioned reinforcers, such as, money. For example, McSweeny (1978) reported the effect of charging a fee to consumers who used a telephone directory assistance system more than the number of times that were allowed as part of the monthly service charge. For some time, there were no changes for dialing directory assistance within the local calling area. Such services have been altered, however, due to rising costs associated with this service. Typi-

cally, consumers are now allowed a limited number of directory assistance calls per month before a charge is levied.

In 1974, Cincinnati Bell Telephone initiated charges for local area directory assistance calls in an attempt to reduce these requests and to reduce costs associated with this service. Telephone subscribers were allowed three local directory assistance calls for each telephone line per month. The subscribers were charged 20 cents each for additional local directory assistance call. Figure 14.8 shows the number of local and long-distance direc-

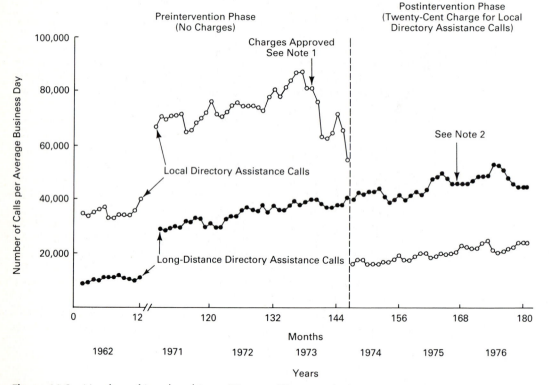

Figure 14.8 Number of Local and Long-Distance Directory-Assistance Calls Placed Per Average Business Day before and after Charges Were Introduced.

Note 1. Charges for local directory-assistance charges were approved by the Ohio Utilities Commission on August 19, 1973.

Note 2. Long-distance directory-assistance calls from another city were added to Cincinnati Bell's area. This city averaged 3,000 calls per day.

Source: From McSweeny, 1978, p. 49. Copyright 1978 by the Society for the Experimental Analysis of Behavior, Inc.

tory assistance calls placed per month over a 15-year period.

The vertical dashed line indicates when the 20 cent charge per call was imposed. The frequency of calls dropped by approximately 60,000 calls per day after the charge was introduced. The requests for directory assistance for long-distance calls, which were not fined or associated with monetary loss, were not reduced. In this example of the use of response cost the positive reinforcer that was removed was money.

Examples of the Use of Response Cost

Response cost is rarely used alone as a behavior management strategy. In fact, in most instances response cost is used in combination with other procedures that have been shown to have differential effects upon behavior in and of themselves. One such example was reported by Marholin and Gray (1976). Small businesses are faced with many personnel problems that might effectively be solved by applications of behavioral procedures. One problem is employee theft, with estimated losses reported as high as $6 billion annually (Lykken, 1974). Marholin and Gray sought to reduce such losses associated with a family-style restaurant located in Champaign, Illinois. They subtracted from six employees' salaries cash shortages that exceeded 1 percent of the total daily sales. The effect of this group response cost procedure was immediate and dramatic. Response cost was used only three times throughout the study, with a maximum cost of $18.70 per employee over approximately a two-month period. The response cost procedure was accompanied by verbal and written instructions.

Walker, Hops, and Fiegenbaum (1976) evaluated the combined effectiveness of praise, token reinforcement, and response cost in modifying the classroom behavior of five boys ranging in age from 6 to 9 years. These boys displayed high rates of disruptive classroom behaviors, such as being noisy and aggressive. The educational program included a token reinforcement system based on dispensing

points. The students could earn points for appropriate social and academic behavior, which could later be exchanged for such tangible reinforcers as model cars and airplanes, games, books, chess sets, toys, and sports equipment.

Each student could earn a maximum of 35 points per day. At the end of the day, points could be exchanged for the tangible reinforcers. These reinforcers ranged in value from 25 to 500 points. The cost contingency (response cost) involved the loss of earned tokens (points) contingent upon the occurrence of specific deviant behavior. Talking back to the teacher, talking out of turn, not attending, being out-of-seat, disturbing others, and playing with objects cost one point each. Defying the teacher cost two points, and swearing and harsh language cost three points. Fighting and throwing objects resulted in the loss of four points. When a student behaved inappropriately the teacher immediately placed a mark on a record sheet located on the student's desk beside the behavior. Thus, the child knew when points were lost, as well as what behavior resulted in response cost.

The results of the use of praise and tokens for appropriate responses and response cost for inappropriate responses were dramatic. All five students significantly increased their appropriate social and academic responding and decreased their display of inappropriate behavior. In fact, disruptive verbal statements, physical aggression, and inappropriate classroom movement were virtually eliminated. Although the results of the response cost contingency were not studied apart from praise and token reinforcement, there is ample evidence to suggest that response cost is a procedure that contributes greatly to the reduction of inappropriate behavior (Kazdin & Craighead 1972).

In a similar study, Rusch, Sowers, and Connis (1978) sought to increase the amount of time a mildly mentally retarded woman bussed tables in a restaurant setting. As in Walker et al. (1976), social reinforcement (praise), token reinforcement, and response cost were applied. Each of the three procedures, however, were introduced in summative fashion over time. That is, praise was first introduced, then praise and token reinforcement, and finally praise, token reinforcement, and lastly response cost. The simultaneous application of all three procedures was shown to be far superior to combinations of less than all three procedures.

Guidelines for Correct Application

As discussed, response cost is most often used in combination with other behavioral procedures. Because applying more than one procedure, particularly to young children, persons who are mentally retarded, and older people, may be confusing, efforts should be made to carefully explain and demonstrate how the combined procedures work. Along with verbal explanations, identify specific behavioral or academic responses and even role play the use of response cost. Always discuss the number of points, tokens, or units to be lost. When assigning values to the behaviors that will result in response cost, the seriousness and point value of the behavior should be determined jointly, when possible, by the students and other teachers.

When applying response cost *always* tell the student (a) when response cost has been used, (b) which behavior resulted in response cost, and (c) how many points were lost. Construct a visible and straightforward point delivery and feedback system. In the classroom this may be accomplished by taping 4 inch by 6 inch index cards on the student's desk. Rusch et al. (1978) used chalk scoreboards placed in clear view of the busperson in the restaurant mentioned previously. List the behaviors on the scoreboards. Tally the inappropriate responses on one matrix while using another matrix for appropriate responses. Tally cards can be placed on the student's desks in order to accomplish the same outcome in the classroom.

The ratio of fines and points is important. Several studies have used response cost where fines range from 10 to 10,000 points and the students could earn 1,000 points per day. At the other extreme, a low of 3 and 15 points may be lost and 65 points earned per day. Basically, there are no standard rules, but these guidelines should be followed: (a) Point totals should never be reduced below zero. (b) The administration of response cost should be consistent. (c) Verbal interaction between teacher and student should be kept to a minimum. (d) Teachers and students should not argue (in fact, the student should be fined for arguing).

Two final considerations in the use of response cost should be entertained in the classroom as well as in everyday occurrences. First, taking points or privileges away is quite easy. One problem that often arises when a cost contingency has been introduced is that the student, child, or employee looses all of his or her points, earnings or privileges quickly. Once all the points, earnings, or privileges have been lost, it is no longer possible for the individual to be punished.

Second, the rules associated with response cost should be made very explicit and should not be changed over time, except by concensus. The student, child, or employee should be given a clear warning of the results of his or her misbehavior. The opportunity to be reinforced for appropriate behavior must also be present. Along similar lines, reinforcers should be earned before they are removed. Do not dispense all the points to the students at the beginning of a school day noncontingently and then spend the remainder of the day punishing the students for misbehavior. Response cost is a procedure that works well when combined with healthy schedules of positive reinforcement for a variety of appropriate responses.

Summary. Response cost is a negative punishment procedure that seeks to reduce the likelihood of an inappropriate behavior through removal of reinforcing stimuli. The procedure itself is defined by the withdrawal of specific amounts of positive reinforcers contingent upon inappropriate responding. Although the procedure is common in everyday school, home, and community life, it is often applied in combination with other behavioral procedures that have acquired certain reinforcing or punishing value.

Time-Out

Time-out from positive reinforcement is a popular and effective negative punishment procedure. Indeed, time-out procedures have been applied across a variety of behavior problems, situations, and people. Technically, *time-out refers to removal of an individual from a situation in which positive reinforcers are available to a situation which contains minimal opportunity for positive reinforcement.* In actual practice the misbehaving student is removed from a reinforcing situation, such as the classroom or playground for anywhere from 3 to 30 minutes.

Recently, an effort has been made to categorize time-out according to the method that is used to deny the individual access to reinforcers. Alberto and Troutman (1982) introduced two categories, nonseclusionary time-out and seclusionary time-out. *Nonseclusionary time-out* refers to the procedure of denying the student access to reinforcers through manipulation of the setting. This procedure is common and describes instances where a student (a) is told to rest his or her head on the desk, (b) is told to turn away from a group activity, or (c) when participating students are told to not talk with a target student. In one of the more interesting applications of nonsclusionary time out, Foxx and Shapiro (1978) required students to wear a ribbon when they were eligible to receive praise and edibles and to remove the ribbon after any instance of misbehavior, resulting in a momentary loss of any opportunity to earn reinforcers. This procedure was applied to five preschoolers who were severely mentally retarded and who attended a special education classroom. After a week-long baseline period, the reinforcement condition was implemented. Each student was given a different colored ribbon to wear as a tie and received edibles and praise every few minutes for good behavior and for wearing the ribbon. When time-out was intro-

duced, the ribbon was removed and the opportunity for teacher attention and participation in activities discontinued for 3 minutes or until the misbehavior ceased. Overall, these students misbehaved from 30 percent to 40 percent of the time before application of the time-out ribbon. This nonexclusionary time-out procedure resulted in the students misbehaving only 6 percent of the time.

Another form of nonseclusionary time-out involves removing the person from the setting in which he or she is misbehaving. For example, a student may be removed from the immediate instructional setting to a corner of the classroom where he or she is asked to sit on a chair facing a corner, or the student may be placed in an area that has been partitioned off from the classroom (Baer, Rowbury, & Baer, 1973).

Seclusionary time-out refers to removing the person from the reinforcing setting altogether to a room identified for total social isolation. Parents are the most frequent users of seclusionary time-out; few parents have not sent their children to their rooms for misbehavior. The secluded room denies the student, for example, any access to potential reinforcers. Wasik, Senn, Welch, and Cooper (1969) used seclusionary time-out in an elementary classroom. Two 7-year-old girls in a second grade classroom were disruptive during academic and nonacademic sessions. The objective of time-out was to facilitate positive social and academic development. The students were placed into a quiet room for periods of five minutes. Both students improved their general social behavior during academic and nonacademic periods.

Parents' use of time-out has been reported in the applied literature since the 1960s. Waher (1969), for example, trained two sets of parents in the systematic use of differential attention and time-out to control their children's oppositional behavior. Two children, ages 5 and 6, were reported by their parents to be stubborn, negative, destructive, and noncompliant. In these two parental applications, a 5-minute time out period was used whereby the child was sent to his bedroom. If a tantrum occurred while in time-out, the time-out period was extended. The procedure proved to be very effective.

Examples of the Use of Time-Out

A critical time-out component is identifying the time period whereby reinforcement is unavailable. In the ideal situation, during this time-out period all sources of reinforcement are withdrawn. Typically, however, this ideal situation is not always attained. For example, if a student is sent to a partitioned area of the classroom, this does not preclude the target student or other students in the classroom from engaging in any number of reinforcing activities such as yelling to one another or listening to ongoing instruction. Despite this problem with nonseclusionary time-out, the results of numerous studies demonstrate this procedure to be indisputably effective. In fact, the applied literature does not contain many recent illustrations of the use of time-out because it is a long proven behavioral procedure.

One fairly recent example of the use of time-out was reported in the speech and hearing literature. The clinical management of stuttering has been advanced considerably by the application of the principles of applied behavior analysis. Stuttering has been decreased or eliminated through the contingent use of white noise (Flanagan, Goldiamond, & Azrin (1958), delayed auditory feedback (Goldiamond, 1965), verbal statements (Martin & Siegel, 1966), shock (Daly & Cooper, 1967), and response cost (Halvorson, 1971). More recently, time-out has been used. James (1981) introduced a "time-out from speaking" procedure to an 18-year-old stutterer. This procedure was based upon the notion that speaking was self-reinforcing. The general procedure of time-out from speaking involved the presentation of a stimulus contingent upon stuttering, which signaled the person to stop speaking. The period of time-out was very short (for example 10 seconds). In an earlier study by James (1976), no significant differences in the effects of duration ranging from

1 second to 30 seconds was noted. In the more recent application (James, 1981), the time-out procedure produced reliable reductions in disfluencies across all observed settings.

Ford and Veltri-Ford (1980) studied the effects of time-out from auditory reinforcement. Music was established as an auditory reinforcer for an 8-year-old boy and an 11-year-old girl who displayed inappropriate levels of verbal behavior and out-of-seat behavior, respectively. Figure 14.9 shows the percent of observations of inappropriate verbal and vocal behavior.

A multiple-baseline design was used to assess the effects of time-out from auditory reinforcement. During the intervention phase a 30-second time-out from music followed the student's inappropriate verbal behavior. Music was immediately recommenced upon termination of the target behavior, independent of the 30-second criterion. In this application of time-out from reintroduced, the results indicated a reliable relationship between contingent music and behavior.

Guidelines for Correct Application

Time-out from reinforcement assumes that removal from an ongoing activity or stimulus (for example, music) is a form of negative punishment. Thus, the setting or stimulus must be reinforcing for it to be effective. In some instances it may be important first to establish the reinforcing effects of the stimulus. For example, if the removal of music is considered for time-out, the effects of music when presented should first result in increased performance. If this precondition exists, then its withdrawal should be effective as a punisher.

The area that is used for isolating the person, whether the area is a corner of the room or a separate room altogether, must be free of reinforcing value. The area should not contain toys, pictures, or other stimuli that may inadvertently reinforce the student.

If seclusionary time-out is used, such as with aggressive behavior, it is essential that

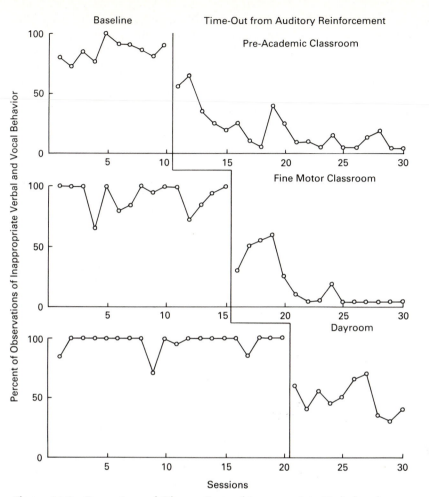

Figure 14.9 Percentage of Observations of Inappropriate Verbal and Vocal Behavior for Subject 1 in Three Locations.
Source: From Ford & Veltri-Ford, 1980, p. 30. Reprinted by permission.

the person be supervised. If a separate room is used, the room must be well lighted, well ventilated, and meet all fire code regulations. When at all possible use areas within the classroom or in the office or health room within the school. In the home, be willing to use nonseclusionary time-out for minor behavior problems. In all situations, however, the area should be dull and uninteresting. Once the time-out period is over be sure to reinforce the student as soon as possible.

Look for every opportunity to say something positive.

When considering the duration of time-out, use periods that are briefer, such as 3 and 5 minutes. White, Nielsen, and Johnson (1972) studied the duration of time-out on reducing aggression, tantrums, and self-abuse. One-minute, 15-minutes, and 30-minute time-outs were evaluated. Nielsen et al. found that each time period was effective, however, if the shorter periods followed the longer periods they were less effective. The one-minute period was the most effective if used first. There were no differences between 15-minute and 30-minute periods. As a rule, time-out periods are shorter for minor behavior problems and longer for such behaviors as aggression. Always keep in mind that if a student is secluded from instructional activities for long periods of the school day, he or she is missing important instruction and opportunities to learn, which may compound the problems being punished. For example, there have been cases reported where students have been sent home from school for misbehavior. Shier (1969) reported a student missed 26 out of 83 days of school over a 5-month period. This excessive use of time out should be avoided.

SUMMARY

Positive punishment should always be combined with a procedure that simultaneously seeks to increase the future probability of alternative forms of behavior. Rarely has a positive punisher, which requires the application of an aversive stimulus, been used in a special education setting without attention being give to simultaneously increasing an alternative behavior. For example, although early applications of restitutional overcorrection typically required students to overcompensate for misbehaving, teachers also involved students in appropriate educational behavior as part of the procedure.

This chapter presented two relatively common negative punishment procedures, response cost and time-out. Both procedures involve the removal of positive reinforcers after a response occurs. Removal of the reinforcing stimulus with corresponding decreases in responding defines the operation. In the first section of this chapter discussion centered upon the delivery of an aversive stimulus. The second section of the chapter centered upon the removal of a reinforcer. In all cases there are several issues that warrant consideration. First, there should be clear ethical standards that direct the use of punishment procedures. Indeed, punishment has been the topic of numerous litigious actions. Even the use of one of the most commonly used punishment procedures, time-out, has received extensive judicial considerations. *Wyatt* v. *Stickney* (1972) addressed the right to be free from isolation. According to *Wyatt* v. *Stickney*, if seclusionary time-out is used with persons who are mentally ill, the following guidelines must be followed:

1. The individual should not be placed in time-out for excessive periods (for example, 60 minutes) without consulting qualified mental health professionals.
2. The effects of time-out must be assessed in relation to the behavior targeted for reduction.
3. If the time-out period is continued in duration, then a written rationale of the procedure must be provided. The written rationale is in effect for only one day (24 hours) only.
4. The person placed in time-out must be supervised at all times and written records of the person's behavior while in time-out must be kept.

In a set of guidelines prepared for professionals working with mentally retarded persons, May, McAlister, Risley, Twardosz, and Coz (1976) recommended that time-out and all other forms of punishment be applied with consideration paid to reinforcing incompatible, more socially accepted behavior. Clearly, the intent of punishment is not to only suppress undesirable behavior but to also promote desirable behavior.

In addition, when applying punishment procedures there exists a strong and compelling reason for collection of data that supports its use. There are known side effects to punishment and our willingness to consider using punishment must be based upon our knowledge of these costs (for example, emotional reactions) versus the benefits (that is, the reduction of an inappropriate behavior).

Punishment has been used for centuries in our society because of its immediate impact on behavior. Over the past several decades our instructional technology, however, has developed rapidly, partly due to applied behavior analysis. Because of our developing methodology and emerging principles we must continue to ask questions relative to the effectiveness of one procedure over another. This is ever so important when considering utilizing any one of the positive or negative punishment procedures introduced in these two chapters. Finally, be imminently aware that rarely, if ever, has a single procedure been exclusively used on preferred modern behavior analysis. Typically, combinations of procedures, each possessing unique value, are applied to problems that are equally unique and complex.

REFERENCES

AGOSTA, J. M., CLOSE, D. W., & HOPS, H., & RUSCH, F. R. (1980). "Treatment of self-injurious behavior through overcorrection procedures." *Journal of the Assocation for the Severely Handicapped, 5*(1), 5–12.

ALBERTO, P. A., & TROUTMAN, A. C. (1982). *Applied behavior analysis for teachers: Influencing student performance.* Columbus, OH: Charles E. Merrill.

AZRIN, N. H., & FOXX, R. M. (1971). "A rapid method of toilet training in the institutionalized retarded." *Journal of Applied Behavior Analysis, 4,* 89–99.

AZRIN, N. H., & HOLZ, W. C. (1966). "Punishment." In W. K. Honig (ed.), *Operant behavior: Areas of research and application* (pp. 380–447). New York: Appleton-Century-Crofts.

AZRIN, N. H., KAPLAN, S. J., & FOXX, R. M. (1973). "Autism reversal: Eliminating stereotyped self-stimulation of retarded individuals." *American Journal of Mental Deficiency, 78,* 241–248.

AZRIN, N. H., & POWERS, M. (1975). "Eliminating classroom disturbances of emotionally disturbed children by positive practice procedures." *Behavior Therapy, 6,* 525–534.

AZRIN, N. H., & WESOLOWSKI, M. D. (1974). "Theft reversal: An overcorrection procedure for eliminating stealing by retarded persons." *Journal of Applied Behavior Analysis, 7,* 577–581.

BAUER, A. M., ROWBURY, T., & BAUER, D. M. (1973). The development of instructional control over classroom activities of deviant preschool children. *Journal of Applied Behavior Analysis, 6,* 289–298.

BLOUNT, R. L., DRABMAN, R. S., WILSON, N., & STEWARD, D. (1982). "Reducing severe diurnal bruxism in two profoundly retarded females." *Journal of Applied Behavior Analysis, 15,* 565–571.

BORNSTEIN, P. H., HAMILTON, S. B., & QUEVILLON, R. P. (1977). "Behavior modification by long-distance: Demonstration of functional control over disruptive behavior in a rural classroom setting." *Behavior Modification, 1,* 369–380.

DALY, D. A., & COOPER, E. B. (1967). "Rate of stuttering adaptation under two electro-shock conditions. *Behavior Research and Therapy, 5,* 49–54.

EPSTEIN, L. H., DOKE, L. A., SAJWAJ, T. W., SORRELL, S., & RIMMER, B. (1974). "Generality and side effects of overcorrection." *Journal of Applied Behavior Analysis, 7,* 385–390.

FLANAGAN, B., GOLDIAMOND, I., & AZRIN, N. (1958). "Operant stuttering: The control of behavior through response-contingent consequences." *Journal of the Experimental Analysis of Behavior, 1,* 173–177.

FORD, J. E., & VELTRI-FORD, A. (1980). "Effects of time-out from auditory reinforcement on two problem behaviors." *Education and Training of the Mentally Retarded, 15,* 299–303.

FOXX, R. M., & AZRIN, N. H. (1973). "The elimination of autistic self-stimulatory behavior by overcorrection." *Journal of Applied Behavior Analysis, 6,* 1–14.

FOXX, R. M., & SHAPIRO, S. T. (1978). "The timeout ribbon: A nonexclusionary timeout procedure." *Journal of Applied Behavior Analysis, 11,* 125–136.

GOLDIAMOND, I. (1965). "Stuttering and fluency as manipulatable operant response classes." In L. Krasner and L. P. Ullman (eds.), *Research in behavior modification.* New York: Holt, Rinehart & Winston.

GOODMAN, L. S., & GILMAN, A. (1965). *The pharmacological basis of therapeutics* (3rd ed.). New York: Macmillan.

GREENE, R. J., & HOATS, D. L. (1971). "Aversive tickling: A simple conditioning technique." *Behavior Therapy, 2,* 389–393.

HALL, R. V., FOX, R., WILLARD, D., GOLDSMITH, L., EMERSON, M., OWEN, M., DAVIS, F., & POR-

CIA, E. (1971). "The teacher as observer and experimenter in the modification of disputing and talking-out behaviors." *Journal of Applied Behavior Analysis, 4,* 141–149.

HALVORSON, J. A. (1971). "The effects on stuttering frequency of pairing punishment (response cost) with reinforcement." *Journal of Speech and Hearing Research, 11,* 560–566.

JAMES, J. E. (1976). "The influence of duration on the effects of time-out from speaking." *Journal of Speech and Hearing Research, 19,* 206–215.

JAMES, J. E. (1981). "Behavioral self-control of stuttering using time-out from speaking." *Journal of Applied Behavior Analysis, 14,* 25–37.

KAZDIN, A. E. (1971). "The effect of response cost in suppressing behavior in a pre-psychotic retardate." *Journal of Behavior Therapy and Experimental Psychiatry, 2,* 137–140.

KAZDIN, A. E. (1980). "Acceptability of alternative treatments for deviant child behavior." *Journal of Applied Behavior Analysis, 13,* 259–273.

KAZDIN, A. E., & CRAIGHEAD, W. E. (1972). "The token economy: An evaluative review." *Journal of Applied Behavior Analysis, 5,* 343–372.

KOHLENBERG, R. J. (1970). "The punishment of persistent vomiting: A case study." *Journal of Applied Behavior Analysis, 3,* 241–245.

KUSHNER, M. (1968). "The operant control of intractable sneezing." In C. D. Spielberger, R. Fox, & B. Masterson (eds.), *Contributions to general psychology.* (pp. 361–365). New York: Ronald Press.

LINSCHEID, T. R., & CUNNINGHAM, C. E. (1977). "A controlled demonstration of the effectiveness of electric shock in the elimination of chronic infant rumination." *Journal of Applied Behavior Analysis, 10,* 500.

LOVAAS, O. I., & SIMMONS, J. Q. (1969). Manipulation of self-destruction in three retarded children. *Journal of Applied Behavior Analysis, 2,* 143–157.

LYKKEN, D. T. (1974). "Psychology and the lie detector industry." *American Psychologist, 29,* 725–739.

LUCE, S. C., DELQUADRI, J., & HALL, R. V. (1980). "Contingent exercise: A mild but powerful procedure for suppressing inappropriate verbal and aggressive behavior." *Journal of Applied Behavior Analysis, 13,* 583–594.

MADSEN, C. H., BECKER, W. C., THOMAS, D. R., KOSER, L., & PLAGER, E. (1970). "An analysis of the reinforcing function of 'sit down' commands." In R. K. Parker (ed.), *Readings in educational psychology* (pp. 265–278). Boston: Allyn & Bacon.

MARHOLIN, D., II, GRAY, D. (1976). "Effects of group response cost procedures on cash shortages in a small business." *Journal of Applied Behavior Analysis, 9,* 25–30.

MARTIN, R. R., & SIEGEL, G. M. (1966). "The effects of simultaneously punishing stuttering and rewarding fluency." *Journal of Speech and Hearing Research, 9,* 466–475.

MAY, J. G., RISLEY, T. R., TWARDOSZ, S., FRIEDMAN, P., BIJOU, S. W., & WEXLER, D. (1976). *Guidelines for the use of behavioral procedures in state programs for retarded persons.* Arlington, TX: National Association for Retarded Citizens.

McSWEENEY, A. J. (1978). "Effects of response cost on the behavior of a million persons: Charging for directory assistance in Cincinnati." *Journal of Applied Behavior Analysis, 11,* 47–51.

O'LEARY, K. D., KAUFMAN, K. F., KASS, R. E., & DRABMAN, R. S. (1970). "The effects of loud and soft reprimands on the behavior of disruptive students." *Exceptional Children, 37,* 145–155.

PHILLIPS, E. L. (1968). "Achievement Place: Token reinforcement procedures in a home-style rehabilitation setting for 'pre-delinquent' boys." *Journal of Applied Behavior Analysis, 1,* 213–223.

PHILLIPS, E. L., PHILLIPS, E. A., FIXSEN, D. L., & WOLF, M. M. (1971). "Achievement Place: Modification of the behaviors of 'pre-delinquent boys within a token economy." *Journal of Applied Behavior Analysis, 4,* 45–59.

POWELL, J., & AZRIN, N. (1968). "The effects of shock as a punisher for cigarette smoking." *Journal of Applied Behavior Analysis, 1,* 63–71.

RUSCH, F. R., & CLOSE, D. W. (1976). "Overcorrection: A procedural evaluation." *The American Association for the Severely/Profoundly Handicapped, 1,* 32–45.

RUSCH, F. R., CONNIS, R. T., & SOWERS, J. (1978). "The modification and maintenance of time spent attending using social reinforcement, token reinforcement, and response cost in an applied restaurant setting." *Journal of Special Education Technology, 2,* 18–26.

SAJWAJ, T., LIBET, J., & AGRAS, S. (1974). "Lemon-juice therapy: the control of life-threatening rumination in a six-month-old infant." *Journal of Applied Behavior Analysis, 7,* 557–563.

SCHUTZ, R. P., RUSCH, F. R., & LAMSON, D. S. (1979). "Evaluation of an employer's procedure to eliminate unacceptable behavior on the job." *Community Services Forum, 1,* 4–5.

SHIER, D. A. (1969). "Applying systematic exclusion to a case of bizarre behavior" In J. D. Krumboltz & C. E. Thoresen (eds.), *Behavior counseling: Cases and techniques.* New York: Holt, Rinehart & Winston.

STOKES, T. F., & BAER, D. M. (1977). "An implicit technology of generalization." *Journal of Applied Behavior Analysis, 10,* 349–367.

TANNER, B. A., & ZEILER, M. (1975). "Punishment of self-injurious behavior using aromatic ammonia as the aversive stimulus." *Journal of Applied Behavior Analysis, 8,* 53–57.

THOMAS, D. R., BECKER, W. C., & ARMSTRONG, M. (1968). "Production and elimination of disruptive classroom behavior by systematically varying teacher's behavior." *Journal of Applied Behavior Analysis, 1,* 35–45.

VAN HOUTEN, R., NAU, P. A., MACKENZIE-KEATING, S. E., SAMEOTO, D., & COLAVECCHIA, B. (1982). "An analysis of some variables influencing the effectiveness of reprimands." *Journal of Applied Behavior Analysis, 15,* 65–83.

WAHLER, R. G. (1969). "Oppositional children: A quest for parental reinforcement control." *Journal of Applied Behavior Analysis, 2,* 159–170.

WALKER, H. M., HOPS, H., & FIEGENBAUM, E. (1976). "Deviant classroom behavior as a function of combinations of social and token reinforcement and cost contingency." *Behavior Therapy, 7,* 76–88.

WASIK, B., SENN, K., WELCH, R. H., & COOPER, B. R. (1969). "Behavior modification with culturally deprived school children: Two case studies." *Journal of Applied Behavior Analysis, 2,* 171–179.

WHITE, M. A. (1975). "Natural rates of teacher approval and disapproval in the classroom." *Journal of Applied Behavior Analysis, 8,* 367–372.

WHITE, G. D., NIELSEN, G., & JOHNSON, S. M. (1972). "Time-out duration and the suppression of deviant behavior in children." *Journal of Applied Behavior Analysis, 5,* 111–120.

WILSON, G. T., LEAF, R. C., & NATHAN, P. E. (1975). "The aversive control of excessive alcohol consumption by chronic alcoholics in the laboratory setting." *Journal of Applied Behavior Analysis, 8,* 13–26.

WYATT, V. STICKNEY, 344 F. Supp. 373, 344 F. Supp. 387 (M.D. Ala. 1972) affirmed *sub nom.* Wyatt v. Aderholt, 503 F. 2nd 1305 (5th Cir. 1974).

chapter 15

Decreasing Behavior Using Positive Reinforcement and Stimulus Control

In this chapter we consider procedures for reducing behaviors that are based on positive reinforcement and stimulus control. These procedures are alternatives among the class of punishment procedures for reducing inappropriate behaviors discussed in Chapter 14. Reinforcement and stimulus control procedures are of particular interest because they are both effective and generally accepted by most parents and professionals in special education. The reinforcement procedures include: (a) differential reinforcement of other behavior (DRO), (b) differential reinforcement of incompatible responding (DRI), (c) differential reinforcement of low-rate behavior (DRL), and (d) differential reinforcement of alternative behaviors (DRA). These procedures share in common the fact that appropriate behaviors are strengthened using reinforcement procedures and inappropriate behaviors are weakened. Stimulus control procedures focus on (a) the identification of

stimulus events that cue the problem behavior and (b) the modification of this controlling function. As a result, the target behavior is systematically selected out of the student's repertoire using differential reinforcement and stimulus control procedures.

With DRO, the student is reinforced when he or she does anything but the target behavior for a specified period of time. In DRI, the student is reinforced for doing something that is topographically incompatible with the target behavior. For example, an employee might be reinforced for working on a task which can not occur while wandering around the job site. The third procedure, DRL, reinforces the student if the individual decreases how often he or she performs the target behavior. Differential reinforcement of alternative behaviors (DRA) focuses upon reinforcing a behavior that is an alternative to but not necessarily incompatible with the behavior that is considered inappropriate. In this concluding chapter we introduce each of these four reductive procedures and provide examples of their use. In addition, we overview a procedure that may be used to identify patterns of behavior through the use of a graph called a scatter plot (Touchette, MacDonald, & Langer, 1985). A scatter plot can reveal patterns of responding and thus suggest stimuli that appear to control these patterns. This assessment technique is important because it may help to identify stimulus controls and lead to reducing the inappropriate behavior by either eliminating or altering the stimuli that control the behavior.

Differential Reinforcement of Other Behavior (DRO)

Differential reinforcement of other behavior (DRO) is a procedure in which any behavior other than the behavior targeted for reduction is directly reinforced. In DRO the target behavior is weakened relative to the other behaviors being strengthened. There are two important considerations that apply to the effective use of DRO. The first is selection of the target behavior to be weakened. The second consideration is the period of time that must elapse before the individual is reinforced. Regarding selection of the target behavior, typically the individual is allowed to perform *any other behavior* except the target behavior. For example, if a student frequently looks around the room and "fidgets" with school supplies located on his table, the teacher would differentially reinforce any other behaviors than the two target behaviors (looking around the room and fidgeting). In this example the teacher might reinforce the student for working on his assignment, for completing his assignment, or for raising his hand to ask a question. Ultimately, however, the teacher would only reinforce behavior other than the target behavior.

The second consideration important to the use of DRO is the time interval for reinforcement. The opportunity for differential reinforcement of the other behavior must be greater than the opportunity for reinforcement of the target behavior. In the case discussed above, we might have determined that the student looks around the classroom and fidgets with his supplies more than 50 percent of the time during a 60 minute academic period. If the student is reinforced every time he looks around the room or fidgets, then he is probably being reinforced once every 2 minutes. Therefore, if we want to reinforce the student for appropriate seat work instead of looking around the room, then we would have to at least reinforce him for appropriate behavior once every two minutes. After dividing a session into intervals, reinforcement can be delivered at the end of each of these intervals in which the target behavior has not occurred. Typically, the intervals are gradually lengthened until the student performs other behaviors for the entire session. In this classroom example, the 60 minute academic session would represent the full-session; the 2-minute intervals would represent the period of time that one would expect the student to be reinforced during the initial stages of the DRO. In the final DRO stage all reinforcement would come after the entire 60 minute interval.

DRO has been studied by a number of investigators, and a very broad range of behaviors have been successfully reduced. For example, rocking, lid flapping, and inappropriate hand motions were completely reduced using DRO in a study reported by Repp, Deitz, and Speir (1974). In this study, DRO was added to the use of an unsuccessful "reprimand" (that is, saying "No!") which had been used during a baseline phase. The combination of the verbal reprimand and DRO was effective after the student was reinforced as frequently for not responding inappropriately as he was for responding appropriately. In this case, the student displayed one of the target behaviors 27 times per minute. Consequently, the initial DRO interval was set at 2 seconds (60 seconds divided by approximately 30 responses per minute).

Parents and a teacher were taught to implement a DRO procedure for a 10-year-old girl with severe mental retardation (Friman,

Barnard, Altman, & Wolf, 1986). The behavior targeted for reduction was pinching. Prior to the intervention the mother had unsuccessfully used corporal punishment (spankings). At school, the teacher had attempted a program in which hot air from a hair dryer was blown into the child's face contingent on pinching. These procedures, *dangerous to the child*, had had little effect on the target behavior. During DRO at home, the child was praised and touched gently by the mother when she did not pinch for a specific time interval during a daily play session between the parent and child. Initially, DRO was set at 20 seconds, but was advanced to 10 seconds because of continued pinching. Each time the mother reinforced her daughter she recorded it on a counter. The DRO for 10 seconds resulted in an initial reduction in the target behavior. Typically, pinching did not occur during the DRO interval, but pinching did occur as the parent reached to reinforce the child after the interval of time had elapsed. It appeared that reinforcer delivery was setting the occasion for the child to pinch her mother; the mother's reaching was serving as a discriminative stimulus. Consequently, time-out and response prevention procedures were used in addition to DRO. The addition of the response prevention to the DRO procedure was most effective and was replicated by the classroom teacher during a play period at school. Response prevention involved gently holding the child's arm to her side for two minutes after the child pinched. The mother and the teacher were taught to gently hold the child's arms, using the least amount of pressure necessary.

Repp, Barton, and Brulle (1983) sought to demonstrate that DRO effects could be produced using a momentary interval criterion rather than a whole interval criterion for reinforcement. Momentary interval DRO requires that the teacher observe the student only at the end of the interval, rather than throughout the entire interval. If the student is engaged in any other behavior at the moment the interval ends, then the student is reinforced. Repp et al. (1983) found that

DRO was consistently more effective in reducing the target behaviors when the whole interval criterion was used. Figure 15.1 displays the effects of the DRO procedures. As can be seen from these data, light-gazing, head-weaving, and hand-flapping were each reduced significantly following the initial baseline phase. The bottom panel displays the use of an ABAB reversal design within the multiple-baseline design. In all cases, the target behaviors reversed to higher levels of occurrence when the whole interval DRO procedure was discontinued. In the bottom panel, the reinstatement of whole interval DRO resulted in a dramatic decrease in hand-flapping as compared to levels attained in the initial intervention phase.

In a second study with three elementary school students, momentary interval DRO was used following whole interval DRO in order to assess the ability of momentary interval DRO to maintain low levels of responding produced by whole interval DRO (Barton, Brulle, & Repp, 1986). The students were nonverbal, ambulatory, and had secondary handicaps including vision or hearing impairments. The targeted behaviors for reduction included noncompliance, head-weaving, light-gazing, hand-flapping, and finger-moving. The DRO procedure was designed so that each student initially received reinforcement from the teacher only after entire intervals of appropriate responding occurred. Whole interval DRO resulted in large reductions in the rate of responding for all six students, which was then maintained by momentary interval DRO.

Differential reinforcement of other behavior is a relatively easy procedure to administer and is considered a positive approach to changing behavior. As such, DRO should be considered a treatment of choice when the target behaviors are relatively discrete and occur fairly infrequently. Indeed, the procedure can be used to reduce and eliminate a wide range of behaviors, and it has been used with frequently occurring behavior.

However, a number of considerations apply to the use of DRO programs. First,

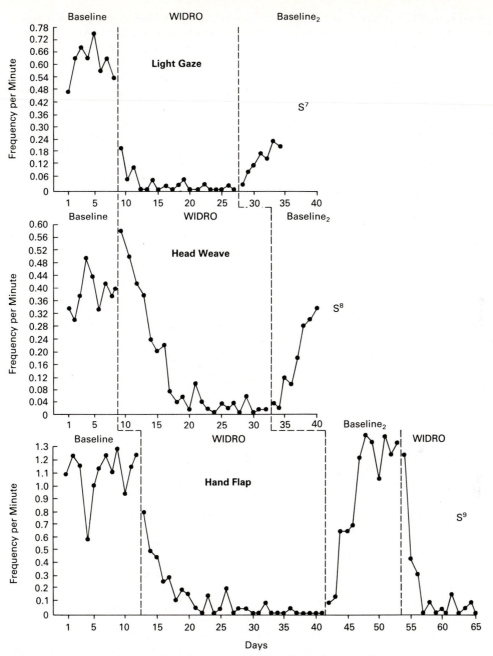

Figure 15.1 Rate of Responding during Baseline and Whole-Interval DRO (WIDRO).

Source: Taken from Barton, Brulle, & Repp, 1986, Figure 2, p. 281.

while it is possible that DRO will be sufficient to reduce or eliminate a target behavior, many studies have combined it with other intervention strategies, including verbal reprimands (Repp et al., 1974), time-out, and response prevention (Friman et al., 1986). Second, the interval size used for reinforcing other behavior responding must be considered carefully. As a rule of thumb, shorter interval lengths are best for initial reinforcement, followed by longer intervals to establish maintenance (Poling & Ryan, 1982). The interval size should be set based upon baseline levels of performance. The more frequently the behavior occurs, the shorter the initial interval length should be. Third, it appears that momentary interval DRO may be used as a maintenance strategy, particularly if it follows the use of whole interval DRO.

Differential Reinforcement of Incompatible Responding (DRI)

The differential reinforcement of incompatible responding (DRI) is a procedure whereby a response that is topographically incompatible with the target behavior is reinforced. In this case, *incompatible* refers to the physical impossibility of the target behavior and the desired behavior occurring at the same time. By strengthening one, the other is reduced. Additionally, by selecting either a socially—or educationally—appropriate incompatible behavior for strengthening, the risk of reinforcing undesirable behaviors is eliminated. For example, a student cannot simultaneously make stereotypic hand movements and play appropriately with toys (Favell, 1973); slap his face and play with a ball at the same time (Tarpley & Schroeder, 1979; or wander around a classroom while participating in an outside project (Patterson, 1965).

DRI has been used successfully with *rocking* (Baumeister & Forehand, 1971; Cone, Anderson, Harris, Goff, & Fox, 1978), *bouncing* (Cone et al., 1978), *hand-flapping* (Weisberg, Passman, & Russell, 1973) and *mouthing*

(Cone et al., 1978). One of the earliest applications of the DRI procedure was reported by Hall, Lund, and Jackson (1968). Hall et al., (1968) worked with a classroom teacher who was having difficulty with two students who were disruptive. They defined the problem behavior as behaviors that included pounding the desk with a pencil, "chewing and licking pages of books" (p. 7), moving a chair back and forth, banging a chair on the floor, blowing bubbles while drinking milk, gazing out of the window, and looking around the classroom, and making statements such as, "This is too hard," "I can't do this," and "How did you say to work it?" (p. 7).

In this particular example, studying was selected as the behavior that was topographically incompatible with the students' disruptive responses. The teacher differentially reinforced studying, the incompatible response, every 10 seconds. The 10 second intervals were cued by a classroom aide; however, these intervals could have been signaled by a second hand on a large clock or by an electronic timer. If 10 seconds elapsed and the student was studying, the teacher would move to the student's desk and make a verbal statement that commended his studying, and she would often touch or pat the student's back. DRI resulted in immediate and marked decreases in all disruptive behaviors.

Two additional examples of DRI strengthened toy play in order to reduce self-stimulation. Cone et al. (1978) taught children to toss a ball, which reduced self-stimulation. Eason et al., (1982) strengthened toy-play and suppressed rocking, hand-flapping and other self-stimulatory behaviors.

There are several considerations that must be addressed when deciding whether or not to use DRI. First, similar to DRO, reinforcement may be delivered after a predetermined period of time. DRI may also be used after a certain number of responses occur. The use of an interval period of time is easier for a teacher to administer than a criterion that focuses upon a number of responses occurring. If the teacher, for example, is responsible for 20 students, he or she would be more capable of administering a DRI program based upon time intervals than one based upon responses that would require careful monitoring. As with DRO, the schedule of reinforcement should be set so that the opportunity for reinforcement for appropriate responding is equal to or greater than the opportunity for reinforcement of the target behavior. In the Dietz et al. (1976) study, the period of reinforcement was initially set at 3 minutes and extended to 15 minutes within 12 days.

Finally, DRI does not allow the administrator to combine its use with a punishment procedure. By definition, the incompatible behavior *replaces* the target behavior. Consequently, teachers, parents, and others may wish to use this procedure instead of DRO, which has often been combined with a punishment contingency (for example, verbal reprimands, time-out, and response prevention) contingent on the behavior targeted for reduction.

Differential Reinforcement of Low Rates of Responding (DRL)

Differential Reinforcement of low rates of responding (DRL) is a procedure in which the student receives reinforcement for periods of time in which a lower frequency of responding is accomplished after a few intermediate steps or criteria are met. The student is reinforced "if the number of responses in a specified period of time is less than or equal to, a prescribed limit" (Deitz & Repp, 1973, p. 457). This "limit" is typically set at a level lower than the original baseline rate of responding. DRL is typically carried out in the context of a changing criterion design in which reinforcement follows progressively lower levels of responding once prior levels of responding have been met. Thus, the target response is "shaped" out of the student's repertoire.

DRL has been applied to individuals and to groups. For example, Deitz, Repp, and Deitz (1976) worked with a 12-year-old boy with mild mental retardation and who was considered the most disruptive student in the classroom. The behaviors in which he engaged were [a] "talking when not called upon by the teacher, [b] talking about a subject other than classwork, [c] leaving his seat, and [d] yelling at other students in the class" (p. 157). In an ABAB study, the baseline phases constituted no special treatment, whereas the intervention phases allowed the student to go to the library for 10 minutes if he emitted two or fewer disruptive responses during the class period. In the library, he was allowed to watch television, play games, read comics, or engage in similar preferred activities. The results, shown in Figure 15.2, indicate that in the two treatment phases, the student exceeded the DRL limit of two responses on only one occasion (refer to upper panel).

A second study reported by Dietz et al. (1976) dealt with a classroom of 14 students whose average age was 13 years. The students engaged in no dangerous behaviors, but the target behaviors constituted what both the teacher and the principal described as the most disruptive in school. The disruptive behaviors in which they engaged were [a] "talking aloud, [b] being out of one's assigned seat, [c] making loud noises, [d] hitting or shoving other students, and [e] throwing objects" (p. 159). An ABA design was used (refer to Figure 15.2, bottom panel), and in the second phase points were earned when the students had a disruptive rate of less than 1.3 responses per minute averaged over the subject period. The class was already on a token program, so the same tokens and back-up reinforcers were used to reinforce the lowered rates of disruptive behavior. The back-up reinforcers were activities rather than tangible items and included going to the library, reading in the classroom, playing games in the classroom, and playing supervised games outside. The class met the DRL limit on 60 percent of the days, and on the other days the disruptive behaviors were very near the criterion.

Rotholtz and Luce (1983) applied DRL to reduce gazing at the ceiling in two students with autism. The DRL procedure for the first student consisted of reinforcement following progressively lower rates of ceiling-gazing.

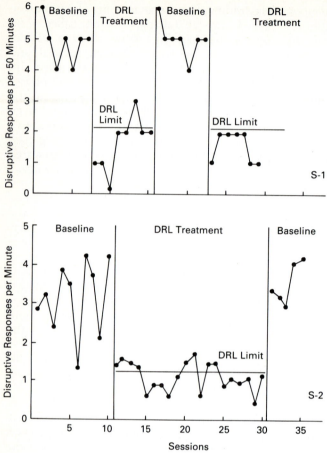

Figure 15.2 Disruptive Responses Per 50-Minute Session for S–1 (top) during Four Phases of DRL Experiment 1. During treatment, staying below the DRL limit earned S–1 10 minutes free time in the library. Disruptive responses per minute for Ss–2 (a group of 14 EMR students) during three phases of DRL experiment 2 (bottom). During treatment, staying below the DRL limit of 1.3 rpm earned Ss–2 exchangeable tokens.
Source: Deitz, Repp, & Dietz, 1976, p. 157.

These lower rates were 13 per minute, 7 per minute, and no ceiling-gazing. The first criterion, 13 per minute, was half of the initial baseline rate for this behavior. Rotholtz and Luce (1983) selected a reinforcing stimulus, playing and looking at a spinning gyroscope, that was thought to be topographically similar to the target response of ceiling-gazing which was preferred by the student. As can be seen in Figure 15.3, ceiling-gazing was reduced to below the criterion as the criterion was decreased over the sessions. The withdrawal of treatment during the second baseline (BL2) resulted in an increase in gazing, which dropped to near zero during the next two criterion phases.

For their second student, inappropriate vocalizations were targeted for reduction. *Inappropriate vocalizations* were defined as any "phrase, word, or sound, including the repetition of words or phrases, not appropriate to the situation" (p. 370). The DRL procedure again consisted of three criterion levels of low-rate vocalizations. These criterions were set at 61, 29, and 15 per minute, respectively, during a 30-minute period. As in the prior example, the initial criterion was set at 50 percent the rate of responding that was measured during the baseline phase. The student averaged 123 vocalizations during baseline. A "star card" was used to aid implementation of DRI. Mario was told that if he had one star

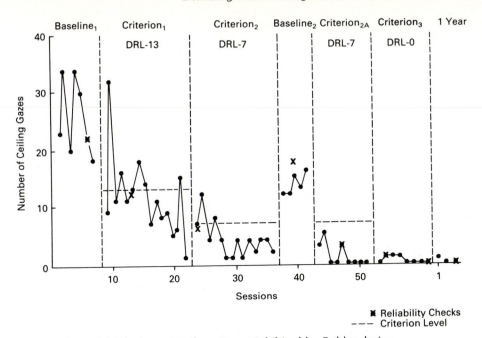

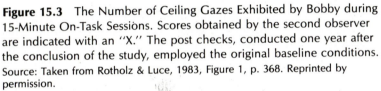

Figure 15.3 The Number of Ceiling Gazes Exhibited by Bobby during 15-Minute On-Task Sessions. Scores obtained by the second observer are indicated with an "X." The post checks, conducted one year after the conclusion of the study, employed the original baseline conditions.
Source: Taken from Rotholz & Luce, 1983, Figure 1, p. 368. Reprinted by permission.

left at the end of a session he would earn the reinforcer. One star was removed by the teacher following each vocalization during the session. Results indicated that the procedures produced a systematic decline in the rate of vocalization. A reversal phase demonstrated that the behavior accelerated when DRI was withdrawn.

There are several advantages to the use of DRL over both DRO and DRI. First, in the DRL contingency the absence of responding is reinforced. In DRO and DRI, however, specific responses are reinforced and strengthened. Second, with DRL a changing criterion is used which serves as a means of reinforcing performance. This procedure is useful as the behavior is shaped out of or eliminated systematically from the student's behavioral repertoire.

A disadvantage of DRL is not having a distinct appropriate behavior that is to be strengthened. As a result, and in similarity with DRO, it sometimes is not entirely clear with DRL what behaviors will actually replace those being eliminated. Thus, it is possible with DRL and DRO that other inappropriate behaviors may emerge.

Differential Reinforcement of Alternative Behaviors (DRA)

Differential reinforcement of alternative behaviors (DRA) is a procedure identical to DRI except that the appropriate response to be reinforced is not physically incompatible with the target behavior. In this case, strengthening an alternative behavior simply occupies the time of the individual to the extent that the target behavior is functionally reduced. The primary difference between DRI and DRA is the possibility of the co-occurrence of the behavior selected for strengthening (that is, the appropriate behavior) and the inappropriate target behavior. In DRI co-occurrence with the target behavior is impossible. For example, high rates of disruptive behavior may be reduced by providing contingencies for task engagement (Greenwood, Hops, Delquadri, & Guild, 1974) or correct academic responding (for example, Ayllon, Laymen, & Burke, 1972). When using DRA, interest is focused upon selecting alternative behaviors from an analysis of the situation in which the problem behavior (that is, the target behavior) is occurring. For example, Carr and Durand (1985) taught students communication skills as a means of reducing their disruptive behavior during their engagement with very difficult tasks. Students were taught to respond to the query "Do you have any questions?" with either "Am I doing good work?" or "I don't understand." Functionally, these responses were trained as a means by which the students could obtain increased reinforcement for trying harder on the task and more frequent teacher help. These behaviors served as functional alternatives to disruptive behavior (the target behavior).

In a very early demonstration of DRA, Ayllon, Layman, and Burke (1872) selected four students from a class who were considered to be "the most unmotivated, undisciplined and troublesome in the school" (p. 316). These students displayed such behavior as walking or running around the classroom; throwing objects; talking out loud to other students; calling out to the teacher; whistling; tapping or pounding objects, feet, or fingers; dropping objects; and snapping fingers. One way to have dealt with these target behaviors would have been to punish them directly. The authors, however, selected appropriate behaviors for reinforcement. The authors chose reading and arithmetic as alternative behaviors to be reinforced. In the first phase of the study, the teacher engaged in her regular routine. During these days, the students were disruptive in 98 percent of the time in which they were observed. In the next phase, the teacher divided the class time into two consecutive 30-minute periods. In one, the teacher instructed the students in math for 5 minutes, then presented them with a 2-minute test, and then repeated the instruction-test cycle four times. In the next 30 minutes, the teacher distributed materials to the students to be read. At the end of each 5 minute period, a 1.5 minute timed test was given over the material just read. This cycle was also repeated until it had occurred four times.

During this second phase, the disruptive behaviors were reduced to 17 percent of the baseline observations. Then four phases occurred in which either the math or the reading answers were reinforced. The results were astonishing and demonstrated the value of this (DRA) approach: (a) disruptive behavior remained at low levels, and (b) academic performance increased. "Within less than 20 hours of the reinforcement procedures, two children improved in reading from preprimer to second grade. The other two children improved from first to fourth grade" (p. 321). In addition, the children continued to perform quite well when reinforcement was no longer used for the math performance.

The results of this early study are very important for several reasons. First, these children had been labeled mentally retarded, but they had been allowed to function at a much lower academic and social level than was necessary. Perhaps if a program like this had been provided for them before they reached the ages of 12 or 13, they could have functioned in a less restrictive environment and at a much higher level. Second, if DRO, DRL, or DRI procedures had been used, the disruptive behaviors may well have been decreased, however, academic achievements would never have been directly reinforced. The two-fold benefits of this approach, the reduction of target behavior and increase in specific academic behavior are substantial and make it a very attractive alternative to punishment alone. As Ayllon, Layman, and Burke (1972) have noted,

The impressive progress made by all four children suggests that the time has come for [special educators] to be satisfied with nothing less than academic objectives. If academic progress, such as that reported here, can be made with these (children) then it is time for the same procedure to be applied to assist in the education of [similar children]. While disruptive behavior and discipline in the classroom are the major, and often the immediate, objectives of the classroom teacher, behavioral applications cannot in good conscience be exploited to foster classroom conformity. On the contrary, the classroom teacher must come to realize that behavioral techniques enable the teaching of important alternative behaviors. (p. 322)

DRA is an attractive behavior reduction procedure because it allows one to focus upon specific appropriate behaviors, whether they are academic or otherwise. The primary disadvantage is that the target behavior may not be entirely eliminated, only reduced. For example, a disruptive student could conceivably continue to disrupt the classroom occasionally and complete his assigned work.

Summary of Differential Reinforcement Procedures

Differential reinforcement procedures can clearly be an effective and acceptable means of reducing problem behaviors. However, the procedures may be technically difficult, time-consuming, and generally slower to take effect when compared to the punishment procedures discussed in Chapter 14. Interestingly, differential reinforcement procedures have been used most frequently by special educators. One of the values of these procedures compared to punishment is that the procedures are less likely to result in unintended and unwanted side effects, such as students avoiding a teacher or a parent, as may happen with a punishment program. These procedures, therefore, are more likely to be accepted by special educators than other punishment procedures, as appears evident in the applied literature.

Stimulus Control

Stimulus control refers to the ability of a stimulus or several stimuli to set the occasion for a response to occur. When there is a high probability that a response will occur in the presence of a particular stimulus and no others, we say that stimulus control has been demonstrated or that the stimulus has "controlled" the probability of responding. According to the laws of operant conditioning, a stimulus is able to set the occasion for a given response if that response has been previously reinforced in the presence of the stimulus. As applied to the reduction of target behaviors, the use of stimulus control involves (a) assessing the natural conditions under which the problem behavior occurs, (b) identifying a stimulus or stimuli that appear to set the occasion for the response, and (c) removing or modifying these stimuli while noting the effect on the target behavior.

An early application of stimulus control interventions to reduce the problem behaviors is represented in the work of Patterson (1982). As a means of decelerating problem behaviors in the home, Patterson assessed parent-child interactions. In one study, it was noted that a child's crying and yelling was correlated to mother's instructions and commands (Patterson, 1974). By advising the mother to reduce her instructions and commands, it was possible to immediately and reliably reduce the target behavior. Patterson referred to this procedure as a "precision" intervention because it was based on the assessment of the natural controlling and reinforcing properties operating within parent-child interactions. Using a procedure that assessed the sequence of events within interactions, Patterson reduced the problem immediately allowing time to implement a standard contingency-based intervention as a second treatment step that could be used to teach the child to actually comply with parental commands.

Stimulus control has been increasingly used in the design of interventions for the most severe behavior problems, such as self-injurious behavior. Iwata, Dorsey, Slifer, Bauman and Richard (1982) described procedures for assessing the relationship between specific environmental events and self-injurious behavior. These stimulus events included various levels and types of play materials, experimenter demands, and social attention. Results indicated that for some children higher rates of self-injury were reliably related to specific combinations of these factors. For example, some students were more self-injurious when alone; others more self-injurious when included in academic sessions. The authors speculated that self-injury when alone may have functioned as self-stimulation; whereas, in academic sessions it may have functioned to terminate academic demands.

The work of Patterson (1982) and Iwata et al. (1982) represents efforts to assess and manipulate existing stimulus control. Typically, these investigators assess the sequence of events that occur over periods of time. Analyzing stimulus control has also recently been reported by Touchette et al. (1985). Based upon an entire day assessment of the frequency of inappropriate behaviors and the activities in which they occurred, they intervened by revising a student's daily schedule. Their data for this student is displayed in Figure 15.4.

Joan was 14-year-old girl with a history of serious aggression, which was first noted when she was 4 years old. She had repeatedly injured staff and peers. Utilizing a graph called a "scatter plot" Touchette et al. (1985) found that assaults were most frequent between 1:00 and 4:00 in the afternoon, Monday through Thursday. Assaults were least likely during weekends, in the morning, at lunch time, and during evening periods. On Friday afternoons, her schedule was different; it included field trips or swimming. Joan's weekday mornings were spent in one-on-one instruction, suggesting that demands and training alone did not provoke assaults.

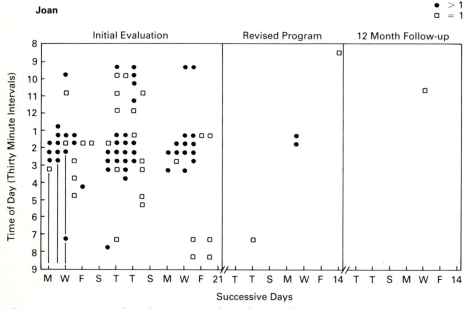

Figure 15.4 Scatter Plot of Joan's Assaults. Filled circles indicate 30-minute intervals during which more than one assault occurred. Open boxes represent intervals with only one assault
Source: Taken from Touchette et al., 1985, Figure 3, p. 347.

These data were used to revise Joan's daily schedule. Activities during the day associated with assaults were replaced by activities that did not result in assaults. In the morning, she continued to receive one-on-one instruction as usual, but her afternoon "group participation" was eliminated. In replacing her afternoon group participation, the schedule was made to approximate her weekend schedule, when she was able to interact with individual staff members. The staff members told her stories, and engaged her in play, etc. These activities were changed every 15 minutes.

As the data under the Revised Program indicate in Figure 15.4, her assaults were dramatically reduced. During the last phase of the program, elements of her former schedule were gradually reintroduced during the afternoon. Increasingly, more time was spent in academic sessions and under increasing response requirements. During the follow-up period under the original schedule only one assault occurred.

The analysis of stimulus control as a basis for intervention with problem behavior, while relatively new in the literature, promises to be an important applied procedure. By using information on stimulus control (Patterson, 1982, Touchette et al., 1985) as the basis for problem identification and treatment design, problem behaviors can be rapidly reduced.

The advantage of identifying stimulus control in the reduction of behavior lies in the discovery and application of the naturally existing relationships controlling the behavior. Assessing controlling stimuli provides a basis for altering stimulus events, either by removing them or by replacing them with other stimulus events that set the occasion for appropriate responding. The disadvantage of this approach is the increased demands placed upon a teacher's time and the complexity of assessment process. In terms of assessment instruments, a means for measuring both the environment and the behavior is required. To date, there is only a small literature to elucidate these assessment procedures.

Other researchers have demonstrated that problem behaviors are often more likely where task demands are frequent (Durand, 1982), where the level of task difficulty is high (Carr & Durand, 1985), and where the pacing of a lesson is too slow (Carnine, 1982). These researchers reduced problem behavior by reducing task difficulty and increasing pacing. Based upon the available literature, the following considerations seem important: First, direct observations must be designed to reveal environmental conditions that are temporally related to the problem behavior. Second, from these data suggestions must be formed about stimulus events that control positive and negative responses. Third, an experimental design should be used to evaluate the effect of the intervention. Interventions can be applied in at least two apparent ways. The first is molar, in which controlling events are modified and effects on behavior are noted (Touchette et al., 1985). The second is molecular in which a single specific event (for example a parent's command) is manipulated at one time (Patterson, 1974). At the molar level, Touchette et al. (1985) suggested using a grid with a key or legend to indicate response frequencies, such as the scatter plot shown in Figure 15.5.

Vertically, the grid segments reflect the time of day. These times may be representative of hours, half hours, quarter hours, or any other period of time appropriate to the analysis. The horizontal segments of the grid represent successive days or sessions. In this example, and also as shown in Figure 15.4, a blank cell represents no responses. A filled cell reflects the occurrence of the response, which may be denoted as low-occurrence (filled box) or high-occurrence (filled circle) responses. As the scatter plot is filled with observations, each unit of time reflects whether the target behavior occurred at a high or low rate or not at all. After several days of plotting the occurrence of behavior, "patterns" or responses become evident. In Joan's case, she was aggressive only in the afternoons, four days a week.

Stimulus control procedures for reducing problem behaviors are a promising new area of study. Unlike differential reinforcement procedures, which provide consequences for

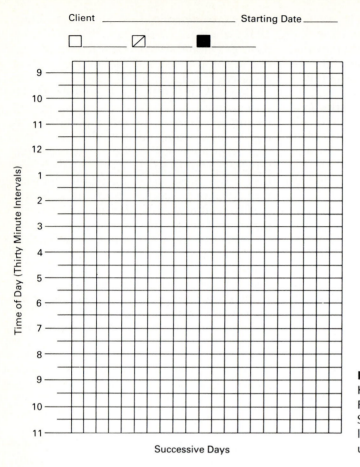

Figure 15.5   Scatter Plot Grid with a Key at the Top to Indicate Response Frequencies Corresponding to Filled, Slashed, and Open Boxes. Each location on the grid identifies a unique time interval on a given day.

responding, stimulus control procedures focus on the antecedent events that appear to set the occasion for a response. By identifying these antecedents stimuli and removing or modifying them systematically, it is possible to produce immediate and long-term reductions in problem behaviors.

SUMMARY

In this chapter we have discussed procedures for reducing problem behaviors using differentiated reinforcement-related methods and stimulus control. These procedures included (a) using differential reinforcement schedules (DRO, DRI, DRL, and DRA) and (b) modifying a stimulus that controls the problem behavior. The first procedure has a long history of application in behavior analysis; stimulus control, on the other hand, has only recently begun to yield practical methods. Nevertheless, both approaches represent useful interventions that reduce problem behaviors rapidly if applied correctly. They also represent procedures that teachers, parents, and others will most often find acceptable for use in the classroom and the community.

REFERENCES

AYLLON, T., LAYMEN, D., & BURKE, S. (1972). "Disruptive behavior and reinforcement of academic behavior." *Psychological Record, 22,* 315–323.

BARTON, L. E., BRUELLE, A. R., & REPP, A. C. (1986). "Maintenance of therapeutic change by momentary DRO." *Journal of Applied Behavior Analysis, 19,* 277–282.

BAUMEISTER, A. A., & FOREHAND, R. (1971). "Effects of extinction of an instrumental response on stereotyped body rocking in severe retardates." *The Psychological Record, 28,* 586–590.

CARR, E. G., & DURAND, V. M. (1985). "Reducing behavior problems through functional communications training." *Journal of Applied Behavior Analysis, 18,* 111–126.

CONE, J. D., ANDERSON, J. A., HARRIS, F. C., GOFF, D. K., & FOX, S. R. (1978). "Developing and maintaining social interaction in profoundly retarded young males." *Journal of Abnormal Child Psychology, 16,* 351–360.

DIETZ, S. M., & REPP, A. C. (1976). "Decreasing classroom misbehavior through the use of DRL schedules of reinforcement." *Journal of Applied Behavior Analysis, 6,* 457–463.

DURAND, V. M. (1982). "Analysis and intervention of self-injurious behavior." *TASH Journal, 7,* 44–53.

EASON, J. J., WHITE, M. J., & NEWSOM, C. D. (1982). "Generalized reduction of self-stimulatory behavior: An effect of teaching appropriate play to autistic children." *Analysis and Intervention in Developmental Disabilities, 2,* 157–169.

FRIMAN, P. C., BARNARD, J. D., ALTMAN, K., & WOLF, M. M. (1986). "Parent and teacher use of DRO and DRI to reduce aggressive behavior." *Analysis and Intervention in Developmental Disabilities, 6,* 319–330.

FLAVELL, J. E. (1973). "Reduction of stereotypes by reinforcement of toy play." *Mental Retardation, 11,* 21–23.

GREENWOOD, C. R., HOPS, H., DELQUADRI, J., & GUILD, J. J. (1974). "Group contingencies for group consequences: A further analysis." *Journal of Applied Behavior Analysis, 7,* 413–425.

HALL, R. V., LUND, D., & JACKSON, D. (1968). "Effects of teacher attention on study behavior." *Journal of Applied Behavior Analysis, 1,* 1–12.

IWATA, B. A., DORSEY, M. F., SLIFER, K. J., BAUMAN, K. E., & RICHMAN, G. S. (1982). "Toward a functional analysis of self-injury." *Analysis and Intervention in Developmental Disabilities, 2,* 3–20.

PATTERSON, G. R. (1965). "An application of condition techniques to the control of a hyperactive child." In L. P. Ullmann & L. Krasner (eds.), *Case studies in behavior modification.* New York: Holt, Rinehart & Winston.

PATTERSON, G. R. (1974). "A basis for identifying stimuli which control behaviors in natural settings." *Child Development, 45,* 900–911.

PATTERSON, G. R. (1982). *Coercive family process.* Eugene, OR: Castalia.

POLING, A., & RYAN, C. (1982). "Differential reinforcement of other behavior schedules: Therapeutic applications." *Behavior Modification, 6,* 3–21.

REPP, A. C., BARTON, L. E., & BRULLE, A. R. (1983). "A comparison of two procedures for programming the differential reinforcement of other behaviors." *Journal of Applied Behavior Analysis, 16,* 435–445.

REPP, A. C., DEITZ, S. M., & SPEIR, N. C. (1974). "Reducing stereotypic responding of retarded persons by the differential reinforcement of other behavior." *American Journal of Mental Deficiency, 79,* 279–284.

ROTHOLZ, D. A., & LUCE, S. C. (1983). "Alternative reinforcement strategies for the reduction of self-stimulatory behavior in autistic youth." *Education and Treatment of Children, 6,* 363–377.

TARPLEY, H., & SCHROEDER, S. (1979). "Comparison of DRO and DRI on rate of suppression of self-injurious behavior." *American Journal of Mental Deficiency, 84,* 188–194.

TOUCHETTE, P. E., MACDONALD, R. F., & LANGER, S. N. (1985). "A scatter plot for identifying stimulus control of problem behavior." *Journal of Applied Behavior Analysis, 18,* 343–351.

WEISBERG, P., PASSMAN, R. H., & RUSSELL, J. E. (1973). "Development of verbal control over bizarre gestures of retardates through imitative and nonimitative reinforcement procedures." *Journal of Applied Behavior Analysis, 6,* 487–495.

Index

Gottlieb, J., 269, 309
Gould, S. J., 112
Graduated guidance, 300
Graduate programs, 10
Graf, S., 320
Grain-size, 125
Grant, L., 297
Grant, M. D., 218
Graphing, 67, 156–62, 198
Graubard, P. S., 254
Graves, A. W., 333
Gray, D., 353
Gray, R. M., 235
Green, D. R., 219
Green, K. D., 224
Greene, B. F., 192
Greene, R. J., 344
Greenwood, C. R., 69, 85, 87, 95, 105, 106, 113, 121, 135, 142, 148, 150, 152, 168, 189, 204, 208, 254, 294, 330, 370
Greer, R. D., 169, 254
Gresham, F. M., 85
Grimes, L., 310, 312
Group contingencies, 69–70, 232, 255–57
Group designs, 168–69, 189–92
Growth period, 10–13
Guess, D., 145, 319–20
Guidance, 299–300
Guild, J. J., 69, 85, 148, 189, 201, 370
Guilford, J. P., 107
Gunter, P., 149
Guralnik, M. H., 299
Guthrie, E. R., 26

Haavik, S., 142
Habit formation, 27
Hake, D. G., 222
Halasz, M. M., 179
Hall, R. V., 35, 36, 95, 121, 133, 135, 168, 178, 192, 194, 195, 202, 203, 235, 252, 257, 294, 330, 331, 340, 366
Hallahan, D. P., 49, 331, 333
Halle, J. W., 300
Halvorson, J. A., 356
Hamblin, R. L., 256, 257
Hamilton, J., 168
Hamilton, S. B., 350
Hammill, D. D., 315
Handleman, J. S., 60
Handraising, 82
Handwashing, 122, 145, 182
Hanline, M. F., 89, 173
Hansen, C., 310
Hanson, M. J., 89, 173
Haring, T. G., 89, 121, 189, 325
Harris, F. C., 366
Harris, J., 114
Harris, M. B., 147
Harris, V. W., 257
Hart, B., 35, 36
Hartmann, D. P., 140, 192, 194, 195, 198
Harvard University, 4, 27
Hasazi, J. E., 218, 235
Hasazi, S. E., 218, 235
Hathaway, C. H., 256
Hawkins, R. P., 315
Hayes, S. C., 134, 136, 198
Head-banging, 344
Heads, T. B., 233
Heal, L. W., 17
Heart, 37–39
Hendrickson, J., 310
Heredity, 6, 7
Heron, T. E., 292, 326
Hersen, M., 170
Heward, W. L., 231, 292, 315, 326
Hickey, K., 224

High-density reinforcement, 70–71
High rates, 275–76
Hill, A. D., 235
Hill, D. W., 145, 185
Hill, S., 257
Hill-Elliot Act, 10
Hines, D., 254
Hippocrates, 1
Histograms, 156–57
Histories, 105
Hoats, D. L., 344
Hogan, T. R., 101
Holland, A., 224, 227
Holt, J., 225
Holvoet, J., 145
Holz, W. C., 222, 343
Home safety program, 192
Homework completion, 88
Homme, L. E., 234
Honesty, 332
Hoogeveen, F. R., 293
Hopkins, B. L., 224, 233
Hops, H., 48, 69, 73, 94, 105, 106, 139, 148, 150, 168, 189, 204, 212, 348, 350, 351, 353, 370
Horizontal axis, 157
Horner, R. D., 195, 196, 198, 315, 316, 318
Horner, R. H., 93, 95, 319, 328
Howard, J. S., 298
Howe, S. G., 405–12
Howell, K. W., 318
Hoyson, M., 179
Hughes, V., 90, 204
Hull, C. L., 26, 27
Hulten, W. J., 133
Human behavior, 33–34
Humphrey, L. L., 332
Hundert, J., 331, 332
Hunt, P., 135
Hurlburt, M., 218
Hutchinson, R. R., 222
Hutton, S. B., 148
Huxley, A., 36
Hygiene, 231

Icing, 340
Idiocy and Its Treatment by the Physiological Method, 4
Idiot, 4
Idol-Maestas, L., 310
IEP (*see* Individualized Education Plan)
Illustrations, 288
Imitation, 298–99, 310–13, 332
Immediate effect, 170
Immediate reinforcement, 246
Immigrants, 6
Implosive therapy, 26
Imprecise reinforcement, 286
Inappropriate response, 218–20
Income, 11
Incompatible responding, 366–67
Increasing assistance approach, 297
Increasing behavior, 221
Increments, 197–98
Independence of baselines, 192
Indiana University, 33
Indirect measurement, 70, 71
Individualized Education Plan (IEP), 15, 16, 78, 90, 120–21
Individuals, 5–7, 13, 44–46
analysis of, 37, 69–70, 167–68
assessment of, 46–47, 138–39
designs for, 169–70, 187–89
Industrial education, 6, 7
Inhelder, B., 23
Inman, D. P., 319
Institute of Child Behavior, 34
Institute of Human Relations, 27

Instructional procedures, 58–65 (*see also* Teaching procedures)
Instructions, 292, 295–96
Instrument referencing, 109
Integrated settings, 56–57
Intensity of behaviors, 147
Interactions, 153 (*see also* Social skills)
Intermittent assessment, 100–131
criterion-referenced, 114–29 (*see also* Criterion-referenced assessment)
data use in, 108
information sources in, 101–5
instruments of, 105–8
norm-referenced, 109–14
Intermittent reinforcement, 268–72
generalization and, 330
natural contingencies and, 252
Interobserver agreement, 137–38, 140
Interresponse latency, 86–87
Intersections, 61, 209
Interspersal training, 70–71
Intersubject comparison, 110, 161–62
Interval recording, 134, 137, 148, 149–52
Interval schedules, 277–81
Intervention effects, 38
Intrapsychic approach, 53
Intrasubject comparisons, 160–61
Inversion error, 325
Irvin, L., 84
Itard, J., 2, 4, 12, 51
Iwata, B. A., 70, 142, 146, 182, 195, 227, 372

Jackson, A. T., 173, 208
Jackson, D., 133, 135, 252, 309, 366
Jackson, R., 312
Jacobsen, L., 11
James, J. E., 356
James, V., 297
Jamieson, B., 179
Jarvis, R., 257
JEAB (*see Journal of the Experimental Analysis of Behavior*)
Jenkins, J. R., 218, 224, 309
Jensen, W. R., 152
Johnson, C., 298
Johnson, G., 296
Johnson, M. R., 333
Johnson, S. M., 73, 252, 356
Johnston, G. T., 253
Johnston, J. B., 253
Jones, M. C., 26
Jones, M. L., 237
Jordan, L. J., 8
Jorgensen, S., 78
Journal of Applied Behavior Analysis, 38, 45, 57, 155
Journal of the Association for Persons with Severe Handicaps, 153
Journal of the Experimental Analysis of Behavior (JEAB), 34
Journal of Learning Disabilities, 133
Judicial years, 13–18
Juniper Gardens Children's Project, 36, 294

Kallikak Family, The, 7
Kanner, L., 4
Kansas City Times, 113
Kaplan, J. S., 318
Kaplan, S. J., 350
Kaplin, J., 119
Karlin, G. R., 85, 146
Karoly, P., 332
Kass, R. E., 341
Kasteller, J., 235
Kauffman, J. M., 49, 310, 312
Kaufman, A., 101, 112, 114

379